Protestantism and Politics

in Eastern Europe and Russia

Protestantism and Politics

in Eastern Europe and Russia

The Communist and Postcommunist Eras

Edited by Sabrina Petra Ramet

CHRISTIANITY UNDER STRESS

Volume III

Duke University Press   Durham and London   1992

© 1992 Duke University Press
All rights reserved
Printed in the United States of America
on acid-free paper ∞
Library of Congress Cataloging-in-Publication Data
appear on the last printed page of this book.

To Herb Ellison, friend,
to whom I am indebted for so much

Contents

Preface

This is the final volume in a three-volume work, *Christianity Under Stress*, which deals with contemporary issues in church-state relations, focusing on the communist world. The first volume, *Eastern Christianity and Politics in the Twentieth Century*, was published by Duke University Press in 1988. The second volume, *Catholicism and Politics in Communist Societies*, was also published by Duke University Press in 1990.

This set of essays is primarily intended to provide an up-to-date, comprehensive survey of Christian religious life and church-state relations in Eastern Europe and the Soviet Union, although other case studies from outside the area were included in volumes 1 and 2. The country chapters in all three volumes include statistical Fact Sheets to give the reader some idea of the strength of these churches. Chapter 3 ("Protestantism in East Germany, 1949–1989") was originally published in *Religion in Communist Lands* (Winter 1991). Chapter 8 ("Protestantism in the USSR") was originally published in Sabrina Petra Ramet (ed.), *Religious Policy in the Soviet Union* (Cambridge University Press, 1992). Chapter 10 ("The New Church-State Configuration in Eastern Europe") was originally published in *East European Politics and Societies*, vol. 5, no. 2 (Spring 1991). I wish to thank the editors of these journals and the editor of Cambridge University Press for their kind permission to reuse this material here.

I am very grateful to the following scholars who provided feedback and suggestions on several chapters: James Felak, William C. Fletcher, Dionisie Ghermani, Trond Gilberg, Jure Kristo, Spas T. Raikin, Gerd Stricker, and Peter F. Sugar. Throughout this entire 3-volume project, it has been a great pleasure to work with Reynolds Smith and the entire staff at Duke University Press.

I also wish to thank the Graduate School of the University of Washington for its generosity in providing a publication subsidy for this book.

Special thanks to my spouse, Christine Hassenstab, who prepared the index for this book.

The first two volumes appeared under the editorship of "Pedro Ramet," and this third volume, under the editorship of "Sabrina Ramet." Pedro and Sabrina are one and the same person. Few people can really understand what it means to be born convinced that one is female, and to find that one's body is male. Years of anguish and struggle against oneself go nowhere. Ultimately, there was only one route to peace of mind: adaptation of my body to conform to my psychic gender. Since taking that decision, I now sail on calm waters.

Sabrina Petra Ramet

Protestantism and Politics

in Eastern Europe and Russia

1

Protestantism and Communism

Patterns of Interaction in Eastern Europe and the

Soviet Union

Sabrina Petra Ramet

True theology is not theoretical or speculative. Its aim is rather action, i.e., a godlike life.—Protestant reformer Martin Butzer

Theory becomes aimless if it is not connected with revolutionary practice, just as practice gropes in the dark if its path is not illumined by revolutionary theory . . . for it, and it alone, can give the movement confidence, the power of orientation, and an understanding of the inherent connection between surrounding events.—Josef V. Stalin, *The Foundations of Leninism*

When social institutions subscribing to divergent programmatic theories (or theologies) come into contact, the result is apt to be some mixture of conflict and accommodation. And to the extent that one or more institutions have to accommodate their ideologies and behaviors in conditions of coexistence, those institutions are likely to modify and revise these theories in the light of prevailing conditions. To the extent that ideology can be described as a kind of *secular theology,* and thus subsumed under the rubric of theology, one may say that while theology is the starting point for an understanding of an institution's goals, resources, and optimal strategies, theologies may expand and contract and shift emphases as changing political realities impose strategic imperatives.

The coexistence of Protestantism and communism in Eastern Europe and the Soviet Union provided unmistakable examples of political accommodation and theological adaptation. In the German Democratic Republic (GDR), the concept of a "Church in Socialism," first articulated in 1971, came in the wake of the creation of a separate Federation of Evangelical-Lutheran Churches in the GDR and signified the Evangelical Church's acceptance of the communist order. In Hungary, likewise, the now-defunct Theology of Diakonia owed its birth to the communist order's influence. This theology, which characterized both the Reformed

Church and the Lutheran Church in Hungary, was defined by a leading Hungarian theologian as entailing "active cooperation with the Marxists and practical participation in the development of the socialist society."[1] Its best-known advocate was Lutheran Bishop Zoltán Káldy, who explained that in opting for a Theology of Diakonia (or service) the church was consciously adapting itself to the existing social order and embracing the goals of the state as its own.

But if some churches found it necessary to adapt to communism, so some communist regimes found it necessary to adapt to Christianity. In the GDR, for instance, authorities long allowed that the churches had a positive role to play at a given stage of development, while in the USSR under Mikhail Gorbachev there were repeated signs of a reexamination of religion and even of a new willingness to concede a positive role to religion.[2] Indeed, in September 1990 *Literaturnaia gazeta* reported the opening of the first Sunday school in the USSR.[3]

Patterns of adaptation are complex and heterogeneous—partly because of differences between countries and systems, and partly because of differences in the self-comprehension of different churches. In the postcommunist era, both the directions and the rates of change may vary, and even if there is already considerably greater freedom for religion, there also is the presence of continued (or perhaps even greater) heterogeneity in church-state relations across the region. In the eastern half of reunified Germany, for example, citizens became subject to the state-imposed church tax in January 1991—a burden unlikely to be imposed elsewhere in the region.[4]

It is formidable enough to attempt to discern patterns of thought and behavior within the Orthodox Church or the Catholic Church, and it is similarly difficult to understand patterns in those churches' relations with communist states.[5] Neither church is a monolith, and the diversity of currents within each of them was an important source of complexity in their dealings with communist regimes. Protestantism is altogether more complex, and for obvious reasons. To begin with, differences of opinion may exist as to just which churches should be counted as "Protestant" and which should not. And among those that *are* counted as Protestant, there may be considerable differences in theology, organization, and political orientation. In spite of these obstacles, one may at a minimum characterize Protestant churches as placing a greater emphasis on scripture than do the Orthodox and Catholic churches, and correspondingly placing less emphasis on dogma, law, tradition, hierarchy, sacrament, and monasticism.[6]

In addition, there has been a tendency in Protestantism to emphasize the laity while deemphasizing the clergy. Seventeenth-century Harringtonian legal scholar William Sprigge, for example, rejected any distinction between clergy and laity, which is to say he did not see a need for any special clergy, while Baptist thinker Gerrard Winstanley (1609–76), known for his association with the Diggers movement, argued for the primacy of individual spiritual experience over church institutions and doctrines.[7] The idea of the "priesthood of all believers" has evolved over time and in the twentieth century has come to signify not so much prerogative as a duty to others, not so much individual self-sufficiency as the indispensability of parish life.[8]

Finally, despite Calvin's theocracy and Luther's belief that the state should serve divine ends, despite Puritan millennarianism and Butzer's argument that the civil magistrate should establish and promote "true religion," Protestantism sowed the seeds for the separation of church and state. Luther considered the idea of a Christian state impracticable and even allowed that a non-Christian could fulfill the role of magistrate just as well as a Christian, provided only that he be guided by the voice of reason.[9] Adolf von Harnack (1851–89), a Lutheran theologian who lectured at the University of Berlin and enjoyed tremendous influence in his day, taught that it was erroneous to deduce maxims for the conduct or regulation of secular affairs from gospel and that the gospel should not be exported into law. As Wilhelm Pauck notes, "Harnack believed that the reformers had to renounce in some way the Roman Catholic ideal of building a visible Kingdom of God on earth and of penetrating the realm of nature with the power of grace and holiness."[10] In this manner, Harnack completed the divorce of church from state begun by Luther.

Protestantism and Communism

From one perspective, Protestant churches were more "troublesome" for the communists than the Orthodox Church or Catholic Church. The communists traditionally preferred to settle their relations with churches through negotiations with their appropriate heads. But where certain religious bodies, such as the Christian Community or the Baptists, declined to appoint heads of their organizations or to give their leaders effective jurisdictional power, the communists had to face dealing with what, to them, seemed like amorphous and unpredictable (hence, perhaps, uncontrollable) "movements." For this reason, in part, the communists long preferred Orthodox, or even Lutheran, churches to Baptists or Mennonites or other "amorphous" denominations. Consistent with this strategy, the Soviets tried, beginning in 1944, to force as many Protestant groups as possible to merge into the All-Union Council of Evangelical Christians and Baptists, facilitating state supervision and control of them.[11]

Yet, in the GDR, Poland, Czechoslovakia, and Hungary, the smaller Protestant churches clearly benefited from the disestablishment of former "state churches" and from the communists' interest in redressing the balance by favoring the smaller churches in certain ways. In Poland, for instance, church buildings that had been lost to the Catholic Church in the interwar period were restored to the Protestants, while in Czechoslovakia the party's central committee issued secret instructions to cadres that the Czechoslovak (Hussite) Church and the Evangelical Church were to receive privileged treatment.[12]

For some Protestant clergy, the advent of communism was even welcome. Czech theologian Josef Hromádka argued that the Christian nations had been responsible for the century's two world wars, that Christianity had therefore not been an effective brake against mass extermination and suffering, and hence this should be kept in mind before criticizing communism. For Hromádka, it was pointless to hope for the old order's return, and, accordingly, he believed that the clergy's opposition to socialism was not only perilous but wrong-headed.[13] But Hromádka was in fact consciously sympathetic toward communism. In his memoirs, he recalled his first approach to socialism:

> At the beginning of February 1948, just before our socialist revolution, we gathered at the Philosophy Department of Charles University and tried to understand and convince each other. I no longer remember all the details, but I still recall the basic theme because I have never abandoned it. It was: As a Christian theologian I have nothing against socialism. Even from a religious standpoint it is much closer to me than is bourgeois liberal democracy. I am ready to help in the construction of a socialist society. But I warned that the fundamental problems of socialist man would still weigh heavily upon us, even after our society has been politically, socially and economically rebuilt. The basic human problems remain, whatever the structure of society.[14]

Nor was his an isolated viewpoint. In Hungary, Calvinist professor Elemér Kocsis told a scholarly symposium in October 1983 (commemorating the quincentenary of Martin Luther's birth) that Protestants and

Marxists shared a common humanist heritage and that Protestants must "choose" socialism as the "most progressive" system available.[15]

This volume focuses on the themes of dissent and pacifism, dialogue, and ecumenism. *Dissent*, as the *Oxford English Dictionary* reminds us, is merely the practice of holding a different opinion, whether this entails disagreement with a church, with the dominant opinions in society, or with the values and policies of a regime. Churches are political to begin with, since their moral codes and social values to retain meaning and potency cannot be divorced from the social and political contexts to which they relate. Under communism, the church's political character is accentuated insofar as it is the sole remaining independent institution in most countries ruled by communist parties, so that the church not only finds itself strategically "alone" in its confrontation with the communist party, but finds that the numerous interested groups that inevitably seek expression in any complex society tend to look to the churches for sympathy, advice, inspiration, assistance, or alliance. The church thus was drawn into pacifist, ecological, trade unionist, nationalist, and other concerns. This course entailed some risk since the communist party typically would arrogate the prerogative of exclusive adjudication in matters social, political, economic, and informational. Hence, the challenge for the church, as Lutheran Bishop Werner Krusche of Magdeburg put it so well, was to find "the narrow space between opposition and opportunism."[16] Ultimately, the churches of Eastern Europe made an important contribution to the pressure that culminated in the "Great Transformation" of 1989.[17]

The involvement of a church in dissent remained, clearly, a matter of choice (though numerous examples testify to the fact that congregations may exert pressure on their clergy to "radicalize"). Hence, as Michael Bourdeaux pointed out, "membership [in] a sect does not of itself in any way imply opposition to the [communist] state."[18]

Christian-Marxist dialogue in communist Eastern Europe bloomed in the early 1960s on the initiative of the communists when and insofar as they felt it could be useful to them; the public meetings of Christian and Marxist philosophers and sociologists could create an impression of openness and liberality for Western audiences and create new opportunities in the church-state relationship.[19] From the beginning, it was Catholics and Protestants who responded to the invitation to dialogue rather than Orthodox, Muslims, Jews, or other religious groups.[20] In Hungary, Lutheran Bishop Káldy gave dialogue theological status, identifying it as an organic part of the Theology of Diakonia.[21] In the GDR, on the other hand, the Evangelical-Lutheran Church saw dialogue as a forum in which the church might carry on constructive criticism of the regime and articulate its specific views on issues of the day. In every case, dialogue was something distinct from either collaboration or confrontational debate, although the possibility always existed that dialogue could degenerate into one of these antipodes.

Christian-Marxist dialogue has had two possible forms: *academic* and *practical-political*. The former, especially characteristic of the 1960s but which continued—until the collapse of communism—in Hungary, Yugoslavia, and elsewhere, typically involved public forums in which distinguished specialists engaged in sophisticated discussions of abstract problems. In Hungary, for example, a long-range project involving Protestant theologians and Marxist researchers of Protestantism was launched with a colloquium in Debrecen on 25–26 September 1981. Such dialogue could win advocates on either side, but it had little chance of producing direct effects on policy since those participating on the Marxist side were usually academicians rather than policymakers. The latter form of dialogue, which characterized the Evangelical-Lutheran Church's relationship with the East German regime, for instance, was politically more to the point, even though it was a quieter, less glamorous process.

Ecumenism may be defined as dialogue and cooperation among churches, founded on mutual respect. Sometimes viewed as the aspiration for ecclesiastical unity,[22] ecumenical forums have come to concentrate on pooling resources to address issues of mutual concern. The starting point for ecumenism is the willingness to grant that another religious body may have as much legitimacy as one's own and be engaged in work no less useful. This prerequisite accounts for the fact that some churches (for example, the Apostolic communities) have no interest in ecumenism; since they view other churches as the tools of Satan, they cannot conceive of any reason to launch ecumenical contacts. Churches such as the Methodists, the Mennonites, and the Free Christian congregations have been enthusiastically ecumenical, however. Ecumenism, of course, has fared differently in different lands. In Hungary the ecumenical spirit has been weak, and the small, ecumenical-minded Free Christian sect has been repeatedly attacked by the Reformed and Baptist churches despite its size.[23] In Czechoslovakia, by contrast, ecumenical contacts have been lively, taking place chiefly within the context of the Ecumenical Council of Churches in Czechoslovakia and the Christian Peace Conference. Similarly, in the GDR organized institutional forums (the Association of Evangelical Free Churches, the Evangelical Alliance, and, above all, the Working Community of Christian Churches in the GDR) serve as the primary arenas for ecumenical contacts,[24] although inter-church cooperation at the parish level also has been pursued.

Ecumenism is not new. Sixteenth-century Calvinist reformer Jan Laski aspired to unite all Protestant churches in Poland in a single Reformation church that would be recognized by the state, and he sought to achieve this goal through negotiation and compromise. Throughout the sixteenth century, contacts took place—between the Lutherans and the Czech Brethren in Poland, for example, in February 1570 when the latter took part in a Lutheran synod in Poznań.[25] But it was only toward the end of 1942 that preliminary approaches were made in the direction of setting up the Polish Ecumenical Council; the body was finally established after the war's end in late 1946.[26] In Hungary, a Working Community for Ecumenism among Hungarian Young People was created as early as 1936 within the framework of the Protestant Student Union. The Hungarian branch of the World Council of Churches held its first session on 25 June 1943 at the height of World War II. In 1954 this body renamed itself the Ecumenical Council of Churches in Hungary. Since then, ecumenical contacts in Hungary have been intense.[27] Ecumenical bodies also exist in Czechoslovakia and in other countries of Eastern Europe. In addition, the Conference of European Churches and the Christian Peace Conference in Prague have served as arenas for contacts among East European churches. The Christian Peace Conference, although born within a communist womb, has survived the collapse of communism and has expressed a determination to adapt to new conditions and carve out a new role.

Protestantism and Culture

In his classic book, *The Spirit of Protestantism*, Robert McAfee Brown argues that Protestantism has been indifferent to culture (hence, by extension, to national heritage and nationalism). He charges that Protestants have been indifferent to the beauty of cathedrals and to achievements in art, literature, drama, sculpture, etc.[28] The picture is overdrawn. In Eastern Europe, Protestantism, while not as closely identified with nationalism as either Catholicism or Orthodoxy, has nonetheless made its contribution to the development and defense of national culture.

In Transylvania, for instance, the Lutheran Church became established among Saxon communities in the mid-sixteenth century and became the central institution of Saxon cultural and social life. It was partly because of the Lutheran Church that the Saxons were better able than nearby Romanians to resist pressures for Magyarization in the late nineteenth century—pressures most forcefully expressed in the educational system.[29] The Lutheran Church played a similar role in nineteenth-century Slovakia, where the leaders of anti-Hungarian Slovak protests were generally Lutheran pastors.[30] Even in Poland, as difficult as it may be to comprehend in the late twentieth century, Protestantism once contributed to the support of national culture. As early as the fifteenth century, humanist Jan Ostorog (1436–1501) had demanded dissolution of ecclesiastical ties with Rome as a prerequisite for establishing a genuinely *national* church.[31] It was on the initiative of Calvinist Jan Laski that the Bible was translated into Polish and made available to the public.[32] In this spirit, Jan Jozef Lipski wrote in a 1981 essay:

> There is no lack of Protestants among our national heroes, no lack of Protestant ministers among our Polish activists. It is true that the Catholic Church played a great part in the perseverance of "Polishness," particularly after partitions in the Prussian part of Poland and the distant borderlands of the Russian part of Poland. But in the Cieszyn areas of Silesia and in Mazuria, "Polishness" was fostered by the Evangelical Church and its ministers. The final act in this heroic drama was the martyrdom of the unflinching Protestant occupation. The contribution of Polish Protestants to Polish culture and to the struggle for independence is so great that all attempts to exclude them from our Polish national community must provoke sharp opposition.[33]

And in Hungary, the failed revolution of 1848–1849, the partial triumph of the *Ausgleich* period, and the subsequent loss of much of the Hungarian patrimony in the Trianon Treaty of 1920 all drew the Lutheran and Reformed churches into nationalist causes.

But if Protestantism in Eastern Europe has indigenous roots (at least for Poland, Czechoslovakia, Hungary, and Slovenia), Protestantism in Russia and Ukraine, not to mention the Balkans, is very much an import from the West. Soviet evangelicals trace their origins to the 1867 baptism of Nikita Voronin outside Tbilisi,[34] while in Poland, the small Baptist community (three thousand members) is the offshoot of missionary work conducted by Baptists from East Prussia in the mid-nineteenth century.[35] Insofar as they are late arrivals in their countries, neo-Protestants have sometimes been viewed with suspicion and distrust, even by fellow believers (of more "traditional" churches). But neo-Protestants are not necessarily "foreign" in outlook and have, at times, explicitly indicated a desire to adapt and contribute to their national communities. In 1945, for

example, *Bratskii Vestnik*, the journal of the Soviet evangelical community, addressed the concept of *rodina* (homeland), calling it

> that country where we were born and grew up, where we walked and
> where our fields are spread out; here are our families and the families
> of those close to us; here is our people which we must love especially
> deeply and strongly from the heart and according to the glorious
> teachings of our Savior, since Jesus himself loved his people Israel. . . .
> In like fashion, we must have a great love for our country, in order to
> give to it all our strength, our abilities and means, and, if necessary,
> also our life.[36]

A New Era

As the twentieth century draws to a close, some Protestant churches in
Eastern Europe and the former USSR are in decline—among them the
Lutheran and Reformed churches in Hungary, the Lutheran Church in
Latvia, the Evangelical-Lutheran Church in the GDR, and in fact most
churches in the GDR. Other Protestant groups are making gains: the
Baptists (especially in Romania and Ukraine), the Pentecostals in several
countries, the Methodists and Lutherans in Estonia.[37]

Perhaps because of communism, churches in Eastern Europe and the
former Soviet Union have remained more traditional, more conservative
in outlook than their West European counterparts. Officially sponsored
secularization has had different effects from the more spontaneous processes of secularization that have affected the West. But as communism
slid ever deeper into crisis and finally crumbled, and as these countries
begin to grapple toward new institutional approaches in managing social
and political life, religious organizations find themselves faced with new
challenges and realities. As Douglas Durasoff has noted, "prior systems
have legacies—some transient, some deep."[38] Among communism's legacies are a tendency to blame problems on the government, a tendency
to look to the churches for resistance to communist programs, and a
tendency to view religion as an essential part of the community's *independent* life, needing to be defended against siege, subversion, and en-
croachment. These tendencies have bred habits of mind, perhaps most
of which will surely fade—how fast is difficult to say. Will decommunization strip religion of its character of oppositional/dissent, or will it simply
shift that character to another plane? Will decommunization lead to a
situation in which the religious profile of Eastern Europe is no different
from that in Western Europe, that is, weaker, more secularized, less

political? Will religion in this region retain its association with nationalism, and to what extent will democratization attenuate or sublate or
simply erode that linkage? These are some of the questions that confront
us at the dawn of the postcommunist era. It is too early to know what
answers history will offer. At this point, it may be enough if we can pose
good questions.

2

Protestantism: Theology and Politics

Sape A. Zylstra

This chapter deals with issues that, however colored they may be by the particularities of the Reformation and the modern era, have many precedents in the church's earlier history. At no time are religion and politics completely divorced. From the time of Constantine (ca. A.D. 300) to that of Pope Boniface VIII (ca. 1300), they were hardly distinguishable whether emperor or pope was supreme. In most places and for half a millennium afterward, church and state were not even formally thought of as separate. Society's increasing secularization finally brought about this change. In what follows I will attempt to trace the theme of the church-state relationship by specific examples in Protestantism's history. For the time of Luther and Calvin, this relationship is examined by looking at (1) the Reformers' use of the sacraments and (2) their reaction to the problems posed to them by, respectively, the Peasants' Revolt and Michael Servetus. Next (3) is a discussion of the concept of Natural Law in Reformation theology, which laid the groundwork for an increasingly secular understanding of political power. (4) The English Reformation receives a section of its own, and after a brief look (5) at developments on the Post-Reformation Continent, there is a relatively long discussion (6) of the peculiarities of church-state relationships in North America, beginning with Colonial times. Because the thought (7) of Karl Barth and Reinhold Niebuhr is central in twentieth-century controversies concerning the relationship between church and state, the chapter closes with a section that focuses on them.

Martin Luther and John Calvin: Sacramental Politics

A. G. Dickens wrote of the sixteenth century that "if one avoided political intrigue and the more delicate issues of sacramental dogma, many things damaging to ecclesiastical prestige and custom might still be written with impunity."[1] He might have added that to raise questions about the sacraments was a form of political intrigue in both Catholic and Reformed territories.

By reducing the number of sacraments from seven to two, the Reformation lessened the pervasiveness of the ecclesiastical hold on people. The Reformers had their theological reasons for maintaining baptism and the Lord's Supper: they were instituted by Christ. Most importantly, they rejected the interpretation of the Mass as sacrifice.[2] This had profound political repercussions. A person's salvation depends on Christ's sacrifice, the only access to which is the Mass that reiterates it. Hence, excommunication means damnation. Baptism brings one into the church where one can partake of the Body of Christ and outside of which there is no salvation. The absence of the sacrificial nature of the Mass (and, redundantly, of the *extra ecclesiam nulla salus*) in the Reformation churches potentially undermined their political clout. However, this does not mean that they did not wield such clout, nor that they did not use baptism and the Lord's Supper as a means to gain leverage, although perhaps indirectly.

The religio-political significance of baptism can be illustrated with the story of the early Anabaptists. When J. W. Allen wrote that they "were persecuted as anarchists rather than heretics,"[3] he overlooked what he was otherwise well aware of, namely, the ambiguity of the distinction between the two in the sixteenth century and long after. The modern sense of separation of church and state (with its own ambiguities) could not be conceived of then. For the Anabaptists, separatism meant life in separate communities within which there would not be a state and a church, but one communal Christian life. Some were revolutionaries or secessionists; most were pacifists.[4] The one who had the most lasting effect, Menno Simons, strove for accommodation with the powers that be as long as his followers were allowed their pacifism.

Allen is right insofar as the Anabaptists' heretical ideas seemed to their contemporaries to disturb the foundations of civil order. Since the Anabaptists turned their backs on civil religious ceremonies and military participation, they must have looked to others what Christians had seemed to the Romans in pre-Constantinian times.

Ever since Karl Marx, the economic question has to be asked, and it should therefore be mentioned that most Anabaptists believed in holding goods in common, indubitably a strike against them.

To return to Dickens's remark, the main reason for the persecution of the Anabaptists, or at least the prima facie evidence against them, was that they refused to allow their children to be baptized and that they practiced adult baptism or rebaptism. Whether in Lutheran Germany or Zwinglian Zurich (or, for that matter, any Catholic territory), the ruthlessness of the persecution[5] for a violation of one of "the more delicate issues of sacramental theology" is remarkable and hard to explain, especially in view of the lack of scriptural proof texts against it, except for the politico-religious implications: One was baptized into a Christian society. To refuse baptism to a child was a political act of separation. For the Anabaptists, the church consisted of a remnant, a chosen few, and could not be associated with the state, which contained everyone.[6] Luther agreed and did not agree.

Within Roman Catholicism, there was more consistency related to the mixture of sacramental theology and the idea of *respublica christiana*, but the matter involved the Reformers in contradiction. Whatever the complexities of Luther's Zwei-Reiche-Lehre,[7] he believed "there are few true believers, and still fewer who live a Christian life, who do not resist evil and indeed do themselves no evil," and "the masses are and always will be un-Christian, even if they are all baptized and Christian in name." He admitted that "heresy can never be restrained by force" and that the temporal government's laws concern external affairs.[8] True, he later seems to have changed his mind and expected government action in matters of doctrine. Even early on, he asked the civil government to call a church council, the way that Constantine did the Nicene.[9]

Similarly, Calvin spoke of two kingdoms (regimes), one pertaining to the soul and eternal life, the other "only to the establishment of civil justice and outward morality." Yet, he went on, "civil government has its appointed end . . . to cherish and protect the outward worship of God, to defend sound doctrine of piety and the position of the church. . . ."[10] Generally, Calvin expressed himself more positively, Luther more negatively about the task of government as it pertains to the church,[11] but both confounded in conclusion what they separated in premise. Augustine preceded them in this confusion. In practice, Calvin inclined toward theocracy and Luther toward caesaropapism.

The Church of Rome, however, had its two-tiered hierarchy in society: clergy and laity, Christians all by baptism, the former directing the latter, who, because of their lower status, could perform worldly acts necessary to maintain the unity of faith and order. Heretics could be handed over to the magistrates for punishment. The church sanctioned the sword. True, bishops might take on direct civil powers, but the confusion existed on a practical level and not, as with the Reformers, in principle. The explanation lies in habits of thought. The Reformers were still partial captives of the spirit predominant in the millennium after Constantine.[12] Their writings, however, contained the seed that would grow to destroy this spirit. The trend was aided by secular factors: the demise of feudalism and its hierarchical structure, the growth of cities and universities not completely under the tutelage of castle and cathedral, and nationalism with its creation of centripetal forces competing with Rome for resources and allegiance. The trend was strengthened by the skepticism of nonbelievers and the convictions of radicals. The successes of the Counter-Reformation were a pyrrhic victory whose lack of staying power was in direct proportion to the level of the accompanying violence by the Inquisition and Philip II, for example.

If baptism was the sacrament most divisive within Protestantism, the Mass was the single most schismatic issue between the Church of Rome and the Protestants. The Reformers rejected its sacrificial nature. Luther called it "an atrocious carnival" and Calvin "idolatry." Yet, like baptism, the Lord's Supper had its political uses for Protestants.

In 1537, Calvin recommended a monthly communion from which those who were found unworthy would be barred. When the council decided a year later to admit all to the Lord's Supper, Calvin left Geneva. The point is important. Calvin wanted to establish the independence of the church in ecclesiastical matters, something that the council's decision contradicted. At the same time, he wanted a Christian society, upheld by his system of discipline, which was undermined if none could be denied access to the sacrament.[13] Here again, as in the case of baptism, contradiction arises. Things took a wrong turn in Geneva, and Calvin returned on request in 1541. Through the interaction of city council and church consistory, whose memberships overlapped, Calvin linked church and state.[14]

In the long and complicated history of the Reformation in England of the sixteenth and seventeenth centuries, the Lord's Supper also was prominent. Politically, its use was indirect: not belonging to the Church of England entailed civil disabilities. Membership was contingent on the correct view of the Last Supper, generally not held by Catholics and Nonconformists. The Acts of Uniformity show that the correct view changed repeatedly: its nonsacrificial but presence-in-body-and-blood nature, close to Luther's interpretation (1549); its more Zwinglian, commemorative concept (1552); both of the above in a purposely ambiguous wording under Elizabeth (1559); its 1549 understanding again (1662); and again, under the Test Act (1673), with an explicit declaration against transubstantiation. The sacrificial idea of the Mass was revived in the Anglo-Catholic movement under John Henry Newman and Edward B.

Pusey in the 1850s, but by this time the Nonconformists had finally been admitted to take degrees at Oxford and Cambridge—that is, establishmentarianism's last bastion had crumbled. In England of the sixteenth through eighteenth centuries, one's social status and rank were partly determined by one's stated convictions concerning the Lord's Supper.

Martin Luther and John Calvin:
The Peasants' Revolt and Michael Servetus

By consensus, the black page in Luther's life was his reaction to the Peasants' Revolt of 1525;[15] in Calvin's life, his execution of Servetus in 1553. This needs to be qualified by saying that these pages were not aberrations, but consistent with the general tendency of Luther's and Calvin's politico-religious views.

As elsewhere in Europe, the lot of the peasant in Germany had grown worse during the fourteenth century. This was primarily due to rising taxes and the shortage of land caused by an increasing population. The latter part of the fifteenth century had seen many peasant uprisings, but this time their cause was linked in their own minds with the Reformation. Its excesses were in part precipitated by the preaching of Thomas Müntzer, who wanted to establish the Kingdom of Saints through violent means. This was not reflected, however, in the peasants' "Twelve Articles." In their introduction to these articles, the peasants denied the charge that the gospel leads to rebellion.[16] The twelfth article stated that if any of the preceding ones "is not in agreement with the Word of God," it would be withdrawn. The articles primarily asked for correction of economic abuses and, in effect, for an end to the peasants' state of virtual slavery.

Luther's three writings in answer to the Twelve Articles and the peasant disturbances were consistent with his "Temporal Authority" of two years earlier in which he held the following:[17] (1) Temporal authority is from God and should be obeyed, but God should be obeyed above all. (This expresses a belief generally held throughout most of Protestantism's history and was mainly based on passages in Romans 13 and 1 Peter 2.) (2) Those who belong to the Kingdom of God do not resist evil and suffer injustice cheerfully. (Luther refers here to the Sermon on the Mount.) (3) Because not all of mankind lives accordingly, the sword of the magistrate keeps society from chaos. (4) The Christian should assist that sword: "No Christian shall wield or invoke the sword for himself and his cause. In behalf of another, however, he may and should wield it and invoke it to restrain wickedness and to defend godliness." (5) The laws of temporal government "extend no further than to life and property and external affairs on earth," and not to the soul. "Heresy can never be restrained by force." (6) A wise and upright prince is rare. (7) Passive resistance and the confession of truth are called for when the prince's command goes against God's word.

Here are all the ambiguities of Luther's position. However, Luther's treatise had to be stretched beyond its evident intention to support the peasants' position—namely, that they were justified in their demands for social justice if these demands were not contrary to Scripture. Therefore, his three writings against the peasants were not ad hoc reactions, but followed from his view that the Christian does not actively seek justice on his own behalf.

That Luther, though he changed, was more systematic and consistent than is generally supposed[18] is not saying very much, considering the inherent ambiguity of his original statements. The two focal questions concerning his position are (1) at what point does obedience to the prince become disobedience to God? and (2) where is the borderline between the two kingdoms? If on my own behalf I should not actively resist injustice, should I do so on behalf of the church? No. For Christians suffer cheerfully. Yes. For if my confession of the truth convinces the prince and he commands me to persecute heretics, I must be his constable and hangman. Is my group's (church's, nation's) behalf not my own behalf? Is godliness not my cause? In soul I belong to the Kingdom of God, in which I can be guided by the Sermon on the Mount in my relationship to others; as a temporal, natural person (*Weltperson*) I belong to the kingdom of the world, which has laws that regulate my relationship to others. How do I reconcile the two kinds of relationship?

There is nothing new in these dilemmas. The tension between Christ's law of love and the exigencies of law and order is as old as the church. The proof is finally in the pudding: the many different directions Luther might have taken after the early 1520s could be explained as "consistent" with his views in "Temporal Authority." The tension is partly resolved once the prince favors Lutheranism, since Luther favored suppression of divergent views. When the secular ruler commands one to side with the pope, one must disobey; when the ruler uses the sword against blasphemy (in support not only of the Second, but also the First Table of the Law), he does what is right. If a change took place in Luther, it was concerning the heretics and, thereby, concerning the differentiation of the two kingdoms. As with most other Reformers, he continued in the medieval view. Ultimately, this meant that the state supported the true religion with the sword. Public confession of divergent views became a civil crime.[19]

John Knox, in his arguments with Queen Mary, was therefore no extraordinary fanatic. When the queen asked, "Ye interprete the Scripturis in one manner, and thei [the pope and the cardinals] interprete it ane other; Whome shall I believe? And who shalbe judge?"[20] Knox had no doubt, and neither did Rome, Geneva, or Wittenberg. In the matter of revolt, Knox took matters further than Luther and Calvin, and agreed with Rome. Luther came to hold that the Lutheran prince is allowed to disobey the Catholic emperor. Calvin also made exception to the rule of obedience to the highest secular authority in his ephor argument, based on Greek and Roman precedent.[21] Knox's view was that the people should revolt if the prince is of a false religion, say, Catholicism. However tyrannical Knox's own full realization of political power might have become, there was a seed of democracy in his views. His tyrannicide differed from Rome's in that it knew no authority but Scripture, which Knox thought spoke plainly to every citizen.

One need not disagree with those historians who say that Luther was not Erastian or caesaropapist[22] to see in his writings a growing tendency toward a statist ecclesiastical authoritarianism and in Lutheranism in general a strand of absolutism that, in a time of crisis, could render the church *at best* politically impotent,[23] if not collaborationist, as was the case with the German National Church in the 1930s. This tendency was closely related to Luther's increasing political pessimism and Pietism. Pietism was neither original with nor limited to Lutheranism, which may have given it its major boost. It has its roots in medieval mysticism and is one of the many patterns in the history of Protestantism. In it, the tension between otherworldliness and political responsibility seems to be resolved: one is a good husband, father, and church member, as well as a patriotic citizen, pledging full allegiance to the state.

As to Calvin's Geneva and Michael Servetus, the other "black page" to be discussed—here, too, there is no aberration, as if it were a case contrary to expectation. Servetus's case is important, because in its notoriety it was a test that Calvin passed or failed according to whether one thought it right or wrong for an ecclesiastic to prevail on the secular ruler to condemn to death a person found guilty of strictly theologically heretical views. Servetus's burning was approved by other Reformed Swiss cities[24] and would have been approved by most rulers in Europe.[25] In addition, it strengthened Calvin's hand in the city. Servetus's crime was his heretical writing concerning the Trinity and infant baptism. His identity as the author was betrayed to the Catholic authorities in France by a friend of Calvin's. Servetus was arrested and, with further proof supplied by Calvin through his friend, sentenced to burning. When it came to great issues like the Trinity and baptism (although not, of course, the Eucharist), Calvin and Rome cooperated in seeing to it that heretics common to both would come to their just reward. Servetus escaped from the Inquisitors' hands and fled to Geneva, where he thought he could take on Calvin, who once again was in conflict with the city rulers. Calvin's earlier temporary exile from Geneva had been caused by his dis-agreements with the city council, which wanted to order certain religious practices. When he returned, he used his consistory (composed of minis-ters and prominent laymen) to conduct the godly life of the citizens, which included all dimensions of their moral life. The consistory made use of informers. The state-church distinction of the *Institutes* thus be-came blurred or, perhaps more accurately, the ambiguities of the church-state relationship in the *Institutes* are here resolved: the state is the executive, the church the legislative branch of government.[26] Geneva was somewhat of a city-state instance of Rome's *Unam Sanctam* universal Holy Empire.

With variations, this would be the theme played by the Puritans in England (against Erastianism) and New England (against other Dissent-ers, such as Baptists; and separatists, such as Quakers) and by Knox in Scotland (against the rival theocracy of Catholicism).

The Reformation and Natural Law

Reinhold Niebuhr concurred with Ernst Troeltsch that only with the aid of rationalistic political thought did religious idealism ever arrive at equalitarian political ideals. Niebuhr added that the idea of "the tran-scendent worth of all human personality" in Christian thought can be "transformed into the ideal of equal worth of all personalities."[27] Troeltsch wrote, more specifically, that "to a remarkable extent Calvin-ism more than Catholicism, and far more than Lutheranism, had pre-pared the way for the gradual emancipation of those theories [concern-ing Natural Law and democracy] from their connection with Christian thought, even though the Baptist movement was more radically effective in this direction."[28]

The sociopolitical question is complicated by the Weber-Tawney thesis concerning the relationship between Calvinism and capitalism. Briefly, Max Weber's thesis is that capitalism grew under the favorable influence of Calvinist/Puritan socioethical thought.[29] Troeltsch seems largely in agreement with Weber, but he qualified this by saying that "it was just because the economic conditions at Geneva were so bourgeois, and on such a small scale, that Capitalism was able to steal into the Calvinistic ethic, while it was rejected by the Catholic and Lutheran ethic."[30] Tawney criticized Weber's work because it did not take into account that the "capitalist spirit" was present in sixteenth-century territories that were Catholic, that Renaissance political thought (for example, Machiavelli's) was as potent a force as Calvin's, and that English seventeenth-century Puritanism (Weber's main source) cannot be equated with sixteenth-century Continental Calvinism.

Tawney instead put the relationship in largely negative terms: Protestantism in England maintained an attitude of dualism between the secular and religious aspects of life and judged economic behavior by different standards from those applied to spiritual well-being.[31] To speak of a Weber-Tawney thesis is to point to the fact that both men saw Calvinism as providing at least a stimulus to the spirit of capitalism.[32] In history there are few necessary causes and hardly any sufficient ones. Instead, there are mutually reinforcing conditions. J. W. Allen put it well: "The Reformation was part of the process by which Europe was resolved into a series of independent, secular, souvereign states."[33] Since the process itself remains undefined, it is perhaps best to see all terms in the formulation as interrelated and in turn related to such factors as economic emancipation, urbanization, and scientific and geographic discoveries.

The concept of Natural Law is an important thread in the changing political-religious tapestry under consideration here. Troeltsch pointed out that the Reformation idea of a natural order of sociopolitical relations differed from the medieval view, which held that these were under the church's control. Rather, the Reformation conceived of these relations— like "rain, storm, and wind"—as appointed by God as part of creation and known by reason. Luther, according to Troeltsch, increasingly saw government as a positive institution appointed by God and arising from Natural Law, and less and less in negative terms, as "due to sin."[34] This did not imply greater optimism or liberality on Luther's part. His natural sociopolitical state is Hobbesian.[35] He argued against the peasants that, aside from the scriptural admonitions of Romans 13 and 1 Peter 2, there is "the natural law of all the world, which says that no one may sit in judgment in his own case. . . ."[36]

Beyond the consensus that Natural Law equals the Second Table of the Decalogue, Luther held that authority is from God, is therefore a matter of Providence, and is therefore part of Nature. His co-Reformer Philipp Melanchthon justified the persecution of the Anabaptists by appeal to Natural Law, which desires the protection of religion. He thereby came close to identifying the First Table with Natural Law as well.[37]

Whatever the political practices favored by the Reformers, their thought expressed a new direction that did not lie in their view of the possibilities of human reason itself, for in this they could hardly outdo Thomas Aquinas, but in connecting reason, Natural Law, and Providence outside of an absolutized interpretation by the church. In theory at least, it thus became possible to advocate, say, freedom of religion on a purely nontheological basis, without thereby necessarily contradicting the ecclesiastical establishment. When Calvin wrote that "the law of God which we call the moral law is nothing else than the testimony of natural law and that of conscience which God has engraved upon the minds of Man,"[38] he undoubtedly thought that human conscience and Scripture are congruent. The same assumption underlies the arguments of John Knox and John Ponet when they appeal to the "Ethnicks" or "Ethnikes" (that is, the nations, the gentiles). Knox argued that princes (Mary, Queen of Scots in this case) are responsible for keeping their subjects in "equity and justice" and for maintaining "God's honor."[39] Ponet held that tyrannicide has historically occurred "by inward motion of God," although he cautions that it "cannot be maintained by God's Word, that any private man may kill."[40] Ponet was the first to advance the idea that Romans 13 should be interpreted to mean that one is subject to the powers that are from God and of which the princes are the executors.[41] That is to say, it is the office, not the person, that carries the authority. He believed that the Anabaptists went too far in their quest for the liberty of the Christian, forgetting thereby the Fall of man, while the "English papists" did not consider proper degrees of power.[42] A few years later, Christopher Goodman summed it up: "Therefore if the Magistrates would wholly despise and betray the justice and laws of God, you which are subjects with them shall be condemned except you maintain and defend the same laws against them, and all the others to the uttermost of your powers."[43]

The connection Reformation–Natural Law–democracy is now coming to the surface, but in practice it was partly submerged again under theocratic governments, as was the case in Puritan New England. The growth of democracy was aided by increasing secularization, which in turn is related to the idea of Natural Law, at least as it developed in Protestant regions. When Calvin discussed forms of government, he did so under the aegis of "divine providence" (seen in Natural Law and human conscience): "divine providence has wisely arranged that various countries should be ruled by various kinds of government." However, he believed that "a system compounded of aristocracy and democracy far excells all others."[44]

Like the Reformers, Oliver Cromwell also believed that the Law of Nature is expressed in the Second Table of the Decalogue. According to Troeltsch, "Cromwell believed that it was possible to combine the *salus publica* of the Natural Law with the Christian idea of salvation, and with this idea of the Christian state he combined a relatively modern and liberal and utilitarian system of politics."[45] The neo-Calvinism of Abraham Kuyper in nineteenth-century Holland held a liberal Natural Law conception of secular affairs, quite unlike Calvin and, of course, after de facto democratization.

Instead of democracy, however, post-Reformation Europe saw royal absolutism in most of its states most of the time during the seventeenth and eighteenth centuries. Theology often acquiesced or supported the monarchies, as was the case with Catholicism in the France of Louis XIV, XV, and XVI, Anglicanism in Restoration England, and Lutheranism in Germany under Friedrich the Great. But there also were marked changes from earlier times. The major change was the increasing emancipation of political thought from theology and the utilitarian view of religion in regard to the state. One reason Machiavelli's *The Prince* (1513) was so ill-received was that in his time political theory was considered a branch of theology. During the Enlightenment, religion was seen as a branch of statecraft. Whereas one can only guess at the degree of theological commitment in the political deliberations of, say, Elizabeth I or Philip of Hesse, in the case of Friedrich the Great or Napoleon the attitude was, if not cynical, purely utilitarian. The concept of Natural Law provided the starting point, although it was, of course, not meant as such by Aquinas or the Reformers.

Natural Law, of course, was a concept central to John Locke's ethical theory and figured in *The Reasonableness of Christianity*.[46] Published in 1665, when political absolutism was past its peak in England, the book argued that if theology can no longer validate political practice, then the "divine right of kings" has no basis. This meant that the political absolutism of the Enlightenment was rootless before it had even ripened.

Jean-Paul Sartre has said it well that the nonbelieving philosophes thought they could inherit the moral structure of Christian tradition without its theism.[47] The idea of Natural Law carried Christian conceptions of the state into a secularized political world. Combined with natural religion, it justified deistic notions of a civil religion. But the existence of God was not the issue; rather, it was that politics had its own reasons, and a despot would be more or less tolerant, more or less latitudinarian, according to the necessities of the state. The long-lasting establishmentarianism in republican or parliamentarian systems was partly due to this perception, as well as to the vested interests of the castes. The civil disabilities attending improper religious belief in England for more than three centuries after the Reformation were increasingly based on hypocrisy, although the worst times for Nonconformists or Dissenters were those when the establishers of belief were perhaps least hypocritical.

England

William Tyndale, the Bible translator, wrote *Obedience of a Christian Man* (1528), in which he argued that the pope and his bishops had taken the sword from the king and made magistrates "hangmen unto the pope."[48] The fact that Henry VIII had changed matters by declaring himself "Supreme Head of the Church" did not help Tyndale because his Bible translation and reformed ideas were not welcome in England. He was strangled and burned at the stake by "hangmen unto the pope" in Brussels.

The English Parliament ratified Henry's declaration in the Act of Supremacy (1534). The Reformation did not get very far in England under Henry VIII because his views were altogether Roman Catholic. The supremacy theory was explained by his apologists in such language as: the Church of England is a national branch of the Church Catholic (Stephen Gardiner); and the people of a realm constitute the church, and the prince speaks for that church and interprets Scripture (St. Germain). Thomas More did not concur and on account of that was accused of high treason and beheaded.

Tyndale's importance for the Puritan cause was his view that Scripture should rule the church, a view that recurs time and again, the assumption being that Scripture is plain and not what the Church of England adheres to. Under the brief reign of Edward VI (1547–53)—that is, the Protectorate of Somerset and Northumberland—it seemed that the Reformation would get under way, but the equally short reign of Mary I turned things Catholic again, with papal authority restored by Parliament. Church property, however, was not restored.

In the long reign of Elizabeth (1558–1603), a temporary equilibrium was achieved. A new Supremacy Act made the queen supreme governor of the church. It was a step down from Henry's supreme head, but she still appointed bishops who were responsible to her. Puritans were allowed to preach as long as they did not meddle in matters of politics or church polity. The Elizabethan Settlement interlaced church and state. Apologists for the status quo, like Richard Hooker, attempted to show that the Christian Commonwealth is in effect the church, and that Parliament is its representative. Only if the law of the land is *demonstrably* against the law of God and the law of reason is there cause for dissent. Hooker came close to equating the two laws, in the manner discussed in connection with Natural Law. Other than by such demonstration, dissent is a crime against the state.

But the Elizabethan Settlement was no settlement, because the Puritans were not appeased and the contradiction between episcopacy and royal supremacy remained.[49] Perhaps Allen was asking too much: Puritans would not be satisfied until they had their own settlement. In addition, in one form or another the contradiction was as old as Constantinian Christianity, whether the pope crowned the king or the king appointed the bishops, or both.

The Puritans were not separatists. They wanted a Church of England where authority rested in Scripture, that is, in themselves who read what Scripture plainly said. One of their grievances concerned the liturgy, especially the use of "idolatrous gear" (vestments). Six of them were called before the Ecclesiastical Commission in London in 1567, because they did not worship in their parish churches.[50] The six claimed that parish services were papist and idolatrous. The bishop, the mayor, and the dean in the commission responded that the things pertaining to ceremony were "indifferent," neither prescribed nor proscribed by Scripture, and that the queen had authority to order them. The accused said that the "things indifferent" darkened the light of the gospel. The dean replied: "But who will you have to be the judge of the word of God?" The Puritans said: "This is what the papists in Queen Mary's time said." They concluded by saying: "We will be tried by the best reformed churches. The Church of Scotland has the word truly preached. . . ."

The crux of the matter was the same as in the debate between John Knox and young Mary, Queen of Scots. Knox and the Presbyterians succeeded (where the Puritans in England failed) because in Scotland, Mary's marital ties with French Catholicism were unacceptable, both on nationalistic and religious grounds. Elizabeth's "settlement" worked in that she kept the upper hand for the length of her nearly half-century reign. This was partly a result of the relative weakness of the Presbyterian-inclined Puritans and the leeway Elizabeth allowed them in preaching and pamphleteering. For the separatists (the Brownists), things were more precarious.

Robert Browne, in *A Treatise of Reformation Without Tarrying Any* (1583), demanded a break with the church's traditional hierarchical organization. The Brownists were the first Congregationalists. In many ways they wanted to separate the church and the state; yet they maintained that it was the magistrate's duty to suppress false religion.[51] In sixteenth-century England, the contradiction (again) seemed to go unnoticed, except by the Anabaptists.

The early seventeenth century saw the emergence of the Baptist separatist movement under the leadership of John Smyth. Congregationalism of a Calvinist, nonseparatist character also had its beginnings then. The pressures at home eventually led three different groups to seek a haven in the New World. The Puritans, who rejected royal supremacy but in principle recognized the Church of England, settled the Massachusetts Bay colony. The separatist Pilgrims settled in Plymouth. The Baptists went to Rhode Island. The form of church government in all of New England was Congregationalist. (These American developments will be considered later.)

From its establishment under Henry VIII on, the Church of England prevailed, with the exception of the last six turbulent years of the reign of Charles I (1643–49) when Parliament against the wishes of the crown exchanged the episcopal system for the synodical one. In the first year of the Commonwealth (Cromwell) it reversed itself, fearing a Presbyterian-Puritan takeover that, in its view, would have landed England from the Erastian frying pan into the theocratic fire. The fact that many in Cromwell's army were independents and Baptists had much to do with the decision, forcing Parliament to a greater amount of tolerance than the Presbyterians had in mind.

James Nichols wrote: "The Dutch were to the seventeenth century what the English were to the eighteenth and the Americans to the nineteenth—the working model of free institutions."[52] As to the Netherlands, that model was shaky in the first quarter of the seventeenth century when religious controversy between orthodox Calvinists and Arminians[53] became explicitly political and eventually led to banishment of the Arminians and imprisonment of Grotius, one of their spokesmen. Although the death in 1625 of Maurice of Orange, the political leader of the national Calvinist party, meant greater toleration, the religious consequences of his coup d'état were an inauspicious beginning of that working model. Comparatively speaking, Holland was perhaps a "political oasis of constitutional liberties," and out of the struggle between "the theocratic predestinarians and Arminian Erastians was evolved at last the confessional neutrality of the state."[54] Nonetheless, the Arminians had to wait till 1795 for official recognition.[55] Still, Holland was a refuge for religious dissenters, especially Puritans and separatists from England and Huguenots from France. Descartes fled there too, as did Spinoza.

As to eighteenth-century Georgian England, Parliament gained in strength, but the ties between episcopacy and monarchy were strong and had long historical precedent. Political offices and sinecures may have more and more accrued to the laity, but the bishops' bench in Parliament kept a voting eye on the ecclesiastical preferments and benefices bestowed by the monarchy.[56] Nichols's "working model" here sits under the long shadow of an aristocratic-oligarchic alliance of landed gentry and bishops, the latter usually being part of the former. There was greater toleration for some, but not for all. Nonconformists of any stripe suffered second-class status.[57] The Occasional Conformity Act of 1711 lasted only seven years and was meant to prevent Dissenters from circumventing the Test Act (in order to hold government posts) by receiving the sacrament in the Church of England (thereby occasionally conforming). King George I also repealed the Schism Act, which forbade Dissenters to have their own schools.

Despite the Enlightenment views that were a prominent part of the intellectual life of eighteenth-century England in the form of Latitudinarianism[58] and Deism, in 1771 Parliament rejected a petition asking that reason and conscience rather than creed interpret the Bible.[59] One notable opponent to the petition was David Hume. His *Dialogues Concerning Natural Religion* was an attack on Deism, but his philosophy was thoroughly skeptical. His opposition can be regarded as an expression of his doubts concerning a reasonable approach to Scripture. He did support an attempt to have the Test Act repealed, but the motion failed to pass Parliament. In England's age of reason, then, the Church of England was firmly established, and church and state were as far from separation as ever.

The Methodist and Evangelical reactions against the formalist ecclesiology and theological liberalism in the Church of England can be characterized, respectively, as Pietist and literalist movements. The influence of the brothers Wesley and George Whitefield was profound. Whitefield, during his preaching journey in the United States, was a considerable force in the Great Awakening. John Wesley, like his fellow Pietists in Germany, was politically conservative (a tory) and supporter of the Hanoverian Church of England. Yet he had doctrinal differences with that church which primarily concerned his belief in perfectionism of motives. Tied to this belief was his Arminianism, which conflicted with Whitefield's Calvinism. Methodism was eventually split off from the Anglican

communion, while the Evangelicals under the leadership of William
Wilberforce remained within it. Methodists provided the main impetus
to home and foreign missions. Home missions were important in reaching the increasing number of urban industrial workers, although, again
as in Lutheran Germany, many workers were alienated from the church's
political conservatism. Foreign missions went hand in hand with the
growth of England's world empire.

The Post-Reformation Continent

The post-Reformation developments on the Continent took many forms,
but they were basically a three-way contest between Catholic, Lutheran,
and Calvinist forces, either for dominance or, if that could not be had, for
tolerance. The Peace of Augsburg (1555) settled the war between the
Lutheran princes and Charles V, the Holy Roman emperor. The principle
cujus regio ejus religio (whose the region, his the religion) generally meant
banishment for those whose religion was not the prince's. At that peace,
Calvinists were excluded, but a century later they received the same
rights at the Peace of Westphalia (1648), which ended the most devastat-
ing intra-Christian religious war of modern history. A significant episode
of the earlier war was Luther's and Melanchthon's approval of Philip of
Hesse's bigamy; they did so with theological rationalization of Old Testament polygamy and political pragmatism that the Lutheran cause could
not afford to lose Philip's allegiance, for he was the protagonist in the
struggle against the emperor's attempt to extirpate the Lutheran heresy.

    The Thirty Years War was indubitably a contributing factor in the rise
of Pietism, which was a reaction against dogmatic disputes, academic
theology, and external ritual. It aimed for a religion close to the heart and
home, emotionally warm, confessionally simple, and ethically pure. It
gained particular momentum in the later seventeenth century and early
eighteenth century under the stimulus of P. J. Spener and A. H. Francke.
It was generally apolitical, which in practice meant that its acquiescence
tended to support the conservative status quo. In the mid-eighteenth
century, Count Zinzendorf brought into Pietism a note of pride in German national consciousness, and after the turn of the nineteenth century, Schleiermacher (who also must be reckoned in the Pietist tradition) preached enthusiastic sermons to the soldiers called up to fight
Napoleon.[60]

    K. S. Pinson claimed too much when he wrote that "the growth of a
political philosophy of nationalism would hardly be possible without the

previous growth of an intense spirit of individualism,"[61] but there are certainly links between Pietism and Romanticism, and between Romanticism and nationalism.

In the eighteenth century, Friedrich the Great tightened his control over the Prussian Lutheran church. Pietism's emphasis on inwardness left politics, and often church polity, to the princes. Thus, Schleiermacher wrote:

> That a Church is nothing but a communion or association relating to religion or piety, is beyond all doubt for us Evangelical Christians, since we regard it as equivalent to degeneration in a Church when it begins to occupy itself with other matters as well. . . . We would not keep the leaders of State from fixing the outward relations of the religious communions according to the principles of civil organization—which, however, in no means implies that the religious communion is a product of the State or a component part of it.[62]

A century later, there was an echo of this sentiment in Wilhelm II's exclamation: "Political pastors—an absurdity. . . . 'Social Christianity' is nonsense. . . ."[63]

The other side of the coin is that Pietism was a force against civil religion. Besides, as Pinson pointed out, in Wesleyanism and German Pietism there was a concern with social welfare and education, which coincided with the increasing lack of these in the growing cities. The channels for social improvement, however, were apolitical.

Repression or tolerance in the eighteenth and nineteenth centuries was largely a matter of political expediency. In Germany the "absorption of the church into the civil bureaucracy" continued to increase during those centuries. By the mid-nineteenth century, "German Protestantism was identified almost wholly with political absolutism and economic landlordism. The new social classes, on the other hand, and the new movements of liberalism and constitutionalism, as well as of socialism and communism, were forced into an antichurch position."[64] Schleiermacher objected to the episcopal rights of the territorial princes, but the tendency continued of a state-controlled church imposed by police power.

Under the Catholic Habsburgs, the Reformed church in Hungary and Transylvania was persecuted, especially during the reign of Maria Theresa. After her death in 1780, there was toleration. But in the mid-nineteenth century, persecution was resumed in the Austrian half of the Dual Monarchy.

In the sketchy portrayal thus far, there is little to support the notion that either tolerance or democracy was a *direct* result of the Reformation.

When religious equality before the law became constitutional in the United States, the Deists and the minority offshoots of the Reformation were its main proponents.

United States

Georg Jellinek of Heidelberg wrote in 1901: "The idea of legally establishing inalienable, inherent and sacred rights of the individual is not of political but religious origin. What has been held to be the work of the Revolution was in reality the fruit of the Reformation and its struggles. Its first apostle was not Lafayette but Roger Williams, who, driven by powerful and deep religious enthusiasm, went into the wilderness in order to found a government of religious liberty, and his name is uttered by Americans even today with the deepest respect."[65]

Jellinek gave Roger Williams too much credit, but in the case of disestablishment and separation of church and state, Williams was preeminent in the American colonies. His book *The Bloudy Tenent of Persecution* was published in 1644, the same year as John Milton's *Areopagitica* (in defense of freedom of the press) and five years before Milton's *The Tenure of Kings and Magistrates* (in defense of the cause of independents). Williams objected to the Puritan state-church system: the oaths required to keep dissidents in check and civil enforcement of the Ten Commandments. He compared the church, whether of true or false worship, to a college of physicians or the East India Company:

> which companies may hold their counts, keep their records, hold disputations; and in matters concerning their society, may dissent, divide, break into schisms and factions, and implead each other at the law, yea wholly break up and dissolve into pieces and nothing, and yet the peace of the city not be in the least measure impaired or disturbed; because the essence or being of the city, and so the well-being and peace thereof is essentially distinct from those particular societies; the city courts, city laws, city punishments distinct from theirs.[66]

He compared the church to a ship on which the magistrate is a passenger and the church officers are the captain and sailors.[67] John Cotton's answer to Williams's initial writing against persecution for the sake of conscience was included in *The Bloudy Tenent*, and the book was addressed to the English Parliament in a dedication. It was a long response to Cotton.[68]

After having been banished from the Massachusetts Bay colony by Cotton, Williams settled Providence, Rhode Island. He was the apostle of toleration and separatism in the colonies. Before Milton, precedent was set in England as early as 1611 when the Baptists wrote in a Confession of Faith: "The Magistrate is not to meddle with religion or matters of conscience. . . ."[69]

According to T. G. Sanders, Williams's views were close to the Mennonite belief that a Christian should shun participation in civil government and that the government in turn has no stake in religion.[70] If Sanders is correct, Williams therefore also contributed to the religious tradition in the United States that wants to keep the church out of politics. This assessment would limit Williams's influence to the American political ideal of the right to religious freedom, which is no small matter, but less than Jellinek claims for him.

The Puritans had set up their state church in Boston. They had not been separatists in England (unlike the Pilgrims in next-door Plymouth with whom they united in 1692) and wanted to establish the church as the Anglican church was established in England, but according to their own views. For most of the colonial period, the region was a theocracy, with this difference—that the elders could not be magistrates and vice versa.[71] The meetinghouse was both church and town hall. Only church members had suffrage rights. Nonchurch members had to pay taxes for the church's support and had to attend church services. When four Baptists were hanged in Boston in 1661, King Charles II protested.[72] After 1689, Dissenters could appeal to England's Toleration Act, and in the eighteenth century there was, in effect, toleration for most. The Anglican establishment in seventeenth-century Virginia was equally intolerant. The difference was that whereas "in Virginia the state controlled the church, in Massachusetts the church tended to control the state."[73]

Because of his policy of toleration, William Penn, a Quaker, made Pennsylvania the most religiously diverse colony. In his Frame of Government of 1682, he wrote: "All persons who profess to believe in Jesus Christ the Saviour of the World, shall be capable to serve this government in any capacity, both legislatively and executively."[74] That, of course, left out Deists and Jews, but since there was no establishment, it went beyond the toleration of most colonies in the eighteenth century, where civil disabilities still attended nonconformity. Disestablishment came to Massachusetts last, in 1833. By this time and ever since the Revolution, establishment had become a dead letter, except for the matter of a tax-supported ministry.

Tolerance, then, came first by way of the Baptist Williams and the Quaker Penn in colonies that had no established church. But nowhere in the colonial period was there ever the assumption that the country was not Christian or that non-Christians had the same rights as Christians or that the state could not legislate laws against blasphemy or the disturbance of the sabbath.

In Virginia first, under the leadership of Thomas Jefferson and James Madison, religious freedom and equality before the law were put into a Bill of Rights (1785). Madison wrote: "The right of every man is to liberty—not toleration." The distinction had been preached before by the Presbyterian John Witherspoon and the Baptist Isaac Backus; by Witherspoon (a Calvinist) in resisting the Anglican establishment in Virginia, by Backus in refusing to pay taxes to the Congregationalists (Calvinists) in Massachusetts.[75]

Virginia's constitution became the model for the federal one, whose Sixth Article reads in part: "no religious test shall ever be required as a qualification to any office or public trust under the United States" (1789). The First Amendment in the Bill of Rights states: "Congress shall make no law respecting an establishment of religion, or prohibiting the free exercise thereof; or abridging the freedom of speech, or of the press; or the right of the people peaceably to assemble, and to petition the Government for a redress of grievances" (1791). The clause, "no person religiously scrupulous shall be compelled to bear arms," proposed by Virginia and Carolina, was not included.

Estimates vary, but only a small proportion of the population of the United States at the time of the Constitution's framing were members of a church.[76] The separation of church and state was due to Deists (who were in the majority among the writers of the Constitution) and the pressure of churches in most places where they were not part of the established church. The Puritans' contribution in this respect is at best indirect. Their part in the political ideals embodied in the Constitution and its amendments is in their tradition of the right to rebellion and its implications. Thomas Hooker (no relation to Richard Hooker) can be taken as an example. He fled England and by way of Holland joined the Massachusetts Bay colony in 1633. He advocated general suffrage and anticipated Rousseau in his compact (contract) theory of the state and the idea of popular sovereignty. In the matter of church and state relations, Hooker was traditionalist: "Civil power has a nourishing and preserving faculty of Ecclesiastical Orders, Officers, and their several operations. . . . Civil power may compel Ecclesiastical persons to do what they ought in their offices, but does not confer their Offices upon them."[77]

With the Constitution and the Bill of Rights, a chapter ended resoundingly, but the story of church and state, religion and politics in the United

States continued. The issues became more ambiguous now that the letter of the law had made the break clear. Strangely enough, New York denied public office to Catholics till 1806, North Carolina to atheists till the late nineteenth century; New Hampshire, Connecticut, and Massachusetts kept their establishment well into the nineteenth century.

It soon became clear in the new nation that the state would have to become involved in church-related affairs. Thus, when Richard Allen founded the African Methodist Episcopal Church in 1816, in the Bethel Church of Philadelphia (the church building having been financed with funds Allen raised), the Methodist denomination claimed the church as part of itself and its jurisdiction. The U.S. Supreme Court ruled in favor of Bethel.[78]

Many cases that came before the Supreme Court dealt with religion in the public schools. In the landmark case *McCollum* v. *Board of Education* (1948), the Court ruled in favor of McCollum and against the use of public school buildings and time for religious instruction. In *Zorach* v. *Clawson* (1952), the court allowed for release time for pupils to be given religious instruction in other buildings by nonpublic school instructors.[79] *Engel* v. *Vitale* (1962) became the precedent for banning prayer from public schools. The Court ruled in *Everson* v. *Board of Education* (1947) that a state can finance bus transportation to parochial schools.

The Everson and Zorach rulings, and the fact that at about that time President Harry S. Truman sent an ambassador to the Vatican, contributed to the founding of Protestants and Other Americans United for Separation of Church and State (POAU). The organization's name and the title of a book by Paul Blanshard, one of its associates, *American Freedom and Catholic Power* (1949), indicate the real issue behind the stated one of separation. Up till the pontificate of John XXIII, the Catholic Church maintained that when in the majority it favored establishment, when in the minority separation. This did not make things easier for Catholics like the Jesuit John Courtney Murray, who fought for an interpretation of Catholic doctrine allowing for freedom of religion.[80] He was not greatly appreciated by Rome.[81]

Martin Marty observed that "Americans succeeded in creating a legal nonestablishment, even as they saw to the development of a *de facto* establishment whose security lay in the ethos, customs, habits, and practices of popular government."[82] The "Righteous Empire" in the title of Marty's book refers to "a kind of public and semi-political counterpart to the religious ideal of the Kingdom of God." One might add that this counterpart is a civil religion. The pervasiveness of this civil religion accounts for the fact that the matters of prayer, Bible reading, and (Protestant) religious instruction in public schools were not brought to court until the mid-twentieth century. Marty noted that the sociopolitical ethos of Protestantism in the United States expresses a pseudo-separatist position, which in fact rests on the understanding of a fundamental fusion of religion and culture in an Americanism of values that are capitalist, individualist, pro-Social Darwinist, anti-Darwinist, etc. Thus, the POAU took no issue with Sunday laws, prayer in public schools (or in sports arenas, Congress, and civic conventions), the national motto "In God We Trust," the mention of God in the Pledge of Allegiance, and other manifestations of the prevailing religious ethos.[83] The POAU's separatism was an attempt to keep alien (say, Catholic) influences separate from the mainstream. Earlier, such motivations can be found in the Alien and Sedition Acts passed by Congress in 1798, when there was a great influx of Irish immigrants, and in the nativist and Know-Nothing movements of the 1850s.

T. J. Sanders characterized the situation in the nineteenth century as follows:

> The vitality bestowed on the churches by the legal status of disestablishment and the religious commitment to voluntarism expressed itself in the evangelical and social fervor of the nineteenth century, making it the "great century" of Christianity. But there was a fateful flaw in this development. For the churches looked back to the fleshpots of Egypt, their established status, and acted on the assumption that this was a Protestant nation by symbolizing their religious commitment in political form and by imposing Protestant moral norms on the nation as a whole. Not only did the churches try to recover the privileges eliminated by the First Amendment, but government as well sought a religious sanction for its ambivalent enterprises by promoting public religion.[84]

And there was—and to a degree still is—such a public religion, whether the country was largely unchurched as in 1800, or churched as in 1900. Its effect was felt in what Alexis de Tocqueville called the tyranny of the majority:

> I am not so much alarmed at the excessive liberty which reigns in that country the United States, as at the inadequate securities which one finds there against tyranny. . . . I know of no country in which there is so little independence of mind and real freedom of discussion as in America. . . . In America, the majority raises formidable barriers around the liberty of opinion: within these barriers, an author may write what he pleases; but woe to him if he goes beyond them. . . . It seems at first sight as if all the minds of the Americans were formed upon one model, so accurately do they follow the same route.[85]

Other visitors saw it too. Harriet Martineau wrote about the clergy's "idolatry of opinion . . . self-exiled from the great moral questions of time," and Francis Trollope observed in 1830 that the absence of a national religion in America did not mean the absence of religious tyranny.[86]

A concrete example is the fate of the Mormons.[87] The Church of Jesus Christ of Latter-Day Saints was founded in 1830 by Joseph Smith, who claimed that the *Book of Mormon* was a supplementary revelation to the Bible. The Mormons were hounded from place to place. In Missouri in 1834 their printing shop was burned and their bishop tarred-and-feathered. When their appeals to the government and to President Andrew Jackson failed, they set up a militia and in a clash four years later, seventeen Mormons were killed. The *Book of Mormon* enjoined monogamy, but Joseph Smith claimed that a new revelation in 1843 established polygamy. The persecution due to popular hostility dated from before that revelation, although Smith's practice of polygamy (he had twenty-eight wives) probably added to the furor. He and his brothers were killed by a mob in 1844. Brigham Young led the Mormons to Utah, and President James K. Polk appointed him governor of that territory. In 1878 the U.S. Supreme Court ruled against polygamy, stating that "to permit religious beliefs to justify polygamy would be to make the professed doctrines of religious belief superior to the law of the land and would in effect permit every citizen to become a law unto himself."[88] Subsequent rulings forced the Mormons to abandon polygamy. The matter of polygamy may illustrate the knottiness of the question of how far the law is guided by a prevailing ethos in deciding what is the social good, but the state's reluctance to protect the safety of a sect far outside the mainstream exemplifies the power of opinion over legal separation.

In the nineteenth century, "Protestantism presented a massive, almost unbroken front in its defense of the social status quo," while social, economic, and political issues were professed to be of no concern to the churches.[89] The Scopes trial of 1925 proved that the trend continued into the twentieth century. In the socioeconomic realm, according to Marty, "the minister and theologian of evangelism progressively identified with competitive individualism at the expense of the community."[90] Liston Pope's study of the 1920s showed that virtually no ministers had made clear and definite statements concerning child labor, the mill village system, wages and hours, or other social questions.[91] There is, then, a kind of civil religion that crosses denominational and interfaith boundaries and that, insofar as it does not completely identify with its host culture, draws quietistically inward. Thus, Billy Graham wrote *Peace with*

God, Bishop Fulton Sheen *Peace of Soul,* and Rabbi Joshua Liebman *Peace of Mind,* indications of a premillenarian escape from the world "even as they implied that serene souls would help to transform it."[92]

An opposing but far less pervasive trend in American Christianity is what H. Richard Niebuhr called "Transformationism." The Puritan roots of this lie in theocratic New England. In the late nineteenth and early twentieth centuries, Transformationism's most prominent spokesman was Walter Rauschenbusch. This is somewhat ironic because he was in most ways not the theological heir of orthodox Calvinism. In *A Theology for the Social Gospel,* he wrote: "The individualistic gospel has taught us to see the sinfulness of every human heart and has inspired us with faith in the willingness and power of God to save every human soul that comes to him. But it has not given us an adequate understanding of the sinfulness of the social order and its share in the sins of all individuals within it."[93] Rauschenbusch argued against a Christianity that had aligned itself with autocratic capitalist organization. As James Nichols noted: "While churchmen and theologians urged charity, they were careful also to warn any businessman who might be tempted that charity should not adulterate the competition for property or the determination of the wage level. So Horace Busnell expressed himself. The *Presbyterian Quarterly* considered that since poverty was generally the consequence of vice, it should be treated as a crime. Henry Ward Beecher was confident of the general truth that no man suffered from poverty in the United States except as a result from sin."[94]

This attitude runs counter to what Paul Tillich called the Protestant Principle, which, in the vein of the Old Testament Prophets' attack on the religious and social order of their times, continually seeks to reveal the ideological underpinnings of the prevailing religio-political viewpoint. Tillich stressed in particular the alienation of the proletariat from a Protestantism that had become an ideology of the bourgeoisie.[95] Reinhold Niebuhr, both in connection with the Depression in the United States and the rise of Nazi Germany, criticized the failure of Protestantism in its defeatist attitude vis-à-vis social and political problems.[96] After World War II, one "Transformationist" voice was the journal *Christianity and Crisis,* edited by John Bennett of Union Theological Seminary. It sought to assert a theological stand in matters of public policy.

In a wide theological spectrum of social activism, churches participated in the civil rights and peace movements of the 1960s. The state responded by infiltrating church groups with undercover agents. The pretext was presumed illegal activity by these groups, but the government acted in the spirit of the prevailing civil religion whose tradition of separatism was one-sided. In 1986, a civil lawsuit was filed in the federal district court in Phoenix by six Lutheran and Presbyterian churches. It alleged that the federal government behaved unconstitutionally in its undercover investigation of these churches. The judge of the district court ruled against the plaintiffs. The issue related to the Sanctuary movement and went on to a court of appeals.[97]

Thus the story continues.

Karl Barth and Reinhold Niebuhr

In the late nineteenth century the German Chancellor Otto von Bismarck wanted the church to leave politics alone. But he did not want the state to leave the church alone. The May Laws of 1873 regulated the education and placement of ministers. This was part of the Kulturkampf whose main target was the Catholic Church, which Bismarck perceived as an impediment to German unity because of Catholic support for the rights of the individual principalities. He received much opposition from Rome, but later on came to an understanding with Pope Leo XIII on the basis of their common hatred of socialism. As to the Lutherans, in 1879 the Supreme Church Council ordered all ministers to refrain from political activity. Adolf Stoecker and Friedrich Naumann, both political activists, resigned their pastorates. Stoecker identified with the Junker class of landowners against the rising industrial leadership. Naumann was a Bismarckian militarist who encouraged the armaments program in preparation for World War I. Others, like the Swiss social reformer and pacifist Leonhard Ragaz,[98] were active in the Christian socialist movement, akin to England's Church Socialist League and Rauschenbusch's social gospel in the United States.[99]

Hitler's rise to power and his dealings with the churches have to be seen in the light of the national and nationalistic Landeskirchen (Lutheran, Reformed, and United Evangelical), which were generally inclined to an apolitical stand or, in the case of the inception of World War I, an enthusiastic support of the monarchy's war effort: "Für Gott und König." In the early 1930s the Nazis organized a church party, the "Evangelical Nazis" or "German Christians," which began to nationalize the churches into one united arm of the state, purified of all Jews and Jewishness. For this effort to work, the Old Testament had to be dropped and the New Testament somewhat revised. The new national church proclaimed: "In Hitler Christ, God the helper and redeemer, has become strong among us." It was in the context of these events that representatives of a sizable minority opposition (the Confessing Church) to the German Christians met at Barmen in 1934, under the leadership of Hans Asmussen and Martin Niemöller. Karl Barth had been appointed to write a declaration, which was approved.[100]

The Barmen Declaration theologically affirmed the Reformation principle of gospel authority as attested in the Bible. It rejected the following doctrines: (1) there are other sources of proclamation, (2) there are areas of life under other lords than Jesus Christ, (3) the church can change its message according to "currently reigning ideological and political convictions," (4) apart from its ministry, the church has special leaders, (5) the state can absorb the functions of the church, or the church the functions of the state, (6) the church can be put at the service of arbitrarily chosen purposes.

Reinhold Niebuhr criticized Barth for his early Lutheran politico-theological pessimism and passivity, which rendered the German churches vulnerable to Nazi domination.[101] The criticism may be justified, but the rise of National Socialism provided Barth with the impetus for a number of positive essays: "Gospel and Law" (1935), "Church and State" (1938), and "The Christian Community and the Civil Community" (1946).[102]

In "Church and State," Barth observed that Luther and Calvin had spoken clearly about the independence of the two spheres of church and state, but not about their relationship. He criticized the post-Reformation phenomena of both Pietism and its failure to engage theology in the problem of social issues, and the secular Enlightenment gospel of justice.[103] He wrote: "For us the fulfilment of political duty means rather responsible decision about the validity of laws, responsible care for their maintenance, in a word, political action, which may and must also mean political struggle."[104] Here, and in "Christian Community and Civil Community," he stressed that the concept of the Kingdom of God implies neither a Christian withdrawal from politics, nor a promise of the identification of the Kingdom of God and the state, but rather that the state is an analogue of that Kingdom of God which the church proclaims. In that understanding, "the poor, the socially and economically weak and threatened, will always be the object of its primary and particular concern, and it will always insist on the State's special responsibility for these weaker members of society."[105] As other consequences of this understanding, Barth mentioned equality before the law for all (he explicitly mentioned women); the lack of secret policies and diplomacies; the rule of *ultima ratio regum* for violent solutions of any conflict; democracy; and ecumenicity in politics as in theology (against nationalist or ecclesiastic parochialism). Against those who want "to keep the church out of politics," he wrote: "It is a bad sign when Christians are frightened by 'political' sermons—as if Christian preaching could be anything but political. And if it were not political, how would it show that it is the salt and the light of the world?"[106] Barth's statements concerning church-state relations, however, were not always unambiguous, and he was particularly criticized for his refusal to condemn Soviet communism under Stalin.[107]

From the sixteenth century through most of the eighteenth, the central question in state-church relations was freedom of religion. After separation and disestablishment, the emphasis shifted to matters of conflict or agreement in civil and religious responsibilities. Theological debate began to focus on action in the realm of political freedom and justice. In Barth's work, the early and late concerns were linked: his central demand is that the church be left free, but it needs to be free so that it can be the salt of the world.

At all times, the command of obedience to secular authority has been qualified by *nisi cum jubent peccare* (unless they command to sin) or that one should obey God more than man. However, for Luther this might mean the keeping of a Bible in a German translation, while for Knox it might demand a popular uprising against a "papist" regime. In the twentieth century the question is raised whether a church's acquiescence in economic colonialism or in apartheid, for example, is not actually obeying man against God. Still, what is there that acquiescing does not entail?

It was Reinhold Niebuhr's opinion that it is useless to try to prove that Jesus' ethic is one of nonviolence, but not nonresistance: "What could be more futile than to build a whole ethical structure upon the exegetical issue whether Jesus accepted the sword with the words: 'It is enough,' or whether he really meant: 'Enough of this'?"[108] Elsewhere, Niebuhr wrote: "Violence and revolution are usually ruled out as permissible instruments of social change on *a priori* grounds. The middle classes and the rational moralists, who have a natural abhorrence of violence, may be right in their general thesis; but they are wrong in their assumption that violence is intrinsically immoral. Nothing is intrinsically immoral except ill-will and nothing is intrinsically good except goodwill."[109] Niebuhr may be right in his general thesis, but the last sentence in the quotation solves very little: it leaves nothing for the discriminating judgment, for who is to say whether the Dominican inquisitor or Bucer's theocrat did not torture the heretic with all of his heart's goodwill for the deliverance of the errant soul? James F. Childress contended that violence is related to intention and that, hence, there is no such thing as structural violence. This is ironic in view of Niebuhr, who would agree with the premise but deny the conclusion.[110]

Niebuhr set the tone in his pre-World War II writings for the debate after the war, especially in the distinction he drew between direct and indirect violence. He wrote: "Once we admit the factor of coercion as ethically justified, though we concede that it is always morally dangerous, we cannot draw any absolute line of demarcation between violent and nonviolent coercion . . . the immediate consequences of violence cannot be differentiated as sharply from those of non-violence, as is sometimes supposed."[111] This also was the point made in a resolution by the conference of the South African Council of Churches in 1974: "The Conference maintains that it is hypocritical to deplore the violence of terrorists or freedom fighters while we ourselves prepare to defend our society with its primary, institutionalized violence by means of yet more violence."[112]

Niebuhr sought to reason his way out of the impasse by citing the distinction between religious and political morality. In this regard, his roots are in the Lutheran tradition, a tradition he castigated for its political passivity. He posed, on the one hand, the religious ideal, which "in its purest form has nothing to do with social justice. It makes disinterestedness an absolute ideal without reference to social consequences. It justifies the ideal in terms of the integrity and beauty of the human spirit. While religion may involve itself in absurdities in the effort to achieve the ideal by purely internal discipline, and while it may run the peril of deleterious social consequences, it does do justice to inner needs of the human spirit."[113]

Here, Niebuhr went beyond even Luther, who was willing to concede the justice of active disobedience for the sake of one's neighbor, although not for oneself.[114] It is difficult to find in the Christian tradition or in the Bible such a manifestation of abstract religious idealism as Niebuhr portrayed. In the collective or political sphere, on the other hand, he posed that "if a reason of violence can establish a just social system and can create the possibilities of its preservation, there is no purely ethical ground upon which violence and revolution can be ruled out. This could be done only upon the basis of purely anarchistic ethical and political presuppositions."[115] Here, he seemed to bank on the possibility of foreseeing the consequences of violence. In this respect, Allan Boesak remarked that violence is always a poor solution and never justified, although there may be situations wherein retaliatory violence is forced on the oppressed.[116] Barth's *ultima ratio regum* may beg the question, but, as with all ethics, the ethics of violence are contextual. *Ultima ratio regum* is neither a rule nor a reason, but an "I can do no other and may God have mercy on me."

The issue of violence is one of the foremost problems faced by today's churches, especially those in South Africa and Latin America. Liberation theology in particular has addressed the question. It is in this theology that Protestants and Catholics come closest to true ecumenicity.[117] A detailed account would take this chapter too far afield, but it is perhaps not too much to say that the nearly five hundred years' separation finds here a bridge.

3

Protestantism in East Germany, 1949–1989

A Summing Up

Sabrina Petra Ramet

Here [in the GDR] the clergymen sound like revolutionaries, and the officials like clergymen.—Stefan Heym (1982)

The reunification of Germany in October 1990 brought an end to an era. For the forty years of the German Democratic Republic's existence, Soviet military occupation of East Germany was a fact of life; the state attempted to construct a communist system on the Soviet model; and—where religion was concerned—the Protestant churches played an ever greater role in harboring political opposition to the regime and its policies. With the dismantling of the GDR, however, the churches, which had been invigorated by their politicization, lost their unique political role and watched helplessly as their congregations rapidly shrank.

The GDR (1949–90) had the distinction of being the only communist system in which Protestantism was clearly the predominant religious force. This, combined with the division of Germany, made for an almost unparalleled intensity of interaction between the GDR churches and churches in the noncommunist world, particularly in West Germany and Austria. Clergy enjoyed an exemption from the general proscription against travel to noncommunist countries and frequently visited the West for ecclesiastical and ecumenical meetings.

At first sight, church life in the GDR in the late 1980s looked vigorous. In particular, the public forums organized by the Evangelical Church drew large and interested crowds. Services were regularly attended; vocations revived; and the churches themselves operated an impressive number of hospitals, old age homes, and other facilities, and, thanks in part to subsidies from sister churches in the West, were relatively comfortable in financial terms.

Yet East German pastors were aware that secularization was eating away at their base. The Evangelical Church, which numbered 14.2 million adherents in 1946, had only 10.1 million in 1964, and as of 1986 claimed only 6,435,000 members. A 1984 publication of the Institute for Marxism-Leninism suggested an even lower figure, estimating real membership of the Evangelical Church at 5.0–5.5 million.[1] Statistics for the Evangelical Church in Anhalt province may illustrate the trend. In 1955 the province counted 422,800 members and recorded 56,591 communions, 5,406 baptisms, and 6,311 confirmations. In 1975 the province could tally only 221,000 members, recording 31,684 communions, 628 baptisms, and 1,161 confirmations. Ten years later, the province numbered 130,000 church members, recording 32,531 communions, 588 baptisms, and 549 confirmations. Or again, in Berlin-Brandenburg the church lost more than half of its members between 1962 and 1987. In villages, as much as 90 percent of the population may still be Christian, while informed sources estimate that only 10 percent of the population in big cities is Christian.

Pastors also were aware that while the church's ability to attract non-believers to its events enhanced its prestige, in the long run the church cannot prosper on the basis of nonconverts who attend specific events out of specific interests. To survive and prosper, a church must, at a minimum, maintain its base if not actually expand.

The Religious Sector: An Overview

In every respect, the Evangelical-Lutheran Church dwarfs all other denominations in what is now eastern Germany. Maintaining 7,347 parishes, it had 4,161 active clergy (in 1988) and operated 44 hospitals (with a total of 6,244 beds), 105 homes for the mentally and physically disabled, 200 old age homes (with about 11,000 places), 19 orphanages, 310 communal service outlets, and 278 kindergartens and day nurseries.[2] In addition, in 1988 the Evangelical-Lutheran Church maintained three ecclesiastical training missions (in Berlin, Naumburg, and Leipzig), two schools for preachers (in Berlin and Erfurt), and one pedagogical institute (in Potsdam). Six of the state universities included theological faculties whose salaries from 1949 through 1989 were paid out of the communist state budget (at the universities of Berlin, Halle, Leipzig, Jena, Greifswald, and Rostok). These faculties are specifically Protestant and are used essentially by members of the Evangelical and Reformed churches. And finally, the Evangelical-Lutheran Church was able to publish five regional newspapers: *Die Kirche* (Berlin, circulation 42,500; and also in a Greifswald edition), *Der Sonntag* (Dresden, circulation 40,000),

Mecklenburgische Kirchenzeitung (Mecklenburg, circulation 15,000), *Glaube und Heimat* (Jena, circulation 35,000), and *Potsdamer Kirche* (Potsdam, circulation 15,000).[3] All of these periodicals were printed on state presses, which made it easy for state authorities to check copy before its publication. This proved important in 1988 when the state repeatedly censored or banned specific issues of these newspapers. There also was the monthly journal, *Standpunkt*, which for years was viewed as no more than a tool of the regime, operated by pro-regime Protestants. In the last years of the GDR, however, *Standpunkt* published a number of probing articles, and as a result, its standing has improved somewhat.

The only other denomination with more than a million members is the Roman Catholic Church, which claimed some 1.05 million in 1990, with 1,083 priests and 1,753 members of women's orders (as of 1987).[4] Its most important periodical publication was the *St. Hedwigsblatt*, published in Berlin, although as in the case of the Protestants there was a pro-regime monthly journal (*Begegnung*).[5]

Leaving aside the Russian Orthodox Church, which maintains its headquarters for the Central European Exarchate in Dresden, the remaining Christian denominations can be divided into three broad groups. *Traditional Protestants* would include the Evangelical-Lutherans as well as Methodists (28,000), members of the Baptist Federation (20,000), Reformed (15,000), Old Lutherans (7,150), Evangelical-Lutheran Free (3,200), Moravians (Unity of Brethren, 2,600), Free Evangelicals (1,000), Mennonites (250), and Quakers (52). There also are *Apostolic Communities:* the New Apostolic Church (80,000–100,000 members), the Apostolate of Jesus Christ (12,000–14,000), the Shepherd and Flock (7,000), Community in Christ Jesus (Lorenzianer, 5,000), the Apostolate of Juda (3,000), Catholic-Apostolic (2,000), and Reformed Apostolic (2,000). And finally there is a heterogeneous collection of *other Christian churches* including the Jehovah's Witnesses (not legally registered in GDR times, but numbering 25,000–30,000 adherents), Seventh-Day Adventists (9,000), Christian Community (*Christengemeinschaft*, 5,000), Mormons (4,700), the Church of John (*Johannische Kirche*, 3,500), Old Catholics (1,000), Anderson Community of God (200), Reorganized Mormons ("a few"), and Darbyists (figure not reported).[6] In addition, there are reportedly a number of Christian Science members in eastern Germany who were placed under ban by the SED in 1951 and remained illegal until November 1989 when they belatedly reacquired legal status.[7]

Finally, there are some non-Christian religious groups, specifically the Muslims (2,000), the Jews (250 in 1988), and the Rastafarians (15, and as of the summer of 1988, awaiting registration). There may be a handful of Satanists in Berlin and Leipzig, but this is hard to verify.

Traditional Protestants

Two churches bear a special relationship to the numerically preponderant Evangelical-Lutheran Church. These are (1) the Federation of Evangelical Reformed Communities in the GDR and (2) the Unity of Brethren. There was no "Reformed Church in the GDR" per se, but there were Reformed parishes, organized in one of two ways. Most parishes exist as parts of the Evangelical district churches—a legacy of the Union Church created by King Friedrich Wilhelm III of Prussia in 1817. In some cases (for example, in Berlin-Brandenburg), the separate origin of the Reformed parishes is recognized by according them the right to reject synodal decisions that contradict their teachings. Three parishes, Dresden, Leipzig, and Bützow, are autonomous units not integrated into district churches. All Reformed parishes, whether separate or integrated, were represented in the Federation of Evangelical Reformed Communities in the GDR, established in 1970. These communities share theological training institutes with the Evangelical Church in Berlin, Leipzig, and Naumburg and take advantage of the theological faculties attached to the state universities.

The Unity of Brethren (Moravian Church) is distinguished by having become an associate member of the Federation of Evangelical Churches in 1969. Associate membership left the Brethren Church theologically and financially independent, but enabled it to take part in Evangelical Federation deliberations and to associate itself with the Evangelical Church's posture vis-à-vis the state. Church life centers on the village of Herrnhut (population 2,000), where about one-fifth of the church's 2,600 members live. In 1970 the community experienced a brief crisis when a Pastor Werner Morgenstern announced that he and his family had been rebaptized and started to build a small circle of born-again Christians. Unity of Brethren parishes in Herrnhut, Niesky, Kleinwelka, and Ebersdorf were affected by his preaching, and for a while the issue of rebaptism was hotly discussed. The debate ended with Morgensterns' expulsion.

The largest traditional Protestant church in the GDR, after the Evangelical, was the Methodist. With some 120 active pastors and more than a thousand lay workers, the Methodist Church, although a minority denomination in the GDR, played a larger role in Saxony where many of its adherents are concentrated. (Saxony, in fact, is confessionally the most diverse province in eastern Germany, and a number of groups that have no other base operate there.) The Methodist Church was actively involved in ecumenical activities in the GDR, and the secretary of the Working Community of Christian Churches in the GDR (*Arbeitsgemeinschaft Christlicher Kirchen in der DDR*), the country's most important forum for ecumenical activity, in 1988 was a Methodist (Martin Lange). Pacifism is strong among Methodists, and some 40 percent of young church members volunteered for the construction brigade in preference to regular military service. The Methodist Church operates a theological seminary at Bad Klosterlausnitz and has published 10,000 copies of a biweekly bulletin, *Friedensglocke*.

With some 20,000 members, the Federation of Evangelical-Free Church Communities in the GDR united three distinct denominations: the Baptists, the Evangelical Brethren, and the Elim Community. The Baptists and the Elim Community combined in a joint Baptist Federation in 1938. The Brethren joined three years later. All three groups are lay movements in which ordained ministers do not enjoy anything like the authority exercised by priests of the Catholic or Orthodox churches, or even like pastors of the Evangelical Church.[8] For all three groups, emphasis is on parish life. But there also are some differences in orientation. (The Baptists are somewhat more concerned than the others about developing parish life in accord with a strict interpretation of the New Testament; the Elim Community places greater emphasis than the others on the role of the Holy Ghost.) Like many church organizations, the Evangelical-Free Church Federation has experienced a decline in membership, down from a postwar level of 30,000–35,000. Retreats for young people are regular events and emphasize Bible study. The federation operates a four-year theological seminary at Buckow, a one-year Bible school for lay people at Burgstädt, a nursing home for the mentally disturbed (140 beds), and three homes for the aged (Berlin-Hirschgarten, Crivitz, and Sonneberg). The federation also issues 12,000 copies of a monthly periodical, *Wort und Werk*, and publishes eight to ten books a year.

Of the remaining traditional Protestant churches, only the Old Lutheran Church has more than five thousand members in eastern Germany. Formed by Lutherans who refused to go along with the administratively decreed amalgamation of the Lutheran and Reformed churches in 1817, the Old Lutheran Church became skeptical of ecumenism, fearing that in searching for "common ground" Christian doctrine becomes reduced to just Christ and love. A representative of the church attended an ecumenical meeting in Dresden in early 1988 and found he objected to some of the conclusions: peace and justice, he felt, cannot be the church's *primary* tasks. The Old Lutheran Church (affiliated with the Missouri synod) views itself as extremely conservative and criticizes the main Evangelical Church for having modified its doctrines. The church's twenty-seven parishes were organized into three dioceses, served by twenty-five pastors.[9] For a number of years, it sought permission to publish a newspaper—without success until the communist regime collapsed. State permission, however, was not required to print its informational bulletin "for internal use only."

The Free Evangelicals, with a thousand members, work closely with the Baptists, sending potential ministers to the Baptist seminary at Buckow for theological training. The Free Evangelicals are actively involved in social work, concentrating efforts on the psychologically disturbed, alcoholics, the aged, and the socially isolated (for example, those recently released from prison). Some 1,700 copies of a church bulletin for internal use only, *Glaube und Dienst,* appears seven times a year.

The Mennonites did not inhabit the territory of the former GDR until after World War II when their communities in East and West Prussia were forced to leave their native lands. Most of them settled in West Germany, but about a thousand remained in the GDR. Today, about 250 Mennonites in eastern Germany are dispersed across two hundred different towns and villages. Normal parish life is impossible. But the Mennonite community holds monthly religious services in Berlin and additional services two to three times a year in Halle, Erfurt, Schwerin, Rostok, Torgau, Potsdam, and Dresden.[10] The community publishes 240 copies of a monthly bulletin, *Gemeindebrief,* for internal use.

Finally, there is the small Society of Friends (Quakers), able to survive with scarcely more than four dozen adherents because of its independence of any hierarchy or structure. Considering their numbers, the Quakers have been surprisingly active on social issues, supporting the initiative to introduce the construction brigade in 1964 and backing the drive for a social service alternative to military conscription.

Apostolic Communities

The bulk of this chapter will be concerned with those churches I have listed as "traditional Protestants" and their experiences under communism. However, a few words should be said about churches in the other two groups.

The Apostolic churches trace their inception to the early nineteenth

century when sentiment among some European Christians that the
churches had decayed spiritually gave rise to a hope that a new age was
dawning. Between 1832 and 1835 these impulses took institutional shape
in England, where twelve men were named "Apostles." They built up a
community, which soon spread to the Continent, and taught that other
churches had become the tools of Satan and that it was therefore necessary to resurrect the "original" church. The new community professed to
be that church. Members of the Apostolic community also were convinced they would see the Second Coming within their lifetimes, specifically during the apostolate of the twelve. By 1861 six of the apostles had
died, and the community experienced a sense of crisis in which some
members favored electing new apostles to replace the deceased, while
others considered this approach unthinkable. The debate led to a schism,
with those favoring the election of new apostles forming what is now
the New Apostolic Church. The original group, known today as the
Catholic-Apostolic Community, continued to refuse to elect new apostles, even after the original apostles had died (the last of them in 1901).
Since the community is hierarchically organized, with apostles required
to consecrate bishops, bishops required to ordain ministers, and so on,
it has steadily atrophied, and as of 1988 its highest-ranking official in
the GDR was a lower deacon (*Unterdiakon*). In the 1960s the Catholic-
Apostolic Community still numbered 8,000–10,000 adherents in the
GDR, but by the late 1980s this number had shriveled to about 2,000. The
other Apostolic communities resulted from splits within the New Apostolic Church. The first of these gave birth in 1902 to the Apostolate of
Juda, which split again in 1923, giving rise to the Apostolate of Jesus
Christ.

All Apostolic churches believe that the Second Coming is a historical
fact and will occur soon. A prominent community member told me his
church expected the Second Coming in the year 2000. All members are
socially and political conservative and view other churches (even within
the Apostolic movement) with condescension. The Apostolic churches,
therefore, with the sole exception of the Apostolate of Jesus Christ,
essentially have no interest in ecumenical dialogue.

As for relations with the communist state, the Apostolic churches had
correct relations but were not given to the kind of effusiveness that
occasionally characterized, say, the Evangelical Church's post-1978 relationship. They view earthly government as a reflection of the divine
monarchy and organize their own churches on a monarchical basis. This
seems to have colored the New Apostolic Church's orientation to the
GDR in the early years when it was openly critical of the proletarian and

social-democratic tendencies unleashed by the new regime.[11] But this criticism never assumed a political aspect, because, like the other Apostolic communities, the New Apostolic Church has completely avoided politics. This, of course, also has consequences for the regime's Christian Democratic Union. As a member of another Apostolic community told me in 1988: "A Christian cannot be in a party. A Christian party is, in our eyes, not possible. Christian teaching teaches one to love one's neighbor; and party life is narrowed to serve partial interests."

Other Christian Communities

If clergy from diverse churches are asked whether they consider other churches to be Christian, one finds that various churches which see themselves as Christian—particularly the Church of John, the Church of Jesus Christ of Latter-Day Saints (Mormons), and the Jehovah's Witnesses—are often not recognized as Christian by the clergy of other Churches. Of the six "larger" churches listed in this category, one (the Jehovah's Witnesses) never succeeded in obtaining legal registration from the GDR's communist authorities and was granted legal status only in March 1990 by the coalition government of Lothar de Maiziere.[12] The Jehovah's Witnesses therefore were unable to engage in ecumenical contacts (which it surely would have spurned in any case). Two other churches (the Old Catholic Church and the Mennonites) joined the Working Community of Christian Churches in the GDR, which was dominated by the Evangelical and Methodist churches. In addition, the Seventh-Day Adventists enjoyed observer status in the Working Community (alongside the Roman Catholic Church, the Central European Exarchate of the Russian Orthodox Church, the Quakers, and the Apostolate of Jesus Christ). The small Christian Community (*Christengemeinschaft*) thinks of itself as ecumenically oriented, although it does not take part in the Working Community; its clergy argue that ecumenism is better fostered at the parish level, between individual pastors and laypersons, than among the leadership.

These churches vary considerably in their degree of social engagement. The Seventh-Day Adventists, for example, mobilized their ranks in 1972 when a law legalizing abortion was being passed and contacted the state secretary for church questions. The Adventists also have been interested in environmental questions, but chiefly in an ecumenical context, taking part in the assemblies devoted to "Peace, Justice, and the Integrity of Nature" and at one time sending medical supplies, automobiles, and other items to Angola, Mozambique, Ethiopia, and Tanzania. The Adventists also reported profitable contacts with the East German CDU—one of the few religious organizations to express this view. GDR authorities allowed the Adventists to publish 6,000 copies of a monthly newspaper, *Adventgemeinde*.

The Church of John is treated as a kind of pariah by most other churches because it teaches that God the Father manifested himself through Moses, God the Son through Christ, and God the Holy Ghost through Joseph Weissenberg (1855–1941), the church's founder.[13] As a result, it did not take part in the Working Community and has no official ecclesiastical contacts with the Evangelical Church, although its clergy have personal contacts with individual clergy of various churches. On social issues, the Church of John considers military duty a matter of individual conscience, and it showed its ecological commitment by organizing volunteers to clean up the long-polluted Blankensee tributary.

In contrast, the Christian Community and the Mormons decline to become involved in environmental issues and other social questions, arguing that "this is the sphere for the state, not the church." The Mormons also do not object to military service per se, although some members opted for alternative service in the GDR's construction brigade. The Mormons have kept their distance from other churches in eastern Germany, abstaining from the ever-increasing ecumenical forums—unlike the Christian Community, which, incidentally, accepts the Church of John as a fellow Christian church.

The Structure of the Evangelical Church

The Evangelical Church in the GDR was not a unified body but a federation of eight district churches (*Landeskirchen*) having somewhat different traditions. In five districts (Berlin-Brandenburg, Görlitz, Greifswald, Anhalt, Saxony-Magdeburg), it is heir to the Union Church, established by the Prussian government, unifying Evangelical and Reformed churches. These district churches are influenced in part by the Reformed tradition, which translates into a greater tendency to become involved in social and political affairs. The other three district churches (Mecklenburg, Thuringia, and Saxony-Dresden) are purely in the Lutheran tradition and have inherited Luther's view that church and state have different tasks and that the church should acknowledge the state as God's instrument in the secular realm (a sentiment that contributed to the state's enthusiasm over Luther during the 1983 quincentenary celebrations).[14] In concrete terms, this attitude was illustrated in an intra-church controversy in 1988.

Bishop Gottfried Forck of Berlin, of the "Union" tradition, responded to pressures from East German citizens seeking emigration by opening his offices to consultations with would-be emigrants. Others in the church criticized him, saying that he had overstepped the bounds of legitimate church activity.

There are some differences in style among the bishops of the district churches, which at times can translate into differences in posture vis-à-vis the state, or differences in orientation and effectiveness vis-à-vis local congregations. Bishops Werner Leich (of Thuringia) and Horst Gienke (of Greifswald)[15] were described as more conservative than others, while Bishops Forck, Christoph Stier (of Mecklenburg), and Christoph Demke (of Magdeburg) were more liberal—which sometimes translated into a greater readiness to confront authorities over social issues. But Stier and Bishop Rogge (of Görlitz), the latter a trained historian with expertise on Martin Luther, were described as very ecumenical-minded and open to dialogue.

The Federation of Evangelical Churches in the GDR was created in June 1969 and lasted until February 1991.[16] Its highest organ was the synod, consisting of eighty members: seventy-two from the eight district churches, and eight from the Conference of Church Leaderships, which was responsible for the federation's administrative and business affairs. In 1970 the Unity of Brethren became affiliated with the federation, and after that it was represented in the conference. Much of the responsibility for coordinating operations fell to the secretariat, which oversaw eleven standing commissions. These commissions were responsible for theology, parish work, social questions, information, radio and television, ecumenism, work with children and candidates for confirmation, work with adolescents, training of pastors, administration, and finances. Beginning in 1971 the federation, along with its district churches, belonged to the Ecumenical Council of Churches and took an active part in its work.[17]

The Evangelical Church in the Early Postwar Period

The Nazis destroyed the institutional structures of the churches, which had to be rebuilt after World War II. But many clergy emerged from the war with great prestige because of their resistance to the Nazis and to the so-called German Christian movement, which came to be called the "Confessing Church" (Bekennende Kirche). New synods had to be elected, although the Confessing Church had maintained an illegal Council of the

Brethren to hold synods and carry out administrative tasks parallel to the administration being conducted by Nazi-controlled church offices.

After World War II, the traditional district church structures re-emerged, and all of the Evangelical churches in the Soviet zone of occupation reestablished episcopal offices (or, in the case of Anhalt, the office of church president). Otto Dibelius, ousted as general superintendent of Kurmark by the Nazis of 1933, had been active in the Confessing Church throughout the Nazi period, and on 7 May 1945 (when Germany surrendered) he took the lead in establishing the church's consistory in Berlin-Brandenburg.

Pastors and communists had been together in Nazi concentration camps, and strong personal ties developed. These contributed to a kind of honeymoon that lasted from 1945 to 1948. During this period, a Conference on Culture, sponsored in January 1947 by the Socialist Unity Party (*Sozialistische Einheitspartei Deutschlands*—SED), declared:

> the brave conduct of a part of the clergy in the struggle against the barbarism of Hitler has also earned the recognition and respect of socialist laborers. Faith and socialism are not the antagonists that some would arbitrarily make them. The position of the party toward religion is one of absolute tolerance. That which Christianity seeks from faith, socialism seeks from knowledge. In their efforts to achieve their eminently secular objectives, the socialists have no desire to misuse the Church in a propagandistic manner.[18]

The church began eliminating Nazis from its ranks immediately after the war and was able to carry out its denazification without interference from any of the occupation authorities. In this weeding-out process, the church was particularly concerned with removing pastors who had been involved in the German Christian movement.

At times, pressure was exerted on local pastors to endorse the new communist authorities. In July 1946 the Evangelical Lutheran Church of Saxony responded by issuing a circular letter to its pastors, asking them to refrain from open political activity lest their spiritual-pastoral role be compromised.[19] The church's position was "that Christian life would only be possible at all if the state were constructed on democratic principles of organization and if the churches received constitutionally anchored guarantees that they could fulfill their Christian mission."[20]

By 1948 there was a change in the atmosphere. Villagers and townspeople in many municipalities were ordered to report for work on farms and in factories on Sundays, thus preventing them from attending church; in addition, the authorities interfered with religious instruction in some communities. The churches grew apprehensive. In a Pentecostal letter dated 1 June 1949, Bishop Dibelius wrote: "More than anything else, we are concerned with the fact that the pattern of the state which is arising here is already showing signs of the same things which we struggled against under Nazi rule: power which overrules law, inner deception and untruth, and enmity to the Christian Gospel."[21] Shortly after the GDR's establishment in October 1949, two "progressive" pastors, Mehnert and Kehnscherper, were foisted on the church's weekly radio broadcasts—as a result of which the church decided to withdraw from the program. Subsequently, the government issued orders forbidding schools to commemorate Christmas and requiring them to celebrate the birthday of Josef Stalin on December 21. Christmas vacation was renamed winter vacation, and the Christ child was renamed the "Solidarity child."[22] At one point, a history textbook was issued in which one passage denied that Christ had ever existed; in the face of strong remonstrations from church officials, a revised edition was issued in 1950 with this passage deleted.

About this time, schoolteachers began requiring children to write essays expressing the materialist point of view. In response, Bishop Dibelius repeatedly protested to Prime Minister Otto Grotewohl, as did bishops in the district churches. But such expressions of concern were unavailing, and in the summer of 1952 state authorities went further and banned almost all Bible study groups.[23] The authorities obstructed the church's work with young people on the grounds that it involved an "illegal" youth organization; this was vigorously denied by the church. And systematic discrimination against Christians took place at all levels of sociopolitical life.

On the other hand, no state interference occurred in religious services or diaconical work. There were no show trials of bishops, as in other communist countries. And relatively few believers had to suffer imprisonment for their faith (although more than seventy Evangelical pastors and lay workers were imprisoned beginning in January 1953, some after show trials, such as Erich Schumann and Manfred Klain—an ardent young Catholic—both without just cause).

The SED was intent in the early 1950s on breaking the inter-German links of the churches and on pressuring the Evangelical Church into docile cooperation. In particular, the SED wanted the church to cooperate with its National Front and to give prominence to "progressive" pastors. In 1950 the SED press published a series of defamatory articles, alleging that Bishop Dibelius was a Western agent. Until then, the SED had faithfully honored the obligations assumed by the state in the nineteenth century to make regular payments to the churches. But in 1952 payments to the Church of Brandenburg were reduced by 20 percent, and in early 1953 all subsidies to churches were (temporarily, as it turned out) discontinued. Lest the churches turn elsewhere to make up the difference, they were hindered from making street collections (for which a special permit was required) and barred from making house collections. In addition, several West German church periodicals, which up to then had freely entered the GDR in the mails, were banned, including the official Lutheran Church organ, *Evangelisch-Lutherische Kirchenzeitung*.

In these years, state authorities regularly interfered in church events, harassed student congregations and student pastors at the universities, and at times published defamatory articles in the press. But on 10 June 1953, Grotewohl promised an end to reprisals against Christian students, the reinstatement of teachers fired for their support of expelled students, and a retraction of certain limitations on religious instruction. These assurances improved the atmosphere temporarily, but by July 1954 the situation was souring again, and pastors were being subjected to police surveillance. Even as church publications experienced difficulties in obtaining adequate paper supplies, a new religious monthly magazine printed on high-quality paper, *Glaube und Gewissen*, made its appearance; the magazine was produced by East Germany's "progressive pastors."

The SED was especially interested in weaning young people from religion. It introduced a requirement that schoolteachers had to be Marxists; then, under pressure in 1953, it dropped the requirement, only to reintroduce it later. In 1954 the SED held a youth dedication ceremony (*Jugendweihe*), at the culmination of which each adolescent was presented with a book, *Weltall, Erde, Mensch* (The Universe, the World, Humanity), which explained that religion was a tool for "holding down the masses and oppressing them."[24] The SED exerted strong pressure on young people to take part in the nominally voluntary dedication ceremony, widely interpreted as an atheist alternative to the sacrament of confirmation. By 1958 the *Jugendweihe* had established itself as a norm for young people.

On 15 February 1956, the city council of East Berlin issued the so-called Fechner Decree, forbidding the conduct of religious instruction *before* school, requiring at least a two-hour interval between regular school and any after-class religious instruction, and requiring parents who wanted their children to obtain religious instruction to secure written permission, renewable on a three-month basis. About the same time, Hilde Benjamin, the minister of justice, issued a decree making the payment of church taxes voluntary. (Up to then, the GDR state machinery had enforced individual payments of this tax!)

In these years, the state's relationship with the churches was entrusted to Deputy Prime Minister Otto Nuschke, head of the CDU-East, who also was a member of the Evangelical Church. Nuschke presided over a special Office for Church Relations, established within the framework of the CDU. But in March 1957 this office was eliminated, and a new State Secretariat for Church Affairs was created, headed by Werner Eggerath, former GDR ambassador to Romania. This organizational change was accompanied by intensified pressure on East German clergy to sever their organizational connections with their West German counterparts. More specifically, the government announced that it no longer would consult with clergy who were not GDR residents. Dibelius, who as bishop of Berlin-Brandenburg had been living in West Berlin, was suddenly ostracized and barred from entering the GDR. The same applied to Heinrich Grueber, the EKD representative to the East German government, who was likewise a West Berlin resident. Dibelius was not merely ostracized, but vilified: posters were put up, linking him with Hitler's henchman, Heinrich Himmler, and with a convicted sex criminal named Balluseck. But for the time being, the Evangelical Church refused to divide itself along state lines.

In his first letter to all bishops in the GDR, Eggerath asked them to devote their Easter sermons to a rejection of the atomic bomb and to advocacy of the peaceful use of atomic energy: compliance would have signified subservience to the government. Bishop Moritz Mitzenheim of Thuringia, as the senior Evangelical bishop resident in the GDR, replied that the church had long ago rejected the use of atomic weapons and that he construed Eggerath's request as an attempt to discredit the leadership and divide the church.

But not only bishops were pressured. Police put pressure on pastors to report on parishioners' political attitudes, and at least one attempt was made to persuade a pastor visiting West Germany to observe and report on Western military installations and troop movements.[25]

On 5 April 1957 came the arrest of the popular Siegfried Schmutzler, a pastor at the University of Leipzig. After a show trial, he was imprisoned for five years on the charge of "agitation to boycott the republic."[26] He also was accused of expressing sympathy for the Hungarian revolt and of favoring the Evangelical Church's agreement with Bonn to establish a chaplaincy in the West German military.

Meanwhile, the *Jugendweihe* was creating a crisis within the Evangelical Church. Some members suggested that the church simply abandon confirmation since it had no biblical basis; others suggested postponing confirmation until the more mature age of seventeen; while still others suggested splitting confirmation into its component parts, foregoing the completion of instruction, vow-taking, and the granting of constitutional rights. A rift emerged within the hierarchy over its posture toward the *Jugendweihe*. Dibelius led the majority who felt that church confirmation and the *Jugendweihe* had to remain mutually exclusive, even if that meant a reduced membership base. Mitzenheim was the principal voice of a group which felt that refusing confirmation to those taking part in the *Jugendweihe* would needlessly contribute to church shrinkage; he recommended tolerance of the atheist youth dedication ceremony.

This controversy adumbrated a deeper rift between Mitzenheim and most of the hierarchy. Mitzenheim believed the church had to choose between a prophetic/critical role and an effective protective role, and he felt that only the latter choice could be justified. He thus tried to maintain cordial and supportive relations with the regime and to seek concessions from it through persuasion and consultation. Typical of his controversial style was his acceptance of an invitation in October 1959 to attend a CDU rally in Dresden, even though the local bishop had declined. The bishop of Dresden was angered and took "revenge" by refusing to allow Mitzenheim to speak in one of Leipzig's large Lutheran churches. Mitzenheim, who served as bishop of Thuringia from 1945 to 1970, would be rewarded by the regime in August 1961, when it decorated him with the Order of Service to the Fatherland in Gold.

However, Mitzenheim was terribly isolated and had little following outside Thuringia. He spoke of a "Thuringian path" (*Thüringer Weg*), and his concessions were said to be calculated to preserve the strongly Christian character of village life. While he was bishop, a number of church people from Thuringia joined the CDU, and Mitzenheim's son, the director of the district church office, became a member of the *Volkskammer* (People's Chamber). In 1964 Mitzenheim was elected an honorary member of the CDU-East.

By the late 1980s (let alone in post-GDR Germany), Mitzenheim was no longer so controversial, chiefly because the controversies of the 1950s and 1960s were no longer relevant. Once branded in some circles as the "red bishop," he was honored years later by the Thuringian church. In fact, the street leading up to the district church office in Eisenach is named for him. Some clergy in Thuringia told me in 1988 that Mitzenheim was a precursor of the "Church in Socialism" concept developed in the 1970s. Outside Thuringia this assertion was disputed. Some recall theologians Günter Jakob and Johannes Hamel who in the 1950s and 1960s spoke about the need for critical solidarity with the state—with a strong accent on *criticism*, and with no attempt to obtain special concessions for the church (on which Mitzenheim placed his emphasis). They represented an opposition to Mitzenheim, who, as noted, felt the church had no critical role to play. Some argued, thus, that the "Church in Socialism" concept could be more accurately traced to the ideas of Hamel and Jakob. Yet it was Mitzenheim who as early as 1964 said: "We don't want to be a Church against socialism, but a Church for the people who want to be Christians in a socialist order."[27]

Mitzenheim's efforts also brought about the church-state accord of 21 July 1958, which produced a softening in party secretary Walter Ulbricht's church policy. In the communiqué issued then, Mitzenheim signed a text that declared: "the Churches . . . are in fundamental agreement with the peace efforts of the GDR and its regime."[28] The communiqué was controversial within the church. But it was quite a change to hear Ulbricht declare in its wake that "Christianity and the humanistic ideals of socialism are not in contradiction."[29] Again, it was Mitzenheim whose efforts led to the granting of permission in 1962 for pensioners to travel to the West. And on 18 August 1964 Ulbricht and Mitzenheim met in Wartburg Castle (in Eisenach) and signed a follow-up document on church-state understanding. Ulbricht commented on that occasion: "We have no basis for differences. . . . In the basics, in the questions of securing the peace and building socialism, we are of one mind. . . . The common humanist responsibility unites us all."[30]

Splitting the Churches from the West

As long as the question of German reunification remained open, it was reasonable to argue that there was no point in hurrying to make organizational changes to conform to what might prove to be transient political realities. But with the creation of the GDR in 1949 and the failure of the last Soviet initiative on German reunification in 1957,[31] it became clear to all concerned that the division of Germany would last for some time. Perhaps the first church to adapt to the new situation was the German Unity of Brethren, which in 1945 divided in two, establishing one organization for the Soviet zone of occupation and one for the other three zones. The Federation of Evangelical-Free Church communities soon followed. And shortly after the GDR was established, the Federation of Free Evangelical Communities severed its ties with congregations in

West Germany and, in 1950, established a separate organization for the
GDR. In 1954 the Old Lutheran Church in the GDR likewise set up a
separate organizational structure.

The authorities, of course, were most interested in splitting the Evangelical-Lutheran Church. In 1967 they stepped up the pressure. At a
conference of the CDU-East in Jena on 10 February, CDU Chairman
Gerhard Götting spoke of an "independent" Evangelical Church in the
GDR that could "not be mentioned in the same breath" with the Evangelical Church in West Germany.[32] This sounded like praise, perhaps,
but church leaders reacted with alarm. Church President D. M. Müller of
the Evangelical Church of Anhalt wrote a letter to Götting, dated 4 March
1967, in which he said that the supposed ecclesiastical division was only
wishful thinking on Götting's part and argued that the GDR churches'
abstention from the West German chaplaincy agreement of 1958 could
scarcely be interpreted (as Götting seemed to think) as evidence of
ecclesiastical secession. Bishop Hans Joachim Fränkel of Görlitz was of
the same mind and declared: "We would be repudiating God's call for
Christian unity if we were to allow ourselves to be separated from our
sister Churches in the Fatherland."[33] An Evangelical Church synod was
convened 2–7 April in Fürstenwalde, and on 5 April it issued a statement
rejecting pressures to split the German organization in two. In a key
passage, the Fürstenwalde synod stated: "We Evangelical Christians in
the GDR have no reason to destroy the community of the EKD. We have
good reasons to preserve it."[34]

The new GDR constitution of 1968 specified that the churches had to
conduct their activities in conformity with the GDR's legislative and
administrative limitations. This seemed to narrow the churches' options.
In April 1968 the district churches of Saxony, Mecklenburg, and Thuringia dissolved organizational ties to the churches of the United Evangelical Lutheran Church of Germany and on 1 December established a new
association, the United Evangelical Lutheran Churches in the GDR. For a
while, the five churches of the Evangelical Church Union held back from
conforming. But by mid-1969 the separation was complete, and a new
organization, the Federation of Evangelical Churches in the GDR, was
set up on 10 June. The Quakers, Reformed, and Methodists likewise
separated from their West German coreligionists about this time.

Organizational adaptation led to ideological adaptation. Meeting at
Eisenach in July 1971, Evangelical Church leaders accepted the programmatic formula—associated with the Evangelical Federation's chairman at
that time, Bishop Albrecht Schönherr—that the church did not want to

be a church alongside socialism, or a church against socialism, but a church *in* socialism.[35] What this statement meant was, to some extent, left vague. It clearly signified a pledge of loyalty, while at the same time implying that some reciprocation was expected. It did not entail "ideological coexistence," as the church made clear.[36] Even so, some clergy and believers initially feared that the church was somehow "selling out," and the concept stirred brief controversy. The other Protestant churches divided over the idea. Some (such as the Unity of Brethren, the Baptist Federation, and the Seventh-Day Adventists) applauded the formula. Others were skeptical. (The Catholic Church repudiated the concept altogether.)

Shortly before the Eisenach synod of July 1971, Bishop Schönherr met with the state secretary for church questions, Hans Seigewasser, who had succeeded Eggerath in 1960. Schönherr complained at the meeting of continued discrimination against young Christians in entering the universities and of the fact that people fulfilling their military service in the construction brigade were barred from university education altogether.[37] Discrimination against believers, both in these forms and in hiring and promotion, remained an issue as long as the SED was in charge. The church might have been *in* socialism, but in a number of ways its believers were made to feel they were only *alongside* socialism.

The Social Engagement of the Church

After the massive destruction of World War II, widespread pacifist sentiments arose, especially among young people. The church responded to these sentiments, and as early as 1962 it became engaged in political debate by promoting the idea of a social service alternative to the newly introduced military conscription.[38] Introduction of the construction brigade in 1964 was the state's reply to this pressure. On the surface, things seemed calmer after that response. But voices were raised within the church—such as that of Heino Falcke, Evangelical provost in Erfurt, at a Dresden meeting in 1972—urging involvement in society's concerns.[39] In fact, Falcke became deeply involved in promoting pacifist and ecological activism on the church's part and addressed an assembly in Buckow (28–29 January 1978) on the subject of a "Theology of Nature," arguing that the Old Testament lies within the environmentalist tradition.[40]

Ironically, it was on the eve of the church's dramatically escalated involvement in peace-related and ecological concerns that Bishop Schönherr was received by General Secretary Erich Honecker for a kind of summit meeting on 6 March 1978. The meeting came at the church's suggestion and was carefully prepared in negotiations between responsible parties for months in advance to assure that it would be more than a formal ceremony and have some substance.[41] The church wanted access to television and radio. The church wanted a pension for clergy over the age of sixty-five. The church wanted to construct church facilities in so-called "socialist cities" (churchless cities built after the war). There also was a more specific issue: ownership of the Augustine Monastery in Erfurt was divided 50/50 between church and state, and the church wanted full ownership. All of these requests were granted. In addition, the meeting created an atmosphere of trust between church and state and led directly to a routinization of contacts in which questions came to be resolved on an issue-by-issue basis. The State Secretariat for Church Questions increasingly came to see itself as a go-between for the state apparatus and the church. Secretariat officials were highly knowledgeable, understood the needs of the churches, and liked to think they were of use to the churches. Other churches benefited from the new atmosphere, and almost every clergyman with whom I talked in 1988 said that his church was an indirect beneficiary of this March 1978 meeting.

What did the state gain? First, the meeting represented the culmination of Honecker's efforts to set church-state relations on a new footing. Honecker wanted to break with the confrontational policies of his predecessor, Walter Ulbricht, and to see church-state relations become more tranquil. Second, the authorities already were planning to introduce obligatory "pre-military" training in the ninth and tenth grades in September 1978. They may have welcomed the chance to work out a kind of modus vivendi with the church before embarking on a course that was certain to inflame many church people. And third, the Honecker regime already was showing a new approach toward the German past, "rehabilitating" long-denigrated giants of German history. Martin Luther was central to this project. The state planned to celebrate the Luther quincentenary in 1983, and Honecker would chair the official Martin Luther Committee of the GDR, which was established on 13 June 1980. The modus vivendi achieved in March 1978 established a kind of trust, on the basis of which church-state cooperation in celebrating Luther would become possible.

Meanwhile, the church reacted quickly to the announcement of the introduction of pre-military training. At a national conference on 14 June 1978 the Evangelical Church Federation warned that the planned educational changes would encourage young people to think in terms of "enemies," cultivating prejudice and hatred in them. In July the Conference of Church Leaderships adopted an "Education for Peace" action program, underlining the church's duty to work for peace, broadly conceived. And in September 1978 a church synod at Berlin-Weissensee urged the regime to scrap its pre-military training program and introduce a "peace education" program instead, with emphasis on independent thinking on moral questions.[42] The SED was not interested.

In 1980, on the initiative of young people in the church, the first "Peace Decade" was organized under the auspices of the Evangelical Church. This ten-day event mobilized Christians and non-Christians each November for discussions and seminars on peace, environmentalism, the arms race, and other social issues. Small groups of pacifists began forming spontaneously in late 1981 in the GDR's larger cities, and by 1983 they numbered 2,000–5,000 activists and 30,000–50,000 sympathizers and supporters. Perhaps as many as 95 percent of these groups were church-linked (until late 1989) because, with the sole exception of church-associated activities, the authorities (up to late 1989) required citizens to register in advance for any "large" get-togethers, which applied even to regular meetings of half a dozen persons. Despite depending on the churches for the use of premises, 30–50 percent of the members of these groups were non-Christians, some of the activists in fact antipathetic to the church in general terms, and some of the groups themselves with no particular Christian character. In this respect the church was quite receptive to independent initiatives. In 1987 a group of so-called punks came to Berlin's Church of the Samaritan and asked for use of a room to set up a punk club. The church turned down the request. However, some members of a peace group already making use of the Church of the Samaritan's premises were sympathetic and allowed the punks to join their group.

In 1981 the Evangelical Church commissioned an East German graphic artist to design an emblem with the scriptural words, "Swords into Plowshares" (*Schwerter zu Pflugscharen*). The resulting emblem was used on shoulder patches distributed by the church at its second "Peace Decade" in November 1981. Authorities initially seemed to approve of the emblem, but in April 1982 banned the patch and ordered the police to stop young people from wearing it.[43]

Other churches, including the Methodist, the Reformed, the Seventh-Day Adventists, and the Church of John, likewise became active in environmental concerns and organized volunteers to help clean up polluted streams and to plant trees. The environment came to be a central theme of ecumenical meetings in the GDR; it thus involved all churches taking part in such meetings. Some churches, such as the Apostolic communities and the Mormons, have not been interested in ecumenism or the environment. The Evangelical Church itself, however, made the environment a focus of its "Peace Decades" in the late 1980s.

As the peace work of the Evangelical-Lutheran Church developed, it became clear there were six bones of contention between church and state. First, the church remained opposed to what it termed the militarization of East German society, and in particular to programs of pre-military training in the schools. Yet the regime repeatedly extended and expanded these programs, both in the schools and in the Pioneers youth organization (for boys and girls ages six to fourteen).[44] Second, the church continued to plead for introduction of a social service alternative to military service, as it had protested in the past against discrimination toward young people who fulfilled their military duty in the construction brigade. In 1984 a panel discussion in St. Sophia's Church in Berlin revealed that more than a hundred former members of construction units had been admitted to university study and concluded that discrimination against veterans of the construction brigade was no longer a problem.[45] Third, the church continued to remonstrate against broader discrimination against Christians—whether in education, jobs, or other areas. Fourth, the church continued to plead for the right of emigration, and in Berlin a consultation service was established for those seeking to leave.[46] Fifth, the church's protection of independent peace groups opened it to the charge of harboring political opposition and made it more complicated to hold onto what Bishop Werner Krusche once called "the narrow space between opposition and opportunism."[47] Sixth, the church increasingly addressed environmentalist concerns and identified itself with those who believed that the s ED's economic policy was leading to ecological disaster. Peter Gensichen of Wittenberg played a special role here; the head of the Wittenberg Church Research Center, he edited an irregular series of information bulletins about environmental questions.[48]

When Honecker received the then chairman of the Federation of Evangelical Churches, Bishop Johannes Hempel of Dresden, for a meeting in February 1985, the conversation centered on the church's peace activism and the s ED's policy on peace. Honecker pointedly reminded Hempel of the GDR's alliance with the Soviet Union and acknowledged the contribution of East German Christians to the building of GDR socialism.[49] The compliment implied a warning.

The Luther and Müntzer Celebrations

In the early postwar years the SED drew a sharp contrast between Martin Luther and his contemporary, Thomas Müntzer. Luther was criticized for serving the interests of princes and nobility, while Müntzer, a chiliastic zealot who stirred up a peasant revolt in Germany in 1525, was hailed as "the true representative of the revolutionary forces" in Reformation times.[50] In a 1947 publication, Luther had been cast as the spiritual ancestor of Hitler,[51] while another East German historian, writing in 1946, had charged Luther with being "counterrevolutionary."[52] By the mid-1960s, however, Luther was being credited with contributing to the early "bourgeois" revolution against "feudal" Roman supremacy— which thus conceded that he had been progressive, relative to his time and context. As Luther's star rose in East German historiography, Müntzer's declined somewhat. In 1967, as the GDR prepared to commemorate the 450th anniversary of the Reformation, consensus was reached in elite circles:

> it is neither scientifically nor politically justified to content ourselves with this "Babylonian captivity" of the progressive Luther heritage. Marxist historical research has, on the contrary, through the exposition of the legitimate [*gesetzmässig*] interrelationship of the Reformation and Peasant War as phases of the bourgeois revolution, uncovered the progressive meaning of the Lutheran Reformation and with it has created the scientific basis for the national jubilee marking the passing of 450 years since the Reformation, which appreciated Martin Luther as belonging to the good traditions of our republic.[53]

The decision to celebrate the Luther quincentary in 1983 entailed his further rehabilitation, even though the SED continued to insist that he had been unable to perceive the full social ramifications of the revolutionary upheaval that he helped to inspire. The state's new interest in him provided a basis for a deepening of church-state rapprochement, although some church officials were critical of the SED's transparent attempt to adopt him as a forerunner of socialism.[54] Indeed, Luther was now described as "one of the greatest sons of the German people."[55]

For the SED, celebrating Luther reinforced its more general effort to reclaim its German past and to establish historical precedents and roots for the socialist system. In this way, the SED hoped to convert German nationalism, which long had been a source of contempt for the East German state, into a source of support. Moreover, Luther's theology explicitly traced temporal authority to divine ordinance, leading him to preach obedience to secular authorities under most circumstances. (He preached passive resistance to authorities whose actions were contrary to Christian teaching.) Thus, Luther could be reinterpreted as a forerunner of "progressive" thinking, even of socialism, and also as an advocate of rendering unto Caesar's what was Caesar's.

Church representatives took part in the official Martin Luther Committee's work, and the state provided funds for restoring a number of churches and sites of historical importance. The state even provided logistical support for church-sponsored events connected with the celebrations. In the wake of the festivities, a new trust had developed in relations between the state and the Evangelical and other traditional Protestant churches. (Since the Apostolic and other Christian churches placed no particular importance on Luther, the quincentary had no effect on their relations with the state.)

Thomas Müntzer was a very different matter. A utopian and political radical who entertained dreams of realizing far-reaching equality in an earthly republic, Müntzer has far less importance for the church than Luther. Indeed, both church and SED tended to see him as a "theologian of revolution"[56]—which explains the SED's interest, and the slighter interest of the church, in commemorating his birth. In a three-page set of "Theses on Thomas Müntzer" the party organ, Neues Deutschland, declared that Müntzer "aspired, on the basis of his revolutionary understanding of Christian teachings, to bring about a radical transformation of society in the interest of the exploited and subjugated people. He developed a theology of revolution with the goal of overcoming every form of class rule. He perceived in simple people the agent and revolutionary instrument of this transformation."[57] Honecker was even more explicit, claiming that Müntzer's legacy lived on in GDR socialism and that this legacy was "especially valuable" for the SED.[58]

The Evangelical Church established a committee to organize its commemoration of Müntzer's quincentary in 1989 and appointed three "observers" to attend the state committee's sessions (headed, as in the case of the Luther celebrations, by Honecker).[59] Following the model established in 1983, the state commissioned a number of biographies of Müntzer as well as musical and dramatic works celebrating him, prepared a series of conferences and ceremonial events to honor him, and renamed the town of Stolberg Thomas-Müntzer-Stadt Stolberg. Yet the celebrations had no particular impact on church-state relations because the church by and large viewed Müntzer as a "Schwärmer" (a fanatic) on the fringes of its tradition.

Trends and Developments in the GDR's Final Years

The church's increased involvement in pacifist and ecological concerns after 1978 was associated with grass-roots mobilization. Indeed, the bishops often have taken stands because of pressures generated from below. In 1986 this mobilization of the grass roots reached the point where one could speak of a rebellion at the base—a rebellion aimed at the laicization of the church. In October, a group of pastors, church workers, and laypersons issued a declaration setting forth the principles of a "Solidarity Church." The laity, according to the authors of this declaration, could not allow themselves to become passive objects of the church's pastoral care but should take an active role in formulating programmatic church statements.[60]

In June 1987 the Evangelical Church convened a synod in Berlin on the theme of Christian-Marxist coexistence. Supporters of the "Solidarity Church" decided that they wanted to hold an opposition synod, which they called the "Church Congress from Below" (Kirchentag von unten). Charging that the church hierarchy had become too quiescent vis-à-vis the state, advocates of the Church Congress from Below were nonetheless ultimately dependent on the church's benevolence since the only places they could legally meet were on church premises. Bishop Forck decided to make church facilities available to them, and the "Counter-Synod" was held at Berlin's Church of the Pentecost, attended by some 1,200 persons, mostly young people.[61] In general, the Church Congress from Below was dominated by the idea that the concept of a "Church in Socialism" had become obsolete and should be replaced by a new "grass-roots movement for a different socialism." That is to say, some movement adherents did not see Western parliamentary pluralism as attractive, but hoped instead to refashion socialism in accordance with certain humanist ideals.[62] The "Church from Below" also aspired to restructure the church—from below.

Church from Below groups appeared in other cities, although the strongest was the original group in East Berlin. In general, these groups saw themselves as presenting an alternative to the Evangelical hierarchy's traditional methods. But in Erfurt, the local Church from Below group enjoyed good relations with the hierarchy, and the two sides cooperated in putting on a critical exhibit about the reconstruction of downtown Erfurt after World War II.

In Berlin, the Church of Zion became deeply involved in environmental concerns, putting together an environmental library. The library published the samizdat journal, *Umweltblätter*, and the Church of Zion organized the first unofficial peace march in the country in September 1987. On 25 November 1987, East German security police raided the library, confiscating copying machines and various publications and materials of a critical nature. Twenty-one persons were arrested, and similar actions were carried out in Rostok, Dresden, Jena, Weimar, Wismar, and Halle. The raid on the Church of Zion marked the first time that church premises were searched in the GDR since the 1950s. Widespread protests took place in East Germany, including protests from Bishop Werner Leich, chairman of the Federation of Evangelical Churches.[63]

Two months later, an official parade in honor of Rosa Luxemburg and Karl Liebknecht, founders of the German Communist Party, sparked new tensions between church and state. Some 200,000 persons taking part in the official parade were joined by unofficial protesters who unfurled a banner bearing a quotation from Luxemburg: "Freedom is always only the freedom to think differently." These activists were quickly rounded up and imprisoned, and the church loudly complained. Evidently, the party had had enough, and Bishop Leich was invited to a private meeting with Werner Jarowinsky, a member of the Politburo. In that meeting Jarowinsky allegedly told the bishop:

> Recently, the number of occurrences and events in the sphere of [the] Evangelical Churches has increased, which cannot be left unchallenged and in some cases exceed the limit of what can be tolerated. These events must be taken very seriously. They are in direct contrast with the form and understanding of togetherness which has proved its worth for a long time, respect for what is due the state, the parties, and the social organizations, and respect for the Church's constitutional tasks and duties. It must be clear that in the Church, too, there cannot be any zones exempt from [the] law. We must take very seriously such occurrences as the provocations on the fringes of the Rosa Luxemburg demonstration, and the obstructionist and virulent campaigns against the GDR, that are connected with the Church of Zion and the subsequent series of events in some Berlin churches. . . .
>
> Churches are organizing purely political agitprop events, and anti-state slogans and calls for riots and confrontation are being tolerated there. . . . The limit of what can be tolerated has been surpassed, the opposition groups have gone too far.
>
> We cannot allow things to continue like this. In a number of cases, events are organized without the knowledge of the allegedly competent municipal church councilors, under pressure from the outside and from above, over which the "well-meaning" initiators no longer have control in the end. These are indeed signs of a disintegration of church structures, which, according to the wishes of people acting in the

background, should apparently be replaced by different structures. If even Church representatives openly admit that real substructures are forming, that there is discernible logistic control from outside and corresponding cooperation, this must be an occasion for reflection, for a reversal, for a necessary clarification, and for a change on the part of the responsible bodies. Attempts are being made to turn the churches into tribunals, lawyers' offices, or prosecutors' offices. At official offices, people answer the phone saying "contact office," "Solidarity office," or "coordination center."[64]

Tensions developed in the relationship between the Evangelical Church and the state beginning in September 1986 when clergy attending the Erfurt synod sharply criticized the regime's policies in education and, once again, demanded a social service alternative to military service. Klaus Gysi, state secretary for church questions from October 1979 to July 1988, finally agreed to take up these issues with appropriate church representatives. But he was overruled by higher authorities, and no meeting took place. In 1987 a state official attending one of the church congresses was asked about the prospects for Gorbachev-style democratization in the GDR. When the official ruled it out, he was loudly booed.

The example set by Gorbachev in the Soviet Union was probably responsible in great part for encouraging church leaders in their outspoken course. In early June 1988, in a document circulated at the church congress in Görlitz, activist cells of the Church from Below said that "current events in the Soviet Union have prompted us to consider certain fundamental questions concerning a social and political renewal."[65] The six-page letter called for initiating action to bring about democratization from below. Later that same month, another regional church congress held in Halle saw explicit calls for the introduction of Gorbachev's programs of glasnost and perestroika in the GDR.[66] Participants in the congress also raised the key question of what the churches might do to "alleviate the glaring injustice of the division of our fatherland."[67] Subsequently, at a synodal meeting in Dessau (16–20 September 1988), Bishop Leich criticized what he called a two-class system developing in the GDR that consisted of people allowed to travel to the West and people denied that prerogative, and he called for a society with a "human face"[68]—a phrase strikingly reminiscent of Czechoslovak reformer Alexander Dubček's calls in 1968 for "socialism with a human face." Other congresses in 1988 took up other sensitive issues.

The authorities responded by barring West German television crews from taping or filming the proceedings in Dessau and by censoring issues of church newspapers that sought to report on the various church assemblies. This marked the first time since the early 1980s that church publications had been censored. All five regional church papers, as well as the Evangelical Church news service, were affected. On one occasion, the Berlin newspaper *Die Kirche* was banned because it attempted to reprint in German translation an article on religious policy in the Soviet Union, originally published in *Moscow News*.[69]

On 24 June, Bishop Leich met with representatives of the State Secretariat for Church Questions to discuss these interventions. But the meeting failed to resolve anything. Subsequently, Bishop Leich made a formal protest to East German Prime Minister Willi Stoph. Meanwhile, two independent groups (a peace group and a working circle of the "Solidarity Church") likewise sent a letter of protest to state authorities. As the censors' intrusions continued, Berlin Pastor Wolfram Huelsemann led a silent protest march of some two hundred people on 10 October; the march was forcibly broken up by security police on the grounds that it was an unregistered and hence illegal assembly.[70] During 1988 alone, the authorities censored *Die Kirche* fifteen times, and other Evangelical Church papers also were affected.[71]

As tensions grew, the GDR authorities banned an international church congress scheduled for East Berlin on 12 November. Sixty-five representatives of Evangelical churches from ten European countries had planned to discuss peace issues and Moscow's reform policy. Authorities said the meeting would put "pressure" on the church-state relationship in the GDR.[72]

The Church and the Revolution

Meanwhile, the formula Church in Socialism came under fire within the Evangelical Church itself in 1988. Writing in the West Berlin periodical, *Kirche im Sozialismus*, East German theologian Richard Schröder criticized the formula for suggesting that the church was somehow incorporating socialism into its self-image. He suggested that "Church in the GDR" might be a more appropriate and politically less loaded formula.[73] But the latter also would have been politically less useful to both church and state. Moreover, although developed within Evangelical Church circles, the formula was widely accepted among other Protestant churches as well as by the Church of John, although not by the Apostolic churches, the Mormons, or, of course, the Catholic Church. By March 1989 Schröder no longer was a "voice in the wilderness," and Thuringian Bishop

Werner Leich, chair of the Evangelical Church Federation, called the concept Church in Socialism "rather worn out." Leich had come to agree that the concept suggested the church was *for* socialism.[74] On the contrary, the church was becoming, ever more decisively, a leading force in the growing opposition to the SED regime. The church began to distance itself from the concept,[75] but the entire idea of the Church in Socialism would soon be overtaken by events.

On 7 May 1989, elections were held in the GDR. Opposition groups sheltered by the Evangelical Church closely monitored the vote, and when the GDR announced the results, the opposition charged the regime with fraudulent underreporting of negative ballots. In East Berlin's Prezlau Hill district alone the opposition said that some 2,659 negative votes had been confirmed; yet the regime had reported only 1,998 such ballots in all of East Berlin.[76] About two hundred young people demonstrated against the elections in front of the St. Sophia Church; GDR security forces roughed them up, arresting 120. Under church pressure, the arrestees were released.

In the summer of 1989, Hungary opened its borders with Austria and announced it no longer would honor its earlier agreement to return to the GDR those East German citizens seeking foreign asylum. Within weeks, hundreds of thousands of East Germans fled to West Germany—most of them via Hungary and Austria, but some by scaling the walls of West German embassies in Warsaw and Prague. An Evangelical Church synod held in Eisenach in September declared that fundamental political and social reforms were "urgent"; in particular, it demanded the introduction of a multiparty system in the GDR.[77] The regime refused. Church officials then sent a letter to the Honecker leadership requesting bilateral talks on political and social reforms. The authories "took note" of this request but—until events forced their hand—shelved it.[78]

The GDR's fortieth anniversary celebrations on 7 October 1989 proved to be the final curtain on the East German experiment. The Evangelical Church organized peace prayers and vigils in support of reform in Berlin, Leipzig, and Dresden, to which hundreds of thousands of people came. The vigils ultimately brought the regime down. Honecker, secretary of the SED since 1971, was forced to resign (and ultimately fled to the USSR), and Egon Krenz briefly took the reins. His first day on the job, Krenz met privately with Bishop Leich—a clear sign of the church's political power at that juncture. Later, in December, when roundtable talks on East Germany's future were convened in Berlin, Bishop Forck of Brandenburg-Berlin was chosen to chair the discussions.

New elections were held in East Germany in March 1990, bringing into office a coalition government headed by Christian Democrat Lothar de Maiziere and committed to German reunification. De Maiziere viewed himself as a caretaker for the brief transition prior to eventual reunification on 3 October 1990. His cabinet included four Protestant pastors, among them Rainer Eppelmann (minister of defense and disarmament) and Markus Meckel (minister of foreign affairs). Fourteen of the four hundred members of the transitional parliament were pastors.[79]

The transition government restored several church holy days (including Christmas and Easter) as state holidays, removed pressures on the church, and released internal documents revealing State Security's strategies for undermining and subverting the churches, including the coercing of Evangelical pastors into cooperation.[80] The reunification of Germany also made reunification of the divided Evangelical Church possible, and this process, started in September 1990, was by and large accomplished by February 1991.[81] Thus ended the independent existence of the "East German Church."

Robert Goeckel, a seasoned American observer of the East German religious scene, noted, however:

> despite its ideological conflict with the SED regime, the Church is ironically more likely than other institutions to retain elements of its past experience of socialism. Little appears likely to remain of "real existing socialism" in much of GDR society. . . . The *Wende*, or transformation, has left no segment of society unaffected, even "non-political" areas like sports and the music scene. Yet because the Church was less affected by the Leninist system, its rejection of the GDR legacy is less sweeping than in these other institutions. There have been few purges in the Church leadership and the Church's calls for social justice stand in stark relief to the popular embrace [as of mid-1990] of West German-style capitalism. . . . Nor is the resurgence of religion after the collapse of the Nazi regime likely to be repeated in the post-communist regime. The collapse of the Leninist system in the GDR was due in no small part to the Evangelical-Lutheran Church. It too will fall prey to the greater diversity of German tradition and the pluralism of liberal democracy. Yet, more than other institutions in the GDR, the Church is likely to embody elements of the past in the new Germany.[82]

Conclusion

During the era of communist rule from 1949 to 1989, the Evangelical Church to some extent, by virtue of its preponderant size, set the general tone for church-state relations. But there were important exceptions to this rule. In the early postwar period, while the Evangelical Church's relations with the state were thorny, other churches that had been banned under the Nazis or had suffered severe limitations felt relief at being able to organize anew. Moreover, whereas earlier German governments had favored the Evangelical Church, the SED treated all registered religious organizations more or less equally. The result was that the smaller churches often took a more positive view of SED policy (a perspective encouraged by circumspection).

The Schönherr-Honecker meeting of March 1978, on the other hand, produced positive effects for all churches. Religious life became more normal, communities generally found it easier to build churches, and the entire church-state climate improved. By contrast, the falling out after 1986 was specific to the Evangelical Church's relationship with the state and did not affect other churches. Only the Evangelical Church's publications were censored. And officials of other churches insisted there was no particular tension in their relations with the state during the GDR's last few years. In fact, as tensions were growing between the Evangelical Church and the state in 1988, the Church of John sent an open letter to Honecker, warmly commemorating the March 1978 meeting and noting the "positive effect of the separation between state and church and of equal respect to all churches and religious communities in our state." The letter gratefully acknowledged the "expansion of the publication of church materials" and underlined acceptance of the principle that the church is "neither a political nor a social organization."[83]

The churches discussed in this chapter are highly diverse; their theologies, ecclesiologies, and perspectives on politics all have differed considerably. Even within the Evangelical Church there have been debates—some traceable to differences between the Lutheran and Reformed traditions, some associated with differences of personality or differences in the experiences of regional churches. But the regime itself generally succeeded in presenting a unified front.

Reunification presents the churches of the former East Germany with a powerful challenge. Unlike churches in the western portion of the country, their ranks have been dramatically depleted by regime-sponsored secularization. Until reunification, their political role assured them of a continued role in society. Now shorn of that role, churches in the former East Germany will find it far more difficult than their sister churches in western Germany to maintain a visible presence.

FACT SHEET*

	Number of members	Number of parishes	Number of pastors
Protestants			
Evangelical Church (Werner Leich, chairman)	6,435,000 (1986)	7,347 (1986)	4,161 (1986)
Methodist Church (Rudiger Minor, Bishop of Dresden)	28,000	400	140
Baptist Federation (Manfred Sult, president)	20,000	222	130
Reformed Church (Hans-Jurgen Sievers, chairman)	15,000	24	20
Old Lutheran Church (Johannes Zellmer, president)	7,150	27	22
Evangelical-Lutheran Free Church	3,200 (1983)	?	?
Unity of Brethren (Christian Muller, chair of the directorate)	2,600	9	25
Apostolic			
New Apostolic Church (Fritz Schroder, president)	80,000–100,000	750	6,000 lay preachers
Apostolate of Jesus Christ (Waldemar Rhode, presiding)	12,000–14,000	130–200	1,600 lay preachers
Shepherd and Flock (Gunter Hain, presiding)	7,000	150	?

	Number of members	Number of parishes	Number of pastors
Community in Christ Jesus (Lorenzianer) (Gottfried Borner, chair of the executive committee)	5,000	60	60
Apostolate of Juda (Horst Glaser, presiding)	3,000 (1981)	14	more than 40
Catholic-Apostolic Church (Werner Zander, lower deacon)	2,000	35	1 lower deacon
Reformed Apostolic Church (Kurt Kretzschmar, chairman—1983)	2,000	56	70

Other

Jehovah's Witnesses	25,000–30,000	illegal	unknown
Seventh-Day Adventists (Lothar Reiche, president)	9,000	280	160
Christian Community	5,000 (1981)	45 (15 regular parishes; 30 affiliate parishes)	40
Mormons (Henry Burckhardt, president)	4,700	27	79 (22 Melchisedek priests; 57 Aaron priests)

Sabrina Petra Ramet

	Number of members	Number of parishes	Number of pastors
Church of John (Frieda Muller, superintendent)	3,500	40	21

---

*Groups with 2,000 or more members as of 1988 unless otherwise noted.

4

Protestantism in Czechoslovakia and Poland

Paul Bock

The coming of communism to Czechoslovakia and Poland presented a great challenge to Protestant churches in both countries. In both lands, Protestants are a minority, much more so in Poland than in Czechoslovakia. In both, they had to struggle for their rights against the dominant Roman Catholic Church long before they had to struggle against communism. In both, they suffered persecution during the Nazi era. Thus, their struggle for survival and influence is not new.

There are, of course, differences in their pasts. In Czechoslovakia, Protestants experienced complete freedom and legal equality with Roman Catholics during the twenty years between the two wars; in Poland, legal equality did not come until after World War II, but in the meantime the Polish Protestant population had been decimated by out-migration.

Unlike Catholics, Protestants do not have a strong international power such as the Vatican to back them in their conflicts with communist governments. However, they do have ties with fraternal churches abroad through world confessional bodies such as the Lutheran World Federation and interdenominational bodies such as the World Council of Churches. But such ties could be both blessings and handicaps in a communist state. They gave the government a pretext to accuse the churches of alliance with the "capitalist" West.

Thus, Protestants constantly were faced with the challenge of remaining true to their faith and at the same time demonstrating loyalty to their government. This was no easy task. Basically, they had three options: (1) to become apolitical, focusing strictly on preaching the gospel, avoiding any involvement in politics; (2) to collaborate with the government, making favorable pronouncements and thus gaining the government's favor; (3) to demonstrate their loyalty to the government in areas where conscience permits them to do so, but voicing criticism in other areas, such as violations of human rights.

Polish Protestants have faced an additional problem. They have had to prove they were loyal Poles. Since in the pre-World War II era most Protestants residing within Poland's boundaries were of German nationality, even those who were Polish nationals have been viewed as foreigners. In the opinion of many people, to be a Pole has meant to be a Catholic.

Czech and Slovak Protestants have not faced this particular problem. They are much more deeply rooted in the national heritage. Such historical realities must be recognized when evaluating the positions and actions of Czechoslovak and Polish Protestants in their dealings with a communist government's power.

The Struggle for Religious Liberty
in Czech and Slovak Lands

In Reformation times, all three of the provinces that make up present-day Czechoslovakia became predominantly Protestant. The two western provinces, Bohemia and Moravia, were mostly Hussite, and Slovakia in the east was predominantly Lutheran. The Counter-Reformation drastically changed this situation.

After the Battle of White Mountain in 1620, Bohemians and Moravians had the choice of becoming Roman Catholic or leaving the country. Later in the century, Slovak Protestants also experienced a severe setback at the hands of the Habsburgs, although it was less severe than in the western provinces. Some Lutheran nobles exerted influence and gained permission for Lutheran worship in several towns.[1]

The Edict of Toleration, issued by Emperor Josef II of Austria in 1781, allowed some freedom for the Lutheran and Reformed churches. Hussitism, viewed as being too revolutionary, was not allowed.[2] The subsequent Protestant Patent of 1861, issued by Emperor Franz Josef, granted more rights to Protestants.

Prior to 1918 the Slovaks were under Hungarian rule (within the framework of the *Ausgleich* system, which divided the Habsburg Empire into autonomous Austrian and Hungarian sectors), and the Czechs in Bohemia and Moravia were under Austrian rule. The Slovaks suffered consistently under Magyarization. The Czechs, especially in the seventeenth and eighteenth centuries, struggled against Germanization.

After World War I, Czechs and Slovaks came together in one state. In the western provinces, the Lutheran and Reformed churches merged to form the Evangelical Church of the Czech Brethren, a body that blended

Hussite, Lutheran, and Reformed traditions.[3] In Slovakia, the Lutheran and Reformed churches remained separate. The Reformed Church was predominantly Hungarian, while the Lutheran Church in Slovakia was the largest of that Confession in the Slavic world. In the late nineteenth and early twentieth centuries other Protestant churches, including Baptists, Methodists, and Brethren, emerged in both parts of the country. The Unity of Brethren (Moravians), an important branch of Hussitism, also reemerged.

A "free from Rome" movement accompanied the liberation from Habsburg rule, and many people left the Roman Catholic Church. Several former Roman Catholic priests who had unsuccessfully sought to modernize the church led a movement to form a new church known as the Czechoslovak Church, later renamed the Czechoslovak Hussite Church. It combined certain Catholic, Orthodox, and Hussite elements with an extremely liberal theology. By 1930, about 10 percent of the population was traditional Protestant, and an equal number could be found in the Czechoslovak Church.

In general, the German Lutherans had organized separately from the Slovak Lutherans and the Evangelical Church of the Czech Brethren. They disappeared from the scene after World War II when Germans were expelled by the Czechs—a response to their role in bringing about Hitler's occupation. In September 1938 Hitler annexed the Sudetenland region of Bohemia and Moravia to Germany, and in March 1939 the remainder of Bohemia and Moravia was annexed. Hungary then annexed the southern rim of Slovakia and Ruthenia, and what was left of Slovakia was reorganized as a clerico-fascist Nazi puppet state under the presidency of a Catholic priest, Father Josef Tiso. Wartime Slovakia thus collaborated with Hitler. On the other hand, Slovak Lutheran ministers were active in the resistance and a number were imprisoned. After the war, Hungary exchanged 150,000 Slovaks for 150,000 Hungarians, which caused a membership decline in the Reformed Church of Slovakia.

Although Roman Catholicism is the dominant religion in Czechoslovakia, its situation, especially in the western lands, is different from that of neighboring Poland. Whereas the church in Poland has long been a champion of national culture, the Czech Roman Catholic Church was identified with the Counter-Reformation, with Habsburg domination, and with the accompanying Germanization of Czech culture. Alan Scarfe states that "in all of Eastern Europe, only in the Czech lands did the Catholic Church become divorced from a traditionally Catholic people."[4]

The religious situation in Slovakia is different. There, the Roman Catholic Church, like the Protestants and especially the Lutherans, was strongly identified with the Slovak struggle to develop its own national culture against Hungarian oppression. Conservative Slovak Catholicism has a much stronger hold on the people than Czech Catholicism does. Czech Catholicism is more secular, less indigenous, less influential, while Slovak Catholicism is closer to Catholicism in Poland.

Vicissitudes of Polish Protestants

There was no period of Protestant domination in Polish history such as there was in Czech history. During Reformation times, there were many Protestants in Poland, especially among the German minority, and for a period in the sixteenth century Poland offered more religious liberty than any other country in Europe. Protestantism was strong among the nobility and the bourgeoisie, but it did not gain a footing among the masses and, furthermore, was badly divided. During the Counter-Reformation, which was spearheaded by the Jesuits, Polish Protestantism virtually disappeared. Early in the eighteenth century, the erection of Protestant churches was forbidden and public Protestant worship greatly restricted. During succeeding decades, the kingdom of Poland was repeatedly partitioned by its neighbors—Austria, Russia, and Prussia—until it disappeared entirely, not to regain statehood until 1918. In the nineteenth century, however, Protestantism persisted and grew, especially in the Prussian section of divided Poland. Increasingly, Protestants were granted more rights both there and in the other two sectors. The Polish branch of the British and Foreign Bible Society, founded in 1816, aided this growth, and by 1914 about 5 percent of the population was Protestant.

Most Polish Protestants were Lutherans. Others were Reformed, Moravians, Baptists, Plymouth Brethren, and Seventh-Day Adventists. Although the Polish language was used in some congregations, Protestantism was identified as a religion of Germans. Here is a clear difference from the situation in Czechoslovakia, where Protestantism has never been seen as a foreign element.

During World War I, Polish Protestants, like Poland's Catholics, suffered at the hands of both Germans and Russians. Many Germans were deported from Poland to Russia, many church buildings were destroyed. The Germans burned many churches and even whole villages. After the war, the Polish National Catholic Church, which had been established in the United States among Polish émigrés who wanted to break with Rome, began a mission in Poland, and by 1939 it numbered 50,000 adherents. Also after the 1918 Armistice, a Protestant theological faculty was created at the University of Warsaw.

World War II and its aftermath brought much suffering to the Protestant minority. Many people were killed, and again many church buildings were destroyed. After the war, boundaries were changed, causing mass population movements. The reduction in size of the largest Protestant church, the Lutheran, was drastic.

> This Church is the small Polish remnant of a largely ethnic German and mainly Lutheran constituency of Evangelical Christians who in 1940 totalled about one million. In the wake of World War Two and the withdrawal or expulsion of the ethnic Germans, their number in 1946 was about 270,000; by 1963, only 120,000. With a renewed egress of ethnic Germans during the early 1970s, by 1976 it had fallen below 80,000. This Church thus represents vividly the effect of harsh forces creating a dispersed Church and the determination of its remaining members to be steadfast.[5]

Other Protestant churches also suffered losses during and after the war. Some Protestants paid a price for their involvement in the resistance movement, where, for example, Baptists conducted underground activity in concentration camps and helped people whose lives were in danger, including Jews.[6]

For the decimated Protestant churches, the main concern after 1945 was survival. That included help for suffering people through relief work financed mostly by churches abroad; establishing parishes; and training ministers, for many pastors and priests had died in concentration camps. Polish Protestants joined the newly formed World Council of Churches and received the spiritual and material support of a worldwide Christian movement.

Confrontation with Communism in Czechoslovakia

In Czechoslovakia the immediate postwar period also was a time of restoration and reconstruction. There, too, churches received help from abroad and became members of the World Council of Churches. In the late forties the churches in both countries faced the new task and challenge of working within communist systems. The Stalinist era was particularly difficult.

If one looks at the history of Czechoslovakia since 1945, one sees a conflict between advocates of a distinctly Czechoslovak social democracy, which would have drawn on the thought of Jan Hus, Tomáš Masaryk, and Karl Marx, and advocates of a strictly Marxist-Leninist-Stalinist model of socialism. The brief democratic period from 1945 through 1948, under the leadership of Eduard Beneš, was a time when many people believed that a distinctive Czechoslovak social democracy could be formed and that the nation might serve as a bridge between East and West.

Then came the communist takeover in 1948, and from that point on, except for the Prague Spring of 1968, the Leninist-Stalinist view was strictly imposed. There no longer was any place for the humanistic democratic philosophy of Masaryk and Beneš. Hus, however, continued to be honored and was interpreted as a forerunner of communism.

The churches had to adapt themselves to Stalinism. The religious pattern imposed on the country was that previously applied for many years in the Soviet Union. The state placed strict controls on the church in an effort to abort any interference with the formation of the new socialist man along Leninist-Stalinist lines. A Secretariat for Religious Affairs was formed within the Ministry of Culture and was given the right to approve or disapprove many aspects of church life—appointment of clergy, acceptance of students into theological seminaries, etc. In the past, clergy of most churches were paid by the government. Now all clergy were paid by the government, including pastors from free churches such as the Methodist and Baptist that had not received support. Since the government had taken the churches' lands as well as their social and educational institutions, payment to the clergy was viewed as a compensation. In time, it became apparent that pastors and priests were among the most poorly paid people in the country.

Church publications were carefully censored; it was difficult to write about current events, safer to write about church history. Youth work was severely restricted. Church youth camps were taken over by the government and turned into communist youth camps. Church institutions such as homes for the aged were seized by the state. Evangelism or other activity outside church walls was severely restricted. Limited amounts of paper were available for church publications. Universities discriminated against Christian youth, especially children of pastors. Spies were present at church gatherings, and pressure was placed on church people to spy on each other.

Shortly after the takeover, the government launched a strong attack on the Roman Catholic Church, confiscating its lands and nationalizing its schools. Perhaps the group that suffered most was the Greek-Rite Catholic Church (Uniate), which was particularly strong in eastern Slovakia adjoining the Ukraine. In 1950 it was banned and its priests and parishes were forcibly united with the Orthodox Church. Many of its priests were incarcerated; some died in prison.

Protestants, being a minority and not duty-bound to a foreign office such as the Vatican, were not viewed as so great a threat as Roman Catholics; yet they were equally pressured to fit into the new system and placed under the same controls. The Czechoslovak Hussite Church was perhaps the most uncritical in its support of the new government.

Immediately after the communist takeover on February 25, 1948, Patriarch Kovář had reassured President Gottwald of the Church's support. About a year later, the General Synod of the Czechoslovak Church, meeting in Prague on February 20–22, 1949, sent this message to President Gottwald: "We solemnly affirm our determination to give full moral support to our people in their efforts for the building of the socialist society in this country. We condemn all reactionary tendencies, and we are determined not to let them be established within the organism of the Church."[7]

Reformation Protestants indicated their willingness to work for socialism, but they were unwilling to blend Marxism and Christianity or to support dialectical materialism. Before long, Protestants too were in difficulty. Three Baptist ministers in Czechoslovakia were charged with spying for the United States, tried, and sentenced to long prison terms. They were accused of using World Baptist Convention funds to establish an espionage network.[8] The Salvation Army was outlawed. Two bishops of the Evangelical Church of the Augsburg Confession (Lutheran, Slovakia) were replaced with men who had demonstrated their loyalty to the government, yet the new bishops' support of government policy did not prevent their local Lutheran congregations from experiencing the same difficulties that other churches were having. Some Lutheran pastors were imprisoned for a time.

That all clergy were suspect in the government's eyes is evident from a document issued in 1949 by the secret police, indicating what to watch for in surveillance of pastors and priests. Among the items: Is he deeply involved with people or withdrawn, and if involved, with what kind of people—reactionaries or progressives? What interests or hobbies does he have? Does he take an interest in political issues? Has he ever worked with the Communist Party or other organizations in the National Front? What is his relationship to the working people, to the rich? What is his relationship to the USSR, to the West? What is his relationship to the church hierarchy—a fanatic supporter or a critic? How did he react to the takeover in February 1948?[9]

Stalinism in Poland

If Protestants in Czechoslovakia were seen as less of a threat to the
government than the Roman Catholic Church, this was even more true
in Poland, where Protestants had dwindled to less than 1 percent of the
population and where their churches were struggling for survival. From
the postwar period until today, Protestant churches in Poland have
found themselves caught between two great powers—the communist
state and the Roman Catholic Church.

Unlike Czechoslovakia's government, the Polish government brought
about a separation of church and state in its constitution of 1952.[10] This
was a boon to Protestants because, for the first time in modern history,
they were legally on a par with Roman Catholics. Discrimination by
Catholics was not entirely eliminated, but the change was clearly an
advance toward equality. Unlike their Czech counterparts, Polish Protestants received no financial support from the government. This was nothing new; they had never received assistance. Also, unlike their Czech
counterparts, Polish Protestants were able to keep their homes for the
aged, although their hospitals were taken over by the state.

Shortly after the war, the non-Roman Catholic churches, sensing
a need for mutual support, drew together in an ecumenical council.
This involved churches other than Protestants: that is, Orthodox, Polish Catholics, and Mariavites. In 1970, non-Roman Catholics composed
about 3 percent of the population.[11] A Christian Theological Seminary
was formed, and it, too, was ecumenical, including Protestant, Orthodox, and Old Catholic sections.

In general, Polish Protestants did not become as involved in political
affairs as did the dominant Roman Catholic Church. They concentrated
on worship, evangelism, religious education, the training of ministers,
and securing facilities. Their public statements were essentially positive
toward the building of socialism.

Yet, in spite of that, they did suffer in the Stalinist era. Charged with
being agents of Western imperialism, many pastors were imprisoned.
Those receiving money from Western churches were particularly suspect. Commenting on that difficult period, Methodist superintendent
Adam Kuczma wrote:

> In the years 1949–1956, our Church was [subjected] to the most diffi-
> cult trial. That was the gloomiest period in the history of the Methodist
> Church in Poland. During that time we lost about 50 percent of our
> Church members as a result of various pressures. A lot of our ministers

resigned from work in the Church in consequence of intimidation or out of fear for their future survival. Some of them emigrated to the West, looking for better living conditions. Those who have endured have come out of the crisis victorious. On those remnants, the renewal of the Church was started.[12]

The Polish government set up a Department of Church Affairs, one section dealing with Roman Catholics and a second with non-Roman Catholics. In the early years the department exercised more control than later, but it never was as severe toward Protestants as the comparable office in Czechoslovakia. From the late 1950s onward—after Władysław Gomułka came to power—the state decreased its interference in church life, and the churches accordingly no longer viewed the Department of Church Affairs as a serious threat.

In a study of East European Evangelicals, Walter Sawatsky makes a number of points that apply to the small Polish Protestant denominations. Many of these churches are rooted in continental Pietism and therefore stress the need for a personal experience of rebirth, a commitment to the authority of the Bible, and a sense of urgency in seeking the conversion of sinners to Christ. In their view, the most important contribution they can make to society is to provide more born-again Christians. They seek to provide a close-knit Christian community; they are not as concerned as the larger churches about being the nation's culture bearers. They have a strong tendency to be apolitical.[13] Their church leaders have participated in peace movements, notably the Christian Peace Conference, doing so partly out of loyalty to the state. They have not been deeply involved in the Christian-Marxist dialogue. In many cases, they lack the academic credentials. Their theologies are often conservative and out of touch with major trends of the twentieth century.

The Role of Josef Hromádka

The best-known and most influential Protestant leader in Eastern Europe in the postwar era was Josef L. Hromádka, a theologian of the Evangelical Church of the Czech Brethren and a member of the Central Committee of the World Council of Churches. An outspoken Christian socialist and antifascist, he found it necessary to flee from the Nazis and spent the war years teaching at Princeton Theological Seminary in New Jersey. After the war, he returned home and became dean of the Jan Hus Theological Seminary in Prague. When the communists took over in Czechoslovakia, he decided to remain, viewing communism as a dynamic social force and expressing the view that Christians could work within a communist system. He often said that the church needed to express penitence for its frequent past alliances with conservative or reactionary forces and that it should be progressive in its social outlook. If it is to be persecuted, he argued, it should be for its faith and not for its reactionary views. He did not seek to blend Christianity and Marxism; their conflict in worldviews was obvious. But he felt the church would support the building of socialism. He saw violations of people's rights in the new regime and sought to get them corrected by contacting the appropriate government office rather than by public denunciation. The government, of course, was pleased to have a leading churchman supporting socialism.

When the World Council of Churches held its initial assembly in Amsterdam in 1948, the day devoted to international affairs was designed to exemplify the fact that the church transcends East-West political conflicts and is not identified with any social system. The speakers for the occasion were John Foster Dulles, an eminent Presbyterian layman, later to become U.S. secretary of state, and Hromádka. Hromádka spoke about the crisis of Western civilization. The West, he said, had won World War I but had lost the peace. It had not lived by its ideals but had sought to perpetuate its privileges. Now, he said, a world revolution was taking place. He viewed anticommunism as sterile and unavailing. The West needed to recover its own ideals and to contribute from its heritage to the world revolution for social justice. Hromádka distinguished between communism and the Soviet system. He did not deny the oppressiveness of the Soviet system but tried to explain it in terms of Russian history. He also expressed the hope that the system might change as Russians and other Soviet citizens drew on their own literary and Christian heritage.[14]

Many churchmen in the West considered Hromádka to be naive in his attitude toward the Soviet Union, and many church people in his own country thought he collaborated too much with the government. Yet the depth of his thought, the power of his commitment, and his evident sincerity evoked wide respect.[15] He greatly influenced a whole generation of theological students. He exemplified the hope that Czechoslovakia could serve as a bridge between East and West and help lay the foundations for a peaceful world.

In the 1950s the government restored the Bethlehem Chapel, the place where more than five hundred years earlier Jan Hus had preached his fiery reform sermons to enthusiastic crowds, attacking the church for its wealth and immorality. The restoration of this building reflects the proclivity of Czech communists to portray Hus, in some sense, as a forerunner of communism. A Czech Marxist historian, in the conclusion of a book on the Hussite movement, wrote:

> the Czechoslovak Socialist Republic, embodying the centuries-old struggle of the Czech and Slovak people for a just social order, acclaims the Hussite tradition. Annual celebrations are held in memory of Jan Hus. The Bethlehem Chapel in Prague has been restored on its original site and a Liberation Memorial has been erected on Vi'tkov Hill, the site of Žižka's victory at Prague. The Czechoslovak people value the Hussite tradition not only as an inspiration for their revolutionary and patriotic struggle and a treasury of national culture, but also because it shows the importance of peaceful cooperation among the nations.[16]

It is interesting that Czech humanists (for example, Masaryk), Czech Protestants, and Czech communists can all draw on the Hussite tradition. However, humanists and communists have tended to ignore or downplay that tradition's religious content.

In 1955 the Ecumenical Council of Churches in Czechoslovakia was formed, consisting of nearly all the non-Roman Catholic churches—Protestant, Orthodox, and Old Catholic. It aimed to foster cooperation among the country's churches and to strengthen relations with churches in both East and West. It has worked closely with the World Council of Churches.

In 1958 the council, together with the Comenius Theological Faculty in Prague and the Slovak Evangelical Theological Faculty in Bratislava, called a meeting that led to formation of the Christian Peace Conference. The conference elected Hromádka its president and chose Prague as its headquarters. Its office was in the same building that housed the offices of the Evangelical Church of the Czech Brethren. In subsequent years, it held a number of assemblies. The Christian Peace Conference brought together church leaders from Eastern Europe and other parts of the world to discuss theological and social issues. Approved by East European governments, it gave churchmen an opportunity to have fellowship with each other under the banner of peace. One reason for its establishment was the conviction of some East Europeans that the World Council of Churches was dominated by Westerners and Western views and that an Eastern-oriented peace movement was needed. In addition, the Christian Peace Conference could be manipulated for Soviet-bloc peace propaganda and was therefore useful to the communists. There was no official connection between this organization and the World Council of Churches, although there were some individuals, such as Hromádka, who were active in both organizations.

The Russian Orthodox Church's participation in the Christian Peace Conference helped to open the way to further ecumenical involvement. In 1959 the Russian Orthodox Church began to take part in the Conference of European Churches, and in 1961 it joined the World Council of Churches at its assembly in New Delhi.[17]

The Christian Peace Conference has been strongly criticized in the West for its one-sided pronouncements. Quite often it simply endorsed positions taken by East-bloc governments. There have been some Western participants in the conference, but they usually have taken part as individuals rather than as representatives of their churches. In the 1970s and 1980s the conference secured a greater involvement of church leaders from the Third World.

Although the 1950s and 1960s were difficult years for the churches, there were some positive developments. Church membership declined, but the commitment of those who remained was deep. There was nothing to gain socially or politically by belonging to a church; in fact, there was much to lose. So a kind of sifting of the congregations occurred. Bible studies increased in importance, and lay people were led by clergy into serious theological studies.

Christian-Marxist Dialogue

In the 1960s a Christian-Marxist dialogue developed in several parts of Europe, often begun by the Roman Catholic Paulus-Gesellschaft, headquartered in Munich. In Czechoslovakia the initiative came from Protestants. Hromádka was active on the Christian side, and Milan Machovec, a philosophy professor at Charles University, played the leading Marxist role. According to Hromádka, Christians could bring biblical insights to the dialogue, and Marxists could help Christians see the need for radical changes in society. Hromádka often pointed out that economic change alone does not change human beings and that Marxists would need to turn to religion to help people become fully human. He insisted that even in a communist system, there would continue to be greed, envy, and struggles for power.

Machovec identified three conditions in Czechoslovakia that aided in the emergence of dialogue: (1) the Czechoslovak self-identity as a people bridging East and West; (2) their consciousness of having started the first reformation in Europe and their continuing concern for reform; and (3) the fact that Czechs took seriously Masaryk's statement that "democracy is discussion."[18]

In 1967 an international Christian-Marxist Congress took place in Mariánske Lázně (Marienbad). It was cosponsored by the Czechoslovak Academy of Sciences and the Paulus-Gesellschaft. This was the only international Christian-Marxist congress that occurred in a socialist country, and its theme was "Creativity and Freedom." The presence and participation of 170 people from the West, predominantly theologians and ministers, had an electrifying effect on participants at the meeting and on public opinion. The congress served as a visible sign of the profound changes that were taking place in Czechoslovakia.[19]

Christian-Marxist dialogue gained momentum during the liberal phase of the 1968 Prague Spring. On one occasion, some 2,000–3,000 people convened for a public dialogue in Prague. Theologian Jan Lochman, who was actively involved in the dialogue, points out in his book *Church in a Marxist Society* that seminarians in the Comenius Theological Seminary were intensely studying the young Marx.

> In the early fifties, our Comenius Faculty in Prague was probably the only place in Eastern Europe where this deep humanistic philosophy was dealt with—as a challenge to that Stalinist form of Marxism which was then the only form recognized. We did it not against the Marxists—as an ideological battle; on the contrary, we did it for them—or better, in our common interest of humanization of our society and as a presupposition for future dialogue.[20]

Lochman taught in the Comenius Theological Seminary until 1968, then spent a year at Union Theological Seminary in New York, and was thereafter at the theological seminary in Basel.

Hints of Dialogue Among Polish Protestants

While Czech Protestants were creatively engaged in dialogue, Polish Protestants were feeling more secure. In 1963 the presidium of the Polish Ecumenical Council said that the country's Protestants had a positive attitude toward the system and the changes it had effected, adding specifically that they had "a different assessment of possibilities of cooperation between Church and State" from the Catholic Church.[21]

On the twentieth anniversary of People's Poland, Bishop Andrzej Wantula, head of the Lutheran Church in Poland and vice president of the Lutheran World Federation, praised state authorities for assuring

> peace, justice, equality. . . . Within the framework of the new system, People's Poland has guaranteed religious freedom to all Churches. Our

country has made it possible for our Church to rise up from the terrible ruins and destruction of war and reorganize its religious life. Moreover, it has given us material assistance to rebuild our churches. We may state, in joy and gratitude, that we now have the necessary conditions not only for our existence but for further development as well.[22]

The Prague Spring

Democratic ideals did not die in Czechoslovakia. Between the two wars, Czechoslovakia developed a functioning democracy. In the 1960s writers and artists helped focus attention on human rights and human values and prepared the way for the Prague Spring under the leadership of First Secretary Alexander Dubček between March and August 1968. During this period, liberal reforms brought to fruition what many people had hoped for—political and civil rights under a socialist system, "socialism with a human face." Under Dubček, freedom of the press, freedom of speech, and freedom of religion were restored. For Josef Hromádka and others it was the fulfillment of a dream and vindication of the belief that communism could be influenced from within. A new vitality swept the churches. In Slovakia there was a gathering of Lutheran pastors, including those who had been in prison. It was a time of joy, but also a time of questioning the policies of church leaders in the previous era. Some people felt that church leaders had been too ready to cooperate with the regime, even to the point of collaboration.

During the Prague Spring, Christian-Marxist dialogue flourished, a huge gathering in Prague took place, and church leaders and members supported Dubček's efforts at democratization, seeing it as a unique renewal within the socialist movement. The enthusiasm of the times was reflected in the Third Assembly of the Christian Peace Conference, held in Prague in April 1968.

Late in the Prague Spring, Erika Kadlecová, a sociologist, was appointed director of the Secretariat for Religious Affairs. She took a somewhat pluralistic view of society and was relatively open-minded in matters of church and religion. She had served as a key leader in the dialogue at Marienbad.

The Warsaw Pact invasion of Czechoslovakia in August 1968 not only ended the experiment with a more open form of socialism, but terminated Christian-Marxist dialogue. Machovec and others lost their positions at the university. Many Protestant pastors, especially in the Evangelical Church of the Czech Brethren, had been active Dubček supporters, and in time a number of them lost their state licenses to preach and were forced to do manual labor.

After the Warsaw Pact invasion, Jaroslav Ondra, the Czech general secretary of the Christian Peace Conference, was removed from office under Soviet pressure, and Hromádka himself resigned from the conference. He wrote a letter to the Soviet government protesting the invasion: "My deepest feeling is of disillusionment, sorrow, and shame," he wrote. "In my lifetime, there has been no greater tragedy than this event. . . . The bond of friendship between Czechoslovakia and the Soviet Union has been destroyed. . . . The moral weight of socialism and communism has been shattered for a long time to come."[23]

After this letter became known, many members of the Evangelical Church of the Czech Brethren breathed more easily. They saw that Hromádka was capable of criticizing the Soviets, and their trust in him, shaken at times by some of his actions, was now stronger than before.[24]

At the time of the Prague Spring, the Slovak desire for greater autonomy came to the fore, and steps taken in that direction were completed in the "normalization" period when a federation of the Czech and Slovak states came into being. After the invasion, the Czech leadership of the Christian Peace Conference was replaced with Russian and Hungarian leaders, and the conference followed the Soviet line more closely than before. A number of European and American churchmen protested and withdrew. For a time, the Evangelical Church of the Czech Brethren did not participate, even though offices of the two bodies were in the same building. At this point, the Slovak Evangelicals (Lutherans) came into prominence in the conference. Their leader, Bishop Jan Michalko, had been consistently uncritical of whatever government was in power. Following Hromádka's death in December 1969, Michalko prepared a eulogy. He expressed appreciation for what Hromádka had done but criticized him for his weakness in resigning. He attributed Hromádka's action to his illness. Many people from Czechoslovakia and abroad attended the funeral, while Russian Orthodox Church dignitaries were noticeably absent.

Normalization in Czechoslovakia

The Prague Spring showed that twenty years of Leninist-Stalinist indoctrination had not been sufficiently effective. Thus, during the normalization period a far more thorough effort was made to develop "the socialist man" and to indoctrinate him with atheist thought. The campaign to spread atheism and reduce the influence of religion was manifested in varied efforts. There was a campaign to reduce the number of children signed up for religious instruction in the schools or enrolled in catechism classes, and the enrollment process was made more difficult and the penalties for doing so were increased. Another form of atheist indoctrination included the regular distribution of questionnaires to school pupils. One questionnaire's introduction said that some people, despite scientific education, still had illusions about life after death and about the existence of supernatural beings. Among the questions the pupils were asked were:

Did the school instruction through the building

of a scientific worldview give you enough insight and help in the battle against religion, against its burdensomeness?

In case you are religious, do you know that

your religious affiliation will be a great hindrance to you in the realization of your future vocation?[25]

Church leaders continued to make clear their loyalty to the government and to testify to their willingness to "build socialism." This was especially true of the Slovak Lutherans. Professors at the Lutheran seminary made a number of public addresses, eulogizing the Russian revolution and the new path it offered mankind. In 1975 Michalko gave an interview at a meeting of the Christian Peace Conference held in Budapest in which he claimed that the laws affecting the church had not changed and that the churches could still engage in significant Christian activity without breaking the law. His church, he said, had developed a Theology of the Diaconate that focused on serving people in their situation, that is, in a socialist society.[26] This was similar to what Hungarian Lutherans were teaching. It appeared to be a modified version of the Lutheran concept of the Two Kingdoms—the view that the Kingdom of God relates to the individual Christian and the church, but not to society; political and economic laws are sovereign in the societal realm. It followed that socialism might be the appropriate form for society and that it is the state's business to say how society should be administered. The church's task, then, was to produce loyal, hard-working citizens.

After the invasion, when Kadlecová was removed from her post as secretary for religious affairs, Karel Hrůza took over the position and expressed his philosophy in an article published in the Czech press:

socialist man, active and conscious creator of the new society, must be freed from prejudices and obscurantism. To these belongs religion,

which for centuries has been identified with social oppression. . . .
Therefore, it is important to carry on a program of atheistic propaganda and education, the purpose of which is to free the believers from
spiritual oppression and to deepen in them the consciousness of their
own power, ability, and understanding. . . . During the whole period
of the building of socialist society, we will engage in a battle for the
conscience of man, so that he may become an active creator of his
future. In this realm, there is and always will be an unbridgeable
difference between the ideology of communism and the ideology of
the Churches and of religion. This battle we will patiently fight, and we
will do all that is necessary so that in the course of building socialism,
atheism will be established in the conscience of each Czechoslovak
citizen.[27]

By the mid-1970s, normalization had presumably taken place. Life
looked "normal" in Czechoslovakia, and the economy was reasonably
healthy. People seemed to be satisfied; consumer goods were in good
supply. But writer Václav Havel warned in 1975 that the system encouraged feelings of hopelessness and apathy, killing the spirit and provoking a spiritual and moral crisis.[28]

Apathy also afflicted the churches, as evinced by an appeal issued by
the Rev. Jakub Trojan, a minister who lost his preaching license in the
early 1970s. He originally got into trouble for conducting the funeral
ceremony for Jan Palach, the university student who immolated himself
in 1969 to protest public acquiescence in "normalization" and who immediately became an important symbol of resistance. Trojan was accused of
having influenced the student to set himself on fire. In his appeal, Trojan
accused church people of taking one of two unsatisfactory paths. Either
they adapted uncritically to society or they withdrew from public activity
and assumed a ghetto mentality.

For the time being, the situation looks unsatisfactory, because the
official Christianity in our country has chosen either the path of cheap
adaptability, whereby it only exacerbated the sickness of socialism
without being able to prevent harsh antagonism toward itself on the
part of the system, or denied solidarity to its atheistic surroundings
and proclaimed its faith so to say "defiantly," i.e., conscious of its
sectarian differentiation and superiority. In my opinion, both represent
a blocked path which aggravated the crisis of the Christian communities as well as of the whole society.[29]

Trojan belonged to a group of young pastors in the Evangelical Church
of the Czech Brethren known as the "New Orientation" group. Its stated
purpose was to draw lessons from the theology of Hromádka, Karl Barth,
and Dietrich Bonhöffer and, responding to the biblical message and the

guidance of the Holy Spirit, to develop a social interpretation of the gospel for society and the world. In the late 1960s and early 1970s the group stimulated the church synod to speak out against injustices, but later the synod became more compliant and failed to respond to its requests.

It seems that this group, although following Hromádka, was going one step further. While Hromádka had indicated that the church had to demonstrate its social progressiveness before it could be in a position to criticize the failings of socialist society, this group felt the church had demonstrated that concern and the time had come to be critical. In this respect, it was taking an approach more akin to the Evangelical churches in East Germany, less like that of the Reformed Church in Hungary, and certainly quite different from the Christian Peace Conference's approach.

Protestants and Charter 77

That some of the spirit of the Prague Spring continued to live after 1968 became evident a decade later when the dissident group known as Charter 77 appeared. It circulated a document calling for the government's observance of the guarantees to human rights provided in the Czechoslovak constitution and recognized in the final act of the Helsinki Agreement. The document bore 241 signatures. Later, other people signed, bringing the total of signatories to more than a thousand. Among them were several ex-communists and several Catholic and Protestant clergymen. The Protestants were from the New Orientation group. Few signers were from Slovakia, reflecting the Czech-Slovak bifurcation. Czechs desired democratization; Slovaks sought some form of autonomy.

The original charter pointed out many violations of human rights in Czechoslovakia. Regarding religious liberty, the document stated:

> Freedom of thought, conscience, and religious conviction, emphatically guaranteed by Article 18 of the International Covenant on Civil and Political Rights, is systematically curtailed by despotic arbitrariness, by restrictions imposed on the activities of clergymen who are under constant threat of revocation or loss of the state permission to perform their function, by reprisals affecting the livelihood and other aspects of life of those persons who express their religious convictions by word or deed, by suppression of religious instruction in [the] schools, etc.[30]

The Czechoslovak government placed great pressure on church leaders to disown the charter and its signers, and, to a large extent, the church leaders compiled. Some denounced the charter; others simply stated that they had had nothing to do with it and were reaffirming their loyalty to the state. Some church leaders were forced to rewrite their statements several times to make them acceptable to the authorities, while others defended their capitulation by saying their churches would have been closed if they had refused to disown the charter.

The government punished the declaration's signatories. Those clergy who had not already lost their preaching licenses lost them now. By 1978, at least 162 signatories had been dismissed from their posts, another thirty were in exile, and twenty were tried and sentenced for alleged offenses against the state.

In spite of the persecution, Charter 77 proceeded to prepare additional documents giving further details of human rights violations. Document no. 9 dealt with religious freedom. It pointed out, among many criticisms, discrimination in employment against religious people, restrictions on the importing of religious literature, denial of religious education, interference with and prevention of religious retreats and conferences, and interference with admission to theological schools. The document began with a quotation from Jan Comenius, the great seventeenth-century Czech educator and churchman: "May everything flow freely. Let there be no violence anywhere." The essential philosophy of the document is stated in this paragraph:

> Freedom of conviction, freedom of thought, freedom of conscience and freedom of religion, together with other freedoms and human rights, must become an object of interest and respect not only because they represent certain citizens' privileges (for instance, freedom of religion); as a matter of fact, without them the whole society cannot become a genuine human community. Therefore, neither the people nor the state have the right to restrain any expressions of freedom of thought, conviction and conscience. On the contrary, their task and obligation are to contribute as much as they can to liberate man to the fullest extent, so that he might develop as a free being, use his freedom in creative endeavors of his choice, and participate actively in the political activity of the country, in the administration of his state and in the economic and cultural development of his society.[31]

Several clergy who signed this document issued an open letter explaining their reasons for doing so. Also, in 1977 a document signed by thirty-one members of the Evangelical Church of the Czech Brethren was presented to the government. It called attention to violations of religious liberty and listed specific cases of infringement of civil rights. The introduction stated flatly that atheism as the government's official philosophy was being administratively forced on the people and that churches were simply tolerated communities, designed to be reduced and eventually liquidated. Ten types of violations of religious liberty were listed: (1) Reduction of congregational activity. Permission for church activities had to be obtained at the State Office for Religious Affairs and was often denied. (2) Reduction of ecumenical activity. Seldom were churches allowed to do anything together. (3) State permission for the discharge of pastoral work. The names were given out of pastors whose preaching licenses had been revoked, of seminary graduates to whom preaching licenses had not been issued, and of prospective theological students whose right to study had been canceled. It noted eight hundred theological students in Czechoslovakia in 1969, but only four hundred in 1977. (4) Harassment of pastors in active service. They were visited by secret police, constantly watched, pressured to give information, and their contacts with foreigners restricted. (5) Restrictions and pressures in religious education. In 1969 there were 10,700 Czech Brethren children in religious education in the schools; in 1977 there were only 576. (6) Discrimination in occupations. Christians were discriminated against in industry, the civil service, and public education. (7) Opportunities for education. Children from Christian homes were often denied entrance into universities and high schools. (8) The New Orientation. This informal pastors' group for the study of theological and ethical questions was being persecuted. (9) Restrictions of church publication activity. Church publications were censored, financially restricted, and hampered in many ways. (10) Lack of freedom at assemblies and synods. These meetings were constantly watched, and government pressure was brought to bear on them to take action against various dissident groups within the church. At the end, the document listed the cases of discrimination against Protestants.[32]

One violation of religious liberty was quickly illustrated. Pressure was brought to bear on church leaders to discipline signers of the document and on the theological seminary to point out the error of their ways. The seminary did make a vague disclaimer, which angered the signers as well as many theological students and other church people. Church leaders were caught between government and dissenters. Like the endorsers of Charter 77, the thirty-one signatories of this document suffered discrimination, hostility, and loss of jobs.

The types of discrimination listed in the Brethren Church's petition existed in other churches as well. In 1973, for instance, more than 500 of 3,500 Catholic priests lacked state-issued licenses to serve in their parishes and had to find other employment—for example, as unskilled manual workers. In this way, some 1,600 Catholic parishes were left without priests.[33]

One of the charter signatories, the Rev. Miloš Rejchert, a pastor of the Evangelical Church of the Czech Brethren who had been deprived since 1972 of permission to exercise his pastoral duties, wrote an angry letter to the theological faculty criticizing it and the church synod for "disowning" those who signed the charter and related documents. He charged the faculty with being more interested in making peace with the state than with remaining true to their Reformation heritage. He further accused the faculty with being untrue to the beliefs taught to students, beliefs that inspired the charter signatories to take their action. Similarly, a group of twenty-two members of the Evangelical Church of the Brethren wrote to the Christian Peace Conference asking it to express concern for the eleven church people who were in prison. The letter gave the basic facts in the case. Rejchert then wrote a letter to Hungarian Bishop Károly Tóth, the conference's secretary general, accusing the conference of turning a blind eye to instances of gross injustice in Czechoslovakia.[34]

Church publications continued to serve the churches. In 1988 there were twenty-seven of them compared with 151 in 1948, and they had to carry on their work under strict censorship. Yet, while censorship of journals was severe, greater freedom was allowed for the publication of Bibles and hymnbooks.

A highly significant development in publications took place in the 1970s. Both Czech and Slovak Protestants produced new versions of the Bible, and the Czech version, prepared by an ecumenical committee, was being published and distributed also by the Roman Catholic Church in Czechoslovakia. The United Bible Society's world report noted that the most dramatic increase was in Czechoslovakia, where distribution rose from 21,000 Bibles in 1979 to 131,000 in 1980. This resulted from new versions being completed.[35] New hymnbooks also were prepared in both parts of the country with the financial help of Western churches.

Polish Protestants and Solidarity

In Poland in the 1970s there were signs of growth in some of the churches—the Baptist Church in particular. A highlight for the Baptists was the visit of the Rev. Billy Graham in 1978, the first trip to Poland by a major Western evangelist. Roman Catholic churches cooperated. The visit enhanced ecumenical cooperation and gave Polish Protestants some unaccustomed public recognition.[36]

In the early 1980s Poland experienced the rise of the Solidarity trade union movement, which was seeking to do for Poland some of the things the Prague Spring had sought to accomplish in Czechoslovakia. While standing for the right of free labor unions, Solidarity also pressed for a number of social reforms and human rights. At first, Protestants gave Solidarity their full support; later, they were more withdrawn as they saw the movement's close identification with Roman Catholicism.

According to the leader of the Polish Ecumenical Council, Andrzej Wojtowicz, Protestants felt that Roman Catholics were using the weakness of the Communist Party to gain certain rights for the church—access to radio and permission to build new buildings—with little concern for the rights of Protestant and Orthodox churches. Therefore, even while approving what it was doing, non-Catholic denominations kept some distance from the movement since they were not interested in seeing a further Catholicization of Polish society.[37]

Between the end of World War II and the 1980s, conflicts arose between Roman Catholics and Lutherans over church buildings in the area taken from Germany and given to Poland. Most Germans moving westward were Protestants, while virtually all of the people moving in were Roman Catholics. The government gave many unused Protestant churches to Roman Catholics. Conflicts arose in various circumstances, one of them an instance in which a growing Lutheran congregation wanted to reclaim some of the confiscated churches. Most conflicts were resolved by 1990, but some bitterness remained.[38]

In 1981 martial law was declared. The great dialogue initiated by Solidarity was stopped. Although martial law was lifted in 1983, new government regulations brought the opposition under tighter control. Polish society remained in deep tension. Efforts were made to establish a new concordat between the government and the Catholic Church—efforts that culminated in establishing diplomatic relations between the Vatican and the Polish state in July 1989.[39] As deliberations about a concordat with the Roman Catholic Church unfolded, Protestants expressed concern whether such an agreement would have a negative effect on their rights and interests.

In 1982, Polish Protestants obtained access to the media. Baptists were the first to broadcast. A schedule was worked out that allowed broadcasts on alternating Sunday afternoons to member denominations of the Polish Ecumenical Council.[40]

Although Jehovah's Witnesses were illegal in Poland, their activities were tolerated. In 1983 they were allowed to hold forty-one public meetings attended by some nine thousand people. Passports were issued to five thousand Jehovah's Witnesses for travel to Austria for a religious congress.[41] Witnesses were imprisoned for failure to perform military service; offers of alternative service were made to them, but these were not accepted.[42]

The work of the churches in Poland was greatly aided by the services of the Polish Bible Society. In 1975 a new translation of the Bible was published in Catholic and Protestant editions. By the end of 1980 more than 130,000 copies of the new Protestant edition had been printed. The Polish Bible Society also printed Bibles for export. In 1986, 50,000 copies of the New Testament with colored illustrations were printed for churches in Czechoslovakia. Bibles also were sent to French-speaking parts of Africa. In 1985 and 1986 some 1.8 million copies of the Bible, the New Testament, or the Psalms were published.[43]

Polish Protestant churches have had many exchanges with and considerable financial support from Protestant churches in West Germany. Beginning in the 1970s, these contacts have contributed toward reconciliation between Germans and Poles. Polish Protestants also exchanged visits with Russian Orthodox churches and deepened relationships with church leaders in the Soviet Union.

Cooperation between the Ecumenical Council and the Roman Catholic Church increased in the late 1980s. A mixed commission met regularly to discuss matters of mutual concern. When Pope John Paul II visited Poland in 1987, he met with the representatives of the council and told them: "The cooperation between the Roman Catholic Church and the Polish Ecumenical Council has already been developing for many years. The experience and attainments up until today encourage us to continue the dialogue in spite of the difficulties, which we ought to overcome on the way to fuller fellowship."[44]

For the most part, Protestant services have been held in Polish. Yet Protestants continued to be viewed by many Poles as foreigners. A visitor to Poland in 1984 reported:

> According to the national mind-set, Lutherans who claim to be Poles are actually "Germans," Baptists and Methodists who claim the same are considered "Americans." The Orthodox—and the Marxists—are branded as "Russians." The Marxist-Leninist state and the Protestant Churches therefore end up having strong common goals: both of them combat the Catholic episcopate's attempt to portray Poland as a monolithic Catholic nation. Both Protestants and Marxists fear the increasing power of the Catholic Church. The communist state has therefore always attempted to elevate the significance of the Protestant Churches at the expense of the Catholic majority. . . . Most of the Protestant Churches never received any legal status prior to 1947. As a result, it is

not uncommon for the Protestants of Eastern Europe to claim that they fare better under communist rule than was ever the case under a Catholic or Orthodox regime.[45]

Witold Benedyktowicz, a Polish theologian, discussed the dilemma of Polish Protestantism in a speech delivered at the European Conference of Evangelical Churches on Confessional Affairs, which met in Wisla-Jawarnik, Poland, 23–27 April 1987. He pointed out that Polish Protestants faced "two giants"—Catholicism and the Marxist state—and went on to say that Protestants cannot simply be absorbed by Catholicism; neither should they be uncritically submissive to the state.[46]

Continued Pressure in Czechoslovakia

Although the 1980s were some years from the Prague Spring, the Czechoslovak government did not relax strictures instituted during the normalization period. In 1982, Charter 77 issued document No. 22, which returned to the subject of religious freedom, especially criticizing the administration of religious affairs. According to the document, countless regulations undermined religious liberty, and the religious affairs officers were free to arbitrarily interpret what religious freedom was and was not. Normally, an avowed atheist has the best chance of getting the religious affairs position, while a church member has the poorest chance. Many state regulations concerning religion were not even published,[47] and people were punished for disobeying rules they knew nothing about. For example, a group of eight laypersons gathered in someone's weekend cabin to read the Bible and pray; they were arrested for having a religious meeting without a permit. Many other examples were given. All in all, the document concluded, the administration of religious affairs was chaotic, bureaucratic, and arbitrary.[48]

According to Keston College, the authoritative British center for the study of religion in the communist world, half of the Charter 77 members were practicing Catholics and Protestants. Thirteen were Catholic priests, and fifteen Protestant pastors. Their presence gave the movement influence, moral responsibility, and greater credibility among believers.[49] The ministers who signed the charter were in a minority, and they usually were not supported by their own churches. Furthermore, they all lived in the western provinces. Czechs were much more involved than Slovaks.

In the early 1980s Pentecostals, some of whose members had experienced trials and imprisonment, were given legal recognition.[50] However, some Adventists were placed in psychiatric confinement and diagnosed as suffering from "paranoia religiosa adventistika."[51] Some Slovak Lutheran ministers were charged with smuggling Bibles, others with distributing illegal literature, and still others with conducting unofficial Bible and song meetings. A Baptist minister lost his license because he was too active in evangelistic work. A Czech Brethren minister lost his preaching permit because he held a summer Bible school outside his church building.

The worst charges were made against the illegal Jehovah's Witnesses, who were being jailed for refusing army service. The Minister of the Interior Jaromír Obzina said of the Witnesses:

> This sect is the most anti-communist, anti-progressive, and anti-scientific Church denomination we have, and that despite the Witnesses' [claims] that they are totally apolitical. . . . It is precisely because they refuse to support any government that they do not acknowledge our state symbols, refuse to take oaths, to take part in elections or the voluntary brigades of socialist work. Their passivity has only one aim, which is the disintegration of the mobilization of the masses and the defense-readiness of the country.[52]

It is generally known that church participation has declined since 1948. This, of course, was true in both Eastern and Western Europe. A number of the churches suffered from shortages of pastors, which could be attributed to government quotas set for theological seminaries, to the loss of preaching licenses by a number of pastors, and to the unattractiveness of the profession to young people. The ministry was very poorly paid, and it was a profession that easily could bring someone into conflict with state and society.

Still, some signs of increased interest in religion were noticeable in Czechoslovakia in the 1980s. Erika Kadlecová, the sociologist who served as commissioner for religious affairs during the Dubček era, gave some of the reasons for this increase. In an article published outside the country, she stated that a greater world interest in religion was partly due to a disenchantment with science, with secular societies, and with the promises of social reformers.[53] She then commented on the Czech situation. There, she found much hopelessness and apathy. Disillusionment was greater because hopes were so high. People lived under a system where they were forced to pretend that they believed pronouncements that obviously contradicted all reason and daily experience. Religion had been suppressed, but those remnants that survived were gaining new respect. Churches had become religious diasporas. This transition was difficult for the Catholic Church, which was accustomed to being the state church. It was no novelty for Protestants, for whom the diaspora was familiar.

New Laws in Poland

In Poland in the late 1980s, the declining power of communism and the increasing democratization resulted in changes in church-state relations. In May 1989 the Sejm (parliament) passed a law entitled "Concerning the State's Attitude toward the Catholic Church in the Polish People's Republic," which gave a legal status to the Roman Catholic Church. The church had had no legal status since 1934, when the government had abrogated the existing concordat. The other main Christian denominations, however, had received legal recognition shortly after World War II. In deliberations leading to enactment of the new law, representatives of the Catholic Church and the Polish Ecumenical Council took part. The law restored many liberties to the Roman Catholic Church, without giving it a de jure privileged position.[54] Two months later, the government signed a new concordat with the Vatican.[55]

Also in May 1989 the Sejm passed the Law Guaranteeing Freedom of Conscience and Belief. Members of the Polish Ecumenical Council were consulted in connection with this law, which defined all citizens' duties and rights that follow from the constitutional principles of freedom of conscience and creed, separation of church and state, and equality of all denominations. The rights were spelled out in some detail. For instance, there was a provision for supplementary service if military service contradicted someone's religious convictions or professed moral principles.[56]

Speaking for the Polish Ecumenical Council about this law, Bishop Wiktor Wysoczanski of the Old Catholic Church stated: "the act will constitute an important legal and political document for all Churches and religious organizations in Poland, including those which were discriminated against in the inter-war period. The act would place the legal situation of all Churches and religious organizations in Poland on an equal footing for the first time in the country's history."[57]

Although the bishop's statement represented the views of nearly all of the council members, one church leader, Lutheran Bishop Janusz Narzynski, disagreed. In his report to the Lutheran synod, he asserted that favoritism was still being shown to the Roman Catholic Church. This was reflected, he said, in the procedures adopted in devising the laws. Several years of preparation took place before the law regarding the status of the Roman Catholic Church was adopted, but only a short time was spent preparing the law on freedom of conscience. Protestants were not always fully informed about the law pertaining to Catholics. As he saw it, such procedures "create an impression of true division of believers in Poland into a privileged majority and a tolerated minority, in accordance with the anachronistic principle, 'first among equals.' "[58]

Yet another relevant law was passed in May 1989, this one providing social security for clergy of all denominations. Thus, the last exception to social security coverage disappeared.[59]

In October 1989 Poland's Council of Ministers officially dissolved the Office for Religious Affairs. The office was felt to be unnecessary in light of the laws passed in May, which regulated the situation of the churches. The remaining task and duties of the office were taken over by the minister in charge of the Office of the Council of Ministers. That made Jacek Ambrozials the first noncommunist dealing with religious matters. Keston College commented: "this should ensure that for the first time in the post-war history of Poland, religious matters will be dealt with on an administrative rather than an ideological basis."[60]

In May 1990 the Roman Catholic Church called for religious instruction to be introduced in public schools. The laws passed the previous year allowed for religious schools, for religious instruction in churches, and for cooperation of schools with churches regarding scheduling, but they did not include religious instruction in public schools. This new demand caused deep concern among non-Catholics. "They fear that non-Catholic children may face discrimination and that already cool ecumenical relations could be worsened. They would prefer religious instruction to continue to take place on church premises, as has been the case since 1961," the Keston College report stated.[61] It was apparent that Protestants felt nervous in their new situation, that of being a religious minority in a democratic Catholic society.

Reform and Revolution in Czechoslovakia

In the late 1980s changes were taking place in the countries touching Czechoslovakia—Poland, the Soviet Union, Hungary—but the Czechoslovak government remained rigidly communist. However, some signs of change were visible, as was obvious from various petitions signed by large numbers of citizens and by several large demonstrations. Also, the government began to prepare a new constitution. At this point, some Protestant leaders engaged in conversations with government officials and made proposals for constitutional changes, particularly in the area of greater religious liberty.

The Baptists offered proposals that advocated equal rights for all church bodies, an end to discrimination in state schools against children of religious families, alternatives to military service, and an end to capital punishment. They expressed the desire for stricter abortion laws, freedom to broadcast religious programs, and the right of Christians to become teachers.[62]

The Evangelical Church of the Czech Brethren called for freedom of religious expression, the right to enter any occupation, the right of churches to engage in social welfare work, the opportunity for alternative service for conscientious objectors, the abolishment of capital punishment, and a cultural policy not based on ideology. Besides making these proposals for the new constitution, the same church also recommended work on revision of the penal code. It called on the legislative committee to eliminate laws pertaining to state supervision of churches and for the addition of laws protecting people whose freedom of conscience was denied and who were frequently punished more than once for the same offense (such as refusal to serve in the armed forces).[63]

While these discussions were under way, dramatic changes took place in neighboring East Germany, culminating in the tearing down of the Berlin Wall. Those events were soon followed by a change in Czechoslovakia—the "Velvet Revolution," which erupted on 17 November 1989. The synod of the Evangelical Church of the Czech Brethren was meeting in Prague at the time of the student demonstrations that led to the government's downfall. On hearing eyewitness reports by students of police brutality against the demonstrators, the synod sent a telegram to the prime minister, protesting the violence and demanding that he use his influence to resolve the situation by nonviolent means and order the release of those arrested. The synodal senior, Josef Hromádka, a distant relative of the late theologian of that name, made a number of unsuccessful efforts to talk directly with high government officials, but he had to communicate the synod's wishes in writing. The synod also issued a statement calling for equality before the law, for the right of assembly, the right to freedom of expression, the need to use nonviolent means, and the need to release prisoners of conscience.[64]

Speaking in his capacity as chair of the Ecumenical Council of Churches, Hromádka addressed one of the huge demonstrations in Wenceslas Square, turning particularly to young people. He appealed to them to recover values that had been missing in society—love, truth, compassion, faithfulness, sacrifice.[65] Partly as a result of his activity in the Velvet Revolution, Hromádka was offered a position in the new postcommunist government as deputy prime minister with responsibility for education, culture, and religious affairs. After consulting with other senior church officials, he accepted the position, took a leave of absence from his church, and served until the next governmental election the following July. One of his first acts was to persuade the government to issue a proclamation that all state organs must abide by the obligations of Czechoslovakia's international agreements, even though they were not yet incorporated into law. Among the documents to which he referred was the Helsinki Accord, as implemented in the Vienna Concluding Document.[66]

In January 1990 the Czech National Council Presidium abolished the Secretariat for Church Affairs. Its task was turned over to the Ministry of Culture until a new church law could be promulgated. With the invalidation of communist legislation, all pastors and priests who had lost their sacerdotal licenses were free to serve their churches once again, political control of seminary enrollment came to an end, and clergy were once again allowed to visit prisons and hospitals. Symbolic of all these changes was the fact that church bells, silent for forty-one years, could ring once more. The new Section for Church Affairs, replacing the old secretariat, had quite different duties, according to Karel Hais, its administrator:

> The main mission of the new office is to mediate relations between the state and the Churches, to help in the legal settling of property issues, to provide—if and where appropriate—financial services for the activity of the Churches, to attend to it that believers' rights are respected during the performance of their military service, to promote foreign contact, and the like.[67]

Regular religious broadcasts by various church bodies began in February 1990. A religious editorial board with representatives from different religious groups was established to plan and coordinate broadcasts.[68]

Continued State Financial Support for Churches

In January 1990, parliament, after discussion with church leaders, prepared a bill pertaining to financial provisions for the churches. According to the bill, the state would continue to pay salaries of clergy of the country's twenty recognized denominations. However, as Hromádka pointed out to parliament, financial support would no longer mean state control. The appointment of clergy would be purely an internal church affair.[69]

There has been much discussion among Protestants regarding the separation of church and state. In general, the feeling prevailed that state financial support was still needed, but that it should be handled as it had been in the precommunist era, that is, without state control. Funds should be given to church headquarters with no strings attached, and church headquarters should directly pay the clergy.

One result of the Velvet Revolution was a change of leadership in some churches. One writer put it this way: "In the Churches too, dramatic situations have been occurring, since numerous compromised persons are trying to preserve their privileged positions of power at any cost, while some other persons are attempting to acquire positions of power. This, however, is a natural phenomenon accompanying any profound social change."[70] In Slovakia, Jan Michalko, general bishop of the Evangelical Church of the Augsburg Confession (Lutheran), known for his rather uncritical support of the communist government, resigned. A group within the church had been campaigning for reforms and for resignation of the old leadership.[71]

Students in the theological seminaries were active in bringing about changes in the faculties. In the Jan Hus Theological Faculty (Czechoslovak Hussite Church), Zdeněk Kučera became the new dean, while in the Comenius Theological Faculty (Evangelical Church of the Czech Brethren), the position went to Jakub Trojan, a signer of Charter 77. Students in the Lutheran faculty in Bratislava made demands on the church for greater freedom and greater openness in dialogue. Both the Hus faculty and the Comenius faculty were incorporated for the first time into the prestigious Charles University, and the Roman Catholic faculty was reincorporated into it.

An indication of the new freedom was the return of the Salvation Army, which had been banned since the end of the 1940s. The Netherlands branch of the Army was given permission to reestablish the group in Czechoslovakia.[72]

Prior to his visit to Czechoslovakia, Pope John Paul II received a letter of welcome from the Ecumenical Council, indicating that prayers were being offered for God's guidance to him during his visit and inviting him to take part in an ecumenical service. However, the pope did not accept the invitation.[73] In March 1990 the working committee of the Christian Peace Conference met in Prague and engaged in some soul-searching. This organization, which in the past had strongly tied Christianity to socialism, decided to continue to work for social justice without being bound to a socialist social order. It admitted that at times it had compromised itself, had made mistakes, had collapsed under pressure, and that it needed to repent and to rethink its role within the newer and freer conditions.[74]

Conclusion

In both Poland and Czechoslovakia, Protestants are a minority, but in Poland much more so. There, they make up 1 percent of the population; in Czechoslovakia, by contrast, Protestants constitute about 10 percent of the population. The Czech Protestant minority is much more indigenous than the Polish, being heirs to the Hussite tradition. Polish Protestants, in contrast, are often viewed as somehow "foreign."

Under communism, Polish Protestants suffered in the Stalinist era along with everyone else, but since that time they have experienced little direct persecution. They are too few to be a danger to the state and also too few to noticeably influence society. In the postwar years they struggled for survival, having been reduced from 3 percent to 1 percent by the war and its aftermath. To a large extent, they have been apolitical, due to a Pietist heritage, to numbers, and to satisfaction with the equal status they have achieved for the first time in modern history. In Poland, church and state were separated after World War II.

Protestants have cooperated well with other non-Catholics, namely Orthodox and Old Catholics, especially in the theological seminary and the Ecumenical Council. Relations with Roman Catholics have improved. During the communist era, Protestants were concerned about being overrun by either or both of the two giants—the Roman Catholic Church and the communist state. In the postcommunist era, they continue to fear the power of the Catholic Church.

In Czechoslovakia, the communist state supported the churches financially. Control and supervision of the churches were much tighter there than in communist Poland. Communists found it difficult to view churches as constructive agents in building socialism. Persecution of the churches increased after 1968 because during the Prague Spring church leaders had manifested their support for a democratic socialism.

The larger Protestant denominations developed different approaches in their dealings with the state. Both the Czechoslovak Hussite Church and the Slovak Evangelical Church of the Augsburg Confession (Lutheran) showed more signs of uncritical loyalty to the state than did the Evangelical Church of the Czech Brethren, especially a group within that church which exhibited a critical loyalty akin to that of the East German Protestants. Some members of the group were involved in Charter 77. As a result, the Brethren Church suffered more than others. For example, a greater number of its ministers lost their preaching licenses. The smaller churches tended to be apolitical, much like the Polish churches.

The Christian Peace Conference, headquartered in Prague, strongly supported the governmental policies of the East bloc. That was the price it paid for the privilege of having meetings with East European Christians, Third World church leaders, and, to some extent, First World church people. Since the conference essentially identified Christianity with socialism, its reason for being came into question after the East European social changes. It has been undergoing self-examination to determine what future course to follow.

While church participation has declined since World War II, the decrease is not noticeably worse than in Western Europe where even with complete religious liberty, a similar decline has taken place. Despite restrictions on the churches in Czechoslovakia, Protestants continued to carry on their worship, religious education, theological education, publication of Bibles, hymnbooks and journals, and other aspects of church life.

The postcommunist era has opened up new opportunities for all churches. One sign is the increased enrollment of theological students. Roman Catholics may benefit more from the new situation than Protestants since the Catholic Church suffered more under the communist regime, gaining admiration for its resistance. There are no clear indications that ecumenical cooperation will increase under the new conditions. In fact, cooperation may decline as the threat of a "common enemy" fades. The new government leadership has supported the churches and spiritual values in general. The churches, for their part, have been engaged in self-examination to see what they have learned through their experience under communism.

The challenge to the churches in the new situation of freedom was discussed by the Rev. Josef Hromádka, then a pastor in Prague, in an address given in early 1990 in the United States. While rejoicing in the end of the "Babylonian Captivity," he felt that people should not succumb to euphoria in view of the great tasks ahead. He said that the churches, now working in a pluralistic society, need to make their contribution without becoming attached to any political power. Operating in a secular society, churches must work out a new model for pastoral care. He concluded:

The Gospel—good news for the human being—is the only one which opens human eyes, so that the human being may see the way to salvation and hope. Our church in its witness to our country does not hold in contempt any struggles of the world, that is of our renewed society, for a new order and form. We only want to bring into those struggles the desire for a more profound righteousness, for a more genuine beauty of life, for a closer mutual service, through which the human being will consider her/his neighbor more dignified than her/himself.[75]

FACT SHEET*

	Number of members	Number of churches	Number of pastors
Czechoslovakia (1988)			
Czechoslovak Hussite Church (Bishop Vratislav Štěpánek)	500,000	343	296
Slovak Evangelical Church of the Augsburg Confession (Bishop Pavel Uhorskai)	369,000	380	350
Evangelical Church of the Czech Brethren (Moderator Pavel Smetana)	230,000	272	268
Reformed Church in Slovakia (Bishop Eugen Mikol)	100,000	300	150
Silesian Evangelical Church of the Augsburg Confession (Bishop Vladislav Kiedron)	48,000	41	21
Church of the Brethren (Jaroslav Kubový)	6,000	35	31
Moravian Church–Unity of Brethren (Rudolf Borsky, chairman)	6,000	17	16

	Number of members	Number of churches	Number of pastors
United Methodist (Josef Červenák, superintendent)	5,200	19	19
Baptist Union (Vlastimil Pospíšil)	4,000	28	27
Seventh-Day Adventists	8,000	173	15
Unitarian Church	2,000	?	?
Czech Apostolic Church (Rudolf Bubík)	2,000	(registered 25 January 1989)	
Poland (1988)			
Lutheran Church of the Augsburg Confession (Bishop Janusz Narzynski)	70,000	305	99
United Evangelical Church** (Eduard Czaejko)	10,000	222	180
Methodist Church (Edward Puślecki)	8,000	49	29
Baptist Church (Konstanty Wiezowski)	7,000	54	24
Seventh-Day Adventists	7,910	174	60
Reformed Church (Zdzislaw Tranda, bishop)	4,000	8	7

---

*Groups of 2,000 or more members.
**In June 1989 the United Evangelical Church split into four parts: the Church of Congregations of Christ, the Church of Christians of the Evangelical Faith, the Pentecostal Church, and the Church of Evangelical Christians. The Polish Ecumenical Council said that the dissolution was caused by "problems connected with growing difficulties within individual groups, and tendencies towards becoming independent," mostly among the Pentecostals. See *Keston News Service*, no. 328 (22 June 1989): 15.

5

Protestantism in Hungary:

The Communist Era

Joseph Pungur

The Protestant churches in Hungary with their 2.5 million members represent one of the largest groups of churches of the Reformation tradition in Central Europe. Out of 10 million Hungarians, some 2 million belong to the Calvinist Reformed Church, some 400,000 to the Evangelical-Lutheran Church, and about 100,000 to the Free Churches. The Roman Catholic Church is the largest Christian denomination in Hungary with some 5 million members. Both the Reformed and the Evangelical churches have a checkered history, with glorious and tragic periods, progress and recessions, orthodoxy and revivals. There was a triumphant beginning in the sixteenth century. After the Turkish conquest (associated with the Battle of Mohács, 1526), the country was divided into three parts and the population was extremely receptive to the ideas of the Reformation, 90 percent of the people joining Protestant churches. In the sixteenth and seventeenth centuries the Protestant churches became the national churches of Hungary by providing spiritual leadership to those living under Turkish or Habsburg domination or to those living in Transylvania, an independent principality in the eastern region. The Protestant churches were guardians of the nation's identity, the preservers and promoters of national language and culture. They preached the gospel in the national language, organized scattered groups of people, and encouraged them by providing ethical principles as well as hope for the future. On a national level, these churches organized the first network of schools available to everyone. They printed and published large numbers of books, among them the Hungarian translation of the Bible (1590), hymnbooks, prayer books, theological treatises, and textbooks. And Protestant churches were the most outspoken advocates of Hungary's political and cultural independence from threatening powers such as Turkey and Austria. Hungarians considered the Protestant churches—particularly the Calvinist church—as their own. To be a good Hungarian meant to be a Protestant, particularly a Calvinist. People felt that the church protected them, helped them, and guided them, and they in turn supported and protected the Protestant churches, sometimes with great sacrifices.

Then came a period of vigorous Counter-Reformation led by the kings of the ruling Habsburg dynasty. Hundreds of Protestant churches were confiscated and handed over to the Roman Catholic Church, and thousands of Protestants were forcibly re-Catholicized, Protestant pastors were dismissed and persecuted. The peak of the wave of Counter-Reformation came during the so-called "Decade of Mourning" (1671–81). In 1673–74, all Protestant pastors were summoned to a special court and accused of high treason. They were tortured, and eighty-nine of them were condemned to galley slavery. Two years later, M. De Ruyter, a Dutch admiral, freed the surviving twenty-six at Naples.

A long and bitter struggle for religious freedom for the Protestant churches ensued, culminating in a series of reform national assemblies during the first half of the nineteenth century. Finally, the National Assembly of 1848–49 passed legislation guaranteeing freedom of religious faith and granting the Protestant churches full equality. A repressive period reoccurred after the defeat of the independent republic in 1849; this period actually ended with the Ausgleich of 1867.

The Treaty of Trianon in 1920 painfully dismembered the country and its churches. The so-called "Christian Course" between the two world wars was favorable to the Protestant churches, while the postwar decades brought tension, trial, and restriction under various communist regimes—with a ray of hope in 1956. In the following decades, the Protestant churches became collaborators of the communist state. During the 1980s, however, they had a greater chance for freedom under a troubled communist-socialist government.

Protestantism Between 1867 and 1918

In 1867 an agreement was struck between the Austrian monarch and the Hungarian nation that paved the way for political, economic, and cultural development of Hungary in the framework of the Dual Monarchy. With this agreement, political conditions were provided for development of the Protestant churches and for the birth and limited life of the small Free Churches.

It also was the time of a new organizational framework for the Protestant churches. The Reformed Church achieved three important things at the general synod of Debrecen in 1881. First, where the organizing pattern of the church districts had been diverse, the synod created a unified structure of the entire church. Second, it gave a new role to the general convent of the church, upgrading it from an office of information to the church's executive body. This office was provided with limited power to represent the church and act during periods between the general synods, which were held according to particular needs of the church. Third, the general convent set up a so-called "domestic"—a general fund for the entire church's use.[1] For these actions, the synod of 1881 can be regarded as the beginning of the modern Reformed Church in Hungary.[2]

The Evangelical Lutheran Church held a general synod in 1891 and accepted a constitution similar to the Reformed Church's. The tiny Unitarian Church also followed the example of these churches and introduced a new constitution.[3]

Toward the end of the nineteenth century a revivalist movement spread among the Protestant churches. The Scot Mission and the German-speaking Reformed Congregation in Budapest were instrumental in bringing it about. Alexander Neil Sommerville led a crusade of evangelization in 1887–88. This evangelist, who belonged to the Church of Scotland, visited thirty-seven churches and sometimes preached to crowds of 8,000–10,000. John Mott, the leader of the Christian World Student Federation, paid several visits to Hungary and helped organize the Christian Student Federation in 1904.[4] Other important movements, such as the Home Mission Evangelization, Sunday schools, Bible study groups, the YMCA, and the Bethania Fellowship, were begun. Institutional charities multiplied; homes for handicapped children, orphanages, and hospitals were established. The Philadelphia Diaconess Training Institution and the Zsuzsánna Lórántfi Association, among others, were organized during this period. Aladár Szabó and Aladár Szilassy and their circle were particularly active and successful with the Home Mission.[5] Another important event of these years was the formation of a handful of smaller Protestant groups—the so-called Free Churches.

The beginning of the Baptist Church in Hungary goes back to the mid-nineteenth century. János Rottmayer (d. 1901) was a young carpenter who, while working in Hamburg, was the first Hungarian to join the German Baptist Church. He was sent back to Budapest to start a Baptist mission. The first Baptist congregation was established at Óbuda in 1873. Police harassment occurred because the Baptists were not an accepted religion of the state; to pursue such acceptance they formulated a standard of faith, the so-called Ócsa Confession. Eventually, in 1906, they were granted permission for religious activity.[6]

The formation of the Nazarene sect also took place during this period. Its full name was the Christ-Believer Nazarene Congregation. In the United States this community is called the Apostolic Christian Church; in Switzerland it is known as Evangelisch Taufgesinnten. Heinrich S. Fröhlich, who lived in the first half of the nineteenth century and was a minister in Thurgau, Switzerland, founded the sect. He preached strict ethics and Anabaptist doctrine. This teaching was brought to Hungary by János Denkel and János Kropacsek in 1839. They baptized Lajos Hencsey, a blacksmith, who wrote a summary of the Nazarenes' doctrines. He is regarded as the founder of Hungarian Nazarenism. The sect's first congregation was organized at Pacsér in 1848 and met with many difficulties from state authorities because its members refused military service. Their situation eased by 1894.[7]

The Seventh-Day Adventist Mission was begun in Hungary on 22 May 1895. On that date, János Rottmayer and his wife—both Baptist pioneers—converted to Adventism. The Rev. József Szalay, a Reformed minister, translated into Hungarian Elaine G. White's book, *A Road to Jesus*, which was a tremendous help to the Adventists' work. Because of their initial success, European Adventist leaders sent a minister, John F. Huenergardt, to Hungary to head the missionary work, which he successfully pursued. In 1890 he was able to send István Kelemen to the seminary of Friedensau, Germany. Kelemen became the first ordained Hungarian Adventist minister. Because of the church's rapid growth, the Austro-Hungarian-Balkan Mission, of which the Hungarian union was a part, was organized in 1902. In July 1912 the Danube Union was formed at Budapest. The Adventists experienced many forms of religious intolerance. For example, minors were forbidden to attend services, which were held under police surveillance; sermons had to be submitted to authorities; and, at times, all religious activities were banned.[8]

Methodism also established itself in Hungary in the first years of the twentieth century. The first congregation was organized in 1900. Otto Melle, the Methodists' first pastor, was called by the congregation from Dresden in 1905. Although he worked successfully, Methodists in Hungary remained a tiny minority.

Protestantism Between Two World Wars

At the outbreak of World War I, the historical Protestant churches supported the war policy and war efforts, but gradually turned toward opposition. In October 1917 the Association of Reformed Ministers (ORLE) launched a peace initiative by means of the Association of the Swiss Reformed Ministers.[9]

Out of the chaos of war's end, a communist regime emerged in Hungary. After 133 controversial days in power the communists resigned, giving way to the formation of a government under Miklós Horthy, who remained head of state for the next twenty-five years.

On 4 June 1920 Hungary had to sign a harsh peace treaty at the Grand Trianon Palace in Versailles. The treaty partitioned historical Hungary, with two-thirds of its territory ceded to neighboring countries. Sixty percent of its population was submitted to foreign rulers—without plebiscite. Romania was awarded Transylvania, together with 2.5 million ethnic Hungarians. The southern part of the country, Bácska-Bánát, was ceded to Yugoslavia with another half million. The Northern Highland with 1.5 million Hungarian ethnics became a part of newly formed Czechoslovakia. Croatia had dreamed of independence, but became part of Yugoslavia.

With the Treaty of Trianon, the Hungarian Reformed Church lost 1,012 churches out of 2,073. Of 2,621,329 church members in Hungary, only 1,632,852 remained. The Hungarian Evangelical-Lutheran Church lost 484 out of 770 churches and 485,219 of 1,340,143 members. The Unitarian Church lost 111 of 115 congregations, and the smaller Protestant churches lost 9,000 members from a total of 17,000.[10] The Treaty of Trianon was always regarded by Hungarians as a national catastrophe.

The treaty set the tone for secular and church politics in Hungary for the next twenty-five years. The Christian Course can be characterized as nationalist—revisionist with a Christian coating—and the churches, primarily the Roman Catholic Church, had a leading role in it. The ruling political ideology was "Christian nationalism," a type of neonationalism. The right-wing parties blamed the leftists and the Jews for losing the war and for postwar hardships. The Roman Catholics went so far as to blame the Protestants by saying that their liberalism opened the way to revolution, socialism, and communism in 1919.[11] Anti-Semitic feeling became dominant, leading to passage of two anti-Jewish acts in the late 1930s that paved the way for persecution and deportation of Jews during the final years of World War II. Bishop László Ravasz of the Reformed Church and Lutheran Bishop Sándor Raffay, members of the legislature's upper chamber, protested the Jewish persecution. Bishop Ravasz in a letter to Roman Catholic Archbishop Jusztinián Serédi suggested common action in this matter, but the leading Catholic clergy rejected the proposal. Albert Bereczky, Reformed minister in Budapest, and his co-workers did an outstanding job of saving many Jews, as did many Protestant ministers.

Because of Roman Catholic hegemony, the Protestant churches, especially the smaller ones, found themselves at a disadvantage. At the beginning of World War II, permission for church activity was withdrawn from the Baptists, the Seventh-Day Adventists, and the Nazarenes. The Reformed Church and the Lutheran Church continued to have a cordial relationship, despite a neoconfessionalist trend among the Lutherans. In fact, the so-called Agreement of Nagygeresd, struck as early as 1883 and confirmed in 1914, regulated co-celebration and inter-communion between the two churches, including ways in which they could help each other in the diaspora. Good relations made the progress of ecumenism possible among Protestant churches. There were unity movements among youth organizations such as the YMCA and SDG. The Unity Movement of the Hungarian Youth was set up on 25 June 1943. That body, the Committee of Church Aid organized in the same year, and other smaller churches constituted the kernel of Hungary's ecumenical movement in 1943.[12]

The Reformed Church grew steadily following World War I. For example, within twenty years in the Danubian district alone, 2 new presbyteries were founded, and 56 new churches, 75 schools, 71 manses, 41 teachers' homes, and 85 church halls were erected. In the suburbs of Budapest in 1921, there were only 8 congregations in 4 church buildings. In 1941 there were 22 congregations with 20 churches, 7 of them recently constructed.[13] The diaconial work of the church was enriched. The organization Alliance of Love had 6 homes for aged people, 14 orphanages, 2 homes for handicapped children, and 1 home for the destitute.

Three theological trends dominated the Reformed Church during these years. First, the so-called General Christians, with János Victor as leader, emphasized the importance of evangelization and spiritual awakening. This movement reflected Anglo-Saxon theological influence. Second, there was the Historical Calvinism movement, led by Jenö Sebestyén. This trend was inspired by the Dutch Reformed theologian Abraham Kuyper. With the advent of the German neo-Reformation theology, Barthianism, the third trend, made itself known during the 1930s. Its main representatives, such men as Sándor Tavaszy, Barna Nagy, István Török, Sándor Czeglédy, Jr., and later Bishop Tibor Bartha, were professors at the theological academies.[14]

The Lutheran Church also held a general synod between 1934 and 1937. It accepted a new statement of faith collected in the Book of Concord and a new set of canon laws. Emphasis was placed on the role of sessions. The leading theological trend of this time among Lutherans was confessionalism—the rediscovery of the values in Lutheran standards of faith.

Protestant Churches at the End of the War and in the Early Postwar Period

By 1943 it had become clear that the Axis powers were losing the war. Thus, the question of Hungary's future came to the forefront in the thinking of the intelligentsia. Between 23 and 30 August 1943, a series of conferences were held at Balatonszárszó, a lakeside resort, organized by the Reformed student organization Soli Deo Gloria Alliance. Here, under the spiritual guidance of Protestant ministers, some democratic writers, scientists, and antifascist politicians discussed the future. Many participants were to play a leading role in postwar Hungary.[15]

Fighting on the Eastern Front approached Hungary's border by the beginning of 1944. On 19 March the German army unexpectedly occupied Hungary to secure a hinterland. With this move, persecution of leaders and members of leftist political parties, deportation of Jews, and a demand for more severe sacrifices to the war effort began. These measures intensified after 15 October 1944 when Regent Miklós Horthy's attempt to pull Hungary out of war failed, and Ferenc Szálasi, leader of the ultranationalist Arrow Cross Party, formed the government; once again Hungary's fate was tied to a crumbling Germany.

By Christmas 1944 the siege of Budapest began, ultimately ending on 13 February 1945. The war was over for Hungary on 4 April 1945. Fierce fighting and deprivation had scoured Hungarian territory for six months.

The fighting soldiers of the Red Army usually were helpful to the civilians. But the occupation contingents inflicted much pain. They confiscated animals, foodstocks and valuables. The menfolk and even women were taken for forced labor to the Soviet Union—most of whom were never seen again. There was large-scale raping of women.[16] Walking on the streets in the darkness of the evening was risky because of hold-ups.

It was significant that at this stage, except for a few atrocities, no harm usually came to the clergy and churches. A Lutheran minister from Budapest wrote to his bishop: "General Tseanisov told us that the expressed wish and strict order of Generalissimo Stalin is that the Red Army should not hinder Church life in the countries occupied during the war [and] let the priests wear their clerical robes that they should not suffer any harm because each Russian soldier knows that it is not allowed even to touch a clergyman."[17] Red Army personnel together with communist workers' brigades helped restore church buildings damaged during the war. Out of 1,265 Reformed churches, 417 were ruined during the fighting.[18] Stalin's benevolent attitude toward the clergy and churches was politically calculated. The war was still going on, and he was unsure of the Western powers' intentions after it ended. Moreover, he wanted to establish communist rule in all Eastern European countries, and to this end he needed the people's sympathy. Stalin evidently was convinced that the time soon would arrive for a communist showdown with the churches.

On 21 December 1944, a Provisional National Assembly was held at Debrecen. The assembly's first meeting was at the oratorium chapel of the Reformed College, the same place where Hungary's independence was declared and the Habsburg dynasty dethroned in 1849. The government of Premier Béla Miklós made radical changes, annulling all agreements with Germany including the Vienna Treaties, and acknowledging the country's borders as they had been on 31 December 1937. The government signed an armistice in Moscow on 20 January 1945 and declared war against Germany. Among other acts of the provisional government was a radical agrarian reform enacted on 15 March 1945, which affected 35 percent of the country's land. As a result, 660,000 improvised agrarian workers received modest amounts of farmland, and 350,000 families obtained free house lots.[19] The agrarian reform affected the churches as well. In 1935 the churches had owned more than 1.3 million acres; 86 percent of those holdings belonged to the Roman Catholic Church.[20] Most of these church lands were confiscated by the state, and only 18 percent of the original estates remained in the hands of the churches. With this act, the churches lost a significant source of revenue to finance their activities, including schools.[21]

A democratic election was held in Hungary on 7 November 1945. Besides the Communist Party, slates were put forward by the Social Democrats, the Peasant Party, the Smallholders' Party, and two smaller parties. The communists expected a breakthrough, but ended up with only 17 percent of the vote. The winner was the Smallholders' Party, which captured 57 percent of the ballots. It seemed that a truly democratic future was on the country's horizon. Hungary was declared a republic on 1 February 1946, with Zoltán Tildy as its first president and Ferenc Nagy as prime minister. Both men were from the Smallholders' Party. Tildy had been a Reformed minister before his gradual involvement in politics. His secretary was János Péter, a Reformed minister, later bishop and foreign minister and finally vice president of parliament. The new government was invited for talks with Stalin. Tildy's audience with Stalin lasted only ten minutes, while the dictator spent some thirty minutes with Péter.

Despite the absolute electoral majority of the Smallholders' Party, the Communist Party managed to get three government portfolios, one of them the powerful post of minister of home affairs, which the communists easily obtained because of the Red Army's presence. With this key ministry in their hands and the Red Army behind them, the communists were in an excellent position to make a new bid for supreme power. Their opportunity arrived in 1947. Shortly thereafter, Hungary signed the Paris Peace Treaties. This was actually a copy of the Trianon Treaty with a slight difference—now the Soviet Union was rewarded with Carpathian Ukraine (Rusinsko), a former part of historical Hungary. With this land, the Soviet Union had direct access to Hungary—and to the West— through the strategic Carpathian Mountains.

Despite all these calamities, a promising revivalist movement was unfolding in the Protestant churches in the postwar years. The Roman Catholic Church, under the leadership of Prince Primate József Cardinal Mindszenty, vehemently opposed nationalization of church lands. Many members and leaders of the Protestant churches felt the same way. As early as 27 May 1945, leaders of the Reformed and Lutheran churches sent a memorandum to the provisional government, to which they made known their claims, and warned: "On the basis of the resolutions of the Conference of Crimea [Yalta] the mandate of the Provisional Government is not to make radical changes but only to call together a National Assembly democratically elected."[22] Bishop László Ravasz, president of the general synod of the Reformed Church and the church's most outstanding preacher in the twentieth century, declared in his New Year's address of 1946: "Let it be emphasized that in this part of the world, only the Reformed Church may stand with a clear conscience, because everybody else kept silent, only the Church spoke up."[23] Andor Lázár, chief curator of the Reformed Church's Danubian district, said on 26 April 1946: "We are expecting from our rulers that they too should accept the ideas of forgiveness, grace and mercy. Let the state listen to the good advice of the Churches."[24] Bishop Ravasz openly called on the Reformed Church for a Western orientation: "In the great question of East and West our predestination tells us what we should do here and now. With all our spiritual contacts we belong to the West, but because of our situation, we are charged with an Eastern mission. Our mission to the East can only be achieved provided that our relationship with the West is undisturbed and complete."[25]

There were sharp voices from the Lutheran churches as well. The Association of Evangelical-Lutheran Ministers suggested setting up an interdenominational committee for "defense against anti-Church and anti-religious tendencies."[26] The Lutheran Alliance created a Committee for the Defense of the Church. Baron Albert Radvánszky, general inspector of the Lutheran Church, aired controversial views at the general synod of 1947: "There is no reason for repentance in our Church with regard to the Jewish question as there is no reason for us to have penitence for the sin of others."[27] Amidst these political struggles, the moral standard of the people fell dramatically. A country town newspaper wrote in 1947: "After sunset it is not advisable to walk alone either in the capital city or in the countryside. There is corruption and embezzlement everywhere. Syphilis and free love chase our children into premature death."[28]

In the meantime, antireligious and atheist propaganda had grown considerably. Its prime targets were Cardinal Mindszenty and the Roman Catholic Church. The attack of the communists grew and in it the MADISZ—the Hungarian Democratic Youth Federation—played an instrumental role. For example, King S. István, the founder of Hungary, was denounced as a "criminal blinded by incense." In the Roman Catholic diocese of Veszprém, out of 304 churches 172 were ransacked.[29]

In the summer of 1947 a political crisis broke out. Premier Ferenc Nagy of the Smallholders' Party was accused of partaking in an anti-state plot. He was in Switzerland at the time and did not return to Hungary but emigrated to the United States. In this situation the Communist Party demanded new elections, which were held on 31 August 1947. It was rigged by the communists. Despite this, they could only muster less than a quarter of the votes. But the communists were in coalition with other parties, and the coalition captured 61 percent of the total votes. Mátyás Rákosi, the communist party leader, as the leader of the coalition, became the "legal" ruler of the country; Hungary fell under communist rule.[30]

Communist Takeover and the Protestant Churches (1948–1956)

Communist historians call 1948 "The Year of Spin," and they are right. In that year, the Communist Party submitted Hungary to communist dictatorship. Non-leftist political parties were dissolved, as were religious organizations. Banks were nationalized. The Social Democratic Party was cajoled into merging with the Communist Party, from which the Hungarian Workers Party emerged.

On 16 June 1948, church schools were nationalized. The Roman Catholic Church suffered the greatest loss, but nationalization was extremely painful to the Protestant churches as well. They had made great sacrifices from the time of the Reformation, maintained and expanded a network of schools on various levels, and some of their colleges had earned a high reputation. The Roman Catholic Church was allowed to retain eight high schools apart from their seminaries. The Reformed Church retained four high schools and four seminaries; in 1952, three remaining high schools and two seminaries were nationalized, finally leaving only one school and two seminaries. The Lutheran Church lost all of its high schools and retained only one seminary. By nationalizing church schools and appropriating them for the state, the Communist Party wanted to undercut the social roots of the churches and educate the younger generation without religion's influence. The party's goal was to educate according to its materialistic-atheistic ideals to create a "socialist man and woman," and by doing so secure communism's future.

Soon after nationalization of the church schools, the communists pressed for an "agreement" with the churches. The party was well aware that church leaders would not cooperate. Consequently, suitable church leaders who were ready to sign an agreement had to be found. With the eventual conclusion of this agreement, a covert interference in the life of the churches began and continued for many years.

The Reformed Church stood first on the communist agenda because the conditions for such an agreement were more favorable to it than to any other churches. It was obvious that Bishop Ravasz would not sign an agreement with the state that would curtail the church's work, and the proposed agreement had exactly that aim. Consequently, Ravasz had to go. According to one version, Mátyás Rákosi summoned him and bluntly told him to retire. Ravasz had two options: either leave the country and settle in Switzerland, or remain in the countryside. He chose the latter. According to another version, Rákosi sent János Péter, who was trained in the Reformed ministry and at that time secretary to the state president Zoltán Tildy, with a message that contained the same plan.[31] Ravasz resigned in April 1948.

Albert Bereczky (1893–1966) was elected as his successor. Bereczky seemed the most suitable person to lead the Reformed Church during those stormy times. One of the most respected revivalist preachers and minister of a new church in Budapest, he not only was Tildy's former colleague but his friend. Tildy was father-in-law of Bereczky's daughter, and, more important, they shared the same vision in politics. Bereczky had actively participated in rescuing Jews at the end of the war and had close contact with the anti-Nazi resistance movement. Prior to his election as bishop, Bereczky had been the undersecretary of the Ministry of Cults, dealing with Protestant affairs. After his election, he convinced church leaders of the inevitability and usefulness of an agreement with the state. Even Karl Barth, who visited the Hungarian Reformed Church in March and April, shared Bereczky's view that an agreement was inevitable. On 7 October 1948, a document was signed by both parties that provided the following.

(1) New laws affecting religious matters will be drafted by a permanent joint commission.

(2)The Government regards the following activities as pertaining to the free function of church life—the holding of divine services in church buildings or in other suitable public buildings, in homes and in open spaces, the holding of bible classes in church buildings, in schools and in private homes, in church halls; the colportage of Bibles and tractates; the holding of congregational or national church conference evangelistic meetings, the compulsory religious instruction in public schools and the charitable work of the Church.

(3) The Church has the right to the maintenance and development of charitable institutions and to collect money for this purpose, within the bounds of existing legal regulations.

(4) The Government takes cognizance of the expressed intention of the Reformed Church to realize the principle of "a Free Church in a Free State." During the time of the transition, in the course of which the Reformed Church will develop her material resources, the Government declares its readiness to pay State subsidies on the following conditions:

a)The Hungarian Republic ensures for five years the payment of State subsidies for the maintainance of church personnel on the existing basis which is assessed in relation to the scale for civil servants. This figure of State aid for salaries will be reduced by 25 percent on 1 January 1954, by a further 25 percent in January 1959, by a further 25 percent on 1 January 1964, and it will cease on 31 December 1968.

(b) The Government will continue to pay solely for the purposes of the construction, reconstruction and maintainance of church buildings, church halls and parsonages as well as for the furnishing of these structures, according to the subsidy paid during the period 1 August 1946 to July 1948. This payment will be reduced by 25 percent at five-yearly intervals and will cease at the end of 1968.

(5) Following the plain commands of Scriptures, the Hungarian

Reformed Church in her Order of Worship will provide for intercession for the Hungarian Republic, for the Head of State, for the Government, and for the welfare and peace of the entire Hungarian people, as well as for Divine Service on State holidays, in conformity with the Word of God and the Confessions of the Church. She states that a new Hymnary, which is about to be published, contains hymns appropriate to these occasions.

(6) The Government's decision to nationalize all church schools, apart from four colleges with strong historical traditions, was ratified, but the Church is to be left free to organize the religious instructions in State schools.[32]

The agreement was regarded as a relatively good one under the circumstances. The problem was that some of its basic provisions were disregarded by state authorities. For example, three of the remaining colleges and two of the four seminaries were nationalized in 1952—a clear violation. To add insult, the Cistibiscan church district—one of only four—was abolished by attaching it to the Transtibiscan district. To eliminate religious classes from state schools, strong administrative methods were applied against parents who registered their children for religious classes and against the children themselves. For fairness' sake, let it be mentioned that a continuous subsidy for the church's budget was paid by the state. Without it, the church could not have met its financial commitments. For example, in 1988 the Reformed Church alone received 120 million forints (about $300,000) from the state, toward its 150 million forint budget.[33]

Soon a new breed of church leaders appeared. Bishop Imre Révész, who as president of the general synod had signed the agreement, retired and János Péter was elected his successor. Péter had an excellent education; before the war he was on scholarship in Germany, Scotland, and France. He was in contact with the antifascist resistance movement. He wavered between an ecclesiastical and political career. As bishop, he was not as visible as Bereczky, perhaps because Bereczky was president of the general synod from 1949. However, Péter, while occupying bishopric office, was heavily involved in politics. After 1956, he resigned, left the church, and assumed a political career.

In the Transdanubian church district, the bishop was Elemér Györi, an aged man in fragile health, but a benevolent person who somehow managed to avoid the deep waters of church politics. A leading theologian of this period—besides Bereczky—was János Victor. But a handful of younger theologians made themselves known during these years. Originally members of the Reformed Free Council formed in 1946 at Nyiregyháza, they followed the theological line of Bishop Bereczky.

Among them were Benö Békefi, Péter Hajdu, József Farkas, József Ador-
ján, and Sándor Fekete.

Bishop Bereczky organized the Reformed Free Council from those
theologians and ministers who were interested in church renewal. The
council's first meeting was held from 14–17 August 1946 at Nyiregyháza.
Here a document, "The Church and the Hungarian Present," was issued
that recommended a new direction for the church by realizing its God-
given opportunity in the new form of state—that is, in the democracy of
the Republic of Hungary. At the second meeting of the free council, held
in March 1947, participants endorsed the concept of the separation of
church and state. The council's third and final meeting took place from
19–21 August 1947. Among other issues, it dealt with the relationship
between Christianity and Marxism. While the council did not accept the
Marxist worldview, it pointed out a possible partnership on practical,
social, and cultural issues.[34]

With the resignation of Ravasz as president of the Reformed Church's
synod, the new trend in the church's theology, represented by Bereczky
and the Reformed Free Council members, was officially adopted and was
spelled out by the synod council on 30 April 1948. It plainly indicated that
the "Church offers its whole willingness for every service in the new
state and social order which can be done in the name of Jesus Christ and
in the power of the Holy Spirit."[35] It marked the first appearance of the
central idea of the "Theology of Service" in an official church document;
since that time such offers to the state in church declarations were
constantly present.

At its initial stages, Bishop Bereczky played a vital role in inventing,
developing, and propagating this new theology. He had been one of the
first theologians to describe World War II as the judgment of God on the
world and the church. With prophetic insight, he called on the church for
penitence and repentance, and he pleaded for its humble acceptance of a
curtailed role in a new society. He was convinced that, if accepted, the
judgment of God on the church would turn into the mercy of God,
expressed in a hope for the church's future. In the new social order, the
church would face a "Narrow Way" that must be accepted in the obedience of faith.[36] This model was accepted by a handful of theologians,
professors, ministers, and laymen. It was the Reformed Church's official theology from 1948 to 1956. This "Theology of the Narrow Way"
was suitable to justify nationalization of church properties, lands, and
schools, the signing of an agreement with the state, and the endorsement of all party and state activities. The advocates of this theology
actually became supervisors over the whole church.

Bishop Bereczky's "Brotherly Message" on 1 January 1951—after a lengthy theological discourse replete with theological jargon such as "obedience in faith," "fruitful thanksgiving," and "active contrition"— arrived at these concrete tasks for church ministers: no special meetings, in any form, of members of the disbanded religious associations (for example, Bethánia C.E.) or any other special activities; and full integration into local congregations but not as leaders of church meetings.[37] Behind this pastoral letter can be detected the worries of party and state authorities that the disbanded religious organizations might regroup under the church's protection. To prevent this from taking place, a leading bishop seemed to the civil authorities to be the best controlling agent available.

This new church leadership went even further in serving the goals of the party and government. They encouraged church ministers and elders to actively help in the campaign for collectivization of farmlands. These church leaders kept silent when a propaganda campaign was launched against wealthy farmers who were in many cases arrested and imprisoned. They were silent in the face of official excesses and lawlessness when the politically unreliable were massively deported from Budapest to the countryside; the church raised not even the faintest protest against this inhuman act, and individual ministers who offered help were punished by church authorities. For example, the ministers of the Fasor Church in Budapest, Imre Szabó and Károly Dobos, were immediately posted to remote parishes. During the years of the Rákosi regime—the Stalinist era in Hungary—the state secret police (ÁVO, later ÁVH) had a free hand to arrest, persecute, torture, and even liquidate those who were stamped "enemies of socialism." The news of these acts steadily spread among the terrified population. Church leaders again remained silent. At the same time, these leaders, incredibly, lauded Mátyás Rákosi in the familiar fashion of the personality cult as "the best Hungarian disciple of Stalin." Here is what Bereczky wrote on Rákosi's sixtieth birthday: "Since the liberation we have learned and are continuously learning a new lesson taught to us primarily by his life, teaching and example [and] we are increasingly aware of the great gift which was and is given to us by his wisdom, humaneness and knowledge. [He is] the great statesman whose wise and strong hand leads the life of our country."[38] The agreement fostered by the Communist Party stipulated the church's intercessions for the country, for the head of state, and for the government. However, no regiment was instituted for praising an atheistic dictator who grossly misused his power, or to award him with the aura of a demigod by offering him such idolatry. One of Bereczky's favourite accusations against subordinate ministers was that they were "blind." After this tirade of praise for a bloody-handed dictator, what can one say? The whole theology of this new breed of church leaders can be understood only as a desperate attempt to justify theologically the political decision of the Communist Party and state leaders.

In this context, it is understandable that Karl Barth, who visited Hungary in 1948 and approved the search for a new direction in theology, was alarmed by this deterioration of Reformed theology. He sent an open letter to Bereczky in September 1951. Barth spoke in a straightforward way:

> You are at the point of making an article of faith of your agreement with Communism, of making it part of the Christian message. You are at the point of wandering into an ideological Christian wonderland. How is it that you put socialism on your banner as if it were a perfect thing? How can you dare to put it on the banner of Jesus Christ? How can you claim in your propaganda that socialism is heaven on earth and is thus identical with what you find in reality in the Hungary of today and throughout the countries of the Eastern Bloc? Why do you have to get mixed up in this business of Eastern propaganda of painting everything black and white? Why do you accept the dubious Stockholm Peace Movement, with its dove that shows its claws, as a genuine peace effort? Why do you bestow upon it your ecclesiastical blessing without any reservation? I can explain your attitude only from the theological, or let me call it philosophical, presupposition of which I spoke above. I am very much concerned about this and ask you to rethink your theology radically.[39]

Of course, this open letter was never published in Hungary. Until this controversy, Barth had stood in good stead with Bereczky and his circle, and one of his works, *Dogmatics in Outline,* was even translated and published for use in the Reformed Church. On his death in 1968, however, the entire Hungarian Reformed Church was represented at his funeral by only one person—László Márton Pákozdy.

The Narrow Way Theology of Bereczky and the Reformed Church's new leaders cannot be totally accepted or rejected. Basically, it contains three major elements. The first can be accepted because it consisted of a call for national confession of sin, repentance, and penitence for the sins committed during the war in which Hungary participated with the churches' full consent. Similar acts of confession and repentance were performed by other European churches. The second element of this theology was its acceptance of the church's restricted role in the socialist system. This "Narrow Way of the Church," however, did not come out of nowhere. At least three motivations were behind it, which, after theological reflection, led the church to an acceptance of socialism. This outcome was quite opposite to what Mindszenty was trying to realize: an open confrontation with the regime. Bereczky, instead, maintained excellent relations with Tildy and with other high-ranking government officials, and he himself was an undersecretary at the Ministry of Cults. His unique position secured him access to vital information from inside and outside the country. For example, he learned how Tito had planned to eliminate all Yugoslav clergymen.[40] He also was informed about the trial of Protestant ministers in Bulgaria.[41] He knew about the negotiations between Marshal Voroshilov, commander of the occupation forces, and Stalin regarding Voroshilov's radical plan for the clergy. Both Bereczky and Tildy rightly feared that because of Mindszenty's staunch resistance against a forced agreement with the state, a tragic fate would befall the Hungarian clergy and churches.[42] It is now known that Tildy and Bereczky, after careful preparation, secretly went to see Arthur Schoenefeld, the American member of the Allied Control Commission, to inform him of the situation and to ask whether the United States would be willing to help "if inadvertently something would happen here." The answer was a categorical "no." The commission's English member also answered negatively.[43] Under the circumstances, it can be understood why Bereczky and the new theologians decided to come to an agreement with the communist regime and even to offer a helping hand to the state. The agreement secured a restricted life for the church, and under the circumstances little more could have been achieved.

Despite these conditions, a third element of the new theology can be criticized. This is the servile attitude of church leaders toward the party and the state. In the early 1950s, the church behaved as if it wanted to be a party auxiliary and state collaborator. The church joined the choir of those opportunists who praised party and state leaders without reservation or good taste. The church arrived at a point where its most important objective, apparently, was not the furtherance of the Kingdom of God but the building of Socialism. This is what Barth criticized so sharply. While church leaders offered cheap praise to the political leadership, it is unforgivable that they were mute in regard to state oppression, disrespect of laws, and adventurism. They also failed to read the signs of a gathering storm.

In contrast to the case with the Reformed Church, an agreement between the Evangelical-Lutheran Church and the state was not so smoothly accomplished. Bishop Lajos Ordass (1901–74) was not a person to cave in easily to regime demands. Ordass had achieved an excellent education in Hungary, Germany, and Sweden; he spoke seven languages. He was consecrated on 15 August 1945 as a bishop of the

Bánya district, which included 53 percent of Hungary's Lutherans. In 1947 he was elected second vice president of the Lutheran World Federation.[44] Unlike Mindszenty, he did not oppose the new regime; Ordass simply wanted a honest agreement between church and state. There were two important issues on which the bishop and the state could not agree: the nationalization of church schools and the church's autonomy. Bishop Zoltán Turóczy was ready for some kind of compromise, but not Ordass. He firmly opposed nationalization of his church's schools. Probably this is why the Lutheran Church was without any high schools in 1991. Ordass soon became the target of increasing accusations by state authorities and the media. The government demanded his dismissal. Finally, he was arrested for fabricated "foreign currency offenses" on 8 September 1948 and persecuted and sentenced to two years of imprisonment. (Similar fates befell the general inspector and the general secretary of the Lutheran Church.) Before Ordass's release from prison on 30 May 1950, a church court refused to dismiss him from the bishopric. What happened is characteristic of those times. Rákosi sent an emissary to Bishop Turóczy with a threatening message: if Ordass were not removed from office by the church court, then he would be indicted on high treason and sentenced to death.[45] Actually, Ordass nurtured a vision of a "Confessing Church" in the fashion of the German and Norwegian churches during the war.[46] After his removal and the removal of his circle—the main opponents of a forced agreement—the road was free for a deal. On 14 December 1948, an agreement was signed between the Lutheran Church and the state. It was similar to the Reformed Church agreement. New and more agreeable leaders were installed. The Rev. Lajos Vetö, once a Russian interpreter, was elected bishop. After Turoczy's resignation, the Rev. László Dezséry, a former student pastor, was elected bishop. One more important administrative change took place; the number of church districts was reduced from four to two—north and south. With these measures, the state created a subservient Evangelical-Lutheran Church.

To gain control over the smaller churches, the state suggested that a supervisory council of free churches be formed. As a result, the Alliance of Free Churches of Hungary was set up in 1945, with Ferenc Kiss as president; it was joined by the Baptists, Seventh-Day Adventists, Old Catholics, and the Salvation Army. They supported nationalization of church schools and abolition of compulsory religious classes. The Free Churches were in an unfavorable situation before 1945. Considered "sects" by the traditional churches and dangerous groups by the state, they were neither recognized nor protected by laws, except for the

Baptist Church, which became an official religion in 1905. The remainder came under the supervision of the Ministry of the Interior. Young people (under age eighteen) were not allowed to attend worship services, and even the services themselves were controlled by police. Most sects were banned on 13 December 1939. No wonder that the Alliance of Free Churches, soon after its founding, sent a memorandum to the government, demanding new laws on religion. With Act No. 33, 1947, parliament abolished discrimination against "non-accepted religions." In the same year, the state recognized the Methodist Church and created a legal basis for activities by smaller denominations and for setting up the Council of Free Churches. The Free Churches did not sign an agreement with the state,[47] probably because the state was confident of handling them without a formal agreement.

After having made agreements with the historical Protestant Churches, the time had arrived for dealing with the Roman Catholic Church. Prince Primate József Cardinal Mindszenty was not a friend of the new regime; he even protested against the confiscation of church lands and schools. He wanted a negotiation, not a forced agreement with the state. The communists regarded him as the embodiment of anti-communist reactionary political forces; he had to go one way or the other. After a massive propaganda campaign he was arrested, tortured, indicted, prosecuted in a show-trial, and sentenced for life for his alleged crime of treason, espionage, and foreign currency offenses.[48] An agreement was finally ironed out on 30 August 1950, after the state applied pressure to the church by sending 3,000 monks and nuns to concentration camps on the nights of June 18 and 19.[49] Even Msgr. József Grösz, Archbishop of Kalocsa, the signatory of the agreement, was sentenced to fifteen years of imprisonment on 28 July 1951.[50] While the negotiations on the agreement were still ongoing, the "Priestly Peace Movement" came into existence prompted by the state, which was to be the source of several headaches for the bishops of the Roman Catholic Church. A similar movement had also commenced in the Protestant Churches, with the difference that the Protestant Church leadership welcomed it.

A new constitution was introduced by parliament on 18 August 1949; with it, Hungary became a people's republic. The new constitution "guaranteed for all citizens the freedom of conscience and the right to a free exercise of religion." To ensure freedom of conscience, "the Hungarian People's Republic separated the Church from the State." However, this important article was conditioned by the next one, which said: "The Hungarian People's Republic guarantees freedom of speech, of the press and of associations, as long as this freedom does not interfere with

the interests of the working masses."[51] In the following years, the constitution's article on freedom of conscience and religion often was disregarded by party and state authorities in their ardent effort to weed out
church influence and religious "idealist ideology."

Here are some acts and orders of this period that clearly show how the
socialist state fought against the churches:

> Act No. 23, 1948 ordered nationalization of church schools. Declara-
> tion No. 5, 1949, of the presidential council, abolished compulsory
> teaching of religion in state schools.[52]
> Act No. 1, 1951 established the state's right of inspection over the
> churches, which was executed by the State Office for Church Affairs.[53]
> An order of the minister of the interior, 24 April 1952, said that
> religious affiliations must not appear in the register.

The State Office for Church Affairs needs further elaboration. Regarded by some as successor to the defunct Ministry of Cults, which
dealt with church affairs before the communist takeover, this office was
the visible means of state control over the churches. Its tasks were
manifold. First, it was responsible for state-church relations. It supported activities of loyal church leaders and sought ways of curtailing
other church activities. Through this office, the state provided financial
assistance to the churches and to preserving a few old churches as
historical sites. Church requests to the state were submitted to this office,
which represented the will of the state in ecclesiastic matters. The office
monitored church activities and church influence on society. In addition,
it made recommendations to higher state authorities regarding policies
connected to the church and to church personnel. It was continuously in
touch with similar institutions in other socialist countries, exchanging
views, and sharing experiences. This agency's president held the rank of
undersecretary of state, and participated in meetings of the Council of
State Ministers. Furthermore, the office had a close relationship with
Communist Party headquarters and the security police. Its main office in
Budapest had branches in countries, towns, and villages, in each of
which at least one person was responsible for church affairs. By means of
a so-called "K" telephone hot line, the agency's officers could be reached
anywhere at any time. The agency supervised church life, the church
press, and pastors, and with the help of informers, it acquired information about church activities such as what messages were preached by
pastors, their relationships to church members, and their visitors. If a
pastor posed a problem, primarily political, the office intervened directly
with the pastor or through his superior. One of the secretary's duties was

politically to screen pastors at every level, seeking those who could be made into informers by promising ecclesiastical promotion.

The State Office of Church Affairs paid particular attention to the selection of church leaders. Toward the end of World War II, when Hungarian soldiers were taken prisoner in large numbers, they were screened by Soviet military authorities in search of war criminals. However, the Soviets had an ulterior motive: to find some highly intelligent and competent people who were offered freedom if they worked as agents of the communists in Hungary. These people were soon released and sent back to Hungary—among them former military chaplains. At home, they talked about miraculous escapes from captivity. Through these agents, the communists were able to penetrate all levels of postwar Hungarian society, including, of course, the churches. Some postwar church leaders fell into this category. The Office for Church Affairs also continued the practice of obtaining agents and informers from the clergy in other ways. First of all, they were looking among the clergy for "idealists," usually younger men. It was relatively easy to trap them and profit from their idealism. They became convinced that only communism had a future. Some church leaders also belonged to this group. But the office was searching for other church leaders who could be manipulated and used to benefit the state's political objectives. These men were clergy who were involved in illegal activities or committed crimes, mainly moral ones. When caught, they were offered the alternative of becoming informants or facing the consequences of their deeds. Some of these blackmailed unfortunates climbed high in the church hierarchy. Then there were clergy who could be called careerist, men driven by personal ambition. They easily fell prey. In more recent years, another method was used to select future church leaders. Candidates for the ministry— that is, theological students—were exempted from military service. Obviously, state authorities considered them unreliable. However, this policy was changed, and as a result seminary students were submitted to compulsory military service. Among the reasons for this change was one not even mentioned: drafted theological students could easily be screened by political officers (commissars), and suitable persons willing to cooperate could be selected and trained as future church cadre.

The second level of the state supervisory system was made up of church leaders. These men provided regular reports to the State Office of Church Affairs, such reports playing a major role in the planning of short- and long-range policy toward the churches. Similarly, reports were compiled of church leaders' activities abroad.

The third level of supervision was the state security police. A special division of that organization dealt with affairs of the church and clergy, monitoring their activities with information from the State Office for Church Affairs and from their independent network of clerical and lay informers. If both church leaders and the state office found a case to be unmanageable, the security police would act.

This threefold security system woven around the churches allowed the party and the state to establish a highly controlled and curtailed church life. The system was fully developed by 1951; since that time, churches in Hungary were held in a modern Babylonian Captivity.[54]

The Revolution of 1956 and the Protestant Churches

A movement of renewal began in the Protestant churches in the spring of 1956. A latent crisis of confidence toward the Reformed Church's leadership came into the open when a statement of faith surfaced called "Confessing Church of Hungary in 1956." From the title, it was apparent that the writers had in mind the German Bekennende Kirche and its Barmen Confession of 1939. The writers were young pastors, elders, and church members opposed to the church government, and they expressed their concern on a spiritual basis. They characterized as false the philosophy that the Marxist social order would bring salvation to the world, and they confessed their belief that salvation was the church's evangelization task. They stated that the church could not surrender such an undertaking, whether the world wanted to hear the gospel or not. The Confessing Church was anxious over the church government's closing of mission stations, which forbade missionary activities by the laity and did not live up to the opportunities allowed by the 1948 agreement to continue mission work for children, young people, unbelievers, and addicts. The Confessing Church was deeply aware of its missionary responsibility. Obedience to the rulers as ordained by God was declared in Romans 13:1 within the limits of Acts 5:29. The writers were not in favor of reactionary politics; they even opposed them. They were, however, anxious to note that the church exercised only half of its prophetic function: approving the government's action for social justice, while remaining silent in offering creative criticism of some of the state's actions. The church thereby became subservient, rather than a ministering body. Finally, they expressed their belief that Jesus Christ was head of the church, and they condemned the church government for its dictatorial rule by a privileged clique that applied scare tactics in church courts and removed ministers by autocratic means, while always supporting its acts with seemingly authentic scriptural theology. They disapproved of the leadership's luxurious living and frequent world travels, especially when the lower ranks of ministers often lived below poverty level.[55] The criticism voiced in this letter grew louder at various church meetings, and further letters were sent by presbyteries to the Office of the General Convent demanding radical changes. One protest was signed by 160 ministers. The church leadership replied with empty promises, and the tension mounted.

In addition to this crisis, the church was virtually without leadership in these critical days. Bishop Bereczky was seriously ill, while bishops Péter and Györi behaved passively. Imre Kádár, leader of the general convent, was a cautious person by instinct, and because of the lack of clear direction from the State Office for Church Affairs, he was paralyzed to act. Only one person in authority looked after church affairs, László Pap, the deputy bishop of the Danubian district. Pap did not belong to the leadership clique and therefore enjoyed high esteem among church ministers; he conducted his life along puritan lines and was a man of wisdom and experience.

In the feverish days of the revolution, the Reformed Church's previously underground forces surfaced and set up a National Action Committee of the Reformed Church at Budapest on 1 November 1956. Its purpose was to provide interim leadership for the church in the official leadership's absence and to prepare a general church election. The committee called Bishop Ravasz and chief curator János Kardos back to active service. Both men had resigned under political pressure in 1948. They and Pap provided leadership for the Renewal Movement. This move was announced by Pap in a broadcast of Free Kossuth Radio on 30 October, at which time Ravasz spoke. In his radio message he called on the people for soberness, calmness, and maturity. Cardinal Mindszenty, who was set free from his captivity by insurgents, broadcast a message in which he envisioned a full restoration of the prewar social order, and Bishop Ordass of the Lutheran Church gave a short radio speech that identified the Lutheran Church with the freedom fight. Exponents of the compromised church leadership sent a letter of resignation.

The action committee continued its work after the second Soviet armed intervention, which—after a few days of bitter street fighting in Budapest—crushed the Hungarian Revolution. On 13 November the action committee sent a circular to the sessions calling on them to decide whether or not they adhered to the Renewal Movement. Within a short time, more than a two-thirds majority expressed their wish of joining in. They also aired their distrust toward leaders of the general synod,

Joseph Pungur

the general convent, and the presidium of the church districts because of their growing faults, lack of prophetic courage, and their failure to point out and correct their shortcomings. However, the action committee made clear its support of the church-state agreement of 1948.[56]

After 4 November 1956, under Soviet occupation and the return of the communist dictatorship, in a milieu of deportation and imprisonment, tortures and executions, the brave efforts of the sessions and the action committee rapidly faded away, and, backed by state authorities, the resigned members of the previous church government—except for Péter and Roland Kiss, lay president of the Danubian church district—were installed in office again, as if nothing had happened. The revitalized State Office of Church Affairs used administrative means to paralyze the Renewal Movement's activities. For example, permission was required for meetings and even for typing and duplicating; Bishop Ravasz was sent back into retirement; Pap was given a leave for vacation. Later, from his chair of Old Testament studies at the Budapest Theological Academy, Pap was posted to a remote village church as assistant minister, and at age fifty-five was sent to early retirement. He died in late 1984. László Kardos also was silenced.

Events involving the Evangelical-Lutheran Church were not as stormy. A process of rehabilitation of Bishop Ordass had been completed by 5 October 1956, just before the outbreak of hostilities on 23 October. He was reinstated in his former bishopric office on 31 October. The resignation of the church leadership—Bishop Lajos Vetö, Bishop László Dezséry, and lay leaders such as József Darvas and Ernö Mihályfi—actually hastened the return of Bishop Ordass and Bishop Zoltán Turóczy. The case of Ernö Mihályfi is characteristic. He was so deeply involved in procommunist politicking that in fear of retribution he left the country for Vienna; after 4 November—the second invasion of Soviet troops—he came back at the Kádár regime's urgent request.

In this period of the restoration of communist power, the strategy of János Horváth, president of the State Office of Church Affairs, was twofold. First, he sought to alleviate the grave situation in the Reformed Church while keeping the Lutheran Church at bay; second, he attempted to deal with the Lutherans. The authorities tried to bend Ordass to their official line and to manipulate him to become a puppet. Here is an excerpt from the bishop's letter to president Horváth, written on 25 October 1957:

> You, Mr. President, mentioned many times that our Church Press is over-cautious and timid in regard to the state authority and it would be

good if it would relate to the State in a more "positive way." Simultaneously the censorship of articles written to our weekly became more
strict. Those promises I was given, when after a long persuasion I
reluctantly accepted the responsibility [for] the Church Press [an information bulletin in English and German, sent to churches abroad], were
not kept at all. This situation forced me to resign as Publisher . . .
believe me, Mr. President, that I can make a better judgment of what
should be printed in the Church Press than a clerk at the Office of
Church Affairs.

In this letter, Ordass talked about two of his pastors who applied for
passports promised by the State Office for Church Affairs, but who did
not receive them. Finally, the bishop made an inquiry into the case on his
own, and to what he found he added his opinion. "They [the state office
clerks] received such information from pastors which indicates that they
[the two applying pastors] do not relate well to the People's Democracy. I
am worried that in collecting information the words of unknown informants have more weight than the words of a bishop of the Church." He
went on to criticize the state's new terror tactics. "In my opinion the
retaliatory measures of the Government result in strong reaction in a
very wide circle. This is enhanced by its overzealous execution." One of
the church's pastors was taken from his village together with ten villagers. He was treated inhumanly and severely beaten. When the interrogators learned that he was a priest, they forced him to recite the "Ave
Maria." He answered that he did not know it, then was forced to recite an
"Our Father." As he did so, the interrogators cursed and humiliated
him.[57] It was no wonder that after this letter and similar ones, the state
office was convinced that Ordass could not be manipulated. Despite his
rehabilitation in October 1956, despite his readiness to work with state
authorities in an honest way, and despite his election as a vice president
of the Lutheran World Federation, he was forced into retirement on
19 June 1958. He died on 14 August 1974.

In March 1957 the Decrees of Law No. 22 came into force. This spelled
out that state permission was necessary in filling certain church vacancies. Its validity was extended retroactively 1 October 1956, and it virtually abolished the autonomy of the Hungarian churches.[58]

The official evaluation of the role of the Protestant churches in the
tragic events of 1956 was that it was a "rebellion" prepared and in-
stigated by the meeting of the central committee of the World Council of Churches at Galyatetö in the summer of 1956 and that only a
"few" clergymen participated.[59] After two turbulent years, the Protestant churches ended up as tightly restricted as they had been before 1956.

The Theology of Service and Theology of Diaconia

By early 1958, the State Office of Church Affairs effectively controlled
the Protestant churches. Now the time had arrived for some changes in
the churches' leadership. In the Reformed Church, only Bishop Elemér
Györi survived the storms of history. The synod council at its meeting on
21 December 1956 pronounced the resignation of Bereczky and Péter as
invalid and wanted to reinstate them as bishops in office. However,
Bereczky was incapacitated, and because of his serious illness was unable to resume his role. Péter did not want to continue his service as
bishop in spite of the district's request. He soon became president of the
Institute of Cultural Relations; then, after the resignation of Endre Sík,
he was appointed minister of foreign affairs. His successor was Bishop
Tibor Bartha, who was elected in 1958 and resigned at the end of 1986.
Bishop Bartha was Péter's former secretary. He was educated in Germany, and his doctoral thesis was on "The Homiletics of Barth." After
serving as a pastor at Munkács, he became minister at Debrecen, then
professor of theology at the Debrecen theological academy and secretary
to Bishop Péter. Having been elected bishop of the Transtibiscan district,
he also was chosen as president of the general synod. Soon he was
elected a member of parliament and a member of the presidential council. He held high positions at the Christian Peace Conference and within
leading bodies of the World Council of Churches. For three decades,
Bartha provided leadership to the Reformed Church. After Bereczky's
resignation, István Szamosközi was elected bishop of the Danubian
district in 1958 and retained this position until his resignation in 1978.
The Cistibiscan district—which was annexed to the Transtibiscan district
in 1952—was restored with Lajos Darányi as its bishop. After his death,
Bishop Sándor Ráski succeeded him. Bishop Elemér Györi was followed
by Bishop Benö Békefi, and he by Bishop Lajos Bakos in 1964.

The new leadership of the church continued the tradition of Bishop
Bereczky's and Bishop Péter's theology and church politics. While the
Kádár government acknowledged and condemned the faults and excesses of the communist leadership prior to 1956, the new church leaders
failed to do the same. They kept silent about the excesses committed by
church leaders between 1948 and 1956. Instead of confessing their own
shortcomings and serious mistakes, the new leaders belittled the imprisoned leaders and ridiculed them as a tiny group of troublemakers
within the church. They simply forgot that more than two-thirds of the

congregations had stood behind the National Action Committee in 1956. To counter the influence of Bishop Ravasz, the State Office for Church Affairs commissioned Imre Kádár to write a critical book on his theology and church policy. This book was translated into English and published as *The Church in the Storm of Time*. It was so poisonously written that after several years the state office considered it useless and condemned the entire lot of remaining copies to be destroyed.

The church's new leadership was busy devising and working out an acceptable theological basis for their unconditional support of the state. The effort involved a group of bishops and professors, including Bartha and to a lesser extent other bishops; also taking part were such academics as László M. Pákozdy, László A. Szabó, Zsigmond Varga, Imre Jánossy, and Elemér Kocsis. They succeeded in inventing and constructing the so-called Theology of Service, the roots of which can be found in the Narrow Way Theology of Albert Bereczky. Bereczky introduced the theological term Serving Church as opposed to Ruling Church. In one of his 1950 sermons, he said: "I saw the vision of a renewed Hungarian Reformed Church, which has the joyful privilege of service on Hungarian soil, it can work with happy heart for the furtherance of the material and spiritual wealth of the motherland and it has no other claim except to follow the Lord, who did not come to be served but to serve."[60] Some scholars, however, insist that this concept can be traced in the works of Imre Révész, János Victor, and Sándor Makkai, as well as in the avant garde theology of the National Free Council of the Reformed Church.[61]

Between the declaration of the synod council (1958) and the instruction of the synod (1967), the basic features of the Theology of Service had been systematically worked out. The synod instruction, released on the Reformed Church of Hungary's four-hundredth anniversary, provides a good summary of the Theology of Service. The title of the instruction is "Our Heritage and Task Is Reformation." Among other things, it states: "In the centre of the attention of our Church stands the source of service. It is not only a meditation on the vision of the Serving Church but the good works in the name of Christ and in fellowship with Christ. We gladly recognize that our task is obedience to the Great Commandment of love God and Man." In practice, this statement meant that the Christian congregation had to stand before the world offering patient, helpful, and useful love in every dimension of life. By actually practicing social responsibility among all facets of family, economy, and state and social life, it could be "demonstrated that we are really Christians and members of Christ's earthly congregation."[62] The instruction was actually an ecclesiastical expression of the church's role in a socialist state. With it, the church not only accepted the socialist-communist system, but offered its assistance both at home and in propaganda abroad.

The Theology of Service skillfully used all of the paraphernalia of a genuine theology, from scriptural references to basic confessional writings—for example, the Heidelberger Catechism and the Helvetic Confession. However, in practice it became an ideo-theology that made the church the collaborator with an atheist secular authority. In reality, this theology was faulty from its inception. It was true that Christ came to serve the sick and the ill and the sinners who were willing to repent. But Christ never offered his help and service to the occupying Roman imperium; had he offered political help to Pontius Pilate, Jesus never would have died on the Cross. On the other hand, the Theology of Service was superfluous simply because members of the church, as citizens of the country, had to take part in building the new society. They were properly instructed by party organs and propaganda about the merits of the new society. Why then did the church feel it was necessary to tell its members what they already knew? If the church tried to play the role of a commissar, then who would fulfill the church's task of proclaiming the Good News of the Kingdom of God? Barth was right in his criticism of Reformed Theology in Hungary. In his never-published letter, he had said: "You are at the point of wandering into an ideological wonderland."[63] Neither leaders nor theologians of the Reformed Church heeded his warnings. Barth's prophecy was fulfilled as theology became ideologized and was transformed into a political theology—an idol that its creators were even proud of. Géza Boross, a theologian of a younger generation, hit the mark in characterizing the Theology of Service by saying that its "tone is that of the Standards of Faith, its immediacy is that of the Pietists, its boldness is that of Stauffer, its message in many respects is that of Barth, and it is not at all a mix of all these."[64] It turns out that the Theology of Service was not even an original theology, but one borrowed from other systems.

The protagonists of the Theology of Service soon ran into difficulties. Leaders of the church who proclaimed service to others themselves behaved like tyrants. Three cases illustrate the point.

In 1965–66 Peter Hajdu was perhaps the closest coworker of Bishop Bereczky and a staunch follower of the bishop's theological ideas and leadership line. Hajdu was the senior minister of the seniorate (presbytery) of Buda-South. He criticized Bartha and his clique, first, for a growing personality cult that was nurtured by Bartha and his inner circle of faithfuls, careerists, and opportunists. This group of lackeys came with Bartha from Debrecen to Budapest, where the office of the convent, later the office of the general synod, was located. Members of this group were appointed leaders of almost every department; they filled key positions and were the bishop's confidants. They even decided who could get an audience with Bartha. They created and nurtured a personality cult of Bartha, who apparently accepted and used it to cover his authoritarian style of leadership. In some respects it was a replica of the dictatorial conduct of party and state leaders. Without the consent of the State Office of Church Affairs, such a leadership style was impossible. It was entirely possible, however, that the state office suggested such a strong-hand policy. Hajdu was bold enough to challenge the bishop's overblown power and suggest a return to the classical Presbyterian Church government; instead of bishops elected for life, let the church have periodically elected moderators. Second, Hajdu pointed out that church finances were administered in secret by the bishop's inner circle and that corruption and misuse of funds was suspected. Third, a concern that Hajdu shared with many colleagues was that all church ministers, even members of the church judiciary, were completely dominated by the church government; consequently, an independent church court of appeal did not exist. Fourth, Hajdu expressed his concern about the unhealthy alliance between the Bartha clique and some high officials of the state office, which promoted individual interests rather than the interests of the church or the state. As a consequence of this alliance, the state office tried to cover up manipulations by church leaders that it should have prevented. Hajdu was spared the full rage of the Bartha clique because of public awareness of his charges. However, he was forced to resign from his senior post. And nothing changed. The Hungarian Reformed Church was the only Presbyterian church that elected bishops for life. Therefore, it was easier for the state office to work with bishops that it selected than to deal with moderators or clerks of the general synod who were elected yearly.

The second case is the story of the Rev. József Éliás. In his younger years, Éliás worked at the Budapest-based Good Shepherd Mission converting Jews to Christianity. During World War II, he, together with others, did everything he could to save them from persecution and death. In 1947 he published a book entitled *Christianity and Politics,* and in 1958 he was called to be minister of a church in Debrecen. Soon, he became the confidant of Bishop Bartha. In 1962, Éliás pleaded with the bishop to stop the despotic behavior of one of his ministers. Instead of disciplining that person, however, the bishop distanced himself from Éliás and did something strange: he sold his church building to the state and allegedly spent the money for renovation of the Reformed College of Debrecen. When Éliás learned of the deal and spoke out, he was disciplined and sent into retirement. To save Bartha's reputation, the state office finally gave permission for construction of a new church on a new lot. Almost at the same time, Bartha also sold to the state the only remaining high school building in Debrecen, using the money for further renovation of the college.

The third case is the so-called Turós affair. The Rev. Aladár Turós, leader of the department of Diakonia of the general synod office, was an important member of Bishop Bartha's entourage, mainly for two reasons: he was able to raise funds, and by devious means he could provide town apartments for the cronies of the leadership in a city with a chronic housing shortage. Turós was held in high esteem by the bishop, who made him counsellor of the general synod and helped to rescue him from a lawsuit. All of these things could not go on without the tacit toleration of the State Office of Church Affairs.

In addition to these problems, the church's leadership style gave reason for concern. Bishop Bartha and his circle introduced and exercised a two-faced, neo-baroque style of government. One face showed an autocratic attitude, the other a sympathetic, "democratic" one. This stance contributed to widening the gap between the church leaders and the ministers, elders, and congregations whom they were supposed to lead. Toward the end of this period, an icy atmosphere pervaded the entire church.

In the Evangelical-Lutheran Church, the restoration after the 1956 revolution was complicated. In the tense days of the revolution itself, the entire church leadership resigned, which opened the way for Bishop Ordass and Bishop Turóczy to resume their service as leaders. Ordass was rehabilitated by the state after his trial and imprisonment. However, after the revolution was crushed, the presidential council refused to accept the earlier resignations. Consequently, Bishop Lajos Vetö returned to his post in December 1957. After the second dismissal of Bishop Ordass, even Bishop László Dezséry returned for a short time in June 1958. Then Dezséry resigned again, this time for good, to become a commentator for the state-run radio broadcasting system. His successor was Bishop Káldy, who was installed in December 1958. After Vetö's final retirement, Ernö Ottlyk was elected as his successor in 1966.

With the return of Bishop Káldy, a new chapter began in Evangelical-Lutheran history and lasted until his death on 17 May 1987. He was bishop president of the church, a member of parliament, and, from 1984, president of the Lutheran World Federation. He devised the outlines of the so-called Theology of Diaconia, which had a close link with the Reformed Church's Theology of Service. These two theologies are indeed twins; they have the same roots, the same purpose, and the same context.

The main tenets of the Theology of Diaconia were presented in a 1958 article by Bishop Káldy, "How Can We Go Forward?" After discussing several temptations of the church—its negative attitude toward socialism, a church uninterested in the world, and an unconditional accommodation of the church with the state—Káldy envisaged another choice. This was the way of Diaconia, that is, the "Church must be a Church in a socialist society"—preaching, administering the sacraments, and rendering the service of love to society. Under Káldy's guidance, a group of theologians worked out and systematized the concept's tenets. These theologians were: Gyula Nagy, Miklós Pálfy, Ernö Ottlyk, Károly Pröhle, Gyula Groó, József Vámos, Tibor Fabinyi, and Bishop Lajos Vetö. The biblical foundation of this theology was to be found in Matthew 20:28, where Jesus Christ said: "The Son of Man came not to be served, but to serve." Its practical consequence was that the church offers full and unconditional support to the building of socialism and to the state's sovereign policy objectives.

Although the Theology of Diaconia was the official theology of the Evangelical-Lutheran Church,[65] it was not unanimously accepted and followed by all pastors. Critical voices questioned its tenets. Zoltán Dóka, the pastor of Hévizgyörk, in an open letter to the executive committee of the Lutheran World Federation at its meeting at Budapest in 1984 offered sharp criticism. He insisted that "Diakonia" is not a central theme of the New Testament, where it simply means the service around the table; on that table is the Life of Christ—the elements of Holy Communion—as a ransom for many.[66] In Dóka's opinion, it was a subjective theology of church leaders, which they wished to force on the church. He wrote later:

> I have often re-thought Káldy's "new road," but I always came to the same conclusion: that it is, in fact, the always tempting wrong way of Theology on which the "German Christians" have travelled at other times and in other contexts. Their criteria are always the same: (1) They place the Gospel under a historical and political situation and they use it as a springboard for a certain concept of politics and Church politics. (2) In accordance with it, theology is downgraded, loses its freedom, and deteriorates into an ideology which justifies the political manipulation of the Gospel. (3) The secret of the Church is the communion with Christ; this now becomes unimportant and insufficient and the apparent basis and standard of this communion will be a political

concept. The representatives of the "new way" regard themselves as prophets, and under the umbrella of the existing regime they live well in security and in the Church they rule with tyranny. This arbitrary behaviour which crushes all critics is especially controversial when at the same time the beautiful word of the New Testament "Service" is written on the flag.[67]

Vilmos Vajta also, more recently, criticized the concept. He insisted that the Diakonia was taken in a broad sense and transformed into a "social-ethical Diakonia," which included the questions of society and humankind. This theological thinking led to a situation in which the "Theology of Diaconia is subjected to a social-ethical conception. This ethical ideologization steals away from the sinners the merciful Word of God. This false theological basis of the Theology of Diaconia makes the theological thinking and the preaching of the ministers uncertain."[68] Dóka added another criticism, namely, that the Theology of Diaconia lacked a means of critical self-examination. Only this would prevent it from slipping toward the concept of "good works."[69]

The smaller Protestant churches were on the state's periphery of interest. In the early 1950s, the time had come for the state to subject them to strict control. The Baptist Church, the Evangelical Pentecostal community, the Assembly of the Living God, the Seventh-Day Adventists, the Church of God, the Christian Brethren congregation, the Methodist Church, the Ancient Christian congregation, and the Free Christian congregation all belonged to the Council of Free Churches, formed in 1947 as successor to the Alliance of Free Churches founded two years earlier. The Council's purpose was to represent the common interest of the smaller churches. However, the council was relatively inactive until the State Office of Church Affairs realized that it could become an instrument of the state's higher control over the smaller churches and Christian groups. Under the presidency of Sándor Palotay, the Council of Free Churches joined the state-supporting policy of the traditional Protestant churches, and the state office could effectively exercise both its influence and control role over the Free Churches.

Two general synods signified a turning point in the life of the Protestant churches. The Evangelical-Lutheran Church held a general synod in 1966 to legislate the church's service in socialist society. The Reformed Church, in the Jubilee Synod, held in Debrecen in 1967 to commemorate the four-hundredth anniversary of the church's founding, also offered its services to the state.

The synod declarations clearly enunciated the essential principles of the Theology of Service and the Theology of Diaconia. Gyula Nagy, now bishop-president of the Evangelical Lutheran Church, in his books *Dogmatics* (1965) and *Church in Today's World* (1967), expounded the doctrinal basis and the socio-ethical consequences of the Theology of Diaconia. Elemér Kocsis, now bishop of the Transtibiscan District, in his *Dogmatics* (1976) and *Christian Ethics* (1975, 1979), did the same for the Theology of Service. The fifth volume of *Studia et Acta Ecclesiastica* (1983) also deals with the genesis and development of the Theology of Service. Studies of this new theology also can be found in books by leading bishops—the pioneers of this theological trend—such as A. Bereczky's "Narrow Way" and "Door-Opening," and "Between Two Judgements"; Z. Káldy's "On a New Way," and "He Came to Serve"; T. Bartha's "Word, Church, People," K. Tóth's "Good News, Message of Peace," and "Roots and Perspectives," and L. Bakos's "I Believe and Confess." In these and other writings, great efforts were made to justify the tenets of the new theologies, which led the respective churches to unconditionally support the ideological twists and the capricious acts of the ruling regime as if these were some new kind of divine revelation.

The Praxis of the Serving Church (1968–1988)

The Protestant churches in Hungary always offered services to society beyond their work of preaching and witnessing, teaching, and comforting and encouraging. Yet these efforts gradually degenerated into open collaboration with a totalitarian state. This meant that the Protestant churches' responsible leadership continuously offered assistance for building up an atheist-socialist society at home and promoted communist state's abroad. The state, which asked and demanded such services, in return tried everything to reduce the churches' influence on society and its social roots by applying administrative methods, antireligious propaganda, and atheistic education. State authorities, in furthering the policy of the Communist Party, applied a dialectic method to the churches—that is, on one hand, they fought the churches and, on the other, they tried to gain maximum advantage from the churches' willingness to collaborate.

The churches offered help in building a socialist-communist society in Hungary by trying to enhance patriotism and obedience to authorities, by supporting and promoting the transformation of society, by justifying party directives and resolutions, by participating in every level of work of the Patriotic Front (a noncommunist organization under communist leadership) to support the party's politics, and by participating in the work of the National Peace Council. The churches tried to strengthen the people's working morale.

In foreign relations, Protestant church leaders rendered an important service to the state in supporting the Soviet bloc's objectives. The main intent of the church diplomats was to influence church leaders abroad by winning them over and through them exercising influence on governments and church bodies.

The Christian Peace Conference, based in Prague, was the most important church-related organization for realizing such objectives. This movement was started by the initiative of a handful of Czech Protestant theologians such as Josef Hromádka, Hans-Joachim Iwand, Bohuslav Pospisil, and Heinrich Vogel in 1958, with the honest aim of promoting world peace by calling on the superpowers to disarm. Soon, the leading theologians of the Eastern bloc joined them. However, the peace conference had been transformed into an auxiliary of Soviet bloc diplomacy. Initially, the organization was dominated by Czechs, but after Warsaw Pact troops occupied Czechoslovakia in 1968, the organization's leadership changed. Károly Tóth was appointed general secretary to replace the dismissed Jiri Ondra. Metropolitan Nikodim of the Russian Orthodox Church became the new president after Josef Hromádka's death in 1968. Under the leadership of Tóth, the organization was transformed into an "Eastern European Ecumene." Tóth became the organization's president in 1978. With its regional conferences, the Christian Peace Conference established itself on five continents. Although it was regarded with much suspicion—not unfounded—the conference managed to hold spectacular, highly publicized assemblies, world conferences, with pre-prepared resolutions and communiques. Hungary's Protestant church leaders and their theologians actively participated in the movement's theological and diplomatic work. And the churches regularly contributed to its budget.

Since the mid-1960s, the state-suggested unwritten policy of church leaders was to stage an offensive to capture and occupy as many positions as possible in such organizations such as the World Council of Churches, the Conference of European Churches, the World Alliance of Reformed Churches, the Lutheran World Federation, and others, and to develop bilateral relations with sister churches abroad. As a result of the offensive, which coincided with similar efforts by Soviet-bloc diplomats, a handful of church leaders were elected to executive and staff positions with these organizations. By being present, they could influence policy, decision-making, and activities.

The Protestant churches were well aware of the importance of organizing conferences of international and interdenominational bodies on Hungarian soil. The central committee meeting of the World Council of Churches at Galyatetö in the summer of 1956 did not yield the expected results; instead, it was blamed for encouraging the outbreak of revolution in Hungary—an unfounded accusation. International conferences were not allowed again until 1964, when as a trial balloon the Working Committee of the Christian Peace Conference held a meeting in Budapest, to the trepidation of state officials. Then in 1967 a Jubilee Synod was held in Debrecen, with many foreign guests, which started a series of international gatherings that grew in number and importance. For example, in 1984 alone these important events took place: the seventh assembly of the Lutheran World Federation, which elected Bishop Káldy its president; a Christian-Marxist international conference; an Orthodox-Reformed dialogue; the visit of leaders of the Christian-Jewish Council; the visit of a delegation from the Reformed Church in Romania; the visit of a delegation from English churches; the visit of leaders of the HEKS, Switzerland; and a conference of the Hungarian Reformed Churches in Diaspora. Among the foreign visitors were Alan Boesak, president of the WARC; Claire Randall, general secretary of the National Council of Churches of Christ in the United States; and Bishop Ting from the People's Republic of China. As far as Hungarian churches visiting abroad, Bishop Károly Tóth was the star diplomat. In 1984 Tóth visited President Gustáv Husák of Czechoslovakia, General Wojciech Jaruzelski of Poland, and Kenneth Kaunda, president of Zambia. He visited churches in Sweden, Norway, Finland, France, England, East Germany, the United States, and Egypt. Tóth was not alone among Hungarian church travellers; Bishop Káldy, bishops, professors, senior ministers, and department leaders of synod offices took part in many international conferences. No wonder that the state acknowledged the serving church by rewarding its leaders. In doing so, the government always emphasized that church-state relations were "good, orderly and fruitful."

A Crisis Situation

Since the late 1970s some important improvements occurred within the churches and in church-state relations; these gradually developed into a crisis situation for both the state and the churches.

During the seventies, a new generation of church leaders replaced the old guard. These younger leaders had been carefully selected, nurtured, and trained. At the beginning, everything possible was done by the state so that they would carry on the theologies of Service and Diaconia. The new leadership of the Reformed Church included Bishop Kürti of the Cistibiscan district (since 1977), Bishop Tóth of the Danubian district (since 1978), Bishop Kovách of the Transdanubian district (since 1979), and Bishop Kocsis of the Transtibiscan district (since 1987). In the Lutheran Church three new bishops were elected in rapid succession for two bishoprics: Bishop Gyula Nagy of the North district (1982–89), Bishop Béla Harmati of the South district (since 1987), and after the resignation of Gyula Nagy, Imre Szebik took charge of the North district bishopric (1990). János Viczián was president of the Council of Free Churches from 1988 until its dissolution in 1990. The general secretary of the Ecumenical Council of Hungarian Churches was László Lehel (since 1988). Members of the communist parliament were Tóth, Gyula Nagy, Kürti, and János Viczián. In 1990 new democratic elections were held, and none of the former leaders won a seat; instead, ten ministers were elected.

Most of the new leaders had been selected much earlier for leading roles. Tóth, Kürti, and Kovách belonged to Bishop Bartha's circle. Kürti and Kovách were brought by the bishop from Debrecen to Budapest where they worked at the general synod office's Department of Foreign Relations; Kovách became its chairman and Kürti became a professor at the theological academy in Debrecen. Elemér Kocsis also was a professor there and became a leading supporter of the Theology of Service. Nagy, a former professor and former follower of Bishop Ordass, became one of the leading theologians of Káldy's Theology of Diaconia. He worked for years at the European Conference of Churches in Geneva. For a while, Béla Harmati was foreign secretary in Káldy's administration. He also spent years at the study department of the Lutheran World Federation in Geneva. Bishop Tóth in his early years as a theology student was chosen by Imre Kádár, the gray eminence of Bereczky's leadership team, and appointed to the Department of Foreign Relations of the general synod; he soon became the Reformed Church's top diplomat, occupying that position for fifteen years. He also became general secretary of the Christian Peace Conference and later its president, vice president of the World Alliance of Reformed Churches, and member of the executive committee of the World Council of Churches. In 1988 Bishop Tóth was elected to parliament and appointed to the Presidential Council of Hungary. He became president of the general synod of Hungary's Reformed Church, and he also was elected president of the Ecumenical Council of Hungarian Churches. In all respects, he appeared to be Bishop Bartha's successor. But in the general synod of 1989, in a secret ballot, Bishop Kocsis was elected church president.

At the same time, many politically uninvolved theologians and ministers remained faithful to their calling to preach the gospel in harmony with the evangelical tradition of the Protestant churches during a difficult period. From this group came representatives of an underground movement within the Reformed Church in the late 1970s and of renewal groups in the Evangelical Lutheran Church in the mid-1980s. In 1978 an eight-page memorandum, "Confession and Opinion," on the sad state of the Hungarian Reformed Church was secretly published.[70] This document was born out of a sense of responsibility for the church's life and witnessing. The writers discovered the faint outlines of the plan to liquidate the church—a plan that had gone on since 1948. They criticized the government policy of using sermons for political agitation, and they claimed that the government applied immoral methods of taking over the churches in order to promote its aims through control and transformation of the real church into a make-believe one, replacing efficiently serving ministers with false priests, and turning church leaders into state officials. The memorandum protested the state's arbitrary interference in church elections, which rendered the churches unable to select their own officials. Because state approval was given to only one candidate, the electorate was forced to play out an election comedy. The document's authors sharply criticized church leaders for assisting the state in this fraud in violation of the 1948 agreement. Church leaders, it was claimed, were fighting against church interests and made the government's church-liquidating steps appear as magnanimous deeds. Such leaders removed those ministers who raised their voices to defend the church, its ministry to youth, and its programs for religious education. These leaders likewise reinforced the government's political decisions with their "solemn" declarations. As a consequence, the church was a dying institution. The document demanded a genuine separation of church and state, dissolution of the clerical movement and the State Office of Church Affairs, and resignation of church leaders.

Since the late 1970s, there had been economic and political crisis in Hungary that in the summer of 1988 culminated in the dismissal of János Kádár, general secretary of the Hungarian Socialist Workers' Party since 1956, and the emergence of Károly Grósz as the new party leader, with Miklós Németh as the new prime minister. In this crisis, the churches were given greater freedom. Behind this move, however, lay other calculations. First, there was an alarming decline in membership of the historical Protestant churches since the late 1960s, especially in urban areas.[71] At the same time, new members had joined the Free Churches. From the state's point of view, it was an undesirable development because the Free Churches were not under the state's complete control. Second, membership in Protestant churches decreased faster and in greater numbers than had been anticipated. This posed an inherent danger to the success of the church leaders' propaganda campaign abroad, namely, that they might end up with no sizable church behind them. Third, by allowing greater church freedom, state leaders scored points both at home and abroad in a situation where they badly needed them.

Greater freedom for the churches meant more conferences could be held for elders and young people. The churches' publishing activity broadened; besides weeklies, official bulletins, an ecumenical press service, and an ecumenical theological review, permission was given to publish two quarterlies: *Confessio* (Reformed) and *Diakonia* (Lutheran). Aside from these ventures, Bibles, hymn books, and pamphlets were published. Permission was given to open two bookstores, one in Budapest, the other in Debrecen. New church buildings, conference centers, and charitable institutions could be erected and older ones renovated. Ráday College in Budapest added a new wing, and the old wing was modernized. The new policy also allowed the churches to reclaim all institutions and other facilities illegally confiscated by the state after the 1948 agreement. State permission was granted for the formation of church-related associations. This was how the Collegium Doctrum, an association of theological doctors in the Reformed Church, came into existence. The Reformed Church's missionary activity also grew after 1970; two missionaries were sent, one to Africa, and the other to Latin America. Theology students from the Third World and from the West were enrolled in Hungarian theological academies, and Hungarian theology students and ministers were given a chance to study abroad—if they were selected by authorities. A leprosy mission became active, as did a mission among the blind. In the later 1980s, a mission was begun among the growing number of ethnic Hungarian refugees from Transylvania, which was under Romanian rule. Since then, more than 40,000 ethnic Hungarians have obtained political asylum. The refugees escaped the forced "homogenization" policy of the Romanian communists, which entailed the extinction of the language, customs, and culture of 2.5 million ethnic Hungarians. This policy included bulldozing 7,000 mostly Hungarian-inhabited villages. The state allowed the churches to help the refugees, and church leaders brought the oppression of Hungarian and other minorities to the attention of international forums such as the

World Council of Churches, the Christian Peace Conference, and the European parliament. For the first time since World War II, two candidates were allowed to contend for the office of bishop. At Easter of 1988, a worship service was televised from the Calvin Square Reformed Church in Budapest. A law to determine the churches' role in society was passed by parliament in 1990. Discussions of church activities clearly showed that for forty years there were dark sides to state-church relations. In the past, both state and church leaders had talked of Hungary's full religious freedom. Now it turned out that not even the concept of church was defined by law, let alone its activities. Sometimes the churches were regarded as "social entities," at other times as "persons," depending on which was more favorable to state authorities. Other grievances also were raised, such as the churches' place and role in society and their works of charity, art, and education. For the first time it was revealed that for forty years the state had denied licenses for forming and operating religious societies. Suggestions were raised that such organizations in the future should not be supervised by state authorities, but only by the church. Similarly, discrimination against religious persons or religiously educated young people was called into question.[72] In light of these grievances, it was asked, how could church leaders report full religious freedom in Hungary during the past four decades? That church leadership did not admit the full truth about the lack of religious freedom in socialist Hungary was convincingly proved by their own complaints in a nationally televised interview, which was later published in the Reformed Church weekly.[73] During these revelations, a growing number of demands were raised in the Protestant churches. In the Reformed Church, members wanted to see different theological trends emphasized other than the official line.[74] Others advocated restitution of chaplaincies in the army.[75] A communique revealed the State Office of Church Affairs allowed church leaders to duplicate circulars without previous permission; however, the leaders had to take full responsibility for the content of such materials.[76] From these examples, conclusions could be drawn about the real situation of the Hungarian churches since the late 1940s.

When this question of the church leaders' responsibility was raised to Bishop Tóth, his answer was elusive. He mentioned only the Narrow Way Theology of the late Bishop Bereczky, but he would not criticize it. He also cited the Theology of Service in such a way as to indicate that it should be attributed to Bereczky as well. In fact, this theological concept was closely connected with Bishop Bartha, whose name was not mentioned. Bishop Tóth's selective amnesia was not accidental; it was purposeful because he and the church's three other bishops at the time were among the chief theoreticians, advocates, and executors of the concept that ruined the Reformed Church theologically and morally.[77]

In the Evangelical Lutheran Church, too, tensions were building. The first sign of them was an open letter from Zoltán Dóka to the leadership of the Lutheran World Federation in 1984, in which he sharply criticized the Theology of Diaconia. In the autumn of 1985, a Renewal Movement came into existence as the result of work by the Fraternal Word Community.[78] The movement strongly criticized the corrupt theology of the past forty years. Dóka, a prominent member, said that this theology deviated from the classic Lutheran Theology of Gospel and Law (or the Theology of the Two Realms), and as a result politics had replaced the gospel. Consequently, political concepts such as "progressive" and "reactionary" received theological support. Church leaders turned against the church, their pastors, and the people and became advocates of official state policy. Moreover, the leaders assumed political roles on various levels. This participation in itself could not be criticized, provided that the leaders had acted as individuals, but they had taken part on behalf of the church. They forgot that the church was not a political entity, and consequently could not have a purely political program.[79] The authors of the letter also criticized the personality cult in the church, the deterioration of fraternal relations among pastors, and the declining quality of theology, preaching, religious life, and publishing activities.[80] Positive suggestions for change were put forward. Among other things, the movement demanded detailed, truthful information from church leaders and abolition of the church press monopoly. Movement members questioned the practice of filling church vacancies at the national level with tiny cliques that monopolized important decisions. They also demanded that the church's financial management be brought to light. It was suggested that an independent reform committee should be set up to oversee church life, the activities of church leaders, and the process of renewal. Finally, it was suggested that if church leaders continued to use empty words regarding renewal, then renewal must be brought about independent of them.[81]

A New Beginning

The radical political changes in the former Soviet Union under Mikhail Gorbachev and the advent of glasnost and perestroika offered a unique possibility for political changes in the East European satellite states.

Accumulating problems and general disappointment finally led to the communist system's collapse throughout the region in 1989. In Hungary, the collapse occurred despite last-minute maneuvering of reform communists. Communist rule had left the country in economic, ideological, and moral disarray, saddled with a burdensome debt of $22 billion.

In response to these mounting difficulties, a silent revolution took place that marked the end of socialism's costly experience and the beginning of a new, post-communist era. The year 1989 carried great significance in Hungary's history. The Iron Curtain came down, and the martyrs of the 1956 revolution were honored with a state funeral on 16 June. János Kádár, the communist strongman for thirty-three years, died, but not until the crushed revolution's ideals were resurrected. Political pluralism was introduced; political parties mushroomed. The State Office of Church Affairs was dismantled. With it, the controlling and manipulating arm of the party-state disappeared. Ten percent of its original mandate survived the death of that notorious office, but this partial agenda was divided among three new administrative agencies. A secretariat for church policy (of the council of ministers) was organized, its leader to be Barna Sarkadi Nagy, formerly vice president of the defunct State Office of Church Affairs. The National Religious Council, a new organization, also was formed. A consultative body, it had as its president the prime minister of the state; its members were church representatives. Each interested ministry formed a department to deal with church-related issues.[82] These measures signaled an important step toward realizing the principle of a "Free Church in a Free State." In the midst of these changes and developments, Billy Graham's third Hungarian evangelization campaign took place in Budapest's People's Stadium on 29 July 1989. This single event attracted more than 90,000 people.

National elections were held on 25 March and 8 April 1990, resulting in a sweeping victory for the noncommunist opposition parties, specifically the Democratic Forum, the Alliance of Free Democrats, the Smallholders' Party, the Christian Democratic People's Party, and the Social Democrats. A coalition government took over, with József Antall as prime minister. The new government pleaded to create a free and democratic Hungary that would abide by its constitution and laws, with a market economy and a Western orientation in foreign policy.

Since the early 1980s, an additional concern had developed, slowly but steadily, over the persecution and oppression of the 2.5 million Hungarian ethnic minority in the western Romanian territory of Transylvania, which until the end of World War I had belonged to Hungary. This

territory had been ceded to Romania by the Treaty of Trianon forced on
Hungary in 1920. After World War II, the Hungarian minority in Transylvania enjoyed limited autonomy. They had schools, a university, theaters, and libraries, and they freely used the Hungarian language—their
mother tongue. Nicolae Ceaușescu, the last Stalinist, while fostering
Romanian nationalism, wanted to eliminate all ethnic minorities by his
plan of "homogenization." This policy affected not only Hungarians, but
Germans, Jews, and Bulgarians. Gradually, the autonomy of Hungarian
ethnics was taken away, and with it their cultural facilities. The Hungarian language was banned, historical documents confiscated, villages
with Hungarian names were Romanianized, even cemeteries with Hungarian pasts were bulldozed. The Hungarian ethnic population was dispersed throughout Romania, and the influx of Romanians into formerly
Hungarian regions was encouraged. Finally, an insane plan of "systematization" was put into effect, which meant that some 8,000 villages,
mostly in Hungarian-populated areas, would be demolished. The evict-
ed inhabitants were moved into poorly constructed apartment buildings
in agro-industrial centers. In the meantime, the whole of Romania suffered hunger, misery, backwardness, food rationing, and shortages of
fuel and electricity.

The news of this "cultural genocide" of ethnic minorities in Romania
reached Hungary and alarmed the people. But not the communist rulers.
The Kádár regime did nothing to defend the victimized ethnic minorities'
most basic human rights. As a consequence of Ceaușescu's minority
persecution policy, some 40,000 ethnic Hungarians from Transylvania
fled to Hungary and asked for political asylum. In this crisis, Hungarian
church leaders asked for the help of world church organizations such as
the Vatican, the World Council of Churches, the Lutheran World Federation, and the Alliance of Reformed Churches. Even the European parliament was called on to protest the Ceaușescu regime's atrocities. Romanian church leaders were kept silent. Only a young Reformed minister,
Lászlo Tökés, pastor of the Hungarian Reformed Church in Timisoara,
decided to speak up on behalf of his oppressed people. As an outspoken
critic of their regime, the Romanian authorities wanted to silence him at
any cost. When Tökés's staunch resistance created a showdown, Hungarian Church leaders did their best to defend him. The crisis finally ex-
ploded in a revolution that toppled the Ceaușescu regime at Christmas.
In early 1990, Tökés paid an official visit to Hungary at the Reformed
Church's invitation. He was received everywhere as a national hero—by
the church, by state authorities, and by the people. Huge crowds greeted

him. He was not hesitant to reprimand Reformed Church leaders in Hungary for failing to provide effective support for the Reformed Church in Romania and for the Hungarian ethnic minority during their years of trouble.[83]

Hungarian church leaders responded cautiously to the developing changes. Their stance was understandable. All church leaders were appointees of the defunct communist regime with which they had collaborated to some degree. In times of trouble, the communist regime had expected the help of church leaders, and the leaders had often been ready to provide it. In the late 1980s, when the crisis reached a serious level, church leaders had suggested a "new national consensus" between the party and the people—a more effective "pulling together" in "difficult times" to preserve "national unity."[84] In exchange for this action, the regime offered the church greater latitude in national life. The government was even ready to return some illegally nationalized church property, including gymnasiums and conference centers. Some religious orders and religious groups—for example, ministers, youth, and women—were permitted to reorganize. A ban on religious orders was lifted, and nuns and monks from sixty-three religious communities indicated their intentions to resume their activities. The state promised that the monastic groups would get back confiscated monestaries and convents. The churches also were retrieving schools. The Evangelical Church reopened its gymnasium in Budapest, while the Reformed Church reopened a second gymnasium in Budapest, the old Baár Madas, in September 1990. The historical reformed colleges of Sárospatak and Pápa were again in church possession. The Reformed Church in 1991 had a gymnasium in Kecskemét and a teachers' training school at Nagykörös. The theological academy of Debrecen again became part of the University of Debrecen. The Péter Pázmány Roman Catholic Theological High School returned as a unit of Loránd Eötvös University in Budapest. Religious instruction in public schools was possible, and religion almost became a part of the curriculum. A serious debate in parliament took place over this question: should religious classes be compulsory in public schools? The answer: compulsory religious classes were voted down.

Recognition of the churches and their restoration into the life of the nation reached their peak in the Law of Freedom of Conscience and Religion voted by parliament on 24 January 1990. The law spelled out, inter alia, that freedom of religion was a basic human right, and that church activities were useful to society. The churches' new autonomy from the state did not interfere with their operations. The law guaranteed the churches' right to work in education. In full accord with international agreements, this legal act placed the church-state relation on a new basis.[85]

The new law superseded agreements between state and churches made in 1948 and 1950. Agreements between the state and the Reformed and Evangelical churches were cancelled on 19 March 1990, and the agreement between the state and the Roman Catholic Church, made in 1950, was erased on 6 February 1990.

As part of these radical changes, the question of rehabilitation within the churches was raised. The Catholic Church officially requested rehabilitation of the late Cardinal Mindszenty. After his posthumous reinstatement, a square in front of the archbishop's residence in Esztergom, where Mindszenty had resided was named after him. Rehabilitation of the late József Grösz also was granted. Besides such prominent leaders, many clergy of lower rank were restored.

In the Reformed Church László Pap, István Török, and the late Bishop László Ravasz were rehabilitated together with 104 ministers. The Evangelical Church rehabilitated the late Bishop Lajos Ordass together with other clergy who suffered during the communist era.

In these two churches a groundswell had developed for theological and institutional renewal, and the movements generated by this impetus were the driving forces behind changes that occurred during recent years. A Renewal Movement of the Reformed Church was formed secretly in the late 1970s. Ministers who were not collaborating with the communists agreed to cooperate in working for the renewal of the church *in capite et in membris*. The Renewal Movement regarded itself as successor to a similar movement in 1956. In 1978 the movement published a memorandum, "Confession and Opinion," which revealed in plain language the tragic state of the church under communist rule.[86] The authors sharply criticized the communists for the practice of forcing ministers to preach political sermons; for turning church leaders into state officials; for the comedy of church election practices. Blame was placed on church leadership for working against the interests of the church and, in doing so, for offering a helping hand in the church's liquidation.

The underground movement was active in organizing resistance among clergy and laity alike to collaboration between church leadership and the regime. Links were established with other renewal movements: The Bush in the Roman Catholic Church, led by Father György Bulányi; and Pastor Zoltán Dóka, leader of the Lutheran Church's renewal efforts. These movements also had close ties with secular political resistance groups.

In the summer of 1989, the Renewal Movement came into the open. Among its leaders were István Török, Lóránt Hegedüs, Géza Németh, and Tivadar Pánczél. Besides demanding church renewal on every level, the movement raised the issue of church leaders' moral responsibility during the communist era, and it asked them for public confession of past sins. In response, church leaders also talked about renewal, but only on the congregational level, and they did not want to hear about personal confessions of sin. Instead, the leaders wanted to carry on as usual, holding onto their former positions and clinging to power.

The strategy and tactics of the pro-communist church leadership were similar to those of reform-communist leaders. The reform-communists wanted to regain the political initiative, recapture the voters' lost confidence, and win the coming election by introducing radical reforms such as allowing the participation of political parties other than the communists, abolishing censorship, accepting the political heritage of the 1956 revolution, state burial of the revolution's martyrs, and restoration of religious freedom. Similarly, the church leadership wanted to preserve its role by reclaiming schools confiscated by the state; allowing the formation of religious associations for the elderly, young people, and ministers; giving permission for printing more religious literature; and voicing concern over the oppression of Hungarian minorities in neighboring states, particularly in Romania. Church leaders even promised new elections, but delayed them and did everything possible to undermine the opposition's credibility.

Although a new, democratically elected government replaced the reform-communists in elections during the summer of 1990, church leaders resisted making concessions. Great efforts were required of the Renewal Movement to force the election of a new general synod, which in turn ordered a new leadership election. Also, it abolished the life-time tenure of the bishops; they were now elected for a six-year term. In the fall of 1990, voting took place; all four incumbent bishops ran for reelection, but only one was reelected.[87] The Renewal Movement also demanded that the church dissociate itself from the Christian Peace Conference based in Prague, although this was a delicate issue since the conference president was Bishop Tóth. Importantly, the Renewal Movement's effect on the Reformed Church helped in the country's political rebirth by providing ethical guidelines to a chaotic campaign before the general elections.[88]

In the Evangelical Church, the renewal process started relatively early with demands for change in both theology and personnel. The official Theology of Diaconia was criticized and resisted in the work of the church's Renewal Movement. During the Lutheran World Federation's general assembly, which elected Bishop Káldy president in the summer of 1984, a letter from Zoltán Dóka, the Lutheran pastor of Hévizgyörk, was circulated among the delegates. In it, he criticized the Theology of Diaconia and Bishop Káldy. The letter's impact was explosive. After this incident, a group of Lutheran pastors demanded theological reforms. Bishop Káldy died in 1987, and Bishop Gyula Nagy, an exponent of the Theology of Diaconia, resigned amid growing criticism and pressure at the end of 1989. The two new bishops, Béla Harmati and Imre Szebik, were ready to listen to pastoral concerns.[89] A new general synod was held in June 1991. In the opening address, Bishop Harmati emphasized: "We came together for the opening of a legislative general synod. After twenty-five years we would like to commence something new in the life of our Church. We determined ourselves for a radical renewal. There are hundreds of issues before us such as: church membership, new church schools, church and state relations, youth organizations, women ministers, refugee policy, the care of elderly and drug abusers, training of pastors and teachers of religion, the service of pastors, senior pastors, bishops and elders."[90] This synod became a milestone in the Evangelical Church's history.

On another front, the Council of Free Churches, a highly political organization, was dissolved, and the smaller Protestant churches went through a process of soul-searching similar to that of their larger counterparts. On 24 June 1988, the Church of Jesus Christ of Latter-Day Saints was finally recognized by the state.[91]

Signs of theological renewal became visible in all of the churches. In the Protestant churches, the era of post-Theology of Service and post-Theology of Diaconia had arrived. Besides an ongoing criticism of these political theologies, the dawning of a new era of theological pluralism had begun. The Reformed Church witnessed a serious debate on the political role of ministers—that is, whether ministers should be allowed to participate in political life. In the past, some bishops and priests were permitted election to parliament. In the new, democratic parliament, no bishops were elected, but eight parish ministers were successful. Altogether, twelve clergy were voted into parliament. However, the Evangelical Church did not allow its pastors who became members of parliament to function as ministers during their political tenures.

The renewal of the churches also could be seen in a new understanding of ecumenism. The Reformed Church organized the second World Conference of Hungarian Reformed Churches, held on 21–30 June 1991. This conference promoted unity of the church, which had four million members and twelve bishops worldwide. The church also renewed its responsibility to assist oppressed Hungarian Reformed minorities in neighboring countries. The Pope's visit to Hungary in August 1991 occasioned a unique expression of renewed ecumenism. Pope John Paul II held an ecumenical prayer service at the main Reformed Church in Debrecen, the "Calvinist Rome," and laid a wreath of reconciliation to memorialize those Protestant ministers who were condemned to galley slavery by eighteenth-century Roman Catholic courts. The Reformed bishops presented a memorandum to him in which they asked for a solution to the painful problem of mixed marriages and for his attention to Hungarian minorities in neighboring states.[92]

At the end of the 1990s a "velvet revolution" swept across Eastern Europe, including Hungary. The people of Hungary, too, overthrew the communist political, ideological, and economic system, and by the restoration of democracy the country entered into a new era of its history.

This means both a new beginning and a new challenge for the churches. The forty-two years of "Babylonian captivity" of the church, under the communist regime, is over. The church, together with other churches in the region, survived systematic and tenacious persecution by the communist regimes over a period of forty years. Miraculously, not the victim but the persecutor—the communist system—left the stage of history.

The task facing the Protestant Churches is multifaceted and enormous. They would like to regain the influence they had enjoyed in the pre-communist era and reshape society according to Christian values. To this end, the churches reclaim their confiscated schools and institutions together with some estates necessary for the upkeeping of colleges. The churches set out to re-Christianize the secularized society. To this end the churches are involved in a massive evangelistic campaign. A renewed ecumenism also characterizes the new situation. The churches in Hungary learned a lesson that divided they fall, while united—at this stage, in essential issues—they can successfully carry out their mission.

FACT SHEET

Reformed Church of Hungary

Current strength of the church (1988)
1.9 million believers
1,506 ministers

Number of churches and church facilities (1991)
    1,201 " Mother" churches
    240 "Filiale" churches
    200 diaspora churches
    3 theological academies (2 are university faculties)
    1 teachers' training college
    5 high schools
    2 elementary schools
    The number of schools reclaimed from the state is growing.

News organs (1991)
    Reformátusok Lapja (weekly)
    Református Egyház (monthly)
    Confessio (quarterly)
    10 nationwide weekly, monthly, and quarterly publications
    Seniorates, congregations, and church organizations also publish
    periodicals; their number is growing.

Present bishops (1991)
    Lóránt Hegedüs (1991–), presiding bishop, Danubian district
    Elemér Kocsis (1987–), Transtibiscan district
    Mihály Márkus (1991–), Transdanubian district
    István Mészáros (1990–), Cistibiscan district

Evangelical Lutheran Church of Hungary

Current strength of the church (1988)
    430,000 believers
    430 ministers

Number of churches and church facilities (1991)
    323 churches
    1 theological academy (university faculty)
    2 high schools

News organs (1991)
    Evangélikus Élet (weekly)
    Lelkipásztor (monthly)
    Diakonia (quarterly)
    4 nationwide weekly, monthly, and quarterly publications

Seniorates, congregations, and church organizations also publish periodicals; their number is growing.

Present bishops
    Béla Harmati (1987–), presiding, South district
    Imre Szebik (1990–), North district

Baptist Church of Hungary

Current strength of the church (1988)
    20,000 believers
    96 pastors

Number of churches and church facilities
    500 churches
    1 theological seminary

News organ
    Békehírnök (weekly)
Present president
    János Viczián

Methodist Church of Hungary

Current strength of the church (1988)
    2,000 believers
    11 ministers
    6 lay preachers

Number of churches and church facilities
    10 churches
    41 preaching stations

Present moderator
    Frigyes Hecker

Council of Free Churches

Member churches
    Baptist Church
    Methodist Church

Seventh-Day Adventists
Evangelical Pentecostal community
Assembly of the Living God
Church of God
Christian Brethren Congregation
Ancient Christians
Free Christians

Current strength of the churches (except Baptists and Methodists)
    10,000 members (estimated)

Present president
    János Viczián (1988–)

Ecumenical Council of Hungarian Churches

Member churches
    Reformed Church
    Evangelical-Lutheran Church
    Baptist Church
    Methodist Church
    Free Council of Churches
    Hungarian Orthodox Church

News organs
    Hungarian Church Press (biweekly)
    Theological Review (monthly)

Present president
    Elemér Kocsis

6

Protestantism in Romania

Earl A. Pope

In the Socialist Republic of Romania there were fourteen officially approved religious communities regulated by the 1948 Law of Cults; the Roman Catholic Church had de facto recognition on the basis of a license, but it did not have its own statute because of a number of unresolved tensions.[1] There were nine fully recognized religious communities according to the 1928 Law of Cults, but one of these, the Romanian Byzantine Catholic (or Uniate) Church, had no legal existence from 1948 to 1989. The other eight were the Romanian Orthodox, which with the Uniate Church had been the national church in the interwar period; the Latin Rite Catholic Church; the Armenian-Gregorian Orthodox Church; the Jewish and Muslim communities; and the Hungarian Reformed, German Lutheran, and Unitarian churches.[2] The 1948 law officially recognized an independent Hungarian Lutheran Church, the Lipovenians (Russian Old Believers), and four Protestant bodies that had struggled without success for full recognition during the interwar period.[3] Scholars frequently state that there were approximately sixty official religious communities in Romania before World War II,[4] but records do not begin to justify that claim.

The Romanian Orthodox Church, obviously the most prominent of these sanctioned bodies, has claimed the allegiance of approximately 70 percent of the country's population at approximately 16 million followers. This church has been well-organized and effectively administered with a highly trained clergy (a core of whom have studied in the West), distinguished theological scholars, an abundance of candidates for the priesthood, extensive ecumenical relationships, and some of the finest journals within the Orthodox world. Presumably, it had no special privileges within the Romanian socialist state; in practice, however, its position amounted to a virtual establishment vis-à-vis the other religious communities.[5] The Orthodox Church was closely monitored by the state, which was extremely sensitive to any evidence of internal dissent within this community. No member of the church's hierarchy was officially recognized without the approval of state officials. Unquestionably, restive elements existed within the church over this modus vivendi with the state, but there was an obvious absence of the creative leadership (on the part of both the state and the church) that could have brought about a far more constructive relationship.

The Latin Rite Catholic Church has had its stronghold in Transylvania and has claimed more than a thousand churches. It is considered to have about 1.3 million members, the majority of them Hungarians, but it also has strong German and Romanian constituencies. Relationships between the Roman Catholic Church and the Romanian Orthodox Church have been among the most complex and difficult in the millennial-old controversy between Catholicism and Orthodoxy; this stems in large measure from the dispute related to the Romanian Uniate Church (Eastern Rite Catholic Church), whose union with Rome dated back to 1700 and profoundly divided the Transylvanian Romanian community. The Romanian Orthodox Church had tenaciously held the position that the "reintegration" of the Uniates into the Orthodox Church in 1948 was a historic moment of profound significance and constituted reparation of an ancient "injustice."[6] The Catholic Church has maintained that the "reunion" was brought about by sheer political power and that most of the Uniate clergy and many of the faithful were in radical opposition to the move.[7] Frequent discussions took place between Romanian state authorities and representatives of the Vatican in an effort to improve the Catholic Church's situation and to resolve the Uniate crisis. It appears that Vatican officials had given up any hope of the Uniate church's resurrection, but the inconceivable was to occur in December of 1989.

Two other Orthodox communities in Romania are related to ethnic minorities: the Armenian-Gregorians, connected with the Oriental Orthodox; and the Christians of the Old Rite, descendants of the Old Believers Schism in Russia. The Armenian community dates back to the fourteenth century and at one point had approximately 50,000 members with its own schools and social institutions. Since World War II, it has lost most of its members through emigration and, according to Bishop Dirayr Mardikian, "is breathing its last breath" with only about 2,000 members remaining.[8] Many of those who left Romania were descendants of the refugees from the massacres in Turkey. The Lipovenians fled to Moldavia to escape the persecutions in their native land in the later seventeenth century and moved into the Danube delta where they are concentrated to this day. This community, with about 45,000 members, always assumed a low profile, quietly going about its work and following its ancient traditions, speaking Russian at home and using Slavonic in worship services and Romanian in the community at large.

The Jewish community with a history that goes back to the Roman era was decimated, first by the Holocaust and then by massive emigrations to Israel. The remnant of approximately 20,000, however, reported a relatively active and free Jewish life, although anti-Semitic references appeared in officially sanctioned publications during the Ceauşescu era. The Muslim community, mostly found along the Black Sea coast, goes back to the fourteenth and fifteenth centuries when Turkish armies invaded Romania. It has about 50,000 members in ninety religious communities, with its center in Constantsa.

The Protestant communities, which constitute a lively and formidable bloc of churches, have presented an unique challenge to the Romanian nation. It has been suggested that their followers may number as high as 2.5 million, approximately 10 percent of the population.[9] The Protestant churches may be viewed in two major categories: (1) the traditional or historic churches (Lutheran, Reformed, Unitarian) emerging out of the sixteenth-century Protestant Reformation and largely concentrated in Transylvania and (2) the so-called neo-Protestant[10] bodies (Adventist, Baptist, Christians According to the Gospel, and Pentecostal) entering Transylvania and the Old Kingdom in the nineteenth and twentieth centuries.

The convictions and protests of Martin Luther, John Calvin, and Huldreich Zwingli reached Transylvania at an early period. The German community (popularly called the Saxons) was deeply moved by Luther's profound religious faith focusing on justification through grace by faith, coupled with his scathing indictments of the corruptions of the medieval Catholic Church. By 1547, the Saxon community as a body declared its adherence to the Augsburg Confession and became known as the Evangelical Church of the Augsburg Confession. Almost simultaneously, the Hungarian community gravitated toward the teachings of the Swiss reformers with their emphasis on the sovereignty of God.[11] The Lutheran and Reformed churches that emerged represented the right wing of the Protestant Reformation, which preferred a close relationship of church and community, developed its own confessions of faith, and placed strong emphasis on a professional ministry and the importance of the institution of the church and the sacraments. Both churches tended to view their ministry as the gradual permeation of society by the truth of Christianity. The Reformation protests coupled with an emphasis on the unqualified oneness of God, the ethical way, and the Scriptures to be followed under the guidance of reason and conscience culminated in Unitarianism and found a deep response within the Szekler community, now regarded as a subgroup of the Hungarian people. Thus, Unitarianism also spread rapidly in Transylvania at an early period and at one point held the allegiance of a large percentage of the population. It still maintains serious doctrinal differences with the Lutherans and the Reformed, although it has cooperated closely with them and in many ways may be identified with them in their cultural concerns. In the Reformation era, however, the Unitarians (particularly because of their anti-Trinitarianism) were identified with the radical wing and regarded as heretics by right-wing Protestant churches and by the Roman Catholic Church.

There is a long and tragic history of controversy among the various Reformation bodies in addition to the controversy between them and the Roman Catholic Church during the Counter-Reformation period that led to persecution, oppression, and bloody confrontations. Kenneth Scott Latourette writes that the deep divisions among the Protestants were the major cause for the resurgence of Roman Catholicism.[12] The edict of Turda in 1568 finally brought about some measure of peace to troubled Transylvania with official recognition of four religious groups—Lutheran, Reformed, Roman Catholic, and Unitarian—at a time when wars over religion raged in other parts of Europe. The Romanian Orthodox were merely tolerated, even though they constituted the majority of the population.[13] Schöpflin points out that "this unusual religious dispensation has meant that religious adherence has come to be identified with national and cultural loyalties, that churches have tended to be regarded as national institutions which have helped to underpin national cultures and that attacks on religious life have been interpreted in national as much as in religious terms."[14] A simultaneous assault directly on national cultures as such immeasurably intensified these tensions since the national cultures were inextricably interwoven with the religious communities.

Over the course of centuries, and particularly since World War I, the preservation of cultural heritage has become a primary responsibility of these religious traditions, so much so that they could be described as "cohesive, culturally insulated, and inward looking communities."[15] The Reformed faith became closely identified with a large segment of the Hungarian community, and the church that emerged is still regarded as a unique vessel for the preservation and transmission of "Magyar religion" in Transylvania.[16] The Lutheran Church of the Transylvanian Saxons perceived itself as the bearer of German culture. The Unitarians developed their cultural concerns, as did a segment of the Hungarian community that accepted the Lutheran tradition. Attempts were made to establish ethnic Romanian Lutheran and Reformed churches, but with little success.

The second category of Protestant religious bodies in Romania consists of the neo-Protestant churches; in a sense, they are the left-wing descendants of the Protestant Reformation with less emphasis placed on the institution of the church, its creeds, a professional ministry, or the sacraments, and more on a biblically oriented community consisting of dedicated individuals transformed by divine power, committed to the ethical way, and waiting for the Day of the Lord. These churches also held firmly to a separation of church and state and strongly criticized the territorial forms of right-wing Protestantism.[17] Within the Romanian context, these were the Baptists, Christians according to the Gospel (popularly called the Brethren), Pentecostalists, and Seventh-Day Adventists. Related to them are a number of unofficial religious bodies such as the Reformed Adventists, the Nazarenes, the Pentecostal Dissidents, and the Army of the Lord, which is an evangelically oriented movement within the Orthodox Church. The Jehovah's Witnesses also are included among this group since they had a Protestant origin, even though they have radically deviated from it.

Until the establishment of the Greater Romanian State in 1918, the Orthodox faith had been the nation's official and almost exclusive religion. The acquisition of Transylvania, Crisana, Banat, Bessarabia, and Bukovina brought about serious political predicaments and important changes in the country's religious configuration; with the inclusion of large numbers of Reformation Protestants with their strong ethnic identifications as well as Roman Catholics of the Latin and the Uniate traditions, problems were created that still have not been resolved. The new situation was formalized in the Law of Cults in 1928 in which all the major religions enjoyed freedom in spiritual matters with the exception of the "sects" (Baptists and Seventh-Day Adventists); the state reserved the prerogative to censor teachings "contrary to the interests of the nation and to public mores." The state also exercised administrative control over all religious bodies, with the exception of the Roman Catholics for whom relations were dictated by the 1927 Concordat with the Vatican whereby the church and its educational and philanthropic institutions were given virtually total freedom from the state. The concordat was abrogated unilaterally by the communist state in 1948.[18]

The union of Transylvania with Romania following World War I unquestionably represented the culmination of long-cherished Romanian

hopes and dreams, but this union has remained a focal point of controversy between Hungary and Romania. Transylvania indisputably is perceived to have a central role in the national mythologies of both Hungarians and Romanians. Schöpflin defends the thesis that "a mythicized
concept of Transylvania, which may have little to do with existing realities, plays a central role in the national consciousness of both nations,
most particularly in that it is seen as having safeguarded the survival of
the nation in the most critical epoch of its history."[19]

During the interwar period, there were reports of serious problems,
particularly regarding the treatment of the Hungarian religious communities in Transylvania, and numerous complaints charging discrimination were registered with the League of Nations and other international
organizations.[20] There are different versions of what in fact did occur, but
there appears to be little question that in religious matters the Romanian
Orthodox Church was unquestionably favored. The minority religions,
however, "were clearly better off in matters of faith, practice and status
than the Orthodox Church had been under Hungarian rule," but the
minority religions were definitely hampered by the land reforms of the
early 1920s that divested them of a large part of their income.[21] The
Romanians responded that the complaints were totally false; indeed,
it was the Romanian Orthodox Church that was being discriminated
against and in its own land at that![22] The German Lutheran community
was relatively silent during this period.

The leaders of the various ethnic German groups decided in favor of
Romania rather than Hungary at the end of World War I "because they
wanted to end magyarization and to seek far-reaching privileges for
themselves." They were granted virtually unlimited freedom of assembly and organization, and the great majority "reciprocated the relative
toleration of their ethnic freedom with loyalty to Romania, while retaining strong connections to their country of origin."[23] The religious situation was compounded by the tension between the Hungarian and Romanian states, which once again surfaced openly and continues to this day.

World War II was a period of incredible suffering for all the religious
communities in Romania, and its aftermath brought about a radically
different situation for each of them. The international ecumenical agencies attempted to come to the rescue of the Romanian churches following
the war. The Lutheran, Reformed, and Orthodox churches were deeply
involved with various phases of the ecumenical movement in the interwar period, and there was a profound sensitivity to their situation. In
1945 J. Hutchison Cockburn, a former moderator of the Church of Scotland, became the first director of the Department of Reconstruction and

Inter-Church Aid of the World Council of Churches. He faced an incredibly complex challenge in attempting to address the needs of churches in the lands devastated by the war.[24] In July 1945 he sent identical letters to Patriarch Nicodim Munteanu of the Romanian Orthodox Church, Bishop Friedrich Müller of the German Lutheran Church, and Professor L. Gonczy of the Hungarian Reformed Church. He informed them that his department had been created so that the Christian church might be able to play its ecumenical role of mutual service and regard. He specifically requested that they respond as to whether or not they were willing "to consult with the leaders of the other churches in Romania including Transylvania about setting up a Joint-Board of all the Churches." He emphasized that no church should be overlooked and that agencies such as the YMCA, the YWCA, the Student Christian Movement, and other organizations should be invited to participate.[25] Because of the official "silent response" to his requests, Cockburn finally concluded from other sources that something needed to be done quickly; he therefore sent two representatives to Romania. Robert Tobias, an American Lutheran, made the first visit in August 1946, and Gote Hedenquist, a Swedish Lutheran, traveled to Romania in October 1946. Both men presented comprehensive and perceptive reports on their visits.[26] They called attention to the serious food shortages, the overwhelming poverty, the widespread disease, and the "scandalous inflation." A primary objective for both Tobias and Hedenquist was to assist in forming an internal ecumenical committee to develop the immediate priorities for all Romanian churches so that the international community could respond in the most effective way. Both men were shocked by the lack of any real trust among the leadership of the Christian communities. Tobias had an extensive meeting with the Protestant clergy, but it was clearly evident that ecumenical cooperation was out of the question. He came to the conclusion that Magne Solheim and Richard Wurmbrand, the dynamic and able leaders of the Norwegian Mission to the Jews in Bucharest, should be appointed to coordinate the work of the WCC and be given "every color and kind of legal document and stamp of authorization."[27]

The WCC was to channel extensive shipments of desperately needed relief items to Romania; many of the supplies came from the United States. The political, social, and economic situation, however, was deteriorating rapidly; tensions also were running high between East and West. In October 1947 Solheim through the Swedish legation reported in a terse communication to Geneva that the WCC was regarded as a "political agency" supported by the Americans and "suspected of smuggling in money in order to help build up a resistance movement against the government."[28] In his last report dated 15 November 1948, he wrote about the terror that had gripped the society, the allegations that "reactionary imperialistic powers" were using the ecumenical movement, and the concern that the religious institutions he had been trying to assist were having serious difficulties or were being shut down on every hand.[29] By the end of 1948, it was apparent that Romania was closed to any assistance by Western ecumenical agencies. A constellation of factors in the end subverted the efforts of the WCC in its attempts to assert its solidarity with the suffering people of Romania and to channel the resources of food and clothing so desperately needed. The ecumenical bodies were deeply disappointed that the Romanian religious leaders were unable to transcend their rivalries, suspicions, and animosities to coordinate their efforts for the common good. There is bitter irony in this whole situation. By the time the ecumenical community was fully mobilized to send substantial aid and was sensitized to the destructive internal tensions, political decisions had been made that irrevocably closed the door and sealed the fate of many thousands.

The year 1948 was critical for all Romanian churches. A communist government with its Marxist-Leninist ideology was now in full control, and a new Law of Religious Cults was established that carefully delineated the relationships between church and state. The Reformation bodies found themselves losing control of the educational and social institutions that they had developed over the centuries and that had enabled them to maintain their identity. The educational reform in 1948 provided for the transfer of all ecclesiastical and private schools to the state. This was, of course, a particularly serious problem for the Germans and the Hungarians for whom the ecclesiastical school system had been tremendously important. The German Lutheran community was particularly devastated by the war. It had been deeply divided by Nazism, and after the war the homes and property of its members were confiscated and many church members were reduced to abject poverty. Almost eighty thousand German Lutherans were taken to the Soviet Union to work in factories and mines; many perished, and large numbers eventually emigrated to Germany.[30] Despite these hardships, the church and its members made a remarkable recovery, but they never fully overcame the traumatic events of the war and its immediate aftermath.

The period between 1948 and 1961 involved only minimal contacts between the Protestant churches in Romania and their colleagues in other countries, although there was considerable contact between the Romanian Orthodox Church and the other Orthodox churches of Eastern Europe.

Unquestionably, Marxist atheism with its militant Leninist focus had the most important influence on the nature of church-state relations in Romania, but there were other important considerations that throw light on the contradictory policy of "Ceauşescuism":[31] the durability of ecclesiastical institutions, the persistence of religious convictions and practices, the concern for political survival, modern means of communication that could call almost immediate attention to church difficulties, the sensitivity to allies and critics outside Romania, the temptation—indeed the perceived necessity—to maximize the usefulness of the churches to achieve economic, political, and social objectives at home and abroad. In the 1948 Law of Cults, freedom of conscience and religious freedom presumably were guaranteed by the state, and "confessional hatred" of any kind was repudiated. The law further asserted that one's religious faith could not jeopardize civil and political rights.[32] It also made provision for religious communities to organize themselves "according to their own norms," provided "their practices and ritual be in harmony with the constitution, security or public order, and good morality." The state's power was clearly enunciated here because to receive official approval each religious cult had to "send in, for examination and approval through the Ministry of Cults, its own organizational and administrative statute, together with the confession of the respective faith."[33] Then, too, no religious body was permitted to maintain relations with agencies outside the country without official approval. Furthermore, no member of the hierarchy of any religious body would be recognized without receiving the government's prior approval and without taking an oath of loyalty to the state.[34] The law clearly stated the right of the churches to use the "mother tongue" of the believers in their worship and to organize seminaries and institutes for the training of clergy. Subsidies could be provided by the state to the churches, but clergymen who had an "antidemocratic attitude" could be deprived of such support. All citizens were free to change their religious faith, but it was mandated that official notification of such transfers be made through the proper authorities, and churches were forbidden to enroll new members if proper notification had not been made.[35] This stipulation created serious problems for the neo-Protestant communities in addition to compounding the statistical dilemma.

The law on religious cults spelled out what were considered to be the constitutional rights of freedom of conscience and religious practice under the communist regime, and it established a comprehensive—and at times ruthless—system of state control over all religious communities. The churches were under the direct jurisdiction of what was called the

Department of Cults, a very important agency run by a nationwide network of highly skilled personnel. This agency had impressive resources at its command whereby it could be certain that the religious legislation and a variety of even more stringent oral interpretations, which often blatantly subverted the constitutional freedom of believers and their communities, were carefully followed.[36] Indeed, it has been considered little more than an agency of the dreaded Securitate, or secret police.

The Romanian constitution stated unequivocally in Article 17 that all citizens, "irrespective of their nationality, race, sex, or religion, shall enjoy equal rights in all fields of economic, political, juridical, social and cultural life."[37] It also affirmed that the "co-inhabiting nationalities shall be assured the free use of their mother tongue, as well as books, newspapers, periodicals, theatres and education at all levels in their own languages."[38] Soon after the law took effect, charges were made that a tremendous gap existed between theory and practice as far as the cultural and religious rights of the minorities were concerned.

The Traditional Protestant Churches

The Reformed Church was organized in Transylvania in 1564; its congregations are mostly descendants of the Catholic parishes in Transylvania, Crisana, and Banat. There was an early identification with the Swiss Reformation, and relationships were set up with Geneva, Zurich, and Heidelberg.[39] It now has close to 1 million members organized into 732 parishes, thirteen presbyteries, two dioceses with two bishops, more than 900 churches, and more than 700 clergy. It has attempted to conduct its own inner life and activities in the Hungarian language. This church hosted the World Alliance of Reformed Churches' European Assembly in September 1980. Edmond Perrett, former general secretary of the alliance, announced at that time that Romanian authorities had approved a presentation of 10,000 Hungarian Bibles to the Reformed Church on this historic meeting. The WARC had sent the same number of Bibles to this church in 1971. These Bibles became the focal point of much controversy regarding their use or final destination. Alexander Havadtoy maintained that he had irrefutable proof that the Bibles were recycled into toilet paper;[40] Metropolitan Antonie of Transylvania, joined by the two Reformed bishops in Romania, claimed this was absurd and called it "another item of anti-Romanian propaganda."[41]

The Hungarian Lutheran Church is regarded as a diaspora church with approximately 35,000 members in thirty-six parishes, including five Slovak parishes and a Romanian parish that was related to what had once been a Jewish mission in Bucharest. This church has been highly dependent on its international relationships and has received substantial assistance from the Lutheran World Federation.[42] The Evangelical Church of the Augsburg Confession, also known as the Church of the Transylvanian Saxons, is the oldest of all the German-speaking Lutheran churches in Eastern Europe.[43] Until the beginning of World War II, it had approximately 240,000 members, 260 elementary schools, and a large number of social institutions. When speaking about their history, the Saxons have used terms like "God's miracle," "God's guidance," or "God's plan" to explain their survival for more than eight hundred years in Transylvania. They have perceived their community as "the outpost of Western European civilization" against the assaults of the Mongols and Turks, and they survived the threats of the Counter-Reformation, Magyarization, and Romanianization.[44] This group has carried on a vigorous religious life and has endeavored to be a church in the midst of socialism. The church has undergone a profound identity crisis, with one group migrating to the West, and a rapidly dwindling number, led by the late Bishop Albert Klein, maintaining that despite all problems they still had a mission in Romania. The restiveness within the German community was such that an agreement was reached between the Ceauşescu regime and the German Federal Republic whereby up to 12,000 Germans could be repatriated each year. Apparently, this official agreement accounted for approximately two-thirds of all the emigration from Romania during the 1980s. There have been reliable reports of a financial arrangement for each family permitted to leave.[45] The church has been reduced to less than 100,000 members in approximately three hundred churches with fewer than a hundred ministers, and many ministers have applied for emigration permits. In 1988 Bishop Klein stated: "If the present rate of emigration by Transylvanian Saxons continues, the ethnic group and this denomination will cease to exist in Romania in the next quarter century."[46] Following World War II, the two Lutheran churches in Romania were among the most isolated in Eastern Europe; attempts by the LWF to establish closer contacts with them were not especially successful until 1964. Since then, however, the churches have played an active role in ecumenical affairs locally as well as on the international scene.

In 1968 the Unitarian Church celebrated the four hundredth anniversary of its founding. In an official statement at the time, it described itself as radical in its theological system and progressive in its social system. It paid high tribute to its founder, Francis David, who insisted on a return to the Bible and in 1566 denied the dogma of the Trinity. It emphasized that David did not intend to divide the unity of Transylvanian Protestantism, but that the Lutherans and the Reformed churches rejected further necessary and logical reforms.[47] At present, the Unitarian church has approximately 85,000 members in 120 congregations concentrated mostly in the villages of Transylvania. One reliable source suggests almost 100,000 members.[48] The church emphasizes a Christological model similar to the teaching of one of the founders of American Unitarianism, William Ellery Channing.[49] The churches regularly carry out their ancient rites of baptism, confirmation, communion, and marriage, and the sanctuaries are crowded for these occasions. The order of worship is dignified with prayers, scripture readings, hymns, and sermons. The Unitarian Church of Romania is the only Unitarian body in the world with a bishop; its supreme church authority is the synod with a representation of two-thirds laity and one-third clergy. Bishop Lajos Kovacs has served as president of the International Association for Religious Freedom (IARF), the international organization of liberal religious groups in twenty countries. The Unitarian Universalist Association in America is a member of this group. The election of Bishop Kovacs was considered an important step in restoring communication between East European religious liberals and their Western counterparts, and it also was highly regarded by the Department of Cults. The suggestion has been made that the Unitarian Church had certain privileges under Ceaușescu that other minority churches did not have because of its large number of foreign relationships.[50] The other Reformation churches, however, have a greater number of even more powerful allies in the West; therefore, other factors such as the Unitarian Church's leadership, size of the community, its liberal theological and social perspective, and its long legacy of being persecuted and oppressed are factors that need to be explored.

The four traditional Protestant churches received state support for the salaries of their clergy, theological professors, and administrators; they conducted their own traditional worship services each week in their own languages; they held their own catechetical classes; they had their own pension programs and periodicals;[51] and they participated in an ecumenical theological institute[52] that used the Hungarian language in Cluj and German in Sibiu. Each of the three Reformation traditions at Cluj had the opportunity to provide instruction to its own candidates in addition to the general curriculum they shared. The Lutheran and Reformed churches also have endorsed the Leuenberg Agreement of 1973, which established full communion and cooperation between them.

These Reformation communities also participated with the Romanian Orthodox Church in interconfessional theological conferences that date back to 1964, soon after the Orthodox, Lutheran, and Reformed churches joined the wcc and other ecumenical bodies. These ecumenical conferences always were conducted under the leadership of the Romanian Orthodox, with strong state encouragement and presence, and directly involved the Lutheran, Orthodox, and Reformed communities with a significant participation of Unitarians and an increasing involvement of Roman Catholics.

It should be noted that the full depth and meaning of the ecumenical spirit, given the strict surveillance and harassment for anyone who attempted to raise any kind of prophetic voice, was extremely difficult to determine. Published reports invariably conveyed the impression of a marvelous ecumenical harmony transcending the deep-seated animosities of the past. The state unquestionably viewed these conferences as important forums for encounters between the Romanian Orthodox Church and the minority religious communities. In spite of the national rivalries and tensions that separated the minorities from the Orthodox, the religious groups were bound together by common religious mythic structures that presumably transcended their ethnic particularities. It was indeed of interest to see a communist state encouraging religious dialogue in an effort to help resolve sensitive and complex internal problems that defied all solutions, ideological and practical, offered by the new social order. In spite of the obvious secular objectives that the state may have had, religious dialogues of this nature had an intrinsic value of their own. The international dialogues in which all of these religious communities were involved had a profound impact on their consciousness and modes of thought, even though this influence may not have been readily evident at times.

In the late 1980s there were incontrovertible reports of a growing crisis brought about by intensive pressures on Hungarian institutions in Romania. Gilberg gives a careful analysis of the policy that prompted this crisis.[53] During the years after 1948 the Hungarian minority in Transylvania enjoyed extensive political and cultural privileges, but with an increasing focus on nationalism in Romanian politics in the late 1950s, their privileges were gradually suppressed. In 1967 a policy of accommodation appeared to be emerging, but after 1971 pressures for assimilation began to intensify in both passive and active forms. It was inevitable that the religious communities would be deeply involved since they had become the primary vehicles of cultural traditions. As the economic situation deteriorated in Romania after 1980, the Hungarian community could envisage only a very bleak future; consequently, increasing despair about attempts at internal reforms led to a series of appeals and protests to the West, particularly to Hungary, which stirred up paranoias of irredentism among Romanian political leaders. The result was that the Hungarians perceived the internal pressures and discrimination to have reached intolerable levels.[54]

A litany of strong complaints from a wide range of sources documented the radical forms of discrimination directed at the Hungarian minority in Transylvania; these involved the lack of educational opportunities, the deliberate dissolution of minorities, the reduction of bilingualism, the limitation of cultural opportunities, the falsification of history, the confiscation of ecclesiastical archives, and the "special" harassment of the minority churches. These charges were summarized by Bishop Butosi in 1987. It was now the policy of the Romanian state, he said, "to liquidate with all its might, overt and covert, a two and a half million Hungarian ethnic minority." This, he believed, was the fundamental issue.[55] The traditional policy of the Hungarian state and religious leaders regarding these charges had been public silence, and the emphasis had been on quiet diplomacy. It was inevitable that there would be a radical change in this approach in the light of the problems that appeared to defy attempts at negotiation and positive resolution. The conspiracy of public silence was finally broken in Hungary in the summer of 1986 when a plea for religious liberty and national rights in Transylvania was released by an unofficial ecumenical group that included members of the major religious communities. In a document entitled "A Call for Reconciliation to the Caring People of Hungary and Romania," this committee urged the pope, the World Council of Churches, the Soviet Union, and Western human rights activists to work together to encourage Romanian authorities to end repressive policies against Transylvania's national and religious minorities. References were made to the use of police terror, the informant system, brutal beatings, torture, and martyrs.

The committee was convinced that the churches of Romania could play an important role in bringing about reconciliation. It expressed a vision in the light of their common Christian heritage of a Transylvania that "could be the scene of Orthodox, Roman Catholic, Reformed, Lutheran and Baptist brotherhood." Furthermore, it stated that "Orthodox spirituality" could enrich the Hungarian churches, as would the "enthusiasm of our Romanian Baptist brothers and sisters."[56] Here was the recognition of a profound crisis that desperately needed to be addressed and called to the attention of the international community, coupled with a vision of a Transylvania where various religious traditions with their respective cultures could live together in peace and harmony. It was a noble vision, to be sure, and well-intended; it attempted to speak the truth and unequivocally rejected the picture presented by Romanian authorities. Paradoxically, the focus on Transylvania may help to explain some of the emotional nuances of the responses by Romanian leaders. The perceived echoes of "Transylvanianism" with all its implications could only stir up additional dimensions of paranoia among an already confused and insecure Romanian leadership.

The "Call for Reconciliation" set in motion an avalanche of appeals and protests not only from the Hungarian state and churches but also from churches and international agencies around the world. The response from Romanian state and religious leaders was that the picture presented was totally false and was prompted by sinister self-serving motives. The Romanian Orthodox position was that internal ecumenism in Romania was "a living and indisputable reality,"[57] and the Reformed bishops allegedly were "astonished" that such charges could be made.[58] The position of these two bishops remained unchanged in all their public utterances despite the large volume of information reaching the West that disclosed extraordinarily serious problems involving the communities for which they were responsible. The growing controversy brought about a public exchange of views involving two of the foremost ecumenical leaders in Eastern Europe as well as important religious leaders and spokesmen in their respective countries. In a 1987 interview with the *Ecumenical Press Service*, in which he gave written answers to written questions, Metropolitan Antonie of Transylvania, the primary ecumenical representative for the Romanian Orthodox Church and a member of the executive committee of the wcc and of the presidium of the Conference of European Churches, unequivocally denied reports of religious and cultural discrimination against the Hungarian minority in Transylvania.[59]

Károly Tóth, bishop of the Reformed Church in Hungary and a leading member of the executive committee of the wcc and president of the Christian Peace Conference, seriously challenged Antonie, particularly focusing on the serious decline of schools using the Hungarian language. He concluded that he had no desire to reopen past wounds, but that he considered "one-sided and tendentious information to be dangerous because it makes reconciliation impossible."[60] One of Tóth's most dramatic statements was his reference to the official destruction of the Romanian Uniate Church. He could scarcely have touched on a more sensitive matter for both the Romanian Orthodox church and the state.

The neo-Protestants in Romania had raised this issue several years earlier, with extremely serious consequences for those involved.

The official position of Romanian religious leaders regarding the widespread reports of violations of human rights and religious freedom also was seen in the reports of the fiftieth Interconfessional Theological Conference held in Bucharest on 3–4 November 1987. Bishop Gyula Nagy of the Reformed Church reaffirmed his position that his churches had full freedom to preserve and cultivate the "sacred faith" of their ancestors. Bishop Paul Szedressy of the Hungarian Lutheran Church and Bishop Kovacs of the Unitarian Church also stressed the freedom that they had, although they did so in a more subdued manner, as did Hans Hermannstadter, curator general of the German Lutheran Church.[61] In his concluding remarks, Metropolitan Antonie summarized what he felt had been achieved during the history of these conferences, and he reaffirmed some of the notes that he and other Romanian religious leaders had made in response to the severe criticisms being offered. The "old separatist mentalities" had been transformed, and at a level of practical ecumenism they had arrived at "positive positions" in relationship to their "motherland" so that they were no longer "separate and marginalized groups." He challenged the confessions in Romania to advance more courageously toward "the one, holy catholic and apostolic church."[62] Antonie eloquently expressed the ecumenical vision that perhaps inspired and animated him, but he also felt compelled to present it as a reality despite irrefutable signs to the contrary.

At the end of its deliberations, the conference sent a telegram to President Ceauşescu calling attention to what it claimed was "Romania's new and bright image" and rejoicing in the "wonderful achievements" in the "most productive years in the history of the country." With "justified pride," they could call this period "the Nicolae Ceauşescu Epoch" since he had been "acknowledged all over the world as a thinker of genius and an exceptional statesman, a political personality who has definitively marked the age in which we live."[63] These affirmations under carefully controlled conditions did little to prevent a radical escalation of the tensions regarding the minority situation in Transylvania. The flight of thousands of refugees across the border into Hungary in 1987 and 1988 immeasurably compounded the situation. The seriousness with which the problems were now perceived, concurrent with the radical erosion of the credibility of the religious leaders in Romania, was seen in the virtually unprecedented intervention by one of the major ecumenical bodies—the World Alliance of Reformed Churches. Its strategy in the past regarding problems dealing with the Reformed Church had been to consult quietly with local church officials and the Department of Cults to bring about the best possible resolution of issues. The visit of the WARC representatives planned for April 1988 to discuss discrimination issues was cancelled on very short notice at the request of the Reformed Church in Romania.[64] Tensions were raised to a new level by the flood of refugees into Hungary with their tragic reports, coupled with the plan announced by the Romanian state in the spring of 1988 to further its "systematization" of its agricultural land by destroying half of its villages and moving the people into new "urban agro-industrial centers." This plan had tremendous destructive potential in undermining the social roots of religion and the culture of the national minorities.[65] In the light of these events, the WARC concluded that the problems which had erupted were so grave that quiet diplomacy would no longer be effective or meaningful.

It sent its message openly and simultaneously to President Ceauşescu and President Campanasu of the Department of Cults. It noted that the WARC represented 164 churches and 70 million members worldwide and expressed "deep dismay" about plans to destroy the village. It maintained that this decision could "only tear apart the fabric of society, violate human and civil rights, and deprive thousands of their traditions, cultural heritage, and language." The WARC called on the Romanian government to "respect the fundamental rights of all its citizens and, therefore, to rescind its decision to implement this destructive program."[66] The WARC also informed all its member churches of its action and requested that they indicate their support by writing or cabling Ceauşescu.[67] A worldwide response occurred. The Global Mission Ministry Unit of the Presbyterian Church USA expressed its profound concern to the Reformed bishops in Romania regarding the cultural, religious, and social implications of the "devillagization" program.[68] The World Council of Churches and the Conference of European Churches also intervened with a joint message of "deep concern" regarding the Transylvanian situation, but they followed a more traditional course of action in requesting that their member churches (Romanian Orthodox, the two Lutheran churches, and the Reformed) report on the situation in their country. The Central Committee of the WCC was deeply divided on the most appropriate approach to the tragedy unfolding in Romania, but it finally adopted a report at its July 1989 meeting in Moscow recommending that the WCC carefully monitor the situation, promote visits among churches inside and outside Romania, follow the international human rights efforts, and support the churches, especially in Hungary, that were assisting the Romanian refugees.[69] It is difficult to know what

kind of impact these concerns and protests made on state authorities in
Romania. There were reports that the process of "systematization" actually began in the environs of Bucharest, particularly on the road to
Ceaușescu's villa at Snagov. In this case the Romanian Orthodox Church,
which had been the state's most loyal ally, was the initial casualty since
this area was primarily ethnic Romanian with an Orthodox Church at the
center of every village. In May 1989 an appeal for $500,000 was made
by the wcc to support a two-year relief program of the churches in
Hungary for the refugees from Romania. According to Hungarian state
sources, there were then 16,000 registered refugees in addition to 5,000
asylum-seekers and more than 15,000 who were not registered. Reports
indicated that an increasing number of the refugees illegally entering the
country were ethnic Romanians; this posed its own unique set of problems. The funding sought was to be used for counseling and pastoral
support, accommodations, medical assistance, coordination of the refugee program, and training opportunities for volunteer refugee workers.[70]

The Reformation churches of Transylvania, particularly the Hungarian Reformed, found themselves in a crisis compounded by the fact that
they not only were the vehicles of religious faith, but of cultural heritage.
Manifest destiny, Ceaușescu-style, unquestionably subverted the basic
identity of these religious minorities and threatened to sacrifice them to a
strident, ruthless form of Romanian nationalism. Radical changes in the
policy of the Romanian state were necessary if the minorities' full rights
were to be restored. Such changes, given the winds of perestroika and
glasnost in the Soviet Union, were inevitable.

The Neo-Protestant Communities

Concurrent with this crisis was the one brought about by the tremendous growth and persistent challenge of the neo-Protestant churches
that are now found in virtually every community in Romania. This
phenomenon involved another highly sensitive group of churches that
were primarily ethnic Romanian and did not have preservation of the
cultural heritage as a primary concern. As a matter of fact, a primal cause
of the neo-Protestant movement may be disenchantment with the in-
ordinate focus on the ethnic communities and the search for an alternative, not only to Marxist-Leninist ideology but also to the destructive
tensions of the past. Most neo-Protestant communities entered the country through non-Romanian channels. Originally they were accused of

undermining national unity,[71] were seriously restricted or forced underground before 1945, were locked in serious struggles with both church and state authorities in the interwar period, and were imprisoned by the thousands under the fascist military dictatorship of Marshal Ion Antonescu. They were perceived as posing very serious internal security problems, and great vacillation and perplexity always have existed among state authorities regarding the wisest ways to deal with them. These churches received recognition by the communist government in the 1948 Law of Cults, for which they were extremely grateful. The state authorities admired their resistance to, and their suffering under, previous governments, and they may have envisioned the neo-Protestants as valuable allies in controlling the power of the Orthodox and the Reformation churches as well as in providing important bridges to the West. The moral earnestness of these communities and Marxist idealism[72] were perceived as having much in common, and in the early days after World War II they were seen as potential comrades that, once liberated from their "mystical" views, would become full participants in the revolutionary work at hand. The perception also arose that by giving them official status, they could be more easily controlled than they had been as underground churches.

For a number of reasons, statistics vary widely on the membership of these groups. Many people participated within the life of these communities, but they did not officially notify their former churches[73] because of the difficulties entailed. There were reports of continuing resistance from the Department of Cults to counting converts from other communities, even if the converts had gone through the necessary legal process. Furthermore, many of them were active in unofficial churches that had been waiting for years to be approved. Then, too, state authorities underestimated the strength of these communities, although they claimed that neo-Protestant leaders unofficially overstated their followings.[74] It is not unreasonable, therefore, to suggest a total neo-Protestant constituency of close to 1 million people, with a rapid growth rate.[75]

The neo-Protestant communities focus on the Bible as the verbally inspired, infallible word of God. Their favorite version is still the one by the evangelically oriented Orthodox scholar, Dumitru Cornilescu.[76] The neo-Protestants boldly promise a knowledge of God and the ultimate mystery that is available to every individual and that endues one with divine power. The Pentecostalists maintain that this power is received in a commitment experience called the Baptism of the Holy Spirit; the initial physical evidence of this experience is an ecstatic spiritual language referred to as speaking in tongues. Conversion to these communities meant a new moral seriousness and a dedication to a work ethic that did not escape the authorities' attention. The belief in faith healing also is found throughout the neo-Protestant groups and appears to be of special importance within the Pentecostal community.[77] There is a high proportion of lay leadership in these churches, a characteristic born of necessity in many instances, but also founded in the conviction of the universal priesthood of believers.

The typical neo-Protestant church is a "highly cohesive spiritual and social unit" that provides an impressively supportive community for its participants. The new member is immediately made to feel needed, called brother or sister, and incorporated into the life of the church as an active worshiper and servant. The Baptists and the Brethren stress the independence of each church, thus creating serious problems for the authorities in their efforts to centralize power. These groups have a powerful awareness of mission coupled with the conviction that they are living in the last moments of time and that the Second Coming is imminent. Intensified by "the urgency of the eschatological moment," this missionary imperative brought about serious tensions with not only state authorities but also with the Orthodox and Reformation churches. The neo-Protestants' millennial zeal may develop revolutionary dimensions if profound frustration is reached because of continued postponement of the final moment of cosmic liberation and what may be perceived as the total corruption of the present political and social order. Neo-Protestant services tend to be informal, crowded, and lively, with enthusiastic singing and preaching and excellent choirs and instrumental groups. The large majority of neo-Protestants are ethnic Romanians, but the communities have active minority representation, primarily Hungarian and German, and the Pentecostalists seem to have considerable strength among the Ukrainians along the northern Romanian border. The Gypsy population also has been significantly incorporated within some of their communities.

Members of the neo-Protestant churches ran into problems with the communist authorities more often than any other religious group. They were most likely to receive Bibles and religious literature through "illegal" channels and to distribute them throughout the country, most tempted to have religious meetings outside of the officially designated hours, most apt to disagree with or strongly resist ecclesiastical admonitions or discipline, and the least inhibited in calling attention to the imperfections they saw or experienced in their society. They pooled their resources to pay the heavy fines assessed for unauthorized religious activities, and many appeared to have lost their fear of prison. Only a fine line existed between some of their members and members of the country's unofficial groups. Their challenge to the constitutional legality of many of the Department of Cults' rulings was perceived to be provocative and dangerous; such challenges unaddressed could lead to serious disturbances in other areas of society. Furthermore, their rapid growth threatened to be destabilizing, particularly as far as the traditional churches were concerned, and this growth raised serious questions about the Marxist-Leninist analysis of religion and the success of the new social order.

The Baptist movement in Romania goes back to 1856 with the founding of a German Baptist church in Bucharest. In 1864 a group of Russian refugees established a Baptist church in Dobrogea, and by the end of the nineteenth century Baptist churches existed in Transylvania and Banat under the leadership of German and Hungarian evangelists. In 1912 the first Romanian Baptist church was formally organized in Bucharest, and in 1919 the Baptist churches in Greater Romania united as the Baptist Union.[78] In 1921 a Baptist theological seminary was opened near Arad; it was later moved to Bucharest where the Southern Baptist Convention provided funds for the purchase of its property.[79] This seminary had five professors and a total of forty students in 1978, but in the later 1980s enrollment was radically reduced.

Ioan Bunaciu, the former rector of the Baptist seminary, writes of the intense hostility between the Baptist and the Orthodox communities in the 1930s, which culminated in the closing of all Baptist churches from 15 December 1938 to 14 April 1939 when Archbishop Colan of the Romanian Orthodox Church was minister of cults. Bunaciu refers to the World Baptist Alliance's intervention at that time.[80] Grigorie Comsa, bishop of Arad, led the assault on the "sectarian" invasion of Romania—with a particular focus on the Baptist "heresy"—in a series of widely circulated booklets.[81] In 1942 the Baptist churches again were closed under Antonescu but were permitted to reopen in 1944. Petru Groza, presumably a devout Orthodox believer, proudly took credit for the liberation of Baptists from prison. Bunaciu states that in 1939 there were 62,000 Baptists in 420 churches.[82]

The Baptists' difficulties in Romania in the 1930s led to serious problems between Baptists and Anglicans in England. In September 1937 William Temple, archbishop of York who later became primate of England and one of the great ecumenical leaders of his age, sent a letter to Patriarch Miron Cristea that raised serious questions about religious freedom in Romania, particularly as it related to the Baptists.[83] Temple was encouraged in his action by J. H. Rushbrooke, general secretary of the World Baptist Alliance. According to the correspondence, the patriarch was outraged by what he regarded as an insensitive and irresponsible intervention in internal Romanian affairs. He officially responded to Temple in a lengthy document maintaining that Temple had been seriously misled and the Romanian church deeply maligned. Intolerance in Romania! This was incredible nonsense. Romania in reality was "hypertolerant." Cristea maintained that the minority religions were being treated in a privileged manner! He deplored "the perverse propaganda, gross untruths, false mystifications of the Magyars," the "ferocious and barbaric proselytism of the Pope." He exclaimed: "Romania cannot be indifferent in the face of her enemies allowing herself to be undermined by agents paid by foreigners dressed in innocent pseudo-religious garb."[84] Unquestionably, the patriarch had the neo-Protestants in mind.

Temple was embarrassed by the Romanian storm he had caused, and he did his best to calm the troubled waters.[85] Rushbroke, in contrast, zestfully plunged into the controversy, challenging the most formidable of the Anglican Romanian Orthodox apologists to a debate in late 1938 in *Church Times* and the *Manchester Guardian*. Missives were sent back and forth until the editor of *Church Times* declared that he had had enough and would publish no more.[86] Rushbroke charged that Baptists were being persecuted and churches closed—an outrage, particularly in a country whose national church prided itself on its ecumenism.[87] Canon J. A. Douglas, secretary of the Council on Foreign Relations of the Church of England, was so enamored of the ecumenical vision that he refused to accept the realities of the situation and criticized the aggressive, propagandistic ways of the "bands of Baptist crusaders" who he felt were at the heart of the problem.[88] The bishop of Gibraltar suggested that the Baptists were having difficulties for other than religious reasons.[89]

Denton Lotz, general secretary of the World Baptist Alliance, calls attention to the fact that, historically, Baptist relationships with Orthodoxy have been limited and that whatever contact there might have been was frequently in the form of persecution. He points to a continuing legacy of suspicion and hostility, although he did call attention in 1974 to signs of "opening dialogues and respect for one another" that had not previously existed.[90] The Baptist Church was recognized by the communist state and apparently did not undergo serious restrictions during the new regime's early years. In 1954 the Ministry of Cults began to exercise greater control over the church and made strong efforts to develop a cooperative leadership. In the late 1950s, many Baptists, particularly in Transylvania, were perceived as subversives and were imprisoned and then released in the general amnesty of 1964.[91]

The consciousness of the Romanian Baptist movement and the neo-Protestant community as a whole increased in 1973 and 1974 in response to two papers written by the eloquent and dynamic—albeit controversial—Joseph Tson,[92] who had been granted permission to study at Oxford University and had just returned to Romania. In "The Present Situation of the Baptist Church in Romania," he exposed what he regarded as the unfortunate submissiveness of Baptist leaders to the oral instructions of the Department of Cults, which he charged were openly illegal. There was radical, intolerable interference in the life of the church. It could no longer choose its own pastors and executive committees, baptize freely, invite guests to speak without prior approval, decide what to do with its own funds, or accept all who wished to become members.[93] Tson charged that "we have fallen from the legal position in which the Law of Cults of 1948 had placed us and which is still in force, and from the position of a free and autonomous church given us by the *statute* and the *Confession of Faith* of our denomination."[94] He charged that Baptist leaders were "especially guilty" in that they had accepted these new regulations; the pastors were at fault for having been too submissive; and the churches were responsible for not being sensitive to their constitutional rights. He declared that "Baptists in Romania wish to demonstrate that they are loyal citizens, with a high moral standing," and that the state stood only to gain "internally and externally" if it gave them the right to a "free and undisturbed existence."[95] He concluded with the warning that "if faced with a conflict of loyalties, we will be obliged to put our loyalty to God first." Up to that time, this was the most open and forceful challenge presented to the state and its Department of Cults by a leader of an official religious body.

In 1974 Tson sent his second paper, "A Christian Manifesto to a Socialist Society," directly to Ceauşescu, bypassing the powerful Department of Cults. He focused on atheism's destructive impact on morality, called attention to the persecution of the neo-Protestants, and emphasized the critical role that evangelical Christians could play within Romanian society. "Let the evangelical believer enjoy full religious freedom, treat him as a citizen with full rights, and not simply as a tolerated person. Grant him the possibility to show that as a Christian, he has something definite to contribute to society."[96] Tson concluded: "The Christ Revolution will meet the need of the socialist society."

These two papers caused deep unrest within the Baptist community and shocked the Department of Cults. Gheorghe Nenciu, its vice president who was really in charge of the department, called the "Manifesto" counterrevolutionary, but the Baptist community—indeed, the entire neo-Protestant body—found itself in substantive agreement with Tson's concerns. The consensus was that the constitutional rights of churches as stated in the constitution and the 1948 Law of Cults had unquestionably been subverted. Surprisingly, the authorities' response was fairly moderate by Romanian standards. There were extensive investigations and interrogations, but no one was imprisoned, although "people had been reminded of the power of the secret police."[97] Baptist leaders quietly agreed with Tson's analysis, but they felt he had been impetuous and indiscreet. Furthermore, both the Baptist leadership and the Department of Cults maintained that Tson's recommendations had already been under discussion and were on the verge of being implemented. Thereafter, a significant number of Baptists began to insist that their leaders take a more independent stance. This obviously was the beginning of an important movement for greater freedom within the church.

Among the continuing efforts made for increased religious rights was a document circulated following the Congress of Baptist Churches in February 1977. Tson, joined by Pavel Nicolescu and Aurel Popescu, in a document called "Evangelical Believers and Human Rights in Romania," focused on three primary areas of discrimination against the neo-Protestants: education, employment, and the right of religious association.[98] This document found its way into the U.S. Helsinki Commission dossier on Romania for the Belgrade Review Conference in 1977.

In September 1977 the vice president of the Department of Cults was suddenly replaced, and neo-Protestants feared they would now encounter a more difficult time. They felt they had developed a good working relationship with Nenciu and that he had listened to their concerns. No official explanation was ever given for Nenciu's unexpected ouster, but an important factor undoubtedly was a high-level decision to bring the freedom movement under control. Furthermore, a news release in the United States had stated that the Romanian government had granted permission for 100,000 Bibles to be sent to Romania by a consortium of Christian believers and organizations.[99] Apparently, discussions about this matter had occurred, but final approval had not been obtained; further, it was discovered that the consortium's leader was a major figure in the "underground evangelism" movement that had been engaged in smuggling Bibles into Romania. There was consternation in high circles; Nenciu apparently was blamed; and neo-Protestant leaders were scolded for their involvement. The neo-Protestants were correct in their assessment that the Department of Cults would become much more aggressive in its quest to bring the churches under its control, which was revealed by subsequent events.

Tensions within the Baptist Church continued to develop, and in April 1978 an organization was formed calling itself the Christian Committee for the Defense of Religious Freedom and Freedom of Conscience (ALRC). In July it sent an appeal to the Council of State, the minister of justice, the Department of Cults, and the Baptist Union; this contained certain "demands" made of the Communist Party and the state. The primary spokesman for this committee appeared to be Nicolescu, a staunch ally of Tson. The document was signed by twenty-five Baptists, one Orthodox, and one Pentecostalist, with a covering letter from Popescu and Tson acknowledging their approval of the association and its objectives, although they declined to become members. The appellants stated their desire "to make a modest contribution to the defense of man's basic rights, to the respect for constitutional guarantees, and to the raising of Romania's international prestige." They spoke of the necessity to reform church-state relations and charged that the Department of Cults had been "a continuous source of abuses, restrictive measures, and psychological pressure on those who serve the Church," thus bringing about a profound and unnecessary alienation between Christians and the state.[100] They called for "the right of religious associations to exist undisturbed and be recognized by law." In a daring and courageous ecumenical thrust, they demanded the right of the Catholic Church to have "a recognized juridical statute; the official recognition of the Uniate Church, the Reformed Seventh-Day Adventists, and 'the Lord's Army'" within the framework of the Romanian Orthodox Church. They dealt with the whole spectrum of religious concerns such as church appointments, new churches, use of the media, religious literature, censorship, religious instruction, social agencies, ideological discrimination, the oath of loyalty to the Communist Party, and respect for human rights in accordance with international agreements.

This obviously was the most far-reaching statement made up to that time; it challenged the state's authority in matters of the greatest sensitivity that were more than interpretations of the law. The Baptist Union Council, obviously under great pressure, sent a letter in September 1978 to all its churches, expelling a number of this organization's leaders, including Nicolescu and Popescu, charging they were involved in an illegal political group directly attacking the leadership of church and state authorities.[101] The most significant absentee from the expulsion list was Tson, who originally had indicated his approval of the concerns raised. Some of Tson's supporters felt he had come to an understanding with Baptist Union officials much too quickly.[102]

The tensions among the dissidents were profoundly intensified when

Tson remained silent on the imprisonment of Baptists related to the Caransebes controversy in October 1978.[103] His role in this matter was severely criticized in an impassioned letter by Popescu, who charged that his "silence and change of position in favor of the Union" had encouraged the Securitate to persecute those who had been his followers.[104] Tson maintained that because he had tried to keep himself in a "correct and right relationship with the leadership of the denomination and with State authorities," some of his friends turned against him and called him a "traitor." He emphasized that "we must formulate our demands politely, and ask for the things which are ours according to the laws of the country with dignity."[105] He further stressed that he was advocating a policy of legal recognition, not confrontation, between church and state. Tson urged that believers be allowed to exercise the full constitutional freedom of worship and practice and to make their contributions to the building of a socialist Romania. He was supporting what he called "conscientious cooperation," with his focus on preaching, not human rights.[106]

This embittered division seriously weakened the dissident movement, which suffered another blow when some of its primary leaders were strongly encouraged or even forced to emigrate. Nicolescu, Popescu, and Tson were exiled to the United States. Tson became president of the Romanian Missionary Society in Wheaton, Illinois, and involved himself in an extensive program of publishing works to strengthen the leadership of the Romanian Baptist community. For years, BBC carried his ten-minute program to Romania every Saturday and Sunday; on Sunday afternoons he broadcast a fifty-minute program on Radio Free Europe to a large Romanian audience.

In the 1980s the Baptists in Romania made a number of appeals directly to President Ceauşescu. A hope lingered that Ceauşescu really did not know what was going on and would intervene on behalf of their undeniable constitutional rights. Sixty-six Baptist pastors sent a letter, dated August 1982, listing seven points of concern.[107] These had been addressed to the authorities on many occasions, but with what they perceived to be minimal results. Following the appeal, the signatories were questioned by the Securitate and were pressured to remove their names. Ten pastors eventually withdrew their signatures, but fifty-six names remained. No reply came from the president, and awareness grew that Ceauşescu himself was at the heart of the problem.

Meanwhile, in the 1980s from his American sanctuary, Tson continued to support his colleagues in Romania, reiterating their concerns and charging that they had become a "special target" of the communist regime. He called attention to the severe limiting of the number of students in the seminaries and to the restrictions on having foreign visitors speak in Romanian churches. He pointed out that about three hundred Baptist churches, three hundred Pentecostal churches, and fifty Brethren churches (each of which had more than twenty members) had officially applied for state authorization. He claimed that the Department of Cults kept the application forms in a safe and refused to release them. Consequently, these churches' religious services were perceived as illegal and were periodically raided, and the participants were forced to pay heavy fines.[108] Tson unquestionably helped to keep alive in the West the Romanian Baptist cause in particular and the neo-Protestant cause in general.

The Baptist Church in Romania continued its rapid growth at the end of the 1980s before the revolution, with reports of a membership that exceeded 300,000 in more than 1,200 registered churches.[109] Its total constituency was obviously considerably larger. Its most eloquent leaders were in the diaspora, although new leaders had emerged. Fewer than two hundred of its pastors had theological training, but there was a dynamic lay leadership, which is probably a major reason for the church's success.

The Baptists have presented a paradoxical picture to Western observers. On the one hand, there were undeniable reports of serious problems between Baptist communities and state authorities; on the other, there were reports of remarkable expressions of Baptist religious activity obviously tolerated by the state. The Baptist Church has had a considerable impact on both the domestic and international scenes. It has been an active member of the European Baptist Federation and the World Baptist Alliance,[110] and individual churches have developed special relationships with fundamentalist organizations and a complex of Eastern European missions, many of which are to be found in the United States. The differences in strategy among the international organizations supporting the churches in Romania at times have seriously exacerbated the country's internal divisions.

Unquestionably, among the neo-Protestant communities, the Baptists have attracted the greatest share of international attention, but the other three neo-Protestant communities also are important. The Pentecostal body in Romania is the youngest of all the official religious communities, but it has grown remarkably under adverse conditions, propelled by an amazing inner dynamism. Begun in Romania in 1922 with the organization of a thirty-member church by Gheorghe Bradin in Paulis, near Arad,[111] the Pentecostal movement responded to a deep concern for spiritual renewal following the traumatic experience of World War I. The

church grew rapidly, and in 1923 state authorities declared the movement illegal, presumably because there were internal divisions within
the church regarding its basic convictions, which were shared by only a
few "initiated" individuals. The movement continued to attract followers, however; appeals for official status were made and denied in 1924
and 1929. A significant number of Pentecostal churches identified themselves with the Baptist community during this early period for the purpose of being registered with an official religious association as designated by the 1928 Law of Cults.[112]

In 1940 a large number of Pentecostalists and Baptists were imprisoned under Antonescu, and the period from 1940 to 1944 is regarded as
the darkest in their history. They received provisional recognition in 1946
and finally were granted official state recognition in 1950. At this time,
they had a membership of 36,000. A merger took place among at least
three different groups, one of which practiced the ritual of the washing of
feet. They held their first nationwide conference in the fall of 1951, and in
1954 their main administrative offices were moved to Bucharest.[113]

The real strength of the Pentecostal movement is difficult to determine. Its membership was probably in excess of 250,000 in approximately 1,200 registered churches at the close of the Ceauşescu era.[114]
Some reports indicate that the church has been rapidly rivaling or ex-
ceeding the Baptists in numbers. As Tson suggests, there were approximately three hundred Pentecostal churches waiting for state authorization in 1986; a strong possibility exists that at least that many, if not
more, had not even applied for official status. The Pentecostal seminary,
founded in 1976, has enrolled well-qualified students, and Pentecostal
churches appear crowded to this day. Since the Pentecostals have only
about 150 pastors, most of whom are engaged in some form of secular
work to support their families, it, too, has depended on a strong lay
leadership. The church strove to transform its members to become model
socialist citizens of industry and integrity. Its rapid growth has been
claimed to stem from a high birthrate among its members, but its missionary zeal has brought in a steady stream of converts. Third World
students visiting in Romania have been attracted to Pentecostal services.

It should be noted that the Pentecostal community's leaders were
paradigms of cautious discretion in their relationship with the communist state. Pavel Bochian, who succeeded Bradin as church president,
waxed eloquent both at home and abroad regarding the accomplishments of President Ceauşescu and the freedom that his church enjoyed
in Romania. He participated in the fiftieth Interconfessional Theological
Conference held in Bucharest in 1987 and was the only neo-Protestant

quoted by the international press. He declared that the Republic had become "more beautiful and stronger" each year, the Pentecostal denomination was totally committed to a harmonious relationship of all religious communities and nationalities, and many houses of prayer had been built. He expressed special gratitude to the state for the pastoral program and the publications the churches were permitted to have. He called particular attention to an ecumenical dimension of the life of his church that was missing in virtually all the historical churches that were so closely identified with particular ethnic communities. "The members of our denomination, some of whom belong to the coinhabiting nationalities, conduct their religious services in their mother tongues: Hungarian, German, Slovak, and Ukrainian."[115] It is clear that state authorities were perplexed by some views of the Pentecostalists,[116] but they found within these communities signs of the moral qualities as well as the reconciliation of rival ethnic groups that Romanian society so desperately needed. Bochian closed his address with reference to Ceauşescu's "indefatigable work" for global peace, a form of high praise for political leadership that was normative in Eastern European societies.

The Pentecostal Church had reached the stage where it was anxious for better relations with other religious communities, particularly the Orthodox Church from which it had long been estranged. Over the years, the Pentecostalists have had difficulties with the Reformation churches, particularly the Baptists who have severely criticized their focus on glossolalia. Tson is extremely conscious of this Baptist-Pentecostal tension and has attempted to be a reconciling agent. There have been reports of an extensive charismatic penetration of some of the other churches in Romania, particularly the Orthodox. Whether this will assist or inhibit the reconciliation desired by the Pentecostal leadership remains to be seen. There is a Pentecostal-oriented "Gypsy Evangelical Movement," which may be extensive.[117]

Periodic reports continued of Pentecostal believers' difficulties over the smuggling of Bibles, holding unapproved Bible classes, or permitting insistent American missionaries who had not been approved to speak at services.[118] On the whole, however, the official Pentecostal Church did not give state authorities as much difficulty as the Baptist community did. The Pentecostal leaders vigorously sought to promote their views and develop their communities at least formally within the context of the 1948 Law of Cults and the interpretations provided by the Department of Cults. As they perceived it, the privilege of the inner freedom they found in their faith superseded open concern with interference by state authorities, however disliked.[119]

In recent years, the church has been represented at European and world Pentecostal conferences, and their leaders have visited various Pentecostal churches abroad. In particular, the church has close relationships with the Church of God in Cleveland, Tennessee, and the Assemblies of God; Bochian and Sandru have made frequent trips to the United States. The Romanian Pentecostal Church in America has tripled in size in recent years, due in large measure to a steady stream of immigrants from their native land.

The Seventh-Day Adventists were introduced into Romania in 1870 by Mihail B. Czechowski, a former Polish Catholic priest who while in the United States encountered the Adventist views of the personal, imminent, premillennial return of Christ and the observance of the seventh day as the Sabbath. In the winter of 1868–69 he arrived in Pitesti and communicated the Adventist beliefs. In 1890 the Adventist message began to penetrate Transylvania, and the believers made contact with an ancient Sabbatarian movement. Following World War I, the various Adventist communities were organized into a union conference with headquarters established in Bucharest.[120] They were recognized by the state in 1928 under the same provisions as the Baptists. In 1930 they had 7,700 members, sixty-five ministers, and 290 houses of prayer. In 1940 the membership of the community was about 25,000. At the end of 1941 the state closed all their churches and their leaders were imprisoned, but despite the severe persecution, members continued to meet secretly.[121] The churches were reopened in 1944, and in 1946 one observer, very impressed with this community, reported that "they have the best welfare service in Roumania." They had found homes among their members for six hundred children from the "starving districts" in Moldavia, and they also were trying to open a hospital in Bucharest.[122] At present, membership is approximately 70,000, with a constituency of more than 100,000 in more than 500 churches.

In 1973 the Adventist Church was permitted to open a theological seminary with fourteen students, and in 1978 it had thirty-four students enrolled in a four-year program with five professors. Two students were studying abroad during 1977–78, and two had received permission to study abroad the following year. Services were well-attended, and catechetical classes were held on Friday evenings and Saturdays. Hungarian and Romanian were used alternately in the singing and preaching of some services in Transylvania. From time to time, there were reports of Seventh-Day Adventist members having difficulties because of their Sabbatarian views, but the official community developed a form of accommodation with the state that was on the whole acceptable to the authorities. The leadership of this community was reluctant to complain about state interference into church activities if there was a risk of losing any of the "privileges" it had received. In 1980 it was reported that the situation had improved considerably over a twenty-year period, and Adventist leaders were permitted to leave the country to attend international conferences and meetings. The international Adventist community has given careful attention to its churches in Romania and has made every effort to resolve problems in as quiet and responsible a way as possible. A tradition of such involvement dates back to the 1930s.[123]

The Christians According to the Gospel, popularly known as the Brethren, represented a state-mandated merger of at least three different bodies: a group resulting from Plymouth Brethren missionary activity in the later nineteenth century; a deeply pietistic movement called the Tudorites or Christians of the Scriptures, which followed Tudor Popescu and Dumitru Cornilescu in the 1920s; and a splinter group called Christians, which emerged with its center in Ploiesti.[124] The Brethren branch, known as the "Darbyites" after their British founder, was considered illegal in the 1920s and was accused of spreading communist ideas. It stresses a strong biblicism and spontaneous divine leading in its services rather than carefully ordered worship. The members of this group seek a restoration of primitive Christianity and recognize no church hierarchy except the "headship of Christ." They focus on the supreme importance of the inner religious life, and in a world they perceive to be corrupt, the millennial day looms large in their thought. Deheleanu noted that their convictions are similar to those of Baptists and Tudorites.[125] The Tudorite movement inspired by Popescu was regarded as the only "sect" with actual Romanian origins. Popescu, having undergone a profound religious experience, began to proclaim a message of repentance and faith, calling into question the significance of the cult of the saints, icons, and the sacramental way of the Orthodox Church. He emphasized the centrality of the Bible rather than the liturgy. Eventually, he was excommunicated from the Orthodox Church and forbidden to speak to its congregations. J. Howard Adeney of the Anglican Mission to the Jews in Bucharest provided him with an auditorium, much to the consternation of the Romanian Orthodox Church, whereby he was able to firmly establish his work. Popescu was a very popular preacher who drew large crowds.[126] He deeply impressed some of the secular authorities, and his church in Bucharest was granted official status in 1926. This mother church has almost eight hundred worshipers on a Sunday morning to this day. Popescu has been called the Romanian Martin Luther because of his attempts at a reformation of the Orthodox Church.

The three groups were merged after World War II in order to receive official state approval. The community had six hundred churches in 1950, but with a state ruling that a church had to have more than twenty members to be established or continued, a large number of small churches were officially closed; in all probability, however, many of them still continued to meet quietly. In the late seventies, the community claimed to have nearly four hundred churches and approximately 55,000 members, with a number of churches waiting for official registration. A number of scholars suggest a following of 120,000, but this is probably based on strong Tudorite support within the Orthodox Church and also includes a considerable number not listed as actual members because they had not formally transferred their membership.[127] The church does not have a hierarchy, and it totally relies on a lay ministry that appears to be highly effective. Services are informal with biblical readings and expositions, prayers, and fervent singing. There is a spontaneity that leads to considerable participation by the community, and the churches express a great measure of local autonomy. Members have demonstrated their social concern by supporting a leprosy community of ninety people in Romania. The church had a full-time secretary in Bucharest and an executive committee of three members, but there was a great deal of ambiguity regarding the committee's authority. As with the other neo-Protestant communities, this church did not receive any state aid; it supported itself entirely from the contributions of its members. The group practiced both infant baptism and adult baptism, reflecting the Orthodox and the Plymouth Brethren traditions from which it emerged. Its convictions remained closest to those of the Baptists, with whom the group shared a common pension program. It had relationships with churches of the Brethren persuasion in Czechoslovakia, England, Germany, Hungary, and Switzerland as well as with communities in Canada and California. Representatives from these international communities attended the peace conferences allegedly sponsored by the Romanian religious communities in the 1980s, an obvious display of support for their local colleagues. The church had its own publication, through which it expressed its pietistic orientation to life.[128]

Periodically, there were reports of difficulties this movement had with the state. The entire leadership of the church was dismissed in 1984 because it did not exercise the required supervision over its assemblies regarding unofficial religious services. Local and regional officials of the Department of Cults also were replaced because they, too, were viewed as being responsible for permitting these unofficial meetings to take place. Church officials were indicted because of their failure to expel church members who had been convicted by the state of illegal Bible distribution. The Department of Cults intervened and appointed the church's new leadership.[129]

The neo-Protestant groups have been wracked by internal divisions over a number of issues, particularly regarding their most appropriate relationships to the state. The Adventists and the Pentecostalists reportedly had their permanent unofficial wings. Although there were rumors of an unofficial Baptist church, they may have been related to the large number of Baptist communities that had applied for but not received official authorization. There also is good reason to believe there were many more unregistered communities ready to apply for state authorization, but for groups to apply openly or to declare themselves in this manner was to come under the watchful eye of local authorities, even if the local authorities did not really wish to know about them.

Religious communities also exist that never have been officially recognized in Romania and about which little is known. Unfortunately, much of the available information about them has been written by their opponents and therefore must be used with great caution. The most important of these groups are the Jehovah's Witnesses, Nazarenes, Reformed Adventists, and the Pentecostal schism called the Dissidents or "Resistance." For obvious reasons, the size of these groups is difficult to estimate. Tobias wrote in 1946 that the Nazarenes, "Millenialists," and Reform Adventists were forbidden to worship legally, but that he was informed that "tens of thousands" met privately.[130] It should be noted that these same religious communities have been fully recognized in neighboring Yugoslavia. The Department of Cults was well aware of this fact, but bureaucratic inertia coupled with misconceptions about these groups denied them a legal existence in Romania under the communist regime. The department may have felt the need for unofficial groups of this nature to justify its existence and vigilance, although official church bodies in themselves provided extraordinarily serious problems. The Jehovah's Witnesses developed a considerable following and at times caused great paranoia with their vigorous critiques of ecclesiastical, social, and political institutions. The communist authorities probably could have lived with their radical millenarianism, but found unacceptable their opposition to military service[131] and particularly what they understood to be their attitude toward the Romanian state. Witnesses' apocalyptic proclamations sounded threatening to previous Romanian governments and subversive to the communist system. Myths were circulated in high circles indicating that Jehovah's Witnesses were prepared to become personally involved in overcoming the powers of darkness and to bring to a consummation the climatic eschatological moment. The communist state vigorously responded to this community both through the media and through a variety of coercive measures. An authoritative American source reports that in 1975 there were "heavy persecutions" of Jehovah's Witnesses in a number of major cities. "Some of our brothers were brutally beaten, some were questioned continuously for fifty hours or more at a time and subjected to physical torture. There have been many hundreds of house searchings of the homes of Jehovah's Witnesses all through the country and their religious literature has been seized.[132]

The Jehovah's Witnesses originally found their way into Romania through Hungarian missionaries in Transylvania. In 1920 Ioan B. Sima, a former Romanian Uniate, was sent from the United States to organize the community, and in the 1930s this community was divided into four groups. The Witnesses had a rare moment of freedom in 1945–46 when they could openly publish their own literature in the Romanian language.[133] The door was quickly closed, however, and they were not included among the official religious communities in 1948. Metropolitan Antonie stated in an interview for *One World*, the wcc's official monthly magazine, that it would have been very difficult for the Jehovah's Witnesses to obtain official recognition because of their attitude toward the communist state and military service; it would not have been impossible, however, if the state had understood their views better and had been much less paranoid. Antonie maintained that as long as the Witnesses kept a low profile and were not active against the state, the authorities were not concerned about them.[134] It is clear, nevertheless, that communist officials did in fact maintain careful surveillance of this community, that their members suffered intense harassment and discrimination, and that they could be totally divested of their civil rights whenever the moment seemed convenient or opportune. The international Jehovah's Witnesses organization attempted to enter into negotiations with Romanian authorities on behalf of their colleagues, but there was no response to their communications. It is difficult to estimate the Witnesses' membership in Romania, but it was large enough to create considerable apprehension for communist officials.[135]

The Nazarenes had been the object of considerable criticism in Romania amid reports of their continuing survival; they were sharply attacked in a *Scinteia Tineretului* article in 1976.[136] The founder of the Nazarene community was Samuel Froelich, a pietistically inclined Reformed Swiss pastor who became very impressed by Baptist convictions before organizing his own church in 1832. He believed that the Reformed

Church of his day had radically compromised its faith by its relationship to the state, and he envisioned a Christian community that would recover its apostolic identity and separate itself from a world controlled by the spirit of the Antichrist. The Nazarenes arrived in Transylvania and Romania at the beginning of the twentieth century, but they never had an official existence because their views were perceived to be antisocial. Their illegal existence was reaffirmed in the 1938 Law of Cults, which stated that Nazarenes were to be "completely suppressed" along with Jehovah's Witnesses and Pentecostalists. Furthermore, all printers were officially forbidden to publish any religious tracts or books of these groups.[137] The Nazarene Church is considered to have a similar biblical orientation to that of the Baptists, but it holds to a view of perfectionism that prompts its members to strongly criticize the prevailing religious and political order; members refuse to send their children to school, repudiate military service and oaths under any circumstances, and look forward eagerly to the Second Advent with the millennial reign. They are convinced that the final eschatological moment is in their immediate future. They regard the Bible as the infallible word of God and practice a life of self-denial and love. They have only a lay leadership; reportedly each person speaks as moved by the Spirit, but the elders have developed considerable authority.

The Nazarene community has had a long history of intense suffering for its convictions. Strong appeals were made to the Church of England in the 1930s to intervene on behalf of Nazarenes who had been imprisoned for long terms in Yugoslavia for their refusal to perform military service, although they had indicated their willingness to undertake a civil alternative, even a double length of such service.[138] A Romanian Nazarene elder in Yugoslavia estimates that there are about a hundred Nazarene communities in Romania. It is likely that Nazarene sympathizers would attend either the Baptist or the Brethren churches in Romania and then periodically hold their own inconspicuous services. In 1985 Robert H. Michel, Republican leader in the U.S. House of Representatives and a member of the Nazarene Church in America (known as the Apostolic Christian Church), wrote a letter to a congressional hearing on human rights in Romania. He expressed deep concern over the harassment and persecution of members of the Nazarene Church.[139] Efforts were made by Western supporters to adjudicate the Nazarene differences with the Ceauşescu regime, and it was hoped that this community in time would become one of the recognized evangelical bodies, just as it had become in Hungary. The group has maintained ties with Nazarene churches in the United States, Hungary, Yugoslavia, and Switzerland.

There are approximately 3,300 Nazarenes in Hungary and at least 5,000 in Romania, with most members still in the western part of the country.[140]

The Reformed Adventists in Romania are related to a schism within the Seventh-Day Adventist community in the United States brought about by the followers of Margaret Rowen of Los Angeles in the early twentieth century. From the United States, this church spread to Germany and reached Romania during World War I. Central among the group's convictions is the view that if one were to bear arms, he would have abandoned the true way. Members are convinced they are living in the Last Days and should conduct their lives accordingly. They object to oaths and participation in military service, and it has been reported that some members are opposed to marriage,[141] probably because of their fervent belief that they are living at the end of time and must follow the Pauline injunctions to abstain from normal marital relationships. They were involved in a confrontation with both the state and the official Adventist community, to which they were an obvious embarrassment. They felt very strongly that the official church and its leaders were too closely linked with the communist state. Information regarding their existence was extraordinarily limited, but their confrontational posture vis-à-vis the totalitarian state did not change.

The Pentecostal Dissidents were one of the least known unofficial religious communities in Romania. They represented groups of believers scattered throughout the country, some of whom may also have belonged to the official church but who gathered in rural areas for their own unauthorized Bible studies and prayer meetings. Since the official Pentecostal Church tended to be restrained in its public exercise of the "spiritual gifts," this attitude may have been important in bringing about extralegal inspirational meetings. It is entirely possible that this group also may have included a segment of the Pentecostal Church that originally remained outside the union because of what was perceived to be the church's unacceptable relationship to the state. In addition to being concerned over public restrictions on manifestations of the spiritual gifts, the Pentecostal Dissidents expressed a wide range of sensitivities similar to those of the Baptists: difficulties in building new churches, baptism restrictions, registration of church members, evangelism, and approval of pastors. They deplored what they viewed as the "blind submissiveness" of their leaders, the "political elements" that were expected to be embodied in preaching, the censorship of their official publication, the control of visits from abroad, and reports that needed to be made to the secret police. All of these problems had been openly voiced by Baptist leaders. This group has maintained an extraordinarily low profile, and no accurate assessment of its strength can be made. It may be that it experienced considerable growth along with the official Pentecostal church, attracting those who appreciated a more independent stance on the part of their leaders. It is very likely that this group had close ties with East European missions in Western Europe and the United States that strongly supported clandestine communities of this nature.

Two other groups once had, but then lost, legal standing under the communist state and thereafter held unofficial meetings. The first is known as the Lord's Army (*Odsted Domnului*), and the second involves remnants of the once-powerful Uniate Church in Transylvania. The late Monsignor Aloysius Tautu, leader of the Romanian Uniate community in Rome, was convinced that hundreds of thousands of Romanians were still loyal to the Church of the Byzantine Rite and that they were served in a clandestine way by several bishops and approximately six hundred priests. The Lord's Army represented a very successful evangelical awakening within the Romanian Orthodox Church in the 1920s and was founded by Iosif Trifa, a dynamic Orthodox priest from Transylvania. This movement, strongly supported by Metropolitan Nicolae Balan of Sibiu,[142] spread widely throughout the western part of Romania. Members were challenged to become soldiers of Christ and to struggle against the evil in themselves and the world. This movement has been seen as an effort to counter the neo-Protestant influence on the Orthodox Church. The Lord's Army has had an extensive following in the Oradea area.[143] Hedenquist was deeply impressed by his encounter with this group in 1946. He discovered that it still regarded itself as a part of the Romanian Orthodox Church, but he was informed that it was "officially persecuted" by the church. He felt that it was the only religious movement in Romania in which the "Romanian temperament" was allowed "free play." Most of its hymns were sung to melodies taken from Romanian folk music.[144] Estimated millions of Romanian Orthodox members participated in its evangelistic activities and large, open-air meetings in the 1930s. In 1935 a controversy erupted when the Orthodox Church's hierarchy attempted to limit the laity's leadership role. This culminated in the defrocking of Trifa, who was committed to the lay orientation of the Lord's Army. The group's "soldiers" rejected efforts by the hierarchy to control them and developed an independent life apart from the official church, although they still considered themselves members.[145]

The Lord's Army was officially banned in the mid-1950s, probably because of a misunderstanding of its objectives brought about by its very name and the tenacious insistence of its members on holding unauthorized meetings apart from the Orthodox Church's regularly scheduled services. Periodic reports came out of fines having been imposed on participants in these meetings, homes searched for the group's literature, and priests who might have been sympathizers placed under surveillance. The Army of the Lord has had a highly committed lay leadership. Its great poet and hymn writer, Traian Dorz, spent almost twenty years in prison before his release in 1982.[146] Because of the clandestine existence of the Lord's Army, its membership has been difficult to determine, but suggestions of approximately 500,000 participants in its activities have been made. In 1937 it claimed to have the largest selection of religious literature in the country and to have distributed more than 750,000 copies of Trifa's works.[147] Members of the Lord's Army have been accused by the traditional Orthodox of being neo-Protestants in disguise. There have been reports that the Lord's Army was increasing in numbers despite the communist state's censure and that periodic requests had been made for its separate legal existence. It is ironic, after the December revolution, that this group should continue to have difficulties in obtaining legal recognition.

The religious situation in Romania in the 1980s was extremely complex and volatile, involving both the registered and the unregistered Protestant communities. Increased breathing space was a profound concern of the churches, but the communist state showed no signs that it would begin to respect its citizens' civil and religious rights. The Protestant churches along with other religious communities always were carefully monitored by the Securitate because they were perceived as potentially destabilizing forces for socialist society. Because of their basic ideological incompatibility, they remained the only social structures not fully integrated into the Romanian political system.

During the 1980s, the Ceauşescu regime began bulldozing various historic buildings, as well as churches, in downtown Bucharest in order to make room for a gargantuan palace for the ruling family. Orthodox as well as Protestant churches were affected by Ceauşescu's megalomania. Some Orthodox church buildings were moved to new sites. Beginning in late 1983, several Baptist and Pentecostal churches were closed or demolished on regime orders, including buildings in Tîrgu Mures, Aiud, Bistrita-Năsăud, Oradea, and Bucharest. The Baptist church in Oradea had served some 2,000 parishioners. The 1980s also saw an intensification of pressure on Romania's Hungarian-language materials, curtailed Hungarian-language instruction even at the elementary level, and inspired a series of physical attacks on Hungarian clergy.

At the end of the 1980s, astounding changes took place in the Soviet Union and Eastern Europe owing to the revolutionary developments related to Mikhail Gorbachev's programs of perestroika and glasnost. Those years became a time of hope and expectation with the emergence of new respect for human rights and religious practice. Churches suddenly found possibilities for leadership, renewal, and social service thrust upon them. There also were new dangers; old problems could surface once again, and the process of transformation itself was bound to invite its own conflicts. In the light of the bankruptcy of Marxist-Leninist ideology, a search began for new moral values as well as for new economic models and systems of political and social justice.

Until mid-December 1989, Romania appeared to be immune to these monumental changes, or so its president loudly proclaimed. Nicolae Ceauşescu made it clear that as long as he was in charge, Romania would not follow the other East European countries along the road toward democracy and radical social and political change.[148] Ceauşescu appeared to be in complete control of Romania.[149] His large, well-armed security forces had an extensive informant system that penetrated every part of society and seemed to be omnipresent if not invincible. The Romanian poet, Mircea Dinescu, stated in March 1989 that even "the judiciary and the press" had become "instruments of intimidation and terror against the population," thus the "silent revolt" in the streets.[150] In addition to an abysmal human rights record, Romania was undergoing an economic crisis of catastrophic proportions. The crisis provoked by the Ceauşescu regime had gradually developed, and particularly after 1982 people seemed to be the last priority in what was called a "nightmare world."[151]

Two troublesome areas in particular, however, resisted the dictator's total control—the minorities, especially the Hungarians, and the increasingly restive religious communities. The convergence of these two forces provided the spark that toppled Ceauşescu in a spasm of violence that was literally televised around the world despite the imposing security measures that he had taken.

On 16 December 1989 a confrontation took place between local authorities, who were supported by the secret police, and religious believers surrounding a Hungarian Reformed Church in Timişoara in the western part of Romania. László Tökés, the church's minister, was an outspoken critic of the Hungarian minority's oppression and of the Ceauşescu plan to destroy thousands of villages. Tökés had experienced serious difficulties with both church and state authorities for several years.[152] Tensions had been building during 1989, particularly after 24 July when a videotape was shown on Hungarian television of Tökés protesting in his church. The televised statement caused profound concern within

Hungary and shocked the Romanian leadership. The Reformed Bishop, László Papp, ordered Tökés to be transferred to a church in the remote village of Mineu in northern Transylvania. Tökés and his church members strongly protested this decision and accused Papp of "violating the laws of the church and the state."[153] For his defiance Tökés was placed under surveillance by the Securitate, harassed, and beaten. His supporters were terrorized, and one of them died under very mysterious circumstances. Yet, incredibly Tökés was able to survive the ordeal.[154] The conviction that he was a spokesman for God in the midst of the "nightmare world" in which he found himself became his underlying theme.[155] He declared that this revolution could not stop at Romanian borders. His followers viewed him as a modern-day prophet who dared to tell the truth when everyone else was lying. He had the courage to challenge the corrupt, unjust system that tyrannized them.[156]

The Securitate's persecution of Tökés rallied a small but dedicated parish to his defense and evoked tremendous sympathy throughout the ecumenical religious community in Timişoara. This community spontaneously came to his assistance, and just as spontaneously freedom from tyranny became the common cause for thousands who surrounded the Reformed church,[157] particularly after it became clear that the Securitate had abducted Tökés. Tökés was supported in a moment of euphoria by his own faithful parishioners and by an ecumenical community of believers who in turn inspired the community at large to take their destiny into their own hands. In that moment, they transcended their divisions and religious rivalries and united on the basis of their common human dignity in a desperate thrust against overwhelming odds for the freedom that most of them had never known. The citizens of Timişoara concluded that it was better to die with dignity than to continue living in slavery. They found themselves ready to choose death over Ceauşescuism. Their decision electrified the entire country and called the world's attention to their dilemma.[158] The fall of Elena and Nicolae Ceauşescu and their allegedly secret trial were followed by their executions on 25 December with the announcement: "Good news this Christmas Day: the Antichrist is dead."[159] For reasons Ceauşescu never fully understood, the apocalyptic mythology of the ancient books of Daniel and Revelation were very popular with the Romanian churches that had become profoundly disillusioned with his regime. What was perceived as the most powerful dictatorship in all of Europe collapsed in just a few days in the face of an aroused nation. Tökés appeared on national Romanian television just after Christmas and addressed the need for unity between ethnic Romanians and Hungarians if democracy and freedom were to survive in

Romania. He expressed his gratitude for the Romanians who united with the members of his church to protect him. He described that moment as "the greatest honor" while the crowd, the majority of whom were Romanians, sang a national song of unity. He felt himself to be the representative of all religious believers and national minorities in the country.[160]

The international ecumenical agencies such as the World Council of Churches, the Lutheran World Federation, and the Conference of European Churches assisted by the Ecumenical Council of Churches in Hungary responded quickly and in an unprecedented manner to help meet the shocking emergency needs of the Romanian people. They used their ecumenical networks to channel food, medicine, and relief supplies to the destitute Romanian communities.[161] The neo-Protestant communities also were assisted in part by this ecumenical effort as well as by their own evangelical agencies in the West.

The "revolution" brought about dramatic changes within the Romanian society at large and for the religious communities in particular. One of the most significant decisions made by the National Salvation Front, which initially served as the provisional government, was to relegalize the Eastern-Rite Romanian Catholic Church[162] and to permit the other 14 churches which had been recognized under the Ceauşescu regime to have an amazing amount of freedom. For the first time in more than forty years it was now possible for the churches to govern themselves, to set their own agendas, to revise their structures, and to live out their own lives and articulate their own mission in the fullest way. Unparalleled opportunities had arisen for their ministries and for their service; in large measure, they were totally unprepared, although they had helped to pave the revolution's way by keeping alive the spirit of democracy and a belief in the innate dignity of every human being. Since the revolution, they have taken steps to effectively use this freedom in the light of their particular perspectives. There have been extensive restoration and building programs, many new church periodicals and publications, opportunities on radio and television, and ministries in all the state institutions. State subsidies continued to be provided for the salaries of pastors and administrators of the traditional churches but were not considered to be adequate given the economic problems. The neo-Protestants have refused to receive such state subsidies. Understandably, given their historical experience, some groups are using this new freedom in a very cautious way. The neo-Protestant churches have been the most enthusiastic in their attitude regarding the new freedom and the traditional Protestant churches have been more restrained. The formerly illegal groups such as the Lord's Army, Nazarenes, Reformed Adventists, and

Jehovah's Witnesses have all been recognized as legal religious associations.[163]

The old nemesis of the religious communities, the Department of Cults, has been elevated to a ministry and claims to be transformed into a supportive government agency although some neo-Protestant leaders were dismayed to find so little change in its personnel. In all the Protestant churches important leadership changes have taken place at both the local and national levels, perhaps most dramatically within the Hungarian Reformed Church where László Tökés was elected bishop of the diocese of Oradea, replacing an unrepentant Papp who had fled to France where he charged that Tökés was a "megalomaniac."[164] It is important to note that the most sweeping leadership changes came within the neo-Protestant communities where many of the leaders were voted out or retired and replaced by those who had been dissidents in the past; fewer changes were made in the historic churches, especially the Romanian Orthodox Church.

In contemporary Romania the religious situation is very complex and defies any brief or simple analysis. Among the Protestant communities, new forms of ecumenical ventures have emerged concurrent with old, unresolved tensions and new ones brought about by the Ceauşescu tyranny. The Hungarian Protestant churches joined with the Latin Rite Catholic Church immediately after the revolution and adopted a document that calls for a free church in a free society. They called for the removal of the 1948 Law of Cults; the restitution of their archives, libraries, schools, and social institutions; freedom to train their pastors and publish their literature; access to the mass media; and religious education in the public schools.[165] They have met with the new Romanian president, Ion Iliescu, on two occasions to press their demands and they continue to have their own "ecumenical" meetings, thus causing a great deal of sensitivity. These same Protestant churches (with the exception of the Unitarians) together with the German Lutheran Church have formed a National Ecumenical Council with the Romanian Orthodox Church under the stimulus of the wcc and the cec to assess their needs and conduct their mission more effectively among the Romanian people. Their platform has three objectives: (1) helping inter-church dialogue on matters of common concern; (2) providing an ecumenical instrument through which its members can make a public statement; and (3) discussing priorities for ecumenical cooperation and witness. The representatives of these churches recognized the critical importance of developing trust and confidence within the country so that "freedom and democracy" could be fully achieved through "non-violent and reconciliatory means." They also stated as priorities: (1) the development of "national-ethnic reconciliation" whereby the churches would have a special responsibility for providing models for a "multi-racial, multi-cultural society"; (2) issues related to new religious legislation; (3) religious education in the public schools; (4) the reevangelization of the Romanian people; (5) a joint ecumenical witness involving ecological concerns, and the transformation of life for the most underprivileged within the society. In addition, they established a Bible Society and they plan to issue ecumenical translations of the Bible in the languages of the churches.[166] In February 1991 AIDROM, a service agency organized by these churches and coordinated by the Committee on Interchurch Aid and Refugee World Service (CICARWS) of the WCC, began its operations to achieve the social objectives on its agenda.[167] This was later extended to include the appalling needs of the Roma or Gypsies who experience persecution, violence, and injustice in Romania and whose numbers are estimated at 2.5 million, making them the largest minority in the country. An extensive program of assistance has been formulated for the churches.[168] Obviously the priorities set forth by the Council represent a long-term program that will need close cooperation among the churches and the continued creative leadership and support of the ecumenical bodies to help the leaders of the Romanian churches themselves fully to trust and work with one another. Apparently the Council has also invited the Catholic, neo-Protestant, and Unitarian communities to join in some aspects of its agenda, but it has not received the response hoped for although there have been some positive developments. The Council has made slow progress in achieving its ecumenical agenda owing to the controversies in which some of its members are involved, the pressing internal needs that each church has, and the sheer enormity of the problems. Indeed there is the strong feeling within the Council itself that ecumenical cooperation after the revolution has suffered seriously and that "every church in the country now seems primarily concerned with its own internal affairs and there are increased national and confessional tensions."[169]

The Romanian Orthodox Church, the major ecumenical partner, has sent a message to the WCC stating that its involvement in the ecumenical movement had provided it with "great satisfaction" and the opportunity to learn "new values" and reaffirmed its "unfailing commitment" to the ecumenical movement and its Christological confession.[170] Bishop Tökés, however, represents his church to the international meetings of the WCC, and the critiques that he has offered have given clear signals to serious difficulties regarding internal ecumenism. He has been relentless in his criticism of the hierarchy of the Romanian Orthodox Church for its support of the Ceauşescu regime and also of the ruling NSF.[171] Also, the Eastern-Rite Catholic Church and the Romanian Orthodox Church are locked in a complex religio-political struggle that has important property and institutional ramifications as well as psychological dimensions and conflicting myths of infallibility, which is a primary obstacle to participation by the Latin-Rite Church. The neo-Protestants have developed their own agenda and criteria for ecumenical cooperation and do not sense a great need for cooperation, particularly with the Orthodox. The Unitarians have emerged from the Ceauşescu world reasonably intact, have continued their cooperation with the other Hungarian churches, and have been strengthening ties with their own international organizations.

Meanwhile, Tökés was elected honorary president of the Democratic Association of Hungarians in Romania, the second largest party in the country, and is very critical of the policies of the new government. He has been harassed and has received threats on his life but he has refused to be silent. He has consistently maintained that the "spirit of Ceauşescu lives on," that the promises made by the state authorities have never been fulfilled, and that Hungarians are still being vilified and treated as second-class citizens.[172] He has been very forceful in his demands for the restoration of the full, legitimate rights of the Hungarian minority but he has unequivocally denied charges that he is a Hungarian irredentist. He has been deeply concerned with the emergence of "Vatra Romaneasca" (Romanian cradle), the Romanian ultranationalist movement in Transylvania, with its xenophobia and implacable animus against Hungarians, Gypsies, and Jews and for whom national reconciliation was to be only among ethnic Romanians. In September 1991 a "Vatra Romaneasca" manifesto could declare that "unfortunately the holy land (Transylvania) is still soiled by the Asian feet of Huns, Gypsies, and other dregs of society" and urged that measures be taken to drive them out.[173] Tökés does not believe that such movements have been sufficiently condemned by either the ethnic Romanian churches or the state, although he claims that there are individuals "who stand way beyond the average level." At the beginning of 1992, however, he felt that the situation was improving for the Hungarian community, that Hungarians and Romanians got along reasonably well, that the regional elections in February 1992 were a "fair and first step forward" toward democracy, but the right wing nationalists were the ones still "promoting conflict" between the ethnic groups.[174]

There is an unprecedented crisis for the German Lutheran Church owing to the exodus of most of its members to Germany since the revolution, leaving behind a remnant of about 30,000 at the end of 1991.[175] The bishop Christoph Klein, however, emphatically opposes "bilingual German-Romanian" worship services because he feels the German community would become insecure. He stated that the German-speaking church service is often all that is left of their original homeland.

While the Reformation Protestant Churches have engaged in two major ecumenical ventures, inner renewal and strenuous attempts to reclaim their institutions, the neo-Protestants have largely reconciled their differences and have organized and engaged in a literal explosion of religious activities that has startled both the state and the Orthodox church. According to the records of the new Ministry of Cults, 2,500 churches were opened in the eight-month period following the revolution and more than half of them were by the neo-Protestant communities; many new churches have been opened or built since then.[176] It is clear that the neo-Protestants have been the biggest religious surprise in Romania and that they are seeking to evangelize the entire country. Immediately after the overthrow of Ceauşescu, the Baptists formed a committee under the leadership of Paul Negrut, Vasile Talos, and Joseph Tson, who hurried back to Romania from his exile in the United States; they contacted six other religious communities (Brethren, Pentecostalists, Seventh-Day Adventists, the Lord's Army, Lutherans, and Reformed) with a proposal to form an Evangelical Alliance.[177] The Brethren and Pentecostal churches, part of the Lord's Army, and the Romanian Evangelical Lutheran Church of Bucharest, which is affiliated with the Hungarian Lutheran Church, accepted this invitation. The Brethren have lost their Tudorite wing ostensibly over the issue of baptism but the Tudorites, now renamed the Evangelical Church, have also joined the Alliance. The Adventists were very sympathetic to the proposed Alliance but preferred to devote their energies to the development of their own infrastructures. The Lutheran and Reformed churches declined for several reasons, among them ethnic and theological, although there are obvious sympathizers within those churches as well. The alarmed Romanian Orthodox Church has attempted to bring about a reconciliation with the Lord's Army by officially endorsing it and rehabilitating its deceased leader, Iosif Trifa.[178] Part of the Lord's Army has officially accepted the authority of the Orthodox Church but at least half has assumed an independent stance and has identified itself with the Evangelical Alliance. There are reports of at least two other divisions, but the Ministry of Cults lists only one association.

The Alliance has sponsored a large number of Western evangelists such as Luis Palau who attracted 200,000 to his meetings in palace halls and sports stadiums throughout the country in 1990 and returned with considerable success in 1991. The Palace Hall in Bucharest, where Ceauşescu once held many of his party meetings, has become a favorite center for these crusades. Many independent agencies and evangelists have also visited the country. Richard Wurmbrand, long an antagonist of the communist regime, returned to a capacity crowd at the Palace Hall in December 1990, related his prison experiences on national television, and founded a center called Stephanus near the Patriarchate in the center of Bucharest. There is good reason to believe that the crusade held by Billy Graham in Romania in September 1985 may have been an important factor in the emergence of the Evangelical Alliance. Graham's meetings attracted thousands of evangelicals from the various religious communities even though there appeared to be a deliberate plan to keep his itinerary secret.[179] There have been efforts made to bring Billy Graham to Romania for another series of meetings; although these attempts have not been successful, his organization has been active there. Some evangelical leaders feel that they have had too much evangelism from the West and that they will need to develop more creative strategies to reach the Romanian people.

The evangelicals, as the neo-Protestants are increasingly known and prefer to be called, are building a three-story publishing house in Oradea with a grant from the MacLellan Foundation in Tennessee and have begun an extensive program of translating and publishing religious literature with which they plan to saturate the country.[180] They have distributed what, in the eyes of the Orthodox, were vast quantities of the evangelical version of the Romanian Bible. They have also begun to use public radio and television to communicate their message. The Alliance sponsored Pat Robertson's "Superbook" programs on primetime national television beginning in the fall of 1991 and received an astonishing response of hundreds of thousands of letters. Reportedly Orthodox leaders protested directly to President Iliescu and the program was taken off the air in February 1992.[181] With the assistance of the World Christian Radio Fellowship and the U.S.-based Romanian Missionary Society, plans are under way to build eight radio stations at key locations throughout the country to proclaim the evangelical message twenty-four hours a day. The churches that are members of the Alliance have founded their own high schools, Bible institutes, and theological seminaries, and are building a university in Oradea with funds provided by their supporters in the United States with Tson as chancellor. These churches have also developed a large number of associations to meet the needs of their constituencies. They have begun an increasing network of programs to deal with social problems such as assistance for the disabled, orphanages, homes for the aged, and prison ministries. The needs in this area are overwhelming and the state is strongly encouraging all the churches to become involved.

These evangelical churches have also become politically active. Vasile Talos, the first president of the Evangelical Alliance who was elected president of the Baptist Union in May 1991, joined the opposition groups in University Square prior to the first elections in May 1990. The National Salvation Front had declared that it would constitute itself a party and field candidates in the election. Talos read a statement from the Alliance which charged that "the actions of the former nomenklatura since the revolution show that they wish to continue with old Communist practices. We consider our support for those who are demonstrating peacefully against the continuation of Communism and the danger of another dictatorship, [to be] in accordance with God's will to bring spiritual renewal to our country." The NSF, as Ceauşescu before them, labeled their opponents "hooligans" and the university students hailed Talos as a "hooligan with faith."[182] This Alliance statement, the strongest recorded public critique made by any of the predominantly ethnic Romanian religious communities of the ruling NSF, reflected a widespread perception that the revolution had been stolen by former communist officials if not by the Securitate itself. It could also be compared with some of the utterances of Bishop Tökés who continually called for another revolution, but of a peaceful nature, that would bring true democracy to the nation. The Evangelical Alliance held its first national congress in October 1990, with an attendance of 5,000 in the Palace Hall in Bucharest. The representatives of the Alliance expressed their concerns to President Iliescu regarding the "official bias" that they perceived was given to the Orthodox Church; they also stressed the importance of religious education in the state schools; they declared their incontestable right to equal access to the media; and they declared their conviction that more legal restrictions were necessary on abortion.[183]

The freedom of the evangelicals was initially tested in their attempt to register the Evangelical Alliance with the new Ministry of Cults, frequently referred to as the State Secretariat for Religious Affairs. Nicolae Stoicescu, the first head of this Ministry and a militant Orthodox believer, rejected their request until three amendments were made to their constitution: (1) the Lord's Army was to be excluded from the Alliance in that it was regarded not as an independent organization but rather as an integral part of the Orthodox Church; (2) all decisions of the Alliance were to be subject to the approval of the Ministry; (3) all the activities of

the Alliance were to be confined to the church buildings. These conditions were regarded as subversive of authentic religious freedom and
found totally unacceptable by the Alliance representatives. Furthermore,
the representatives feared that there might be additional efforts to undermine their freedom with the announcement by the Ministry that the new
religious legislation would be based on laws governing the religious
institutions in 1928; these had favored the Orthodox Church and had
discriminated against the evangelical communities.[184] Vigorous protests
were made and the Ministry was to quickly grant the Alliance full legal
standing without any conditions. There were calls for the closure of the
Ministry from both the Evangelical Alliance and the Catholic church, but
the Romanian Orthodox Church was to argue strongly for its continuation.

To avoid further conflicts, Stoicescu established a committee in the
spring of 1990 with representatives chosen by the fifteen religious communities to draft the new religious legislation which would then be proposed by the Ministry to the country's new parliament for approval. This
new law was to grant the churches self-determination and freedom of
religion and replace the 1948 Law of Cults which had given the state the
right to intervene in and control the churches' internal affairs. The discussions among the representatives of the religious communities proved
to be very difficult even though on many issues they shared similar
positions. The major controversy was between the representatives of the
Romanian Orthodox Church and the evangelical communities. The Orthodox argued vigorously for a more restrictive law whereas the evangelicals joined by other churches such as the Catholics, Lutherans, and
Reformed supported a version reflecting greater religious freedom. At
one point, the members of the Evangelical Alliance withdrew from the
committee in protest against what they regarded as regulations that were
too restrictive. The controverted proposals were withdrawn or changed
and the evangelicals rejoined the committee.[185] A fifteen-page document
was finally agreed upon that emphasized the freedom of the churches in
a large number of critical areas but did not call for a strict separation of
church and state. The role of the Ministry of Cults still remained important: it ensured that the rights of the religious bodies would be respected
and it also guarded against the abuse of those rights; it would also
mediate, when so requested, between the religious bodies themselves
and also between them and the state institutions.[186] In February 1991, the
document was submitted to the Romanian parliament. Gheorghe Vladutescu, a former philosophy professor at the University of Bucharest,
became the new secretary of state for religious affairs in July 1990, suc-

ceeding Stoicescu, who had alienated both the Catholics and the evangelicals. Vladutescu reported that the most important point on which
there was unanimity was that all of the religious communities were equal
before the law and state and that there would not be a state church. The
proposed religious legislation clearly bears the imprint of the evangelicals' concerns and affirms that the Romanian state "recognizes, respects,
and guarantees the freedom, the autonomy, and independence of the
religious cults" and will not grant special privileges to any one church
and discriminate against the others.[187] Concurrent with the deliberations
by this committee there were vigorous discussions in the Romanian
parliament regarding the proposed national constitution and its clauses
on the freedom of religion. The Baptists, in particular, were very atten-
tive to these proceedings and officially presented several amendments of
their own. They proposed that "by the grace of God" be added to the first
article of the new constitution which then read that "Romania is a national state, sovereign, unitary and indivisible." Their rationale was that
there needed to be a radical break with the official atheism of the past
with the constitutional acknowledgment of the nation's dependence on
divine providence.[188] They were also very uneasy about Article 50, which
stated that "loyalty to the state is a sacred duty" and proposed that it be
changed to read that "loyalty to the state is the obligation of every
citizen," because in their eyes political loyalty was not the ultimate loyalty. They were the only religious community to raise even implicitly the
idolatry of nationalism in which many Romanians were involved. These
amendments did not appear in the constitution approved by the Parliament on 21 November 1991 and by popular referendum on 9 December
1991. Article 29, entitled "Freedom of Conscience," declared that freedom of religious belief could not be restricted in any way; freedom of
conscience was guaranteed but it must be expressed in a spirit of tolerance and mutual respect; the religious communities were free but all
forms of religious controversy were prohibited; the religious communities were autonomous in relation to the state and they enjoyed its
support; parents had the right to provide religious education for their
children.[189] It is interesting to note that parliament appeared to stress the
importance of tolerance, mutual respect, and the avoidance of religious
controversy in the national constitution more than the representatives of
the religious communities did in their document. The religious controversies unquestionably had become a major concern for the state authorities. The constitution also stressed in Article 6 under "General Principles" that "the state recognizes and guarantees for members of the
national minorities the right to preserve, develop, and express their

ethnic, cultural, linguistic, and religious identity,"[190] but the representatives of UDMR did not believe that these rights were sufficiently safeguarded in the constitution as a whole.

Article 32 of the constitution emphasizes "that the state will ensure freedom of religious education in accordance with the specific requirements of each faith. In the state schools, religious education is organized and guaranteed by law."[191] This was similar to the proposal made by the religious communities which had included, however, a wider range of institutions. In the light of the widespread concern to address the ideological vacuum left by the collapse of communism and in anticipation of legislation in this regard, "moral-religious education" was introduced in the elementary and secondary schools of the country in the fall of 1990. This was an optional course taught by teachers appointed by the various religious communities for the students who had declared themselves to be members of those communities.

Open tensions have surfaced between the evangelical communities and the Romanian Orthodox Church regarding the complex issue of proselytism. The Orthodox do not consider Romania as "terra missionis" but rather as a country, people, and culture that are inextricably related to the Orthodox faith from their origins. The evangelicals, however, imbued by a spirit of triumphalism, view all the people of Romania as their legitimate, indeed divinely mandated, mission field. The evangelical success in attracting large numbers of Orthodox believers and nonbelievers to their services is perceived as a serious threat to the self-identification of the Orthodox as the church of the Romanian people and subversive of the unity of the nation. There obviously is a great deal of sympathy among many of the members of the Orthodox Church for the evangelical message with its emphasis on the importance of a "born again" religious experience, but this does not necessarily mean that they will all abandon their ancestral faith. The evangelicals, however, do provide a religious alternative in the new era which many Romanians find attractive. It is ironic that the deepest religious tensions as such in Romania at the present time are to be found among the churches that have primarily ethnic Romanian constituencies.

Unquestionably there is a serious moral void within the Romanian society at large. This is the tragic legacy of the Ceauşescu era, which needs to be addressed. More than forty years of oppression, corruption, paranoia, and social atomization have taken their tragic toll. This is a critical and dangerous period in the history of the Romanian nation. There are great fears that democracy itself will not take root and that a new totalitarianism will seize control and the nightmare will begin anew.

All of the Protestant churches are keenly aware of the dangers they confront, but they are also conscious of the possibilities of positive developments. The evangelical churches, even some of those immersed in apocalyptic forebodings, are deeply sensitive to what they perceive to be an historic opportunity to lay the foundations of a new society. They are deeply aware that the freedom that they advocate can only be preserved and protected in a truly democratic Romania, and many of them appear to be modifying their millennarianism and are becoming militant eschatologists with a this-worldly focus. They are profoundly convinced that they have a critical role to play in making possible a transfigured Romanian world.

There is restiveness among the traditional Protestant churches because they fear that they will not be full partners in the ecumenical venture and that the center will be controlled by the Orthodox leaders and dominated by their agenda. With careful guidance by the ecumenical agencies, however, it could become a focal point for the beginning of meaningful dialogue by the religious communities involving their own relationships and the welfare of their nation. It could be extremely painful but it is a necessary step for authentic reconciliation and cooperation. Bishop Tökés, who with his courageous denunciation of the tyranny of Ceaușescu served as the catalyst for the revolution, could set the agenda for such a dialogue. In his own inimitable way he expressed the problem, hope, and challenge for the Romanian churches in the new age.

FACT SHEET

(It is important to note that there have been serious statistical problems related to the Hungarian churches and the neo-Protestant communities.)

	Members	Churches	Pastors
Traditional Protestants			
Reformed Church	900,000	960	720
Hungarian Lutheran	35,000	46	35
German Lutheran	50,000	200	70
Unitarian	85,000	130	110
Neo-Protestants			
Baptists	325,000	1,700	170
Brethren	65,000	565	—
Pentecostal	300,000	1,600	150
Seventh-Day Adventists	75,000	540	120

	Members	Churches	Pastors
Related Communities— Basically Lay Movements (Unofficial before 1990)			
Nazarenes	10,000	100	
Pentecostal Dissidents	40,000	N.A.	
Reform Adventists	10,000	226	
The Lord's Army	500,000	N.A.	
Jehovah's Witnesses	50,000	350	

7

Protestantism in Bulgaria and

Yugoslavia Since 1945

Paul Mojzes and N. Gerald Shenk

The vast majority of people in Bulgaria and Yugoslavia most likely never heard the term "Protestant" (or its equivalents) and are even less aware that some Protestants live among them. Truly, Protestants in Bulgaria and Yugoslavia are minuscule minorities. They are certainly a numerically tiny minority, being in both countries less than 1 percent of the population; in Yugoslavia, they draw most of their membership from the national minorities that live in the country. Not only is the Protestant spirit alien to these two countries, but over the years efforts have been made to portray Protestants as a foreign element. Except for brief periods of Protestant influence in Bulgaria, mostly in the nineteenth century, it is fair to say that Protestant influence in both countries has been negligible. Perhaps the communities' greatest achievement is their very survival under extremely hostile circumstances.

Generally, there are few points of contact or parallels between the history of Protestantism in Bulgaria and in Yugoslavia (the notable exception being the Methodists of Macedonia whose predecessors were part of the Congregational mission in European Turkey and regarded by missionaries as linked with Bulgaria). In many ways, the history of these two groups under communism is a story of great contrasts. In Bulgaria, Protestants until late 1989 underwent the cruelest possible treatment that led to near extinction and complete subjugation by the state.[1] In Yugoslavia, after initially harsh treatment, the government gradually changed by the mid-1960s to interfere significantly less in Protestant activities. Opportunities for religious work in Yugoslavia during the communist era were among the best in Eastern Europe, although the government liked to be informed about religious undertakings and occasionally hindered them. Bulgarian Protestants had few international ecumenical contacts before 1990; Yugoslav Protestants, in contrast, were actively involved abroad as well as with various ecumenical meetings and agencies inside the country. The Prague-based Christian Peace Conference was one of the few links to the outside world for Bulgarian Protestants, although even this avenue was rarely accessible to them; again in contrast, Yugoslavs assiduously avoided participating in the Christian Peace Conference and had numerous contacts with Western Christians. What both groups had in common was an avoidance of any political dissent in their respective societies; only in a religious sense were they dissenters by being an exception to the majority churches.

Bulgarian Protestants Since the 1850s

Historical Antecedents

The Protestant Reformation never reached Bulgaria. None of the issues, achievements, or problems associated with its history had any impact on the country, which at that time lay deep in the heartland of the Ottoman Turkish Empire.

Protestantism made its first, and nearly its only, impact on Bulgaria through American missionaries in the second half of the nineteenth century.[2] Even those missionary efforts began more as a surprising accident than as matters of deliberate policy.[3] Around the 1850s, the Congregationalist missionaries of the American Board of Commissioners of Foreign Mission stationed in Istanbul—where they were hampered in their work because of the death penalty imposed on Muslim converts to Christianity—turned their attention to contact with Christians of the empire and to educational work. At the bazaar in Istanbul they encountered some villagers who identified themselves as Bulgarians, about whom the missionaries knew next to nothing. These were largely Orthodox Christians, who, from the missionary perspective, seemed only nominally Christian—and thus fitting targets for conversion.

In a matter of a few decades, the Congregational and Methodist missionaries, and later the Baptists and Pentecostals, came to work in Bulgaria, generally creating opposition and uproar among the hierarchy, priests, and most lay members of the Bulgarian Orthodox Church. The missionaries' early years were stressful and sometimes violent, and some American Protestants and Bulgarian converts lost their lives in confrontations with brigands and revolutionaries.[4] Yet this also was the beginning of a "falling in love" by many missionaries who became passionate partisans in the struggle for Bulgarian liberation from the Turks.

Not only did the missionaries vigorously campaign for American governmental and public sympathies for establishing an independent Bulgaria, but they organized some of the first educational institutions of
higher learning that succeeded in educating the first governing elite of
the newly independent nation. From 1878 until about 1920, the tiny
Protestant minority, numbering only a few thousand members, and a
handful of American missionaries had an extraordinary impact on Bulgaria. Some government leaders acknowledged their indebtedness to
the U.S. missionaries for their education and for some notions of modern
statesmanship. These leaders received their training at Roberts College
in Istanbul, but the Protestants later established the American College in
Sofia, the Methodist School for Girls in Lovech, the Pordim Folk School,
and the Plovdiv Boys' School—all examples of pioneering institutions
that left a mark on the young state. None of these institutions were
permitted to remain in church hands after the communist take-over. For
their championing of the Bulgarian cause in Western circles and for providing educational opportunities when few existed, the Protestants (especially the Congregationalists and Methodists) gained gratitude from
the elite and recognition as an important religion.

The Congregational and Methodist boards of missions decided not to
compete against each other in Bulgaria; instead, they divided the country
in two. The Methodists were active in northern Bulgaria, while the
Congregationalists worked in southern regions, with only the capital city
of Sofia having both churches. In the 1930s, an attempt to merge the two
churches failed because of their inability to settle property matters and to
resolve leadership rivalries. The Baptists who did not start their work in
Bulgaria until the late 1920s, and the Pentecostals who also arrived late,
were both only loosely organized. Still later arrivals, the Adventists and
the Church of God, did not enter into territorial arrangements but aimed
to be active throughout the country; these groups also avoided merger
efforts. At the peak of their success, the four Protestant churches seem to
have won over about equal numbers of members, with each church
claiming some three thousand followers.

After World War I, the Protestant missionaries' reputation and influence had dwindled, not for lack of opportunity, but because of financial
dilemmas created by the aftermath of the Great War and by the Great
Depression. Thus, even while Bulgaria developed as an independent
country, Protestant influence waned.

The Bulgarian Orthodox Church had shaken off the centuries-long
domination of the ethnically Greek Patriarchate of Constantinople after

a protracted struggle for autonomy and then autocephaly, and it rein-
vigorated its central position until it became the state church. The ties
between Bulgarian nationalism and the Orthodox Church were, and
continue to be, strong. As Stefanka Petrova, a Bulgarian Orthodox theologian, wrote,

> It should also be stated that making capital out of her position of a
> national church, i.e. of a representative of the people's national iden-
> tity, the Orthodox Church in Bulgaria took a stand against the activity
> of the Protestant missions, accusing them of tending to alienate the
> Bulgarians from their own people and the faith of their fathers. A thing
> which they would easily believe, as they regarded at that time, in the
> second half of the 19th century, their nation bound together by their
> Orthodox religion. To become a Protestant and remain a Bulgarian
> seemed an impossible thing.[5]

This attitude naturally cast an anti-nationalist pall over the non-Ortho-
dox—both the small Roman Catholic and even smaller Protestant communities. Some Protestants had a greater ecumenical vision of working
with the Orthodox and other Christians, as when the YMCA operated
from 1925 to 1940 on a multidenominational basis.[6] But by and large,
they remained confined within their own denomination; and while elicit-
ing respect among an intellectual elite, they never created a basis for
larger support.[7] Years later, this inability resulted in total isolation when
the communists decided to crush them.

   The royal house, of German noble extraction, had no sympathy for
the Protestants either. In both world wars the Protestant community,
because of its strong American links, suffered severe setbacks as a result
of Bulgaria allying itself with Germany. In World War II the presence
of a German missionary among the Methodists may have alleviated
suspicions of Protestants as Allied sympathizers, but in both wars the
churches suffered numerical losses because of deaths and displace-
ments.

   After World War I, Protestants in Bulgaria reported a dramatic rise in
opportunities for various kinds of missionary work. Some work was
devoted to war relief, but most consisted of maintaining and expanding
educational institutions through financial support and missionary teachers from the United States as well as by more modest support from
Bulgarian Protestants. Unfortunately, these advances were nearly wiped
out by the Great Depression when missionary work and financial contributions were virtually terminated. World War II did not cause much
interruption, except for the internment of a few ministers and church
members, because the government continued its policy of toleration.

From 1945 to 1989

If there were any hopes that Protestant church activities would recuperate after the war, such expectations were as short-lived as the aspiration that Bulgaria would become a parliamentary democracy. The Fatherland Front coalition governments created in the war's immediate aftermath turned out to be only provisional when Soviet occupying forces quickly supported the Bulgarian Communist Party's move to monopolize control. By 1948 the power struggle ended with a complete victory for the communists, who wasted no time gaining control over the churches on the Soviet model.

Even under the Fatherland Front, conditions for the churches were difficult, and their future uncertain. Some communication was established between the Congregationalist and Methodist missionary agencies, but the last two American Methodist missionaries were forced to leave in 1948, while the last, very elderly Congregationalist missionary was tolerated until 1950.[8] The Congregationalists had forty-seven places of worship, twenty-seven church buildings, twenty-two ministers (some with little or no theological education), and about 4,300 members. The Methodists were somewhat weaker, with about twelve congregations. These two churches were regarded by the communists as "progressive" and more stable than the Baptists and Pentecostalists. The church pastors worked vigorously under difficult financial circumstances to minister to the people, often to huge crowds, and they even succeeded in uniting all Protestant young people in an ecumenical association, the Union of Bulgarian Protestant Young People's Christian Association.

But after 1947, their situation rapidly deteriorated; by 1950 all ties with Protestant churches outside of Bulgaria had to be severed, while churches inside the country experienced their Calvary without the benefit of a resurrection—despite the changes of the winter of 1989–90.

The state's blueprint for taking complete control of the churches was to intimidate the large Bulgarian Orthodox Church by imposing severe pressure on it while exerting even greater pressure on the smaller Roman Catholic and Protestant communities. This effort amounted to virtually crushing the Protestant churches by sensational public show trials, murders, and long years of labor camp atrocities.[9] The blueprint was implemented so successfully that all subsequent Bulgarian religious activities have been completely controlled by the government. No religious (or political) dissent was tolerated after 1948—a situation that persisted until 1989.[10]

The government's first move was to devise legal provisions that would help it in controlling the churches. In 1947 the government issued "Regulations for the Organization and Administration of the Evangelical Churches in the People's Republic of Bulgaria."[11] Under these rules, the four Protestant denominations were compelled to form the Union of the Allied Evangelical Churches in Bulgaria, under the administration of the Ministry of Foreign Affairs and Cults. The state required the churches to communicate through the evangelical religious representative, elected by the denominations and approved by the ministry. Ecumenical cooperation that was not voluntarily accomplished in earlier years of Protestant existence was decreed by the government, not out of any admiration for ecumenism, but from its desire for more effective supervision, which included requiring the churches to submit to the ministry all annual reports and budgets. The appointment of ministers to congregations had to be approved by the same ministry. Many regulations were enshrined in the restrictive Law on the Churches, adopted on 24 February 1949, during the time of a great show trial against Protestant church leaders.[12]

In July 1948, and in some instances even earlier, mass arrests of Protestant clergy and laity took place. Some Jews, Catholics, and even Orthodox were to suffer similar fates, but the Protestants, being minority communities, were selected as an example of what would happen to others should they not comply with the communist government's wishes. The treatment of Protestant leaders, which sometimes included family members who were in no way engaged in church work, was probably as brutal and as inhumane as that meted out to any Protestant community in Eastern Europe, although many Soviet and Romanian Protestants probably suffered equally intensely. Some of those arrested simply disappeared and were never seen again. Others were tried on trumped-up charges. The government's most important judicial act was the highly publicized show trial of fifteen Protestant pastors that took place in Sofia from 8 February to 8 March 1949.[13]

At the showcase trial, the accused pastors[14] all confessed to the charges. Their court-appointed lawyers did not defend them but merely asked the government for leniency, while the pastors repented and asked for mercy. The trial was a grotesque miscarriage of justice. Observers immediately guessed that physical and psychological torture must have been used to obtain the grovelling confessions. The memoirs of one of the accused, the Pentecostal pastor Haralan Popov, provide the gruesome details of the torture that broke these men's bodies and spirits. It included beatings, physical abuse, hunger, sleeplessness to the point of sickness and fainting, the use of provocateurs, around-the-clock questioning by three teams of interrogators, and psychological manipulations. One of the most successful techniques involved taking the accused, after months of torture, to a field where he was told to dig his own grave, which he did with a sense of relief and hope for martyrdom. Then an empty gun would be placed at his head and the trigger pulled. Immediately thereafter, the accused was informed that the grave was never intended for him, but for his wife and children. This led to a complete breakdown of his resistance, whereupon the prisoner was willing to sign any confession based on random notes he had been asked to write over months of imprisonment. Statements from these notes were then taken out of context and interpreted malevolently. Thus broken, the pastors would admit to high treason, spying for the United States and Yugoslavia (!), black marketing and other financial misdoings, and various acts of immorality. The trial received wide coverage, in which the press and allegedly the public demanded that the pastors be punished. The trial was filmed, engendering a great deal of propaganda for use abroad.

This was not the only trial; several others, less spectacular but equally phony, followed. Protestant church leadership suffered a crushing blow. Even those who did not endure imprisonment were frequently interrogated and occasionally beaten. Such tactics were used against many lay people, some of whom were beaten on a regular basis in the hope of discouraging them from church membership. Only the most committed Christians persisted in their church membership. And to compound the tragedy, some of the released pastors, such as Methodist superintendent Yanko Ivanov, died within months of their release from lengthy imprisonment.

The point was to render the Protestant denominations leaderless and to ruin the moral reputation the churches had enjoyed, as well as to drive fear into all who attended Protestant services. By such means, the government was successful in gaining complete supervision over church life and intimidating the small remnant of members into complete isolation and innocuous semisurvival. From that time onward, the Protestant churches were completely neutralized.

The denominations' ties with their parent bodies also were radically severed by the government, so that no visits, correspondence, or financial aid was tolerated for several decades. The few remaining pastors and lay leaders were continually asked to report to the security organs, were pressured to denounce imprisoned pastors and avoid their families, and were told to constantly reiterate their allegiance to the Fatherland Front.

A new pro-communist leadership was foisted on the congregations.

Some of the new leaders were nearly or completely unknown and had not even been on the clerical registers of their denominations before these events. Some were hastily and irregularly ordained and were probably people catapulted into leadership by communist pressure because they were the most amenable to the party's desire to control the churches. This amenability to communist goals was discovered through the continued process of interrogation and coercion practiced on nearly all leaders and potential leaders. During such sessions, those who were broken were asked to report regularly about internal church affairs. This tactic created intense mutual fear, distrust, and deterioration in church life. In many places, the churches were practically or actually destroyed by such people. It is reported that in 1961 Baptist church attendance in Sofia dwindled from 400–500 down to six people, and the equally large Methodist church to four. Only the Pentecostal churches maintained their previous membership or even grew. The Methodist congregation in Sofia accepted the Pentecostals into their building when the Pentecostal meeting site was closed down by the government, but they were later forced by the government to terminate the welcome.[15] Village churches suffered even worse harassment and some were completely closed down. City churches often survived because communist-approved pastors were foisted on them. The role of these new leaders was filled with ambiguity. Some of them may have tried to do their best under extremely trying circumstances, simply hoping to assist the churches' survival. Others may have been opportunists willing to lead the church into ruin. To the present day, there are controversies about the imposition of certain pastors by the government where the congregation or segments of it feel that the appointee was meant to liquidate the church.[16]

When the churches were forced to sever their relationships with their foreign connections, some strange ecclesiological "innovations" took place. The Methodist Church in Bulgaria once was headed by a superintendent connected to the bishop of the Zurich (Switzerland) episcopal area, but from 1948 to 1990 no bishop was allowed to visit Bulgaria. An unknown person, Metodi Markov, was elevated to the superintendency in 1948 and served in the Albert Long Methodist Church in Sofia. He was considered a communist stooge and nearly destroyed the congregation. At his death in 1964, he was replaced by Ivan Nozharov, who soon took the title "Bishop of the Bulgarian Methodist Church," thereby violating Methodist polity.[17] The Methodist Church continued to regard Bulgarian Methodists as part of their jurisdiction, which was terminated until 1990 when the government acknowledged the bishop of Zurich's jurisdiction and supervision.

Under communist rule, the Bulgarian Protestants were almost completely isolated from Western and even East European churches. The
extent of this isolation was so great that in 1988 an East German theologian, well-traveled in Eastern Europe, stated that he had never met a
Bulgarian Protestant in all his years of activity, and that he wondered
whether there were any of them left. The Bulgarian Protestants' only
contact with Christians outside the country was by means of sporadic
attendance at a few Christian Peace Conference meetings.[18]

Bulgarian Protestant life was irregular, marginal, and most likely
dwindling, despite some reported revivals. Until late 1989, the government blatantly intervened in the churches' internal governance.[19] The
few positive notes—a permit to rebuild a Baptist church building in
Varna, permission for Pentecostals to meet in Plovdiv and Sliven,[20] official registration of the Seventh-Day Adventist denominations—were
offset by the prohibition of religious education for children under sixteen
years of age[21] and by reports of continued harassment and imprisonment
of Protestant pastors and conscientious objectors.[22] Imprisonments were
fewer in the 1980s,[23] but the government still exiled undesirable Protestants to remote villages.[24] The unregistered Church of God, a loose
charismatic association, was particularly targeted for persecution.[25] In
April 1988 the Seventh-Day Adventists, who until then were merely
tolerated, were given official government recognition.[26]

No reliable statistics exist on church membership. No new publications were allowed; publications were discontinued (for example, the
Congregationalist magazine *Zornitsa*); Bibles became unobtainable.[27] The
Methodists published a modest calendar. Others may have had similar
innocuous publications, although much religious literature was usually
disseminated in secret. Dissent was unthinkable until 1989 because repression was so complete. Under such conditions, no real ecumenism
was possible because ecumenism presupposes a free decision to interact.
On the surface, there was politeness and correct protocol between the
various churches, and local congregations even helped each other. But
no real ecumenical discussion or cooperation took place.

Since the Great Transformation of 1989

In October 1989 the first public demonstrations against some government policies occurred, and by 10 November Todor Zhivkov, the Stalinist
leader of the Communist Party, suddenly resigned, unleashing a process
of democratization that led to a multiparty system and the first free
elections in June 1990. Protestants, because of their small numbers and

the repression they had suffered, did not play a major role in the process for change. It is known that a Methodist, Hristo Svatovski, was part of the Independent Association for the Defense of Human Rights in Bulgaria founded in January 1988, but he was harassed and forced to leave the country.[28] Protestants, however, did profit from the political changes. The Pentecostals were able to elect a new leader, Viktor Virchev, and the Baptists succeeded in electing Iordan Gospodinov.[29] The Methodists reestablished their historical connection by recognizing Bishop Heinrich Bolleter of Switzerland as leader.[30] The Seventh-Day Adventists were allowed to import denominational literature, and all Protestants demanded that Bibles be made available for everyone who wanted one.

Most significantly, an "Initiative Committee for Contacts Between Evangelical Christians in Bulgaria," consisting of Baptist, Congregationalist, Methodist, Pentecostal, and Church of God representatives, met in Sofia on 24 December 1989 and passed the following resolution:

1. Evangelical Christians in Bulgaria support "perestroika" which is now taking place in our country.
2. We demand that the new law of religious freedom be enacted and it is the wish of the believers that all restrictions on work with children and youth be discarded.
3. For decades there were many house searches and actions of the secret police. Thousands of Bibles and Christian literature were seized. Also thousands of "leva" [currency of Bulgaria] of church money, as well as video and audio cassettes with spiritual music and films were confiscated. We demand as a small compensation that we officially be permitted to import within the country for church purposes, 10,000 Bibles, 10,000 hymnals, as well as Christian literature.
4. We demand the organization of a new evangelical Christian youth association.
5. We demand permission to print a new edition of the evangelical newspaper [*Zornitsa-Morning Star*].
6. We support the organization of an Evangelical Alliance of Bulgaria.
7. We demand that Christmas and Easter be celebrated in Bulgaria as official holidays.[31]

In December 1990 a new Department for Religious Questions was established in conjunction with the Council of Ministers under the leadership of Lyubomir Popov, the former president of the Committee for the Affairs of the Bulgarian Orthodox Church and Other Cults. All denominations now sent their representatives to advise the department. Nine Protestant denominations were listed among the fifteen in Bulgaria. A round table of religious representatives was convened to discuss whether the religious communities should send their own delegates to the Parliament or be represented at the Council of Ministers.[32]

The political reforms undertaken since the defeat of the Communists at the polls and the establishment of a noncommunist government seem to be genuine. There is now hope that Bulgarian Protestants may recuperate and regroup. But they are not likely to take a prominent place in Bulgarian society partly because of the "sectarian" spirit of some of the Protestants but also because of the historic identification of the Bulgarian people with the Orthodox Church. In times of increased national tensions the Orthodox Church's role is apt to grow and is only more likely to be a barrier to any significant Protestant gains that would have to come at the expense of the bonding of Bulgarian and Orthodox identifications. Protestant church leaders frequently attend international ecumenical conferences when finances permit. The institutional ties with their mother churches have been resumed and normalized. Foreign visitors, including church leaders, come and go freely. Evangelization is permitted and church attendance has picked up dramatically. Services sometimes attract much larger attendance than the actual church membership. Many believe that the Protestants will contribute to a "re-Christianization" of the Bulgarian people. Assertive revival methods are making an appearance and may bring an increase in Protestant church membership, even a dramatic one, but Protestant evangelization is likely to provoke conflicts with the Bulgarian Orthodox Church, and cloud the ecumenical relations for years.

When the first draft of this chapter was written in 1988 we concluded that the prospects for Bulgarian Protestantism were bleak. It is less so now in the spring of 1992, but one could hardly regard their prospects as rosy since there are neither internal resources nor substantial foreign interest to come to their assistance.

Protestants in Yugoslavia Since 1945

Years Before 1971

Historically, Protestantism arrived in the lands that were until recently known as Yugoslavia in three waves. The first occurred during the Protestant Reformation when Lutheran and Calvinist influences were felt in Slovenian and Croatian lands. The Counter-Reformation obliterated nearly all Protestant congregations formed at that time except for tiny remnants of Slovene and Croatian Lutherans, most of them living in

remote villages in the country's northwest region. The second wave
came in the form of ethnic migrations in the eighteenth century into the
northern regions by Hungarian, German, and Slovak Protestants, the
former mostly from the Hungarian Reformed Church with a smaller
number of Lutherans, while the latter were mostly Lutheran. This group
composed the largest segment of the Protestant community, but it was
made up of national minorities. The third wave occurred at the end of the
nineteenth century and into the twentieth, marked by the arrival of the
so-called Free Churches, mostly through the labors of Western missionaries (American, German, and British). Thus, Methodists (who also
include the former Congregationalists in Macedonia), Baptists, Pentecostals, Seventh-Day Adventists, Church of the Brethren, Nazarenes,
Salvation Army, and similar groups—generally numerically small and
not too well-known throughout the country—were added to the Protestant mosaic.

The Protestants tend to be more concentrated in the north of the country. From the outset, there was little cooperation among the various
churches; instead, a sense of rivalry prevailed. More tense, even hostile,
was the relationship between the Protestants, who constituted only
about 1 percent of the population, and the Eastern Orthodox or Roman
Catholic majority churches.

The Protestant community's position before the country's creation in
1919 varied greatly, depending on whether a group lived in Austria-
Hungary, Serbia, Montenegro, or the Ottoman Turkish Empire and on its
legal status. From the creation of the Yugoslav state until the end of
World War II, the Lutheran and Reformed churches were legally recognized and enjoyed whatever protection the state afforded. The other
churches were tolerated, but they did not enjoy the same legal guarantees and were frequently harassed by local authorities. From that perspective, the communists' uniform legalization of all churches in the
reconstituted state after World War II represented a formal improvement
for the Free Churches.

In the immediate postwar period, which lasted until the early 1960s,
the communist government pursued a policy of administrative harassment and persecution of all churches, which had an impact on even the
minuscule Protestant minority. Some Protestant clergy were imprisoned,
beaten, even murdered; all literature was forbidden; churches were
closed; repairs to church buildings were not allowed; the secret police
monitored worship services and controlled the clergy; all religious work
was limited to worship services and voluntary religious education; social

services were nearly eliminated. The pressure varied from region to region and tended to be most severe during the immediate postwar period, gradually relaxing by the early 1960s when the government altered its attitude toward religion.

From 1971 to 1989

From 1971 to 1989, communist Yugoslavia earned a reputation among governments in Eastern Europe for the extent to which constitutionally guaranteed religious liberties were actually realized. The process of defining these liberties was often contentious, with church-state relations frequently making both foreign and domestic headlines. Progress was sporadic, with occasional throwbacks to increased restrictions; yet the cumulative effect over more than four decades was unmistakably beneficial to the churches, enabling them to expand their scope of activities.

Thus, the Protestant communities of Yugoslavia eventually faced fewer political restrictions than was true of their counterparts in other East European communist countries. For their modest numbers, in fact, Yugoslavia's Protestants had made real progress in developing an impressive array of religious activities, including institutional accomplishments for which their colleagues in other East European countries could only yearn. Yet the churches' statistics showed little overall growth in the number of adherents; in fact, some groups witnessed a steady decline not due to emigration alone. For decades, membership hovered at just less than 1 percent of the country's population.

The relatively favorable political situation for Yugoslavia's Protestants thus had to be contrasted with their marginal position in society. Unlike the three largest religious organizations (Orthodox, Roman Catholic and Islamic), Protestants were in the minority in all of Yugoslavia's republics or regions. This peripheral status entailed a more significant limitation on their efforts than did their position vis-à-vis the bureaucrats responsible for regulating social and cultural affairs.

For purposes of this inquiry we shall pursue this contrast between the political and social situation of the Protestant groups, fully cognizant that these dimensions interweave and overlap. The distinction has been pursued by others and had become an important theme in recent theoretical debate on Yugoslavia's future.[33] The further question is how this combination of social and political-environmental factors that has affected the Protestant groups is changed by the onset of the profound economic and social crisis brought about by the collapse of East European communism.

Current Situation: Intensification

Low membership levels easily account for the frequent neglect of Protestants in most reference works on religion in contemporary Yugoslavia.[34] Even the most extensive account of Yugoslavia's church-state relations by long-time observer Stella Alexander ignored the Protestant presence.[35] The overwhelming majority of incidents of church-state tension in reported by the foreign press pertained to the three dominant religious groups, not to the Protestants.

In the late 1980s and early 1990s, Protestants in Yugoslavia faced conditions similar to the turbulent situations in which they had their origins and often had achieved their greatest gains. Lutheran and Reformed groups took root in Yugoslav lands in the sixteenth century amid peasant uprisings; Methodist, Baptist, and Nazarene work began in the nineteenth century with the prolonged decline of aging empires (Austro-Hungarian and Ottoman); Adventist, Pentecostal, and smaller groups spread in the early twentieth century, marked by political instability and economic collapse during the interwar period.

The two largest Protestant groups, like the dominant Orthodox and Catholic traditions, are closely tied to specific ethnic minorities. The chief Lutheran community is found among the Slovak minority that immigrated to Vojvodina (Serbia) from the northern part of the Habsburg dominions toward the end of the eighteenth century. While other Slovaks who were Catholics may have assimilated more easily to either the larger Hungarian or Croatian groups in their vicinity, the Slovak Evangelical-Christian Church of the Augsburg Confession claims the allegiance of some 60 percent of those inhabitants who were still identified as Slovaks in Yugoslavia in the 1980's. The church's membership (given as 51,500) includes about 1,500 in the Hungarian Evangelical seniorate, centered in Subotica. The second largest Lutheran group is the Evangelical Christian Church of the Augsburg Confession in Slovenia, and the third is the Evangelical Church in Croatia, Bosnia-Herzegovina, and Vojvodina, for a total of slightly more than 75,000 adherents.

The Lutheran Church's predominance among the Slovaks means that it plays a role similar to that of the Catholic Church among Croats or Slovenes and that of the Orthodox Church among Serbs, Montenegrins, and Macedonians.

The next largest group, primarily among Hungarian-speaking residents of the Vojvodina region north of Belgrade, is the Reformed Christian Church in the Calvinist tradition. Unlike the Slovak Lutheran group, the Reformed Church does not represent a majority of the larger Hungarian community within Yugoslavia, but it is just as specifically defined within its own ethnic unit, with a membership given at 22,000.

The specific ethnic character of these two groups distinguishes them from the dynamics of the smaller Protestant communities. In particular, the other groups exercised considerable freedom to recruit among any groups they encountered in the ethnic mosaic that made up Yugoslavia. To a varying degree from one group to another, the composition of the Protestant groups approximated the complexity of the country as a whole, so that Serbs, Croats, Hungarians, Romanians, Slovaks, Rom (Gypsies), and others may be found worshiping together in the same congregation.

The smaller Protestant groups include Adventists (11,500 members), Pentecostals (4,350 in three related groups), Baptists (3,400), Evangelical-Methodists (2,600), and Free Brethren (1,100). Another group, the Christian Nazarene Community, is even more reluctant than others in providing estimates of its membership, but outside estimates range from 2,000 to 5,000.

It is significant that each of these groups, with the lone exception of the Methodists in Macedonia, is located predominantly in the country's northern region above the Sava River. A map depicting the location of Protestant congregations would show a large empty band across Yugoslavia's center from the Dalmatian coast through Herzegovina and Bosnia into the central parts of Serbia, all without any substantial Protestant presence. At the same time, the degree to which these groups reflected the country's general ethnic composition was unmatched by any of the larger religious bodies. This resulted from their status as a dual minority in both ethnic and religious identity. At first glance, it seems to be a disadvantage, since Protestants found themselves peripheral to both the country's political realm and to its dominant religious traditions. Yet in some cases this apparent limitation has been turned to an advantage, especially in ethnically mixed regions where none of the larger groups is clearly predominant. Observers note a higher than expected proportion of members who claim family roots in more than one of Yugoslavia's constituent ethnic groups.

Unique Features of the Yugoslav Context

What are the observable consequences of these environmental features for Protestant groups in Yugoslavia? Just how has the Protestant situation differed (1) from that of Protestants elsewhere in Eastern Europe and (2) from that of the large religious groups in Yugoslavia?

The situation for Protestants prior to World War II varied significantly from group to group and region to region. Lutheran and Reformed were officially recognized, while Methodists, Baptists, and Nazarenes were merely tolerated, and Pentecostals and Adventists were suppressed. Officials of the state and the large religious groups often colluded to hinder and harass adherents of new teachings.[36] Suppressed groups had to mask their work as simply the distribution of literature or by acting as cultural organizations. Wartime disruption in the 1940s placed almost all activities in limbo, as foreign occupation and fratricidal domestic strife tore the social fabric apart. Some pastors and priests (like those of the larger groups) ended up in concentration camps. For groups without official recognition or toleration, the transition to a socialist order actually brought an improvement in their lot, with equal treatment before the law.

Nevertheless, the postwar period began with the same kinds of traumas known to small Protestant groups across the entire region: severe disruption of organizational patterns and deliberate harassment of visible leaders, leading some of them to emigrate. Ordinary members faced serious limitations on career advancement. Building permits and property disputes were a frequent concern. In groups where ethnic Germans had played a prominent role during the formative prewar period, their departure was a loss and left a legacy of suspicion. Church life in the new order was drastically limited despite the obvious advantages of legalization.

Yet in comparison with their Protestant counterparts across Eastern Europe, Yugoslavia's groups in the postwar period were among the first to achieve normalized relations with the socialist authorities. More than elsewhere, this meant that within constitutional boundaries defining a narrow scope for religious activities, the churches (since the mid-1950s) were increasingly free to pursue their tasks with little or no intervention in their internal affairs by state authorities.

An expansion of personal liberties in the society at large also brought benefits for the religious communities. After Tito's break with Stalin (1948) and the moves toward worker self-management, the next two decades saw a slow but steady increase in individual freedoms such as access to international travel, openness of communication, possession of foreign currency accounts, and reduction of censorship.

As for domestic comparisons, Yugoslav Protestants found, whether because of or despite their modest numbers, numerous small advantages in relation to the large Orthodox, Catholic, and Islamic groups. Some were able to benefit from free-rider effects: whatever rights the large groups had won, the small ones could lay claim to come under the familiar plank in socialist policy whereby all religious bodies had equal standing before the law. A prime example was the extensive range of religious publications, for no group was without them, and their vitality was remarkable. Another was the privilege of founding educational institutions for training religious workers. Adventists, Baptists, Pentecostals, and Lutherans did so, following the lead of earlier schools among the larger groups.

Where bureaucratic restrictions did impinge on Protestant activity, such as the often tedious and expensive procedure for establishing new places of worship, these restrictions were not devised specifically to hamper Protestants, nor were they applied more stringently to Protestants than to others. They affected all groups, and usually there was no legal basis for Protestants to claim special exemptions. This was particularly true for the obligation of universal military training (discussed below).

Yet in other matters, the small groups sometimes found more leeway (or in local parlance, a willingness to "look through fingers") for their organizational needs, even when the endless regulations would, if enforced in every detail, go against them. Baptist and Pentecostal publishing operations, for example, advanced steadily from mimeograph machines to offset presses and typesetting by computer, while the larger groups, whose production machinery had been nationalized immediately after the war, still needed to contract for printing with public, secular workers' organizations.

If a group is active only among a single ethnic population or a single region, decentralization of political control as practiced in Yugoslavia can work in its favor, depending on the vicissitudes of local officials. Protestants, tending to be active in more than one ethnic unit and several republics, sometimes found ways to make this decentralization of policy work for them. If a particular activity was difficult to register in one region, it would be initiated as a branch of another program already approved elsewhere. In this way, several groups overcame a restriction on "private" summer camping; this activity was not presented in competition with existing public facilities on the attractive Adriatic coast, but as religious education, which, along with the obvious recreational component, fulfilled a vital function for their youth.

Despite their modest numbers, then, Protestant groups discovered numerous strategies for maximizing their effective presence in society. In terms of the political system, their small size usually did not prevent them from taking full advantage of rights and privileges accorded by law. The only method of doing so was an intensive use of personnel and resources appropriate to their nature as voluntary associations of believers.

An obvious incentive existed for pursuing this strategy inconspicuously, always maintaining the crucial distinction between small groups and larger religious bodies. While the larger groups were always suspect for latent tendencies toward support of separatist, "nationalist" fervor among their own ethnic units at the expense of overall Yugoslav unity, the smaller groups had nothing to lose in emphasizing their distinctive position on this point. Rather than lamenting their own political insignificance, they were inclined to make a virtue of it.

Dealing with a Secular System

Are the minor advantages Protestants found in communist Yugoslavia (ending in 1989) perhaps better understood as a peculiarity of the maverick directions taken by the communist party since Tito's break with Stalin in 1948? Or might small bureaucratic concessions be a sign that the Marxist system and its guardians were somehow less hostile, inherently more positive in their inclination toward religious phenomena in general and Protestants in particular compared to neighboring regimes?

This cannot be shown from official documents or pronouncements; on paper, their policies demonstrated just as "strenuous" a secularity as other countries did (with the clear exception of worst-case Albania, where everything religious was forbidden for decades). Since the 1970s, Yugoslavs freely admitted that early constitutional provisions on religion were modeled on Soviet statutes of the Stalinist period.[37] Rather, it was the application of policies and laws in real practice that tended to require greater sensitivity on religious questions, since these questions were so closely tied to the status of nationalities and regional or ethnic minorities.

The vigor of communist Yugoslavia's effort to keep religious life separate from political affairs is best understood as a reaction to the previous order, which had been marked by extensive and mutually reinforcing links between state and religious authorities. It was to prevent a resurgence of these ties in each region that the communist party insisted, to the end, on vigilance.

A further strain on the secularity of Yugoslav public policy on religion is found in the persistent identification of religion with ethnic loyalty among the peoples of the region. This linkage from the outset has presented Protestants with the necessity of distinguishing between ethnic (or national) consciousness and essential religious concerns. In periods when the national questions are heating up because of a general perception that a group's very existence might be threatened, the large religious bodies are quick to stress this traditional identification.

Even without directly objecting to claims by larger religious communities to represent or defend the national interests of their respective groups, Protestants can be seen to benefit from the favorable contrast when their own religious claims are not so conflated with ethnic or political agendas. Their stance is more persuasively religious, to the extent that others' claims are more confused with the contest between religious organizations and other forces in society, often over national identity or institutional privileges for organized religion.

This factor also relates to the Protestants' ability to cast a critical eye on inflated claims stemming from the national history of particular ethnic groups, especially when such claims are mixed with religious elements. Even without emphasizing it, their approach to a region's general history has the effect of desacralizing the partial claims of competing religious traditions.

Are They Political?

In many respects, Protestants in Yugoslavia seem most determined to avoid the impression that they are in any way political. That, after all, is one of their most useful distinctions from their Orthodox, Catholic, and Islamic counterparts. And their relatively small numbers alone usually are taken as sufficient evidence that few political consequences need be expected from their activities. Protestant groups seek room to maneuver in the contest between the dominant religious group of a region and the political authorities. In any region, they are seen as spear carriers in the midst of a battle of titans.

Even so, there is some evidence that each religious tradition, given sufficient time to develop the ramifications of its own beliefs, will run up against boundaries with other groups, or it will encounter resistance from the encompassing political system in such concerns as medicine, education, and cultural expression. Such boundaries defining the appropriate scope of religious influence and intervention are always potential points of conflict; the task of negotiating these limits is inherently a political task. Each group, with varying degrees of explicitness, finds internal reasons for making its position on these issues precise and available for public discourse. Each group in the Protestant minority, therefore, shows some evidence of being aware of its political and social situation, adopting a deliberate stance in relation to each group in its vicinity as the need to do so arises in practice. This need becomes apparent in specific cases such as marriages between members of different groups, use of shared literature, cooperation for educational purposes, etc.

Dissent

Beyond minority consciousness, however, what further constitutes these groups as political actors in strife-torn Yugoslavia? Is there any sign of direct interests in political causes opposed to the ruling parties and coalitions? Do Protestants become a hotbed of dissent in times of general unrest?

The answer is complicated. But it highlights the basic distinction between the political and social situation of the Protestant groups. Some actual advantages are to be found in struggling with monolithic configurations such as the Marxist dominance of political activity and the three large religious traditions' partial monopoly on the religious definition of cultural facts. The mere act of joining and belonging to a dissenting religious group is enough to stake out some position against the prevailing majority. This dissent is implicit in every set of interactions with the surrounding religious and political environment.

The intensity of organizational activity within the small Protestant groups may be misleading to outsiders too easily impressed with their political potential for structuring or channeling dissatisfaction and dissent. Yet the inside picture of these groups is invariably one of dissent focused almost entirely on competing claims of religious, not political, legitimacy. The differences between particular Protestant groups are rehearsed in minute detail, while the chief protest is directed toward the larger religious entity in whose shadow the small group resides.

Thus, a Protestant dissent is primarily defined by its social context and the religious tradition prevailing in the immediate region, which was also within the political context defined by bureaucratic regulation in a Marxist state-party program. Bureaucratic regulation is a matter of laws and permissions and official contacts, both formal and informal; religious tradition is more an affair of public opinion, columns in the press, visible participation in (or nonobservance of) traditional religious ceremonies, and neighborhood relations in the vicinity of the local minaret or steepled church.

Certainly, in the communist era any inclination to use religious communal strength for incipient political opposition to the prevailing Marxist powers was alien to the Protestant minority groups. From time to time, larger religious bodies have exhibited a tendency to harness the force of nationalist fervor on their own behalf, posing as the last defenders of national interests, and, when the general climate allowed it, going so far as to directly oppose official policies for their region. This tactic is widely recognized by supporters and critics alike. Protestants had virtually nothing to gain by emulating such tactics. Nor did they have the strength to withstand the official reaction easily provoked by the threat of separatist loyalties.

Single-issue protest campaigns likewise can expect little support from the Protestant groups. Involvement with ecological, feminist, or peace and disarmament concerns has thus far been evident only on a secular basis, without recruitment geared specifically to minority religious communities. These small groups are more than subconsciously aware that minimal societal tolerance for their dissenting position may easily be revoked if they allow themselves to mobilize in support of causes that do not grow out of their narrowly defined religious mandate.

The most likely exception to this apparent disinterest of Protestant groups would be the question of universal military training. In the late 1980s, a pacifist critique of the state's military establishment and armaments sales emerged, especially in Slovenia, among radically oriented youth publications, provoking a sharp reaction from veterans' and other political organizations. In this environment, a proposal for civilian alternatives to the military service obligation was rejected and hotly denounced as an attack on the armed forces and the very unity of the country. It was not so remarkable that the proposals were initially rejected, but that they gained significant public attention and clearly entered the larger political debate on civil society. Discussions of objections to military training regularly took note of the fact that certain small religious groups had members serving prison sentences for rejecting military training. These were the Nazarene Christian Community (chiefly located in Vojvodina) and the Jehovah's Witnesses. Yet there was no evidence that members of these groups joined the secular campaigns in protest against the military requirement.[38]

Ecumenical activity of the smaller Protestant groups has been minimal, confined primarily to the personal contacts of interested individuals. Josip Horak, long-time president of the Baptist Union in Yugoslavia, wrote of pulpit exchanges and even the sharing of buildings among several denominations after the war.[39] Many groups by design do not cultivate official contacts for the sake of protocol; their own structures show little correspondence with the hierarchical patterns of the larger churches involved with ecumenical dialogue.

It is therefore of more than passing interest that a more egalitarian pattern for ecumenical association was instituted in Croatia (1988) in the form of an Association of Evangelical Religious Workers. Its stated purposes included the "advancement of various activities which we develop in our congregations: evangelism, spiritual growth, education, publications, and resolving the question of the legal status of our congregations." The association's founding members included leaders from Pentecostal, Baptist, and Church of God congregations.[40]

Protestants do cooperate willingly with other social and political forces for certain common goals. Publication activity sometimes reaches across denominational barriers so that Baptists occasionally print Orthodox and Adventist material, and all make use of modern Bible translations done primarily by Catholic scholars. But there is little direct dialogue of the sort organized by themes and conferences and study commissions. Rather, the dialogue of life shared in the same environment and under the same conditions (economic, social, political) draws participants into contact and not infrequent conflict. Increased interaction also can increase tensions unless the wounds of wars (both ancient and recent) are healed, however slowly.

Church Response to Social Crisis

Yugoslavia in the 1980s following the death of Tito experienced a serious economic crisis with profound social consequences. Foreign indebtedness throughout the decade remained over $20 billion (U.S.); annual inflation at one point reached 2,000 percent; unemployment climbed and was moderated only by a further exodus of workers in search of jobs abroad. At home, strikes in troubled industries only hastened the onset of bankruptcy proceedings, while the number of social welfare recipients swelled dramatically.

Given the divergent characteristics of large and small religious communities, we could anticipate differing responses to this social crisis. Large groups tied to specific national units showed a predictable tendency to align themselves with the particular concerns and causes of their own region and ethnic group. The Orthodox Church hierarchs raised their voices in support of efforts to assure the unity of Serbia and to find solutions for the Serbs and Montenegrins living amid a fast-growing majority of Albanians in the province of Kosovo. Catholic figures in westernmost Slovenia supported the activities of human rights monitoring groups and the diversity of cultural expression.

In the midst of such increased involvement with the public agenda, each religious community has had its internal critics who have warned of fateful consequences if the whole religious authority crossed over into active political opposition. The small groups, however, have nothing to gain from outright political opposition. Indeed, events of the day rarely find coverage in their publications. They do not elaborate proposals for recovery and emergence from economic crisis. Nor do they tackle the plethora of political disputes that can arise from general dissatisfaction. If there is any chance of their benefiting from social crisis, it is only through backlash or vacuum effects.

There are at least two ways that small groups might benefit from a backlash against the large groups. If leadership in the large religious communities completely ignored popular dissatisfaction and refrained from any alignment with protest, small groups (as in Romania and the Soviet Union) might preempt that fervor by increasing the militancy of their own confrontation with political authorities.[41]

Yugoslavia's experience is in the other direction, so that increased militancy on the part of the large groups, tied to the twists and turns of daily politics, is seen by some as a neglect of what should be the faith's central religious concerns. If crisis is seen as diverting the larger churches from a spiritual agenda, Protestant groups find increased interest in their own claims to present an alternative on the very terms they already had chosen to emphasize. A crisis is seen as an invitation for Protestants to intensify their specifically religious activity, not engage in broader political action. This response accords with the generally conservative theological orientation and personal piety already prevalent among most Yugoslav Protestants.

The tangible rewards for secularity in individual life, by which religious loyalties have been discouraged from taking more radical forms, are fewer and fewer. For example, employment prospects cannot generally be wielded in favor of ideological conformity if new jobs are simply unavailable and existing jobs produce less and less real income. Thus, the ideological manipulation of economic benefits, a proven tool of effective control during earlier times of economic expansion, is less potent than before in producing prudent moderation (rather than fanaticism) among the ranks of ordinary believers.

In summary, Yugoslavia's Protestants could see in the societal agonies of the late 1980s new opportunities for matching their message to the needs of their neighbors. They did not have the population base to convene their own experts on various problematic areas of social and political life, and they were not found offering alternative solutions as a program for society as a whole. But Protestants did have a distinctive contribution to make, not by hitching their cause to regional tensions and ethnic campaigns, but by redoubling their efforts to build families and communities with integrity at the micro level. Every attempt that bridges the barriers between competing ethnic groups in a fragmenting social situation will have an enduring impact out of proportion to the numbers involved.

The modesty of the Protestants' accomplishments raises several issues for further critical reflection. If large religious groups in their vicinity are diverted by preoccupation with nationalist political concerns, how can Protestant groups clearly bear witness to vital religious pursuits? Further, can they do so in a way that reflects commitment to the common welfare, beyond the partial interests of ethnic group and region?

This analysis has stressed a distinction between political dissent and social or cultural dissent. Is there, rather, a natural affinity to be discerned among dissenters of all hues? That is, are they natural allies at the fringes of a state-party system? Or must the small Protestant groups in relation to secular dissent campaigns be just as cautious as they have been in relation to ecumenical and other relations among religious groups?

Finally, the modest results for Protestants in a Marxist state-party system such as Yugoslavia, whose policies on religion were less repressive than those of neighboring countries, raise a question for evaluating reportedly great gains elsewhere under severe repression. To what extent are those gains in membership a function of protest against unpopular regimes, or, alternatively, a genuine renewal of religious commitments?

Indications from this analysis of the Yugoslav Protestant experience suggest that (1) a normalization of institutional life by their recognition of limits to the scope of religious activity in a secular society and (2) their avoidance of nationalist rivalries represent an effective and prudent means of clarifying the focus of religious dissent while preserving group identity amid social unrest and heightened intergroup tensions.

Conclusion

On 25 June 1991, after a prolonged political crisis, Croatia and Slovenia declared their secession from Yugoslavia. The Yugoslav People's Army

(JNA) immediately attacked Slovenia, but later withdrew its forces to concentrate its strength against Croatia. As the summer wore on, it became clear that the JNA was acting in league with irregular Serbian militias, aspiring to seize large chunks of Croatian territory (including the Slavonian cities of Vukovar, Vinkovci, and Osijek, and the coastal cities of Zadar and Dubrovnik) for annexation to an expanded Serbia. By October, Macedonia and Bosnia had likewise declared their impending secession, and, in a clandestine poll conducted among the Albanians of Kosovo, an overwhelming majority of respondents voted for Kosovo's secession from Yugoslavia and annexation to Albania. More than 250,000 refugees fled their homes in the first three months of civil war, taking refuge in Germany, Austria, Hungary, Czechoslovakia, and elsewhere within what had been Yugoslavia. The war completely disrupted and subverted normal church life for all the faiths. The Serbian Orthodox Church, in particular, loudly endorsed the Serbian military campaign and, in particular, cheered the prospects of a Serbian annexation of Osijek. Some of the refugees from Czech and Hungarian villages in Croatia were Protestants.[42]

By April 1992, the European Community and the United States had decided to extend diplomatic recognition to the newly independent states of Slovenia, Croatia, and Bosnia-Herzegovina, and a large U.N. peacekeeping force began deployment in contested areas of Croatia under a very fragile cease-fire. Serbian inhabitants categorically rejected minority status within the new states, raising the spectre of violent partition and full-scale ethnic war in Bosnia, which is especially vulnerable with Serb, Croat, and Muslim communities closely intertwined.

Protestant voices featured more prominently than ever before in the public discourse on future possibilities, denouncing the violence and insisting on the necessity of repentance, restoration, and reconciliation.[43] An Evangelical pastor in Zagreb called the strife "demonic, and worse than that of World War II"; typical of many others was Reformed Pastor Lang, forced to flee into exile as his home and church were destroyed in eastern Croatia. Noted Protestant leader Peter Kuzmić, whose seminary in Osijek was forced to relocate to Slovenia in 1991–92, was instrumental in bringing at least $850,000 in medical aid to hospitals from churches abroad. Even though travel and communication across the battle lines between Serbia and Croatia were almost entirely cut off, Protestant pastors from both regions were able to meet in spring 1992 in southern Hungary to keep their ties alive. If peace is eventually restored to the region, the Protestant communities are likely to be asked to play significant roles in the reconstruction of their societies.

FACT SHEET

	Number of members		Number of churches		Number of pastors
Bulgaria (1982)*					
Pentecostal Evangelical Church (Viktor Virchev, head)	2,000–9,500 (7,000)	claimed**	160	claimed	?
Congregationalists	1,500–4,500 (5,000)	estimated	20	claimed	?
Methodists (Petar Hriston, head)	632 (1,300)		15		?
Baptist Union (Iordan Gospodinov, president)	700 (800)	estimated	15		?
Seventh-Day Adventists	3,294 (3,000)		56	claimed	17 ordained 9 honorary 11 licensed ministers
Church of God (unregistered)	4,000	claimed	50	claimed	
Yugoslavia (1988)*					
Slovak Evangelical-Christian Church of the Augsburg Confession (Ondrej Beredji, head)	51,500		39		29
Evangelical Christian Church of the Augsburg Confession in Slovenia (Ludvik Novak, head)	20,000		18		10

	Number of members	Number of churches	Number of pastors
Evangelical Church in Croatia, Bosnia-Herze- govina, and Voj- vodina (Vladimir Deutsch, head)	5,000	18	?
Christian Re- formed Church (Imre Hodosy, head)	22,000	85	26
Christian Adven- tist Church (Jovan Lorencin, head)	11,500	280	120
Pentecostal Church of Christ (Dragutin Volf, head)	3,500	90	?
Church of God (Veljko Bog- danović, head)	450	25	23
Christ's Evangeli- cal Church of the Spirit (Josip Ar- nold, head)	400	17	?
Union of Baptist Churches (Zeljko Srnec, head)	3,400	116	70
Methodist Church (Martin Hovan, head)	2,600	24	26

---

*Note: Estimates in parentheses are derived from Janice Broun's *Religion in Eastern Europe* (Washington, D.C.: Ethics and Public Policy Center, 1989). Other figures come from *The World Christian Encyclopedia*, ed. David B. Barrett (New York: Oxford University Press, 1982), or from the churches them- selves.
**Official claims on the part of the churches may be vastly inflated.

***Note: This fact sheet includes only groups with 400 or more members. Other groups not included for reasons of (1) size: Free Brethren, Church of Christ, and the Nazarene movement (indigenous to Switzerland and territories of the former Austro-Hungarian empire, not to be confused with the Church of the Nazarene elsewhere); and (2) historical or theological distinctions: Jehovah's Witnesses, said to number some 3,000 members, but not significantly associated with Protestants. Data have been checked wherever possible with the responsible heads of each church listed. Figures on clergy have been most difficult to define across the variety of denominational polities, and in some cases are simply unavailable. Compiled by N. Gerald Shenk in conjunction with the Biblical Theological Institute, Zagreb.

8

Protestantism in the USSR

Walter Sawatsky

The many disparate groups commonly known as Protestant Christianity do have in common the fact that they are neither Eastern Orthodox nor Roman Catholic. Where Roman Catholics make a strong pretense of structural and doctrinal unity (a stance belied by striking national and individual diversity), Protestants have tended to celebrate pluralism. The result (intended or unintended) of stressing the priesthood of all believers has been a proliferation of denominations and theological schools of thought. Indeed, it is not that uncommon to think of American secular humanism and the many varieties of Marxism as logical progressions from Protestantism. Put simply, it is the story of protest thought from Luther through Hegel to Marx and beyond. That helps to explain why the Marxist-Protestant encounter has been complex, involving alternating stages of respect and cooperation with stages of rather excessive antipathy.

Given the widespread notion that to be Russian is to be Orthodox, the presence of Protestantism in the former USSR as a significant religious movement requires an explanation. It is too easy to dismiss either Protestantism or Marxism as a foreign import. Both are more than imports, having found fertile soil in a long tradition of dissent and sectarianism, developing distinctly Slavic features, and subsequently becoming Sovietized.

Essentially, two stories and two sets of issues are important for Protestants in the former USSR. There is the story of Protestant believers settling in the Russian empire as early as the 1760s. They came as foreign colonists with special privileges of religious freedoms,[1] and their numbers were supplemented by other Protestants added through political annexation, particularly in Estonia and Latvia during the imperial period and after World War II. Then, there is the story of the rise of popular education and the widespread distribution of Bibles, newly translated into the vernacular during the nineteenth century. Just as the vernacular Bible was a key raison d'etre for the rise of Protestantism in Habsburg Europe, so the Bible in modern Russian (finally completed in 1876) triggered the rise of a Slavic Protestant sectarianism.[2] In terms of issues, it is helpful to distinguish the churches of the magisterial Reformers (Lutheran and Calvinist) from those of the Radical or left wing of the Reformation (Anabaptists). Indeed, the intellectual origins of Slavic Protestant sectarianism are more complex than standard Reformation literature would suggest, since the impact of the First, or Hussite, Reformation tended to renew the thought of Soviet and East European Protestantism, especially during the twentieth century.

Still further complicating the story is the reverse immigration of Protestants from the United States at the turn of the nineteenth century, at which time new Protestant movements such as Pentecostals, Seventh-Day Adventists, and Jehovah's Witnesses were introduced. Not only these movements, but Baptists and several related groups were fostered through American and European mission efforts.[3] That influence continued primarily through shortwave religious broadcasting.

Sectarian Protestantism has seemed more suited to a Marxist setting than is true of state churches. Its deep commitment to a separation of church and state as two distinct cultures seemed at first glance to be supported by the Leninist decree of 1918 separating church from state. Indeed, Protestants experienced the first decade of Soviet power as liberating and as a time of religious tolerance. But the Bolshevik understanding of separation was fundamentally different from theirs. Where Protestants wanted to free the church from state interference, the Bolsheviks sought to free the state from church interference, and then to free society from the reactionary burden of religious superstition.

Once the simplistic and often violent atheization campaign took hold (after 1927),[4] the earlier strain of Marxist fascination with radical Protestantism was forgotten. Beginning with Friedrich Engels, Marxist thinkers had regarded the Anabaptist (or Radical) Reformation as a forerunner of their movement, seeing that reformation as expressing the emancipation efforts of the lower classes—mainline Protestantism being a bourgeois religion.[5] Early Russian social democrats also placed their hopes for a social revolution on the Protestant sectarians as being morally more reliable than the Orthodox masses. The last major thinker along these lines was V. D. Bonch-Bruevich, secretary to Lenin.[6] At the end of his career, he organized a new, more scholarly approach to the study of religion (from 1959) that had Protestant sectarianism as its focus. Given the controlled conditions for research in the Soviet Union, most materials published there on the Protestants (as is also true for other confessions) have had an aggressively atheistic tone. The sociological data were collected and used in ways most suited to the antireligious campaign.[7]

In what follows it will be impossible to devote adequate detail to each church normally subsumed under the rubric "Protestant." These churches include formerly established Lutheranism in Latvia and Estonia; German Lutherans and German Mennonites once living in separate colonies in south Russia, in the Saratov region (Volga), and along the expanding frontier east of the Ural and Caucasus mountains, who had developed in considerable isolation from the surrounding population; Evangelical Christians (related to the Open Brethren); and Baptists who (Russian, Ukrainian, Latvian, Estonian, and German) formed the largest and most dominant church union in 1944, the All-Union Council of Evangelical Christians-Baptists (AUCECB). Also included are Pentecostals and Adventists, divided here into a moderate and officially registered group (part of the Pentecostal wing joined the AUCECB in 1945) and an independent union.

There also has been an Estonian Methodist Church since the late nineteenth century—missionary efforts by Methodists in Siberia during the twentieth century having been swallowed up into the subsequent Evangelical Christian-Baptist (ECB) structure. A small number of Hungarian-speaking Reformed churches still exist in the southwestern border regions (Transcarpathia), but little is known of them except that they received a small gift of Bibles in 1988.[8] Even less information is available about New Apostolic Christians (Neutaeufer), whose coreligionists in other East European countries lead a precarious existence largely because of their pacifism. Since the Jehovah's Witnesses are discussed elsewhere in this book, it should be noted only that the difference between them and other neo-Protestants was more keenly felt than might be true in the United States. In a modified way, "Protestant" should include uniquely Russian groupings like the Molokany and the Dukhobortsy. To the degree that they shared the common experience of faith under stress, they are included here, but it is impossible to do them justice on the basis of available information. Instead, we will seek to sketch the broad outlines of a common historical experience and to illustrate the major issues from the viewpoints of those denominations that sensed them most deeply.[9]

Decade of Growth and Subjugation, 1917–1929

Two somewhat contradictory themes dominated the first period of
Protestantism under Soviet power. For sectarian Protestantism or neo-
Protestantism, it was a decade of growth and submission (under considerable administrative pressure) to the new Soviet authorities. For
Lutherans and Mennonites, the first decade represented the final loss of
privilege, an uncertain status as a foreign ethnic element, and then the
breakdown of the colonist system of life through the dekulakization
campaign and the collectivization campaign that followed. The breakdown was aggravated by a major out-migration to North America and
South America.

Statistics for church membership throughout the Soviet era have always been problematic. Organizational structures did not keep pace
with the initial explosive growth; subsequently, it was deemed disadvan-
tageous for both the churches and the state (for different reasons) to
present full statistics. In addition, the statistical base provided by Soviet
sociologists was regarded as incomplete and misleading—indeed, deliberately distorted at times.[10] Membership figures for the majority of Soviet
Protestants also represented adult members only, in keeping with the
practice of adult baptism, thus requiring the addition of children and
nonbaptized adults before comparing them with statistics for Orthodox
adherents.

Scholars accept that in 1905 there were approximately 105,000 Baptists
and Evangelical Christians, their number rising to 150,000 by 1917, then
increasing rapidly to about 350,000 by 1920, and to more than 500,000 by
1929.[11] Adding nonbaptized family members, the latter figure of 500,000
would suggest more than 3 million people identifying themselves as
either Baptist or Evangelical Christian. Some of this growth involved
lateral transfers from other denominations, such as the Molokan Evangelical Christians, and especially from Orthodox villages where people
were dissatisfied with the local, inadequate clergy. The growth of Soviet
evangelicalism coincided with the enthusiasm for grass-roots activism in
local soviets; the evangelical groups represented a religious grass-roots
movement led by people speaking for the peasants and workers. Pen-
tecostalism, which had begun in the United States in 1901 and had
entered the Russian empire a few years later, came to the USSR largely
through the influence of Ivan Voronaev on his return to Odessa in 1921.
A gifted organizer, his wing of the Pentecostals claimed 17,000 members
in 350 assemblies by 1928.

The activity of the evangelicals was singularly focused on expansion—on evangelism. Congregations were urged to send their members to nearby towns and villages to evangelize. Soon, many full-time traveling evangelists were appointed—fifty-six for the Ukrainian Baptist Union in 1927, for example. Baptists, Evangelical Christians, Pentecostals, and some Mennonites developed their own aggressive programs to publish and distribute literature, often with financial aid from abroad. Several Bible institutes were started for leadership training, few of them lasting more than four years, but their graduates were to be the only "theologically trained" leaders till a correspondence course was opened in 1968. There also were women's circles, reading libraries, area rallies, and meetings for children and young people. In a dozen localities, Christian agricultural communes and urban cooperatives were organized, which reflected the evangelicals' desire to contribute to the building of a socialist society, albeit on Christian principles.

For Lutherans and Mennonites, the first decade of Soviet power became an uncertain one, a portent of the loss of independence and privilege that arose with the war's anti-Germanism. As a church, the German Lutherans were divided into several districts with little sense of commonality.[12] The Mennonites had resumed closer cooperation following some denominational splits during the second half of the nineteenth century. The devastation these colonists in Ukraine experienced during the Civil War and famine hastened their desire to emigrate. Approximately one-fourth of the 100,000 Mennonites had been permitted to emigrate to Canada, Paraguay, and Brazil by 1929 when that avenue was closed.[13] Lutherans had experienced a longer process of attrition as far as the church (rather than German culture) was concerned, which was only partially reversed through the impact of regional conferences and participation in the general Protestant revival movement in the mid-twenties. Loss of leadership through emigration and death was severe for both Mennonites and Lutherans. For the Moscow and Petersburg consistories, for example, where there had been 190 Lutheran pastors during the war, there were only ninety by 1922. That figure dropped to sixty-four in 1932, after which Stalinist persecutions achieved a virtual institutional collapse with the arrest of the last two pastors in 1937. As far as total adherents were concerned, of the 1.35 million Lutherans in 1923 (of whom 1 million were Germans), there were only 900,000 left in 1926 (540,000 of them Germans).[14]

As the Soviet state struggled for control and to gain some indications of legitimacy, it began pressuring all religious bodies to make loyalty declarations. The Orthodox Church underwent a desperate period between 1922 and 1927 when most of its hierarchs were imprisoned. Finally, in 1927, the acting patriarch made a public announcement of total loyalty to Soviet power, abandoning as unrealistic the earlier effort at political neutrality.[15] Protestants, who at first had been tacitly encouraged by the authorities because their growth might help weaken the influence of Orthodoxy, began feeling state pressure to submit, especially after 1923. In June 1924, a general synod of the Lutheran Church in the Soviet Union officially declared its readiness to cooperate with Soviet authorities, including acceptance of military service obligations.[16] Baptists, Pentecostals, Evangelical Christians, and Adventists, all of whom had met in separate national congresses between 1926 and 1928, passed loyalty declarations that included accepting military service requirements. The Mennonites, who had met in national conference in 1925 (later known as the "Martyr's Conference"), were still hopeful of getting a list of religious freedoms restored, including the right to conscientious objection. By the time of the loyalty declarations, the Mennonites no longer met in conference and hence retained the distinction of failing to officially declare their loyalty.

Common Persecution and Collapse, 1929–1939

The second decade of Soviet power was characterized by experiences common to all religious bodies. The excesses of administrative persecution and the atheistic propaganda of the League of Militant Godless left an indelible mark. To speak of the commonalities of Soviet Christianity today is to acknowledge the degree to which church institutions and church practice stopped and had to start over fifteen years later.

The details have been widely covered in the literature, although in the last few years we have witnessed an astonishingly candid Soviet reexamination of the record. For our purposes, the basic outline will suffice. There was, first of all, the decision taken by the Communist Party in April 1926 to aggressively foster atheism in all spheres of education and culture.[17] This was followed by the Law on Religious Associations of April 1929, which had the effect of drastically curtailing religious activity. All activities for expansion that the evangelicals had engaged in were now expressly forbidden (especially Article 17), and the wholesale closing of churches quickly followed. Within a year, the evangelicals had dropped to one-fifth of their earlier membership. A series of governmental actions (such as high taxation) culminated in the arrest and imprisonment in labor camps of clergy and other leaders. Of those taken during the wave of arrests in 1937–38, many never returned. After 1930, it became increasingly difficult to communicate with fellow believers abroad, all contact ceasing after 1935. By that year, the Baptist Union was no more, and the Evangelical Christian Union had ceased to exist except for one congregation in Moscow. Pentecostal leaders were all in prison, with Ivan Voronaev never to return from his second imprisonment in 1937. The Lutheran Church collapsed in 1937–38, experiencing only a brief revival during the German occupation of 1941–43, as did the Mennonites in the Ukraine.

Rise of Soviet Protestantism

The rather sudden and surprising national congress of leading Evangelical Christians and Baptists in Moscow in October 1944 to announce their unification into one church union marks the birth of Soviet Protestantism. In August 1945 Pentecostals officially joined what came to be known as the All-Union Council of Evangelical Christians-Baptists. The Smorodintsy wing of the Pentecostals also took part for a few years, and in 1963 the majority of Mennonite Brethren began joining that evangelical union. Official recognition of independent Pentecostals, Mennonites, Lutherans, and Adventists did not come till the late sixties and early seventies.

This union of Soviet evangelicals began to shape a Soviet form of Protestantism in which the historical traditions were a dim memory and an unfriendly, controlling state was not. Early leaders had been active in the Baptist, Evangelical Christian, and Pentecostal unions before their collapse, but they had not necessarily been the primary leaders, since most of those people perished in prison.[18] Many delegates were released from prison to attend the congress of 1944. Thus, for many years members harbored suspicions that these leaders had compromised their faith in order to be released and that this act explained their cautious leadership, their counsels of restraint to energetic pastors, and their loud public pronouncements on behalf of Soviet peace policies.

Although there was a continuing effort at a balance of representation between Baptists and Evangelical Christians (the two competitive unions that had always failed at unity efforts before), it is safe to say that the union came about through the adoption of Baptist polity by the less rigid Evangelical Christian leaders who provided the dominant leadership. The Pentecostal presence was to be a persistent problem. The August agreement spelled out in twelve points what boiled down to Pentecostals agreeing to abandon their distinctive emphases (except in private worship).[19] The evidence points to a state policy to allow one national church structure for Orthodoxy and one for Protestantism. If the Pentecostals wished to be legalized, they had to subordinate themselves to the AUCECB; otherwise, they would remain illegal and subject to harassment. Major conflicts with the Pentecostals developed in 1949, 1957, 1972, and 1979, and in each case the AUCECB reasserted the need to adhere to the terms of the August agreement. As a result, up to one-half of the Pentecostals left the AUCECB and chose to remain independent and unregistered.

A major initial task of the union leadership was to assist in rebuilding a church structure by appointing regional superintendents and facilitating the registration of local congregations. By 1949, such registration was no longer possible, leaving about two-thirds of the worshiping groups unregistered. The leadership also sought to obtain Bibles and songbooks, finally managing a small printing of 10,000 copies of the New Testament in 1956. It became increasingly difficult to hold leadership conferences. As a result, the overall leadership became entrenched and increasingly authoritarian. After 1955, the AUCECB leaders began traveling abroad to defend Soviet peace themes and claims for religious liberty. In 1958 the AUCECB joined the Christian Peace Conference (Prague), and in 1962 it affiliated with the World Council of Churches. These international connections came to be very important and helpful, but they initially seemed politically contrived since the broad membership did not get to vote on the issue, and many rank-and-file members remained decidedly suspicious of the ecumenical movement.

Impact of the Khrushchev Antireligious Campaign

Although there was some ebb and flow in the church-state relationship between 1944 and 1958, for our purposes the next major stage of development was the concerted state effort (1959–64) to eradicate religion from society as it sought to take a major step toward full communism.[20] Closely associated with the reforms of Nikita Khrushchev and his ideologist L. F. Il'ichev, the campaign began with an announced increase in atheist education and propaganda that included the use of recent prominent apostates from the church, but the emphasis soon shifted to administrative measures. Unauthorized religious services were stopped, local vigilante bands broke up authorized meetings, and the organizers of religious groups were arrested. In 1960 the authorities began pressuring the central church leadership (of both the Orthodox and Evangelicals) to use their authority to restrain and reduce religious activity. Both church bodies were required to prepare new governing statutes to bring them closer into line with state legislation on religion.[21] As became clear some years later, the 1929 Law on Cults had been drastically amended, but only in 1962 after the new restrictions on religious practice were already in force.[22] Charges brought against a growing list of local pastors and church activists concerned violations of this secret law.

The AUCECB leaders watched what happened to Metropolitan Nikolai of Krutitsy who lost his position and soon died under suspicious circumstances when he ventured to resist state pressure. That cowed the union's leaders into arbitrarily issuing a new statute (something normally approved by a congress of elected delegates). This statute was sent to the regional superintendents with an accompanying secret letter of instructions on how it could be enforced. The letter stated:

> In the past, due to insufficient knowledge of Soviet legislation on cults, certain of our congregations have violated it. There have been occasions of baptizing persons younger than 18 years, giving material aid from the congregation's treasury, holding biblical and other meetings of a specialist character, permitting declamations of poetry, there were excursions for believing youth, financial accounts for mutual aid were created, meetings for preachers and for training choir leaders were held . . . . All this must now be eliminated . . . and our activities must be conducted in agreement with existing legislation.[23]

This letter precipitated a split in the evangelical union. By August 1961, an initiative group had formed to challenge the Moscow church leadership. Led by A. F. Prokofiev, G. K. Kriuchkov, and G. P. Vins, the group dispatched letters through the Soviet Union, calling for sanctification of the church. This use of samizdat as a means of communication was a key factor in informing the broader church public and marshaling opposition to the instructions from Moscow.[24] Particularly shocking to many were such phrases in the letter of instruction as "harmful missionary tendencies" and the assertion that the chief goal of worship services was "not the attraction of new members but satisfaction of the spiritual needs of believers." The Initsiativniki, as the reformers were soon called, quickly labeled the letter an "antievangelical document."[25]

Initial efforts at dialogue with Alexander Karev, the Evangelical Union's general secretary in Moscow, and with other leaders proved fruitless. The Moscow leaders saw no possibility of obtaining permission to convene a national congress. Instead, they tried to get the reformers— most of whom had only recently been exposed to the restrictions under

which the AUCECB had been permitted to exist since 1944—to be realistic. The reformers then turned to the member churches, appealing for
disciplinary action against those leaders who were cooperating with the
state's antireligious program. Having formed an organizing committee
(*Orgkomitet*) in February 1962, they drafted a revision of the 1960 statute,
called for a day of prayer and fasting for 6 May so that the Moscow
leaders might repent, and in June 1962 issued Protocol No. 7 in which
twenty-seven persons were declared excommunicated, which included
most of the central leadership. They also declared the *Orgkomitet* to be the
temporary leading body till a congress of the Evangelical Christian-
Baptist congregations had been held. State authorities had arrested numerous local leaders who supported the reformers, and the AUCECB
leadership also had responded to the dissenters by arranging to dismiss
or excommunicate local reformers.

What made the reformist movement a significant problem for the
authorities were the concerted actions that followed. There was the
highly effective and widespread distribution of written summaries of
discussions and actions through the laborious and dangerous methods
of samizdat. Arrests of believers stimulated the dissent movement, a
result of the reduced atmosphere of fear after the short de-Stalinization
phase. By 1962, there were ninety-four evangelical activists known to be
in prison, including one of the key leaders, Prokofiev. In early 1964,
relatives of these prisoners met to form the Council of Prisoners' Relatives (CPR) and prepared a list of known prisoners, which included the
names of five persons who had died in prison or exile. Since those
beginnings, the CPR has produced a bulletin on an average of six times a
year, filled with details about arrests, trials, and treatment of prisoners.
This organization, led by women, earned a reputation for reliability and
has made it possible for more information to be known about this group
of Baptists than for any other religious group.[26]

Support for the reformers grew steadily, reaching a peak in 1966 when
perhaps one-half of the evangelicals backed them.[27] In September 1965
the reformers announced the formation of their own national church
union called the Council of Churches of Evangelical Christian-Baptists
(CCECB). Two months later, they issued their own statute. Although
permitted to hold one national congress by state approval, they never
succeeded in securing state recognition, so their leaders were forced to
work clandestinely.

In 1963 the AUCECB was permitted to respond to the Initsiativniki
challenge by calling a national conference and submitting for approval a
revised church statute that borrowed extensively from the Initsiativniki

proposal. These reforms did not go far enough, but the changes registered at a second congress in 1966 turned the tide. The union's president, Jacob Zhidkov, had died. Election of delegates to the congress was more democratic than before, so more delegates with the courage to speak their minds attended. Elections to the council helped to eliminate several leaders who had been widely distrusted and criticized, and more acceptable (and younger) leaders replaced them. By the 1969 congress, this rejuvenation was nearly complete. Perhaps most important, however, was the radical revision of the church statute's content and tone into a more clearly congregational polity with a stronger affirmation of the centrality of witnessing to the gospel.[28]

Between the two congresses, unity talks had been held with the reformers. These produced a clearer understanding of differences in approaches to separation from the state, but reconciliation eluded the negotiators. Another factor causing the loss of support for the reformers after 1966 was the perceived intransigence of Kriuchkov and Vins, who demanded abject apologies from the AUCECB while maintaining that they had nothing to apologize for. In various localities, individual Initsiativniki activists were viewed as problem personalities, too eager for a struggle with the state because of their lack of proper Christian meekness. In other localities, however, the deep spirituality, personal courage, and loving spirit of an Initsiativniki martyr engendered respect and admiration.

Following the ouster of Khrushchev in 1964, the state's antireligious program was reviewed and modified to focus more on education, although the number of religious prisoners continued to rise till 1968. Gradually a policy pattern set in whereby the registered AUCECB with its member churches received concessions to engage in religious practices with less state interference, whereas the CCECB and its churches were subjected to the brunt of state pressure. That pressure included surveillance of leaders, reporting on worship services, and informing school administrators of the names of children who attended church services. It also included threats to deprive parents of parental rights, in several cases actually removing children to state orphanages. Also, there were many cases of physical abuse, a few leading to death.

Thanks to samizdat and increased travel into the Soviet Union during the era of détente, this church-state conflict became more exposed to world public opinion. In 1974, when Georgi Vins was caught (having worked in secret since 1970) and put on trial, a major international campaign developed to appeal for his release and for increased religious rights. The international effort included public letters, statements, and appeals by a number of ecumenical leaders, in contrast to the more muted voice of the wcc after 1961 when the Soviet churches had become members. In 1975 the legislation on cults was revised.[29] Although the laws were still extremely restrictive, this action marked the beginning of a period of stabilization in church-state relations that lasted until the era of perestroika.

One result coming out of the years 1960–75 was the formation of two opposing responses by the Christian public in the West. Dissenters and their so-called underground churches were hailed as the true church that needed support, the AUCECB being labeled a puppet of the regime. Numerous mission societies sprang up, promising to smuggle Bibles and send financial aid. The AUCECB, on the other hand, through its growing contacts at the wcc and among fellow denominational bodies abroad, gained the friendship and support of people who sought to apply quiet diplomacy to improve their situation. The AUCECB's gains included the right to import small quantities of Bibles and to send a few students to theological seminaries in the West.

A further motivation for some Christians in the peace movement was the fostering of closer relations with the officially approved Soviet churches as a way of reducing international tensions. These peace activists felt that support of the human rights campaign served the political interests of the Western anticommunist, or anti-Soviet, lobby. Some writers began to see this dichotomy as necessary; one was either for peace and supported the registered church, or one was for human rights and supported the unregistered church.[30] This partisanship played into the hands of both Soviet and Western political interests. By the mid-eighties, however, the situation had changed when both citizen diplomats and church leaders became active on behalf of both human rights and peace, and the rhetoric of perestroika also began to acknowledge the need for both.

Denominationalism and Stabilization, 1975–1985

Only after the retirement of the long-time chairman of the Council of Religious Affairs, Vladimir A. Kuroedov (in office 1960–84), did his successor, Konstantin Kharchev, publicly acknowledge that neither the churches nor religious belief were likely to disappear in the immediate future.[31] Therefore, a modus vivendi had to be found that went beyond grudging toleration of this "pernicious vestige" of the past; ways had to develop through which communist and Christian citizens could coexist and cooperate on mutual concerns. That was one indicator of a most remarkable change in the church-state relationship under perestroika, but the thinking was not as new as it seemed. This more realistic recognition of the persistence of religion, of the possibility of differentiation between socially progressive and conservative churches, and of the need for dialogue had been evident for several decades in some of the East European states, most notably the GDR and Hungary. Also in the mid-seventies, there was a worldwide recognition that nongovernmental organizations could play a valuable role in Third World development and in education for peace and justice. Finally, it is fair to describe the 1975–85 decade as a period when Soviet policy toward religion was making de facto adjustments to this reality while still retaining its hostile rhetoric.

Normal or stable relations between church and state—true for both Orthodoxy and Protestantism—involved a relationship of hostile state supremacy over the churches.[32] That relationship involved clearly established limits to religious activity, which was basically understood as satisfying the need for religious ritual within the confines of specially designated buildings.[33] For example, regulations assumed the need for a local congregation to submit an application for state registration that accepted a readiness to abide by legislation. The understandings included permission for regularly stated worship in a prayer house that met health and safety standards and did not violate zoning considerations. For evangelicals, services usually consisted of two hours of worship three times on Sunday and three evenings during the week. Locally licensed pastors and regionally licensed superintendents were free to work within their jurisdictions, but they needed permission from the plenipotentiary of the Council of Religious Affairs (CRA) to exercise their office outside that jurisdiction. The CRA usually was informed about baptisms and ordinations. Sometimes that notice required a list of names (certainly with regard to ordination candidates), and sometimes only the number of people involved.

Stabilization also involved a slow but steady granting of small concessions. Every year, a few more congregations were registered, and permission was given to renovate a few church buildings. In most cases, these approvals came through after years of appeal. The number of copies of *Bratskii Vestnik* increased from 3,000 to 5,000 to 8,000, and then to 10,000 at the beginning of perestroika. A modest literature plan became evident as the AUCECB secured permission to publish several thousand Bibles, or New Testaments, then a songbook, then a license to import some Bibles, then the right to again print a few thousand, and so on. It gave the membership (or at least the broader leadership who knew

about the negotiations) a sense of minor but steady progress. Throughout the decade, the membership's expectations and demands increased.
By 1979, members were asking the central leadership for a special department to meet the needs of younger believers. Five years later, they were
more articulate in requesting religious education materials for children.
In this way, the de facto religious activity of the AUCECB churches
stretched well beyond the limits of legislation on religion—state authorities giving tacit approval or else granting special permission for specific
activities.

These concessions need to be understood in light of the state's two-
pronged policy toward religion. Although the policy had emerged earlier, after 1975 there were explicit statements in popular publications
indicating that registered churches (and approved central church organizations) were free to practice their religion, but specific churches were
designated as illegal and their leaders were prosecuted.[34] These illegal
churches included the Initsiativniki (or CCECB) whose general secretary,
Georgi Vins, was in prison (until 1979 when he was deported to the
United States in exchange for a Soviet spy) and whose president, Gennadi Kriuchkov, was hiding. Other illegal churches whose activities were
to be suppressed were dissident wings of the Adventists and Pentecostals, and the Jehovah's Witnesses as a group. These last three denominations began developing their own samizdat, which gained them greater
recognition in world public opinion, but their key leaders were in prison.
Pentecostals in particular demanded the right to emigrate for reasons of
religious freedom. This appeal was dramatized by seven Pentecostals
from Siberia who gained extended refuge in the American embassy
(1978–83) before authorities permitted their gradual departure.[35]

For these illegal Protestant churches, the years 1979 through 1984
became a major time of persecution. With the ouster of Vins in 1979, the
number of Baptist prisoners again began to climb from a low of thirty-
three to eventually reach 150. These groups also suffered as a result of the
new cold war and the fact that Soviet authorities no longer tried to cultivate favorable public opinion in the West, by easing up on dissent, as had
been true under détente.During this period, most dissident movements
were crushed through the imprisoning of their leaders, the forced emigration of other church spokesmen, and the more frightening tech-
nique of incarcerating members in psychiatric hospitals where they were
forced to endure drug injections to induce behavior modification. KGB
interrogation was brutal, and the majority of prisoners returned with
their health broken. Such heavy-handed treatment caused a weakening
in the network of cooperation between dissident and human rights

movements, which created an atmosphere of resignation and hopeless-ness.[36]

The CCECB's situation was affected in another way by this dual-pronged policy. When many Protestant believers continued to resist joining the AUCECB as the only permitted Protestant denomination, but also refused to join the CCECB, authorities began granting registration to locally autonomous congregations. The first group to register was a Men-nonite congregation in 1967, but registration became more generalized in the mid-seventies. An increasing number of Pentecostal congregations registered independently. In both situations, congregations were en-couraged to relate to their cobelievers abroad through the AUCECB's international department, and the AUCECB was encouraged to share its small shipments of literature with these churches, even inviting a few of their leaders to study in a theological correspondence course.

Some CCECB leaders began suggesting registration to their congrega-tions, particularly since the authorities were not insisting on strict ad-herence to the law on cults, provided that a minimal normalization through registration was achieved. Kriuchkov opposed all such adapta-tions and developed a highly authoritarian leadership style. Primarily because of the lack of systematic leadership, nearly all of the original CCECB members over the course of the decade were ousted from the organization or left of their own accord. In 1983 such churches formed an extremely loose association on the basis of a memorandum on principles. They are now known as the Autonomous ones (*Avtonomnyi*), or Autono-mous ECB churches.[37]

The new denominationalism among Protestants during this period had several causes. After the war, Soviet Lutheranism was reintroduced by virtue of the annexation of Estonia and Latvia, republics that included large national Lutheran churches. The Lutherans' church life was per-mitted to continue, but it was controlled by means of ensuring a church leadership selection procedure acceptable to Soviet authorities.[38] This step proved to be comparatively less debilitating to the Baltic Lutherans than to the Baptists, because Latvians and Estonians (and a smaller number of Lithuanian Lutherans) conducted affairs in their own lan-guages, which few Russian officials bothered to learn. Baptist unions in Estonia and Latvia also retained considerable autonomy, and the Ini-tsiativniki split never affected them to the extent that it did in the Ukrai-nian and Russian republics. Nevertheless, all of these groups experi-enced steady, negative pressure from state authorities.

The German Lutherans and Mennonites had a more unusual experi-ence. Following the forcible resettlement of all Germans in Siberia and

Central Asia in September 1941 as a response to the Nazi invasion, a special administration of these deported nations was established, known as the *Spetskomandatura*, or Deportation Regime.[39] Following the war, 280,000 forcibly repatriated Soviet Germans were added to these settlements, making a total of 1.25 million people living under a special command that functioned like forced labor camps. The Soviet Germans lost all civil rights and had to report their location monthly to a special command. Restrictions on movement prevented families from being reunited or any systematic networking between groups. For a generation of children it was common to grow up without a father (who had disappeared in the camps or died during the war) and without education, resulting in a high illiteracy rate among Soviet Germans who are now in their fifties. This Deportation Regime dealt a debilitating blow to German culture and religion. When the *Spetskomandatura* was dismantled in 1956 and the Soviet Germans received identity papers again, they began to reestablish communities through seeking out relatives and fellow church members. Since Soviet Germans were forced to sign a promise never to return to their old homes, their major settlements were to be found throughout northern Kazakhstan (where many had worked in the mines) and southwestern Siberia, as well as smaller groupings in Kirgizia, Uzbekistan, and Tadzhikistan. Forty thousand of the approximately 1.8 million Soviet Germans immediately applied for permission to emigrate to West Germany, but without success. It was long estimated that up to 80 percent of the Soviet Germans would emigrate if they could, and popular discrimination against them as fascists was fostered by the Soviet press till the mid-eighties.

Soviet German Lutherans were in a sorry state, with only two pastors, Eugen Bachman in Tselinograd (1957–72) and Johannes Schlundt in Prokhladnyi (1971–73), to provide services.[40] Both of them were able to emigrate in the early seventies. After considerable negotiation by the European secretary for the Lutheran World Federation, Paul Hansen, the CRA granted permission in 1980 for a Latvian pastor, Harald Kalnins of Riga, to visit the Central Asian German Lutherans and function as their superintendent. From 1957 to 1985, around 250 congregations were registered, and permission to import a few thousand German Bibles and songbooks was secured. After August 1991 the German Evangelical Lutheran Church in the Soviet Union (DELKSU) found itself challenged by a new United Evangelical-Lutheran Church based in St. Petersburg and claiming twenty-six congregations. The latter, headed by Latvian Joseph Baronas and funded by the Russian record firm "Melodia," may not last but pressure is on for the Riga-based DELKSU to move closer to the four hundred congregations (and up to 500,000 members) spread across Russia and Central Asia. DELKSU was able to launch the fifth session of its theological seminary in Riga during October 1991 with eight students from the RSFSR and Kazakhstan appearing, three more expected in spring 1992, and four German Lutherans coming from the Ukraine.[41]

Mennonites attempted to worship wherever they could. Some of them were exposed to the religious revival in the postwar years, but the major religious renewal came in 1956 with the dismantling of the *Spetsko-mandatura* and the return of ordained ministers from the labor camps. The rebuilding of the Mennonites as a denomination proved to be difficult. The Mennonite Brethren came to be the group's larger wing, due in part to many new converts being baptized by immersion (the Baptist way) and fitting in with the general ECB milieu. The Church Mennonites (*Kirchliche*) retained the more traditional form of adult baptism by effusion, a form that the ECB churches refused to recognize. Hence, once the disregarding of denominational differences that had characterized the initial postwar religious revival movement had passed, it became necessary for the Church Mennonites to organize their own churches. Certainly, many clergy returning from prison came with a sharper sense of denominational identity than was true for the average believer.[42]

It was obvious to these leaders that some intrachurch structure was necessary to deal with the task of establishing regular contact with scattered groups. A representative of the Mennonite World Conference who visited the Soviet Union in 1956 was unable to visit local communities but did meet with several Mennonite leaders who came to Moscow. The latter were encouraged to seek needed assistance from the AUCECB and to try to resume contact with Mennonites wherever they might be found. Several *Kirchliche* leaders did meet in Solikamsk (Urals) in 1957 to form a Mennonite Church union, but the authorities ended the effort by arresting the union's leaders.[43] All that remained were individual ministers and elders (bishops), such as Heinrich Voth, Johann Penner, Hans Penner, and Aron Thiessen, who made private visits, secretly baptizing, conducting communion, and giving counsel.

After the Khrushchev era, these independent Mennonite congregations gradually emerged and applied for local registration. The first congregations to receive registration were in Karaganda, Novosibirsk, and Tokmak. Others were granted filial status as part of an ECB-registered congregation that met in the same building. A similar arrangement developed with accommodating Methodist and Baptist congregations in Latvia and Estonia. By 1980, most of these congregations had obtained

their own meetinghouses and separate registrations; in the case of the
Baltic, however, the Mennonite contingent had dissolved because of
emigration to West Germany. There also were several instances where a
local congregation was technically ECB, but included German Lutherans
and Mennonites, all of them agreeing to recognize each other and to
include certain traditional distinctions, such as their manner of conducting communion.

Social Demographic Aspects

If Protestants in the Soviet Union originally included both lower-class
and middle-class strata, this changed after World War II. Although officially all citizens were now either workers or peasants, discrimination
aimed at all religious persons ensured that adherents were almost invariably the least advantaged in society. In contrast to the process of a
congregation's relatively rapid upward movement into the middle class,
as was characteristic of Western neo-Protestant churches such as Baptists, Methodists, Salvation Army, and mainline Pentecostals, in the
Soviet Union Protestantism remained a religion of the lower class. Most
of the intelligentsia who became Christians in the 1980s joined the Orthodox Church since, culturally speaking, the AUCECB churches were
not attractive enough.

Soviet Protestantism as a whole did not significantly differ from the
overall demographic picture of religious concentrations. In terms of
religious denominations, the Western border regions continued to be the
most active. Half of all evangelicals (whether AUCECB, CCECB, or autonomous) were located in the Ukraine, primarily the western half. Another
30 percent were scattered across the vast RSFSR, with pockets of concentration in the regions around Moscow and extending south to the
Ukraine, and on to Rostov and the Caucasus, the Volga region, and the
Novosibirsk and Altai regions. A highly active movement developed in
the twenties in the Far East as a result of the exile system and active
missionary activity. Much of that movement went underground, congregations reemerging after Stalin's death in a much more restrained
climate than in the central USSR. At that time, a major contingent of
independent Pentecostals moved to the Far East. There, they experienced more antireligious excesses of a brutal nature than their fellow
Pentecostals in the central regions. It is from these ranks that the most
persistent campaign to emigrate from the Soviet Union for reasons of

religious freedom has developed; more than five thousand succeeded in leaving the Soviet Union after 1987.[44]

Soviet scholars maintained that the rapid growth of Protestant sectarianism during the first decade of Soviet power came largely from the kulak class of peasants, an argument that supported the claim that the sectarians made up an opposition movement to the communists.[45] Those claims may be modified once scholarship becomes less subject to party interests. It is true, however, that by the communists charging many adherents with being kulaks, the movement was spread across Siberia and Kazakhstan through forced exile or deportation.

The initial spurt in growth in the postwar years was interpreted as a response to the general social and economic crisis occasioned by the war's ravages and traumas. Many returned to the apparent solace of religious groups that retained vestiges of the past. The dominant theme of the literature of the later sixties was to claim that the evangelical movement was aging and younger people were not joining because they had become secularized. Such views caused a part of the leadership to become alarmed and to launch an effort to rejuvenate their ranks by offering more enticements to children and young people. The more law-abiding and established leadership resisted this approach; hence came the Initsiativniki split.

New regional field studies in the mid-seventies forced three inescapable conclusions.[46] It had been thought that urbanization and industrialization would produce a modernized population liberated from religious vestiges. If the Soviet population in 1917 was largely rural (82 percent), by the mid-seventies more than 60 percent were urbanized. The urbanites also were better-educated. Yet regional studies showed that evangelical congregations were primarily urban, and such urban evangelicals were active proselytizers, relying on religious education in the home (Mennonite families apparently being most active in this sphere) and outside musical events designed to attract young adherents. If the growth in the twenties and the fifties had come from Orthodox families, during the late sixties and early seventies families of atheists were the major source of new members. In short, during the seventies the number of male congregation members increased more rapidly than females; the number of younger people and those with middle-level education (high school and trade school graduates) also increased, and this growth primarily occurred in urban congregations.[47]

These conclusions resulted in renewed theoretical work to develop new explanations for the persistence of religion. Such explanations in-

cluded a stronger emphasis on the role of historical tradition in producing sectarian loyalty, an obvious answer for the retention of children
of believing families once those children reached adulthood and had to
initiate baptism for themselves. Further, Soviet society's pace of modernization was seen as contributing to the emergence of new sects that
sought a more satisfying religious experience to compensate for the
strains of keeping pace with progress. One increasingly prominent sociologist of religion, D. M. Ugrinovich, began drawing on Weberian ty-
pologies applied to American denominationalism to differentiate among
the diverse Protestant sects and to locate them along a spectrum between
church and sect types.[48] In terms of structure and degree of accommodation to the surrounding society, he delineated four discrete groups. The
first and most nonconformist included dissident movements such as the
CCECB, Reform Pentecostals, and Adventists. Less aggressive but still
highly nonconformist were the Molokany and Subbotniki. Most of the
autonomously registered societies such as the Mennonites, Pentecostals,
Adventists, and Methodists fit into a third group, thus leaving only
the AUCECB as having reached a stage of social and political conformity sufficient to warrant anticipation of their continued transformation
through the influence of secularization into a church culture of the
socially progressive.

No major work on sectarianism in the former USSR has appeared
since 1980, but further developments have occurred in sociological theory. Ugrinovich began examining the psychology of religion, allowing
for the religious personality type.[49] Studies of the impact of religion on
politics around the world resulted in greater differentiation of not only
religious confessions, but of groups within a specific confession differ-
entiating into more progressive or less progressive wings. Finally, although not yet evident in the academic literature, public acknowledgment since perestroika began of the persecution of believers under Stalin
and Khrushchev and of discrimination under Brezhnev may produce
an even more nuanced treatment of the increasing diversity of Soviet
Protestantism.

Peace and Dialogue

Shortly after the Russian Revolution, many Protestant bodies took an
official position in favor of pacifism. Joint efforts, in which the role of the
Tolstoyan V. G. Chertkov was crucial, resulted in an agreement whereby
members of a religious association could apply for an alternative to mili-

tary service. If their request was approved by a review board (which included leading Protestant church members), then a term in the forestry or similar national service was assigned. This provision did not last beyond 1930, the authorities making it increasingly difficult for anyone to be approved, and the law was officially withdrawn as being unnecessary in 1936. Between 1923 and 1929, the national church congresses of the Baptists, Evangelical Christians, Pentecostals, and Adventists were forced to rewrite their statutes to remove pacifist statements. The state viewed this concession as the litmus test of loyalty. In all three unions, feeling was so strong that a majority vote to reject pacifism was passed only after heavy state pressure was brought to bear. That included the temporary imprisonment of one leader, the removal of a dozen of the most intransigent opponents from the Baptists' congress hall by the secret police, and other private threats. Small schisms developed but did not endure subsequent persecution.[50]

The Mennonites were a historic peace church who had long enjoyed the privilege of freedom from military service. When that option became impossible after 1874, they secured the right to alternative service, with the church financing the forestry service.[51] Unfortunately, the ravages of the Civil War in 1918–19 caused some Mennonites in south Russia to organize an armed self-defense league. This organization saw limited action, proved to be ineffective in defending women and children from marauding bands, and was forced at various times into the Red and White armies. Such resorts to self-defense were subsequently rejected by Mennonite leaders, many of whom had warned against it all along, but the experience served to cast doubt on the integrity of the religious basis of Mennonite pacifism since that conviction had been abandoned when the loss of property was at stake. In 1925 a Mennonite appeal for freedom from military service was rejected. After 1930, Mennonite men were forced to serve except during the *Komandantura* years (1945–56) when they were disenfranchised along with other Germans.

With the new beginning for Soviet evangelicals in 1944 as the AUCECB, its leaders quickly set the tone by stressing the loyal service that evangelicals had rendered to defending the motherland "with weapon in hand," an oft-repeated phrase in the next years. The declaration of 1926 urging members to obey the authorities and to serve when called were regularly reprinted in *Bratskii Vestnik*, and the pacifist affirmations of a few years earlier were officially forgotten. As the cold war settled in, AUCECB leaders joined other Soviet clergy in vociferous affirmations of support for Soviet foreign policy, which they declared to be peaceful, whereas the Western powers, in particular the United States under the leadership of a Baptist president (Truman), were accused of imperialist expansionism. This uncritical support of Soviet foreign policy, which church leaders in the West generally viewed as expansionist because of Soviet domination of Eastern Europe, caused them to doubt the Soviet clergy's integrity. The Soviet clergy, it appeared, had accepted the necessity of mouthing Soviet peace propaganda in exchange for a further lease on church life. This situation began a slow change, especially after 1956 when a visiting National Council of Churches delegation had a frank exchange with Metropolitan Nikolai.[52]

In subsequent years it was commonly expected that including a peace theme in an international conference declaration made it easier for a Soviet delegation to return home. Seldom, however, were issues of war and peace debated theologically and substantively as they applied to the international situation. Gradually, such conferences contributed to making the Soviet Baptist leadership better-informed about the Soviet side of the nuclear armaments race, as well as that of the West. The Vancouver Assembly of the WCC (1983) marks a turning point, coming as it did at the height of a new European peace movement that was drawing peace activists East and West, official and unofficial, into new alignments. Soviet churchmen, including the AUCECB representatives, signed a statement calling for a halt to nuclear armaments on both sides.

This European peace movement involved a major role for the churches, which not only joined the chorus of groups arguing that the current MAD policy had lost political effectiveness, but began to make nuclear pacifism an issue of *status confessionis*.[53] This theological rejection of the East/West nuclear confrontation resonated in Soviet church circles. Their general drift was supported by the shift in Soviet military thinking toward the doctrine of sufficiency, with both Soviet and Western churchmen affirming Gorbachev's published statements calling for "New Thinking" in international relations on the basis of shared universal values to preserve the globe, and also affirming his rejection of nuclear war as an instrument of diplomacy.[54]

Under perestroika, Soviet churchmen, including Protestants, participated in dialogues with Marxist atheists. These dialogues involved church leaders invited to meet with local dignitaries to explain their moral teaching as it applied to personal morality, with the Marxists showing positive interest in the reasons why evangelical families had fewer broken marriages, why their young people rejected drugs, and how alcoholism was avoided. Another approach recognized the necessity for Marxists and Christians to coexist in the nuclear age and to undertake a search for common universal moral values. In other words, a common concern for peace placed dialogue between Christians and Marxists on a different plane than was true in two earlier dialogues involving evangelicals.[55]

In the early twenties, there had been public disputations or dialogues between Christians and atheists which had taken place with the purpose of liberating people from religious bondage by demonstrating the inadequacy of religious belief in a scientific world. No doubt successful on many occasions, there were able defenders of belief in both Orthodox and Protestant circles. One Baptist participant, V. F. Martsinkovskii, was widely respected as an able and eloquent defender of Christian faith.[56] These debates soon were terminated by the authorities.

At the end of the Khrushchev era, several exchanges took place between Baptists and state authorities that have been labeled dialogue, although incorrectly so.[57] Finally, the authorities agreed to receive an Initsiativniki delegation that presented evidence of abuse of their religious freedoms. A number of participants had hoped to present their understanding of the gospel to the authorities, to win them over; instead, some of them were arrested and others were prevented from meeting. Neither of these memories of "dialogue" was positive, which helps to account for the minimal interest that Soviet evangelicals (as well as the Orthodox) showed in Christian-Marxist dialogue. On the other hand, Soviet Marxism was singularly heavy-handed toward any deviation from officially approved lines of philosophy, making its representatives rather uninteresting partners for dialogue with Western Christian scholars.

Religious Perestroika Begins with Millennium Celebrations

Between the death of Brezhnev (November 1982) and the election of Gorbachev (March 1985), uncertainties arose about the future of the churches. A new antireligious drive as part of an effort to rejuvenate community ideology appeared possible.[58] Another disturbing sign was the growing number of cases where a religious prisoner was resentenced on a new charge before completing a term. The appointment of Kharchev as chairman of the CRA (1984) sounded positive, but the first signs of a more friendly policy toward religion involved relatively unimportant matters such as the publication of Gingis Aitmatov's novel in spite of the positive image of a believer in it, or Yevgeny Yevtushenko calling for broader access to the Bible as necessary for understanding world literature. In his bestseller, *Perestroika . . .* , appearing on the eve of his visit to the United States, Gorbachev quoted part of a letter from a Lithuanian Catholic who promised to pray for him. By then, Gorbachev's position seemed increasingly secure, and expectations for applying perestroika to religion grew, with preparations for the millennium of Christianity in Russia now gaining state support.

The celebration of the millennium produced precedent after precedent.[59] It began with the opening of the Danilov monastery as Orthodox headquarters and publishing center, including permission to publish 100,000 Russian Bibles. The Protestants received permission to import 100,000 Russian Bibles, 10,000 German Bibles for Mennonites, 5,000 for Lutherans, 8,000 Latvian Bibles, and permission to publish a new translation of the Bible in Georgian. The AUCECB also received 5,000 sets of the fifteen-volume New Testament commentary by William Barclay in Russian. Next came permission for the Orthodox to receive 10,000 copies of the Lopukhin Study Bible (three volumes), and then a further order for a staggering 150,000 copies of the same. These orders nearly doubled the total number of Bibles printed or officially imported since 1945.[60] Then the AUCECB senior presbyters for the Ukrainian and RSFSR republics began submitting requests for literature. Permission was granted to import 100,000 Ukrainian Bibles, 20,000 songbooks (Ukrainian), and 50,000 concordances in Russian. Also surprising was permission to import 50,000 copies of a children's Bible storybook. When all of this literature was tallied (not counting what was sent privately in the mails), it became evident that in 1987 and 1988 a total of 2.1 million Bibles and New Testaments had been sent or printed.[61]

Whereas the Soviet press and television provided quite amazing coverage of the Orthodox millennium celebrations in Moscow and Kiev, in many other cities there were numerous unheralded celebrations organized by all of the religious groups. For the Protestants, these celebrations included inviting foreign radio evangelists who spoke to large crowds in public squares. There were riverside baptismal services attended by thousands, with fifty to seventy believers baptized at a time, and often more than a hundred new converts resulted from such open meetings. Such events happened in numerous locations and usually included the cooperation of several churches; even AUCECB ministers and autonomous Baptists shared the preaching. In one instance, the evangelicals in Tallinn rented an ice arena seating ten thousand. The arena filled within minutes. Leaders then invited the believers in the crowd to step forward to make room for more of the unbelievers eager to enter. After two thousand stepped forward, the authorities opened the doors and allowed more people to stream in.[62]

The "Process of Evangelization"

It was common in 1989 for Soviet church leaders to preface their remarks about the religious situation by saying that the Soviet Union was now in the "process of evangelization." Mainly, this had to do with Bibles and other literature. After the initial inundation of 1988, people from all levels of society were demanding a copy of the Bible to read for themselves. That is, such new readers were experiencing their first confrontation with the Evangel, and from those reactions everything else flowed. Soviet Evangelicals, especially the loosely organized group of Autonomous ECB churches, and often in local or even national cooperation with the AUCECB, organized preaching missions. These included foreign speakers such as Luis Palau; James Irwin, the American astronaut; and Bill Bright of Campus Crusade. But many other less famous speakers preached in rented stadiums and arenas, or to large masses of people in the open air, inviting the tens of thousands of listeners to respond to a gospel invitation. Gospel tracts or even New Testaments were distributed in massive numbers, and still the appeal for more literature would not let up. Mass baptisms became common throughout the summers of 1989 and 1990.

In April 1989, Soviet postal authorities removed restrictions on individuals receiving packets from abroad that contained religious literature. Very quickly, warehouses in the West containing Russian language literature were depleted. After August 1989 it was no longer necessary to secure special permits to import religious books. One mission society, long associated with the ECB fellowships, started sending one three-ton truck of literature a month. Visitors to church headquarters in Moscow or Kiev found all of the available staff in a nearly constant flurry as they hurried to unload shipments, tried to find storage space in corridors, or in and around the church pews, and then reloaded the literature into cars or suitcases for people from other cities who had been sent to pick up their share of the supply.

By the summer of 1990, church leaders were heard to say that they often felt literally torn apart by people coming to them from all sides to ask questions about faith. A villager, for example, would ask the evangelicals in a nearby city to visit his village and bring along a group of singers and a speaker. Vice president Bychkov and editor Kulikov of the Baptist Union found themselves invited to give ten-minute sermons on Moscow radio on a monthly basis. When in June 1990 the Baptist vice president for evangelism called a national conference, pastors from all over the Soviet Union reported invitations they were receiving to speak on Christianity to university professors or their classes, or to lecture at institutions of higher learning. When many of them expressed their insecurity at addressing the educated of society, Nikolai Kolesnikov reminded them of the intent of those invitations. These poorly trained pastors or simple church members claimed to have a personal relationship with Jesus Christ, and that was what their listeners wanted to hear about, not a scholarly dissertation on the nature of transcendence or proofs for the existence of God. The task of these church people was to explain the differences that their faith in Christ made in their lives.

The process of evangelization, in essence, was acquainting unbelievers with the nature of the gospel; all Christian confessions were involved in explaining their faith to seekers. Many new converts were individuals who now chose to make public their earlier secret belief; others responded to the Christians they met with requests for baptism. Statistically speaking, a minority of the population was converting, and, of these, the vast majority became Orthodox. Soviet evangelicals were highly systematic in outreach and received disproportionate assistance with literature and even personnel from abroad. In October 1990 the Lausanne Committee for Evangelism conducted a congress in Moscow for Soviet evangelists, of whom the majority were Protestants. The influx of new members was already sufficiently large to create an initial anxiety about the capacity of these Protestant congregations to culturally adapt themselves to their new members.

Protestants and Nationalism Under Perestroika

Glasnost and perestroika encouraged new thinking among Protestants. Most surprising was the Rebirth and Renewal movement among Latvian Lutherans.[63] A Latvian theology student named Maris Ludviks who was having difficulty being ordained, apparently because of his religious activism with young people, asked the Lithuanian Lutheran Bishop Kalvanas to perform the ceremony. When a Latvian newspaper attacked Ludviks, calling him a black marketeer and former juvenile delinquent, the rector of the Lutheran correspondence seminary, Propst/Dean Modris Plate (age thirty-six), and four other leading clergymen issued a protest to the paper. They argued that the attack was not in keeping with the new thinking and openness advocated by Gorbachev. The response to their action was that the Latvian Council for Religious Affairs (CRA) pressured the consistory and Archbishop Mesters to dismiss Plate.

At first, the consistory asked the CRA to reconsider, since Plate was popular and respected in the seminary and in the congregation he was pastoring. In March 1987 the consistory did suspend him, whereupon open letters in his support were sent to the archbishop. One letter was signed by nineteen clergymen, another by five, both praising Plate's qualities as a pastor and teacher. The signatories included the seminary rector, four lecturers, and three deans. In spite of this response, the consistory bowed to CRA pressure and reconfirmed his dismissal as both dean and pastor.

In June 1987 Plate and fourteen other leaders (who included the seminary rector, Roberts Akmentins, and two other deans) formally founded a group called Rebirth and Renewal with the declared aim "to defend openly the right of Latvians to lead a Christian life." They presented "a few points" to the archbishop and the consistory, asking them to propose the following revisions to the Latvian Law on Religious Associations. These changes included: "the issue of alternatives to military service for religious believers, religious instruction for children, legal rights for the church, the possibility of religious radio and television programs, the publication of more religious literature and the authorization of religious activities in hospitals and old people's homes."[64]

Further, the group explained its activities as an effort to halt the further decline of the Latvian Lutheran Church. From a prewar membership of more than 1 million, the church had declined to 350,000 in 1980, of which, Rebirth and Renewal claimed, only about 25,000 were regular communicants. A crucial problem was the shortage of clergy. Since this movement also participated in national demonstrations against the annexation of Latvia, and in commemorating Latvians deported by Stalin to labor camps, the consistory refused to identify with it. Plate was dismissed as lecturer as well as pastor; the rector was dismissed; and another dean, Aivars Beimanis, was deprived of his position. To forestall further protests by faculty and students, courses were temporarily suspended. By now, the movement had become known through samizdat so that in addition to pressure on the consistory from local clergy and the CRA, there was pressure from Lutherans abroad, including a visit from the general secretary of the Lutheran World Federation, Gunnar Staalstett, to discuss the matter.

Although some of the first activists on this issue—such as Ludviks—emigrated with permission of the authorities (December 1987), a change in the consistory's attitude occurred. In January 1988 Plate was permitted to resume his duties as pastor. The stern reprimand to the rector, Akmentins, was withdrawn, and Plate was permitted to lecture, although he was not restored as dean. Somewhat later, a sympathizer with Rebirth and Renewal was appointed "pastor of the youth movement" of the Latvian Lutheran Church, a position still illegal according to the old law on religion.

Finally, in April 1989 the general synod of the Latvian Lutheran Church voted the entire consistory and Archbishop Mesters out of office, replacing them with Karlis Gailitis as new archbishop and a consistory of eight persons, all from Rebirth and Renewal. They included Plate and Akmentins. Archbishop Gailitis soon thereafter placed an advertisement in the newspaper inviting young people interested in the pastorate to apply for a new, intensive six-month theology course intended to train pastoral assistants.[65] Still another action of the synod was a resolution to the Latvian government, based on the Christian conviction of overcoming evil with good, to permit conscientious objectors to do alternative service. It is a fascinating story reminiscent of the goals and actions of Orthodox and Baptist dissent during the sixties, but here the apparently positive outcome resulted from appeals to glasnost and New Thinking. Indeed, the newly appointed plenipotentiary for religious affairs, Alfred Kublinskis, gave a lengthy speech in which he indicated that the church would have access to the media, stating that "religion is a social necessity." He concluded by apologizing for all of the injustices that the state and his office had done to the church, promising not to interfere in church affairs again.[66]

Rebirth and Renewal was closely linked to the revival of Latvian nationalism. Those linkages made possible the organization of the Latvian Christian Mission as an ecumenical service agency. Volunteers were soon working in hospitals and prisons as visiting chaplains. A newly appointed director of Sunday school education for children was able to spell out her vision for religious education in the national newspaper. As the de facto independence of Latvia drew nearer, the churches received back confiscated church buildings and the liberty to organize church schools.

The Estonian Lutheran church did not experience as much drama. Nevertheless, at its synod on 12–13 June 1990, major changes were undertaken in contrast to previous years of regimented and controlled debate and excessive state controls.[67] Presiding in addition to Archbishop Kuno Päjula was Propst Einar Soone of Tallinn. The newly elected consistory had only two former members in it. In contrast to a year earlier, the church's ninety pastors in 1989 conducted seven times as many baptisms and confirmations. Pastors no longer had to pay a higher income tax rate. The synod decided to prepare a new church statute without waiting for a new state constitution to guide them. The Peace Fund, for which the state had insisted on voluntary donations, was now redirected to church purposes, with each local congregation able to determine how funds were to be applied. Religious material could be printed without a censor's review—only paper was in short supply. The Estonian Lutheran Church was allowed to broadcast a fifteen-minute Sunday morning prayer on radio, plus church news every second Sunday, and television carried a series on "The Book of Books." In addition, organized worship services were permitted in hospitals, counseling in senior citizen homes, and the first national Estonian Christian youth gathering since 1939 took place in June 1990.

For the approximately 250,000 practicing German Lutherans in the Soviet Union (out of 1.2 million ethnic Germans of Lutheran origin), the new openness encouraged further progress. On 13 November 1988, Harald Kalnins of Riga was ordained bishop of the 250 registered German Lutheran congregations, most of which were located in the Asiatic part of the former USSR.[68] Kalnins had officially begun a ministry as superintendent for these German congregations in 1980. Perhaps more significant than this personal honor was the fact that twenty preachers received some supervisory right that could lead to more networking between locally registered associations.[69] Yet these promising changes came too late for many Soviet Germans. The shift in official attitude and policy toward the emigration of Jews, Germans, and other groups, which began in February 1987, produced a major new wave of emigration. Churches that had grown in membership fairly rapidly during the early 1980s were suddenly reduced to less than half their size. New converts among the Soviet Germans temporarily replaced those who had emigrated, but pastors found themselves baptizing and marrying couples who already had packed to leave for West Germany. Another issue, the renewed sentiment among Soviet Germans to obtain an autonomous German republic, was of little interest to those Soviet Germans who were actively religious, whether Catholic, Lutheran, or Mennonite; observers (Soviet and Western) tended to agree that the trauma of the *Spetskomandantura* was still too recent a memory for them to join in the rebuilding of Soviet society.

Soviet Mennonites also appeared to have begun their final emigration after February 1987. More than 35,000 of their number had left by the end of 1990. Many of their strongest independent churches in Central Asia were reduced to a remnant. In January 1987 the independent Mennonite Brethren Church of Karaganda had more than a thousand members. Yet four years later, only several hundred were left, with only about twenty families not already in the process of applying for emigration. Still, the remaining Mennonites illustrated what was happening elsewhere. The key leaders who remained were young (under forty) and had some professional training in industry as well as fluency in the Russian language. These leaders chose to organize mission and service projects, and in the process they added more of a Russian-language character to their churches, thus making it easier for non-Germanic converts to join.

In August 1989, Soviet Mennonites organized officially approved celebrations of their bicentennial and received positive coverage in the national press. Instead of merely recounting their history, these celebrations were converted into evangelistic events involving closer cooperation with other evangelicals than had been the case before. Similarly, Soviet Mennonites attending the Mennonite World Conference in Winnipeg, Canada, in July 1990 publicly confessed their own shortcomings and the shortcomings of their forefathers in not having shown sufficient concern for the well-being of Soviet society.

Perestroika of Structure

Much of what has just been described goes well beyond what the legislation on religion would allow. Indeed, since the summer of 1987 a revision of that legislation had been expected. The longer it was delayed the more the expectation grew that it would be a major revision, an expectation confirmed by reports of a consultation with religious leaders in March 1988 where authorities were urged to abandon the 1929 law as part of discredited Stalinism, in favor of a shorter statement of principles similar to the 1918 separation decree. In his interview with the press during the millennium celebrations in June 1988, which received front page coverage, then President Andrei Gromyko freely acknowledged that a revision was in process, but that there were strongly opposing views.[70] Officials from the Council of Religious Affairs began speaking at the end of 1988 as if the old legislation had been abrogated, indicating, for example, that increased charitable work would be part of the activities granted to believers by new legislation, soon to be announced. The worldwide response of assistance after the Armenian earthquake further was a stimulus to permitting religious organizations (local and foreign) to become involved in the rebuilding effort. There was also strong resistance to liberalizing the law. Indeed, local enforcement remained diverse even after official promulgation, and in some local regions the plenipotentiary for religious affairs still functioned as if perestroika had changed nothing.[71]

Soviet evangelicals also submitted their recommendations for new Soviet legislation on religion. By the time the new law was printed for public discussion (June 1990) and then approved by the Supreme Soviet (September 1990) the focus had shifted. If in 1989 many religious leaders were regularly saying that none of the changes could be regarded as achieved until they had been anchored in law, Baptist and Adventist leaders, for example, now stated that the new law seemed acceptable for a time of transition; however they already were looking toward the time when the need for special legislation on religion would have withered away. For most churches, including the Protestant groups, the new religious legislation of 1990 meant the following:

1. Specially designated persons had the right to provide religious education for children, but not in public school facilities.

2. All religious institutions from a congregation with a minimum of ten members to regional and central unions, monasteries, seminaries, etc., whose statute was legally registered, would receive full rights of juridical personhood.

3. Such institutions had the right to hold property, usually tax-free, and the right to engage in business subject to normal taxation.

4. Religious bodies had the right not only to conduct religious services on their own premises, but also in hospitals, homes for seniors, etc., if it were requested and suitable scheduling were worked out with the administration; public meetings should be arranged according to normal procedures for use of buildings and organizing demonstrations.

5. Religious bodies received the unrestricted right to produce, distribute, import, and export religious literature and supplies.

6. Religious bodies had the right to engage in charitable activities as a religious body, or as part of a charity society.

7. Relations with religious bodies abroad (individual or group) were permitted, plus travel and study abroad.

8. People working on salary in a religious institution should now be paid according to a contract, be able to join a union, and become part of the national health and pension system.

9. The powers and obligations of the council for religious affairs were spelled out (here there do not appear to be any significant changes).

Whereas the USSR Law on Freedom of Conscience and Religious Organizations was published in final form on 9 October 1990, the Russian parliament's Law on Freedom of Worship was published 10 November. Similar in spirit but differing in how government bodies of supervision and church associations are defined, the Russian legislation (which presumably remained in force in its territory after the dissolution of the USSR) will likely undergo further revision. By the way, it authorizes the teaching of religious philosophy of "an explanatory nature" in the secular state education system.[72]

Even before this legislation was approved, registration of churches was rapidly proceeding. About 2,900 churches (mainly Orthodox) were registered from 1985 to 1989; by mid-1990 the total for the previous five years was 5,500 (4,100 Orthodox).[73] That development pointed to another prime concern of the Protestants and of the other confessions. Alexei Bychkov reported in October 1988 that the AUCECB union had contributed 750,000 rubles to ten or more local congregations engaged in church building projects. Whereas the architecture of evangelical prayerhouses has been more than simple, there is a noticeable shift to erecting buildings that are visually attractive.[74] Hence the Soviet evangelicals were now under great financial strain to carry out local renovations and new building projects while feeling the need to employ more evangelists and teachers.

In February 1990 the largest of the neo-Protestant churches, the AUCECB, met for its regular national congress.[75] As expected, that congress restructured itself extensively. In keeping with the decentralization theme of perestroika, as well as recognizing the de facto shift to more regional and local independence, the AUCECB became a Union of Evangelical-Christian Baptists (UECB). Abolishing the office of general secretary, the UECB was headed by Grigori I. Komendant (a forty-five-year-old Ukrainian) as president and chief executive officer, assisted by vice presidents for theological education, for evangelism and service, and for financial administration. Senior presbyters of republics were renamed president of regional unions of ECB churches. There was much talk of evangelism and training. But the financial report showed an eroding financial base and the official statistics for membership (which many had claimed at 550,000), after subtracting the Pentecostals who had left in June 1989 and the Germans who had emigrated, now claimed only 204,156 members.[76] Throughout the spring and summer the UECB conducted training sessions for leaders—first nationally, then regionally—to enable it to launch in September 1990 a systematic program of Sunday school instruction for children.

The Pentecostals had always chafed under the restrictions of the August agreement of 1945 by which they were brought into the AUCECB. Many of their number left soon after, more left during the 1980s to register as autonomous Pentecostal congregations. A conference of representatives of unregistered Pentecostal fellowships, meeting in Zagorsk on 17 September 1988 with 150 representatives, failed to agree on a common position toward registration.[77] Finally in June 1989 a separation agreement with the AUCECB was worked out, and the CRA agreed to recognize the Pentecostals as a separate denomination. Thereafter, led by Bronislav I. Bilas (formerly key Pentecostal spokesperson on the AUCECB presidium) they sought to establish an independent structure, in which both former AUCECB Pentecostals and the independent and unregistered would participate. They managed to establish temporary offices in Russia, the Ukraine, Byelorussia, and Moldova, while another Pentecostal group claiming 10,000 adherents in Russia established an office in St. Petersburg.[78] With the assistance of western Pentecostals they organized a Bible school.

Several other Protestant churches of the former USSR made gains in organization. After years of illegal and semilegal existence, the Adventists reached an understanding with the authorities to regularize their relationship. The negotiations of the Adventist world body were helpful as was Kharchev's visit to its headquarters near Washington, D.C. In October 1987 Adventists in the United States and the USSR published a joint issue of a magazine called "Is There Faith in God in Russia?", with 35,000 copies printed in Russian. This included the announcement that a theological course by correspondence was to be started in September 1988. In the meantime, permission had been received to obtain a building in the village of Zaoksi (Tula region) to serve as headquarters for the RSFSR. A modern publishing plant initially negotiated as a joint-venture company (51 percent of the stock owned by the Soviet government and 49 percent by the Review and Herald Publishing Association) finally began operations in 1991. This was to serve the 32,000 Adventists, now led by 178 ordained ministers. Although this innovative action produced generally positive responses among Adventists, one of their number, Roy Branson, editor of *Spectrum*, warned about the anomaly of such increased intimacy between Adventist world leaders and the Soviet government when the latter still held eleven Adventist prisoners of conscience.[79] These are members of the unregistered True and Free Adventists, thought to be as large as the registered body. Branson also pointed out that this illegal body of Adventists "undeniably take positions on not bearing arms in the army and not sending their children to school on Sabbath that are closer to the world Adventist church than to the typical practice of the Soviet Union's officially recognized Adventists."[80]

Nevertheless, the success of the Soviet Adventists quickly became a praiseworthy example. Their modern, technologically sophisticated administrative and educational complex erected in the village of Zaokski, complete with red brick student dormitory and greenhouse, attracted up to a thousand visitors a month. Graduates of their seminary with its well-stocked library returned to their home areas with enough practical training to assist in establishing vegetable and fruit farms to fight hunger directly. By the end of 1988 the prisoners of conscience had been released and the Adventist leaders claimed to be in dialogue with the unregistered body.

Perhaps a bigger challenge was the issue of Soviet Baptist unity after so many years of rivalry. Since 1960, there had been two ECB unions (AUCECB and CCECB), but after 1976 the number of autonomous ECB churches gradually increased. Rejecting the authoritarian leadership of Gennadi Kriuchkov and feeling that a policy of negativism toward the AUCECB did not do justice to the presence of many respected Christians active in that union (nor did it conform to biblical admonitions to reconciliation), these churches decided to remain autonomous after they had been rejected by the CCECB. They soon met with AUCECB leaders for unity talks but without the intention of joining that union; they meant to indicate acceptance of each other in Christian fraternity. By 1988, this movement had grown larger than the CCECB, one knowledgeable visitor reporting that they numbered around 115 congregations with about 20,000 members, compared with 15,000–18,000 CCECB members in about ninety congregations. At the end of 1991 the autonomous ECB were estimated to include at least 25,000 members or 75,000 adherents.[81] At the CCECB congress in July 1989, Kriuchkov, who made a dramatic appearance to address the delegates before returning to hiding, indicated that they would continue to reject registration until new legislation provided guarantees against state interference.

Thus far the autonomous ECB churches have resisted forming a competitive union, feeling a deep suspicion of hierarchical structure. In 1980 several of their leaders met in consultation and reached a fraternal agreement (Bratskoe soglasie). A second meeting on 12 November 1983 produced a statement of common principles. There they elected five spokespersons for maintaining intrachurch contacts. They were: Josef D. Bondarenko, A. G. Nazaruk, M. T. Shaptala, F. A. Shumeiko, and P. Ia. Iakimenko. Another major figure in the movement was Nikolai K. Velichko, pastor in Kiev of the largest ECB church (960 members).

This group of Independent ECB churches showed the greatest creativity and initiative in responding to the opportunities of perestroika. They invited several foreign radio evangelists, including Christian preacher and former astronaut James Irwin. They have been open to fellowship with both sides, but still feel that the AUCECB is maintaining too close a link to the state. Indeed, in terms of their approach to the state, the list of leading ECB names indicated that these were all former members of the CCECB who still believed in the principles that prompted the original movement, but who wanted a different structure more suited to changing times.

It was no surprise, therefore, that efforts at a new ECB unity came from their circle. On 17 October 1988, M. T. Shaptala and F. A. Shumeiko drafted a new "fraternal proposal" addressed to all staff members of the ECB unions and associations and to "all persons who love the brotherhood and are zealous for revival and the unity of the children of God in our country."[82] After reviewing the causes of division in the 1960s, the writers proposed a gathering of leading brothers for mutual confession, repentance, and forgiveness. They proceeded to develop a six-point proposal for a new unity that would be more in the form of a facilitating federation than the strong administrative offices now in place.

As a start they called for the creation of a working group consisting of representatives from the AUCECB, the CCECB and the Independents[83] who would collect and then work through suggestions coming from the broad membership of the church. Having done so, this working committee would convene a congress to form a new union with a new constitution and newly elected leaders. The writers wanted to restore unity in order to tackle the major tasks of evangelism, religious education, and literature production jointly, but they also insisted on rejection of the Pentecostals and any contacts with the WCC and "other religio-political organizations."[84] After mid-1990 such efforts at the restoration of ECB unity became increasingly irrelevant as regionalization of church structures followed the breakdown of the USSR and as new Protestant denominations emerged.

The CCECB leadership, on the other hand, has remained rather quiet during the time of perestroika. Its leader Kriuchkov continued to work in hiding. Leaders of its union in Kazakhstan elected to keep aloof from joint evangelistic efforts during summer 1990 because they feared that some of the evangelists were too indiscriminate in cooperating with Orthodox and Pentecostal believers. In short, the CCECB appeared to see their task as keeping free of entanglements by being separatist.

Protestants and the Perestroika of Society

In June 1988 it was announced that members of the Patriarch's parish had been invited to offer voluntary care at a nearby hospital. At the same time about fifty members from the Moscow Baptist church began volunteering at the central psychiatric hospital (Kashenko). In October the chief psychiatrist, Vladimir Kozyrev, and several colleagues attended an evening service at the church where the doctor delivered a speech on the need to combine chemical science and love. There were numerous other beginnings made toward involving religious people in charitable work. Kozyrev and three of his staff, for example, visited the United States in October 1990 as part of an exchange of mental health professionals sponsored by Mennonites and Baptists.

By 1990 approximately 100 to 200 mission or charity societies had been organized by Soviet evangelicals and Protestants. Their statutes or stated programs were quite inclusive. For example, the Latvian Christian Mission (in which Lutherans, Baptists, and Pentecostals cooperated) was sending volunteers to visit or provide care services at seven hospitals and three children's homes, were providing meals on wheels for 200 persons daily, were visiting six prison camps, had begun a Sunday morning newspaper, and had secured land on which to establish a Christian center that would include a 400-bed polyclinic, children's home, rehabilitation center for offenders, home for seniors, and a hostel.[85] Other groups became involved in organizing charity societies to assist the handicapped.

Protestants took part in the politicization of society but were not as prominent in seeking electoral office as were the Orthodox. But everywhere they kept in touch with politicians working for social change to offer their views on legislation or to assist in finding financial aid (also from abroad) for worthy charity projects.

The opportunities to organize cooperatives also resulted in numerous attempts to begin publishing operations. One of the first was *Protestant*, an interdenominational association that began publishing a monthly newspaper in 1988. When it failed to get AUCECB endorsement, it continued on its own, selling a few thousand copies by subscription and the remainder of 25,000 copies by vendors in a few cities. Licensed as a branch of another cooperative company, they were able to obtain buildings, paper, and equipment to establish a publishing company that sold books and other print products for profit. By 1990 there was no longer only the bimonthly AUCECB journal *Bratsky Vestnik*, but also a well-designed and edited monthly paper, *Khristianskoe Slovo*. The editor, Viktoria Mazhurova, was the main force behind a Christian farmers' collective that secured property rights to land near Riazan. The Russian and Ukrainian ECB unions each produced a magazine, and more local church papers were appearing. Often the new mission societies or cooperatives organized Bible schools by extension, working in close partnership with a mission society from abroad.[86]

The growing interest in a market economy provided a stimulus for Soviet evangelicals to facilitate links with businessmen from the West who were interested in combining a financial opportunity with missionary work. In the spring of 1990 the Association of Christian Businessmen (ACB) was organized with Alexei Filev (cofounder of the Light of the Gospel mission) as organizing secretary. A year later he was replaced by the economist Alexander Zaichenko, adviser to Gorbachev and Yeltsin, who had been a closet evangelical the previous decade. Zaichenko began arguing publicly for the rapid protestantization of a significant mass of the population as prerequisite for a capitalist economy, applying the classic Weberian theory.[87] Although a dozen or more entrepreneurs have become wealthy and generous to missionary efforts, the ACB in 1992 was still trying to extend its network beyond its original narrow confines.

Christian missionary work (which had been legally forbidden since 1929) became the primary means for a major new Protestant cultural impact after 1990. Estimates ranged from 100 to 314 mission societies working in the former USSR, some of them legally registered. They included the traditional mission partners, with the best known in Soviet evangelical circles being Light in the East mission (German), Open Doors (Dutch and American), and Slavic Gospel Mission (American and German). Logos mission, formed by Soviet German emigrants in Germany, quickly grew to become a major partner in theological education. The Lausanne Committee for World Evangelization managed to bring eighty Soviet delegates to its conference in Manila in September 1989, following this with a major evangelism conference in Moscow and an ongoing program. The proliferation of parachurch agencies became a cause for anxiety for Soviet church leaders, some of whom rarely got to preach to their congregations because visiting missionaries from abroad occupied their pulpits. In October 1991 Grigorii Komendant, president of the UECB, expressed anxiety about the inattention to church relationships that many of the foreign mission personnel were displaying, asserting that "there can be no mission without ecclesiology."[88]

For the perestroika-era convert to Christianity, the religious options were somewhat restrictive, culturally speaking. One either joined the dominant Orthodox Church, or the dominant church of one's ethnic group (Lithuanian Catholic or Latvian Lutheran), or the evangelical Protestants. Since the latter had developed an ingrown character and were inexperienced in culture and the world of ideas, numerous observers were predicting the likely emergence of new Protestant denominations to provide the needed pluralism. By 1992 there was indeed "growing Protestant diversity" as Mark Elliott put it. Baltic Lutherans were not only reorganizing themselves nationally, their sister denominations abroad helping, but other Lutheran bodies—specifically the Missouri Synod Lutherans—were launching separatist missions, and a separatist German Lutheran church in St. Petersburg was challenging the Latvians for control of the German diaspora. Polish Methodists had become active in the Ukraine again, and Korean Methodists began organizing churches from Moscow to Central Asia. Four other churches that disappeared during the Stalin years (Churches of Christ, Salvation Army, Brethren, and Armenian Evangelicals) all were attempting a comeback. Five new denominations since 1990 were the Word of Life charismatics, Estonian Christian Churches (linked with American Assemblies of God), New Apostolic Church, Presbyterians (especially Korean Presbyterians of which there were four congregations in Moscow alone), and independent Christian Life centers. In addition the American Church of the Nazarene and the Evangelical Free Church announced plans to begin church planting efforts.[89]

Not everything new under religion belongs under the "Protestant" label, however. There was an influx of literature in translation from new religious movements as known in America. The increase in religious freedoms that have always accompanied the Protestant movement, and which now seem so promising in the Soviet Union, can also lead to the excesses of pluralism in faith and practice, epitomized by "Sheilaism" as described in Bellah's recent study of American religiosity.[90] Evangelical leaders that this writer spoke to in Kiev and Moscow were shocked that sports stadiums had been completely sold out four days in a row to hear speakers on occult themes.

Soviet Protestants, though not expecting to become the dominant Christian culture, nevertheless were behaving as if they belonged and had a great deal to offer citizens seeking a road that led to a church.

FACT SHEET

Denomination	Membership	Churches	Clergy	Name of Leader
UECB	204,000	2,260	3,000	G. I. Komendant
CCECB	15,000	90	90	G. V. Kriuchkov
Indep. ECB	25,000	115	115	
Pentecostal	100,000	843	843	B. I. Bilas

USSR

USSR

Denomination	Membership	Churches	Clergy	Name of Leader
Unreg. Pent.	80,000			Ivan Fedotov
Adventists	40,000	445	445	M. P. Kulakov
True Adventist	40,000	—	—	
Church Mennonite	1,100	20	20	Julius Siebert
Ind. Menn. Breth.	2,200	20	20	Viktor Fast
Methodist	1,743	13	13	
Est. Lutheran	50,000	142	110	Kuno Päjula
Latv. Lutheran	50,000 (25,000)	214	100	Karlis Gailitis
German Lutheran	100,000	350		Harold Kalnins
Lith. Lutheran	30,000	27	10	Jonas Kalvanas
Hung. Reformed	80,000	90	21	Pál Forgon
New Apostolic	—	—	—	

(Sources: Data are as of 1990. Much of the statistical data remains at the level of an informed estimate. Data from Trevor Beeson, *Discretion & Valor*, 1984; Konstantin Kharchev's statistics on number of congregations (*Nauka i Religiia*, Nov. 1987), Igor Troyanovsky, ed., *Religion in the Soviet Republics*, 1991; Gerd Stricker, Bill Yoder, and Wilhelm Kahle on Lutherans, Marite Sapiets on Latvian Lutherans; Mark Elliott and the author's own data and assessments on the evangelicals.)

9

Conscientious Objectors in Eastern Europe:

The Quest for Free Choice and Alternative Service

Lawrence Klippenstein

Conscientious objectors rose to general prominence in Eastern Europe only after World War II. That these individuals could become a significant moral force, and in numerous instances bring about even the reshaping of government policies, underscores the vitality of this phenomenon. In a region where a serious search for a more open, free, and satisfying society, including greater religious liberty, had been underway for decades, this phenomenon too merits study. The concern for freedom of conscience and non-military service alternatives is unquestionably an aspect of that quest. Other questions—the concern about human rights, peace and disarmament, dissidence, ecology, and theology have contributed much to the larger picture that the conscientious objector (CO) challenges have created in this region. Such issues point to the need for a very broad perspective, even a wider-ranging survey and analysis of the situation than will be possible here.

Organized churches and denominations have played an important role in this drama. Issues related to personal conscience and religious conviction could hardly make it otherwise. In actual fact, the Christian denominations have not been equally ready to support conscientious objectors in their views and actions. The degree to which they have been prepared to involve themselves actively in this struggle has varied considerably. Traditionally, mainline Protestants and the Catholic Church have not made the tenets of pacifism and non-resistance a prominent point of their theological self-understandings. Most (but not all) of the larger evangelical offshoots of the major denominations currently differ little from their parent bodies in this respect. Some of the exceptions will be discussed in this chapter.

The truth is that pacifism has not respected fixed theological traditions and denominations by and large. It has rooted itself in strange places and sprouted under conditions where one might have thought it could not germinate and flourish. Perhaps it can be claimed that pacifism and conscientious objection have tended to spring more readily from the Protestant side of the post-Reformation church spectrum, and more specifically from what has come to be known as the "free church" tradition of the Protestant movement. Where state and church have cherished century-long and close cooperation, as has often been the case, for example, in the Catholic and Orthodox experience, such dissent has not come to the fore in the same way. However, changing conditions, particularly in the political arena, can significantly impact set patterns and accepted views, as this chapter will show.

What has transpired in the formerly socialist Eastern European countries is seen here as a case in point. In six of the nine nations of this region the question of conscientious objection came to be a matter of public debate, calling for some form of government action and resolution. In two of the remaining three countries it did become a problem to many individuals, although "officially" it was not acknowledged as being a serious problem. This chapter seeks to depict the processes that created these situations, and to understand the co struggle more clearly in the larger context where it has taken place.

By the simplest, popularly understood definition, conscientious objectors are those individuals who view the taking of arms in military forces as unconscionable. Participating in military service is, therefore, an unacceptable form of serving one's country, and must be refused. "Breaking ranks with military tradition" is how one journalist described this characteristic co position.[1] That "military tradition" always was a dominant feature of all the socialist societies of Eastern Europe. Universal conscription and compulsory military service helped to undergird the armies that these regimes required to stay in power. For service-age persons this has commonly called for sixteen months to three years of active duty depending on the country, the branch of service, and other factors (such as education) that can vary considerably.[2]

Military exemptions of certain kinds have usually been available in most if not all of these socialist nations. Such exemptions normally benefited only a few, however, and given the suppression of individualism by these governments one might readily conclude that objection to military service, for conscience' sake or any other reason, could never be officially countenanced in such societies.[3] That is certainly what one would deduce from the military legislation of Marxist/socialist regimes. Typically these laws included very stiff penalties for those who refuse to fulfill their "sacred duty to the Motherland," and to "uphold socialist peace" as defined by their respective constitutions and military regulations.[4]

Until the mid-1970s, almost no one attempted deliberately and openly
to challenge the regular call-ups to military service. Then this general
acceptance of such obligations began to crack in a number of places. The
assumptions of military duty and armed national service came under
increasing criticism including outright rejection in virtually all the countries of Eastern and Western Europe. East Europeans have been well
represented in the independent peace movements, for example, and
among other groups that forthrightly called into question the "givens" of
entrenched militarism and the "obligation" to take up weapons in the
interests of keeping armed forces alert and ready for action.[5] With the
possible exception of Albania, where until recently information was hard
to obtain, every one of the former Warsaw Pact countries and Yugoslavia
have had to deal with the "problem" of conscientious objectors in some
way.

Precedents: The USSR and the GDR

The Union of Soviet Socialist Republics (now the Commonwealth of
Independent States) confronted the question of conscientious objectors
long before it concerned any of its socialist European neighbors. In
Russia, several sectarian bodies that had come into being during tsarist
times showed fairly strong pacifist leanings. For Dukhobors and Mo-
lokans, such inclinations could be traced back to strong antimilitarist
sentiments expressed as early as the eighteenth century when those
groups were formed.[6] When in the nineteenth century some of their
members converted to the teachings of the Stundists, Baptists, Evangelical Christians, and later the Pentecostals, they sometimes took their
pacifism with them. The influence of philosophers like Grigorii Skovo-
roda and Leo Tolstoy (with his followers known as Tolstoyans) caused
still others to accept the pacifist point of view.[7]

Only the Mennonite colonists, immigrants from Poland and Prussia in
the late eighteenth and early nineteenth centuries, managed to negotiate
a legal alternative to service in the armed forces when Alexander II's *ukaz*
universalized military obligations in 1874.[8] These arrangements, effective from 1880 on, permitted young Mennonite recruits to fulfill their
state duties in special forestry camps and, during the Russo-Japanese
War and World War I, in hospital work as well. They were, however, not
alone in holding pacifist convictions.[9] Tsarist prisons inherited by the
Soviets at the time of the 1917 Revolution held hundreds of non-Men-
nonites who had refused to serve under Nicholas II during World War I.

In the spirit of early Bolshevik ideology, which eschewed conscripted military service, and under the influence of people like V. Bonch-Brue-vich, who thought pacifists could be recruited to support the Revolution, the new regime issued military exemption provisions for these groups as early as October 1918.[10] In January 1919, Lenin signed a special decree establishing people's courts to which conscientious objectors could appeal their call-ups to perform military service. During the Russian Civil War this decree allowed tens of thousands of Evangelical Christians, Dukhobors, Baptists, Tolstoyans, Seventh-Day Adventists, and Mennonites to be freed from military service obligations on grounds of religious convictions, that is, for reasons of conscience alone.[11]

About two years after Lenin's death in 1924, the exemption decree was revoked in practice if not in form. All of the pacifist-oriented groups had been pressured even prior to this date to review their positions on military service and therewith enunciate explicit statements of loyalty to the new government. By 1926 both the Baptists and the Evangelical Christians had issued official conference statements rejecting pacifism for their members. Large minorities in both groups (perhaps even a majority) did not support the move. Some of these pacifists went "underground" with their position, while others joined the Pentecostals. Only a year later, however, these congregations were also persuaded to make a loyalty statement and renounce their earlier pacifist stand. The Seventh-Day Adventists came through with their affirmation in 1928.[12]

Mennonites, with their established pacifist tradition, did not yield to this pressure. Until about 1935 they were able to obtain certain types of non-military service alternatives for those who wanted them. A number of the young members had, however, accepted active duty with the Red Army by then.[13] Arrests of ministers, the closing of churches, and general repression directed against all religious bodies seemed to crush all resistance, even among the Mennonites, by the mid-1930s. When the new Stalin Constitution was issued in 1936, authorities explained the absence of exemption provisions by saying that requests for this privilege were no longer being submitted.[14]

Germany's invasion of the Soviet Union in June 1941 evoked enormous waves of deeply rooted patriotic feeling among the Soviet people. Religious groups were now encouraged explicitly to lend their support to the war effort. As a reward for compliance, Stalin promised that they would again be given the right to reconstitute themselves as legal communities. The Russian Orthodox Church and several smaller Protestant bodies, notably Evangelical Christians and Baptists, benefited directly from negotiation that followed Stalin's invitation. The formation of a special Council for Russian Orthodox Church Affairs in 1943, and the All-Union Council of Evangelical Christians-Baptists (AUCECB) a year later, resulted from this "concordat."[15]

Smaller bodies with pacifist backgrounds, such as the Mennonites and Seventh-Day Adventists, both of whom had German ethnic origins, found themselves classed as "unreliable" or, even worse, as "fascist enemies of the state." Some of their young men who had already been conscripted into the Red Army occasionally ended up in German prisons. Most of the remaining men of service age were sent to work in Soviet prison camp work battalions or were consigned to other non-military installations and labor projects.[16]

Nearly 40,000 resident German Russians from Ukraine joined the German retreat from the Soviet Union in 1943. According to German resettlement plans they would be given new homes in recently occupied areas of western Poland. Those families that remained behind were forcibly resettled in Soviet Central Asian communities or in other less-populated areas to the north and farther east. After the war these people lived for a decade or so in restricted residence areas managed by a special regime known as *Spetskommandatura*. These areas were concentrated in the Ural Mountain region, central Siberia, and other sectors of Soviet Central Asia. Conscientious objection to military service was rarely mentioned in public, although instances of it still did occur.[17]

The westward advance of the Red Army during the final months of World War II became an essential prop for the stage on which conscientious objectors would appear in other East European countries. All of these communist regimes came to power in the late 1940s, and military forces dominated by the Red Army remained a crucial element in the survival of these governments until their demise in 1989–1990. The suppression of what Moscow viewed as uprisings against Soviet control in the GDR (1953), Hungary (1956), and Czechoslovakia (1968) highlighted this reality for those who resisted the Soviet "presence" during those years.[18]

A new state, the GDR (German Democratic Republic), founded with Stalin's blessing in 1949, was the first of the subjugated areas where conscientious objection became a public issue in the postwar period. This development achieved prominence partly because the largest church body in the GDR, the *Evangelische Kirche Deutschlands* (EKD, or Evangelical Lutheran Church of Germany), became involved. Its official statements accepted not only the validity of military service; the right to object to such service for conscience' sake was recognized as well. In significant ways the Evangelical Church championed the cause of conscientious objectors throughout the forty-year history of the East German state.[19]

The political creation of the GDR definitely favored those who stood for peace. The wartime Allies took steps after World War II to "convert" the German people into a nation that would never become a military threat again. Some leaders thought that a single neutral German state should be set up with nothing but a home guard to protect itself, like Austria perhaps. But this was not to be. When the talks ended four years later, two Germanys resulted: the GDR and the Federal Republic of Germany. Soviet military administrators ordered the establishment of armed units as a German *Volkspolizei* (People's Police) already in the summer of 1948. Four years later these units were officially incorporated into the *KVP* (*kasernierte Volkspolizei*), a national armed police militia.[20]

Actually, the GDR had no military conscription during the first thirteen years of its existence. The newly formed Socialist Unity Party was radically pacifist in the earliest phases of its rule. Its motto was simply: No German may again take a weapon in hand. Soon, though, these authorities began to denounce pacifism as a deception used by imperialist forces to undermine the masses' resistance to their power (clearly the Soviet line).[21] Evangelical Church leaders in the GDR, who had hitherto been non-pacifist and whose traditional theology basically called for support of the state, viewed the renewed militancy of the early postwar years with some alarm. They publicly documented their concern about dehumanizing militarization at their synods in Eisenach (1948), Berlin-Weissensee (1950), and Elbingerode (1952). At these meetings they also expressed their readiness to support young German service recruits who might decide to resist military service for reasons of conscience, that is, on religious grounds.[22]

The GDR established its *Nationale Volksarmee* (National People's Army) in January 1956, but did not introduce military conscription until 1962. Its new military law now rendered all males between the ages of eighteen and fifty liable for service in the *Volksarmee*. For defense emergencies that regulation was later extended to cover women of the same ages, and also to include men up to age sixty. The initial legislation mentioned only imprisonment as an "alternative" to serving in the armed forces.[23]

Significant segments of the East German public, such as younger parents, registered immediate disapproval of this move. Some EKD leaders publicly announced their deep disappointment in the government's action, especially citing its seemingly total lack of respect for freedom of conscience and individual rights. The government apparently thought it unwise to ignore the EKD, and agreed to hold discussions with the churches in order to deal with the questions that its new military service initiatives had raised.

These church-state conversations led in the spring of 1962 to a *modus vivendi* in which the state agreed to end all its attacks on pacifist forms of thought, and admitted a willingness to validate the views of those persons who might conscientiously object to military service as such.[24] It did not, however, concede to the church's demand for a legal, civil alternative to bearing arms. Even its relatively generous treatment of conscientious objectors in the next few years could not alleviate the unrest and suspicion that had been generated by the military legislation initially.[25]

In 1963, a conference of EKD leaders released "Ten Articles Concerning Peace and Service in the Church," in which the religious hierarchy took responsibility for providing legal protection for conscientious objectors, as well as for giving spiritual guidance to those who did join the armed forces. The creation of noncombatant "construction units" (*Baueinheiten*), ordered by the state on 7 September 1964, seemed to be a direct response to these conference statements.[26]

This rather striking concession by the government was described by the party newspaper, *Neues Deutschland*, not as a compromise, but as a "military necessity," since such construction units integrated with the army would be vital in building up the nation's defense capacity. The need for broader "democratic legitimization" of the new state, still only fifteen years old, has been cited as another reason for this move. It is possible that the disconcerting prospects of having to deal with a potential force of three thousand to four thousand objectors, and the intensified conflict with the EKD that might have been caused, may have been the strongest motivator of all.

Recruits for the *Baueinheiten* (also referred to as *Bausoldaten*, that is, literally "construction soldiers") were given a distinctive uniform carrying the design of a spade as a shoulder emblem. This insignia gave rise to the designation, *Spatensoldaten*, meaning "soldiers with a spade." Their regular work excluded the carrying of arms, although the units remained under military administration. The specified eighteen-month term of service equaled that of regular soldiers. Construction projects were primarily related to military sites and installations. The men were usually stationed in units of fifteen to twenty, although large-scale undertakings such as building the new harbor at Mikran on the island of Ruegen utilized larger groups.[27]

Neither EKD leaders nor the conscientious objectors felt that this arrangement really met their objectives and needs.[28] All units were still fully controlled by the army, the construction of military sites still seemed to involve them directly in military-related activity, and the required oath of commitment to service differed little in substance, they said, from that required of regular servicemen.[29] Almost immediately some objectors protested the requirements of the *Baueinheiten*, both by appeals to authorities and by nonparticipation at the worksites. Others called for an open discussion of all ideas relevant to the search for a meaningful peace service alternative to carrying arms.

By the fall of 1964, the regional synod of Berlin-Brandenburg had prepared and submitted a complaint that "the concerns of the conscientious objectors were not being met." A year later, the Görlitz provincial synod asked for "a form of alternative service which would not force anyone to participate in military building projects against his own conscience." In the spring of 1967 the provincial synod of Saxony registered its anxieties about students who had served in construction units facing discrimination in schools. This meant, the statement pointed out, that career opportunities were being closed to those who refused to serve in the country's active forces.

A civilian form of alternative service is what many church leaders and the conscientious objectors themselves had in mind. The 1967 Saxony synod already had heard the proposal of Bishop Johannes Jaenicke that the government consider alternatives in the fields of health or disaster service. Beyond the GDR itself, the Conference of European Churches, held at Nyborg in 1971, considered the same idea in various propositions on peace service presented there by Bishop Werner Krusche. The conference resolved to encourage churches of its member groups to be sympathetic to conscientious objectors, especially in cases of discrimination or even arrest. Beyond this resolution, it seemed, little more could be done.[30]

In the Soviet Union, even in the early post-Stalin years—that is, the late 1950s and early 1960s—one could not expect to find the degree of church influence on government policies that the EKD was exerting in the GDR. The newly reorganized Russian Orthodox Church, like the EKD, really did not have a traditional pacifist tradition to draw on, and like its Protestant counterpart, the AUCECB (but unlike the EKD), it could hardly risk criticizing or even opposing the policies of the governing authorities at this time.

The Soviet press for its part had kept on fanning wartime Germanophobia, purporting to see obvious connections between the hated "fashisty" of the war years, and the earlier Russian pacifists who also had been Germans (such as the Mennonites and the Adventists). Sociologists and other academics who were pursuing scientific studies of religious groups helped to keep the public memory of "disloyal" conscientious objectors alive.[31] The Mennonite "turning to arms" in their *Selbstschutz* (self-defense) strategies of the Civil War also could readily be used to condemn "hypocritical" views of nonresistance held by some leaders.[32]

Nikita Khrushchev's stepped-up antireligion campaign of 1959–64, and more specifically the Baptist schism of 1961–62, helped to make conscientious objection a more highly visible public issue once again.[33] *Initiativniki* (dissenting) Baptist leaders like Prokofiev, Kriuchkov, and Georgi Vins, as well as others who had withdrawn from the AUCECB or congregations that had refused to join it in the first place, were prepared to challenge more than the registered council officials in their Moscow headquarters. They fearlessly defied the state itself by simply refusing to accept any legislation designed to restrict religious life (such as the regulations of registration) and by willingly paying the price for doing so by accepting harassment, fines, and frequently imprisonment as well.[34]

General religious dissent, that is, opposition to the state's policies on religion, could easily become a psychological and spiritual "home base" for conscientious objectors in the post-Stalin era. In the sixties and seventies a growing number of Soviet COs appeared among the unregistered Baptists and other similarly illegal and dissenting groups. Notably represented among these objectors were the independent Pentecostals[35] who had not joined, or who had left the AUCECB; the True and Free Seventh-Day Adventists, who had parted company with their registered fellow-member congregations, and who were led at this time by P. Matsanov and V. A. Shelkov;[36] and the Jehovah's Witnesses,[37] who were often targeted in press attacks for their "exceedingly intransigent" pacifist stance.

In the early 1970s, samizdat sources began to mention increased harassment and mistreatment of young believers serving in the army. The death by violence of twenty-year-old Ivan Vasilievich Moiseev, a member of the Slobodzeisk ECB church in Moldavia and a Red Army truck driver (as a CO), was widely publicized in the Western media. That Moiseev had refused to take the military oath for reasons of conscience seemed to dramatize for other Soviet young men the option of conscientious objection as an appropriate religious stand against bearing arms in military service.[38]

Quite a few of the new conscientious objectors, especially those from unregistered Baptist communities, launched their protest with a refusal to take the military oath. The required promise of giving ultimate loyalty to the state seemed to these persons to contravene their prior loyalty to God. For some, this contradiction did not necessarily call for rejection of state service as such, or even objection to being a part of the army.[39] As one such recruit put it, "I am a believer, and from purely religious conviction, I cannot take the military oath, or bear arms. I do not refuse to serve in the ranks of the Soviet army, and am prepared to fulfill conscientiously all that my service demands. But with regards to the oath, as a religious believer I cannot alter my thoughts and convictions."[40]

During this period, military authorities commonly viewed the refusal to take the oath as being also a refusal to bear arms. The military statutes in any case forbade the handing of weapons to anyone who would not take the oath. Court proceedings following such a refusal usually resulted in sentencing, not simply for nonswearing of the oath (for which there was no article in the criminal code), but for "evasion of call-up to service." Charges were then laid with explicit reference to Article 249a, namely, attempting to evade the obligation of military service altogether.[41] Punishments under Article 249a typically included imprisonment for three to seven years in time of peace and possibly the death sentence during wartime. A sentence of three to four years served in camps of ordinary regime was the most common punishment given.[42]

Imprisonment was not automatic, however. Granting a service alternative, albeit always to be carried out under military auspices, could occur at the commanding officer's discretion.[43] An émigré Baptist pastor in Germany related in a conversation some years ago that on several occasions he had successfully intervened for a church member who wanted an alternative because of his conviction against bearing arms.[44] Mennonite émigrés describing their experiences in the Soviet Union during the seventies claimed that young men in their communities not infrequently found themselves continuing their civilian trades while completing their service terms. Construction battalions (not unlike the GDR's *Baueinheiten*) could become alternatives too.[45]

The New COs: Hungary and Poland

For other Eastern bloc countries, conscientious objectors were a less-familiar phenomenon. After the Soviet invasion of Czechoslovakia in 1968, COs also began to come forward in these regions. To begin with, a small Protestant minority group, commonly known as Nazarenes, and an even smaller Catholic "base" community calling itself *bokor* (The Bush) brought Hungarian conscientious objectors into the limelight around 1975. They would remain in the public eye for at least the next fifteen years. When the facts are more completely gathered, it may turn out that pacifists in neighboring Yugoslavia, Czechoslovakia, and Poland drew much inspiration from a struggle for alternatives that was headquartered in Budapest.

The 150-year-old Hungarian Nazarene community locates its pacifist roots in the teachings of Samuel Heinrich Froehlich, founder of the Swiss *Neutaeufer* (New Baptizers), who was strongly influenced by the Mennonites of Central and Western Europe. Extant statements in which Fröhlich affirmed such beliefs date back as early as the 1860s. From 1869 to 1875, Hungarian Nazarenes were granted legal exemption from military duty with an option of performing a noncombatant form of service. Members of the group subsequently anchored their pacifist beliefs specifically to a confession of faith drawn up in 1876. They worked persistently to obtain official recognition as a religious body and to regain the privilege of noncombatant army service, which they lost again well before 1900.[46]

Suffering the vicissitudes of all religious groups after World War II, the Hungarian Nazarenes finally regained official recognition in 1977. With it came the privilege of exemption from military service.[47] The concerns of the present-day body of about 3,500 members have not, however, been widely publicized in the West. The granting of such an exemption in Hungary in the late 1970s was, however, also significant for other groups. Its extension to non-Nazarenes such as Jehovah's Witnesses, Seventh-Day Adventists, and eventually also to Catholics is an aspect of the co story of Eastern Europe that must also be included here.[48]

Hungarian Jehovah's Witnesses appear to have received their exemption privileges about the same time as the Nazarenes. Since the Witnesses were then still an illegal sect, the government may have taken a more informal approach about which details were not revealed. It was in fact granting both groups a form of noncombatant service, something which the Nazarenes could accept with appreciation but which Witnesses, who reject any form of military service, would not accept. Refusal to serve almost invariably meant imprisonment of two to three years. Hundreds of young men from Witnesses congregations have sat in Hungarian jails during the past several decades.[49]

The 1977 concessions to the Nazarenes and Witnesses might have reduced the problem to manageable proportions for the Hungarian authorities (that is, kept it out of the media and away from public scrutiny) if the country's Catholics, who are said to make up 60 percent of the population, had not come on stage as well. The growing number of Catholic conscientious objectors, and the publicity which they generated, increasingly exacerbated church-state relations in the late 1970s and 1980s. Catholic involvement in the CO struggle had its roots, in a sense, in the so-called normalization of church-state relations that occurred in Hungary in 1976. This shift included the appointment at that time of László Cardinal Lekai as the new Catholic primate of the country. This rapprochement also included an agreement with the government that the church would receive additional responsibilities and freedom to deal with questions of internal interest while at the same time committing itself firmly to undergird the "legally anchored order of the Hungarian People's Republic, and the government's advancement of socialism."[50]

This new relationship was put to the test very early by the emergence of ad hoc local worshipping groups called "basic communities," which were a decade old by now. Church authorities looked askance at the movement because some of the groups seemed to be straying away from hierarchical control. The communities of greatest concern were those led by Father Görgy Bulányi who had directed one wing of the basic communities (The Bush) as part of a Hungarian Catholic renewal movement after World War II.[51]

When the Catholic bishops met in 1976 to discuss this problem, particularly as manifested in the Bulányist sector of the movement, the newly appointed cardinal warned these base community members about the dangers of disobeying the church's central teachings. One of the controversial emphases of Bulányist doctrine manifested itself in a profession of nonviolence and Christian pacifism that soon would help to create the first Hungarian Catholic COs. Károly Kiszely, the dissident and environmentalist who called himself the "first Catholic CO" may not in fact have been a member of The Bush community.[52] But much sympathy for his stand was expressed in that group, and before long others were following his example. In 1979 The Bush formally adopted nonviolence as a central theological tenet and with that pacifism became a prominent feature in the public profile of the Catholic basic communities movement.[53]

Meanwhile the cardinal had attempted unsuccessfully to have Father Bulányi sent abroad. In the summer of 1981, Lekai suspended a popular youth chaplain and Bulányist contact person, Father László Kovacs of Budapest, from his parish duties. One of the charges laid against Kovacs stated that he was misleading people on the question of pacifism and military service. A number of letters protesting the cardinal's move reached him almost immediately. One of them had been written by a country curate, Andras Gromon, who now also had to terminate his pastoral work.[54]

Some of the Hungarian bishops—for example, József Cserhati—occasionally expressed hopes for a relaxation of tension between the Catholic hierarchy and the Bulányists, both now definitely on a collision course as far as the service issue was concerned. The arrests of Catholic cos continued, however, with the government reaffirming its refusal to change the requirements of military service even a little.[55]

Participants at an international cultural forum held in Budapest in November 1985 learned about the situation from Karóly Kiszely, who offered to any person interested a sheaf of comments that illustrated the difficulties and deprivations suffered by Hungarian cos, Catholics, and others. Even while they were meeting, Kiszely noted, Hungarian prisons were holding about 150 persons for their pacifist convictions. Most of these individuals came from the smaller churches, but at least a tenth of that number were Catholics. Of these the majority came from The Bush.[56] Catholic officials seemed unwilling to intervene. The cardinal could only hope that Rome would take some action against Bulányi for his unorthodox views. At the same time, Bishop Cserhati insisted that the Bench of Bishops could do nothing to give any assistance to cos because "one cannot change the regulations of the state."[57]

The new conscientious objectors who came forward in Poland around 1980 received an official response remarkably similar to the one given in Hungary during the 1970s and early 1980s. In Poland, too, it was the military oath that led a number of young men to publicly protest their service obligations. For many of them a 1976 change of wording in that oath created the crux of the problem. That modification brought into the pledge the words "to safeguard peace in fraternal alliance with the Soviet Army and other allied armies." This seemed to some Polish recruits to be an unwarranted intrusion designed to placate a foreign country. In a compromise of loyalty these words clearly implied a promise to uphold communism, something they found to be against their conscience and thus unacceptable.[58]

The revised oath had already been the concern of the Committee Against Repression for Those Objecting to Military Service, established with Solidarity before the imposition of martial law in 1981. This committee hoped to change Poland's constitution to allow for exemptions to military service, while at the same time offering some form of civilian service "of general benefit" as an alternative to carrying arms. It also sought to improve the lot of those refusing military service by organizing sessions on nonviolent resistance and self-help psychotherapy for those who wished to prepare for imprisonment, by disseminating information on repressive measures against cos, by spreading information on how the question of national defense was dealt with in other countries, and by making pacifist literature available where needed.[59]

It has been alleged by some sources that a 1979 government statute had already provided for civilian service. If true, this law had seemed quite ineffectual, failing to help anyone perhaps because it was too demanding (someone referred to it as the "right to work in coal mines"), and very poorly publicized.[60] Some have pointed out too that any available alternative service provisions would have been rescinded at the time of martial law. It should be added that the extraordinary forcible conscription of many young Solidarity supporters, as well as the military suppression of the union movement itself, brought military recruitment even greater disrepute.[61]

Twenty-two-year-old Maciej Glebocki helped to force the issue when he refused to obey his call to military service in 1982. He was sentenced first to three years' imprisonment, then had the sentence extended by another thirty months. After the 1983 amnesty when the section of his prison that held trade unionists was closed, Maciej was moved to another prison. He was not eligible for amnesty. The Polish episcopacy intervened on his behalf in the autumn of 1983, but could accomplish nothing.[62]

Such problems lay at the heart of a new peace organization, *Ruch Wolnosc i Pokoj* (wiP), established in 1985 and known in the West as the "Freedom and Peace movement." For this group a creative focal point of action came from a protest aimed at assisting Marek Adamkiewicz, who had been sentenced in December 1984 for refusing to take the oath. Hundreds of supportive letters poured in, while a series of petitions, some bearing the name of Lech Wałesa and other well-known figures, were delivered to government offices.

In March 1985, Marek's supporters held a week-long hunger strike at a church in Podkowa Lesna near Warsaw. Prominent intellectual and opposition leaders including Jacek Kuron, Bronislaw Geremek, Jan Jozef Lipski, and Stefan Bratkowski attended. The Freedom and Peace movement in Poland came into being during these discussions.[63]

A month later wiP members drew up a declaration of its broader purposes and objectives. These goals, said its authors, were inspired particularly by the sermons of Pope John Paul II. The declaration noted that it was the aim of the Freedom and Peace movement "to bring the greatest number of Poles to a true unfalsified understanding of the notion of peace . . . [and] to give back to peace activities their moral and political values."[64] A detailed program of the new organization's aims appeared in November, with its two main points enunciated as follows:

1. To take action against the threat of war by calling for a change in militaristic ways of educating young people. Action in this area would involve promoting dialogue and understanding amongst citizens of Eastern and Western Europe, supporting the rights of conscientious objectors, and calling for a change in the form of the military oath.

2. To fight for fundamental human rights, and for freedom of thought, freedom of association and prisoners' rights, a demilitarization of Central Europe, the declaration of a nuclear-free zone to reduce the danger of war, and support for the struggle of national minorities in Poland to obtain an independent cultural life.[65]

Polish authorities kept a sharp eye on all individual and or group peace activities, and vigorously opposed actions that challenged compulsory military service. Several leaders of the Adamiewicz protest were heavily fined, and some were arrested. When Wojciech Jankowski was arrested in November 1985 for refusing military service a judge told him that his prison sentence of forty-two months was to be a deterrent for others who might be contemplating a refusal to serve. The judge went on to note that it also reflected the "socially damaging nature of the offense, and the fact that similar offenses occur with increasing frequency in the area of the court's jurisdiction [in this case, Gdańsk]."[66] To a considerable extent these words fell on deaf ears. The latest call-up around the end of that year led fourteen young men in the district to refuse military service. More protests would follow.

Six women began a week-long public fast in support of Polish cos in March 1986 at the same site where the hunger protest had occurred the previous spring. A demonstration protesting the opening of Poland's first nuclear plant followed on 2 May. Then in September came the announcement by General Wojciech Jaruzelski that all persons sentenced or arrested for crimes and offenses against the state and public order would be immediately released. As it turned out, all but one of the imprisoned Freedom and Peace movement members were among those released.[67]

Later in 1986, the difficult case of imprisoned Jehovah's Witnesses began to gain attention in the West. Altogether, Freedom and Peace sources said, about three hundred Jehovah's Witnesses were serving prison sentences as conscientious objectors. Some put the figure as high as five hundred. wip maintained categorically that the detention of these people constituted an infringement of the Polish constitution, which guaranteed freedom of conscience and religion. The group demanded immediate release of all Jehovah's Witnesses still held in prison.[68] Reports of these events pointed out that the Jehovah's Witnesses had been promised as early as 1980 that imprisonment for refusing military service would cease. If such a promise had in fact been made it had obviously not been kept.

Other Cases: Czechoslovakia and Yugoslavia

The escalating struggles of the Polish conscientious objectors probably made an impact on related groups in neighboring Czechoslovakia. That country, however, had taken some earlier initiatives of its own. At the outset these initiatives flowed in large measure from the Evangelical Church of the Czech Brethren (ECCB). There is clear evidence, though, that some of the smaller religious groups, particularly Seventh-Day Adventists and Jehovah's Witnesses, were adding significant numbers to the objectors' groups as well. Here, too, growing levels of dissidence and protest against the continuing restraints of government policy, both inside and outside the religious communities, formed an important facet of the emergence of COS in the region.

The ECCB, originating in 1918, has been called the most important Protestant group in Czechoslovakia in the past twenty-five years.[69] From the podiums of this church Josef Hromádka promoted reconciliation and peace among nations in the immediate post-World War II years, continuing to do so right up to the Soviet invasion of 1968. Ten years earlier he had organized the Christian Peace Conference, while receiving the International Lenin Peace Prize at about the same time.[70] A number of Christian leaders who hoped to deepen the Marxist-Christian dialogue launched by Josef Hromádka utilized the pre-1968 liberalizing policies to begin a renewal movement within the ECCB. The creation of "New Orientation," as this program was called, drew open rebuke from some of the top synodal leaders and even more vigorous opposition, indeed suppression, from the government.[71] Many pastors involved in "New Orientation" ministries were relieved of their duties and had to find other types of work. Church-state tensions reached new levels of crisis in the decades that followed the "Prague Spring."[72]

In the late seventies, documents from Czechoslovakia stated that "an increasing number of young people have refused to serve as conscripts in the army." Among those mentioned were František Matula, Jaros Vaznias, and Ales Brezina. Brezina's case was widely publicized by Palach Press in London and elsewhere in the West.[73] A member of the ECCB and a signator of the human rights movement, Charter 77, Brezina was tried on 24 June 1977 and sentenced to thirty months imprisonment for attempting to evade military service.[74] In his court speech he mentioned his support of Charter 77 and declared his opposition to the "manipulation" strategies of the Czech military forces, that is, allowing themselves to become a tool of the Soviet Union. He also referred to Albert Camus, Martin Luther King, Jr., Leo Tolstoy, and Peter Chelcicky as his "mentors,"[75] stressing also that a published 1976 Czech law had legalized free choices of conscience and belief (in paragraph 120). One news report referred to Brezina's stand as "the first case of man openly stating that he regarded the army as a potential threat to peace, and therefore felt unable morally to serve in it."[76]

Information about the situation of Tomas Petrivy was released in 1980 by Amnesty International. Petrivy, a student who had been expelled from his university two years earlier, was then called up for military duty and refused to serve. At his court trial he was sentenced to prison and served ten months. His appeal was rejected on 27 October 1980, and he was sentenced to another twelve months in prison "for causing bodily harm to a public agent and for evading military service." The first charge had to do with an alleged scuffle with police at the time of his expulsion in 1978.[77]

Then came the case of Jan Hrabina, also a signator of Charter 77, a member of the ECCB, and charged for evading military service. He received thirty months imprisonment after a trial on 6 June 1981 found him guilty as charged by the state. In his court speech he said: "We are convinced that a legal alternative to military service would enable many of our citizens to live according to their consciences and beliefs, and would ensure respect of our society as well as tolerance of attitudes of life and personal conviction. At the same time it would certainly help to improve the services which are legal alternatives to military service."[78]

The development of the Czech independent peace movement took the question of conscientious objection to a highly public level in the mid-1980s. In Prague, late in 1985, a thousand or more young people marched through the streets shouting peace slogans based on John Lennon's lyrics. Many of the participants had signed a petition rejecting the siting of nuclear arms anywhere in Europe ("scrap the army" was heard repeatedly in the crowd). This demonstration led to the drawing up of a document that incorporated Charter 77's broader disarmament objectives.[79]

Among its proposals the document included a section calling for "more space for the younger generation." Taking the example of Hungary and the GDR, this statement noted that for reasons of conscience some young people were objecting to military service. Because the pressure of moral conflicts would lead to despair and suicide "we propose the introduction in our country of alternative service for conscripts whose

conscience or religious belief conflicts with training in killing people."
The proposal went on to suggest useful alternative work such as forestry
conservation, protection of the environment, and care of the handicapped. Such a move "would be welcomed by young people and the
European public."[80]

Hoping to reach as many sympathetic readers as possible, the authors
of the document also forwarded a statement to members of the Federal
Assembly, the Czechoslovakian Peace Council, and the synodic council
of the ECCB, as well as to František Cardinal Tomášek. The letter maintained that society should respect any person's right to refuse military
service on grounds of conscience. A proposal for various forms of alternative service in such agencies as health services was included. Finally, it
urged the government to endorse a UN resolution of 5 April 1987 regarding conscientious objectors.[81]

Just prior to the Prague demonstrations, Western information centers
had become aware of certain secret government documents that contained officially held views of groups like Jehovah's Witnesses. The
writers of one such article maintained that Witnesses had "only one
aim—the disintegration of the mobilization of the masses, and the defence readiness of the country." That seemed to be a direct reference to
the group's pacifistic views. The writers (two police sergeants) also noted
that the members of these religious groups normally could be identified
only when young men refused to serve in the military.[82]

Two specific cases helped to keep the CO issue alive in the late 1980s.
In August 1988 the courts handed down a sentence of fifteen months in
prison to conscientious objector Vladan Koci, a cellist with the Prague
Chamber Orchestra. He too was charged with evading military service.
His defense counsel, Oktakar Moteji, alleged that Vladan had been
swayed by conscience in making his decision. Moteji also asserted that
the law should take account of people who refused military service for
reasons of conscience.[83] The other incident had to do with the earlier
sentencing of CO Peter Obsil in January 1987 to twenty-two months of
imprisonment for self-mutilation to avoid military service. He would
have to face another call-up and possible further imprisonment in September 1989.[84]

Some ECCB members, particularly those of the "New Orientation,"
hoped the general synod might intervene for conscientious objectors.
That would put theory into practice. On 19 November 1983 the synod
had in fact formulated a broad resolution in which it called for arms
reductions and for the right of COs to do alternative civilian work. A
mandate to intercede in the case of Brother Svoboda (not otherwise

identified) was given to the council at the synod sessions in November 1987.[85] That sixty Czechs signed an appeal to include conscientious objection in the Helsinki process signified clearly that such initiatives remained alive and well.[86]

Yugoslav peace groups seemed less sure of themselves. Details of individual cases for conscientious objectors had been unavailable since the release of a group of Nazarenes imprisoned in the 1960s. One group, calling itself the Ljubljana Peace Working Group, now began to publicize the cause of conscientious objectors in Slovenia.[87] Most of the cases brought to light were of Jehovah's Witnesses who were reluctant to campaign politically on their own behalf.[88]

Resentencing had become the specific issue for a number of individuals who had received a second or a third prison sentence. The matter had become a point of debate in churches as well. A petition of the Church of the Nazarene, issued in April 1986, and protesting "the breach of Tito's decree ruling out the practice of repeated sentences [in October 1960],"[89] reflected this problem clearly. A group of six Jehovah's Witnesses refused to travel to their units after serving their sentences, and then after receiving a second call-up authorities withdrew the call-up papers—only to reissue them in January 1987. Most members of this group went into hiding to avoid arrest.[90]

The Peace Working Group, however, won the support of Joze Smole, the Slovenian Party president, who went so far as to outline civilian service alternatives. But the Presidium of the Socialist Alliance (representing all of Yugoslavia) decided in January 1987 to reject this and all other calls for civilian alternative service. It also declared that "no further debate should be conducted" on such initiatives. In May the Peace Group had its lawyer, Slobodan Perovic, take the case to the Constitutional Court for a ruling on the constitutionality of compulsory military service.

Members of the Peace Group stated that accepting such obligations was contrary to their beliefs and to the freedom of religion guaranteed in the Yugoslav constitution. The court's ruling, handed down on 27 November 1987, was that no one could be exempted from military service on religious grounds. To allow this, the court stated, would be to allow discrimination, that is, to favor some religious groups and not others. Private beliefs should not restrict participation in the country's defense.[91]

At least a dozen COs remained imprisoned in Yugoslavia during 1988. All were members of religious groups. According to reports eight of these were Jehovah's Witnesses from Slovenia (mostly) and Vojvodina, one was a Serbian Seventh-Day Adventist, and one was a Nazarene. Also in this group was Father Don Andro Ursić, the first Yugoslav Catholic and priest to have refused military duty on grounds of conscience. Ursić had been sentenced late in 1987 to two weeks' imprisonment, but faced a much longer sentence if he were found guilty. Another seven persons were known to have been released.[92]

There seem not to have been any independent peace groups of consequence in Romania, Bulgaria, and Albania during the seventies and early eighties. Conscientious objectors did come forth in the former two countries, however, especially among Jehovah's Witnesses, the Nazarenes, Pentecostals, and Seventh-Day Adventists. Some were able to obtain noncombatant military assignments. Romanian authorities claimed that some religious groups were being granted exemptions, although it seemed they were granted in an arbitrary fashion. The Bulgarian government issued a number of decrees that provided the opportunity to fulfill alternative service requirements by working in certain industrial areas for five years. Conscripts working in these areas were not subject to the rights and duties of those serving in the army, but were granted all the rights and obligations of the Labor Code.

A few cases of sentencing Bulgarian COs came to the attention of the West. One was that of Emil Kalmakov, a Pentecostal from Karnobat in southeast Bulgaria who was imprisoned five times for refusing to serve in the Bulgarian army. He was first arrested in 1979, and during the following six years served a total of four and a half years in prison. A subsequent term of three years in prison ended when the authorities announced his release in December 1988.[93]

Up to this point the quest of East European COs for recognition of personal rights and freedom of conscience had been an uphill battle most of the way. Notable achievements had occurred in several countries, but an "old guard," with an almost "Stalinist" frame of mind, remained in Romania, Bulgaria, Albania, and some would have said that the GDR, which had made some provisions twenty-five years earlier, should also be included in this list. But hopes had been raised by the mid-eighties, and it was clear that confrontations would continue and that the search would likely be intensified in the days to come.

By now the yearning for personal rights and freedom of conscience also had become an integral part of the larger peace movements that persisted in most Warsaw Pact countries at that time. Reform requirements of countries like Poland and Hungary, and some positive responses attempted by these regimes, no doubt had a good deal to do with the modest but significant successes registered by peace groups and cos in these areas.

All the independent peace groups did have larger agendas than simply gaining an alternative service opportunity for individual cos. Ecology, disarmament, general human rights, and other causes formed an important part of the widespread protest against bureaucratization, collectivism, and outright suppression of peoples that socialist economies and politics had brought to the region. A different way of life—more open, freer for individuals, with less emphasis on military power and better international relations—was being aspired to not only by conscientious objectors, but also by many others. The struggle of the cos may well have come to symbolize the aspirations of broad sectors of the population, an abiding faith that such efforts were not in vain, and that change and improvements were possible even amid the distressing social, economic, religious, and political conditions that prevailed in Eastern Europe as a whole.

Some saw a need for greater cooperation among the peace groups in various countries, and also for more extensive contacts with sympathetic elements in the European and world community. The East European co declaration of 1988 related to the Helsinki Process pointed in that direction. More than 400 people signed that declaration including prominent figures such as Andrei Sakharov, Charter 77 spokespeople, and Poland's Solidarity leaders. Of the signatories 229 came from Hungary, 60 from Czechoslovakia, 36 from Yugoslavia, 21 from Poland, 15 from the GDR, and 77 from the Soviet Union. It was the first East European initiative to have so much Soviet support.[94]

The appeal began with a statement of support for the 1987 resolutions of the Council of Europe and the United Nations Human Rights Commission. These had acknowledged conscientious objection to military service as a universal human right, while appealing to governments to release prisoners held for resisting military service and to provide an alternative service for them. The statement heartily endorsed these demands, then added: "As Europeans we also protest against the inhuman practices of our governments. It is disgraceful for the whole of the continent that even after Hitlerism and Stalinism, and the evils of the world wars, there are still governments that do not respect an individual's right to follow the dictates of his own conscience. War and the suppression of individuals' rights go hand-in-hand today as well. The nations of Eastern Europe expect the Helsinki process to link European security with the extension of human rights."[95] In their conclusion the authors called all "signatory countries to the Helsinki Accords to recognize conscientious objection and alternative service, and to initiate the formulation of such an agreement at the Vienna CSCE follow-up meeting."

Meanwhile the mutual support programs of independent peace groups in Eastern and Western Europe seemed to be gathering more steam. Still there were hurdles to overcome. The personal involvement of people from the East in meetings held in Warsaw Pact countries and Yugoslavia continued to be restricted, and that was true too for exchanges going the other way. One such meeting was an illegal seminar held in Warsaw on 7–9 May 1987 under the eyes of TV cameras and with reporters present from the international press. The seminar, organized by Freedom and Peace workers, brought together peace and human rights activists from eighteen countries. About twenty Freedom and Peace workers and the same number of Western applicants were denied permission or visas to attend. That still left more than fifty Europeans who did get there to join Freedom and Peace workers from Poland, members of the Ljubljana peace movement in Yugoslavia, people from Charter 77 in Czechoslovakia, and others.[96]

One of the documents unanimously endorsed came from the East German group "Peace and Human Rights" (unable to attend), stressing objection to the use of Warsaw Pact troops in member states and calling for the right of conscientious objection. One journalist wrote that independent activists were thus declaring their own peace agenda, an agenda that took as its starting point the idea that peace was a social question and required radical social change. A British anti-war periodical, *Peace News for Nonviolent Revolution,* could report in the summer of 1990 that "conscientious objection had finally made it into the Helsinki Process." Paragraph 18 of the document formulated at the 1990 Copenhagen Conference on the Human Dimension (of the CSCE) committed all signatory states with conscription (and that included the USSR) to consider ways of exempting COs from military service. In a subsection the statement specified that these should be "forms of alternative service being in principle of combatant or civilian nature, in the public interest, and of a non-punitive nature."[97]

A somewhat similar meeting occurred in Bohinj, Slovenia on 25–28 August 1988. More than thirty people from the international CO movement attended, coming from sixteen countries and including two Czechs, one Hungarian, and an exile from the GDR. Those from Poland and the Soviet Union who had registered did not arrive. A lively discussion took place, especially on the question of "how much is conscientious objection contributing to demilitarization?" Most people thought "not very much" because civilian service often was integrated with military service. Participants were encouraged to treat conscientious objection less as an individual matter and more as a collective objective to promote a real alternative to militarism.[98]

The Yugoslav media were well represented. They saw a connection with the "Trial of Four" held by a Yugoslav federal military court. That trial, which had included the sentencing of Ivan Borstner, an officer in the Yugoslav army, followed reports of plans for a military coup in Slovenia. Slovenian society rallied behind the four with many demonstrations and public statements.[99] The question of the Slovenian co meeting may have been one of the crucial ones that would continue to be asked about conscientious objection. Interested bystanders were possibly hoping for a fuller view of the ideas that informed the peace movements as such. The question of whether conscientious objectors could and would help achieve the broader goals of these movements remained to be asked again.

Breakthrough: The Curtain Rises

East European conscientious objectors could always hope for better times and they were certainly prepared to keep up the struggle if necessary. As late as 1988, though, there were few signs that the situation would change dramatically in the near future. Governments grudgingly gave small concessions here and there, but simultaneously continued to insist that the laws of military service be kept to the letter. Objectors would continue to face confrontations, trials, and imprisonments, as pressures continued wherever these dissidents appeared.[100]

With hindsight one can say now that such pessimism was unwarranted. Poland took the spotlight in the early spring of 1988 when the government announced that a proposal to legalize alternative service would soon be forwarded to the *Sejm*. The new law would include setting up a commission of civilian and military personnel to judge the merits of each individual case. A normal term of civilian alternative service would be three years, somewhat longer than the regular two-year term of military duty. Students who normally served a shorter term of duty would have their civilian service reduced to two years.

The proposal passed in the Polish *Sejm* on 13 July and was scheduled to become law on 1 September. Not many days after the *Sejm*'s July action, eighty-six Jehovah's Witnesses serving sentences for refusing military service were released from prison. Thirteen imprisoned Freedom and Peace activists also were freed. The action resulted, reports stated, from an appeal by the Polish military prosecutor's office to the Council of State made on behalf of ninety-five Jehovah's Witnesses, and nine persons refusing military service for "pseudopacific reasons" (meaning they were Freedom and Peace workers). All those released had agreed to exchange two years of military service for three years of civilian alternative service.

Government spokesman Urban admitted that several hundred Jehovah's Witnesses and about a dozen or more Freedom and Peace workers still remained in prison because of their views. One of the activists, Slawomir Dutkiewicz, received his release on 6 August 1988 after being on a hunger strike since the previous November.[101] It was not clear at that point if and when the remaining imprisoned cos would be freed. The new legislation did not define very clearly who could qualify for exemptions. No national framework for appeals had been set up to control and standardize procedures and practices. Instead, local recruiting commissions were allowed to act arbitrarily in individual cases.

Freedom and Peace leaders appealed to the public to help monitor the new act's implementation. Beyond that, the Catholic primate's social welfare committee was established to give opinions submitted to it by persons whose applications for alternative service were rejected. This group included Father Bronislaw Debowski (deputy chairman of the primate's social welfare committee), Bishop Władysław Miziolek (chairman of the committee), and another committee member, Jan Sikorski. Their findings would not be binding, but the commission hoped to control abuses of the system where it could.[102]

The uneasiness of some observers about how the law would be implemented was warranted. cos would continue to experience difficulties even after the demise of the Communist regime. Many objectors were told by their local boards that they had it wrong. Some of these tribunals would not recognize Catholic cos, and Catholics make up well over 90 percent of the population. Mariusz Szewczyszyn thus became the first post-communist government co to be given a prison sentence in February 1991. On appeal his one-year sentence was suspended. The enormous rise of mass employment had reduced the available jobs that qualify as alternatives for military service. Some objectors have taken a defiant stance, saying they will go to prison if the co program is not administered more efficiently and as proclaimed by law.[103]

In Hungary, a breakthrough in the deadlock appeared imminent when the Catholic bishops and László Cardinal Paskai met with the new prime minister, Károly Grósz, on 14 March 1988 to discuss possible changes in relations between the state and the Catholic Church. In effect, as the bishops outlined their wishes, this meant a new agreement would replace the one signed under duress by Archbishop Grósz in 1950. Besides presenting concerns for greater freedom in such areas as education, religious broadcasting, and rehabilitation of religious orders, the meeting heard a request from the cardinal that the government reconsider its policy of jailing Catholic conscientious objectors and provide for some kind of unarmed alternative service.[104] That meeting resulted immediately in the prime minister's announcement that government ministers were in fact considering a new law that would grant COS what the cardinal had requested.[105] Not long afterward, government spokesman Rezsö Banyasz provided the first official government statistics on the number of COS still in Hungarian prisons. The total of 158, he said, included 146 Jehovah's Witnesses, 6 Catholics, 1 Nazarene, and 1 Adventist.[106]

Information about the new legislation reached the general public soon afterwards. The Munich daily newspaper, *Süddeutsche Zeitung*, reported in August that, from 1989 on, young Hungarian men would be able to choose between active military service and a civilian alternative. The Hungarian government officially announced the new law's introduction on 10 November 1988. It stated that civilian service would be available as an alternative to military service, but it would consist of twice the length of service for regular recruits, that is, thirty-six months. The work would be mainly manual, and be administrated by the Department of Employment rather than the army itself. The new service was made available in January 1989.[107]

Father Bulányi termed the meeting of the bishops with the prime minister as "surpassing our wildest dreams." He noted that twenty-five of "our brethren" had been imprisoned in "recent years" for refusing military service. "Always," he said, "the bishops have opposed them, saying that pacifism was incompatible with Catholicism and patriotism." He and other members of The Bush remained concerned, however, that alternative service would indeed be civilian work and not under the army's auspices. "We are not prepared," they declared, "to perform service in an institution whose task it is to kill the 'enemy.'" If service were not to be a true civilian alternative, Bulányists predicted that the problems connected with conscientious objection would continue.[108]

In February 1989 Justice Minister Kalman Kulcsar announced that all conscientious objectors remaining in prisons (the number given was 73) would have their sentences suspended. He added that legal proceedings against COS would also be suspended while the new legislation for exemptions was being completed. Reports issued in August that year noted that 209 individuals out of 31,800 new army recruits had asked for exemptions. Of these 14 were Jehovah's Witnesses and 2 were Naza-renes. Two other Nazarenes and 27 Jehovah's Witnesses had refused to perform either civilian or military service. It was mentioned as well that most of those choosing civilian alternative service would be employed in the health sector.

Hungarian objectors, still looking for greater freedoms, chose 15 May 1990 to found the Conscientious Objectors League, also known as the Alba Society. Its members hoped to put an end to discriminating differ-ences between the various forms of service, to ensure that everyone would have the right to choose non-military service on demand, and even to end obligatory military service by constitutional means. Perhaps these voices helped to bring about actual changes. In August 1990 mili-tary service was reduced to twelve months plus ten months reservist duty. Noncombatant service was reduced to fifteen months, while civil-ian service was reduced to twenty-two months duration with no further call-up.[109]

A genuine civilian alternative service remained the unreached goal of the COS and their church supporters in the GDR. That had been the substance of a seven-point program set forth in May 1981 by the Dresden Initiative Group *Sozialer Friedensdienst* (Social Service for Peace). This formula had offered a two-year term of work preceded by education preparation on themes of demilitarization, disarmament, peaceful se-curity, and non-violent forms of conflict resolution. It suggested exten-sion of service to that of medical aides, social work, disaster control, and protection of the environment as worthy fields of service. Synods of the Evangelical district churches gave these proposals sympathetic hearings as the bishops continued to warn against militarization in the GDR.[110]

Klaus Gysi, then the GDR secretary of state for church affairs, had no such sympathies and made it clear that such proposals were unaccept-able to the government.[111] That left the problem of the *Totalverweigerer* (that is, total resisters, notably again Jehovah's Witnesses, and some-times Seventh-Day Adventists) unresolved. For those who refused the legal alternative, the only other was imprisonment, that is, a sentence of at least eighteen months. In actual fact it seemed that the sentences were often less severe, and that many individuals appeared to escape call-up altogether.[112]

In 1986, a new civil rights initiative emerged from the independent peace movement; it called itself Human Rights GDR. Among other things, it appealed for demilitarization of society, the creation of alterna-tive civilian service for COS, and an end to travel restrictions for East and West Germans. GDR peace groups had, on the whole, tended to engage in quieter activities to avoid ongoing arrests. The authorities, for their part, tried to cut off contacts with peace activists in the West.[113]

On 12 January 1988, a group of seventy-seven people from the *Umweltbibliothek* (Ecology Library) circle in East Berlin presented a petition to parliament for an alternative "community peace service" to last as long as a term of military service. They asked that cos not be required to take the military oath, or be under military jurisdiction, or to have further military duties. Ecology circles of this type were subject to strict surveillance under the pretext that illegitimate political activity might be part of their agenda.[114]

These efforts seemed not to impress the authorities; the state continued to claim that a number of social concerns were outside of the church's proper sphere. This was in keeping, the church was told, with its doctrine of "two kingdoms" (one the kingdom of Christ and the other the kingdom of this world, for which earthly authorities are responsible). Among the items the state questioned were conscientious objection and alternatives to military service. These matters, said the authorities, along with human rights and problems of the environment, ought to be settled by the state alone.

That the EKD intended to keep the issue alive was apparent from a March 1988 address given by Werner Leich, the new chairman of the Conference of Protestant Church Leaders of the GDR. Seeking to address some "signals for the future" of church-state relations, Leich listed "fields of action, by state and society which would have a significant effect on expectations of the future." He included also these words: "the introduction of a civilian alternative to military service would solve the problem of those who refuse to serve; it would release powerful energies for socialist society among young people, even if they do not actually make use of this alternative."[115]

The GDR did begin to grant a regular civilian service by the end of 1989. In Dresden, for example, a group of twenty-five young objectors, all so-called "total resisters," had been serving as volunteers since 20 November. By that time the Methodist Church, with a membership of 20,000, expressed itself as being in favor of the abolition of military service. It held the view that if such service were to continue, young men ought to be able to choose alternative peace work anywhere in Europe. To that opinion the Conference of Protestant Churches publicly added its conviction: (1) that the type of service performed ought to depend on a declaration made by the conscript, not on the pronouncement of a tribunal; (2) that conscripts should be allowed to serve near their homes;

and (3) that an alternative civilian service ought to be longer than the regular term of military service.[116]

An official announcement allowing alternative service in the GDR was released on 8 February 1990. Recruits would be allowed to choose their own field of civilian work. The term of service would be twelve months whether in the army or in alternative service. Total resisters would not be imprisoned, but asked to pay a fine. That summer GDR officials announced that half of the recruits who had just started their basic training in the army (about 80,000 men) would be opting for conscientious objection. With the uniting of the two Germanys on 3 October 1990, recruits for military service came under the somewhat less generous regulations of the new Federal Republic of Germany *Bundeswehr*. Alternative civilian service had been an option to West Germans for a number of years. The majority of these cos had worked in hospitals as aides or as orderlies. Sometimes objectors would be allowed to go home because not enough alternative work positions could be found. Since 1969 German objectors could do their service in a third world country. Service is for a period of fifteen months in place of a full year of military service. Some peace activists feel that this is a form of discrimination that too must end.[117]

By this time the ending of criminal prosecutions of cos in the Soviet Union seemed to be under active consideration. A leading legal expert, Valeri Savitsky, deputy director of the Institute of State and Law of the USSR Academy of Sciences, announced that possibility in London on 13 June 1988. That announcement followed a published reference to alternative service in the early Soviet period, made by Konstantin Kharchev, chairman of the USSR Council for Religious Affairs.[118] At that point, however, many conscientious objectors still remained in prison. In fact the majority of religious prisoners listed in Western publications such as *Keston News Service* and *War Resisters' International Newsletter* were cos.[119]

Concern about the ongoing problems of Soviet conscientious objectors shifted somewhat to the Baltic republics during this period. A number of new co sentencings occurred in that region, related perhaps to the fact that a large number of recruits for the war in Afghanistan originally came from Lithuania and the neighboring republics. For example, sixteen members of a new, formerly Baptist, group in Estonia that called itself "Word of Life Church" all refused to join the Soviet army.[120]

Meanwhile, the independent peace movement known as the "Group for Establishing Trust Between the Soviet Union and the United States," begun in 1982, experienced much harassment, notably in Moscow. Many of the early members had been scattered by arrest and expulsion to the West. Others took their place and continued the group's peace promotion program. Several people gained some prominence through their pacifist stand regarding military service. Nicholas Khramov and Dmitri Agunov were among them. The former had suffered repeated short-term imprisonments, while Dmitri finally "disappeared," perhaps forced into military service somewhere in the country.[121]

On 19 February 1988, several young Moscow men led a Pushkin Square demonstration calling for the right to obtain exemption from military service and alternative service opportunities. An associate of these men, Lev Krichevskii, was committed to a military hospital in April 1988 after repeated hunger strikes taken to protest military service. In the summer of that year eighteen-year-old Alexander Pronozin declared his objection in an open letter sent to the USSR Minister of Defense. The procurator's office in Moscow opened a criminal case against Pronozin for "evasion of the regular call-up to active military service," but took no other action against him at the time.[122]

Soviet cos remained under pressure in 1989. Rising rates of draft evasions were possibly partly responsible for this, as may have been the impending budget cuts and the army's loss of popularity. Chief of Staff Mikhail Moiseyev told *Pravda* later that 6,647 men had evaded the draft call-up in 1989 compared with 1,044 the previous year. About 90 percent of these were "ethnic objectors"—conscripts from the Baltic republics, the Caucasus, Central Asia, and other national groups who considered conscription into the Soviet Red Army a violation of their national sovereignty. Local authorities often refused to cooperate, so most of the evaders were never prosecuted. Reports of more arrests continued to reach Western research centers, mostly concerning Jehovah's Witnesses.[123]

Disturbances in the Baltic republics seemed to increase in the fall of the year. Such organizations as the pacifist Latvian group For Country and Freedom encouraged resistance. Documents appeared urging people who hesitated to join the Soviet army to become members of the Latvian Popular Front, Helsinki 66, or the Group for the Defense of Human Rights instead. The Popular Front actually sent an open letter to the Presidium of the Latvian Supreme Soviet calling for the introduction of a military service alternative. On 10 November 1989 the Latvian constitution was amended to allow an alternative to military service for persons "whose religious and ideological convictions do not permit them to serve in the armed forces of the USSR." Many activists continued to hope that new legislation on freedom of conscience would provide for conscientious objection as a legal alternative. That did happen on 1 March 1990 when the Latvian Supreme Soviet adopted a labor alternative. The co commission set up to judge cases included a priest and a professor of literature.[124]

Two weeks later Estonia became the second Soviet republic to introduce alternative service. Men of service age were given until 15 April to register. Alternative service would be six months longer than the regular military term. Young men would be allowed to work where a shortage of workers existed, that is, in such areas as the militia, fire brigades, hospitals, railways, public transportation, municipal offices, or simply working as doormen. The legality of the move seemed unclear since the Estonian constitution (in contrast to that of Latvia) had not been amended to allow for such exemptions.[125]

The central Soviet authorities refused at first to recognize the validity of these changes, but later seemed to accept them in practice if not in theory. Young Estonian men were directed to report their intention to seek an alternative service to the newly established Estonian Labor Service Commission. At its first meeting on 9 April the Council accepted all applicants, regardless of the reasons given for refusing military service. In other USSR republics more cos had had to face the courts, and accept prison sentences. A prisoners' list released in March 1990 revealed that at least eight Christian and seventeen Jehovah's Witnesses in a larger group of sixty-seven were in prison as cos. Other names were added to the list in the fall of the year, most of these being Jehovah's Witness cos as well.[126]

Discussion of the implementation of a new "Law on Freedom of Conscience and Religious Organizations" in the army also had raised the issue of conscientious objection. In an interview with Major General N. Grebenko, published in *Izvestiia*, it was claimed that efforts had already been made to arrange for cos to serve in railway or military construction. Generally, however, discussions of new legislation on freedom of conscience did not touch on the matter of conscientious objection. An exception to this was the case of the RSFSR where specific mention of a need for an alternative service did occur in these debates. On 15 June 1990 several deputies of the Moscow city council published the text of a petition on behalf of cos, which they planned to submit to the Supreme Soviet later that year.[127]

A dramatic announcement early in 1991 stated that the USSR as a whole would now grant legal exemptions to military service for conscientious objectors. Spokesman Lieutenant General Anatoli Antonov, the deputy head of the Soviet general staff, also stated that such non-military service would last for three years and have no connection with any of the armed forces of the Ministry of Defense, the KGB, or the Ministry of Internal Affairs. The August coup brought a change of government and much turmoil at high levels. By the end of October 1991 the new law still had not come before the Supreme Soviet.

More republics were now introducing alternative service legislation in their own assemblies. In the RSFSR Alexander Pronozin was invited to serve in a special work group to help draft alternative service regulations. The seven members of this body also included Moscow city councilor Alexander Kalinin, who had already been working on such legislation on behalf of the Supreme Soviet, and a peace group known as The Radical Party. In Moldova such a law was enacted on 10 July. By then Georgia had done so as well, and in October the Ukrainian government followed suit. For the latter it seemed that provisions applied only to those whose religious beliefs precluded military service, and the term of service was thirty-six months to replace two full years of military service.

Reports continued to suggest that a large number of COs, perhaps several hundred, remained in prison even after the August coup. Pronozin, who had been arrested on 14 June 1991, and brought to the Kascenko psychiatric hospital for an examination on 24 July, appeared at the Sovietski District Court of Moscow on 27 December for a ninety-minute hearing. A final verdict was postponed. Amnesty International took up the cause of a dozen or more COs imprisoned in the Soviet Union. One of these had to do with the arrest and sentencing of Sergy Osnach of Shostka in the Sumy region of Ukraine. He was arrested on 4 April 1991 and would be due for release, if he had to serve his full sentence, in October 1992.[128]

Laws for conscientious objectors in Yugoslavia came under review in 1989. An official news agency announced that as of 21 April a form of alternative service would be available, but the term of service would be two years instead of the normal military term of one year. Only those persons refused on the grounds of religion would be considered for such exemptions. Even these still would need to swear the military oath and render service under military direction. This meant that many objectors would find the alternative unacceptable. Since Jehovah's Witnesses, for example, refused to serve in the army in any form, most of those serving prison sentences in 1989 (dozens altogether) represented that group. Some other individuals were released during the year.

The outbreak of war between Serbia and the republics of first Croatia, then Bosnia created chaos in all three republics. Military authorities, although speaking under the sham authority of a defunct government, threatened draft evaders, resisters, and deserters with heavy penalties.

The maximum sentence for leaving the country could be death. Refusal to report for duty became widespread in Serbia. Some peace activists were arrested. Slovenia alone provided a proper debate on conscientious objection, and indeed provided the right to conscientious objection. The Croatian constitution now also recognizes the right of conscientious objection against military service, but the Defense Law provides the right only for recruits, and not at all for men who have served in the Yugoslav People's Army.

As a result Croatian anti-war campaigners have called for more consistency in the regulations, and for aid to help resisters insufficiently protected by law. In the summer of 1991, Amnesty International noted reports that many young men were deserting or refusing to respond to call-up. The organization urged the immediate recognition of the right of conscientious objection for all who would not serve in the military. It also called for the abolition of the death penalty for these and other offenses, allowable under the Criminal Code of SFRJ.[129]

In Czechoslovakia imprisonments were continuing in 1989, even as events were moving rapidly toward the "Velvet Revolution" at the end of the year. One CO case had to do with the 14 June sentencing of nineteen-year-old Libro Frank, who belonged to the Hari Krishna community. Frank later agreed to serve in the armed forces. By that time the Independent Peace Group (NMS) had launched a petition calling on the Czech president, Gustav Husák, to release two other objectors, Vladan Koci and Jan Subrt. The latter, serving a sixteen-month sentence, was in fact released after nine months, and it was thought that the authorities might allow him to work for ten years in the coal mines, then the only existing alternative service available in Czechoslovakia.[130]

In February 1990, Jana Petrova, a representative of the new coalition government created on 10 December 1989, informed a group of workshop participants in Waterloo, Ontario, Canada, that alternative service legislation was being worked out in her homeland. It would allow recruits to submit written applications for alternative service to the military authorities. Civil alternatives to military service would be made available, with requests considered by special committees set up on regional levels. Those not considered eligible might be sentenced to several years imprisonment if they refused to serve. These provisions were enacted by the Federal government on 14 March. Article 12 of the law also provided between six months and three years of imprisonment for those who intentionally avoided civilian service. By the end of 1990 it seemed that all persons imprisoned for refusing military service had been released.[131]

Conclusion

In Eastern Europe the recent struggle for freedom of conscience with respect to state service appears to have registered significant successes. The majority of the countries of the area formerly dominated by Marxist regimes have brought in alternative service legislation after World War II. In several of the remaining states (one must not forget the new ones recently created), conscientious objectors may expect more favorable treatment when the changeovers to new governments and revised laws are completed. To work out an equitable and proper application of these laws so that those seeking alternative service may actually get it as promised may take longer. Political, social, and economic hurdles can still get in the way of solving all the problems cos have faced until now.

Conscientious objectors themselves will be reassessing their positions in the years ahead. With foreign domination gone it may seem less onerous, and eventually no longer a problem, to serve in the army of one's homeland. Not all objectors took their stand on the basis of religious conviction alone, although a very large number have and will continue to do so in the future. A deep cynicism about the relative merits of militarism will remain for many people in the years to come. The views of some religious groups are not linked to the political fortunes of the state; they rest on views of biblical understanding and philosophical attitudes to life and community existence. Politics have been a vital part of the equation, however, and the marked pattern changes of the recent East European revolutions will have their impact on the pacifist community as well.

It may be that cos will find themselves in a lonelier position in the days ahead. Some church groups that have undergirded them in their own institutional struggles for goals no longer so centered on survival alone may want to move on to another agenda. It remains to be seen whether the tenets of pacifism, nonviolence, and nonresistance (or whatever term one wishes to use) will be permanent parts of the doctrinal foundations in the churches that have made a home for conscientious objectors thus far.

Protestants were not alone in standing with the cos, nor always necessarily the most aggressive groups in seeking recognition for the objectors. Groups like the Mennonites of the Soviet Union, holding to a centuries-old pacifist tradition, tended to seek at least some accommodation, to seek their exemption from carrying arms within the framework of the army itself. Jehovah's Witnesses, not clearly part of the Protestant ethos, have demonstrated perhaps the most consistently radical position on this theme. The Catholic-inspired perspective of Polish and Hungarian Catholics is more difficult to categorize. In Poland, the changing of the military oath will no doubt make a difference for some; Father Bulányi's leadership in The Bush bases its self-identity on what some have called a "Protestantized" approach to interpretation. Focussing strongly on "what the Bible teaches," this group has brought a significant critique to its Catholic traditions regarding church and state. Whether its pacifist thrust can be sustained under new conditions remains to be seen.

Czech Brethren and German Lutherans often rooted their pacifism in the varied objectives of the larger peace movements of Eastern and Western Europe. Baptists and Pentecostals sought their rationale in a very personal, and in some ways simple, conviction that killing humans is wrong, and that too is a principle that changing politics and economics do not really affect. The challenge of building a new civil society is daunting in all these countries, and the test of personal integrity may come in the end not so much through what is objected to, but through what is affirmed and attempted in building the better communities many are longing for so much.

It is too early to say whether the common co concerns expressed in various religious groups will actually bring these churches together to discuss peace issues around one table. There still are major differences between the denominations, and recent evidence suggests that greater freedom in Eastern Europe may lead to increased tensions rather than unifying them in some way. The struggle for preserving the rights of the individual must be seen as a struggle that goes beyond a particular group, and even beyond the region studied here. Freedom of conscience and religious liberty are world-wide concerns. Conscientious objectors have sought to focus on some of the central issues on which churches need to work together. It remains to be seen whether their gains will deliver what they have seemed to promise and how the uncompleted agenda fares in the years ahead.

10

The New Church-State Configuration
in Eastern Europe

Sabrina Petra Ramet

The repluralization of Eastern Europe has radically transformed the conditions in which religious organizations functioned. It has changed the relationship of church and state and altered the balance of forces in these countries. Protestants are not the only ones affected, and their situation is fully comprehensible only if placed in the wider context of general religious life. These more general changes are treated in this chapter.

My starting point is the self-evident fact that the political changes in Eastern Europe have opened up significant new opportunities for all churches, and the less evident—but I would argue, clearly documentable—fact that the Roman Catholic Church stands to gain the most.

The essence of these changes is that the regulatory mechanisms of the communists, which, among other things, served to bridle the strength of the larger churches, have been dismantled. In the new, less-regulated environment, the larger churches are now able to flex their muscles. This has quickly led to controversy, above all in Poland but also in Hungary, Croatia, Serbia, and elsewhere. In Czechoslovakia, by contrast, the ascent to power of the Civic Forum in late 1989 opened the door to a revival of an anti-Catholic animus, rooted in the traditional anti-clericalism of Czech intellectuals.[1]

The purpose of this chapter is to assess the changes that already have taken place in the sphere of church-state relations since the collapse of communism in 1989, to assess the effect that these changes will likely have on the role of the churches in politics, and to indicate some probable future effects on patterns of religiosity in the region. The discussion will focus on Poland, Czechoslovakia, Hungary, Yugoslavia, Romania, and Bulgaria. The German Democratic Republic (GDR), which was formally accepted into a reunified Germany on 3 October 1990, and Albania will be discussed only in passing.

Changes in Legislation

The most signal change in the church-state relationship throughout the region is the abolition of the old state offices for religious affairs and the drafting of new, far more liberal legislation governing church-state relations and the exercise of religious faith. Under the old regimes, the state offices were entrusted with the task of supervising, containing, and exploiting religious organizations. These offices were variously attached to the ministry of culture (as in Czechoslovakia), to the secret police, or later placed directly under the council of ministers (as in Poland), to the ministry of foreign affairs (as in Bulgaria), etc. In the Bulgarian case, for example, the Orthodox Church was considered useful in promoting the state's objectives abroad; hence, the church's organizational subordination to the Ministry for Foreign Affairs.[2] These offices maintained a high level of surveillance, including the bugging of homes of outspoken clergy and the bugging of Catholic Church confessionals.[3]

In general, after dissolving the old state offices, the new governments of Eastern Europe transferred some of their functions to new bodies. In Poland, for example, coordinating functions were assigned to a new section attached to the Council of Ministers, while in Hungary, the state office was replaced on 1 July 1989 by a new Secretariat for Church Policy; Barna Sarkadi Nagy, a reputed liberal on religious matters, was initially appointed to head the new secretariat.[4] (The more orthodox Imre Miklós had headed the old state office.) By the end of the year, the secretariat was reorganized as a religious affairs department, attached to the Ministry of Culture, and Iván Plátthy had been appointed to head it. The churches were allowed to deputize representatives to take part in the department's work.[5] But with the electoral victory of a noncommunist coalition in elections held in March 1990, further reorganizations seemed likely. In Czechoslovakia, the Secretariat for Church Affairs, hitherto headed by Vladimir Janků, was simply abolished outright.

The new laws already adopted in Poland, Hungary, Czechoslovakia, and Bulgaria, and taken up more slowly in Romania and Yugoslavia (which was mired in civil war by the summer of 1991), had a number of common features. The laws assured freedom of religion, forbade discrimination on the basis of religious faith, guaranteed the right of parents to obtain religious education for their children, assured that soldiers may practice their faith without obstruction (as the Hungarian law puts it, "as individuals on military premises, and . . . collectively off military premises"), barred the state from controlling religious life, and liberalized

conditions for the reopening of religious orders, the reestablishment of
church orphanages, hospitals, and retirement homes, and the engagement by laypersons and clergy in charitable work.[6] In Czechoslovakia,
the communist regime had used its control of sacerdotal licenses to stran-
gle official church life—thus driving it underground—and had tried to
exploit its provision of salaries to clergy to induce cooperation. Under
Czechoslovakia's new law on religious organizations, the licensing of
clergy became a dead letter, although the noncommunist government
continued to provide financial assistance and salaries to clergy belonging
to the country's twenty recognized churches.[7]

In Poland, new religious legislation was passed on 17 May 1989.
Under this legislation, the Catholic Church obtained the full rights of a
legal person for the first time since the war as well as the sanctioning of
its sundry educational, cultural, and charitable activities, many of which
had operated in communist times in the gray zone of semi-illegality. The
new law also guaranteed the church's right to build facilities, including
places of worship, hospitals, radio stations, and even theaters. The law
also guaranteed the church the legal right to own and operate private
schools, including diocesan and monastic seminaries, and abolished
the military obligation for novices in orders and students in church
seminaries.[8]

In Bulgaria, the Independent Committee for the Defense of Religious
Rights, Freedom of Religious and Spiritual Values submitted a petition to
the Bulgarian National Assembly in October 1989, signed by 240 people,
demanding radical changes in state legislation governing religious affairs, including freedom of communication with religious organizations
abroad and a recognition of the legal validity of church marriage. In
January 1990, Lyubomir Popov, deputy minister of foreign affairs and
chair of the Committee for Affairs of the Bulgarian Orthodox Church and
the Religious Denominations, announced that a draft bill on religious
organizations had been drawn up. The draft law was described as "consistent with the international agreements signed by Bulgaria, and more
specifically with the Vienna concluding document."[9]

In Yugoslavia, the Federal Secretariat for Information convened a
meeting with editors of religious publications from various churches in
July 1990 to discuss proposed legislation. But the subsequent disintegration of Yugoslavia rendered all further talk of federal legislation entirely
gratuitous. Croatia's Catholic bishops had earlier demanded a restoration of religious instruction in the state schools. After June 1991, this
question became hostage to the broader question of whether Croatia, in
which the largest number of Yugoslav Catholics lived, would be able to

consolidate its independence or whether it would be crushed by the Serbian military and annexed to a Greater Serbian state. Certainly, the legislation drafted in the new Croatia in 1990 promised to legally safeguard the liberalized conditions already achieved for publication of religious material and for other religious activities.[10] Officials said at the time that the new legislation would allow the churches to freely engage in areas of health care, education, culture, and even science.[11] In Romania, the government of Ion Iliescu announced that the new legislation on religion would be based on the precommunist laws of 1928. Since these laws discriminated against neo-Protestant communities and treated the Orthodox Church with special favor, Romania's Protestants expressed concern about the regime's intentions in this regard. Both neo-Protestants and Catholics also have been concerned about the evident continuity between the old (Ceauşescu era) Department of Cults and the "new" Ministry of Cults. Many officials in the ministry occupied the same jobs they had held in the old department, and the staff of the new ministry was actually larger than that of the now superseded department.[12]

The churches have moved quickly to establish themselves on surer footing. Their first moves focused on obtaining the return of property confiscated at the time of the communist takeover, expanding their media efforts (both print media and broadcasting), and—as already hinted in the context of Yugoslavia—pressing for the restoration of religious instruction in the state school system.

As the communist regimes collapsed and the reprivatization of the economy acquired high priority, the return of nationalized property inevitably became the focus of wide discussion in all of these countries. This discussion included questions of returning church property confiscated between 1945 and 1952. Hungary perhaps moved the fastest, with the return of school facilities being a top church priority. On 2 September 1989, for example, the Evangélikus Gymnázium of the Lutheran Church in Budapest was reopened; seized by the state in 1952, it was returned to the church after three years of campaigning by Lutheran lay activists. By late 1989 already, there were, aside from the Evangélikus Gymnázium, ten other denominational middle schools in Hungary (eight Catholic, one Reformed, and one Jewish), and a second Reformed middle school was reopened in 1990.[13] A special difficulty developed in Hungary in early 1990 when it was discovered that the owners of confiscated church property were putting their facilities on sale rather than waiting for the state to seize them and return them to the church. This chiefly affected buildings that had been confiscated from such Catholic religious orders as the Salesians. As a result, the Hungarian parliament intervened in

February 1990, imposing a freeze on the further sale of former church facilities. Eventually, on 10 July 1991, parliament approved a law authorizing the return to the churches, within three years, of all nonprofit-making property confiscated by the communists.[14]

In Czechoslovakia, the Catholic Church asked for the return of only basic church facilities and lands, but declined to ask for the return of industrial enterprises previously owned by them. On 19 July 1990, after a heated debate lasting several hours, the Czechoslovak Federal Assembly voted to return to the Catholic Church seventy-four buildings confiscated by the communist government in 1949 and 1950, mostly from the religious orders. Of this number, sixty buildings were in the Czech lands and fourteen in Slovakia. As in Hungary, the return of confiscated property produced complications. Here, controversy centered on property of the Greek Catholic Church that was forcibly turned over to the Orthodox Church in 1950 by the communists when the Greek Catholics were suppressed.[15] The Czechoslovak Orthodox Church protested the decision of the Slovak government to return remaining properties to the original owners, arguing that where the majority of the parishioners were Orthodox, the church should remain in Orthodox hands.[16] Disagreements between the Czech and Slovak republics about federal jurisdiction generally held up passage of all major legislation for months, with the result that the Czechoslovak government finally passed its law on church property only in late July 1991. As passed, the law called for the return of 198 church buildings (in addition to the seventy-four previously returned).[17]

And in Romania the Orthodox Church Patriarchate hinted at compensation by publishing data on church facilities demolished or obstructed since 1977. Specifically, the patriarchate claimed that twenty-two churches had been demolished (including the Vacareşti monastery, and the Cotroceni, Pantelimon, and St. Vineri churches) and that another seven had been "moved and disadvantageously sited, [and] also closed to religious services."[18]

Religious programs—once considered a media anathema—are now commonplace on East European radio. Poland, Czechoslovakia, Hungary, and Yugoslavia have all allowed religious programs to be broadcast, and pressure built up for similar permission to be granted in Bulgaria as well. In Hungary, churches also were allowed to schedule religious programs on television. By May 1990, an agreement was reached that allotted twenty-five minutes per week to the Catholic Church, which could be used for Bible readings, ecclesiastical news, children's catechism, and advice to the laity, while Protestant churches would have fifteen minutes per week to share among themselves.[19] New religious publications also made their appearance, such as the monthly journal, *Protestant Review—World and Thought* (print run of 5,000 copies), which was the first Protestant mass publication in Poland since 1945.[20] In Czechoslovakia the prestigious journal *Teologičke texty*, which had been published underground for some ten years, began "official" publication in March 1990.

But it is in the sphere of education where church gains may have the greatest impact. In Czechoslovakia, Croatia, and Slovenia, theological faculties, which had been separated from the universities in the late 1940s or early 1950s, were allowed to reaffiliate with local state universities that held full faculty status. In the German Democratic Republic, the theology "section" of the University of Rostok was restored to "faculty" status in February 1990. It had enjoyed faculty status from 1432 to 1970, but had been demoted to a section in 1970 as part of the Ulbright regime's efforts to curb religious practice. The restoration of denominational schools in Hungary was discussed above; in Poland the Lutheran Church opened the country's first postwar Protestant high school in the fall of 1990 in Bielsko-Biała.

Potentially far more important, however, were pressures to restore religious instruction in state schools. These pressures already had led to the reintroduction of religious instruction in public schools in Poland, Czechoslovakia, Hungary, Serbia, and Romania, and stirred controversy in Poland, Hungary, Slovenia, and Croatia (where the issue was raised soon after the electoral victory of the noncommunist Croatian Democratic Community in April 1990). The debate heated up in autumn of that year, as some priests argued that religious instruction was stronger when kept strictly voluntary. But this argument did not prevail, and Catholic religious instruction was reintroduced into the state schools beginning in autumn 1991. Because of the war, it was impossible to assure regular school instruction in all districts, let alone introduce religious instruction. But taking that into account, the Catholic weekly *Kana* was able to report, in March 1992, that about 65 percent of all schoolchildren from Catholic families were enrolled in state religious instruction programs.[21] Meanwhile, the controversy continued unabated with resistance and criticism at many of the schools as religious instruction was first introduced.[22] In Poland the churches of the Polish Ecumenical Council (whose members include most Protestant churches alongside the Polish Orthodox Church and two Old Catholic churches) have disputed the desirability of introducing religious education in state schools, claiming that non-Catholic children would inevitably become victims of discrimination. Mass protests in Warsaw featured banners with a picture of a black-robed Catholic priest towering over a throng of openmouthed children, with the words "We didn't struggle for *this!*" inscribed below.[23]

In Hungary, where the Ministry of Culture announced in June 1990 that religious instruction would be introduced in the curricula of state schools in all grades on a voluntary basis effective in September, skeptics were concerned. "Those who don't participate in one or [an]other religious class will be branded [as] . . . heretics," Péter Hanák, a noted historian, said on a Hungarian radio talk show.[24]

The Normalization of Church Life

Almost overnight, much that has been considered "normal church life" in the West revived in Eastern Europe after four decades of suppression. The two most poignant expressions of the new climate were the somewhat vague relegalization of Romania's Greek-Rite Catholic Church on 31 December 1989 (it had been banned on 1 December 1948, at which time it claimed about 1.7 million faithful) and the repeal in Albania on 8 May 1990 of the law banning religious propaganda. Six months later, places of worship were allowed to reopen; Albania's 2,169 churches and mosques had all been closed in 1967.[25] Where Romanian Greek-Rite Catholics were concerned, the 1989 decree lifted the ban on their church's services, but omitted to say anything explicit about the church's legal status or its long-standing claims for restitution of property turned over to the Orthodox Church.[26]

Other changes have included restoration of the religious orders (in Czechoslovakia and Hungary), resumption of diplomatic ties with the Vatican (by Poland, Hungary, Czechoslovakia, Romania, Bulgaria, and Albania), revival of seminary life (in Slovakia, for example, the three Catholic seminaries accepted a record 277 applicants to start training in the fall of 1990), and arrangements to make the Bible readily accessible (in Bulgaria, for example, it was announced in July 1990 that some 300,000 Bibles would be printed by mid-1991).[27] Alongside the resumption of diplomatic ties with the Vatican, the pope has been able to visit several countries in the region, specifically Czechoslovakia in April 1990, Hungary in August 1991, and Poland for his fourth and fifth time as pope in June and August 1991. Ljubljana promised that the pope would be able at some unspecified date to visit Slovenia.[28]

With the collapse of communism, there have been changes in the organizational infrastructure. In Hungary, for example, the Free Church

Council (which performed administrative functions for the State Office for Church Affairs) and the controversial "patriotic priests" organization, Opus Pacis, were both dissolved in late 1989. In Czechoslovakia, Pacem in Terris, the state-sponsored association of Catholic clergy, condemned by the Vatican in March 1982, was disbanded on 7 December 1989; it literally collapsed hand in hand with the communist regime.[29] As of December 1987, only three of Czechoslovakia's thirteen dioceses had resident bishops; state obstruction prevented the church from installing regular bishops in the other ten. Now, all dioceses are manned by resident bishops, and a new bishops' conference was established in March 1990 with subconferences for Bohemia-Moravia and for Slovakia. Meanwhile, the Christian Peace Conference, based in Prague and long tainted by its collaboration with its communist backers, decided to continue its operations, but to try to redefine its role. In Bulgaria, the first Muslim "junior college" opened its doors on 1 October 1990 to some forty-five Muslim students whose curriculum was to include classes in history, the history of philosophy, and foreign languages.

For ordinary believers and clergy alike, official recognition of certain religious feasts (such as Christmas and Easter) as public holidays has been an important breakthrough. Poland, Czechoslovakia, Hungary, and Yugoslavia all restored the status of Christmas as a public holiday. Shortly before its self-dissolution, the GDR also extended recognition to ecclesiastical holidays.[30] Similar measures were taken up in Romania and Bulgaria.

The normalization of church life also has meant discarding theologies of service, which were developed in the communist era. In Hungary, the so-called Theology of Diakonia, under which the late Lutheran Bishop Zoltán Káldy advocated church cooperation with the regime, was successfully repudiated, and a process of theological reexamination was begun.[31] In the GDR's final months, Christians openly began to criticize the slogan "Socialism is the Gospel in action." The church newspaper, *Mecklenburgische Kirchenzeitung*, noted, for example, that the Bible contains no endorsement of a program of public ownership of the means of production.[32] For years, believers throughout Eastern Europe were told that religion was a "private affair." This concept is completely at variance with the social and ethical concerns of religious organizations.[33] Consistent with the new spirit prevailing in Eastern Europe, Poland's Cardinal Glemp declared in September 1991: "Religion is no private affair, it concerns the whole society."[34]

Finally, the collapse of communism opened possibilities for churches to "redress the balance." For example, the Polish Catholic Church went on the offensive with a clear agenda. Among the items to be initiated were restoration of Catholicism as the official state religion of Poland,[35] the introduction of Catholic religious education in public schools, the tightening up of divorce laws, and the banning of abortion. The church succeeded in obtaining tighter divorce laws,[36] and in introducing Catholic religious instruction in the public schools (beginning in fall 1990), albeit amid vociferous protests. But in May 1991, Cardinal Glemp was compelled to withdraw the church's demand for abolishing separation of church and state.[37] And the following month the Polish parliament decisively rejected a bill that would have banned abortion.

Pope John Paul II, visiting Poland soon after the failure of the abortion bill, vigorously denounced abortion, comparing it with the Nazi liquidation of 6 million Jews in World War II.[38] Western Jewish groups did not appreciate this comparison and registered a strong protest.[39] Poland's Catholic Church remains adamant to play a determinative role in the country's politics. In mid-September 1991, the Polish episcopate issued a statement complaining of the absence of "moral teaching" in the mass media. At the same time, Poland's bishops and clergy started to make serious efforts to influence parliamentary elections, promoting those candidates who supported the church's agenda.[40] For that matter, Czechoslovakia's Roman Catholic bishops were said to have interfered vigorously in the parliamentary elections of June 1990.[41]

Ecumenism or Chauvinism?

Liberalization has been a simultaneous spur to ecumenism and to a new chauvinism, often with overtly antiecumenical aspects. For decades the communist regimes either controlled or constricted ecumenical contacts; hence, the new freedom excited various clergy to try to deepen their ecumenical commitments. But communist constriction also gave the churches certain reasons for solidarity—reasons that no longer seemed to exist. Hence, the various resentments accumulated over the years, even over centuries, easily pushed to the surface, especially when there were controversies about the ownership of church buildings or nationalist issues to worry about. One need only think of relations between the Catholic and Lutheran churches in Poland, between the Greek-Rite Catholic and Orthodox churches in Slovakia and Romania, and between the Catholic Church in Croatia and the Serbian Orthodox Church to see the point.

In Yugoslavia liberalization has produced currents in both directions.

On the one hand, despite Catholic Archbishop Franc Perko's confessed "puzzlement" as to why God allowed Islam "to appear and compete with Christianity," Catholic and Islamic theologians have drawn closer and have opened up avenues of active interfaith cooperation.[42] They held two joint meetings in winter 1989–90. The first was a round table discussion of fundamentalism, organized by the Islamic monthly magazine, *Islamska misao,* and the Islamic newspaper, *Preporod,* at Sarajevo's Islamic Faculty of Theology on 20 December 1989. Some nineteen theologians of the two faiths attended the session. Theology students from the Catholic faculties of theology in Zagreb and Ljubljana and from the Islamic faculty of theology in Sarajevo subsequently held a meeting from 31 March through 1 April in Ljubljana and adopted a joint statement calling for more tolerance and dialogue between people of different religious faiths and cultures.[43]

On the other hand, the Serbian Orthodox Church's relations with both of these religious communities have markedly soured. A major reason was the new wave of Serbian nationalism that engulfed the country, stirring paranoia among Serbs about Muslim "invasions" of Orthodox territory, and reviving Serbian tendencies to associate the Catholic Church with the Ustasha terror of the wartime years.[44] Where the Belgrade newspaper *Politika* once condemned any tendency to associate religion and nationalism, or to trace national feeling in any way to religious roots, that same newspaper—now the mouthpiece of the Serbian nationalist government of Slobodan Milošević—declares that the Serbian Orthodox faith is "the basic and most essential component of the national identity" of Serbs, underlining that "its center is not located abroad, whether in the Vatican or in Saudi Arabia, but in Šumadija."[45] The Serbian Orthodox Church's status as the de facto state church of Serbia was signaled at a meeting between Milošević and Serbian Orthodox Patriarch German in June 1990.[46]

Lately, Serbs have taken to writing anti-Muslim graffiti on Islamic religious objects—such as the inscription "Death to Muslims!" on Belgrade's Bajrakli mosque. Muslims have reciprocated these feelings and have decorated the Orthodox Church in Sarajevo with the inscription "Serbs out of Bosnia!"[47] Even the Albanian discontent in Kosovo is sometimes painted in religious hues. *Politika,* again, in a series of articles from 5–8 April 1990 charged that Albanian Muslim fundamentalists were waging a "religious war" against Kosovo's Orthodox (that is, Serbian) population.[48]

As for Orthodox-Catholic relations in Yugoslavia, an appeal by Catholic Cardinal Franjo Kuharić to Orthodox Patriarch German was peremp-

torily rebuffed by the Serbian Orthodox Church synod, with the explanation that it could not forgive the role allegedly played by the Roman
Catholic Church and Zagreb's Cardinal Alojzije Stepinac during World
War II,[49] or the lack of sympathy allegedly shown by the Catholic Church
over the suffering of Orthodox Serbs and Montenegrins in Kosovo in the
postwar years, or the Vatican's cordiality toward the Macedonian Orthodox Church, with which the Serbian Orthodox Church nurtures an
unresolved jurisdictional dispute. After a second interview by Catholic
Archbishop Perko (this time with the Split daily *Slobodna Dalmacija*), in
which the archbishop complained about the strong wave of anti-Catholic
propaganda being generated in Serbia, the Serbian Orthodox Church
synod announced that it was severing all friendly contacts with the
Catholic archdiocese in Belgrade and that it would not attend or participate in any services or other events organized by the archdiocese.[50]
Relations between the two communities have clearly deteriorated, as
further evinced in charges by Serbian Orthodox Bishop Nikolaj of Dal-
matia that vandals (implied: Catholic Croats) had attacked and dese-
crated Orthodox Church property in the Croatian coastal towns of Šibe-
nik, Zadar, Split, and the resort area of Kastela.[51] On 7 May 1991 the new
Serbian Orthodox patriarch, Pavle, finally received Cardinal Kuharić for
friendly talks.[52] But the damage already had been done, and some of it
could not easily be undone. Besides, the Serbian Orthodox newspaper
Pravoslavlje continued to publish overtly chauvinistic, anti-Croatian po-
lemics, among them a strident expostulation on "the contribution of the
Serbian Orthodox Church to the development of the culture of the city of
Osijek," which it saw fit to print precisely as Serbian troops were laying
siege to Osijek.[53]

These ecclesiastical broadsides have contributed to a climate of deep
distrust and hostility in Yugoslavia—a climate dangerous and symptom-
atic of the more general social instability in that country to this day. I have
spent some time on the growth of chauvinism in Yugoslavia because it
has contributed to the disintegration of civil order, erupting into open
civil war in June 1991. But the problem plagues other countries in Eastern
Europe, too.

In Bulgaria, for instance, the Bulgarian Communist Party's decision
on 29 December 1989 to terminate its virulent anti-Turkish/anti-Muslim
campaign and to restore civil and religious rights to Turkish Muslims
stirred strikes and protests by angry Bulgarians who demanded that the
decision be rescinded and the discriminatory policy be revived. Demonstrators at a rally of 25,000 at Khaskovo (25 January 1990) raised banners
with such slogans as "Bulgaria for the Bulgarians," "Turks to Turkey,"

"In Bulgaria only Bulgarian names," "The Central Committee sold Bulgaria," and "General strike till full victory!"[54] In the summer of 1990 Orthodox Bulgarians in the southern town of Kurdzhali, which contains a significant Turkish-Muslim population, formed an Orthodox Christian Union, named for the Holy Trinity. Led by Father Stanimir Todorov, the movement aspired (in Todorov's words) "to combat false prophesy and its bearers," including Muhammad. The movement aimed to promote Christian values, to mobilize Orthodox solidarity (against the Muslims), to introduce Bible classes in secondary and higher education, and to build and restore Orthodox churches and monasteries.[55]

In Yugoslavia and Bulgaria, religious identity is bound up with national identity, and religious intolerance is often inseparable from national intolerance. In Poland and Czechoslovakia, the national link is much less strong, but religious intolerance has been a problem. In Poland, both the Orthodox and the Protestants complained of a new Catholic esprit that they find menacing. In the summer of 1990 the Polish Orthodox Church suffered a series of arson attacks on its property (including a fire at the home of Marian Bendza, professor on Orthodox Church history; a fire at the Orthodox convent at Grabarka in northeastern Poland; and three arson attacks on the Trinity Church under construction in Białystok). Orthodox believers, many of them members of a small Belorussian minority, blamed the arson attacks on Catholic chauvinism.[56]

If there is a nationality link where the Polish Orthodox Church is concerned, there is no such link for Protestants. Here, too, new anxieties have been aroused. Although roughly half of the Polish population was Protestant in the sixteenth century, the subsequent Counter-Reformation succeeded in reestablishing Catholic predominance, and the period of the partitions cemented the identification of Catholicism and Polish identity.[57] This religious nationalism came into full bloom in 1980–81 when the independent trade union Solidarity made its first appearance. There were reports at the time of Lutheran church facilities being seized by Catholics, and Polish Protestants complained of what they called a "negative alliance of party, state, and Catholic Church."[58] Stanisław Dąbrowski, president of the Seventh-Day Adventist Church in Poland, fretted in a 1985 interview that "many instances demonstrate that the Roman Catholic Church has not rid itself of its hegemonist tendencies and practices vis-à-vis adherents of other faiths," but he took consolation in the observation that "the legally privileged standing of the Roman Catholic Church [had] been annulled" by the communists.[59] The same Dąbrowski told a Keston College researcher in 1987 that while his church had excellent relations with the Orthodox Church, as well as with other Protestant churches, relations were difficult with the Catholics. He felt that his church had to defend itself against Catholic pressure.[60] Such fears were not restricted to the Seventh-Day Adventists, and with Solidarity, which has openly avowed Catholic ties, running Poland, many Protestants feared that the Catholic Church might grow too strong. Recall that Prime Minister Tadeusz Mazowiecki's first public statement after being sworn in was to draw attention to his Catholicism and to the importance for him of Pope John Paul II's teachings. Nor is it without importance that Polish President Lech Wałesa's first official state visit took him to Rome to confer with the pope.[61] With these conditions, Tomasz Kalisz, a member of the editorial board of the Baptist monthly, *Mysl Ewangeliczna*, told Keston College: "Not only Protestants, but other religious minority groups are afraid the new Solidarity government could bring us difficulties, because Solidarity is very influenced by the Roman Catholic Church. We are afraid of the attitudes of Catholics at a time when the Catholic Church is becoming very powerful."[62] Kalisz noted, in particular, that while the Catholic Church had easy access to radio and television, such access was far more complicated for the Baptists. (Whether that was appropriate in a majoritarian democracy is another question; but James Madison himself warned in *Federalist Papers* No. 10 about the tyranny of the majority.) Anti-Semitism also was on the rise.

Then there is Czechoslovakia, still affected by legacies of Protestant-Catholic hatred and anticlerical secularism. It is probably too early to become gloomy about religious chauvinism there. But recent Catholic "fury" about sex education in the schools, and Catholic appeals to nationalist considerations in Slovakia as the *chief* reason for opposing abortion prompt some concern.[63]

The new chauvinism also was reflected in a rise in anti-Semitism, not merely in Poland, but in Czechoslovakia, Hungary, and Romania, where numerous periodical publications—most prominently, the weekly newspapers *Romania Mare* and *Europa*—make anti-Semitism their regular fare. In Romania there also were problems between the Uniates and the Orthodox, with the latter falsely accusing the Uniates of supporting Transylvanian separatism, and the former charging the Orthodox with "cultural genocide."[64]

Under such circumstances, it may come as a surprise that well-intentioned ecumenism has sometimes been unwelcome. Here, the case of Hungary is instructive, and the difficulty is familiar—political control. Hungary's senior church leaders have wanted to retain full control of any ecumenical processes; hence, they have frowned on initiatives from the grass roots. When such grass-roots ecumenism started to flourish—drawing together Catholic, Lutheran, Reformed, Jewish, and Baptist parishes—nine leaders of these religious denominations, including Catholic Cardinal László Paskai, Reformed Bishops Elemér Kocsis and Károly Tóth, Lutheran Bishop Gyula Nagy, Rabbi Alfréd Schöner, and Baptist President János Viczián, collaborated in a joint statement criticizing the movement and claiming exclusive responsibility for organizing ecumenical worship and other activities; this sphere, they said, belonged to authorized church leaders. Eight clergymen who had participated in such services, including clergy from all of these faiths, issued a counterstatement a week later, objecting that organizing ecumenical services was not the exclusive right of church leaders.[65] The church hierarchs, however, formed a coordinating advisory body of Hungarian church leaders to suppress future grass-roots ecumenical initiatives.

By contrast with Hungary, ecumenical contacts in Romania and Czechoslovakia have been less controversial. In Romania an initiative was taken by Baptist ministers in late December 1989 to establish an ecumenical forum in which members of the Pentecostal, Brethren, Seventh-Day Adventist, Lord's Army, Lutheran, Reformed, and Baptist churches could cooperate.[66] In Czechoslovakia, despite their troubled history, Protestants, Catholics, and Jews pooled resources to form a new Religious Life Editorial Board with the aim of stirring religious broadcasting and contributing to society's spiritual renewal.

The Future of Religion in Eastern Europe

As the Communist governments of Eastern Europe collapsed or descended into crisis, church leaders became available symbols of legitimation. In Poland, the overt role played by József Cardinal Glemp throughout the country's period of turbulent evolution toward pluralism is unmistakable. Glemp is conscious of the role he plays and at times comports himself as a spokesperson for the nation. In his address to Poland's top politicians in September 1990, he talked politics, not religion.

> Cardinal Wyszyński [he recalled] once said that the Church has never been silent in our history. To prove this, I will cite the words of a modest woman but a great Pole, the Blessed Urszula Ledóchowska, in 1916: "When one loves one's country, one wants to see it happy, free, and prosperous, but most of all, great and noble."[67]

The Polish church's nationalism is its claim to legitimate activity in politics, to spiritual leadership in the *political sphere*.

In Yugoslavia, the new leaders of Serbia and Croatia (Slobodan Milošević and Franjo Tudjman, respectively) have tried to exploit local church leaders for their own purposes. In Serbia, Milošević created the illusion of church-state condominium in politics and posed as a kind of Defender of the Faith; in a small but revealing reflection of the Orthodox Church's favor, Milošević buttons went on sale at the large St. Sava Cathedral in downtown Belgrade. In Croatia, on the other hand, Tudjman's Croatian Democratic Community misled people by falsely claiming that Cardinal Kuharić had sent it a letter of support, had received its representatives, and had held a special mass for its members. In all of these ways the new Croatian ruling party tried to perpetrate the illusion that the Catholic Church was endorsing its rule.[68]

In other countries this tendency was even more overt. In the waning GDR, Evangelical Bishop Gottfried Forck of Brandenburg-Berlin was the leading candidate for appointment to the GDR presidency in April 1990, until he formally withdrew his name from consideration. Similarly, in Bulgaria, Orthodox Metropolitan Pankratii of Stara Zagora was being promoted for the post of president of the Bulgarian Republic by the Workers' Social Democratic Party, until the nomination ultimately went to former dissident Zheliu Zhelev.[69]

The same pattern has been replayed at a lower level in other countries of the region. In Czechoslovakia, Josef Hromádka, synodal senior of the Evangelical Church of Czech Brethren and chair of the Czech Ecumenical Council, became minister of education, culture, and religious affairs. Also, the fiery oppositionist pastor Rainer Eppelmann served briefly in the GDR's final months as minister of defense and disarmament.

On the face of it, all of this would seem to foreshadow a strengthened, if ambivalent, role for religion in Eastern Europe's future. There are, however, several important caveats that bear on this question.

First, forty years of communist rule have left a legacy of widespread ignorance of the faith. Some striking exceptions to this rule (chiefly Poland and Croatia) exist, but in many cases ordinary believers have little knowledge of the tenets of their faith. Their faith is, accordingly, simple and distorted, and often authoritarian. In fact, a sociological study conducted in Poland found a strong correlation between the degree of religiosity and the degree of deference to authority.[70] The absence of unproblematic access to religious instruction in most of these countries in the communist era also has resulted in many cases in a drift away from religion, or in a transformation of religion into mere politics. Hence, the

Table 1. The Proportion of Young People Identifying Themselves
as Religious, or Nonreligious by Confession (1985–86)

	Religious	Nonreligious
	(in percentages)	
Catholics	62.3	31.4
Orthodox	26.2	64.0
Muslims	43.8	45.3
Other faiths	56.6	43.4
Without church link	7.5	82.3

Source: Srdjan Vrcan, "Omladina osamdesetih godina, religija i crkva," in *Položaj, svest i Ponašanje mlade generacije Jugoslavije: Preliminarna analiza rezultata istraživije* (Belgrade, 1986), p. 159.

curious fact that there are more "Catholics" in Poland than "believers." In general, Catholics are probably the best-educated about their faith overall, followed in declining order by Protestants, Muslims, and Orthodox.

Second, forty years of communism has resulted in the thoroughgoing atheization of the populations of Bulgaria, sections of Czechoslovakia, and what is now the eastern part of united Germany. A June 1991 poll in Czechoslovakia, for instance, found that almost 40 percent of the citizens in the Czech Republic had no religion at all (compared with only 9.7 percent in Slovakia).[71] Such figures are most dramatic in the former GDR, where a poll conducted in May 1990 found that only 21 percent of East Germans considered themselves Protestants, and only 3.6 percent Catholics. Three-quarters of the population was atheist.[72] Traditionally, religiosity also was weak among certain groups, for example, Orthodox Serbs. A 1985–86 poll conducted in Yugoslavia found that religiosity among young people from traditionally Orthodox families was markedly lower than among young people from traditionally Catholic or Muslim families. (See Table 1.) Consistent with my earlier observation, religiosity is strongest among Catholics, weakest among Orthodox. In Poland, by contrast, according to a 1989 survey, fully 84 percent of the population were practicing believers.[73] What this means is that religion has less hold on people in many areas in Eastern Europe than in other parts of the region.

Third, where religious organizations seem to be the most active—for example, in Poland, in the GDR during the 1980s, and in Serbia since the accession of Slobodan Milošević to power in 1987—religion has drawn its strength as much from politics as from spirituality. But politics is a fickle mistress. To the extent that religious organizations in the region attracted support through their identification with the struggle for freedom, the achievement of their goals brought that struggle to an end and loosened the bonds that succored religion. Within weeks of the crisis of communism in the GDR in October 1989, attendance at Evangelical Church services fell dramatically. As new forums for politics opened up, the church ceased to be the exclusive venue for the articulation of political positions, and its political audience migrated. In Serbia, on the other hand, where the Orthodox Church has promoted ethnic chauvinism and thereby achieved a kind of "religious" revival, the high psychological, economic, perhaps political, and (I would argue) moral costs of ethnically inspired civil war have the potential to produce a political backlash at some point, and such a backlash would touch the Orthodox Church.

Fourth, under the impact of general modernization, the religious landscape in recent years has become far more heterogeneous than before, and the traditional churches have lost their monopoly. This development has nothing to do with communism per se, but follows similar processes to those that occurred earlier in the West. New religious organizations have sprouted in Eastern Europe, including Hare Krishna, Ananda Marga, adherents of the Rev. Sun Myung Moon's Unification Church, spiritualists, and a host of others.[74]

And fifth, the simultaneous removal of the communist elites and the Soviet shadow are apt to result in the waxing disjunction of church and nationalism and/or the transformation of the religio-nationalist nexus along lines reminiscent of, but not necessarily replicating, the interwar experience. That is to say, if the larger churches of the region become de jure or de facto state churches, as was the case in most of the countries of interwar Eastern Europe, the result is apt to be the further excitation of interconfessional hatreds, the polarization of religious communities, and the stimulation of both fanatical religious zealotry (as in the Romanian League of the Archangel Michael) and militant anticlericalism (ranging, in the interwar period, from the humanism of the Czech intellectuals to the anticlerical demonism of the Polish Church of Satan, to the antireligious proclivity of communist activists). As Krzysztof Kosela notes: "the possible transformation of the Catholic Church into the state Church of Poland has been seen as a threat by the intelligentsia for many decades . . . [and] was clearly perceived [as a threat] by the left-wing intelligentsia who were inclined to promote far-reaching societal reforms."[75] Yet this is one possible future for Poland.

And yet, everywhere one turns in Eastern Europe, there is a new stridency among religious groups. Catholics and Protestants both talk of a reevangelization of the region, while Orthodox clerics have told Catholics and Protestants alike (in March 1992) to keep out of "their" territories.[76] As Earl Pope noted in his chapter above, Romania has been a particular target for American Evangelical Christians, who have arrived well funded, whether by Jerry Falwell's organization or some other. Catholics and Protestants refer to the countries of Eastern Europe as "missionary territories," and have had some success in advancing their positions. In Croatia, for example, the Catholic family weekly, *Kana*, admitted in February 1992 that Croatia's atheists had overnight become invisible and that atheism had been pushed out of public view and into the private sphere.[77] In Poland, the Church's powerful base among both peasants and workers, as well as its well-tuned organization, has enabled it to exert strong pressure in the political sphere. One government official in Lublin, speaking on condition of anonymity, described his feelings in these words: "For 45 years we were scared of the communists. Now it is the Church that is controlling Poland, and again we are afraid, even though we are Catholics."[78]

There are, thus, not only factors for an attenuation of religious belief but also factors that work in the opposite direction. Here, economic factors come into play. Most of these economies are still troubled, burdened by the communist legacy of administrative mismanagement and industrial inefficiency. Of the six countries discussed in this chapter, none can be said to be home free. Surveying the region *as a whole*, eastern Germany and Slovenia have by far the most promise. And there are difficulties even in those two countries: industrial production in Slovenia, for example, declined steadily from November 1990 to January 1992 by an average of 1.1 percent per month, and registered its first modest recovery only in February. Unemployment in this small country reached 75,430 already by mid-1991.[79] Elsewhere the situation remains, at this writing, uncertain—at least in the short term. The Viennese daily newspaper, *Die Presse*, held out some hope (in March 1992) that Hungary and Poland could get their economies on sound footing, but said that the likelihood of their succeeding was "not good." In the other countries of Eastern Europe, the process of economic shrinkage is expected to continue unabated for some time. Even the Czechoslovak economy, which at one time was seen by some experts as the most promising in Eastern Europe, slowed down steadily between 1990 and 1991, and was described in March as "standing at the edge of a collapse."[80] The Balkans offer even less reason for optimism. Of this set, Bulgaria is the best poised economically, while Albania, Bosnia, and Serbia were experiencing, by the early months of 1992, varying degrees of social and economic chaos. In Romania, the economic picture is likewise disastrous. The Romanian GNP sank 10 percent in 1990, with industrial production dropping almost 20 percent that year and exports down by 42 percent. The negative trend continued into 1991, with a 17 percent decline in economic productivity during the first seven months alone.[81] With soaring inflation, creeping rent increases, and recurrent mass protests, the *Daily Telegraph* confidently predicted in October 1991 that Romania was "spiralling into sustained anarchy and social and economic catastrophe."[82] In the region as a whole, industrial production declined 18.9 percent between 1990 and 1991, GNP declined 16.2 percent, personal incomes have plunged at varying rates (58 percent in Bulgaria and 24.2 percent in Czechoslovakia, for example), general indebtedness has risen (from $88.8 billion for the region as a whole in 1990 to $92.6 billion in 1991), and foreign trade has fallen off.[83] Unemployment has risen everywhere in the region. Meanwhile, Western investment has come more slowly than originally hoped, and there has been widespread disappointment with the first year's performance of the European Bank for Reconstruction and Development (EBRD). For example, Ivan Kostov, Bulgarian foreign minister, complained in April 1992 that the EBRD had approved only one investment for his country and had nothing further in the pipeline. "We need the help now," he said. "In two years it might be too late."[84]

Whether or not such pessimism is warranted is, for present purposes, not the point. The point is that present economic difficulties are serious and may reach the state where they have profound social ramifications (as they already have had in Serbia, Croatia, Bosnia, and Albania). Economic disintegration is often associated with burgeoning social chaos and intensified religious proselytization.

Again, the new governments of the region are fledglings. In Czechoslovakia, government officials invited American and British constitutional scholars to educate them on how to draw up a democratic constitution. Almost all of these countries have played host to a series of American and other Western experts, including delegations from the American Bar Association, who have been asked by several governments for counsel on pending legislation. Most of these countries (and prominently Poland, Czechoslovakia, and Hungary) have had to learn the basics of how to establish and operate a free enterprise economic system. As a result, their stability and survival cannot yet be presumed, despite their obvious legitimacy and their creditable record to date. In 1990 there were rumors that Czechoslovakia's communists were dreaming of a return to power, and in the course of 1991 Czechoslovak authorities became increasingly concerned about a wave of brutal attacks on Gypsies and foreigners (including Vietnamese and Turkish guest workers and Arab diplomats) by gangs of skinheads and neo-Nazis.[85] Right-wing national groups also have made an appearance in Romania (in the form of a revived Iron Guard) and in Serbia. Secessionist sentiment is rising in Slovakia, and in Slovenia and Croatia passed the point of no return in June 1991. The latter two secessions have produced confessionally more homogeneous states—and that feature has already had an impact on the church's position in society.

The Rev. Václav Maly of Czechoslovakia, jailed by the communists in 1979 for his dissident activities, said in 1990 that, "psychologically, Christians have been in exile."[86] When a people, or a group, returns from a long exile, it is unrealistic to expect it to shed all at once the psychological effects and habits of mind developed under those conditions. The reintegration of believers on a normal basis, like the rebuilding and reintegration of these societies as a whole, will be a lengthy process.

Now that the homogenizing communist system has been overthrown, the historic heterogeneity of the region is likely to reassert itself. That is likely to include as well a diversity in patterns of religiosity, religious behavior, and church-state interaction.

11

Afterword

Gerd Stricker

At first sight, it is difficult to find consistencies among the multifarious forms of Protestantism in Eastern Europe. That is due, in part, to the fact that the concept of "Eastern Europe," as it has generally been used, has absolutely no geographic or cultural unity; it is a political concept reflecting postwar European realities. "Eastern Europe," in a word, means (until 1990) the communist countries lying in Central, East Central, and Southeast Europe. They represent diverse cultural landscapes, which often have nothing in common. There is the land of the Reformation—Germany's eastern part, which enjoyed independent existence as the German Democratic Republic (GDR) from 1949 to 1990. Poland and Czechoslovakia also are regularly counted as "East" European, even though they consider themselves part of the "West." Add to that Hungary, with its Habsburg tradition. And finally, there are the Balkan states—Yugoslavia, Albania, Romania, and Bulgaria—the latter two largely Orthodox in religion, and all four having experienced centuries of Ottoman rule.

The chapters in this book have undertaken a dual task: to survey the panoply of Protestant churches in Eastern Europe and the Soviet Union, identifying the chief modalities characterizing their religious and ecumenical behavior; and to trace the history of church-state relations in the era of communism. This book caps a three-volume project launched in 1983 by Sabrina Ramet. The first volume, *Eastern Christianity and Politics in the Twentieth Century* (published in 1988), concentrated on the themes of nationalism, opposition, and co-optation. The second volume, *Catholicism and Politics in Communist Societies* (published in 1990), was organized in terms of hierarchy vs. lower clergy, traditionalism vs. modernity, and grass-roots religiosity vs. institutional structure. This third volume, which essentially completes the survey of Christianity in communist states, focuses on the themes of pacifism and dissent, dialogue and ecumenism. Those themes are relevant to all Christian churches and are not unique to Protestants. But they have been lodestars in the post-war experiences of these churches and, as such, are well-chosen.

Some Protestant groups were forced into illegality in the era of communism. The fate of unregistered Baptists in the USSR (described by Sawatsky), of Nazarenes and Jehovah's Witnesses in Romania (outlined by Pope), and of Jehovah's Witnesses again in the GDR (noted by Ramet) illustrate this fact. Other churches—such as the Lutheran and the Reformed in Hungary—were able to enjoy a kind of privileged position, although, as Pungur notes, this privilege had to be purchased at a price. Some churches strove for a middle course, blending cooperation and critical distance. Of the region's larger Protestant denominations, the Evangelical Church in the GDR, as discussed by Ramet in her chapter, was clearly the most successful. Still other churches avoided any semblance of cooperation with the regime and resolved to "tough it out." The Baptists in Romania and the Adventists in Poland—as described by Pope and by Bock—reflect this tendency, but with the difference that while in Romania it was the Ceaușescu regime (1965–89) that created the greatest difficulties for the Baptists, in Poland the greatest threat to the Adventists has been presented (and continues to be presented) by the Catholic Church.

Diversity in the Protestant World

What are we talking about when we speak of Protestantism in Eastern Europe and Russia? To begin with, there are the traditional Protestant churches: the Lutheran, the Reformed, the United Lutheran/Reformed in the GDR, and the Evangelical Church of the Czech Brethren in Czechoslovakia. There are also the products of internal fissures such as the numerous Protestant denominations in Czechoslovakia, the Old Lutheran Church (which broke away from the Lutheran Church in Prussia after 1817), or the Moravian Brethren of Herrnhut (a product of classical German Pietism in the eighteenth century), and there are those churches often designated as neo-Protestant: the Baptists, Adventists, and Pentecostals, among others.

From the start, I would say that in comparison with the Catholic and Orthodox churches—whether one talks of theology or organizational forms or political orientation—Protestant churches are characterized by a greater orientation toward Holy Scripture, by their practice of giving greater weight to the biblical word. The theological intellect can unfold very freely in Protestantism, which has entailed the danger that theological or pseudotheological arguments could be developed to support the principle of cooperation with secular, even antiecclesiastical state systems (for example, the Theology of Diakonia or the Theology of Service developed by Lutherans and Reformed in Hungary, or, arguably, the concept of the Church in Socialism, adopted by the Evangelical Church in the GDR in 1971).

In situations such as those that long prevailed under East European communism, it must be the task of the churches to come to terms theologically with the social environment and perhaps to introduce Christian elements into an un-Christian system—that is, if the church did not want to become totally isolated from the enveloping communist world. In situations of self-imposed isolation, believers were left to cope with everyday problems of anti-Christian communism alone—a reproof made by some Catholics against their church in the GDR.

Leading Christian figures in communist countries (such as Josef Hromádka in Czechoslovakia and Bishop Moritz Mitzenheim and Bishop Albrecht Schönherr in the GDR) tried to find a place for the church in a communist state. They identified a path and attempted to avoid opportunism. Afterward, their followers invoked formulas that, in the meantime, had become empty phrases as well as camouflaging their conformist dependence on state power. For example, the Theology of Service, or Theology of Diakonia, which for decades served as the central feature of church-state cooperation in Hungary and which is closely connected with the name of the Lutheran bishop, Zoltán Káldy, was subjected to intense criticism within Hungarian church circles even before the revolutionary events of 1989. The concept of the Church in Socialism, popularized in the GDR, also came under critical scrutiny after 1987, as the question was raised whether this idea involved a fundamental compromise on the part of church officials.

The Catholic Church in communist countries was better equipped to deal with such dangers. The church's strong attachment to dogma, the tight connection to Rome, and the clear hierarchical organization considerably restricted possibilities for developing transient, ad hoc theologies. Of course, there were instances of co-opted priests' associations (Pacem in Terris in Czechoslovakia, the Berlin Conference of Catholics in the GDR, and "peace priests" in several countries). These associations were isolated institutional formations whose members could not always be accused of having consciously sought to harm their churches. In addition, the communist states could not always obtain the appointment of bishops entirely to their liking—not even with massive pressure on the church. The state had to promote its candidates in the face of resistance from the Vatican, and it was progressively less successful in this regard— as was shown most clearly in Czechoslovakia in the waning 1980s. There, the Catholic Church endured near-paralysis of its operations when eleven of the thirteen episcopal seats were vacant because the communist state would not agree to permit installation of bishops acceptable to the Vatican. The link with the Vatican and with the church elsewhere in the world generally gave the Catholic Church in the communist countries a unique inner independence, a spiritual strength, which provided it with the fortitude to resist by means of delaying tactics or even open defiance. Examples of such resistance are provided by František Cardinal Tomášek of Prague, by the Catholic Church in Lithuania and Poland, and by the Greek-Rite Catholic Church in Ukraine, which was forced to operate underground from its suppression in 1946 until the relegalization of its congregations in December 1989. It is also of some interest that while the Catholic clergy are committed to lives of celibacy, their Evangelical and Orthodox compatriots routinely married and had children, with the result that the state could exert pressure on the latter by threatening their immediate families, while this was not possible in the case of Catholic clergy.

The Protestant (and actually also the Orthodox) churches were in a much more complicated situation in that they were smaller than the Catholic Church and hence more vulnerable against pressures from the communist state apparatus. Secular authorities in the communist countries always had the leverage—and made use of it in considerable measure—to exert their influence through either direct or indirect personal meetings with Protestant and Orthodox church leaders. Church officials were always constrained to prove their loyalty to the state, which could mean in practice to defend antireligious policies and to collaborate in concealing repressions from the world public. All too often they were confronted with the realization that Westerners took their misrepresentations at face value and even saw in them proof that the churches in communist countries did not suffer repression. The Protestant clergy tried to some extent to accommodate themselves to the role prescribed by state authorities in order to secure the survival of their parishes and their own positions. As a result, many in the West inevitably accused Protestant and Orthodox church leaders of opportunism. Furthermore, it was characteristic of the Western (mis)understanding of the situation that Western church leaders and people of a left-liberal orientation took the statements of their Eastern colleagues at face value and entirely ignored—even denied!—the existence of repression at the parish level.

Protestantism in Eastern Europe presents a heterogeneous picture with many regional and national specifics. Until the mid-1950s, the Protestants like adherents of other faiths suffered harsh suppression. For the most part, these repressions reflected direct instructions from Moscow. That religion would die off was the unquestioned axiom of the communists, whose duty it was to promote this natural process through administrative and coercive measures. This proved to be all the more necessary when church leaders refused to allow themselves to be harnessed to the goals of anti-church ideology.

Beginning in the 1960s, however, increasing differences could be seen in the religious policies of the communist states of Eastern Europe, with the sharpest repressions occurring in the Soviet Union, Romania, and Czechoslovakia, and the most toleration being shown in East Germany, Yugoslavia, and, albeit inconsistently, Poland. Yet through all of these events and developments, there were noticeable efforts on the part of Protestant churches—often with opportunistic pseudotheological maneuvers ("critical solidarity with the communist state")—to cooperate with the regimes in the construction of socialism. Church leaders such as Bishop Hromádka in Czechoslovakia, Bishop Mitzenheim and later Bishop Schönherr in the GDR, and Lutheran Bishop Káldy in Hungary guided their churches in the direction of coexistence and cooperation with the communist state. Their goal was "normalization" of relations between church and state. In the countries with large Protestant denominations—the GDR, Hungary, and Czechoslovakia—theological models were developed to legitimate the service of the churches to the communist-atheist state.

Christian-Marxist dialogue followed in due course. It was implemented in Prague, and also in Yugoslavia, in the mid-1960s and bloomed in Hungary in the 1980s. Theologians emphasized that this dialogue should not be understood as a form of struggle against the Marxists, but had to be conducted in the spirit of the common interest of Christians and Marxists in the humanization of communist society. It was predominantly Protestants who conducted this dialogue, while, except for Yugoslavia, Catholics largely avoided it.

In Hungary as early as 1951, the Protestant churches were under stronger state control but experienced during the 1956 Revolution a brief interlude of hope, which was quickly dashed with the revolution's suppression. In the GDR with the luckless uprising of 13 June 1953, the anti-church campaign, which had focused above all on winning the youth, was essentially won for the state. After these events, the churches in the

GDR lost part of their autonomy for some years. In Czechoslovakia the Protestant churches were brought to heel soon after the communist takeover in 1948. Resistance was rendered impossible through the installation of new church leaders and the imprisoning of priests and believers (measures also adopted in other communist countries). And there were men such as Hromádka who expressed the deepest conviction that Christians could live and work in a communist state and had to cooperate in the construction of socialism. He became the first president of the Christian Peace Conference—established in Prague in 1958 as an ecumenical union of churches from the communist countries—with the specific assignment of promoting Christian engagement on behalf of communism and above all on behalf of the foreign policy of the Soviet Union and its partners, which was generally advertised as "peace policy."

Principal Types of Protestantism

Protestantism in the countries of Eastern Europe can be differentiated into three broad groups: the large traditional churches, churches of national minorities, and the neo-Protestant communities.

Among the traditional churches, the Evangelicals are closely associated with the largest national denominations in several states, but in other countries they were not among the largest religious groupings.

The Protestant churches of national minorities are for the most part relatively insignificant in terms of numbers and have naturally been concerned, above all, with sheer survival. The assured replenishment of their pastors is thus their most important task. The training of pastors looms large in the consciousness of these churches, but they typically lacked the intellectual resources to pursue vigorous theological discussion or to engage in exchanges with representatives of the atheist systems. The by no means unproblematic role of leading the struggle for the survival of national minorities has never actually been assumed by Protestant-minority churches, although the Catholic Church provided a model in Lithuania and Ukraine. Protestants in Estonia and Latvia were disappointed for decades with their churches' silence in the face of Russification. Indeed, the church leadership there openly became marionettes of state power. Only recently was there a reorientation of the Lutheran churches in Latvia (1989) and Estonia (1990), when new prelates, more sympathetic to national resistance, took office. By contrast, the Lutheran and Reformed churches of the Hungarians and the Germans of Transylvania and the Romanian Banat have always figured as rallying points for national consciousness.

The neo-Protestant communities constitute the third major grouping. Because of their relatively small numbers, they held no special interest for the atheist state; but because of their missionary activities, they often experienced especially harsh repression.

Traditional Protestant Churches

Traditional Protestantism may be found in Hungary, Czechoslovakia, and the former German Democratic Republic. In these countries, Protestant thinking has been anchored in place since the Reformation, if not even earlier (the Hussites were active in Bohemia in the early fifteenth century). This characterization also applies today to Latvia and Estonia, the Baltic lands first organized by the Teutonic Order and penetrated by the Reformation during Luther's lifetime. A rich theological culture developed under German domination in "Estland," "Livland," and "Courland," as the Baltic provinces were then known. The Balts, moreover, were able to continue development of their theological prowess, after their annexation by the Russian empire in the eighteenth century, with the Lutheran theological faculty of the German University in Dorpat (Tartu) becoming its center. The Estonians and Latvians, alongside the Lithuanians, obtained their political and ecclesiastical independence only after World War I, the Estonian and Latvian Lutherans having been, until then, underprivileged members of the German-led Evangelical-Lutheran Church in Russia (founded in 1832).

In the GDR, after an early phase characterized by rising church-state tensions—particularly over the atheist youth dedication ceremony (the so-called *Jugendweihe*)—the Protestant churches made serious efforts to find an accommodation with the state. As early as 1957, Bishop Mitzenheim of Thuringia favored ecclesiastical cooperation with the communists to obtain concessions for the church. Branded the "Red Bishop" by most church leaders at the time, Mitzenheim was more recently praised, as Ramet notes in her chapter, among church leaders of Thuringia for having anticipated Bishop Schönherr's concept of the Church in Socialism. The state showed itself to be open in certain ways to the wishes of the church, especially after the East German church's separation from what was until then the all-German Evangelical Church Federation. A high point in church-state cooperation was achieved in 1983 with the celebrations of the Martin Luther quincentennial. True, many pastors and parishioners viewed this accommodation as unacceptable familiarity with the unloved state; the self-immolation of Pastor Oskar Brüsewitz in 1976, for example, was intended as a protest against the state's religious policy and against the church's flexibility and readiness for compromise. This self-immolation made evident the estrangement between the church leadership and church members. Yet this accommodation with the state also permitted the church greater maneuvering room and enabled it to protest, for example, against the introduction of premilitary training for youngsters in school. Through such actions, the church came to be taken more seriously by GDR citizens. By the mid-1980s, moreover, the church was providing grass-roots groups (concerned, for example, with pacifism, environmentalism, and human rights) with meeting places and in this way with legal protection. The state even delegated certain social responsibilities to the churches (for example, homes for the physically and mentally disabled, old people's homes). That is why churches in other socialist countries imagined the Protestant churches in the GDR to enjoy a freedom of which they could only dream. In fact, the GDR leadership in certain ways had accepted the churches (or their leaderships, at any rate) as part of socialist society, at least as long as the leadership avowed its loyalty to the socialist order. On the other hand, a large number of believers (for example, the Pietist groups in the Lutheran Church, Mormons, or members of the Apostolic community) who were oriented along biblical and evangelical lines did not consider it appropriate for the churches to be engaged in ecological or pacifist work, or to assist with exit visas, since they were unable to ground these tasks in biblical sources. Moreover, they saw their fears of a politicization of the Evangelical Church confirmed when GDR authorities struck firmly— above all in Leipzig—in the spring of 1988 against members of grass-roots groups that had enjoyed that church's protection, and when the state repeatedly intervened to censor the Evangelical Church press to prevent it from addressing social and political questions of the day.

There is no question that the changes that took place in the USSR after the accession of Gorbachev began to awaken hopes and aspirations in the GDR church circles. Associated with that awakening was a critical reevaluation of some of the church's past positions, and in particular a turning away from the formula of the Church in Socialism, which came to be seen as too strongly identified with socialist ideology, thus coming to be criticized as a veil that concealed the compromise made by the church leadership with the state. The neutral formula "Church in the GDR" briefly came into parlance. Renewed state efforts to circumscribe the churches through attacks and warnings ran aground as the churches felt more self-confident and refused to allow themselves to be bottled up.

Hungary presents the most interesting picture where Protestantism is concerned. The country's 2.4 million Protestants make up something less than one-third of all Christians (6.6 million being Catholics). With the decline and ultimate collapse of communism in Hungary, church circles abandoned the Theology of Service (Reformed) and the Theology of Diakonia (Lutheran). Pastors and church officials (such as Bishop Lajos Ordass of the Lutheran Church) who were not popular with the regime and who had criticized these theological innovations had been barred from their functions by church leaders, even though it was not certain that these expulsions would have been demanded by the state. But I suspect that church leaders in many cases chased such clergy away as acts of self-censorship out of fear that the state would otherwise apply its force. In the Catholic Church of Hungary, the situation was not that different. The Catholic bishops often paid more attention to the State Office for Church Affairs than to the Vatican—which in turn contributed to the emergence of opposition communities such as those associated with Father Gyorgy Bulányi.

Since the moment when Moscow renounced its claim to hegemony in Eastern Europe, reform was introduced at a rapid pace in both political and religious spheres. A new law on religion, guaranteeing full religious freedom, was passed. For the churches themselves, a new era began, marked, for example, by rehabilitation of clerics removed earlier for political reasons (Ordass; Lutheran pastor Zoltán Dóka; Reformed pastor Geza Nemeth) or by the failure of Bishop Károly Tóth, chair of the Prague-based Christian Peace Conference, to obtain reelection as spiritual head of the Reformed Church in Hungary.

For the churches of Czechoslovakia, the Prague Spring had brought a brief respite and stirred hope after years of oppression. After the Warsaw Pact military intervention, a phase ensued of so-called normalization, that included extensive antichurch measures. In the Czech and Slovak Protestant churches, a local variant of the Theology of Diakonia was developed. Other churches during the post-1968 normalization phase fell into a state of passivity and apathy.

Until the communist state's collapse in late 1989, Czech and Slovak Protestant Christians were under greater pressure than their fellow Protestants elsewhere in Eastern Europe to repudiate Western criticism of religious policy and to portray foreign critics as liars. But compared to the situation of the Catholic Church in Czechoslovakia, that of the Protestants was more relaxed in the late 1980s. For these relatively small churches (1.3 million Evangelicals as compared, for example, with Czechoslovakia's 10.4 million Catholics), it did not hurt the state to grant the Protestants some concessions, and sophisticated propagandists could exploit these concessions in their arguments with Western critics. Eventually, with the changes that swept Eastern Europe in 1989, the Prague-based Christian Peace Conference was virtually closed down.

Czechoslovakia's Charter 77 movement, which had set itself the task of defending the Helsinki Act, enjoyed the active support of a number of Evangelical and Catholic clergy. However, these clergy did not enjoy the protection of their churches in this support and were often punished by being deprived of their (state) sacerdotal licenses. While the Slovak Lutheran Church and the Hussite Church ostensibly fulfilled all state demands without even a murmur of criticism, the Evangelical Church of Czech Brethren brought forth a number of courageous pastors who continued to criticize the state's religious policy and the docility of church leaders, even when stripped of their sacerdotal licenses and isolated within their own church.

Protestant Churches of National Minorities

In the GDR, Czechoslovakia, and Hungary, religious policy toward the Protestants was an integral part of communist internal policy. In the other East European communist countries, Protestants found themselves in another, more dramatic situation as objects of nationalities policy insofar as these churches were associated with local ethnic minorities. The church has the capacity of assisting smaller national groups to preserve their cultures, but in the variable conditions under communism it was not always in a position to do so. The communists often pursued policies injurious to national identity and national culture, even in the face of church protests and opposition. Although the church often could no longer be a place for spiritual discussions, it had rarely offered ritual without spiritual pretensions. In short, the level of spirituality has been sinking, there are internal splits, and the pressure on these churches to keep silent on the subject of denationalization caused many believers to leave them—whether to become religiously indifferent or to join newer neo-Protestant groups.

About 1.3 million Protestants live in the USSR. A large portion of them are non-Slavs, such as Latvians, Estonians, and German Lutherans, Hungarian Reformed, Estonian Methodists, German Mennonites, and Lithuanian Lutherans and Reformed. In large measure, their churches were treated as objects of Soviet nationalities policy, which, from Stalin's time until the advent of Gorbachev, meant Russification. In particular, the training of clergy was severely hindered—either proper training no longer was allowed (where Hungarians, Germans, or Lithuanian Lutherans were concerned), or there were only ineffective correspondence courses for Latvian and Estonian Lutherans and for Baptists. The Lutheran churches of Estonia (40,000 active members) and Latvia (50,000) had to refrain from any kind of nationalist expression; in this way, they let their people down and provided no help, until recent years, against the pressure of Russification. And while the Hungarian Reformed Church in Transcarpathia (60,000 believers) or the Lithuanian Lutheran (30,000) and Reformed (10,000) churches could at least build ecclesiastical organizations, this remained impossible for the German Lutherans (100,000) until November 1988 or for German Catholics.

After 1987, Soviet religious policy became friendlier toward the churches, and only now, above all in the wake of the national awakening in the USSR, are the Protestant churches in those regions winning a greater freedom of action. The Latvian Lutherans, for example, replaced their old church leadership on 12 April 1989; up to then, the church's leadership (the archbishop and the consistory) had been installed under state auspices. Now, not a single member of the old leadership remained in office. Even Archbishop Erik Mesters was retired and replaced by Karlis Gailitis. The new church leadership has been engaged in national movements (the people's front and the national independence movement).

In Estonia, things have not been so dramatic, but have proceeded in a pragmatic and effective way. Here, the resistance of church leaders to state influence was somewhat greater than in Latvia, and so the general synod in June 1990 did not have to bring about as great a break with the past as in Latvia. Nevertheless, five of the six members of the consistory were replaced, and the archbishop was reelected only because the synod wanted to signal a degree of continuity in church life. Archbishop Kuno Pajula had been the state authorities' candidate when elected in 1987. In both churches, people apprehended the danger that an exaggeratedly strong engagement in the national movement could entail; with every positive assessment of the national awakening and with every active participation in nationally oriented groups, the Estonian and Latvian Lutheran churches tried to find an independent, ecclesiastical standpoint.

The German Lutherans have been guided—with state permission since 1980—by Pastor Harald Kalnins (in Riga), their bishop since 13 November 1988, and they convened their first diocesan conferences in Karaganda (May 1989) and Celinograd (July 1990), both in Kazakhstan. The "German Evangelical-Lutheran Church in the Soviet Union" is an accredited member of the Lutheran World Council, headquartered in Geneva. The future of this church (250 official parishes and 250–300 small groups and house circles) is highly questionable because of the mass exodus of Germans from Russia, because the younger generation speaks mostly Russian, and because Bishop Kalnins proved unable to provide the integrative leadership needed to unite the diverse parishes and groups.

The United Evangelical-Lutheran Church in Russia, founded by Pastor Joseph Baronas at Easter 1991, now competes with Bishop Kalnins's church. This development makes it clear that the archbishop does not enjoy great authority with believers, who cannot ignore that fact under the new, freer conditions. The Reformed Hungarian Church in Carpatho-Ukraine is likewise able to pursue closer contacts with the mother church in Hungary, after decades of total isolation, and to send young people to Hungary to study theology. The USSR's Hungarian Protestants are also able to import theological and religious literature from Hungary in great quantities.

In Romania, one finds the largest minority churches. Alongside the 15.5 million Orthodox Romanians live 1.4 million Hungarian Catholics, 715,000 Hungarian Reformed, and 32,000 Hungarian Lutherans, as well as 200,000 Germans of Transylvania in 1985 (this number includes some German Lutherans living in the largely German-Catholic Banat). After the great exodus of the "Transylvanian Saxons" in the wake of the Romanian Revolution of December 1989, their new bishop, Christoph Klein, fears that their number will drop to as little as 20,000–30,000 by the end of 1992. Until the end of the 1970s, Hungarian and German Protestants in Romania were able to conduct normal church life, and there were various theological institutes of high quality, at which visiting professors from the respective mother countries would sometimes teach. The "systematization campaigns" of Nicolae Ceauşescu, which aimed at the Romanianization of the minority nationalities, also placed their churches under ever greater stress. The churches tried, without success, to stop the mass exodus of their Hungarian and German congregations.

Protestantism in Poland, which is primarily a Lutheran concern, provides an entirely different picture. In this overwhelmingly Roman Catholic land, with noteworthy Orthodox (850,000) and Greek-Catholic/Uniate (500,000) minorities (among the Ukrainian and Belorussian peoples),

Protestantism constitutes a mini-minority: 100,000 Protestants as against almost 37 million Catholics. Since the expulsion of the Germans from East Prussia, West Prussia, and Silesia, the majority of Poland's Protestants are reputed to be ethnic Poles. The Lutheran and Reformed churches have to struggle, even today, against the negative image that their members are not "real Poles." Most Poles identify the country's 70,000 Lutherans with Germans; and, in fact, even today most names of pastors of the Polish Lutheran Church are German. The uncertain self-consciousness of Polish Protestants is characterized by their always trying to prove they are "real Poles" and that they have no connection with German Protestants. The experience of the interwar period, when Poland's German and Polish Lutherans worked in conditions of open mutual hostility, has not been overcome even today. On the contrary, the decades-long assimilation of those Germans who remained in Poland after World War II only provided a seedbed for reviving this hostility. Only in 1989 did Bishop Janusz Narzynski speak in favor of allowing reintroduction of German as the language of the Lutheran service when the parish so wishes—a great contrast to his statements in earlier years. It is characteristic that in 1990, when Polish politics took on a democratic form, he retired from office, nominally for reasons of health.

The Polish Lutherans and Reformed, of course, are not actually churches of national minorities, but the Catholic majority sees them as such because a "true Pole" can "only" be a Catholic. While the Catholic Church found itself in constant and often successful conflict with the communist state from 1947 through 1989, the Protestants, together with the other non-Catholic minorities, developed survival strategies in their competition with the Catholic Church. In doing so, they often leaned on the state for support. Non-Catholic ecumenism was visibly expressed in the joint training institute named the Christian Theological Academy in Warsaw, where Protestants, Orthodox, and Old Catholics studied together. The non-Catholic churches tried to protect their freedom of action against the Catholic Church and to expand it with the help of the state. This strategy has not brought them any sympathy from Poland's Catholics, and during the period of martial law in the early 1980s the non-Catholics were viewed as traitors when they joined the pro-government Movement of National Rebirth (PRON) in which Barbara Narzynska, the wife of the Lutheran bishop and representative of the Polish Ecumenical Council, held a prominent seat as a presidium member.

One also must note that by comparison with the situation of the powerful and nationally oriented Roman Catholic Church, the position of Polish Protestants is modest and adapted. Polish Protestantism sought a difficult path, defined by its claim to loyalty, and by its aspiration to be seen as authentically Polish. More recent developments involving close cooperation between the new Polish governmental leadership (Mazowiecki, Wałesa) and the Catholic Church augur for further strengthening of Catholicism in Poland. They do not make the way of Protestants in that country any more confident. On the contrary, by April 1991 the Catholic Church in Poland was pushing for an end to the separation of church and state and for its own reestablishment as Poland's official state church. (However, the church subsequently withdrew this demand.) As Sabrina Ramet notes, Protestants fear that the new religious freedom, underpinned with Catholic religious instruction in Polish public schools, gives the Catholics a huge advantage, and they complain that with fewer numbers of schoolchildren, it is logically impossible for them to demand corresponding Protestant religious instruction.

As to Yugoslavia, the Protestant presence in that country—largely German, Hungarian, and Slovak—was in the years before 1945 not insignificant. But after the war, and the exile of most Germans, the Protestants are largely splinter groups with only regional significance. In such small religious communities there can be neither theological discussion nor ideological conflicts with the state or with local authorities.

Neo-Protestants

Since the middle of the nineteenth century, neo-Protestant churches have penetrated Central, Eastern, and Southeast Europe: Baptists, Adventists, Pentecostals, and others. In Bulgaria, these groups are nearly the only representatives of Protestantism. These communities evangelize energetically, and under communism they often were subjected to especially harsh repression. The religious communities often split: one part would adapt to the communist system, try to observe the letter of the law, and advance the church's interests in relations with the state; the other would reject the legal premises of the communist state and operate underground. Wherever they took root, the underground groups were subjected to harsh persecution.

The Baptists and Pentecostals are the most widely dispersed of these neo-Protestant groups, and they were the most disagreeable to the communists. Typical of such underground Protestant groups was the unregistered Baptist community in the Soviet Union, which refused to go along with Khrushchev's plan for increased supervision of the churches and in 1961 went underground. The Pentecostals in the USSR experienced something similar in that most of their groups refused to register with the All-Union Council of Evangelical Christians and Baptists, as ordered by state authorities in 1946, and therefore were forced underground. Many Adventists also preferred to work underground. However, underground Protestantism on the pre-Gorbachev Soviet model was not common in other communist countries, except perhaps in Romania and Bulgaria.

For more than fifteen years, new and legally recognized communities emerged in the USSR from underground: Baptists, Adventists, Pentecostals, German Mennonites, and others. Until then, the price that evangelical Protestants had to pay for legalization was joining the state-controlled ACECB. Special state concessions—in particular, permission to register as autonomous—persuaded them to come into the open. "Autonomy" means that they did not need to join a larger, state-approved, and state-controlled umbrella organization. For them, that was decisive. As late as October 1988, leaders of the autonomous Evangelical Christians and Baptists reproached the ACECB for being overly beholden to Soviet authorities.

On the other hand, the statistically insignificant neo-Protestants also were beneficiaries of spectacular concessions (a new church center for Adventists in the USSR, several Mormon temples in the GDR, etc.), as the waning communist regimes tried to demonstrate their friendliness toward religion. Church representatives, referring to these privileges, presented in visits to the West a rather more harmonious picture of the religious situation than the representatives of the larger churches could do. While the traditional Lutheran and Reformed churches shrank dramatically, the neo-Protestant churches showed a tendency to expand. With their simple message, devoid of abstract academic-theoretical theology, they attract more people; in the process, they produced consternation not only among communist authorities, but among the larger, more traditional churches whose congregations they proselytize.

They have repeatedly come to the attention of the Western press and Western human rights groups because of their refusal to bear arms and their consequent conscientious objection to military service. This subject was explored in Lawrence Klippenstein's chapter. At this stage, the entire issue of conscientious objection has been or is being rapidly transformed in the postcommunist systems of Eastern Europe, and with legalization of conscientious objection, these smaller groups will have one less reason for alienation and one less reason for political engagement.

Church Opposition to the Atheist State

Just as there is no single Protestantism, so too the paths taken by individual Protestant communities in communist countries were necessarily different. There are many paths to choose from between the extremes expressed by Luke 20:25 ("Render therefore unto Caesar the things which be Caesar's, and unto God the things which be God's")—often cited by Eastern Europe's Protestants and Orthodox in hopes of signaling their loyalty to the state—and Acts 5:29 ("We ought to obey God rather than men").[1] Some churches, such as those found in the World Council of Churches, tried to fashion a constructive coexistence with the state, to vouchsafe an official existence in their communist homeland, and to promote a "normalization" in church-state relations. Formulas such as the Theology of Diakonia and the Church in Socialism were attempts in this direction. But the danger of self-compromise was always great, and the churches could not always avert the danger. Nowadays, church leaders in eastern Germany, Czechoslovakia, the former Soviet Union, and Romania are admitting their many errors.

The strength, and likewise the weakness, of Protestantism lies in its openness to the development of relatively individual theologies. More easily than in Catholicism, these can be adapted to diverse situations since individual churches in the different countries are independent and there is no Protestant equivalent to the Vatican.

To some extent, the situation of the individual Protestant churches has reflected the political situation in states of often militant atheist ideology. The formulation of viewpoints running counter to state policy entailed personal danger for their champions. Opposition on the part of legally permitted Protestant churches to regime policies—except for the Evangelical-Lutheran Church in the GDR—was simply not possible. Dissident officeholders risked arrest, and church publications usually preferred to engage in self-censorship.

But if "Protestantism" means many things, the same holds true for "communism." Hence, the general liberalization of religious policy in the region, impelled by mounting economic crises and social pressures, was different from one country to the next. All the same, the permissible boundaries for the churches remained strict right up to 1989, and the Protestant (and likewise the Orthodox) churches in most of these countries made no detectable effort—again with the exception of the Evangelical-Lutheran Church in the GDR—to cross them.

People often recall the Confessing Church of the Third Reich, which set itself in opposition to the Hitler regime and the so-called German Christians, the official Nazi-tolerated Protestant church organization. The Confessing Church (associated with names like Martin Niemöller, Karl Barth, Hans von Soden, Kurt Scharf, and Theophil Wurm) sharply opposed Nazi religious policy from the mid-1930s onward and likewise protested against some of the misdeeds of the Nazis (in particular, the liquidation of the Jews, euthanasia, and the war itself). The Confessing Church came into competition with the official church leaderships, which wanted to avoid confronting the state.

With a retrospective glance at this Confessing Church, some people wonder why there was no equivalent body in the communist countries of Eastern Europe and the USSR. The answer is so simple as to be banal: the repression of the churches by the Nazis was not nearly as destructive as the massive and systematic church persecutions in the communist countries that were carried out until well into the 1960s. The instruments of Nazi authorities were control, licensing, and the selective persecution of annoying critics. However, the question arises as to whether a comparison might be made with the situation in the GDR from the late 1970s to 1989, and why the Protestant churches in the GDR did not give birth to an opposition movement comparable to the Confessing Church. But one must realize that the Confessing Church arose shortly after Hitler's seizure of power, as soon as the general thrust of his policies was clear. In the GDR, by contrast, the general exhaustion after the war probably contributed to a general weakening of institutionally based opposition, and certainly after Soviet suppression of the June 1953 popular uprising and the eventual erection of the Berlin Wall in 1961, the dominant mood was one of resignation. Beyond that, the carrot-and-stick policy applied by the regime—particularly in the earlier period in its persistent seeking to separate the East German Lutherans from their coreligionists in West Germany, and in the later period in the ample rewards for the church stemming from the Luther celebrations of 1983—established clear rewards for compliance.

In many of these countries, the arrest of outspoken church dignitaries served to make the churches pliable. In the GDR, for example, pastors who had been part of the Confessing Church in Nazi times, and who therefore had experience in opposition, were shunted out of active service or retired under communism. The newer generation of church officials by and large grew up and was shaped by the anxieties of the first years of communist terror after 1945; they were therefore psychologically ill-equipped to withstand the seemingly almighty state power.

As long as the Protestant churches stood fast on the principle that the organizational form of the institutional church must be safeguarded, they could only do what communist religious policy permitted. The developments after 1989 in Hungary and Latvia, and in 1990 in Estonia, where Protestant churches took important personnel decisions without consulting the state, did not become possible because of a sudden growth in the Protestant will to resist, but largely because political circumstances permitted such a course of action. This fact was demonstrated by the unprecedented apology of Alfreds Kublinskis, chair of Latvia's Council for Religious Affairs, before the general synod of the Lutheran Church of Latvia (in April 1989) for the state's many injustices, and especially for the council's transgressions during four decades of Soviet rule.

Developments in the GDR in the late 1970s and 1980s would seem to contradict this thesis that official Protestant churches in communist systems could do only what they were permitted, being incapable of mounting a real opposition. Indeed, the Evangelical Church in the GDR increasingly came to serve as a protective umbrella for opposition groups, even if such groups had no specific Christian character. That some of this activity exceeded the bounds of what the Honecker regime considered tolerable was made clear in the late 1980s when arrests, expulsions of dissidents, searches, and censorship measures were imposed.

The Present Situation

The dramatic developments that followed the Soviet abdication of hegemony will not be without consequences for the Protestant communities of Eastern Europe. During the Stalinist era the churches of the region shared a similar fate: drastic losses of members and the decimation of church life. After Stalin's death, diverse paths opened for the churches in communist systems.

Since mid-1989, the political landscape of Eastern Europe and the USSR has been completely remade. East Germany finally was reunited with the rest of Germany. Poland, Czechoslovakia, Hungary, and parts of Yugoslavia introduced multiparty parliamentary systems. Before losing power, Bulgaria's communists were forced to introduce massive reforms. Even in Romania and Albania, there were changes—in Romania of a rather ambiguous nature, and in Albania of a rather dramatic and, looking at the events of 1991, unexpected character.

These changes had necessary consequences for the life of Christian and non-Christian religious organizations alike. The moral-ethical basis of Christianity would be needed in the resurrection of these hitherto socialist societies; in fact, the new state leaderships said as much themselves, albeit with different degrees of intensity. In Bulgaria and Romania the need for moral-ethical renewal received less emphasis than in the other states formerly associated with the Warsaw Pact. But new laws on religion in Poland and Hungary provided a good start in this direction. In other formerly socialist states, new religious legislation also was passed. In the former republics of the Soviet Union, the churches enjoy a much greater freedom of action, although part of that freedom resulted from the general social chaos. For example, Article 6 of the law on religious organizations (1 October 1990) does not provide for religious instruction in state schools. But for some time, religious instruction has taken place after hours in both state schools and universities.

Romania at this point is a kind of exception, both insofar as it considers itself socialist and in that the Orthodox Church remains tightly integrated with the state, its hierarchy cooperating closely with state authorities and enjoying the privileges of a state church. Yet for all that, the situation for Romanian Protestants has improved since the fall of Ceauşescu. For one thing, the Baptists now enjoy more breathing space. Again, pressure on the Hungarians generally (most of whom are either Reformed or Lutheran) has eased considerably, while the Transylvanian Saxons (German Lutherans) have enjoyed essentially full freedom of religion since 1990. What Romania's Germans want now, above all, is to leave Romania and go to Germany.

In the other countries that have officially broken with socialism, virtually complete religious freedom prevails. There are certainly no obstacles to the building of religious life or to its reorganization. On the other hand, a number of entirely new intraecclesiastical problems have arisen under these circumstances; sweeping changes in political leaderships everywhere in the region contribute to this result. One can hardly find anyone who formerly worked for the communists (except in Serbia and Montenegro, and in the Romanian security service). It is a different story where the churches are concerned. Only most reluctantly have the hierarchs of most churches been willing to step down. Aside from the developments in church leadership in the Latvian and Estonian Lutheran congregations, in the Russian Orthodox Church (after the death of Patriarch Pimen), and among Baptists in the former USSR, can one find important changes among Romania's Hungarian Reformed and German Lutheran groups. For example, László Papp, the reigning bishop of the Hungarian Reformed Church, fled to France after the revolution, and the second bishop, Gyula Nagy, finally retired when the authorities belat-

edly allowed him to draw his pension. Meanwhile, after the death of
their bishop, Albert Klein, in January 1990, Romania's German Lutherans had to elect a new head of the church. Interestingly, just after the
Christmas 1989 uprising, Klein had confessed: "We are confronted with
our own guilt, for not having dared to call injustice injustice." Bishop
Károly Tóth of the Reformed Church in Hungary was not reelected
bishop, while Protestant leaders were forced to resign in Poland and
Czechoslovakia.

Everywhere else we find church leaders who have held office for as
long as ten or twenty years. This is especially true of Eastern Europe's
Protestants and Orthodox. A leading church figure from the former GDR
said early in 1990:

> Many of our fellow pastors, who today loudly trumpet the word
> "Revolution" and who play up their supposed role in it, actually took a
> rather different position before and during the transformation. If peo-
> ple in the GDR today look to us Church leaders with trust, then we
> have to hang our heads in shame, because many of us have really not
> earned this trust; we were able to work quite well within the old
> system.

So the Protestant churches, like other churches in the region, must
confront the problems of making a critical reckoning with their pasts.
Church leaders, who only a short while ago were singing the praises of
socialism, now stand compromised as collaborators in the state repression against their own believers. (An extreme example is Bishop Károly
Tóth of the Hungarian Reformed Church or the late Bishop Zoltán Káldy
of the Hungarian Lutheran Church.) They hope to defend their positions
and privileges against the reforms demanded by believers. Now, when
there are no longer external hindrances limiting the churches, it seems
that there are some internal barriers—above all, to the needed self-
purification. The result is internal conflicts within many Protestant
churches in Hungary, Romania, Czechoslovakia, and Poland as reformers try to root out those "for whom the friendly disposition of the state
was dearer to their hearts than the prosperity of our own Church," as
Propst Modris Plate put it at the general synod of the Latvian Lutheran
Church on 12 April 1989. Plate himself had become one of that church's
most popular pastors; he had instituted popular Bible classes, carried out
liturgical reforms in the service, had revived the practice of singing
responsorial psalms, and had organized regular concerts of religious
music. But when a slanderous article appeared in the Latvian newspaper
Padomiju Jaunatne (Soviet Youth) attacking his fellow clergyman, Maris
Ludviks, Plate wrote a letter of protest to the newspaper. For this act of

courage, the Latvian Council of Religious Affairs decided to punish him
and put pressure on the Lutheran consistory to dismiss him from his
sacerdotal duties. The consistory bowed to the council and suspended
him on 18 March 1987. Although not an isolated instance, the Plate
dismissal captured more attention than many other such occurrences
because of his credibility and popularity as a pastor. A group of nineteen
Lutheran clergymen wrote a letter on 31 March to the archbishop and the
consistory, protesting the dismissal:

> We simply cannot understand how unsubstantiated complaints signed
> by local officials (and nowadays the press clearly shows that illegal
> actions are commonplace in local administration) could result in such a
> severe and kow-towing reaction by the Consistory. . . . Try to imagine
> how we feel when, before our very eyes, we see one of the best
> clergymen in Latvia being punished and transferred to another parish,
> so that all the activities he established in the parish of Kuldiga are
> disrupted. His only fault is consistent and uncompromising service
> rendered to God and dedicated to the future of the Evangelical Lu-
> theran Church in Latvia. It is painful indeed to see such goings-on
> [which] undermine our faith in the Consistory. If injustice and lies are
> to win the day in the case of Dean M. Plate, then we must ask: which of
> us will be the next victim?[2]

The docility of church leadership toward the state became a major
topic in several churches and led to several personnel changes. In the
Reformed Church of Hungary, Bishop Tóth failed to be reelected in 1991;
among the Slovak Lutherans, General Bishop Jan Michalko promptly
resigned; Bishop Janusz Narzynski retired in 1990 at age sixty-two, citing
"reasons of health"; and in the GDR Bishop Horst Gienke of Greifswald
committed the serious faux pas of inviting Erich Honecker to join him in
dedicating the newly completed Greifswald Cathedral, praising the regime's religious policy, at a time when East German Lutherans were
becoming highly critical both of the Church in Socialism concept and of
anything that smacked of collaboration with the state.

However, with such complex conditions one must always ask at what
point pastoral care for the community, for the family, or for the institutional church itself will translate itself into silence, inaction, and collaboration. After the December 1989 uprising, a Lutheran pastor from Romania said: "We are all forced to make compromises—but some, instead
of retreating just one step, retreated two or more steps—out of anxiety,
usually for their careers." A purification is needed in many churches in
the former Soviet sphere of influence where Protestants, like Orthodox
and in some cases Catholics (Pacem in Terris, for example), often drew

too close to the atheist state. Such a self-purification can scarcely occur without changes in personnel.

A second problem derives from the new freedom for the churches generally. This new freedom (as Ramet discussed in the preceding chapter) has been repeatedly abused as stronger churches put pressure on weaker ones, giving rise to frictions and conflicts. In this context, the disadvantages of the weaker churches figure as points of vulnerability in the revived rivalry with the larger, more powerful churches. And insofar as some of the Protestant churches of Eastern Europe are the churches of national minorities, they are dragged into ethnic conflicts.

After decades of persecution and repression of individual citizens and of entire groups, the relationships of citizens to each other, to ethnic groups, and to the state are often wracked by distrust. The churches could serve as a bridge in this regard. But after decades of persecution and accommodation, they have not had a chance to accustom themselves to such a task.

The Protestant churches in the former Soviet sphere of influence, like the Orthodox churches in the region, have had to accommodate themselves for so long to the destructive measures of the communists that they confront their new freedom feeling almost "helpless." It will require some time before these churches are able to gather their strength to define new courses and positions, to train new cadres, and to take up the new challenges of the postcommunist era.

Translated by Sabrina Petra Ramet

Notes

1 Protestantism and Communism

1. Quoted in Vilmos Vajta, "The Hungarian Lutheran Church and the 'Theology of Diaconia': Dispute Over the 'Theology of Diaconia'—The Hungarian Version of 'the Church in Socialist Society,'" *Religion in Communist Lands* 12, no. 2 (Summer 1984): 131.

2. See Pedro Ramet, "Gorbachev's Reforms and Religion," in Eugene Shirley and Michael Rowe (eds.), *Candle in the Wind: Religion in the Soviet Union* (Washington, D.C.: Ethics and Public Policy Center, 1989).

3. *Literaturnaia gazeta*, international ed., no. 1 (September 1990), pp. 12–13.

4. *Der Spiegel* (17 September 1990), p. 170.

5. See the two previous books in this series: Pedro Ramet (ed.), *Eastern Christianity and Politics in the Twentieth Century* (Durham, N.C.: Duke University Press, 1988); and Pedro Ramet (ed.), *Catholicism and Politics in Communist Societies* (Durham, N.C.: Duke University Press, 1990).

6. Avery Dulles, *The Catholicity of the Church* (Oxford: Clarendon Press, 1985), pp. 108–9, 112.

7. J. C. Davis, *Utopia and the Ideal Society: A Study of English Utopian Writing, 1516–1700* (Cambridge: Cambridge University Press, 1981), pp. 172, 258.

8. Robert McAfee Brown, *The Spirit of Protestantism* (New York: Oxford University Press, 1965), pp. 94–98.

9. Wilhelm Pauck, *From Luther to Tillich: The Reformers and Their Heirs* (San Francisco: Harper and Row, 1984), pp. 15–17.

10. Ibid., p. 96.

11. Michael Bourdeaux, "Baptists and Other Protestants," in Bourdeaux et al. (eds.), *Religious Minorities in the Soviet Union* (London: Minority Rights Group, 1977), p. 15; and Bourdeaux, *Religious Freedom in Russia: Protestant Opposition to Soviet Religious Policy* (London: Macmillan, 1968), pp. 6–7.

12. Ludvik Nemec, *Church and State in Czechoslovakia* (New York: Vantage Books, 1955), p. 253.

13. Joseph L. Hromadka, *Theology Between Yesterday and Tomorrow* (Philadelphia: Westminster Press, 1957), pp. 50–51, 55.

14. Josef L. Hromadka, *Thoughts of a Czech Pastor*, trans. from Czech by Monika and Benjamin Page (London: SCM Press, 1970), p. 87.

15. Peter Boner, "Ethical Détente: Marxist-Christian Dialogue in Hungary," *Religion in Communist Lands* 13, no. 1 (Spring 1985): 51.

16. Quoted in Gisela Helwig, "Zwischen Opposition und Opportunismus: Zur Lage der Kirche in der DDR," *Deutschland Archiv* 9, no. 6 (June 1976): 578.

17. See Sabrina P. Ramet, *Social Currents in Eastern Europe: The Sources and Meaning of the Great Transformation* (Durham, N.C.: Duke University Press, 1991).

18. Bourdeaux, *Religious Ferment*, p. 1.

19. Interview with Franc Rode, Vatican Secretariat for Nonbelievers, Rome, 11 June 1987.

20. See Paul Mojzes, *Christian-Marxist Dialogue in Eastern Europe* (Minneapolis: Augsburg, 1981).

21. J. V. Eibner, Zoltán Káldy: A New Way for the Church in Socialism?" *Religion in Communist Lands* 13, no. 1 (Spring 1985).

22. See William G. Rusch, *Ecumenism—A Movement Toward Church Unity* (Philadelphia: Fortress Press, 1985).

23. Susan Horvath, "Sects in Hungary: The Free Christian Congregations," *Religion in Communist Lands* 12, no. 1 (Spring 1984): 7–8.

24. See Hans-Martin Moderow and Matthias Sense (eds.), *Orientierung Ökumene: Ein Handbuch*, 2nd ed. (East Berlin: Evangelische Verlagsanstalt, 1987), chap. 7.

25. Tadeusz Wojak, "Historische Traditionen des Okumenismus in Polen," in Gerhard Bassarak (ed.), *Okumene in Polen* (East Berlin: Evangelische Verlagsanstalt, 1982), pp. 124, 128.

26. Karol Karski, "Die Entwicklung der ökumenischen Bewegung in Polen," in Bassarak (ed.), *Okumene in Polen*, p. 140.

27. Mihaly Bucsay, *Der Protestantismus in Ungarn, 1521–1978*, part 2 (Vienna: Verlag Hermann Bohlaus, 1979), pp. 144–45, 185–88.

28. Brown, *Spirit of Protestantism*, pp. 186–87.

29. Michael Shafir, *Romania: Politics, Economics and Society* (Boulder, Colo.: Lynne Rienner, 1985), p. 137.

30. Jan Michalko, "Das Erbe des reformatorischen Werkes Martin Luthers im Leben der Slowakischen Evangelischen Kirche A.B. in der CSSR," in Gerhard Bassarak and Günter Wirth (eds.), *Luther und Luthertum in Osteuropa* (East Berlin: Evangelische Verlagsanstalt, 1983), pp. 130–31.

31. Janusz Narzynski, "Zur Geschichte des Luthertums in Polen von 16. bis zum 20. Jahrhundert," in Bassarak (ed.), *Ökumene in Polen*, p. 56.

32. Ryszard Trenkler, "Die Reformation in Polen," in Bassarak and Wirth (eds.), *Luther und Luthertum*, p. 224.

33. Quoted in Paul Keim, "Polish Protestants: Ecumenism in a Dual Diaspora," *Religion in Communist Lands* 11, no. 3 (Winter 1983): 296.

34. Douglas Durasoff, "The Soviet State and Russian Protestants," in Nicolai N. Petro (ed.), *Christianity and Russian Culture in Soviet Society* (Boulder, Colo.: Westview Press, 1989), p. 54.

35. R. E. Davies, "Baptists in Poland—Past and Present," *Religion in Communist Lands* 18, no. 1 (Spring 1990): 52–53.

36. Quoted in Walter Sawatsky, *Soviet Evangelicals Since World War II* (Kitchener, Ont.: Herald Press, 1981), p. 113.

37. Lorna and Michael Bourdeaux, *Ten Growing Soviet Churches* (Keston, Eng: Keston College, 1984).

38. Douglas Durasoff, "After the Revolution? Modes of Authority in a 'Good Economy' in Post-Communist Systems," paper presented at Fourth World Congress of Slavic Studies, Harrogate, Eng., 21 July 1990.

2 Protestantism: Theology and Politics

1. A. G. Dickens, *Reformation and Society in Sixteenth-Century Europe* (New York: Harcourt Brace and World, 1966), p. 33.

2. "Luther's attack on the sacrifice of the mass and transsubstantiation . . . further undermined the foundations of clerical ideology. For much of the strength of the clergy's claim to be a special caste derived from the belief that the clergy alone had the power to offer up the sacrifice of Christ and that they alone had the power to celebrate the miracle of the mass by which the elements were changed into the body and blood of the Lord." W. D. J. Cargill Thompson, in Philip Broadhead (ed.), *The Political Thought of Martin Luther* (Totowa, N.J.: Barnes, 1984), pp. 29–30.

3. J. W. Allen, *A History of Political Thought in the Sixteenth Century* (London: Methuen, 1928), p. 42.

4. H. Zuck (ed.), *Christianity and Revolution: Radical Christian Testimonies, 1520–1650* (Philadelphia: Temple University Press, 1975). Separatists were, for example, Obbe Philips and Jakob Hutter; revolutionaries-secessionists, Melchior Hoffmann, Bernhard Rothmann, and Balthasar Hubmaier; pacifists, Menno Simons, Conrad Grebel, Michael Sattler, and most of the separatists.

5. The common punishment was drowning, a horribly ironic touch. This was often preceded by torture. The record is sickening: Hubmaier was tortured in 1525 and burned at the stake in 1527 by the Catholic Habsburgs; his wife was executed by drowning in the Danube. The same happened to Sattler and his wife. Felix Manz was drowned in Zwinglian Zurich in 1527. Grebel escaped drowning by dying of the plague before the Zurich council decreed that all Anabaptists be drowned. In Bern, between 1529 and 1571, forty public executions took place. T. G. Sanders calculated that more than five thousand Anabaptists were put to death in Switzerland alone in the first decade of their movement (*Protestant Concepts in Church and State* [New York: Holt, Rinehart, 1964], p. 91). W. Walker sums up the situation as follows: "At the diets of Speier (1529) and of Augsburg (1530), the assembled German estates, both Roman Catholic and Protestant, applied the old Roman law against heresy to them. Henceforth membership in any Anabaptist group was punishable by death. In Roman Catholic territories, particularly Austria and Bavaria, this newly proclaimed law was executed with utmost severity. In Evangelical lands, Anabaptists were not treated as heretics but as seditionists. If they were unwilling to conform to the established ecclesiastical order, they were given the chance to emigrate. If they refused to do so and con-

tinued to profess their faith publicly, they were regarded as disturbers of the peace and punished by imprisonment or death. Only in Hesse, Wurttemberg and Strassburg blood-judgments were avoided" (Cycil Richardson, Wilhelm Pauck, and Robert Handy, *A History of the Christian Church*, rev. ed. [New York: Scribner, 1959], p. 328).

6. Roland Bainton, *The Age of the Reformation* (Princeton, N.J.: Van Nostrand, 1956), p. 43.

7. See Thompson, *Political Thought of Luther*, for a thorough discussion.

8. "Temporal Authority: To What Extent Should It Be Obeyed?" in J. Pelikan and H. T. Lehmann (eds.), *Luther's Works* (Philadelphia: Fortress Press, 1955ff.), vol. 45, pp. 89ff.

9. "By 1536 any subtle distinctions between heresy and blasphemy had disappeared, and Luther called upon magistrates to suppress heresy actively" (Sanders, *Protestant Concepts*, p. 48). In 1520 Luther wrote that if the pope is an offense to Christendom, then someone should call a free council and no one is better able to do this than the temporal authorities, "especially since they are also fellow-Christians, fellow-priests, fellow members of the spiritual estate, fellow lords over all things" ("To the Christian Nobility of the German Nation Concerning the Reform of the Christian Estate," *Luther's Works*, vol. 44, pp. 123–217).

10. John Calvin, *Institutes of the Christian Religion*, trans. Ford Lewis Battles (Philadelphia: Westminster Press, 1960), vol. 2, pp. 86–87.

11. Reinhold Niebuhr, *Christianity and Power Politics* (New York: Archon Books, 1969), pp. 50–59.

12. "All rulers, Protestant included, inherited from the Christian Roman Empire the view that a state cannot thrive without the support of religion. Only one religion can be true and that religion should be upheld by the state" (Bainton, *Age of Reformation*, p. 24). Bainton also pointed out that Zwingli based baptism on Old Testament circumcision and that "increasingly Zurich assumed the form of a chosen people, the elect of the Lord, striving for themselves and their children to achieve under God a holy commonwealth. This idea was to have a profound influence in New England by way of English Puritanism which, at many points, was more influenced by Zurich than by Geneva" (p. 41).

13. Walker, *A History*, pp. 352–53.

14. Allen, *A History*, pp. 64ff.; Dickens, *Reformation*, p. 163.

15. For a brief discussion of the Peasants' War, see James Atkinson, *Martin Luther and the Birth of Protestantism* (Baltimore: Penguin Books, 1968), chap. 17.

16. *Luther's Works*, vol. 46, pp. 8–16.

17. Ibid. "Admonition to Peace: A Reply to the Twelve Articles of the Peasants in Swabia" (pp. 17–43); "Against the Robbing and Murdering Hordes of Peasants" (pp. 49–55); "An Open Letter on the Harsh Book Against the Peasants" (pp. 63–85).

18. Thompson, *Political Thought of Luther*, introduction.

19. See, for example, Martin Bucer, *De Regno Christi*, in Wilhelm Pauck (ed.), *Melanchthon and Bucer*, Library of Christian Classics (Philadelphia: Westminster Press, 1969), vol. 19, p. 181: "I shall indicate how Your Majesty

[i.e., Edward VI of England] can and should establish, foster, and encourage
the full restoration of the Kingdom of Christ among his subjects." Bucer
continued by saying that, by God's command, this should be done by
"beatings, whippings, prison, exile, and various forms of execution." Bucer
was one of the most influential Reformers of the sixteenth century. After
Zwingli's death in 1531, he led the Protestants in Switzerland and the Rhine-
lands. Calvin was with Bucer in Strassburg from 1538–41. After Charles V's
Interim Peace (Augsburg, 1549), Bucer was forced into exile and taught at
Cambridge, where he was much sought after for counsel and advice. He died
in 1551.

20. *History of the Reformation in Scotland,* in David Laing (ed.), *The Works of
John Knox* (New York: AMS Press, 1966), vol. 4, p. 284.

21. "I am speaking all the while of private individuals. For if there are now
any magistrates of the people, appointed to restrain the willfulness of kings
(as in ancient times the ephors were set against the Spartan kings, or the
tribunes of the people against the Roman consuls, or the demarchs against
the senate of the Athenians; and perhaps, as things are now, such power as
the three estates exercise in every realm when they hold their chief assemblies), I am so far from forbidding them to withstand, in accordance with
their duty, the fierce licentiousness of kings, that, if they wink at kings who
violently fall upon and assault the lowly common folk, I declare that their
dissimulation involves nefarious perfidy, because they dishonestly betray
the freedom of the people, of which they know that they have been appointed protectors by God's ordinance" (*Institutes,* vol. 2, p. 1519).

22. Thompson, *Political Thought of Luther,* p. 174; Dickens, *Reformation,*
p. 80; Allen, *A History,* p. 25. Erastianism: after Erastus (1524–83), a Swiss-
German theologian who advocated the supremacy of the state over the
church. This is roughly equivalent to caesaropapism, in which the power of
the pontiff is in the prince's hands.

23. Paul Tillich, *The Protestant Era,* trans. James L. Adams (Chicago: University of Chicago Press, 1957), p. 179; Reinhold Niebuhr, *The Nature and
Destiny of Man* (New York: Scribner, 1949), vol. 2, pp. 190–98. Dietrich
Bonhoeffer's political ideas in ethics are often classically Lutheran: the Christian's "duty of obedience is binding on him until government *directly* com-
pels him to offend against the divine commandment, that is to say, until
government openly denies *its divine commission* and thereby forfeits its claim"
(trans. N. H. Smith, ed. E. Bethge [New York: Macmillan, 1962], p. 307; italics
mine). However, the specific example Bonhoeffer gives ("by making itself
master over the belief of the congregation"), his rejection of the *cuius regio
eius religio* rule (p. 313), and of course his participation in a tyrannicide plot,
show that the crux lies in interpretation and practice, not in dogma.

24. Allen, *A History,* p. 83.

25. Dickens, *Reformation,* p. 164.

26. Sanders, *Protestant Concepts,* pp. 228–29; Allen, *A History,* pp. 64–69.

27. Reinhold Niebuhr, *Moral Man and Immoral Society: A Study in Ethics and
Politics* (New York: Scribner, 1960), p. 59.

28. More specifically, Ernst Troeltsch wrote: "to a remarkable extent Calvinism, more than Catholicism, and far more than Lutheranism, had pre-

pared the way for the gradual emancipation of these theories [concerning Natural Law and democracy] from their connection with Christian thought, even though the Baptist movement was more radically effective in this direction" (*The Social Teaching of the Christian Churches*, trans. Olive Wyon [New York: Macmillan, 1931], p. 640).

29. Max Weber, *The Protestant Ethic and the Spirit of Capitalism*, trans. Talcott Parsons (New York: Scribner, 1958).

30. Troeltsch, *Social Teaching*, p. 643; see also pp. 588ff. and 681–82.

31. R. H. Tawney, *Religion and the Rise of Capitalism* (New York: New American Library, 1947), n. 32, chap. 4, and conclusion.

32. For a discussion of the Weber-Tawney thesis, see Dickens, *Reformation*, p. 178; also see esp. Winthrop S. Hudson, "The Weber Thesis Reexamined," in Sidney A. Burrell (ed.), *The Role of Religion in Modern European History* (New York: Macmillan, 1964), pp. 44–55. It seems to me that neither Dickens nor Hudson sufficiently acknowledged Tawney's criticism of Weber. James H. Nichols summed up the matter satisfactorily: "The relation between Calvinism and Puritanism and the 'capitalist' mentality has been much debated. There does seem to be a correlation of Lutheran, Roman Catholic, and High Anglican ethics with economic traditionalism. Commercial, technological, and industrial leadership, by contrast, have rested with Calvinist and Puritan Dutch, English, and Americans. Free church Calvinism penetrated and became identified with democracy, capitalism, and applied science to a degree unequaled by the other major Christian traditions. And whereas this tradition was secondary to Anglicanism in England, everywhere else in the English-speaking world free church Calvinism has been vastly more numerous and influential than the Anglican communion" (Nichols, *History of Christianity: 1650–1950* [New York: Ronald Press, 1956], pp. 66–67).

33. Allen, *A History*, p. xiv.

34. Troeltsch, *Social Teaching*, pp. 503–8.

35. Martin Luther, *Selected Political Writings*, ed. J. M. Porter (Philadelphia: Fortress Press, 1974), p. 8 in Porter's introduction.

36. Luther, "A Reply," in *Works*, vol. 46, p. 25. Bonhoeffer also wrote in the tradition that holds that natural law equals the Second Table of the Decalogue: "For pagan government the answer [to the question: whence the goodness in political authority] is that there is a providential congruity between the contents of the second table and the inherent law of historical life itself" (*Ethics*, p. 305).

37. Troeltsch, *Social Teaching*, pp. 526–530, 493.

38. Calvin, *Institutes*, chap. 20, sec. 16.

39. Knox, *Works*, vol. 4, p. 481. Here, as elsewhere, I have modernized the diction.

40. John Poynet, *Politike Power*, facs. ed. (Amsterdam: Theatrum Orbis Terrarum, 1972), n.p.

41. J. W. Allen believed that Jean Bodin in *De la République* (1577) was the first to detach the idea of sovereignty from king, pope, or emperor (*A History*, p. 423). It seems to me that Poynet preceded Bodin in this notion.

42. An exile from England during the reign of Queen Mary I, Poynet wrote from Strasbourg.

43. Christopher Goodman, "How Superior Powers Ought to Be Obeyed" (1558), in Zuck, *Christianity and Revolution*, p. 151.

44. Calvin, *Institutes*, chap. 20, sec. 8. The French is more ambiguous: "que la préeminence de ceux qui gouverneront tenant le peuple en liberté sera plus à priser."

45. Troeltsch, *Social Teaching*, p. 675.

46. Gerald R. Cragg, *The Church and the Age of Reason: 1648–1789* (Baltimore: Penguin Books, 1960), pp. 75–79.

47. Jean-Paul Sartre, *Existentialisme est un humanisme* (Paris: Editions Nagel, 1946), pp. 19–20.

48. Quoted in Allen, *A History*, p. 160.

49. Ibid., pp. 180–181.

50. H. C. Porter, *Puritanism in Tudor England* (London: Macmillan, 1970), pp. 90–92.

51. William Haller, *Elizabeth I and the Puritans* (Charlottesville: University Press of Virginia, 1964), p. 21. See also Allen, *A History*, pp. 225–28.

52. Nichols, *History*, p. 56.

53. Arminianism is called after Jacobus Arminius, a Dutch theologian. It differs from Calvinist orthodoxy primarily on the issue of predestination. It was condemned by the Synod of Dort (1618–19), which declared that God predestines some to believe rather than, as Arminius stated, that God elects to save those who believe.

54. Ibid., p. 57.

55. Walker, *A History*, p. 400.

56. Norman Sykes, *Church and State in England in the Eighteenth Century* (Hamden, Conn.: Archon Books, 1962), chap. 2.

57. Cragg, *The Church*, pp. 134–35.

58. Although favoring the forms of worship and liturgy of the Church of England, the Latitudinarians believed them to be "things indifferent" and were tolerant of variant forms.

59. Ibid., chap. 11.

60. Koppel S. Pinson, *Pietism as a Factor in the Rise of German Nationalism* (New York: Octagon Books, 1968). See esp. the introduction and the last chapter, "Christian Patriotism." Pinson marked the beginning of Pietism with the publication in 1675 of Spener's *Pia Desideria oder Wahren evangelischen Kirche*. Spener was born in 1635, Francke in 1663, Zinzendorf in 1700, and Schleiermacher in 1768.

61. Pinson, *Pietism*, p. 63.

62. Friedrich Schleiermacher, *The Christian Faith*, ed. H. R. Mackintosh and J. S. Stewart (New York: Harper, 1963), vol. 1, pp. 5–6. In *On Religion*, he wrote: "It is . . . my strong conviction that it is one of the most essential tendencies of Christianity to separate completely church and state, and I can just as little agree that the church should evermore and more be absorbed in the state" (*On Religion: Speeches to Its Cultural Despisers*, trans. John Oman [New York: Harper, 1958], p. 18).

63. Nichols, *History*, p. 249.

64. Ibid., p. 161; see also chaps. 12 and 13.

65. Quoted in Anson P. Stokes and Leo Pfeffer, *Church and State in the United States*, rev. ed. (New York: Harper, 1964), p. 16.

66. Roger Williams, *The Complete Writings of Roger Williams*, ed. Samuel L. Caldwell (New York: Russell and Russell, 1963), vol. 3 (facs. ed.), *The Bloudy Tenent of Persecution*, p. 73.

67. Williams, *Bloudy Tenent*, p. 378.

68. The dedication begins: "Next to the saving of your own souls (in the lamentable shipwreck of mankind) your task (as Christians) is to save the souls, but as Magistrates, the bodies and goods of others" (p. 5). Cotton wrote: "We acknowledge that none is to be punished for his conscience, though mis-informed, as has been said, unless his error be fundamental and seditiously and turbulently promoted, and that after the conviction of his conscience, that it may appear he is not punished for his conscience, but for sinning against his conscience" (p. 47).

69. Ibid., editor's preface, pp. x–xi.

70. Sanders, *Protestant Concepts*, p. 179.

71. Stokes and Pfeffer, *Church and State*, p. 5.

72. Nichols, *History*, p. 72; Walker, *A History*, p. 473.

73. Stokes and Pfeffer, *Church and State*, p. 7.

74. Ibid., p. 18.

75. For Witherspoon, see ibid., p. 41; for Backus, see Paul T. Dieffenbach, "Isaac Backus and the Separation of Church and State," in Ronald C. White, Jr., Louis B. Weeks, and Garth M. Rosell (eds.), *American Christianity: A Case Approach* (Grand Rapids, Mich.: Eerdmans, 1986), pp. 30–41.

76. "1 in 8 to 1 in 20," according to Stokes and Pfeffer, *Church and State*, p. 23. "Less than ten percent," according to John Dillenberger and Claude Welch, *Protestant Christianity* (New York: Scribner, 1954), p. 148.

77. Thomas Hooker, *A Survey of the Summe of Church-Discipline*, facs.ed. (New York: Arno Press, 1972), p. 13. The book was first published in 1648, a year after Hooker's death. An elegy by John Cotton was included. The last four lines read:

> Now blessed Hooker, thou art on high,
> Above the thankless world, and cloudy sky:
> Do thou of all thy labor reap the Crown,
> Whilst we here reap the seed, which thou has sown.

78. Ronald C. White, Jr., "Richard Allen and the Birth of the African Methodist Episcopal Church," in White, Weeks, and Rosell (eds.), *American Christianity*, pp. 57–62.

79. Stokes and Pfeffer, *Church and State*, pp. 131–34, 142.

80. See Roger A. Couture, "John Courtney Murray, The American Experience, and Religious Freedom at Vatican II," in White, Weeks, and Rosell (eds.), *American Christianity*, pp. 156–70.

81. John Courtney Murray was vindicated. He is the one principally responsible for the section "Religious Freedom," in Walter M. Abbott, S.J. (gen. ed.), *The Documents of Vatican II* (New York: Guild Press, 1966). The first chapter of this section begins "This Vatican Synod declares that the human person has a right to religious freedom" (p. 678).

82. Martin E. Marty, *Protestantism in the United States: Righteous Empire,* 2nd ed. (New York: Scribner, 1986), p. 41.

83. The motto was sanctioned for coins by Congress in 1865, for all paper money in 1955. It was made the official national motto by an act of Congress in 1956 (Stokes and Pfeffer, *Church and State,* p. 570).

84. Sanders, *Protestant Concepts,* p. 219.

85. Alexis de Tocqueville, *Democracy in America,* ed. Richard D. Heffner (New York: New American Library, 1956), part I, book 1, chap. 12, pp. 115–20.

86. Marty, *Protestantism,* pp. 73, 88.

87. A brief sketch is found in Stokes and Pfeffer, *Church and State,* pp. 262–63, and Walker, *A History,* p. 516.

88. *Reynolds* v. *United States,* in Stokes and Pfeffer, *Church and State,* p. 109.

89. Marty, *Protestantism,* p. 147. Marty quotes Henry May.

90. Ibid., p. 115. Marty quotes Theodore Parker: "The merchants build the churches and endow theological schools; they furnish the material sinews of the church" (p. 122).

91. Ibid., p. 225.

92. Ibid., p. 250.

93. Walter Rauschenbusch, *A Theology for the Social Gospel* (New York: Abingdon, n.d.), p. 5.

94. Nichols, *History,* p. 277. The opinions are from about the turn of the century.

95. Tillich, *Protestant Era,* pp. 161–80.

96. Niebuhr, *Moral Man* (1932) and *Christianity* (1940).

97. *Why Churches Fight Government Infiltration,* Office of Church and Society, American Lutheran Church and the Program Agency, Presbyterian Church (U.S.A.), January 1987. See also no. CIV 86-0072 PHX CLH: Plaintiffs' Response to Defendants' Motion to Dismiss. The gist is that the government labels political refugees as illegal aliens. The government's position evidently is that persons from a noncommunist country cannot be political refugees because they move between ideologically similar political systems. The Sanctuary movement maintains that these people are fleeing military dictatorships.

98. In 1906 Leonhard Ragaz (1868–1945) published *The Gospel and the Present Social Struggle.* He was a pacifist and with Hermann Kutter gave a theological interpretation of socialism that influenced the young Karl Barth.

99. For this paragraph and most of the following, see Nichols, *History,* chaps. 17–20, 29.

100. For the making and the text of the Barmen Declaration, see Rolf Ahlers, *The Barmen Theological Declaration of 1934: The Archeology of a Confessional Text,* Toronto Studies in Theology, vol. 24 (Lewiston, N.Y. and Wuensten, Ont.: Edwin Mellen, 1986).

101. Niebuhr, *Christianity,* p. 58.

102. Karl Barth, *Community, State, and Church,* ed. Will Herberg (New York: Doubleday, 1960).

103. Ibid., pp. 102–5.

104. Ibid., p. 144.

105. Ibid., p. 173.

106. Ibid., pp. 175–83, 185.

107. See Herberg's introduction to ibid., pp. 11–67. Barth was taken to task by Reinhold Niebuhr in "Why Is Barth Silent on Hungary?" in *The Christian Century* (23 January 1957); by Charles West in *Communism and the Theologians* (SCM Press, 1958); and by Emil Brunner in "An Open Letter to Karl Barth," in Barth, *Against the Stream* (New York: Philosophical Library, 1954).

108. Niebuhr, *Christianity*, pp. 9–10.

109. Niebuhr, *Moral Man*, p. 170.

110. J. G. Davies, *Christians, Politics and Violent Revolution* (Maryknoll, N.Y.: Orbis Books, 1976), pp. 131–33.

111. Niebuhr, *Moral Man*, p. 172.

112. In Charles Villa-Vicencio, *Between Christ and Caesar: Classic and Contemporary Texts on Church and State* (Grand Rapids, Mich.: Eerdmans, 1986). The statement was made in the context of the debate on conscientious objection and the conference's stand that the taking up of arms is never (if at all) justified in Catholic and Reformation theology except for a "just war," which excludes the defense of an unjust and discriminating society. J. Moltmann and J. G. Davies maintained that conscientious objection is (at least) justifiable in view of nuclear war, because there can be no just nuclear war when it destroys the world and hence the possibility of establishing justice (Moltmann, *On Human Dignity*, p. 122, and Davies, *Christians*, p. 148).

113. Niebuhr, *Moral Man*, p. 263.

114. Luther, "Temporal Authority."

115. Niebuhr, *Moral Man*, p. 179.

116. Allan Aubrey Boesak, *Farewell to Innocence: A Socio-Ethical Study on Black Theology and Black Power* (Maryknoll, N.Y.: Orbis Books, 1977), p. 70. See also Dorothee Soelle, *Political Theology*, trans. John Shelley (Philadelphia: Fortress Press, 1974), pp. 59–61.

117. See, for example, Gustavo Gutierrez, *A Theology of Liberation: History, Politics and Salvation*, trans. Sister Caridad Inda and John Eagleson (Maryknoll, N.Y.: Orbis Books, 1973), and Jürgen Moltmann, *On Human Dignity: Political Theology and Ethics*, trans. M. Douglas Meeks (Philadelphia: Fortress Press, 1984).

3   Protestantism in East Germany 1949–1989

This chapter is based in part on interviews conducted in East Germany, 20 June–12 July 1988. Interviews were conducted with appropriate clergymen and responsible officials of seventeen religious organizations as well as theologians and responsible state officials in Berlin, Dresden, Herrnhut, Leipzig, Halle, Erfurt, and Eisenach. I am grateful to the International Research Exchanges Board (IREX) for providing funding in support of this research.

1. Wolfgang Kaul, *Kirchen und Religionsgemeinschaften in der DDR—Eine Dokumentation* (Rostok-Warnemunde: Institute for Marxism-Leninism, 1984),

pp. 5–6; and *Zahlenspiegel Bundesrepublik Deutschland/Deutsche Demokratische Republik: Ein Vergleich,* 3rd ed. (Bonn: Federal Ministry for Inter-German Relations, 1988), p. 97.

2. *Zahlenspiegel,* p. 97.

3. *Frankfurter Allgemeine* (23 April 1988), p. 12, trans. in JPRS, *East Europe Report,* no. EER-88-040 (23 May 1988), p. 2.

4. *Keston News Service,* no. 279 (9 July 1987), p. 19.

5. For detailed discussion of the Roman Catholic Church, see Robert F. Goeckel, "The Catholic Church in East Germany," in Pedro Ramet (ed.), *Catholicism and Politics in Communist Societies* (Durham, N.C.: Duke University Press, 1990).

6. Most of the figures given here come from interviews with responsible church representatives or with state officials in East Germany, June–July 1988, or from Kaul, *Kirchen und Religionsgemeinschaften.* Some statistics were taken from Hubert Kirchner (ed.), *Freikirchen und Konfessionelle Minderheitskirchen* (East Berlin: Evangelische Verlagsanstalt, 1987); and Helmut Obst, *Apostel und Propheten der Neuzeit: Gründer christlicher Religionsgemeinschaften des 19.20. Jahrhunderts,* 2nd ed. (East Berlin: Union Verlag, 1981).

7. *Christian Science Monitor* (6 November 1989), p. 3.

8. Ulrich Materne, "Der Bund Evangelische-Freikirchlicher Gemeinden in der DDR," in Kirchner (ed.), *Freikirchen,* p. 51.

9. Werner Klan and Johannes Zellmer, "Die Evangelisch-lutherische (alt-lutherische) Kirche," in Kirchner (ed.), *Freikirchen,* p. 134.

10. Knuth Hansen and Hubert Kirchner, "Die Mennoniten-Gemeinde," in Kirchner (ed.), *Freikirchen,* p. 32.

11. Christian Pietsche, "Im Benehmen mit dem Staate: Die Neuapostolische Kirche in der DDR," *Kirche im Sozialismus* 12, no. 3 (June 1986): pp. 123–24.

12. DPA (Hamburg) (19 March 1990), trans. in FBIS, *Daily Report* (Eastern Europe) (20 March 1990), p. 33.

13. For an account of Weissenberg's life and the early experiences of his community, see Obst, *Apostel und Propheten,* pp. 326–44.

14. See Dan Beck, "The Luther Revival: Aspects of National *Abgrenzung* and Confessional *Gemeinschaft* in the German Democratic Republic," in Pedro Ramet (ed.), *Religion and Nationalism in Soviet and East European Politics,* rev. and expanded ed. (Durham, N.C.: Duke University Press, 1989).

15. Bishop Gienke aggravated the members of his church in 1989 by joining Honecker in reaffirming the continued validity of the "Church in Socialism" concept at a time when church members were increasingly critical of the idea. As a result, the district synod took a vote of no confidence in November, voting 32–30 against him. The vote impelled the bishop to resign his office in the same month. See ADN International Service (East Berlin) (14 November 1989), trans. in FBIS, *Daily Report* (Eastern Europe) (14 November 1989), p. 27.

16. See *Neue Zürcher Zeitung* (28 September 1990), p. 3, (24–25 February 1991), p. 4, and (27 February 1991), p. 4; and *Süddeutsche Zeitung* (Munich) (23–24 February 1991), p. 5.

17. For details, see Hans-Martin Moderow and Matthias Sense (eds.),

Orientierung Ökumene: Ein Handbuch, 2nd ed. (East Berlin: Evangelische Verlagsanstalt, 1987), esp. chap. 7.

18. Quoted in Richard W. Solberg, *God and Caesar in East Germany: The Conflict of Church and State in East Germany Since 1945* (New York: Macmillan, 1961), p. 30.

19. Ibid., p. 57.

20. Horst Dähn, *Konfrontation oder Kooperation? Das Verhältnis von Staat und Kirche in der SBZ/DDR 1945–1980* (Opladen: Westdeutscher Verlag, 1982), p. 28.

21. Quoted in Solberg, *God and Caesar,* p. 74.

22. Ibid., p. 90.

23. Dähn, *Konfrontation oder Kooperation,* p. 44.

24. Quoted in Solberg, *God and Caesar,* p. 196.

25. Ibid., p. 234.

26. Ibid., p. 235.

27. Quoted in Florian Ehlert, " 'Suchet der Stadt Bestes!': Bischof Mitzenheims Bemühungen um Einvernehmen mit dem Staat," *Kirche im Sozialismus* 14, no. 3 (June 1988): 97.

28. Quoted in ibid., p. 98.

29. Quoted in ibid., p. 99.

30. Quoted in ibid.

31. Stephen R. Bowers, "East German National Consciousness: Domestic and Foreign Policy Considerations, *East European Quarterly* 13, no. 2 (Summer 1979): 148.

32. Quoted in Peter Fischer, *Kirche und Christen in der DDR* (East Berlin: Verlag Gebr. Holzapfel, 1978), p. 28.

33. Quoted in ibid., p. 87.

34. Quoted in ibid., p. 89.

35. See *Kirche als Lerngemeinschaft: Dokumente aus der Arbeit des Bundes der Evangelischen Kirchen in der DDR* (East Berlin: Evangelische Verlagsanstalt, 1981), pp. 161–62.

36. Ibid., pp. 202, 206.

37. Ibid., p. 169.

38. Theo Mechtenberg, "Die Friedensverantwortung der Evangelischen Kirchen in der DDR," *Deutsche Studien* 19, no. 74 (June 1981): 176.

39. *Kirche als Lerngemeinschaft,* p. 208.

40. Ibid., p. 255.

41. See Albrecht Schönherr, "Nach zehn Jahren: Zum Staat-Kirche-Gespräch am 6. März 1978," *Kirche im Sozialismus* 14, no. 1 (February 1988): 5.

42. *Frankfurter Allgemeine* (27 September 1978), p. 1.

43. For further discussion, see Pedro Ramet, "Church and Peace in the GDR," *Problems of Communism* 33, no. 4 (July–August 1984): esp. 51–53; also reprinted as chap. 5 in Pedro Ramet, *Cross and Commissar: The Politics of Religion in Eastern Europe and the USSR* (Bloomington: Indiana University Press, 1987).

44. *De Tijd* (Amsterdam) (16 December 1983), trans. in JPRS, *East Europe Report,* no. EPS-84-015 (30 January 1984), p. 20; and Ulrike Enders, "Erziehung zum Hass: Zum staatlichen Erziehungsprogramm für Kindergarten," *Kirche im Sozialismus* 13, no. 2 (April 1987).

45. *Frankfurter Allgemeine* (5 September 1984), p. 3.

46. Ibid. (9 February 1988), p. 2.

47. Quoted in Gisela Helwig, "Zwischen Opposition und Opportunismus: Zur Lage der Kirche in der DDR," *Deutschland Archiv* 9, no. 6 (June 1976): 578.

48. Wolfgang Büscher and Peter Wensierski, *Null Bock auf DDR: Aussteigerjugend im anderen Deutschland* (Hamburg: Spiegel Verlag, 1984), p. 42; also *Glaube und Heimat* (Jena) (18 May 1986), p. 4, trans. in JPRS, *East Europe Report*, no. EER-86-103 (17 July 1986), pp. 98–99.

49. *Neues Deutschland* (12 February 1985), p. 1.

50. *Mittelalter, Beginn der Neuzeit* (Berlin: Volk und Wissen Volkseigener Verlag, 1958), a history textbook for senior schools in the GDR, as quoted in Arvan Gordon, "The Luther Quincentary in the GDR," *Religion in Communist Lands* 12, no. 1 (Spring 1984): 78.

51. Wolfram von Hanstein, *Von Luther bis Hitler* (Dresden, 1947), pp. 22–23, as cited in Stephen P. Hoffmann, "The GDR, Luther, and the German Question," *Review of Politics* 48, no. 2 (Spring 1986): 250.

52. Alexander Abusch, *Der Irrweg einer Nation* (Berlin, 1950), as cited in Hoffmann, "The GDR." First published in 1946.

53. Gerhard Brendler, "Reformation und Fortschritt," in Leo Stern and Max Steinmetz (eds.), *450 Jahre Reformation* (Berlin, 1967), p. 67, as quoted in Hoffmann, "The GDR," p. 256.

54. Robert F. Goeckel, "The Luther Anniversary in East Germany," *World Politics* 37, no. 1 (October 1984): 119.

55. Quoted in ibid., p. 121.

56. Friedrich Winterhager, "Thomas Müntzer und die Gegenwart in Beiden Deutschen Staaten," *Deutsche Studien* 24, no. 96 (December 1986): 386; and Arbeitsgruppe *Thomas-Müntzer-Gedenken 1989* des Kirchenbundes, "Orientierungshilfe zum Gedenken des 500. Geburtstag von Thomas Müntzer im Jahre 1989," *EPD Dokumentation*, no. 52 (1987): 44.

57. "Thesen über Thomas Müntzer," *Neues Deutschland* (30–31 January 1988), p. 9.

58. Ibid.

59. Roland Hahn, "Müntzer ein Sozialrevolutionär? Die SED und die Kirche vor dem 500. Geburtstag Thomas Müntzer," *Kirche im Sozialismus* 14, no. 4 (August 1988): 141; also *Thomas Müntzer Ehrung der DDR 1989* (East Berlin: Dietz Verlag, 1988).

60. Rita Hermanns, "Auf der Suche nach Freiräumen: über die Initiative 'Kirchentag von unten,'" *Kirche im Sozialismus* 13, no. 4 (August 1987): 145.

61. *Frankfurter Allgemeine* (24 June 1987), p. 5; (29 June 1987), p. 5.

62. "Grössere Freiräume für Basisgruppen" (Rüdiger Rosenthal, interviewed by Matthias Hartmann), *Kirche im Sozialismus* 13, no. 5 (October 1987): 189, 191.

63. *Die Welt am Sonntag* (Bonn) (29 November 1989), pp. 1–2; and *Frankfurter Allgemeine* (31 December 1987), p. 2.

64. *Frankfurter Allgemeine* (14 November 1988), p. 7, trans. in FBIS, *Daily Report* (Eastern Europe) (17 November 1988), pp. 19, 21. The statement was

allegedly read to Leich and distributed in written form to only the first secretaries of SED *Bezirk* and *Kreis* leaderships.

65. Quoted in Barbara Donovan, "Church Groups Call for Democratic Reforms," *Radio Free Europe Research* (10 June 1988), p. 1.

66. *Frankfurter Rundschau* (27 June 1988), p. 1.

67. Quoted in *Die Welt* (7 June 1988), p. 10, trans. in FBIS, *Daily Report* (Eastern Europe) (8 June 1988), p. 36.

68. *Frankfurter Allgemeine* (20 September 1988), p. 3; and Matthias Hartmann, " 'Hier ändert sich nichts'—Zur Synodaltagung des Kirchenbundes," *Deutschland Archiv* 21, no. 10 (October 1988): 1025.

69. On this case, see *Frankfurter Allgemeine* (20 June 1988), p. 1.

70. *Süddeutsche Zeitung* (5 July 1988), p. 2; *Die Welt* (5 July 1988), p. 1, trans. in FBIS, *Daily Report* (Eastern Europe) (6 July 1988), p. 29; *Frankfurter Allgemeine* (23 July 1988), p. 4, and (9 August 1988), p. 3; and *Süddeutsche Zeitung* (18 October 1988), p. 2, trans. in FBIS, *Daily Report* (Eastern Europe) (19 October 1988), p. 18.

71. Vienna Domestic Service (30 December 1988), trans. in FBIS, *Daily Report* (Eastern Europe) (30 December 1988), p. 25; and Michael Burg, "Es geht nicht um die Kirchenpresse," *Kirche im Sozialismus* 14, no. 6 (December 1988): esp. 218.

72. *Die Welt* (14 November 1988), p. 1; DPA (Hamburg, 14 November 1988)—both trans. in FBIS, *Daily Report* (Eastern Europe) (15 November 1988), p. 27.

73. Richard Schröder, "Was kann 'Kirche im Sozialismus' sinnvoll heissen?," *Kirche im Sozialismus* 14, no. 4 (August 1988): 137.

74. *Frankfurter Allgemeine* (13 March 1989), p. 4, trans. in FBIS, *Daily Report* (Eastern Europe) (17 March 1989), p. 22.

75. Heino Falcke, "Stellvertretendes Handeln: 'Kirche im Sozialismus' am Beispiel der DDR," *Kirche im Sozialismus* 15, no. 6 (December 1989): 232–37.

76. *Frankfurter Rundschau* (13 May 1989), p. 2.

77. *Frankfurter Allgemeine* (21 September 1989), p. 2; also *Neue Zürcher Zeitung* (24/25 September 1989), p. 3.

78. *Die Welt* (16/17 September 1989), p. 4, trans. in FBIS, *Daily Report* (Eastern Europe) (19 September 1989), p. 28.

79. *New York Times* (18 May 1990), p. A5.

80. On the last point, see *Frankfurter Allgemeine* (3 September 1990), p. 12; (24 September 1990), p. 14.

81. *Neue Zürcher Zeitung* (27 February 1991), p. 4.

82. Robert Goeckel, "The Evangelical-Lutheran Church and the East German Revolution," *Occasional Papers on Religion in Eastern Europe* 10, no. 6 (November 1990): 43.

83. *Neues Deutschland* (31 May 1988), p. 2.

4 Protestantism in Czechoslovakia and Poland

1. Ludwig von Gogolak, *Beiträge zur Geschichte des slowakischen Volkes*, vol. 1 (Munich: Verlag R. Oldenbourg, 1963), pp. 118, 119.

2. Kamil Krofta, *Dějiny Československé* (Prague: Sfinx, B. Janda, 1946), p. 554.

3. Jiří Otter, *The Witness of Czech Protestantism* (Prague: Kalich, 1970), pp. 44–50, 55–69.

4. Alan Scarfe, "National Consciousness and Christianity in Eastern Europe," in Pedro Ramet (ed.), *Religion and Nationalism in Soviet and East European Politics*, 1st ed. (Durham, N.C.: Duke University Press, 1984), p. 34.

5. "Lutheran Churches in the World," *Lutheran World*, nos. 2–3 (1977), p. 261.

6. R. W. Davies, "Baptists in Poland—Past and Present," *Religion in Communist Lands* 18, no. 1 (Spring 1990): 54.

7. Ludvík Němec, "The Czechoslovak Heresy and Schism: The Emergence of a National Czechoslovak Church," *Transactions of the American Philosophical Society* (Philadelphia, March 1975), p. 36.

8. *Christian Century* 70, no. 30 (29 July 1953): 861.

9. Bohumil Jiří Frei, *Staat und Kirche in der Tschechoslowakei* (Munich: Verlag Robert Lerche, 1973), pp. 268–88.

10. Adam Piekarski, *Freedom of Conscience and Religion in Poland* (Warsaw: Interpress Publishers, 1979), pp. 65, 80.

11. David Barrett, *World Christian Encyclopedia* (Oxford: Oxford University Press, 1982), p. 570.

12. *News from the Polish Ecumenical Council*, nos. 1–2/19 (January–July 1987), p. 24.

13. See Walter Sawatsky, "Evangelicals in Eastern Europe Compared," *Occasional Papers on Religion in Eastern Europe* (hereinafter, *OPREE*) 6, no. 4 (August 1986): 1–3, 6.

14. See Paul Bock, *In Search of a Responsible World Society* (Philadelphia: Westminster Press, 1974), pp. 130–31.

15. Among Hromádka's books in English are *Theology Between Yesterday and Tomorrow* (Philadelphia: Westminster Press, 1957); *Thoughts of a Czech Pastor* (London: SCM Press, 1970); and *Doom and Resurrection* (London, 1945). During my numerous visits to Prague over the years, Czechoslovak Protestants have repeatedly told me of their great respect for Hromádka.

16. Josef Macek, *The Hussite Movement in Bohemia* (London: Lawrence and Wishart, 1965), pp. 88–89.

17. J. A. Hebly, *The Russians and the World Council of Churches* (Belfast: Christian Journals Limited, 1978), p. 91.

18. Paul Mojzes, *Christian-Marxist Dialogue in Eastern Europe* (Minneapolis: Augsburg, 1981), p. 118.

19. Ibid., pp. 120–21.

20. Jan Lochman, *Church in a Marxist Society* (New York: Harper and Row, 1970), p. 179.

21. Jerzy Walicki, *Religious Life in Poland* (Warsaw: Interpress Publishers, 1970), p. 29.

22. Ibid., p. 39.

23. "An Open Letter of Prof. Hromádka to the Soviet Ambassador in Prague," *Religion in Communist Dominated Areas* 7, nos. 17–18 (15/30 September 1968): 148–49.

24. Dorothea Neumärker, *Josef L. Hromádka: Theologie und Politik im Kontext des Zeitgeschehens* (Munich: Chr. Kaiser Verlag, 1974), p. 146.

25. Adalbert Hudak (ed.), *Staatsatheismus in der Tschechoslowakei* (Zollikon: Institut Glaube in der 2. Welt, 1980), p. 21.

26. *Church Within Socialism* (Rome: IDOC, 1976), pp. 167–70.

27. Hudak, *Staatsatheismus*, p. 24.

28. *ČSSR. Zur Lage der Evangelischen Kirche der Böhmischen Brüder. Eine Dokumentation* (Zollikon: Institut Glaube in der 2. Welt, 1978), p. 5.

29. Jakub Trojan, "Christian Existence in Socialist Society or The Theology of Conflict," *Religion in Communist Dominated Areas* 16, nos. 10–12 (1977): 162–63.

30. "Charter 77," ibid., vol. 16, nos. 1–3 (1977), p. 5.

31. "Charter 77—Document No. 9: On Religious Freedom," ibid., vol. 16, nos. 4–6 (1977), p. 54.

32. *ČSSR. Zur Lage der Evangelischen Kirche der Böhmischen Brüder*, pp. 7–18.

33. Milena Kalenovská, "The Religious Situation in Czechoslovakia," *Religion in Communist Lands* 5, no. 3 (Autumn 1977): 152.

34. "Czech Pastor Protests," in ibid., vol. 6, no. 3 (Autumn 1978): 173.

35. *Keston News Service* (hereinafter *KNS*), no. 118 (27 March 1981), p. 6.

36. Paul Keim, "Polish Protestants: Ecumenism in a Dual Diaspora," *Religion in Communist Lands* 11, no. 3 (Winter 1983): 302.

37. Andrzej Wojtowicz, "Katholischer Sozialismus, Polen aus protestantischer Sicht," *Evangelische Kommentare* 14, no. 7 (July 1981): 403.

38. Grazyna Sikorska, "The Polish Roman Catholic Church and the Fate of Former Lutheran Churches in the 'Recovered Lands,'" *Religion in Communist Lands* 16, no. 3 (Autumn 1988): 206.

39. *Christian Science Monitor* (19 July 1989), p. 6.

40. *KNS*, no. 143 (29 March 1982), p. 3.

41. Ibid., no. 191 (26 January 1984), p. 6.

42. Lawrence Klippenstein, "Conscientious Objectors in Socialist Poland, 1980–1987," *OPREE* 7, no. 5 (October 1987): 26.

43. *News from the Polish Ecumenical Council*, nos. 1–2/19 (January–July 1987), p. 16.

44. "Address of Pope John Paul II to Polish Ecumenical Council," *News from the Polish Ecumenical Council*, nos. 1–2/19 (January–July 1987), p. 19.

45. Bill Yoder, "Poland in mid-1984," *OPREE* 5, no. 1 (February 1985): 16.

46. Witold Benedyktowicz, "The Place of Polish Protestants on the Denominational Map," *News from the Polish Ecumenical Council*, nos. 1–2/19 (January–July 1987), p. 23.

47. "ČSSR: Ausführungsbestimmungen zum geltenden Recht verletzen die Religionsfreiheit," *Glaube in der 2. Welt* 11, no. 3 (1983): 28–32.

48. Ibid.

49. *KNS*, no. 125 (6 July 1981), p. 3.

50. Ibid., no. 197 (19 April 1984), p. 5.

51. Ibid., no. 196 (5 April 1984), p. 2.

52. Ibid., no. 234 (19 September 1985), p. 5.

53. Erika Kadlecová, "The Causes of Increased Interest in Religion," *Religion in Communist Dominated Areas* 25, no. 1 (Winter 1986): 5–10.

54. Bogdan Szajkowski, "New Law for the Church in Poland," *Religion in Communist Lands*, vol. 17, no. 3 (Autumn 1989): 196–200.

55. *KNS*, no. 330 (20 July 1989), p. 2.

56. "The Law on Guarantees of Freedom of Conscience and Belief," *News from the Polish Ecumenical Council* (Warsaw), nos. 1–4/22 (January– December 1989), pp. 31–42. The full text is provided here.

57. *Slowo Powschechne* (6 April 1989), pp. 1, 6, trans. in Foreign Broadcast Information Service (FBIS), *Daily Report* (Eastern Europe) (10 May 1989), p. 45.

58. "The synodical report of Bishop Janusz Narzynski," *News from the Polish Ecumenical Council* (Warsaw), nos. 1–4/22 (January–December 1989), pp. 22–23.

59. *Polityka* (Warsaw) (6 May 1989), p. 6, trans. in FBIS, *Daily Report* (Eastern Europe) (17 May 1989), p. 41.

60. *KNS*, no. 337 (2 November 1989), p. 5.

61. Ibid., no. 351 (31 May 1990), p. 15.

62. *Ecumenical Press Service* (1–10 November 1989), nos. 89, 11, 5.

63. For further discussion, see Paul Bock, "Czech Protestants Propose Reforms," *OPREE* 10, no. 1 (February 1990): 33, 34.

64. *Kostnické Jiskry* (Prague) (29 November 1989), pp. 1, 2.

54. *Kostnické Jiskry* (6 December 1989), p. 1.

66. *Český Bratr* (Prague) 66, no. 5 (May 1990): 50.

67. *Pravda* (Bratislava) (12 January 1990), p. 2, trans. in FBIS, *Daily Report* (Eastern Europe) (22 January 1990), p. 35.

68. ČTK (Prague) (4 February 1990), trans. in FBIS, *Daily Report* (Eastern Europe) (6 February 1990), pp. 23–24.

69. *KNS*, no. 343 (8 February 1990), p. 8.

70. *Czechoslovak Ecumenical News* (10 January 1990), p. 1.

71. *KNS*, no. 350 (17 May 1990), p. 14.

72. *Kostnické Jiskry* (14 March 1990), p. 4.

73. Ibid. (28 March 1990), p. 4.

74. Ibid. (24 January 1990), p. 2.

75. Josef Hromádka, "Church-State Relationship in Changing Society," *OPREE* 11, no. 1 (February 1991): 10.

5 Protestantism in Hungary

1. Albert Bereczky, *A Keskeny Út* (Budapest, 1953), p. 369.

2. Mihály Bucsay, *A Protestantizmus Története Magyarországon 1521–1945* (Budapest: Gondolat, 1985), p. 216.

3. Ibid., p. 217.

4. Sándor Biró, M. Bucsay, E. Tóth, and Z. Varga, *A Magyar Református Egyház Története* (Budapest: Kossuth, 1949), pp. 321ff.

5. Kálmán Tóth, *The Church of the Glorious Lamb* (Ottawa, Ont., 1982), pp. 15–16.

6. Ferenc Bajusz, *Az Ökumenikus Mozgalom Története és Problémái: A Keresztyén Felekezetek* (Budapest: Református Theol. Akadémia, 1972), pp. 136ff.

7. Ibid., pp. 118ff.

8. József Szakács, "A Magyarországi H.N. Adventista Egyház 75 éves Jubileuma," Theológiai Szemle 11–12 (1973): 377.

9. János Csohány, "Református Békekezdeményezés 1917-ben" Theológiai Szemle 7–8 (1975): 227–30.

10. Bucsay, A Protestantizmus, p. 236.

11. Ibid., pp. 236–37.

12. Ibid., pp. 243–45.

13. Biró et al., A Magyar Református, p. 412.

14. Bucsay, A Protestantizmus, pp. 252–53.

15. Ibid., p. 245.

16. Camille M. Cianfarra, The Vatican and the Kremlin (New York: Dutton, 1950), p. 150.

17. Jenő Szigeti, "Az Egyezmény és a magyarországi egyházak új irányvétele" Theológiai Szemle 11–12 (1973): 325.

18. Bucsay, A Protestantizmus, p. 258.

19. István Barta, P. Hanák, L. Makkai, M. Lackó, Zs. Nagy, and Gy. Ránki, A Magyar Nép Története (Budapest: A Kultura Világa, 1965), p. 596.

20. Szigeti, "Az Egyezmény," p. 325.

21. Cianfarra, The Vatican and the Kremlin, p. 151.

22. Szigeti, "Az Egyezmény," p. 326. He quotes from the Minutes of the Transtibiscan District.

23. Ibid.

24. Ibid.

25. Ibid., p. 327.

26. Ibid., p. 329.

27. Ibid., p. 326.

28. Ibid., p. 329.

29. Cianfarra, op. cit., pp. 155ff.

30. Ibid., p. 158.

31. József Poór, A Protestáns Theológia Magyarországon 1945–1985 (Budapest: Kossuth, 1986), p. 30.

32. Trevor Beeson, Discretion and Valour (London: Fontana Press, 1974), pp. 236–37.

33. These figures were mentioned by Bishop Tóth in an interview, Reformátusok Lapja (18 September 1988), p. 4.

34. Jenő Szigeti, Az egyházak új irányvétele a felszabadulás után (Budapest ". . . És emlékezzél meg az útról . . . ," 1981), pp. 226–27.

35. Ibid., p. 227.

36. Albert Bereczky, A Keskeny Út (Budapest: Református Egyetemes Konvent, 1953), pp. 321–23.

37. Ibid., pp. 330–36.

38. Ibid., pp. 297–99.

39. Beeson, Discretion and Valour, p. 244.

40. Against Stalin's advice. See József Éliás, Lehulló Álarcok (n.p., 1988), p. 30.

41. Albert Bereczky referred to it in his lecture to the ministers at a continuing education conference in Tahi (Summer 1954).

42. Éliás, *Lehulló Álarcok*, p. 12.

43. Ibid., p. 14.

44. István Szépfalussy, in Lajos Ordass, Válogatott Irások, ed., *Utószó* (Bern: I. Szépfalussy, E.P.M.Sz., 1982), p. 365.

45. Ibid., p. 367.

46. Vilmos Vajta, *Die Diakonische Theologie im Gesellschaftsystem Ungarns* (Frankfurt am Main: Verlag Otto Lembeck, 1987), p. 21.

47. Szigeti, "Az Egyezmény," pp. 231–33.

48. József Mindszenty, *Memoires* (New York: Macmillan, 1974), pp. 98ff.

49. Jenő Gergely, *A Katolikus Egyház Magyarországon, 1944–1971* (Budapest: Kossuth, 1985), pp. 97–98.

50. Ibid., pp. 122, 125–27.

51. Beeson, *Discretion and Valour*, p. 239.

52. J. Gergely, *A Katolikus Egyház Magyarországon, 1944–1971* (Budapest: Kossuth, 1985), pp. 84, 132.

53. Ibid., pp. 122, 125–27.

54. Joseph Pungur, "The Relationship Between the Hungarian State and the Hungarian Reformed Church," *Occasional Papers on Religion in Eastern Europe* 6, no. 1 (February 1986).

55. Tóth, *Church of the Glorious Lamb*, p. 17.

56. Gyula Bárczay, *Megújulás—Megdermedés—Megmozdulás*, in Bethlen Naptár, 1988, pp. 102–8.

57. Lajos Ordass, *Válogatott Irások* (Bern: I. Szépfalussy, E.P.M.Sz., 1982), pp. 203–14.

58. Bárczay, *Megújulás*, p. 111.

59. József Poór, *A Protestáns Theologia Magyarországon, 1945–1985* (Budapest: Kossuth Press, n.d.), p. 73.

60. Albert Bereczky, *Ajtónyitás* (Budapest, 1951), p. 19.

61. Elemér Kocsis, "Az Egyház Ébredésétöl a szolgáló egyház teológiájáia," *Confessio* 1 (1977): 39–47; *Confessio* 2 (1977): 143–51.

62. "Our Heritage and Task Is Reformation," *Hittel es Cselekedettel* (1970), pp. 87ff.

63. Beeson, *Discretion and Valour*, p. 244.

64. Géza Boross, "Milyen teológiai trányzatokat tükröz a magyar igehirdetés," *Theológiai Szemle* 1–2 (1964): 78–79.

65. The social and ethical aspects of Theology of Diaconia are expounded in Gyula Nagy, *Egyház a mai világban* (Budapest: n.p., 1967). It is available in German translation, *Kirche in der heutigen Welt* (Budapest: n.p., 1967).

66. Vajta, *Die Diakonische Theologie*, pp. 43ff.

67. Letter from Zoltán Dóka to Bishop Gyula Nagy (17 May 1985).

68. Vajta, *Die Diakonische Theologie*, pp. 50–51.

69. Ibid., pp. 72–110.

70. Published in *Hungarian Reformed News* (New York) (October–November 1978 and March 1979).

71. Bishop Tóth wrote about it in *Reformátusok Lapja* (20 November 1988).

72. *Reformátusok Lapja* (Budapest) (28 August 1988).

73. Ibid.

74. Ibid. (9 October 1988).

75. Ibid. (16 October 1988).
76. Ibid. (6 November 1988).
77. Ibid. (18 September 1988).
78. Zoltán Dóka, "*Javaslat*," unpublished manuscript, 1988, p. 1.
79. Zoltán Dóka, "*Summa Summarum*," unpublished manuscript, 1988, pp. 1–2.
80. Ibid.
81. Dóka, "*Javaslat*," pp. 1–2.
82. *Reformátusok Lapja* (9 July 1989), p. 3.
83. *Kecskeméti Lapok* (23 February 1990), p. 5.
84. *Reformátusok Lapja* (29 January 1989), p. 3.
85. Ibid. (4 February 1990), p. 1.
86. *Hungarian Reformed News* (New York) (October–November 1978, March 1988).
87. The only reelected bishop was Elemér Kocsis in the Transtibiscan district (Debrecen). The new bishops elected were Lóránt Hegedüs in the Danubian district, replacing Károly Tóth (Budapest); István Mészáros in the Transtibiscan district, replacing László Kürti (Miskole); and Mihály Márkus in the Transdanubian district, replacing Attila Kovách (Veszprém). Among international Reformed churches, only the Hungarian Church had the office of bishop elected for life—until the general synod in 1990. This synod limited the tenure of bishops to six years. There was an overture to replace the office of bishop by the office of moderator, but the effort failed for at least three reasons. First, during the persecutions of the seventeenth and eighteenth centuries, it was imperative to have a church bishop to make quick decisions in vital cases. Second, the Catholic Habsburg kings of Hungary would not recognize a church without a bishop. Third, along with noblemen and aristo-crats, only bishops could occupy seats in the Upper House of the legislature of royal Hungary. The communist government skillfully used the bishops for their own purposes. To avoid such a situation in the future, the general synod limited bishops' tenure.
88. Géza Németh, *Felkiáltójel* (Budapest, 1990), pp. 85–87.
89. *Evangélikus Élet* (Budapest), 1 April 1990, p. 1.
90. Ibid. (Budapest, 2 June 1991), synod news, p. 1.
91. *Reformátusok Lapja* (10 July 1988), p. 1.
92. Ibid. (1 September 1991), p. 1.

6 Protestantism in Romania

1. An official statement on church-state relations in socialist Romania was written by Metropolitan Antonie of Transylvania, "Church and State in Romania," in Lukas Vischer (ed.), *Church and State: Opening a New Ecumenical Discussion* (Geneva: WCC, 1978), p. 102.
2. *Lege pentru Regimul General al Cultelor* (Bucharest: Imprimeriile Statului, 1928), p. 8. It should be noted that the term "cult" is not used in a pejorative way as is frequently the case in the West, but rather it is used to designate a religion, church, creed, or form of worship.

3. *Legea Si Statutele Cultelor Religioase Din Republica Populara Romana* (Bucharest: Ministry of Cults, 1951), pp. 393–444.

4. Michael Shafir, *Romania: Politics, Economics and Society* (Boulder, Colo.: Lynne Rienner, 1985), p. 151; an important analysis of the religions before 1938 is provided in Olimp Caciula, "Cultele in Romania," *Enciclopedia Romaniei* 1 (1938): 417–42.

5. Earl A. Pope, "The Orthodox Church in Romania," *Ostkirchliche Studien* 31 (December 1982): 297–310.

6. *The Romanian Orthodox Church* (Bucharest: Bible and Orthodox Missionary Institute, 1968), p. 17; Mircea Pacurariu, *Istoria Bisericii Ortodoxe Romane* (Sibiu: Metropolitanate, 1972), pp. 359–60.

7. P. Delroy, "The Church in Romania," *Pro Mundi Vita Dossiers* (November–December 1978), p. 23.

8. Edward K. Bogosian, "Armenian Community in Romania Dwindles to Insignificant Numbers," *Armenian Reporter* (10 August 1978).

9. George Hancock-Stefan, "Cind Spunem Biserica—ii putem include pe ortodocsi, catolici, si protestanti?" Paper presented at the American-Romanian Academy of Arts and Sciences, Portland State University, May 1988, p. 3.

10. This is the official designation for this group in Romania to distinguish it from the Reformation churches. They also have been referred to as evangelicals, Free Churches, fundamentalists, and sectarians.

11. John Butosi, "The Reformed Church in Romania—In a Historical Perspective," *Reformed Review* 60 (Winter 1987): 117–19.

12. Kenneth Scott Latourette, *A History of Christianity* (New York: Harper, 1953), pp. 741–42.

13. Trond Gilberg, "Religion and Nationalism in Romania," in Pedro Ramet (ed.), *Religion and Nationalism in Soviet and East European Politics,* rev. and expanded edition (Durham, N.C.: Duke University Press, 1989), pp. 328–30; Butosi, "The Reformed Church," p. 171. Butosi in his otherwise excellent statement on this period overlooks the severe discrimination against the Romanian Orthodox that Gilberg points out.

14. George Schöpflin, *The Hungarians of Rumania,* report no. 37 (London: Minority Rights Group, 1978), p. 8.

15. Vladimir Socor, "Romania," in Vojtech Mastny (ed.), *Soviet/Eastern European Survey, 1983–1984* (Durham, N.C.: Duke University Press, 1985), p. 366.

16. Butosi, "The Reformed Church," p. 119.

17. Roland Bainton, "The Left Wing of the Reformation," *Journal of Religion* 21 (1941): 124–34.

18. Stephen Fischer-Galati, "Religion," in Stephen Fischer-Galati (ed.), *Romania* (New York: Mid-European Studies Center, 1956), pp. 132–35.

19. Schöpflin, *The Hungarians,* p. 7.

20. *Struggle and Trials of the Magyar Reformed Church in Transylvania under the Roumanian Heel* (Budapest: Foreign Churches' Committee of the Hungarian Reformed Synodus, 1921), pp. 7–20; *The Religious Minorities in Transylvania* (Boston: Beacon Press, 1925).

21. J. H. Jensen, "State-Building, Nation-Building or National Imperial-

ism: The Romanian Experience, 1918–1940," paper presented at AAASS, Honolulu, November 1989, pp. 12–14; Butosi, "The Reformed Church," p. 131. Butosi emphasizes that the Reformed Church faced the problems "with renewed confessional and theological vigor." The church turned to Calvin, republished the Heidelberg Catechism, edited a new hymnal, and responded positively to the theology of Karl Barth. The parochial school system was revitalized, and a wide range of social and religious institutions was sponsored.

22. Patriarch Miron, *Cultele in Romania: Referat pentru raspuns Em. Sale Dr. William Temple* (Bucharest, 1937), p. 12.

23. Anthony Komjathy and Rebecca Stockwell, *German Minorities and the Third Reich* (New York: Holmes and Meier, 1980), pp. 107, 109.

24. Ruth Rouse and Stephen Charles Neill, *A History of the Ecumenical Movement, 1517–1948* (Philadelphia: Westminster Press, 1968), p. 714; W. A. Visser't Hooft, *Memoirs* (Philadelphia: Westminster Press, 1973), p. 175; Earl A. Pope, "International Aid and the Romanian Churches," paper presented at the annual conference of the Society for Romanian Studies at Emerson College, November 1987.

25. Letter from J. Hutchinson Cockburn, senior secretary, Department of Christian Reconstruction and Inter-Church Aid, to Pastor Friedrich Müller, Sibiu, Romania, 13 July 1945 (Archives, WCC, Geneva).

26. Gote Hedenquist, "Report on Trip to Roumania," 24 October–24 November 1946 (Archives, WCC, Geneva); Robert Tobias, "Report—Rumania," 13–29 August 1946 (Archives, WCC, Geneva).

27. Tobias, "Report–Rumania," p. 18.

28. Letter from Magne Solheim to Hutchinson Cockburn, before 24 October 1947 (Archives, WCC, Geneva).

29. Magne Solheim, "Report on the Situation in Romania," 15 November 1948 (Archives, WCC, Geneva).

30. Tobias, "Report–Rumania," pp. 6–7.

31. Gilberg, "Religion and Nationalism," p. 338.

32. *Legea si Statutele*, p. 7.

33. Ibid., pp. 8–9.

34. Ibid., p. 10.

35. Ibid., pp. 11–14.

36. For an early official interpretation of the Romanian state's attitude toward the religious bodies, see Stanciu Stoian, "Attitudinea regimului de democratie populara fata de culte religioase," in *Cultele Religioase in Republica Populara Romana* (Bucharest: Ministry of Cults, 1949), pp. 69–103.

37. Gilbert H. Flanz, "Romania," in Albert P. Blaustein and Gilbert H. Flanz (eds.), *Constitutions of the Countries of the World* (New York: Oceana, 1987), p. 9.

38. Ibid., p. 10.

39. *The Reformed Church in Romania* (Cluj, 1976), p. 6; Caciula, "Cultele in Romania," pp. 429–32.

40. Alexander Havadtoy, "The Hungarian Reformed Church in Romania," *Most-Favored-Nation Trading Status for the Socialist Republic of Romania, the Hungarian People's Republic, and the People's Republic of China*, hearing before

the Subcommittee on Trade of the Committee on Ways and Means, House of Representatives, 10 June 1986 (Washington, D.C.: U.S. Government Printing Office, 1987), pp. 281–84.

41. Metropolitan Antonie, "The Church in Romania," *Ecumenical Press Service*, 86.03.41. It should be noted that the *Ecumenical Press Service* of the World Council of Churches has provided very responsible coverage of the controversy over the Romanian religious situation that erupted within the ecumenical movement.

42. Bishop Paul Szedressy, "The Synodal Presbyterian Evangelical Superintendency A.C. of the Socialist Republic of Romania" (Kolozsvar-Napoca, May 1978), p. 1.

43. Friedrich Teutsch, *Geschichte de ev. Kirche in Siebenbürgen*, 2 vols. (Hermannstadt: Berlad, 1921–22). This is the definitive history of the German Lutherans until 1917.

44. Paul Hansen, "The Lutheran Churches in Rumania," February 1966. Hansen, for many years the Lutheran World Federation's secretary for Europe, had a special interest in the churches of Eastern Europe.

45. Nestor Ratesh, "The Rise and Fall of a Special Relationship," in Paul Quinlan (ed.), *The United States and Romania* (Woodland Hills, Calif.: American-Romanian Academy, 1988), p. 171.

46. "End of Romanian Lutheran Denomination Seen," *EPS*, 86.08.19, 88.09.61.

47. "The Foundation of the Unitarian Church," official statement on the 400th anniversary of the church's founding.

48. Janos Erdo, "Biserica Unitariana din Republica Socialista Romania" (1975), manuscript.

49. Arpad Szabo, "Principiile de Credinta ale Religiei Unitariene" (Cluj-Napoca, 7 October 1975).

50. Elemér Illyes, *National Minorities in Romania—Change in Transylvania* (Boulder, Colo.: East European Monographs, 1982), p. 233.

51. The Reformed Church publishes a bimonthly journal, *Reformatus Szemle;* the Unitarian Church publishes a quarterly, *Kereszteny Magveto;* and the German Lutheran Church publishes a monthly magazine, *Kirchliche Blätter*. The Hungarian Lutheran Church shares the Reformed publication.

52. *Reformed Church*, p. 34.

53. Gilberg, "Religion and Nationalism," pp. 176–86.

54. George Schöpflin, "National Minorities in Eastern Europe," in Schöpflin (ed.), *The Soviet Union and Eastern Europe* (New York: Facts on File, 1986), pp. 309–12.

55. Butosi, "The Reformed Church," pp. 133–34.

56. "Hungarian Plea for Religious Liberty in Transylvania," *Keston News Service* (hereinafter *KNS*), no. 263 (13 November 1986), pp. 9–10.

57. "Romania: Bishop Takes Issue with Charges About Minorities," *EPS*, 87.02.84.

58. Ibid., 87.07.12.

59. Metropolitan Antonie of Transylvania, "Minorities in Romania," *EPS*, 87.04.116.

60. Károly Toth, "Ethnic Minorities in Romania," *EPS*, 87.06.45.

61. "Excerpts from Speeches," *Telegraful Roman*, no. 41–44 (15 November 1987), pp. 3–4.

62. Ibid., 2.

63. "Telegram to Nicolae Ceauşescu," ibid., p. 1; Paul Booth, "Loyalty to the President, Romanian Style," *Frontier* (January–February 1987), pp. 8–9.

64. "Romania: Reformed Trip on Minorities Cancelled," *EPS*, 88.04.89.

65. "Transylvanian Refugees in Hungary," *Religion in Communist Lands* 16 (Winter 1988): 360.

66. Letter from Edmond Perret, w a r c general secretary, to President Nicolae Ceauşescu, Geneva, 14 June 1988; *EPS*, 88.06.110. A virtually simultaneous announcement was made through the official *Ecumenical Press Service* that the w a r c believed the destruction of the villages is the "latest and most dramatic move" in a policy that has intentionally eroded the rights of minorities in Romania. ("World Reformed Alliance Scores Romania Policy on Minorities," *EPS*, 88.08.110.) The two Reformed bishops in Romania predictably dismissed the w a r c's negative judgment as "contrary to the truth" (*For Disarmament and Peace: An Assembly of the Religious Cults in Romania* [Bucharest: Publishing House of the Bible and Mission Institute, 1984], pp. 26–27). Perret attended the 1984 peace assembly in Bucharest and made the strongest statement on human rights of all of the speakers. He stated prophetically that peace was threatened by discrimination and repression.

67. Letter of Edmond Perret to w a r c member churches (Geneva) 14 June 1988.

68. *Presbyterian Survey* (November 1988), p. 33.

69. *EPS*, 89.08.19.

70. Letter from Klaus Poser, director of the Commission on Inter-Church Aid, Refugee and World Service of the w c c, to refugee secretaries of c i c a r w s-related agencies (12 May 1989).

71. Petru Deheleanu, *Manual De Sectologie* (Arad: Tipografia Diecezana, 1948), p. 44. This is a major work on the "sects" in Romania and was reportedly being revised by Marxist scholars in an effort to help stem the neo-Protestant tide. Deheleanu aired a charge frequently made by Orthodox scholars that the Baptist Church was a Hungarian-sponsored movement to undermine Romanian nationalism by a subversion of Romanian Orthodoxy.

72. Tobias, "Report-Rumania," pp. 10–11.

73. Grigorie Comsa, *Cheir Sectele Religioase din Romania* (Arad: Tipografiei Diecezane, 1930), p. 190. This was a stipulation for the Baptists and Seventh-Day Adventists, according to the 1928 Law of Cults.

74. Consiliul Consultatir al Cultelor din Republica Socialista Romania (ed.), *Viata Religioasa in Romania* (Bucharest: Tipografia Institutului Biblio si de Misiune, 1987), p. 47. This work, edited under the careful supervision of the Department of Cults, lists only 75,000 Baptists and 87,000 Pentecostalists.

75. Stoian, *Cultele Religioase*, pp. 40–42. Stoian, first president of the Ministry of Cults after 1948 (reorganized as the Department of Cults in 1957), estimated that the total number of neo-Protestants did not reach 100,000 in 1949. I am indebted to Professor Kilian McDonnell for clarifying my views on some of the basic components of the neo-Protestant movement. See "The

Ideology of Pentecostal Conversion," *Journal of Ecumenical Studies* 5 (1968): 105–26.

76. Alexandru Maianu, *Viata si Lucrarea lui Dumitru Cornilescu* (Vienna: Emanuel, 1981), p. 5. Maianu claims that 5 million copies of this Bible have been published. The refusal of the neo-Protestants to accept the Orthodox version has been a source of tension between the two groups.

77. Trandafir Sandru (ed.), *Biserica Lui Dumnezeu Apostolica Penticostala Din Romania* (Bucharest: Editura Cultului Penticostal, 1982), pp. 13–14.

78. Alexa Popovici, *Istoria Baptistilor din Romania* (Chicago: Bisericii Baptiste Romane, 1980), vol. 1 (1856–1919), pp. 45–51. This is the best work at present on the early history of the Baptist Church in Romania. Popovici points out the importance of Tulca and Salonta as early Baptist centers in Transylvania. Two young Romanians were baptized in Tulca in 1893, Alexandru Pop and Craciun Vidican, and they became important leaders during this early period (*Biserica Noastra si Cultele Minoritare* [Bucharest: Ziarului Universal, 1928], p. 149).

79. Ioan Bunaciu, *Propovaduirea in Bisericile Crestine Baptiste* (Bucharest: Uniunea Comunitatilor Crestine Baptiste, 1976), pp. 43–54.

80. Ioan Bunaciu, "Scurta Privire Istorica Asupra Cultului Baptist Din R. S. R." (Bucharest, 1975), p. 6. This brief but accurate summary of the Baptist movement does not hesitate to present the difficulties.

81. Grigorie Gh. Comsa, *Lupta Baptistilor Impotriva Preotimei Romane* (Arad, 1926); *Combaterea Catehismului Baptistilor* (Arad, 1926); *Primejdia Baptismulu* (Arad, 1928); *Pedepsirea Pacatosilor si Scoaterea din Adunarile Baptiste* (Arad, 1929); *Censua de pe Capul Baptistilor* (Arad, 1931); *Ura Baptistilor Impotriva Noastra* (Arad, 1932); *Eurptia Vulcanului Baptist* (Arad, 1932). Comsa served as general director of the Ministry of Cults before his election as bishop of Arad in 1925.

82. Bunaciu, "Scurta Privire Istorica," p. 7; Alexa Popovici, "Curs de Istoria Baptistilor din Romania" (Bucharest, 1955), p. 274. Popovici states that as of 28 December 1942 the Baptists had 1,684 churches (337 in Bessarabia) and 90,843 members with a constituency of 120,645 (24,434 in Bessarabia).

83. Letter from Leonard Hodgson to Archbishop Temple, 16 October 1938 (Lambeth Archives, William Temple Papers, vol. 60, Oxford 3091, p. 66).

84. Miron, *Cultele in Romania*, p. 30.

85. Letter from Archbishop of York to Your Beatitude, 24 October 1938 (Lambeth Archives, William Temple Papers, vol. 60, Oxford 3091, p. 67).

86. "The Sects in Romania," *Church Times* 120 (25 November 1938).

87. J. H. Rushbrooke, "The Sects in Romania," ibid.

88. John A. Douglas, "Baptists in Rumania," ibid. (11 November 1938).

89. Harold Gibraltar, "The Sects in Rumania," ibid. (25 November 1938).

90. Denton Lotz, "Eastern Europe," in James Leo Garrett (ed.), *Baptist Relations with Other Christians* (Valley Forge, Pa.: Judson, 1974), p. 39.

91. Alan Scarfe, "Romanian Baptists and the State," *RCL* 4 (Summer 1976): 15. The Baptist Church was regarded as an agent of American imperialism in the *Dictionar Enciclopedic Romin* 1 (Bucharest: Editura Politica, 1962): 297. This reference has been deleted in *Mic Dictionar Enciclopedic* (Bucharest: Editura Enciclopedica Romana, 1982), p. 91.

92. This is the spelling that Tson now uses in the United States; it conveys the original Romanian pronunciation.

93. Joseph Tson, *The Present Situation of the Baptist Church in Romania*, RCL supplementary paper no. 1 (November 1973): 15–16.

94. Ibid., p. 16.

95. Ibid., p. 18.

96. Joseph Tson, *A Christian Manifesto to a Socialist Society*, RCL supplementary paper no. 2 (1976), pp. 15–16.

97. Alan Scarfe, "Romanian Baptists and the State," *RCL* 4 (Summer 1976): 18. The interrogations centered on Tson, Pavel Nicolescu, and Aurel Popescu, although many others were to be included.

98. Society for the Study of Religion and Atheism, "A Call for Truth," *Romanian Report* (April 1979), pp. 3–5.

99. "Freedom of Worship Breakthrough Seen," *Atlanta Constitution-Journal* (8 September 1977).

100. "ALCR's Programme of Demands," *RCL* 7 (Autumn 1979): 171–73.

101. "Baptist Union Punishes Dissidents," ibid., pp. 173–74.

102. Alan Scarfe, "A Call for Truth: An Appraisal of Romanian Baptist Church-State Relationships," *Journal of Church and State* 21 (Autumn 1979): 448; and Alan Scarfe, "Dismantling a Human Rights Movement," *RCL* 7 (Autumn 1979): 166–70.

103. Arthur King, "Religion and Rights: A Dissenting Minority as a Social Movement in Romania," *Social Compass* 28 (1981): 118–19. King develops a highly intriguing thesis that the ALCR may be seen as a "vehicle for ideological distress and protest," and the Cransebes affair served as its unifying legend.

104. Aurel Popescu, "Open Letter to Brother Joseph Tson—Who Are You? Brother Joseph Tson?" (Scappose, Oreg., 20 February 1979).

105. Joseph Tson, "My Position in the Baptist Union and Regarding Some Recent Events and Tendencies in the Baptist Denominations," Oradea (25 November 1978).

106. King, "Religion and Rights," p. 116.

107. *KNS*, no. 182, 8 September 1983, pp. 12–13.

108. Joseph Tson, "Persecution of the Neo-Protestants in Romania," paper presented at Marymount College, Arlington, Va. (May 1986).

109. Denton Lotz, "Baptist Witness in Eastern Europe," *American Baptist* (July–August 1976), p. 16. Lotz estimated more than 200,000 Baptists in 1976.

110. Ioachim Tunea, "Cuvintarea," *ICP* 38 (1973): 5–6.

111. Trandafir Sandru (ed.), *Biserica Lui Dumnezeu Apostolica Pentecostala Din Romania*, pp. 26–28; Trandafir Sandru, "Cultul Penticostal" (Bucharest: March 1975).

112. David D. Bundy, "The Roumanian Pentecostal Church in Recent Literature," *Pneuma: The Journal of the Society for Pentecostal Studies* 7 (Spring 1985): 20.

113. Trandafir Sandru, *Indrumatorul Pastorului* (Bucharest: Cultului Penticostal, 1976), pp. 130–33. This is a major work used in the Pentecostal seminary. It summarizes the church's basic convictions, focusing on the

work of the Holy Spirit; it includes a biblical introduction and courses in homiletics, church history, pastoral theology, and Christian ethics. Sandru became a member of the church in 1941, cosponsored the request for official recognition in 1945, and served as general secretary, editor, and director of the Pentecostal seminary in Bucharest (Steve Durasoff, *Pentecost Behind the Iron Curtain* [Plainfield, N.J.: Logos, 1972], pp. 65–73). This book contains a popular account of the spread of the Pentecostal movement in Romania.

114. Ioan J. Buia, *Romanian Pentecostal Church of God* (Detroit: Editura Propovaduitorul, 1987); Comsa, *Cheir Sectele Religioase*, pp. 50–60. Grigorie Comsa, bishop of Arad and probably the foremost Orthodox polemicist against the Pentecostals, writes that in 1930 the Pentecostals had more than three thousand members, recruited primarily from the Baptists but also from the Christians after the Gospel and the evangelical movement within the Orthodox Church known as the Lord's Army. He was concerned because they continued to meet secretly after they had been denied recognition by the Ministry of Cults.

115. Pavel Bochian, "The 50th Interconfessional Theological Conference, Bucharest, November 3–4, 1987," *Telegraful Roman*, no. 41–44 (15 November 1987), p. 4.

116. "Anticazania: The Degradation of Human Reason," *Scinteia Teneretului*, RCL 4 (Autumn 1976): 57. In this critique of the Pentecostal movement, reference is made to the "Dissidents," an unofficial Pentecostal group.

117. Bundy, "The Romanian Pentecostal Church," p. 37.

118. *KNS*, no. 324 (27 April 1989), p. 17; "Foreign Visitors Bring Closure to Romanian Pentecostal Youth Church," *KNS*, no. 310 (6 October 1988), p. 15.

119. Allegedly on 26 December 1985, President Ceauşescu signed Decree 408, which was not published and which imposed new restrictions on Romanian churches in their contacts with foreign visitors unless there was approval by the official leadership of the churches. The Pentecostal Union apparently was implementing the ban much more strongly than the Baptists. "Foreign Speakers in Romanian Pulpits," *The Voice of Truth* (May–June 1986), p. 6.

120. Dumitru Popa, "Scrisori den Ungaria," *Curierul Adventist* 56 (January–February 1978): 16–17; "Scrisori Transilvane," ibid., pp. 8–9; Deheleanu, *Manual De Sectologie*, pp. 47–49.

121. Simultaneously with the drive against the Baptists and Pentecostalists, Romanian Orthodox leaders conducted an intense campaign against the Seventh-Day Adventists. Galaction D. Cordun, *Ce este Adventismul?* (Bucharest: Tipografiei Romana Noua, 1919); I. N. Davravescu, *Feriti-Va de Adventisti si de toti Ratacitii Vremurilor Noastre* (Arad: Tipografiei Diecezane, 1930).

122. Hedenquist, "Report on Trip to Roumania," p. 25.

123. Letter from Jean Nussbaum to the Archbishop of Canterbury, 24 January 1938 (Archives of Lambeth, London, Lang Papers, 1938).

124. Alan Scarfe, "The Evangelical Wing of the Orthodox Church in Romania," RCL 3 (November–December 1975): 15–18.

125. Deheleanu, *Manual De Sectologie*, pp. 57–59.

126. Letter from J. H. Adeney to J. A. Douglas (9 September 1924) (Archives of Lambeth, London, J. A. Douglas Papers, vol. 52, pp. 77–80).

127. Scarfe, "The Evangelical Wing," p. 17; Trevor Beeson, *Discretion and Valour* (Philadelphia: Fortress Press, 1982), p. 357.

128. "Copii Ai Lui Dumnezeu," *Calea Credintei* (January–March 1978), pp. 5–8; "Despre Planul De Mintuire" (April–June 1978), pp. 18–21.

129. "Romanian Brethren Leaders Dismissed," *KNS*, no. 201 (7 June 1984), pp. 7–8.

130. Tobias, "Report-Rumania," p. 8.

131. A young man who had belonged to the Pioneers organization and the Union of Communist Youth became a member of Jehovah's Witnesses and refused to be drafted. He was held up as the antithesis of the new socialist person. "The Impossibility of Being a Conscientious Objector in Romania," RFE/RL Rumanian Situation Report/18, p. 9.

132. Letter from N. H. Knorr, president of the Watch Tower Bible and Tract Society of Pennsylvania, to Earl A. Pope (30 September 1975).

133. J. B. Rutherford, *Domnia Pacii—Speranta Lumii* (Bucharest: Cartea de Aur, 1946).

134. Metropolitan Antonie, "Romanian Ecumenism," *One World* (May 1986), p. 17.

135. S. Reli, *Curs de Istoria Biserica Romane,* vol. 2 (Cernauti: Universitatea "Regele Carol II," 1938), p. 471. Reli suggests a following of 1,000–2,000 in Cluj and Oradea in 1930.

136. H. Culea, "Anticazania: Pocainta . . . pocaitilor," *Scinteia Tineretului* (4 March 1976).

137. "The Secretary of State for Cults and Arts, Law of Cults, No. 26208, June 11, 1938," *Gazette* (14 June 1938) (Public Record Office, London, F0371-22454-07058).

138. Letter from Lord Allen to Prince Paul (18 December 1936); letter from J. A. Douglas to A. C. Don (17 February 1938) (Archives of Lambeth, London, Lang Papers, 1938, no. 1).

139. Hon. Robert H. Michel, *Human Rights in Romania,* hearing before the Subcommittees on Europe . . . of the Committee on Foreign Affairs, House of Representatives (Washington, D.C.: U.S. Government Printing Office, 1985), appendix 4, p. 138.

140. Reli, *Curs de Istoria,* p. 471. Reli estimates a following of 6,000–8,000, primarily in Banat and Transylvania, in 1930.

141. Comsa, *Cheir Sectele Religioase,* p. 105; Deheleanu, *Manual De Sectologie,* pp. 49–50; Grigore Leu Botosaneanu, *Sectele din Romania* (Chisinau: Tipografia Eparhiala Romaneasca, 1931), p. 51.

142. Metropolitan Nicolae, "'Oastea Domnului' Si Biserica," *Mantueste Doamne Poporul Tau* (Sibiu, 1945), pp. 121–25. This is an impassioned defense of the Lord's Army delivered in 1941 at its ninth congress in Sibiu.

143. "Congresul Asociatiei Religioase Oastea Domnului din Eparhia Oradea," *Legea Romaneasca* 15, no. 10 (Oradea) (15 May 1939): 79–91.

144. Hedenquist, "Report on Trip to Roumania," p. 6.

145. "The Lord's Army Movement in the Romanian Orthodox Church," *RCL* (Winter 1980): 314.

146. "News of Lord's Army Leader," *KNS,* no. 179 (28 July 1983), pp. 6–7.

147. *Catalogul Periodic Al Librariei Oastea Domnului, Isus Biruitorul* (Sibiu: Tipografia Oastea Domnului, 1937), p. 1.

148. Mary Dejevsky, "Romanian Leader Scorns Reforms," London *Times* (21 November 1989), p. 24; "In Romania, the Old Order Won't Budge," *New York Times* (25 November 1989), p. 17; U.S. Commission on Security and Cooperation in Europe, *Revolt Against Silence: The State of Human Rights in Romania* (Washington, D.C.: U.S. Government Printing Office, 1989), p. 26.

149. U.S. Commission on Security and Cooperation in Europe, *Revolt Against Silence*, pp. v–vi.

150. Ibid., p. iii.

151. Ibid., p. 1.

152. "Renewed Pressure on Transylvanian Pastor," *KNS*, no. 337 (2 November 1989), p. 2.

153. Ibid., p. 2.

154. "Securitate Threaten to Put Tökés in Prison," *KNS*, no. 339 (30 November 1989), p. 3.

155. Laszlo Tökés, *The Fall of Tyrants* (Wheaton, Ill.: Crossway, 1991); Oivind Ostang, "Romanian Pastor Laszlo Tökés Says He Was Let Down by International Church Organizations," *Lutheran World Information*, no. 11/90 (15 March 1990), pp. 12–13.

156. William Echikson, "Father of Romania's Revolution," *Christian Science Monitor* (25 January 1990), p. 14.

157. "Countdown to the Collapse of a Dynasty," London *Times* (23 December 1989), p. 6.

158. Dessa Trevisan, " 'Hundreds fell' as Timisoara Police Opened Fire," ibid. (19 December 1989), p. 9; "Witnesses Describe Massacre of Children," ibid. (20 December 1989), p. 8.

159. Radek Sikorski, "Christmas Day in Romania," *National Review* (22 January 1990), pp. 22–24.

160. "Laszlo Tökés Alive And Well," *KNS*, no. 341 (11 January 1990), p. 2.

161. "Ecumenical Aid Team Visits Churches in Romania," *LWI*, no. 1/90 (11 January 1990): p. 3; "Report of the Second Ecumenical Team Visit to Romania" (representing wcc, lwf, warc, and cec), (2–8 February 1990); "Ecumenical Appeal of One Million U.S. Dollars for Romania," *EPS*, 90.03.77 (21–25 March 1990).

162. "Greek-Catholic Church Legalized in Romania," *KNS*, no. 341 (11 January 1990), p. 6.

163. "Associatii Religioase," (Bucharest: Secretariatului de Stat pentru Culte, 1990), p. 3.

164. "Reformed Bishops Leave Office," *KNS*, no. 341 (11 January 1990), p. 3–4; "New Romanian Pentecostal Committee Replaced Old Leadership," *KNS*, no. 345 (8 March 1990), p. 16.

165. "Report of the Second Ecumenical Team Visit," p. 11.

166. "Romanian Churches Meet to Set Ecumenical Priorities," *LWI*, no. 26/90 (12 July 1990), p. 16; Robert C. Lodwick, "Romanian Trip Report and Romanian Roundtable Meeting" (18–25 June 1990); "National Ecumenical Platform Set Up in Romania," *KNS*, no. 356 (9 August 1990), p. 11; "Romania: Eastern Orthodox, Lutherans, Reformed Plan Cooperation," *EPS*, 90.11.04.

167. Henk van Apeldoorn, "What is AIDROM?" (Bucharest, February 1991).

168. N. Barney Pityana, "The Plight of the Roma," *One World*, no. 170 (November 1991), pp. 14–15.

169. "Romania's Bishop Says Flood of Emigrants is Over," *LWI*, no. 21 (4 July 1991), p. 10.

170. "Romanian Orthodox Church Pledges 'Unfailing Commitment' to Ecumenism," *EPS*, 92.01.19 (January 1992).

171. "Bishop Tokes Speaks at WCC Assembly," *KNS*, no. 370 (7 March 1991), pp. 2–3; "Romania's Tökés Accuses WCC of Lack of Credibility," *LWI*, no. 10/91 (21 March 1991), p. 11.

172. "Hungarians Treated as Second-Class Citizens in Romania, Bishop Says," *LWI*, no. 26/91 (22 August 1991), p. 9; "Romania Bishop Says Ethnic Minorities Still Oppressed," *LWI*, no. 38/91 (12 December 1991), p. 4; "Bishop Tökés Warns of Ethnic Conflicts," *Foreign Broadcast Information Service: Daily Report Eastern Europe* (13 February 1992), pp. 24–25.

173. "Daily Condemns Vatra Romaneasca 'Manifesto,'" *FBIS-EEU*, no. 174 (9 September 1991), p. 23.

174. "Tökés Views Support for Hungarians," *FBIS-EEU*, no. 1 (2 January 1992), pp. 28–29; "Elections Were First Step on Romania's Path of Democracy, Hungarian Bishop Says," *LWI*, no. 14/92 (30 April 1992), pp. 14–15.

175. "Romania's Lutheran Congregations Face Disbandment," *LWI*, no. 9/92 (12 March 1992), p. 6.

176. "Cultele Neo Protestante" (Bucharest: Ministry of Cults, 1990), p. 5.

177. "Romanian Baptists Seek to Unite Evangelicals," *KNS*, no. 342 (25 January 1990), p. 6.

178. "The New Statutes of the 'Salvation Army' Association," *Romanian Orthodox Church News*, vol. 21, no. 1 (January–February 1991), pp. 32–34.

179. "Reflections on Billy Graham's Trip to Romania," *RCL*, 14 (Summer 1986), pp. 224–227.

180. "RMS to Build Publishing Headquarters in Oradea," *Voice of Truth* (July 1991), p. 10.

181. "Ban Hits Bible TV after Big Response," *The Free Romanian*, vol. 8, no. 4 (April 1992), p. 2.

182. "Romanian Evangelical Alliance Calls for Day of Prayer and Fasting for Romanian Elections," *KNS*, no. 350 (17 May 1990), p. 8.

183. "Romania: Evangelicals Unite, Present Demands to President," *EPS*, 90.11.168.

184. "Evangelical Alliance to Register Despite Minister's Refusal," *KNS*, no. 346 (22 March 1990), pp. 3–4.

185. "Romania Creates New Religious Laws," *KNS*, no. 367 (24 January 1991), p. 9; Berthold Kober, "Churches Unite to Draft New Law on Religion in Romania," 8/91 (28 February 1991), p. 9.

186. "Legea Cultelor si Libertati Religioase din Romania," p. 4, article 19.

187. Ibid., p. 1, article 4.

188. "Teze Pentru Elaborarea Proiectului de Constituie a Romaniei" (Bucharest: Parlamentul Romaniei, 1990), p. 3; *UBBI* (Buletin de Informare al Uniunii Bisericilor Crestine Baptist din Romania) Anul, no. 1 (June 1991), p. 8.

189. "Constitution of Romania," *FBIS-EEU,* no. 246 (23 December 1991), p. 3.

190. Ibid., p. 1.

191. Ibid., p. 4.

7 Protestantism in Bulgaria and Yugoslavia

Paul Mojzes wrote the introduction and the segment on Bulgaria, while Gerald Shenk wrote the segment on Yugoslavia.

1. The treatment of Bulgarian Protestants was so harsh that even scholars who claim to understand Eastern Europe in general without knowing the specific situation of Protestants in Bulgaria are misled by faulty inferences from their knowledge of other contexts. Except for Albania, Bulgaria has the smallest Protestant community since the communist takeover, and the communist government tried to make sure that it became nearly extinct. This is why Protestantism in Bulgaria cannot be viewed through the same prism as other Protestant communities in Eastern Europe. No contemporary articles on Bulgarian Protestantism have been written. A collective study of Bulgaria under the editorship of Zhivko Oshakov, *Protses't na preodolyavaneto na religiyata v B'lgariya* (Sofia: Izdatelstvo na B'lgarskata Akademiya na Naukite, 1968), disregards the contemporary survival of Protestants and points out that at their height in 1934, Protestants made up 0.14 percent of the population. The figure, one presumes, has declined, but no statistics exist. A high estimate is 20,000, but there may be only half as many.

2. There are only a few relatively comprehensive accounts of the work of the Protestant churches. One is Paul Mojzes, "A History of the Congregational and Methodist Churches in Bulgaria and Yugoslavia," 2 vols., unpublished Ph.D. diss., Boston University, 1965. The dissertation covers the history of two Protestant churches from their inception in the second half of the nineteenth century to the early 1960s. The material on Bulgaria in this chapter depends heavily on the information and documentation of that dissertation, but does not repeat the footnote sources. An older book is William W. Hall's *Puritans in the Balkans* (Sofia: Studia Historico-Philologica Serdicensia, 1938). Hall's Ph.D. diss., Yale University, 1937, was entitled "The American Board Mission in Bulgaria, 1887–1918: A Study in Purpose and Procedure." It should be noted that the American missionaries in Bulgaria from the inception of Protestant missions to 1948 took a very pro-Bulgarian stance in American and international circles, for which they were appreciated by all but the communist government.

3. Letters from the American board to its missionaries in European Turkey indicate as early as 1849 that its original intention was to establish churches among Jews in cities like Thessalonica and Adrianople; if Christians from those areas were attracted to Protestant missions, they should be incorporated into these churches.

4. For example, the murder of William Ward Meriam. See James O. Murray, *The Missionary and the Martyr* (Cambridge, Mass.: Riverside Press, 1862), pp. 10–20. While it is customary for some scholars to single out how im-

pressed American Protestant missionaries were by the Bulgarians, there were those who regretted that the many Bibles being bought were used not for reading but for superstitious reasons. See Mojzes, "A History," pp. 59–60.

5. Stefanka Petrova, "Perestroika Without Christ?" p. 2, unpublished paper prepared for a May 1991 conference in Budapest.

6. Ibid., p. 3.

7. Among the outstanding Protestant intellectuals before the Communist takeover were Stoyan Bochev (economist), "Dyado" Georgi Yordanov (former minister of agriculture), Samuil Vasilev and Konstantin Rusev (bank directors), T. Tomov, Todor Shopov, Gavrail Tsvetanov (university professors), Lyubomir Tsanov (industrialist), Bogdan Ikonomov (judge), and Neofit Tsakov and Vasil Zyapkov (editors).

8. It is noteworthy that all three were women, the Methodists Ruth Wolfe and Mellony Turner, and the Congregationalist Mary Haskell.

9. A source of information smuggled out of Bulgaria and provided to the author by Floyd H. Black, former president of the American College in Sofia, was "Po Protsesa na Evangelskite Pastiri v B'lgariya," dated February and March 1949 and probably written by a Vasileff, whose identity had to remain anonymous because of possible reprisals against him and his family. The photocopied document in my possession provides a detailed account of measures undertaken to crush the Protestants.

10. Robert Hoare, "Bulgaria," *Religion in Communist Lands* 18, no. 2 (Summer 1990): 174. Hoare points out that "until 1988 there were virtually no organised dissident groups of any kind in Bulgaria."

11. Mojzes has photocopies of an English translation of the "Regulations for the organization of the Evangelical Churches in the People's Republic of Bulgaria" and a resolution vigorously protesting these regulations by twelve Methodist pastors, both documents typed in Bulgaria, with photocopies in the Board of Missions of the Methodist Church archives in New York City.

12. Ibid. Also Robert Tobias, *Communist-Christian Encounter in East Europe* (Indianapolis: School of Religion Press, 1956), pp. 371–76, provides a translation of the full text of the law on the churches.

13. The Bulgarian government published two books on this trial, *Subversive Activities of the Evangelical Pastors in Bulgaria: Documents* and *The Trial of the Fifteen Protestant Pastors—Spies* (Sofia: Press Department, Ministry of Foreign Affairs, 1949). There also is the typescript, mentioned above, "Po Protsesa na Evangelskite Pastiri v B'lgariya." A primary source providing a detailed account of pretrial tortures and the trial (as well as the subsequent fifteen-year imprisonment) was written by one of the fifteen accused—Pentecostal minister Haralan Popov—which Mojzes obtained originally from Popoff (the way he spells his name in the West) in a Bulgarian handwritten manuscript. This document was later published in slightly revised form: Haralan Popoff, *I Was a Communist Prisoner* (Grand Rapids, Mich.: Zondervan, 1966), and Haralan Popov, *Tortured for His Faith* (Grand Rapids, Mich.: Zondervan, 1970; rev. ed., 1975). The most complete historical analysis of the trial is Paul Mojzes, "A History of the Congregational and Methodist Churches in Bulgaria and Yugoslavia," unpublished Ph.D. diss., Boston University, 1965, vol. 2, pp. 491–554. Another useful secondary source is by an American

minister branded as a spy by the Bulgarian authorities: Tobias, *Communist-Christian Encounter.*

14. The chief defendants were the heads of the four Protestant denominations, Vasil Ziapkov (Congregational; also religious representative of all Protestants); Nikola Mihailov (Baptist); Yanko Ivanov (Methodist); and Georgi Chernev (Pentecostal). The others were Methodists Zdravko Bezlov and Aleksandr Zahariev, the Congregationalist Lambri Mishkov, the Baptists Zahari Raichev, Ivan Stankulov, Georgi Vasev, and Mitko Mateev, and the Pentecostals Haralan and Ladin Popov, Angel Dinev, and Yoncho Drianov. The first four clergy received life sentences, a second group fifteen years apiece, while three others were sentenced to ten years, one minister to six years and eight months, one minister to five years, and two others received one-year suspended sentences; the convicted clergy also had fines and their civil rights suspended. The accused ranged in ages from twenty-eight to seventy-six. Parenthetically, it should be mentioned that Ziapkov was considered a sympathizer of the socialist system and was a representative of Bulgaria at the Paris Peace Conference.

15. Popoff, *I Was a Communist Prisoner*, pp. 272–73. Also "Massnahmen gegen die Pfingstgemeinde in Sofia," *Glaube in der 2. Welt* 11, no. 5 (1983): 4.

16. At Bozavaiski's death in 1984, controversy swirled over who would succeed him as pastor of Sofia's main Congregational church. The congregation first selected Hristo Kulichev as pastor from among their own, but the government intervened, forbidding his appointment. Instead, the government forced the transfer of Pavel Ivanov, an outside pastor not acceptable to most of the congregation. A trusted source from Yugoslavia reported that Ivanov reputedly served as a tool for liquidating local congregations, which he supposedly accomplished three other times. See also "Gewaltanwendung bei der Amtseinsetzung eines reformierten Pastors," *Glaube in der 2. Welt* 13, no. 3 (1985): 4.

17. In 1967, Mojzes paid an unannounced, unofficial visit to the Albert Long Methodist Church and met Ivan Nozharov. He received Mojzes rather coolly, but Mojzes was pleasantly surprised by the quality of his sermon, which showed command of biblical material. Mojzes estimated that fifty to seventy-five people attended church on that Sunday morning.

18. Around 1986 an American reported that she met a Bulgarian Congregational minister at a Christian peace committee meeting—the very person who had been imposed on the Sofia Congregational Church over the congregation's objection.

19. See, for instance, the imposition of a pastor on the Plovdiv Congregational Church, "Plovdiv Congregationalists' Choice of Pastor Frustrated," *Keston News Service* (hereinafter *KNS*), no. 314 (1 December 1989), p. 13. Similarly, the popular Methodist pastor Petar Hristov's dispute with "bishop" Ivan Nozharov ended when the government office for church affairs stripped for life Hristov's license to preach. "Berufsverbot für Pastor," *Glaube in der 2. Welt* 17, no. 9 (1989): 4. Hristov's ban was rescinded by October 1989.

20. "Versammlungserlaubnis für zwei Pfingstgemeinden erteilt," *Glaube in der 2. Welt* 10, no. 1 (1982): 461.

21. "Verbot von Religionsunterricht an Jugendliche unter 16 Jahren,"

ibid., vol. 10, no. 10 (1982), pp. 335–36. This prohibition was based on an interpretation of the Bulgarian Constitution's Article 20, which stated that the "Education and Nurture of youth is exclusively the state's responsibility."

22. *KNS*, no. 267 (22 January 1987), p. 11; no. 283 (10 September 1987), p. 15; no. 291 (7 January 1988), pp. 13, 16; and no. 302 (9 June 1988), p. 11.

23. In 1979, five Pentecostals were tried on currency and black-marketing charges. See "Bulgaria," *Religion in Communist Lands* 8, no. 3 (Fall 1980): 235.

24. "Bedrängte Pfingstgemeinden," *Glaube in der 2. Welt* 15, no. 5 (1987): 3. Harassment of the unregistered Pentecostals was particularly severe. Pavel Ignatev, leader of an association of twenty-five unregistered Pentecostal congregations, was exiled for three years in 1987, but he was released after six months. See *KNS*, no. 280 (23 July 1987), p. 16.

25. "The Bulgarian Pentecostal 'Church of God,'" *KNS*, no. 269 (19 February 1987), pp. 20–21.

26. Ibid., no. 302 (9 June 1988), p. 16.

27. "Bibelmangel," *Glaube in der 2. Welt* 17, no. 10 (1989): 2.

28. Hoare, "Bulgaria," p. 182.

29. Ibid., p. 179.

30. "Bishop Recognized," *United Methodist Reporter* (10 August 1990).

31. *European Baptist Press Service*, bulletin 02/90 (10 February 1990), p. 1. Also Hoare, "Bulgaria," p. 179.

32. "Neues Amt für Religionsfragen," *Glaube in der 2. Welt* 19, no. 2 (1991): 4.

33. See R. N. Berki, "State and Society: An Antithesis of Modern Political Thought," introduction, in Jack Hayward and R. N. Berki (eds.), *State and Society in Contemporary Europe* (New York: St. Martin's Press, 1979), esp. pp. 1–6. The topic of "civil society" also has emerged in Yugoslavia's public discourse; it is closely related to proposals for a civilian alternative to military service. See, among numerous others, the interview with Ivan Prpić, "Društvo i država," in *Naše teme* 32, no. 5 (May 1988): 1147–65; also commentary on Slovenian proposals in *Vjesnik* (15 January 1988), p. 12.

34. See, for example, *Facts about Yugoslavia*, published in Belgrade by the Federal Secretariat for Information: "The Serbian Orthodox Church, the Roman Catholic Church, the Islamic faith and the Macedonian Orthodox Church have the largest number of adherents, there also being several other smaller religious groups" (1985; p. 8). These "several other" groups number more than forty, according to other official publications. See a representative listing in Vuko Pavičević, *Sociologija religije* (Belgrade: Beogradski izdavačko-grafički zavod, 1980), p. 336.

35. Stella Alexander, *Church and State in Yugoslavia since 1945* (Cambridge: Cambridge University Press, 1979), p. xi.

36. See Ivan Lazić, *Pravno-politološki aspekti odnosa crkve i društva* (Zagreb: Institut za društvena istraživanja Sveučilišta u Zagrebu, 1976), p. 63.

37. Ibid., p. 24.

38. A former authority on morality and religious policies in Bosnia and Herzegovina, Todo Kurtović, provides a most intriguing comment on Nazarene "resistance": "Forms of resistance are many, ranging from Nazarene

opposition to national defence and attempts to have this endorsed, even if it is political destruction. Of course, when Nazarene behaviour is in question, their conditions differ from the way they were in prewar Yugoslavia. They are recognized as religious communities but their doctrines on the use of weapons, allegiances, etc., cannot be acknowledged as they clash with the interests of our people and therefore with regulations. Viewed globally, this is an attempt to reduce Man to a helpless being who neither thinks nor criticizes, an object from which absolute obedience and passivity is demanded" (*Church and Religion in the Socialist Self-Management Society*, trans. Irina Mirković [Belgrade: Socialist Thought and Practice, 1980], pp. 244–45). In context, Kurtović is only criticizing uncritical compliance with religious, not secular, authorities.

39. Josip Horak, "Protestantizam i ekumenizam," in Zlatko Frid (ed.), *Vjerske zajednice u Jugoslaviji* (Zagreb: Binoza, 1970), pp. 127–34.

40. From the invitation by the Udruženje (Zagreb, 1 November 1988), to its first regular assembly on 26 November 1988. The association selected Peter Kuzmič (Pentecostal) as president and Stevan Madjarac (Baptist) as secretary.

41. This suggestion is detailed by Pedro Ramet, *Cross and Commissar: The Politics of Religion in Eastern Europe and the USSR* (Bloomington: Indiana University Press, 1987), p. 161.

42. For a helpful account of Yugoslavia on the eve of civil war, see Dennison Rusinow, "To Be or Not to Be? Yugoslavia as Hamlet," *UFSI Field Staff Reports* (Europe) (1990–91), no. 18. For a different interpretation, see Ivo Banac, "The Fearful Asymmetry of War: The Causes and Consequences of Yugoslavia's Demise," in *Daedalus* 121, no. 2 (Spring 1992).

43. See interview in the Zagreb Catholic journal *Kana* with Protestant theologian Peter McKenzie, "Bez pokajanja nema pomirenja" (Without repentance there is no reconciliation), by Suzana Vrhovski, February 1992, pp. 22–23.

8 Protestantism in the USSR

1. Roger P. Bartlett, *Human Capital: The Settlement of Foreigners in Russia, 1762–1804* (Cambridge: Cambridge University Press, 1979).

2. Surprisingly, Jeffrey Brooks in his *When Russia Learned to Read: Literacy and Popular Literature, 1861–1917* (Princeton, N.J.: Princeton University Press, 1985) ignores religious literature.

3. A careful review and evaluation of the role of missionary societies in Russian and Soviet history still needs doing, but a good source on turn-of-the-century efforts can be found in Wilhelm Kahle, *Evangelische Christen in Russland und der Sowjetunion: Ivan Stepanovich Prochanow (1869–1935) und der Weg der Evangeliums-christen und Baptisten* (Wuppertal: Oncken Verlag, 1978).

4. Dimitry Pospielevsky, *A History of Marxist-Leninist Atheism and Soviet Antireligious Policies*, 3 vols. (New York: St. Martin's Press, 1987–88), vol. 2; John S. Curtiss, *The Russian Church and the Soviet State, 1917–1950* (Gloucester, Mass.: Peter Smith, 1965; reprint of 1953 ed.); Joan Delaney, "The Origins of

Soviet Antireligious Organizations," in Robert H. Marshall, Thomas E. Bird, and Andrew Q. Blane (eds.), *Aspects of Religion in the Soviet Union, 1917–1967* (Chicago: University of Chicago Press, 1971), pp. 103–30.

5. In addition to Engels's *The Peasant War in Germany,* both Karl Kautsky and Ernst Bloch were interested in the life of Thomas Müntzer.

6. A. I. Klibanov, "Iz vospominanii o V. D. Bonch-Brueviche (k 110-letiu so dnia rozhdeniia)," *Voprosy nauchnogo ateizma,* no. 31 (1983), pp. 269–95, not only recalls Bonch-Bruevich's keen interest, but reports numerous incidents where Lenin encouraged research and read numerous articles, partly to understand the attitudes of the peasantry. Klibanov is still the most prolific and respected Soviet scholar on sectarianism; see, for example, his *Narodnaiia sotsial'naiia utopiia v Rossii* (Moscow: Nauka, 1978).

7. For a critical survey, see William C. Fletcher, *Soviet Believers: The Religious Sector of the Population* (Lawrence: Regents Press of Kansas, 1981), esp. pp. 13–56; James Thrower, *Marxist-Leninist "Scientific Atheism" and the Study of Religion and Atheism in the USSR* (Berlin-New York: Mouton, 1983); Pospielovsky, *History of Marxist-Leninist Atheism,* vol. 3.

8. Fritz Peyer-Müller, "Reformierte Ungarn in der Sowjetunion. Eine Minderheitenkirche in der Karpato-Ukraine," *Glaube in der 2ten Welt,* no. 11 (1987), pp. 21–30. There are 80,000 believers in ninety parishes with only twenty-one pastors headed by Bishop Pal Forgon.

9. Basic monographs on the different Protestant groups that provide more detail and bibliographical aid are Wilhelm Kahle, *Die lutherischen Kirchen und Gemeinden in der Sowjetunion—seit 1938/1940* (Gütersloh: Gütersloher Verlagshaus Gerd Mohn, 1985); Walter Sawatsky, *Soviet Evangelicals Since World War II* (Scottdale, Pa.: Herald Press, 1981); William C. Fletcher, *Soviet Charismatics: The Pentecostals in the USSR* (New York: Peter Lang, 1985); Marite Sapiets, "One Hundred Years of Adventism in Russia and the Soviet Union," *Religion in Communist Lands* 12 (Winter 1984): 256–73; *Istoriia evangel'skikh Khristian-baptistov v SSSR* (Moscow: Izdanie Vsesoiuznogo soveta Ev. Khristian-Baptistov, 1989), an official, documentary history by S. N. Savinsky, P. D. Savchenko, and I. P. Dyck (hereinafter Istoriia, AUCECB); A. T. Moskalenko, *Ideologiia i deiatel'nost' khristianskikh sekt* (Novosibirsk: Nauka [sibirskoe otdelenie], 1978), a theoretical treatment of chiliastic groups among which he includes Pentecostals and Jehovah's Witnesses.

10. Fletcher, *Charismatics,* chaps. 3 and 4 (printed in Russian in *Sotsiologicheskie isledovanie* [Summer 1988], thereby receiving Soviet endorsement).

11. Where not otherwise indicated, more detail can be found in Sawatsky, *Soviet Evangelicals,* in this case pp. 27–54.

12. Edgar C. Duin, *Lutheranism under the Tsars and the Soviets* (Ann Arbor, Mich.: University Microfilms, 1976); Wilhelm Kahle, *Geschichte der evangelisch-lutherischen Gemeinden in der Sovetunion 1917–1938* (Leiden, 1974).

13. J. B. Toews, *Czars, Soviets and Mennonites* (Newton, Kans.: Faith and Life Press, 1982); Frank H. Epp, *Mennonite Exodus* (Altona: D. W. Friesen, 1963).

14. Wilhelm Kahle, "Die kirchlichen Gemeinden und die nationale Identität der Deutschen. Unter besonderer Berücksichtigung der Zeit zwischen den Weltkriegen," in Andreas Kappeler, Boris Meissner, and Gerhard Simon

(eds.), *Die Deutschen im Russischen Reich und im Sowjetstaat* (Cologne: Markus Verlag, 1987), pp. 104–5.

15. William Fletcher, *A Study in Survival: The Church in Russia, 1927–1943* (London: SPCK, 1965); Dimitry Pospielovsky, *The Russian Church Under the Soviet Regime, 1917–1982* (Crestwood, N.Y.: St. Vladimir's Seminary Press, 1984); Lev Regelson, *Tragediia russkoi tserkvi, 1917–1945* (Paris: YMCA Press, 1977).

16. Kahle, "Die kirchlichen Gemeinden," p. 107.

17. The most recent general survey is Pospielovsky, *History of Marxist-Leninist Atheism*. See also P. S. Fateev and V. V. Korolev (eds.), *O Emel'iane Iaroslavskom: Vospominaniia, ocherki, stat'i* (Moscow: Politizdat, 1988), pp. 199–240.

18. See Sawatsky, *Soviet Evangelicals*, pp. 78–104, for an extended treatment.

19. Fletcher, *Soviet Charismatics*, p. 92–93; Sawatsky, *Soviet Evangelicals*, pp. 93–95, 286–88, 476–77.

20. The literature is extensive, but there is still no definitive treatment. The latest undertaking by Pospielovsky, *History of Marxist-Leninist Atheism*, is too focused on Orthodoxy. For one competent recent review of state policy that provides a guide to some of the literature, see Bohdan R. Bociurkiw, "The Formulation of Religious Policy in the Soviet Union," *Journal of Church and State* 28 (Autumn 1986): 423–38.

21. Metropolitan Filaret (Minsk) acknowledged this openly at the Sobor in June 1988. The speeches and documents of the Sobor appeared in Novosti's monthly news service *Religion in the USSR.*

22. Walter Sawatsky, "Secret Soviet Handbook on Religion," *Religion in Communist Lands* 4 (1976): 24–34; The most relevant parts of the handbook were printed in German translation with annotations as Otto Luchterhandt, *Die Religionsgesetzgebung der Sowjetunion* (Berlin: Berlin Verlag, 1978).

23. Sawatsky, *Soviet Evangelicals*, p. 139; see also Michael Bourdeaux, *Religious Ferment in Russia* (London: Macmillan, 1968), for extensive citation of documents covering 1961–66.

24. Many early Baptist samizdat are available in *Arkhiv Samizdata* (Munich), esp. vols. 14, 15, 16, and 19.

25. The Initsiativniki version of these events was republished by Friedensstimme, *25 Jahre auf dem Weg* (Gummersbach: Missionswerk Friedensstimme, 1987).

26. The CPR was dissolved in September 1987, and the bulletin became part of a CCECB Department of Intercession.

27. G. S. Lialina, *Baptizm: Illiuzii i real'nost'* (Moscow: Politizdat, 1977), p. 51.

28. English translations of the successive statutes and revisions are printed in the appendixes of Bourdeaux, *Religious Ferment*, and Sawatsky, *Soviet Evangelicals*. See *Istoriia* AUCECB, pp. 238–49, for the official AUCECB version of these events.

29. Walter Sawatsky, "The New Soviet Law on Religion," *Religion in Communist Lands* 4, no. 2 (Summer 1976): 4–10.

30. See, for example, Kent R. Hill, *The Puzzle of the Soviet Church: An Inside*

Look at Christianity and Glasnost, rev. ed. (Portland, Oreg.: Multnomah Press, 1991), pp. 159–216; Mark R. Elliott, "How the Churches Have Seen Their Roles in the USSR," *Pulse* 22 (9 January 1987): 2–5; Elliott, "Parachurch Groups Take Different Routes to USSR," *Pulse* 22 (23 January 1987): 2–5, both reprinted in Mark R. Elliott and William Fletcher, *Christianity and Marxism* (Wheaton, Ill.: Wheaton College Extension and Continuing Education, 1987), pp. 115–30.

31. As reported by Father Taska, participant in 1987 NCC Pilgrimage Tour (June 1987).

32. This statement is based on the language of Otto Luchterhandt, *Der Sowjetstaat und die russisch orthodoxe Kirche* (Cologne, 1976), pp. 244, 253.

33. To compare this to regulated prostitution in designated areas and buildings as practiced in some Western countries is a fair approximation of the attitude.

34. G. R. Gol'st, *Religiia i zakon* (Moscow: Iuridicheskaia literatura, 1975), p. 42.

35. The story of the Siberian Seven has been retold in Hill, *Puzzle of the Soviet Church*, pp. 15–72.

36. Ludmilla Alexeeva, *Soviet Dissent: Contemporary Movements for National, Religious, and Human Rights* (Middletown, Conn.: Wesleyan University Press, 1985).

37. Photocopy in author's possession.

38. Kahle, *Die lutherischen Kirchen . . . seit 1938/1940*, pp. 27–37, plus special chapters on each national body. The Latvian and Estonian synods of 1989 and 1990 stated this publicly.

39. Ingeborg Fleischhauer and Benjamin Pinkus, *Soviet Germans: Past and Present* (London: C. Hurst, 1986), esp. pp. 66–91, 103–19. More than 100,000 were placed in a labor army (*trudarmiia*).

40. Johannes Schleuning, Peter Schellenberg, and Eugen Bachman, *Und Siehe, Wir Leben*, 2nd ed. (Erlangen, 1982).

41. Gerd Stricker, "German Protestants in Tsarist Russia and the Soviet Union," *Religion in Communist Lands* 15, no. 1 (Spring 1987): 32–53; Bill Yoder, "Observations on Western Missions in Eastern Europe," *Occasional Papers on Religion in Eastern Europe* (March 1992): 33–38; copy of report by D. Georg Kretschmer, 3 November 1991, supplied by Bill Yoder.

42. Walter Sawatsky, "From Russian to Soviet Mennonites, 1941–1989," in John Friesen (ed.), *Mennonites in Russia* (Winnipeg: CMBC, 1989), 299–337; Gerd Stricker and Walter Sawatsky, "Mennoniten in der Sowjetunion nach 1941," *Kirche im Osten*, Band 27, 1984, pp. 57–98, appearing in an abbreviated English form in *Religion in Communist Lands* (Winter 1984), pp. 293–311.

43. V. F. Krestianinov, *Mennonity* (Moscow, 1967), p. 78.

44. John Pollock, *The Siberian Seven* (London: Hodder and Stoughton, 1979). More recently the so-called Siberian Seventy from Chuguevka received extensive publicity and started emigrating in 1987, with the last of their leaders arriving in Germany in October 1988. Hill, *Puzzle of the Soviet Church*, pp. 15–72.

45. Lialina, *Baptizm*, pp. 60–72.

46. See vol. 24 of *Voprosy nauchnogo ateizma* (1980), a special issue on

sectarianism, with D. M. Ugrinovich apparently writing much of the general text.

47. Summarized and analyzed in more detail in Walter Sawatsky, "Evangelical Revival in the Soviet Union: Nature and Implications," in Dennis Dunn (ed.), *Religion and Communist Society* (Berkeley, Calif.: Berkeley Slavic Specialties, 1983).

48. See also his *Vvedenie v religiovedenie*, 2nd expanded ed. (Moscow: Mysl, 1985), pp. 142–43.

49. D. M. Ugrinovich, *Psikhologiia religii* (Moscow: Politizdat, 1986).

50. Paul D. Steeves, "The Russian Baptist Union, 1917–1935: Evangelical Awakening in Russia," unpublished Ph.D. diss., University of Kansas, 1976, pp. 557–92; Kahle, *Evangelische Christen*, pp. 382–419; Z. V. Kalinicheva, *Sotsial'naia sushchnost' baptizma 1917–1929gg* (Leningrad: Nauka, 1972), pp. 49–85.

51. A definitive treatment is Lawrence J. Klippenstein, "Mennonite Pacifism and State Service in Russia: A Case Study in Church-State Relations, 1789–1936," unpublished Ph.D. diss., University of Minnesota, 1984.

52. For a general survey, see William C. Fletcher, *Religion and Soviet Foreign Policy, 1945–1970* (London: Oxford University Press, 1973).

53. See, for example, Rolf Wischnath, ed., *Frieden als Bekenntnisfrage* (Gütersloh: Gerd Mohn Verlagshaus, 1984).

54. Mikhail Gorbachev, *Perestroika: New Thinking for Our Country and the World* (New York: Harper and Row, 1987), pp. 140–41.

55. For a reliable overview of Christian-Marxist dialogue, see Paul Mojzes, *Christian-Marxist Dialogue in Eastern Europe* (Minneapolis: Augsburg, 1981).

56. V. F. Martsinkovskii, *Zapiski veruiushchego: Iz istorii religioznogo dvizheniia v sovetskoi rossii* (Prague: by author, 1929).

57. Herman Hartfeld's novel, *Irina* (Wuppertal: Brockhaus Verlag, 1980), is an effort to tell the story in dramatized form.

58. Paul Steeves, "The June Plenum and the Post-Brezhnev Antireligious Campaign," *Journal of Church and State* 28 (Autumn 1986): 439–58. In the same issue, Jerry Pankhurst argued for a longer-term view that Soviet society needed the churches for community building ("Soviet Society and Soviet Religion," pp. 409–22); similarly, Walter Sawatsky, "Soviet Evangelicals Today," *Occasional Papers on Religion in Eastern Europe* 4 (March 1984): 1–20.

59. For extended descriptions, see Michael Bourdeaux, *Gorbachev, Glasnost and the Gospel* (London: Hodder and Stoughton, 1990), pp. 42–64; Jim Forest, *Religion in the New Russia: The Impact of Perestroika on the Varieties of Religious Life in the Soviet Union* (New York: Crossroad, 1990), pp. 6–35.

60. See Walter Sawatsky, "Another Look at Mission in Eastern Europe," *International Bulletin of Missionary Research* 11 (January 1987): 14–15.

61. Mark Elliott, "New Openness in USSR Prompts Massive Bible Shipments to Soviet Christians in 1987–1988: A Statistical Overview," *News Network International* (20 March 1989), pp. 24–31. Elliott also presents a chart showing a total of 5,915,000 Bibles/New Testaments for importing or printing in 1989, all legally approved.

62. Viktor Hamm, "Marvellous in Our Eyes: Report on a Visit to the Soviet Union," *Mennonite Brethren Herald* (14 October 1988), pp. 7–9.

63. I am relying here on the helpful reconstruction of events by Marite Sapiets, " 'Rebirth and Renewal' in the Latvian Lutheran Church," *Religion in Communist Lands* 16, no. 3 (Autumn 1988): 237–49.

64. Ibid., pp. 242–43.

65. *Keston News Service* (27 April 1989), p. 2; (11 May 1989), p. 5.

66. Report by Johannes Baumann, Osterholz-Scharmbeck, Germany, 20 April 1989, made available to the author by Gerd Stricker.

67. German language report by Th. Hasselblatt, Hannover, made available to the author by Gerd Stricker.

68. *Frankfurter Allgemeine* (22 October 1988) claims 590 congregations, half of which are smaller groups of twenty to seventy people.

69. Gerd Stricker reports that Kalnins described this function with the words "as if you are deans [*Pröpste*]" in a letter to him of 14 November 1988. I am relying on Stricker's privately supplied data to correct published reports.

70. The reception of church dignitaries and the interview questions and answers were given extensive verbatim coverage in *Pravda* (11 June 1988). For a summary of the background through 1989, see John Anderson, "Drafting a Soviet Law on Freedom of Conscience," *Soviet Jewish Affairs* 19, no. 1 (1989): 19–33; Bourdeaux, *Gorbachev, Glasnost and the Gospel*, pp. 65–74.

71. David E. Powell, "The Revival of Religion," *Current History* (October 1991): 328–332.

72. Full texts in English translation appeared in Igor Troyanovsky, ed., *Religion in the Soviet Republics: A Guide to Christianity, Judaism, Islam, Buddhism, and Other Religions* (San Francisco: Harper, 1991), pp. 23–37.

73. Bourdeaux, *Gorbachev, Glasnost and the Gospel*, p. 57; *Keston News Service*, 13 April 1989, based on *Moscow News*, 9 April 1989; Powell, "The Revival of Religion," p. 328.

74. I am relying on private talks during my visit to the Soviet Union in October 1988 and on discussions with a Mennonite World Conference delegation visiting there a week later.

75. Bourdeaux, *Gorbachev, Glasnost and the Gospel*, pp. 119–20 and 127–28, offers a brief analytical summary. He mistakenly describes Dukhonchenko of Kiev as having been "elected" president of the union in December 1989 by the council of the union (which would be a violation of its statute) when he was merely "nominated" for election at a congress of delegates in February 1990. Dukhonchenko withdrew his candidacy in favor of his deputy, Komendant.

76. The newly revised statute of what he calls the "All-Union League of Evangelical Christian Baptists" [*sic*] was published in English translation in Troyanovsky, 140–150.

77. Bourdeaux, *Gorbachev, Glasnost and the Gospel*, p. 131.

78. Troyanovsky provides an address directory, p. 203.

79. Roy Branson, "Adventist Developments in the USSR," reprinted in *Ecumenical Press Service*, 88.06.118.

80. Ibid. See also Sapiets, "One Hundred Years," passim.

81. Bourdeaux, *Gorbachev, Glasnost and the Gospel*, pp. 128–29 argues for 10,000 members as logical deduction from the number of delegates at its congress in July 1989. See the careful comparison of recent statistical esti-

mates in Mark Elliott, "Growing Protestant Diversity in the Former Soviet Union," in *Pluralism in the Former Soviet Union* (Boston: Institute for the Study of Conflict, Ideology and Policy, Brown University, 1992).

82. Copy in author's possession.

83. A label they seem to prefer for themselves.

84. From author's copy.

85. *Khristianskoc Slovo*, January 1990. Susan Isaacs, "An Introduction to the Soviet Union's Emerging Indigenous Missions," *News Network International Special Report*, 12 February 1991, claimed the Latvian Christian Mission had 30 fulltime and 300 parttime volunteers, whereas Light of the Gospel mission of Rovno and Donctsk had 50 fulltime and 100 parttime. The latter mission also reported the founding of 10 new churches with 20 to 120 members each (Elliott, "Growing Protestant Diversity," p. 15).

86. In addition to ten such regional centers begun by UECB churches in 1990, other such projects involved independent Baptist and Pentecostal churches working with agencies such as the Slavic Gospel Association, Logos, Fuller Seminary, Conservative Baptist Seminary, or East Europe Seminary (Vienna).

87. Alexander Zaichenko, *Christianity As a Means of Economic Renewal of the USSR* (Winnipeg: Soviet Union Network, 1992).

88. Walter Sawatsky, "After the Glasnost Revolution: Soviet Evangelicals and the Western Missions," *International Bulletin of Missionary Research* (April 1992); Mark Elliott, "New Opportunities, New Demands in the Old Red Empire," *Evangelical Missions Quarterly* (January 1992): 32–39; Bill Yoder, "Observations on Western Missions in Eastern Europe," *Occasional Papers on Religion in Eastern Europe* (March 1992): 33–38. Relying also on a thirteen-page report by Steve Weber of the Lausanne Committee, dated 26 August 1991, based on fifty interviews.

89. Mark Elliott, "Growing Protestant Diversity," 9–14.

90. Robert Bellah, et al. *Habits of the Heart: Individualism and Commitment in American Life* (New York: Harper and Row, 1985), pp. 221, 235. In a similar vein, Reginald W. Bibby, *Fragmented Gods: The Poverty and Potential of Religion in Canada* (Toronto: Irwin Publishing, 1987).

9 Conscientious Objectors in Eastern Europe

1. *Christian Science Monitor* (14 September 1988), p. 9. A historical survey of pacifism and conscientious objection in Europe prior to World War I is found in Peter Brock, *Freedom from Violence: Sectarian Nonresistance from the Middle Ages to the Great War* (Toronto, Ont.: University of Toronto Press, 1991). Recent efforts to define such issues for Europeans can be traced in *War Resisters' International Newsletter* (London), and the publications of various peace groups in the Netherlands, Germany, Austria, France, and elsewhere in Western Europe.

2. See Devi Prasad and Tony Smythe, *Conscription, A World Survey: Compulsory Military Service and Resistance to It* (London: War Resisters' International, 1968). A brief updated summary of the East European conscription

requirements appeared in *War Resisters' International Newsletter,* no. 213 (November–December 1986), pp. 7–8; hereinafter *WRIN.*

3. All socialist European constitutions explicitly upheld the right to freedom of conscience in their stated articles. See Jan Triska, *Constitutions of Communist Party States* (Stanford, Calif.: Hoover Institute of War, Revolution and Peace, 1968), pp. 51, 126, 162, 192, 224, 344, 353, 401, 458.

4. All these constitutions declaring the right of freedom of conscience also insisted that it was the duty of citizens to defend their country, if need be, by taking up arms. The GDR's requirements in this regard were clearly set forth in Ernst Legahun, " 'Bausoldaten' und ziviler Ersatzdienst," *Christen drueben,* no. 1 (November 1984): 8–9.

5. *Christian Science Monitor* (14 September 1988), p. 10. The independent peace movements of Eastern Europe were succinctly characterized in Cathy Fitzpatrick, "Into the Public Eye: The Emergence of Independent Peace Movements in the Soviet Bloc," *Sojourners* 17, no. 2 (February 1987): 20ff. The wide-ranging concerns of these peace movements are clearly reflected in Vladimir Tismaneanu, ed., *In Search of Civil Society: Independent Peace Movements in the Soviet Bloc* (New York and London: Routledge, 1990).

6. Peter Brock, *Pacifism in Europe to 1914* (Princeton, N.J.: Princeton University Press, 1972), pp. 442–55. The existence of pacifist thought in Russian Orthodox Church traditions has not been adequately researched. See G. P. Fedotov, *The Russian Religious Mind, Kievan Christianity: The Tenth to the Thirteenth Centuries* (New York: Harper and Row, 1960), pp. 94ff.

7. Brock, *Pacifism in Europe,* pp. 456ff.

8. The definition and maintenance of Mennonite pacifism in Russian and Soviet settings has been studied in Lawrence Klippenstein, "Mennonite Pacifism and State Service in Russia: A Case Study in Church-State Relations, 1789–1936," unpublished Ph.D. diss., University of Minnesota, 1984. See also Brock, *Freedom from Violence,* pp. 153–171.

9. Until 1918 Mennonites were allowed to manage much of the forestry camp program themselves. Under the Soviets, management was placed completely into the hands of appointed Soviet authorities.

10. A. I. Klibanov, *Religioznoe Sektantsvo i sovremennost'* (Moscow: Nauka, 1969), p. 189; Klippenstein, "Mennonite Pacifism," pp. 271ff. On pacifism and the early Soviet period see also Bruno Coppieters, "Die pazifistischen Sekten, die Bolschewiki und das Recht auf Wehrdienstverweigerung," in Reiner Steinweg, ed., *Lehren aus der Geschichte? Historische Friedensforschung* (Frankfurt am Main: Suhrkamp Verlag, 1990), pp. 308–360.

11. Wilhelm Kahle, *Evangelische Christen in Russland und der Sowjetunion* (Wuppertal and Kassel: Oncken Verlag, 1978), pp. 385ff.; and Walter Sawatsky, *Soviet Evangelicals Since World War II* (Scottdale, Pa.: Herald Press, 1981), pp. 115ff. The pioneering study on this topic is Paul Steeves, "The Russian Baptist Union, 1917–1935: Evangelical Awakening in Russia," unpublished Ph.D. diss., University of Kansas, 1976 (see pp. 557–92).

12. The historical experience of Pentecostals in the Soviet Union was traced in William Fletcher, *Soviet Charismatics: The Pentecostals in the USSR* (New York: Peter Lang, 1985). The discussion of pacifism in this treatment, however, is very sketchy (see pp. 114–16).

13. Hans Rempel and George K. Epp, *Waffen der Wehrlosen: Ersatzdienst der Mennoniten in der USSR* (Winnipeg, Man.: CMBC Publications, 1980). This work includes testimonials of many individuals drafted during those years.

14. See John B. Toews, *Czars, Soviets and Mennonites* (North Newton, Kans.: Faith and Life Press, 1982), pp. 151–70. Klippenstein, "Mennonite Pacifism," pp. 315ff.

15. Walter Kolarz, *Religion in the Soviet Union* (London: Macmillan, 1962), pp. 48ff., 303ff.

16. The experience of deportees is described in Joseph S. Height, *Paradise on the Steppe: A Cultural History of the Kutschurgan, Beresan and Liebental Colonists, 1804–1944* (Bismarck: North Dakota Historical Society of Germans from Russia, 1972), pp. 333ff.; and Herta Neufeld, *Im Paradies . . . der Arbeiter und Bauern* (Hannover: Verlag Karl F. Bangemann, 1986), pp. 46ff.

17. Walter Sawatsky, "Mennonite Congregations in the Soviet Union Today," *Mennonite Life* 33 (March 1978): 12–26. Note also Walter Wedel, *Nur zwanzig Kilometer* (Wuppertal: R. Brockhaus Verlag, 1979), pp. 201–2, where one of the main characters mentions his struggle of conscience over serving in the Red Army during this period.

18. The Soviet Union's takeover of countries on its western border was summarized in J. Blum, R. Cameron, and Thomas Barnes, *A History: The European World* (Boston: Little, Brown, 1966), pp. 937ff. See also J. F. Brown, *Eastern Europe and Communist Rule* (Durham, N.C.: Duke University Press, 1988).

19. The broader context of church-state relations is reviewed in H. G. Koch, *Staat und Kirche in der DDR, Zur Entwicklung ihrer Beziehungen von 1945–1975: Darstellung, Quellen, Uebersichten* (Stuttgart: Quell Verlag, 1975). The membership of the EKD declined after the war from 15 million (nominal) members to under 8 million (more active) members. The Catholic Church membership remained more stable, though falling; its current membership is around 1.5 million. See Roger Williamson, "East Germany: The Federation of Protestant Churches," *Religion in Communist Lands* 9, nos. 1–2 (Spring 1981): 6–17, and R. Henkys, ed., *Bund der Evangelischen Kirchen in der DDR* (Witten, Frankfurt, Berlin: Eckart Verlag, 1970) on the background of Protestant developments in East Germany.

20. Koppel S. Pinson, *Modern Germany: Its History and Civilization* (New York: Macmillan, 1969), p. 561; Henry Ashby Turner, Jr., *The Two Germanies Since 1945* (New Haven, Conn.: Yale University Press, 1987). See also "Spuren. Zur Geschichte der Friedensbewegung in der DDR," an unpublished collection of studies presented to members of a seminar, "Frieden konkret VI," held at Cottbus in the GDR in February 1988 (in my files).

21. Kurt and Hildegard Mocker, "Wehrdienstverweigerung in der 'DDR': Rechtsgrundlagen des Wehrdienstes," *Christen drueben* no. 1 (November 1984): 10–12; Peter Wensierski, "Zwischen Pazifismus und Militarismus," *Deutschland Archiv* 15, no. 5 (May 1982): 449–52; and Karl Wilhelm Fricke, "Die Pazifismus-kritik der SED," *Deutschland Archiv* 14, no. 10 (October 1981): 1026–29.

22. Bernd Eisenfeld, "Mit wechselnder Intensitaet: Das Eintreten der evangelischen Kirche in der DDR fuer den waffenlosen Dienst," *Kirche im*

Sozialismus 5, no. 1 (March 1979): 27–28. Lutheran churches had always emphasized obedience to rulers (Romans 13). For a critique of this position see U. Duchrow, *Two Kingdoms: The Use and Misuse of a Lutheran Theological Concept* (Geneva: Lutheran World Federation, 1977).

23. Mocker and Mocker, "Wehrdienstverweigerung," p. 11; Hans-Jochen Tschiche, "Zwischen Traum und Alptraum-Erfahrungen mit der Wieder-bewaffnung in Deutschland," in "Spuren," p. 4.

24. See also Joyce Marie Mushaben, "Swords to Ploughshares: The Church, the State and the East German Peace Movement," *Studies in Comparative Communism* 17, no. 2 (Summer 1984): 123ff.; "Spuren," and Peter Maser, "The Protestant Churches and the Independent Peace Movement in the GDR," in *Studies in GDR Culture and Society 5* (Lanham, Md.: University Press of America, 1985).

25. Mushaben, "Swords to Ploughshares." But see also Bernd Zipperman, "Bemerkungen zur Sozialistischen Wehrerziehung in der 'DDR'," *Christen drueben* no. 1 (November 1984): 13–15, and Gero Neugebauer, "The Military and Society in the GDR," in *Studies in GDR Culture and Society.*

26. Eisenfeld, "Mit wechselnder Intensitaet," pp. 30–31. See also Eisenfeld, "Spatensoldaten: 20 Jahre Bausoldaten in der DDR," *Kirche im Sozialismus* 10, no. 4 (September 1984): 21ff.; and Renate Hackel, "20 Jahre Bausoldaten—Dienst mit den Spaten," *Informationen und Berichte: Digest des Osten,* no. 1 (1985): 16ff.

27. Hackel, "20 Jahre," pp. 16ff.

28. Eisenfeld, "Mit wechselnder Intensitaet," pp. 31–32; Mocker and Mocker, "Wehrdienstverweigerung," pp. 10–12; and Legahun, "Bausoldaten," pp. 8–9.

29. Legahun, "Bausoldaten," p. 9, has the oath's exact wording. It included a pledge to "undergird the defensive readiness of the country" and to do faithful work in the *Baueinheiten* to "contribute to the People's National Army in assisting the Soviet Union and its allied forces to defend the state against all its enemies . . . to obey all orders of the superiors faithfully," and "to uphold the honor of the Republic at all times."

30. Eisenfeld, "Mit wechselnder Intensitaet," pp. 31–32, 35–36.

31. One of these was V. F. Krestianinov who accused Mennonite preachers of encouraging their denomination's young men not to serve in the army. See his *Mennonity* (Moscow: Politizdat, 1967), p. 111.

32. On Mennonites turning to arms see Klippenstein, "Mennonite Pacifism," pp. 235ff., and John B. Toews, "The Origins and Activities of the Mennonite *Selbstschutz* in the Ukraine (1918–1919)," *Mennonite Quarterly Review* 46, no. 1 (January 1972): 5–40.

33. Sawatsky, *Soviet Evangelicals,* pp. 131ff., Michael Bourdeaux, *Religious Ferment in Russia* (London: Macmillan, 1968), and an "insider's" perspective on the emergence of the dissident unregistered Baptists in *25 Jahre auf dem Weg.Kurze Geschichte des Bundes Unabhaengiger Baptisten in der Sowjetunion* (Gummersbach: Missionswerk Friedensstimme, 1987).

34. The *Bulletin* (*Biulletin*) of the dissident Baptists' Council of Prisoners' Relatives (all women) diligently gathered up information about persecuted individuals in their circles and sought to have this material published in the

West. The *Nachrichtenblatt* of a mission organization known as *Missionswerk Friedensstimme*, headquartered in Gummersbach, Germany, sought to be that outlet in the West, along with other publications at information centers such as Keston College, London, and G2W (*Glaube in der zweiten Welt*) in Zollikon, Switzerland. These centers established branch offices in various Western countries, including one in the United States at Elkhart, Indiana, headed by Georgi Vins. A brief history of the Council appeared in Jacob Janzen, *20 Jahre Verwandtenrat.Aus der Not Entstanden* (Gummersbach: Missionswerk Friedensstimme, 1984).

35. Kolarz, *Religion in the Soviet Union*, pp. 330–38. A document reporting the service refusals of 160 Pentecostals in the Rovno region was noted in *A Chronicle of Current Events*, no. 46 (1978): 46. Comments on the later situation are in Oxana Antic, "Obor Polozheniia Piatidesiatnikov v SSSR za 1980–1981," *Radio Free Europe Research*, PC 18/82 (1 February 1982): 1–6.

36. Pacifist thought among Seventh-Day Adventists in the USSR is presented in Marita Sapiets, "One Hundred Years of Adventism in Russia and the Soviet Union," *Religion in Communist Lands* 12, no. 3 (Winter 1984): 256–73. See also "Annotations," *Radio Free Europe Research* 223/84 (5 June 1984); an earlier article by Sapiets, "V. A. Shelkov and the True and Faithful Seventh-Day Adventists in the USSR," *Religion in Communist Lands* 8, no. 3 (Autumn 1980): 201–10, and "Lenin Cited in Support of True and Free Adventist View," ibid., pp. 213–17.

37. Oxana Antic, "Jehovah's Witnesses in the Soviet Union," *Radio Free Europe Research* 39/82 (19 January 1983): 1–2; and Vladimir Kuroyedov, "Church and Religion in the USSR," *Religion in Communist Dominated Areas* 18, nos. 10–12 (October–December 1979): 148.

38. The Moiseev case was discussed in detail in *Religion in Communist Dominated Areas* 12 (January–March 1973): 3–9. Another such case was that of Jurij Burda, an objector to the military oath who died by violent means only five months after entering the army. See *Nachrichten von den Feldern der Verfolgung* 10, no. 48 (January–February 1985): 4ff. This article also includes the text of the Soviet military oath.

39. *Evangelical Times* (January 1985): 1–2; *Prisoners of Conscience in the USSR: Their Treatment and Conditions*, 2nd rev. ed. (London: Amnesty International, 1980), pp. 56–57.

40. Arguments often rested on such biblical texts as Exodus 20:13, Matthew 26:51, or Matthew 5:34. See also *Evangelical Times* (January 1985): 2; *Nachrichten von den Feldern der Verfolgung* 10, no. 48 (January–February 1985): 7.

41. Harold J. Berman, ed., *Soviet Criminal Law and Procedure: The RSFSR Codes*, 2nd rev. ed. (Cambridge, Mass.: Harvard University Press, 1972), p. 197.

42. This conclusion is based on a number of cases in *samizdat* sources received by Keston College, *Glaube in der zweiten Welt*, and *Missionswerk Friedensstimme*, as well as information that these centers and others have released.

43. *Christian Science Monitor* (13 January 1985), p. 12; and *Newspeace* (April 1982), p. 5.

44. Based on conversations held in May 1986 with a Baptist minister, Traugott Quiring, who had served for many years at Tashkent in Soviet Central Asia and then moved to West Germany.

45. Heinrich and Gerhard Woelk, *Die Mennoniten Bruedergemeinde in Russland, 1925–1980* (Fresno, Calif.: Center for Mennonite Brethren Studies, 1981), p. 215.

46. For a short historical sketch of these developments, see Peter Brock, "The Non-resistance of the Hungarian Nazarenes to 1914," *Mennonite Quarterly Review* 54, no. 1 (January 1980): 53–63; and Peter Brock, "Some Objectors in Nineteenth Century Hungary," *Mennonite Quarterly Review* 57, no. 1 (January 1983): 64–72.

47. "Church of the Nazarenes Recognized," *Religion in Communist Lands* 6, no. 1 (Spring 1978): 53. Non-combatant service could include medical, engineering, or other duties. The church amended its statutes to conform with the new state accord. Information on recognition was provided by an Ecumenical Press Service release, 11 August 1977.

48. A reference to exemptions for Jehovah's Witnesses and Seventh-Day Adventists appeared in *Kathpress Beilage* (28 October 1984), p. 8.

49. Membership of Jehovah's Witnesses and Seventh-Day Adventists is probably somewhat over 5,000 for each group. Otto Luchterhandt and R. Bohren (eds.), *Die Religionsfreiheit in Osteuropa* (Zollikon: G2W Verlag, 1984), pp. 241–42.

50. "The Vicissitudes of the Hungarian Catholic Church," *Religion in Communist Lands* 12, no. 2 (Summer 1984): 215–26. See also Stephen Polgar, "A Summary of the Situation of the Hungarian Catholic Church," *Religion in Communist Lands* 12, no. 1 (Spring 1984): 11–38; and Leslie Laszlo, "The Base Community—a Challenge to Peaceful Coexistence Between Church and State in Hungary," *Occasional Papers on Religion in Eastern Europe* 1 (November 1981): 3–4.

51. On the background and activity of Father Bulányi, see a bibliography of published works noted in "Vatican Condemnation of Bulányi's Teaching," *Religion in Communist Lands* 15, no. 3 (Winter 1987): 350; and Lawrence Klippenstein, "Father Bulányi and the Pacifist Controversy in Hungary, 1976–1987," *Occasional Papers on Religion in Eastern Europe* 9 (February 1989): 9–28.

52. *END Journal of European Nuclear Disarmament* 16/17 (Summer 1985): 10. See John Eibner, "A Sectarian Heresy? Conscientious Objectors in Hungary," *Frontier* no. 2 (March–April 1988): 23–24.

53. Miklos Haraszti, "Turning the Other Cheek," *Religion in Communist Lands* 11, no. 1 (Spring 1983): 97–98; *Informationsdienst G2W*, no. 17 (5 October 1981): 16.

54. *Keston News Service* (hereinafter *KNS*) no. 242 (23 January 1986), p. 11; no. 244 (20 February 1986), p. 9.

55. *Kathpress Ausland* (15 October 1985), p. 5.

56. From excerpts of a German translation in my files courtesy of the *Kathpress* office in Vienna. See "Katholischer Waffendienst Verweigerer wendet sich an Europaeisches Kulturforum," *Kathpress Ausland* (5 November 1985), p. 213.

57. *Kathpress Ausland* (15 October 1985), p. 5; *MK Pressedienst*, no. 10 (24 November 1986), pp. 2–5.

58. Gareth Davies, "Conscientious Objection and the Freedom and Peace Movement in Poland," *Religion in Communist Lands* 16, no. 1 (Spring 1988): 4–6.

59. *WRIN*, no. 186 (February 1982), p. 7. The article was translated from Solidarity's magazine *Voice of Solidarnosc*, where it had appeared before the imposition of martial law in December 1981. A brief survey of conscientious objector activity in Poland is Lawrence Klippenstein, "Conscientious Objectors in Socialist Poland," *Occasional Papers on Religion in Eastern Europe* 7, no. 5 (October 1987): 19ff.

60. Karen Schmidt, "Kriegsverweigerung in sozialistischen Staaten— Dargestellt am Beispiel der Sowjetunion und der Volksrepublik Polen," *Berichte des Bundesinstituts fuer Ostwissenschaftliche und Internationale Studien* 43/1972 (Cologne): 1–21.

61. *WRIN*, no. 192 (February 1983), p. 9, and no. 193 (April 1983), p. 4. The latter (taken from *Voice of Solidarnosc*) described in detail the detainees of the conscription program during the martial law period.

62. The story of Maciej appeared in *WRIN*, no. 208 (November–December, 1985), p. 3; also no. 199 (April 1984), p. 13.

63. Davies, "Conscientious Objectors," p. 8. One of the petitions signed by Lech Wałesa is translated in *WRIN*, no. 208 (November–December 1985), p. 3.

64. Irene Korba, "Freedom and Peace: Conscientious Objectors in Poland," *Religion in Communist Lands* 14, no. 3 (Winter 1986): 321. See also an address to the END convention in Amsterdam 14 April 1985, and signed by eighteen people; an English translation is in my files. The speeches of Pope John Paul II were clearly an important element of the movement's intellectual and spiritual dimensions. They were constantly alluded to in Freedom and Peace documents. On other aspects of thought related to nonviolence and peace in Catholic Poland, see Paul Keim, "A Polish Strategy for Nonviolent Change," *Religion in Communist Lands* 11, no. 2 (Summer 1983): 161–69, and *KNS*, no. 259 (18 September 1986), p. 13.

65. Korba, "Freedom and Peace," p. 322. See also Andrzej Tymowski, "Underground Solidarity and the Western Peace Movement," *Poland Watch* (August 1984), pp. 114–130, and *Wolnosc i Pokoj (WiP): Documents of Poland's "Freedom and Peace" Movement* (Seattle, Wash.: World With War Council, 1989).

66. Davies, "Conscientious Objection," p. 17; *WRIN*, no. 209 (February–March, 1986), pp. 3–4. Gdansk was at that time the home of the Alternative Society Movement (RSA), a libertarian movement in the Kropotkin tradition.

67. Ibid., no. 210 (April–May 1986), p. 16, is a translation of a report sent by the women who participated in this protest; their names are attached to the document. The nuclear plant protest is discussed in ibid., no. 211 (June–July 1986), p. 2.

68. *KNS*, no. 260 (2 October 1986), p. 9; no. 264 (27 November 1986), p. 12; no. 269 (19 February 1987), pp. 13–14.

69. On Hromádka's views see Josef Hromádka, *Theology Between Yesterday and Tomorrow* (Philadelphia: Westminster Press, 1957). See also a recent evaluation of his contributions in Charles West, "Josef Hromádka and the

400   Notes

Witness of the Church in East and West Today," *Occasional Papers on Religion in Eastern Europe* 10, no. 2 (March 1990): 13–25. A brief introduction to the ECCB is in Trevor Beeson, *Discretion and Valour: Religious Conditions in Russia and Eastern Europe*, 2nd rev. ed. (London: Collins, 1982), pp. 219–55. It placed the membership then at around 240,000. See also Paul Bock, "Church and State in Czechoslovakia with Particular Attention to Protestantism," *Occasional Papers on Religion in Eastern Europe* 2, no. 2 (April 1982): 9–24.

70. Beeson, *Discretion and Valour*, pp. 241–45.

71. On the founding of and opposition to "New Orientation," see "Pressure on the Churches in Czechoslovakia," *Religion in Communist Lands* 2, no. 2 (March–April 1974): 7–9; and Milena Kalinovska, "Czechoslovakia Ten Years After," ibid., 6, no. 3 (Autumn 1978): 162–78; and Bock, "Church and State in Czechoslovakia," pp. 19–20.

72. The ECCB's distressed situation was depicted in *CSSR. Zur Lage der Evangelischen Kirche der Boehmischen Brueder. Eine Dokumentation* (Zurich: Institut Glaube in der 2. Welt, 1978). For a summary of laws regulating church life see Luchterhandt und Bohrens, *Religionsfreiheit*, pp. 216ff. Other instances of harassment and pressures experienced by Protestant pastors are noted in *KNS*, no. 267 (22 January 1987), p. 3.

73. A Palach Press document in Keston College files (CZ Brezina). Several people who later became conscientious objectors were signators of the leaflet. Matula and Brezina had studied at the Comenius Theology Faculty earlier. "Czechoslovakia Ten Years After," p. 166.

74. On the history of Charter 77, see Milena Kalinovska, "The Religious Situation in Czechoslovakia," *Religion in Communist Lands* 5, no. 3 (Autumn 1977): 148–63, esp. the document "Czech Clergy and Charter 77," signed by Brezina and others. The relationship of Charter 77 to the independent peace movements is suggested in Jan Kavan and Zdena Tomin, eds., *Voices from Prague: Documents on Czechoslovakia and the Peace Movement* (London: Palach Press, 1983).

75. Peter Chelcicky was a fifteenth-century Bohemian church leader of pacifist persuasion who helped lay foundations for the Protestant Reformation in Czechoslovakia. Murray L. Wagner, *Peter Chelcicky: A Radical Separatist in Hussite Bohemia* (Scottdale, Pa.: Herald Press, 1983).

76. See "Trial of Alex Brezina by a Prague Military Court" and "The Trial of Alex Brezina Took Place on 14 June 1977 at the District Military Court," photocopied documents in Keston College files (CZ Brezina).

77. *Amnesty International Newsletter* (December 1980), p. 2.

78. *Bulletin and Summary of Available Documents* (London: Palach Press), no. 17 (June 1981), p. 39, and nos. 18–20 (April 1982), p. 81.

79. *WRIN*, no. 211 (June–July 1986), p. 6, with Charter 77 document No. 7/86, trans. A. G. Brain. The broader peace issue was addressed in another document, "The Prague Appeal" (11 March 1985), and reprinted in trans. in *WRIN*, no. 204 (March–April 1985), p. 13.

80. Ibid., no. 211 (June–July 1986), p. 6. Other issues addressed in this statement were the right to travel, concern for greater freedom of cultural expression, and the right to independent thinking in education.

81. *KNS*, no. 301 (26 May 1988), p. 18.

82. Ibid., no. 234 (19 September 1985), pp. 5–6. Luchterhandt and Bohren estimated the membership of Jehovah's Witnesses in Czechoslovakia to be about 8,000 (in 1980). It is difficult to be precise about Jehovah's Witnesses since they do not publish membership figures. The group is generally believed to be growing rapidly throughout Eastern Europe.

83. *WRIN*, no. 213 (December 1987), p. 7; *KNS*, no. 308 (8 September 1988), p. 8. Koci's release was announced in *KNS*, no. 313 (17 November 1988), p. 10, and his detention for refusing military call-up subsequently was reported in *KNS*, no. 330 (20 July 1989), p. 10. Noncombatant service was available in the army, with three years of working on underground construction regarded as fulfilling military obligations. Evasion of military service was punishable by one to five years in prison. Koci had stressed during his trial in 1988 that he was prepared to serve society in any way as long as it did not conflict with his Christian beliefs.

84. *WRIN*, no. 220 (April–May 1988), p. 13.

85. Milos Rejchrt, "Verfallserscheinungen sittlicher Normen," *Glaube in der 2. Welt* 16, no. 5 (1988): 29. The author had been a strong critic of the synod for compromising its position with respect to government strictures against the church. In this connection see also "Wieder Staat den Kirchen mistraut. Appell an die 25. Synode der Evangelischen Kirche der Boehmischen Brueder," ibid., 16, no. 12 (1988): 13–14, written much in the spirit of Rejchrt's criticisms. He was a member of the ECCB and a spokesman for Charter 77 almost from its beginnings.

86. *WRIN*, no. 220 (April–May 1988), p. 12.

87. An earlier portrait of the situation for COs in Yugoslavia is "Conscientious Objectors: The Situation in Yugoslavia," written by Keston College staff members for *Religion in Communist Lands* 15, no. 3 (Winter 1987): 332ff. Another report appeared in *WRIN*, no. 215 (March–April 1987), p. 8. On the development of an independent peace movement in Yugoslavia, see *WRIN*, no. 203 (January–February 1985), p. 14.

88. *KNS*, no. 297 (17 March 1988), pp. 13–14; no. 309 (22 September 1988), pp. 10–12.

89. Keston College staff, "Conscientious Objectors," p. 334.

90. Ibid.

91. *KNS*, no. 297 (17 March 1988), p. 14.

92. Ibid., no. 291 (7 January 1988), p. 16; no. 314 (1 December 1988), p. 19.

93. Earl A. Pope, "The Contemporary Religious Situation in Romania," in Dennis Dunn (ed.), *Religion and Communist Society* (Berkeley, Calif.: Berkeley Slavic Specialties, 1982), pp. 145ff.; source listed in n. 23; also *KNS*, no. 302 (9 June 1988), p. 11; no. 321 (16 March 1989), pp. 2–3. Emil's father, Kostadin, was also imprisoned, for protesting the punishment of COs. He received a sentence of four years in 1982, with one more added later. He was released in 1988. See also "Conscientious Objection to Military Service," *Amnesty International* (January 1991), pp. 7, 16; hereinafter "Conscientious Objection (AI)."

94. *WRIN*, no. 221 (April–May 1988), p. 12. The UN vote was passed on 10 March 1987. For the wording of the pertinent section on conscientious objectors see ibid., no. 215 (March–April 1987), p. 9. Bulgaria, the Byelorussian SSR, the GDR, the USSR, and Yugoslavia abstained.

402   Notes

95. Ibid.

96. Ibid., no. 216 (July–August 1987), p. 7.

97. Ibid. See also "CSCE moves on objection," *Peace News: Nonviolence in Action*, no. 2332 (August, 1990), p. 3; hereinafter *Peace News*.

98. *WRIN*, no. 221 (August–September 1988), p. 5.

99. Ibid.

100. For a useful analysis of the Eastern European scene just before the changes of 1989–90 see Timothy Garton Ash, *The Uses of Adversity: Essays on the Fate of Central Europe* (Cambridge: Granta Books, 1989). See also Sabrina P. Ramet, *Social Currents in Eastern Europe: The Sources and Meaning of the Great Transformation* (Durham, N.C.: Duke University Press, 1991), which takes the analysis even closer to the present. Neither of these treatments deals much with the peace groups or conscientious objectors as such.

101. *Sueddeutsche Zeitung* (Munich), 22 June 1988, p. 8; *KNS*, no. 306 (4 August 1988), p. 11. One source says that the wording of the Polish military oath also had been changed, omitting the reference to loyalty to fraternal allies. *WRIN*, no. 221 (August–September 1988), p. 4. The Polish Press Agency announcement is quoted at some length in "Polish Government Amends Law Requiring Military Service," *East Europerspectives*, no. 15 (February 1989): 4–6.

102. *KNS*, no. 313 (17 November 1988), p. 16.

103. "Poland local boards play fast and loose with CO rules," *Peace News*, no. 2344 (July 1991), p. 4.

104. *KNS*, no. 299 (28 April 1988), p. 4; no. 302 (9 June 1988), p. 13. Laszlo Paskai became the archbishop of Esztergom on 26 April 1987. A month later, he was appointed a cardinal by Pope John Paul II. He is now primate of the Catholic Church in Hungary. See John V. Eibner, "A New Primate: A New Policy?" *Religion in Communist Lands* 16, no. 2 (Summer 1988): 164–68.

105. *KNS*, no. 297 (31 March 1988), p. 11.

106. Ibid., no. 299 (28 April 1988), p. 17.

107. *Transatlantic Peace Newsletter*, no. 1 (September 1988), p. 6. See also *KNS*, no. 310 (6 October 1988), pp. 8–9. "Cases Against Conscientious Objectors," *KNS*, no. 315 (15 December 1988), pp. 14–15. The same article noted that the August 1988 military call-up included four Catholics (all Bulányists) and ten Jehovah's Witnesses who refused to accept military service.

108. *KNS*, no. 300 (12 May 1988), p. 11; no. 312 (3 November 1988), p. 14.

109. Ibid., no. 320 (2 March 1989), p. 11; no. 333 (7 August 1989), p. 14. "Conscientious Objection (AI)," p. 12. See also "COs group in Hungary," *Peace News*, no. 2331 (July 1990), p. 4.

110. Hackel, "20 Jahre Bausoldaten," pp. 14–15. On the church's reaction to military defense teaching in GDR schools, see Pedro Ramet, "Church and Peace in the GDR," *Problems of Communism* 33, no. 4 (July–August 1984): 48ff., and Norman Thiessen, " 'Defense Training' in the GDR," *East Europerspectives*, no. 11 (April 1987): 2–7.

111. Karl Wilhelm Fricke, *Opposition und Widerstand in der DDR* (Cologne: Verlag Wissenschaft und Politik, 1984), pp. 36–37. Article 23(1) of the GDR Constitution stated that the protection of the peace and the socialist Fatherland with its achievements was the right and duty of all citizens. Legahun, "Bausoldaten," p. 8.

112. Jehovah's Witnesses working illegally in the GDR were thought to number about 28,000 a decade ago, with the Adventists somewhat less than half that number. Luchterhandt and Bohren, *Religionsfreiheit*, pp. 85–86. On *Totalverweigerer*, see Martin Hennig, "Totalverweigerer—Eine schwierige Minderheit," *Was uns betrifft*, no. 3 (May 1983): 12–13.

113. Fitzpatrick, "Into the Public Eye," p. 22.

114. *WRIN*, no. 219 (February–March 1988), pp. 8–9; and ibid., "Petition on COs."

115. *KNS*, no. 314 (1 December 1988), p. 21. The Leich address was published in the *Frankfurter Allgemeine* (8 March 1988), and then in translation in "An Address by Bishop Leich: Two Versions," *Religion in Communist Lands* 16, no. 3 (Autumn 1988): 260–65. A much-abbreviated version had appeared in *Neues Deutschland* on 4 March 1988.

116. *KNS*, no. 342 (25 January 1990), pp. 20–21.

117. A more detailed sketch of military exemption regulations in the FRG is available in "Conscientious Objection (AI)," pp. 9–10. The GDR announcement on alternative service was noted in "Chronik 1990," *G2W Glaube in der 2.Welt 1990* (Zollikon, Switzerland), p. 9; See also "Disappearing army for disappearing state," *Peace News*, no. 2331 (July 1990), p. 4. Here it is reported that total resisters may still be imprisoned in Germany today. See "Berlin Antimilitary Declaration," *Peace News*, no. 2333 (September 1990), p. 5, for a statement from German young men who currently resist all forms of military service.

118. *KNS*, no. 303 (23 June 1988), pp. 7–8.

119. Ibid., no. 297 (31 March 1988), appendix. Out of twenty-five people listed as "New Prisoners," at least thirteen had been charged with "evasion of military service." A number of these also appeared in the lists of *WRIN*, no. 220 (April–May 1988), p. 14; no. 221 (August–September 1988), p. 14.

120. The Word of Life Group totaled about 500 members, largely young people from Tallinn, Tartu, and Parnu. Nearly half of them signed a petition to Reagan and Gorbachev, renouncing Soviet citizenship to emphasize their Estonian identity, and asking for the right to emigrate. *KNS*, no. 297 (31 March 1988), p. 9; *WRIN*, no. 220 (April–May 1988), p. 14. An example of negative response to military service by young Lithuanian men was reported several years earlier in *The Ukrainian Weekly* (8 December 1985), p. 2.

121. *WRIN*, no. 207 (September–October 1985), pp. 5–6; no. 212 (September–October 1986), p. 3; no. 209 (February–March 1986), pp. 1, 4; and *Peace Projections Newsletter* 4, no. 2 (March 1988): 1–4. Another useful summary of the Moscow Trust Group's activities is Fitzpatrick, "Into the Public Eye," pp. 20–25.

122. Bernard Clasen, *Initiative: Vertrauen Ost-West* (19 May 1988): 10; "Demonstrazia za Alternativnuiu sluzhby v Moskve," *Doverie: Informatzionny Biulletenj nezavisimovo mirnovo dvizhenia v SSSR* (Moscow), no. 2 (February 1988): 16–17. See also "Pronozin issuing challenge to old regime's laws on military evasion," *Peace News*, no. 2346 (September 1991), p. 6.

123. *KNS*, no. 324 (27 April 1989), p. 7; no. 328 (22 June 1989), pp. 12–13. See also "Soviet System feels strain of wave of objectors," *Peace News*, no. 2336 (December 1990), p. 8; Beverley Woodward, "Critical Times for Soviet objectors," *Peace News*, no. 2332 (August 1990), p. 5.

124. *KNS*, no. 329 (30 November 1989), p. 10; no. 345 (9 March 1990), p. 5; "CO Law in Latvia," *The Nonviolent Activist and WRI Newsletter*, WRI no. 229 (April–May 1990), p. 18.

125. *KNS*, no. 347 (5 April 1990), p. 10; no. 349 (3 May 1990), p. 80; no. 362 (8 November 1990), p. 13.

126. Ibid., no. 345 (8 March 1990): 5, 20. A list of all known religious prisoners in the Soviet Union appeared in this issue. It seemed that the amnesty of religious prisoners granted at various times did not normally extend to conscientious objectors. See also "Estonian CO Law unchanged," *Peace News*, no. 2331 (July 1990), p. 4.

127. *KNS*, no. 352 (14 June 1990), pp. 5–6; no. 359 (27 September 1990), pp. 15–16; no. 360 (11 October 1990), pp. 13–14; no. 361 (25 October 1990), pp. 15–16; no. 365 (20 December 1990), pp. 17–20; Giovanni Codevilla, "Commentary on the New Soviet Law on Freedom of Conscience and Religious Organizations," *Religion in Communist Lands* 19 (Summer 1991): 119–45. See also "Moscow Call for CO," *Peace News*, no. 2332 (August 1990), p. 5.

128. *KNS*, no. 371 (21 March 1991), p. 15; "Concerns in Europe May–October 1991," *Amnesty International* (November 1991), pp. 11, 37, 62; hereinafter "Concerns (AI)." See also "Moldavia goes for CO Law," *Peace News*, no. 2345 (August 1991), p. 3; "CO Update: Back in the CIS," *Peace News*, no. 2351 (February 1992), p. 3; ibid., "Pronozin issuing challenge," p. 6.

129. *KNS*, no. 323 (13 April 1989), p. 17. This proposal was passed by parliament on 21 April, and Jehovah's Witnesses promptly rejected the option provided by this legislation. The Witnesses' preference was for service completely unrelated to the army. Several additional Jehovah's Witnesses had been sentenced and imprisoned only months earlier. *KNS*, no. 325 (11 May 1989), p. 18; no. 320 (2 March 1989), p. 12. See also "Concerns (AI)," p. 77. On the situation in Yugoslavia seen from a pacifist perspective see "Yugoslavia without a map," *Peace News*, no. 2349 (December 1991), p. 1, and Marko Hren, "Yugoslavia at the funeral of the ideologies," ibid., p. 12; "For genuine CO rights in Croatia," ibid., no. 2351 (February 1992), p. 7; "Stand up to be counted in Serbia and Vojvodina," ibid., p. 6, and "Unorganized resistance to an undeclared war," ibid., p. 7.

130. *KNS*, no. 331 (3 August 1989); no. 337 (2 November 1989), p. 7.

131. This report was given at a conference on "Independent Peace Groups, Pacifism and Civil Society in the Soviet Union and Eastern Europe," at the University of Waterloo, held 16 February 1990. For sketches of events that led to the founding of the new Czech government, see *Christian Science Monitor* (15–21 December 1989), p. 10A; and (5–11 January 1990), p. 10B. See also "Conscientious Objection (AI)," p. 9.

10   The New Church-State Configuration

This chapter is based on a study by Sabrina P. Ramet, prepared under contract with the U.S. Department of State. It was originally published in *East European Politics and Societies* 5, no. 2 (Spring 1991). Reprinted by permission.

1. For an explanation of the origins of Czech anticlericalism in a historical

context, see Pedro Ramet, "Christianity and National Heritage Among the Czechs and Slovaks," in Pedro Ramet (ed.), *Religion and Nationalism in Soviet and East European Politics*, rev. and expanded ed. (Durham, N.C.: Duke University Press, 1989).

2. On the establishment of this arrangement, see Djoko Slijepčević, *Die bulgarische orthodoxe Kirche, 1944–1956* (Munich: R. Oldenbourg Verlag, 1957).

3. An example of the former is the home of Pastor Rainer Eppelmann, reported in *Keston News Service*, no. 321 (16 March 1989), p. 11; the latter was revealed in East Germany by Erich Pätzold, the German official in charge of investigating abuses by East Germany's state security police, and reported in the *Wall Street Journal* (15 October 1990), p. A13.

4. *Keston News Service* (hereinafter *KNS*), no. 330 (20 July 1989), p. 4.

5. Ibid., no. 339 (30 November 1989), p. 15.

6. Ibid., no. 343 (8 February 1990), p. 12.

7. Ibid., no. 342 (25 January 1990), p. 19; no. 343 (8 February 1990), p. 18. The government's financial aid to the churches actually increased from 150 million koruny in 1990 to 559 million koruny in 1991; the increase included a substantial raise in salaries for their clergy, according to Peter Martin, "The New Law on Freedom of Religion and the Churches," RFE/RL Institute, *Report on Eastern Europe* (6 September 1991), p. 17.

8. *Frankfurter Allgemeine Zeitung* (6 May 1989), p. 12; (18 May 1989), p. 6; and *Tygodnik Powszechny* (25 June 1989), pp. 1, 3. See also Vincent C. Chrypiński, "The Catholic Church in Poland, 1944–1989," in Pedro Ramet (ed.), *Catholicism and Politics in Communist Societies* (Durham, N.C.: Duke University Press, 1990), pp. 138–40.

9. BTA (Sofia), 24 January 1990, in Foreign Broadcast Information Service (FBIS), *Daily Report* (Eastern Europe) (25 January 1990), p. 7.

10. *Glas koncila* (Zagreb) (8 July 1990), p. 5.

11. Tanjug (11 January 1990), trans. in FBIS, *Daily Report* (Eastern Europe) (19 January 1990), p. 84.

12. Earl Pope, "The Churches and the Romanian Revolution," paper prepared for the Fourth World Congress for Soviet and East European Studies, Harrogate, Eng., 21–26 July 1990.

13. *KNS*, no. 333 (7 August 1989), p. 7.

14. MTI (Budapest) (10 July 1991), in FBIS, *Daily Report* (Eastern Europe) (12 July 1991), p. 18.

15. It was relegalized in 1968 and obtained the return of some of its former property at that time.

16. *KNS*, no. 350 (17 May 1990), p. 14; no. 355 (26 July 1990), p. 10.

17. *Neue Zürcher Zeitung* (23 July 1991), p. 2.

18. AGERPRES (30 December 1989), in FBIS, *Daily Report* (Eastern Europe) (4 January 1990), p. 89.

19. *KNS*, no. 350 (17 May 1990), p. 15.

20. Ibid., no. 324 (27 April 1989), p. 19.

21. *Kana* (Zagreb), March 1992, p. 37.

22. *Glas koncila* (Zagreb), 15 March 1992, p. 2.

23. *Süddeutsche Zeitung* (Munich) (22/23 September 1990), p. 12.

24. Quoted in *New York Times* (29 June 1990), p. A4.

25. *Daily Telegraph* (London) (14 November 1990), p. 13.

26. Dan Ionescu, "The Orthodox-Uniate Conflict," RFE/RL Institute, *Report on Eastern Europe* (2 August 1991), p. 30.

27. *KNS*, no. 353 (28 June 1990), p. 16; no. 355 (26 July 1990), p. 5.

28. Regarding Slovenia, see *Vjesnik* (Zagreb) (31 July 1990), p. 1.

29. See discussion in *Priestervereinigung "Pacem in Terris"—Eine kritische Analyse* (Munich: Sozialwerk der Ackermann-Gemeinde, 1983).

30. *Süddeutsche Zeitung* (23/24 June 1990), p. 5.

31. Further discussion in Joseph Pungur, "Theological Adaptation in Eastern Europe—The Case of Hungary," unpublished paper, 1991.

32. *Mecklenburgische Zeitung* (17 December 1989), as summarized in *KNS*, no. 346 (22 March 1990), p. 14.

33. For elaboration, see my introduction, "The Interplay of Religious and Nationalities Policy in the Soviet Union and Eastern Europe," in Ramet (ed.), *Religion and Nationalism*, esp. pp. 3–4.

34. Quoted in *Süddeutsche Zeitung* (22/23 September 1990), p. 12.

35. *Frankfurter Allgemeine* (27 April 1991), p. 1; confirmed in *Süddeutsche Zeitung* (27/28 April 1991), p. 9.

36. *National Catholic Reporter* (31 May 1991), p. 7.

37. *New York Times* (15 May 1991), p. A7.

38. *Daily Telegraph* (5 June 1991), p. 10.

39. *Neue Zürcher Zeitung* (12 June 1991), p. 5.

40. Ibid. (3 October 1991), p. 5.

41. Martin, "New Law," p. 19.

42. *Start* (23 June 1990), as summarized in *KNS*, no. 355 (26 July 1990), p. 11.

43. *Glas koncila* (21 January 1990), p. 6; *KNS*, no. 350 (17 May 1990), p. 13.

44. For more detailed discussion, see Sabrina Petra Ramet, *Balkan Babel: Politics, Culture, and Religion in Yugoslavia* (Boulder, Colo.: Westview Press, 1992), chap. 9; and Sabrina P. Ramet, *Nationalism and Federalism in Yugoslavia, 1962–1991*, 2nd ed. (Bloomington: Indiana University Press, 1992), chap. 11.

45. *Politika* (Belgrade), 2 September 1990, p. 18.

46. *Pravoslavlje* (Belgrade), 1 July 1990, pp. 1, 3.

47. Tanjug (28 March 1990), trans. in FBIS, *Daily Report* (Eastern Europe) (29 March 1990), p. 56.

48. Cited in *KNS*, no. 350 (17 May 1990), p. 13.

49. Actually, Stepinac personally arranged for the protection of many Croatian Serbs during World War II and preached vociferously against the Ustasha genocide. He was falsely accused by the communists of collaboration with the fascists in 1946 because the communists wanted to weaken the church. For further information, see O. Aleksa Benigar, *Alojzije Stepinac, Hrvatski Kardinal* (Rome: Ziral, 1974); Richard Pattee, *The Case of Aloysius Stepinac* (Milwaukee: Bruce Publishing, 1953); and Ramet, *Balkan Babel*, chap. 7. See also *KNS*, no. 343 (8 February 1990), p. 15.

50. *KNS*, no. 345 (8 March 1990), pp. 14–15.

51. Letter from Bishop Nikolaj, published in *Pravoslavlje* (1 March 1990), p. 5.

52. Ibid. (15 May 1991), p. 1.

53. Ibid. (15 July 1991), p. 8.

54. BTA (5 January 1990), in FBIS, *Daily Report* (Eastern Europe) (8 January 1990), p. 10.

55. *KNS*, no. 356 (9 August 1990), p. 10.

56. Ibid., no. 355 (26 July 1990), pp. 7–8.

57. *Kościol w Polsce*, vol. 2: *Wieki XVI–XVIII* (Krakow: Spoleczny Instytut Wydawniczy Znak, 1969), pp. 5–35.

58. Andrzej Wojtowicz, "Katholischer Sozialismus. Polen aus protestantischer Sicht," in *Evangelische Kommentare* 14, no. 7 (July 1981): 403.

59. *Rzeczpospolita* (3 October 1985), p. 4.

60. *Frontier* (September–October 1987), pp. 17–18.

61. See the report in *Neue Zürcher Zeitung* (7 February 1991), p. 2.

62. Quoted in *KNS*, no. 334 (21 September 1989), pp. 13–14.

63. Ibid., no. 335 (5 October 1989); no. 351 (31 May 1990), p. 16.

64. Ionescu, "Orthodox-Uniate," pp. 30–31.

65. The statements were dated, respectively, 16 January and 23 January 1990. See *KNS*, no. 343 (8 February 1990), pp. 12–13.

66. Ibid., no. 342 (25 January 1990), p. 6.

67. *Trybuna* (19 September 1990), p. 3.

68. *Borba* (8 March 1990), p. 7; *Vjesnik* (10 July 1990), p. 2.

69. *KNS*, no. 349 (3 May 1990), p. 12; no. 356 (9 August 1990), p. 16.

70. Cited in Ewa Morawska, "On Barriers to Pluralism in Pluralist Poland," in *Slavic Review* 47, no. 4 (Winter 1988): 636–37.

71. Martin, "New Law," p. 18.

72. *KNS*, no. 357 (30 August 1990), p. 11.

73. Cited in *KNS*, no. 337 (2 November 1989), p. 9.

74. For details, see Sabrina P. Ramet, *Social Currents in Eastern Europe: The Sources and Meaning of the Great Transformation* (Durham, N.C.: Duke University Press, 1991), chap. 5.

75. Krzysztof Kosela, "The Polish Catholic Church and the Elections of 1989," *Religion in Communist Lands* 18, no. 2 (Summer 1990): 125.

76. Re. this, see *New York Times* (17 March 1992), p. A5.

77. *Kana* (February 1992), p. 5.

78. Quoted in *New York Times* (19 April 1992), p. 6.

79. *Neodvisni Dnevnik* (Ljubljana), 26 November 1991, p. 5, trans. in FBIS, *Daily Report* (Eastern Europe) (10 December 1991), p. 47; and Radio Slovenia Network (Ljubljana), 17 September 1991, trans. in FBIS, *Daily Report* (Eastern Europe) (18 September 1991), p. 30.

80. Jan Vrba, Czechoslovak Minister of Industry, quoted in *Die Presse* (Vienna), 28/29 March 1992, p. 1. Re. the decline in industrial output in Czechoslovakia 1990–91, see *Hospodarske noviny* (16 October 1991), p. 2, trans. in FBIS, *Daily Report* (Eastern Europe) (22 October 1991), p. 19.

81. *Neue Zürcher Zeitung* (2 October 1991), p. 15.

82. *Daily Telegraph* (1 October 1991), p. 10.

83. *Die Presse* (28/29 March 1992), p. 13. Re. the decline in foreign trade, see also *Frankfurter Allgemeine* (27 March 1992), p. 15.

84. Quoted in *Financial Times* (15 April 1992), p. 14.

85. *New York Times* (14 October 1991), p. A3.
86. Quoted in ibid. (31 July 1990), p. A4.

Afterword

1. King James Version.
2. Quoted in Marite Sapiets, " 'Rebirth and Renewal' in the Latvian Lutheran Church," *Religion in Communist Lands* 16, no. 3 (Autumn 1988): 239–40.

Index

Index

                     429

Plovdiv Boys' School, 211

Plymouth Brethren: in Poland, 76; in Romania, 187, 188

Poland, 4, 99, 141, 297, 310, 325, 330, 347, 348, 349; Catholics vs. believers, 325; and Lutheran Church, 8, 341–342; and power of Roman Catholic Church, 327; and Jan Laski, 7; roots of Protestantism, 8; sixteenth-century contacts between churches, 7; and free enterprise system, 328; Lutheran Synod (1570), 7; and ecumenism, 318; and national culture, 8; and religious schools, 315; and religious holidays, 317; and economy, 327; and proposal to legalize alternative service, 298; resistance by Roman Catholic Church, 333; and state religion, 317–318, 326; visit by Billy Graham, 93; Protestantism in, 76–77, 80–81, 85–86, 93–99, 103–104, 341–343; World War One, 76; World War Two, 77; Protestant legal equality, 73; loyalty of Protestants in, 74; diplomatic relations with Vatican, 94, 316; separation of Church and state (1952), 80; no financial support to Protestant clergy, 80; and repression of religion, 334; Stalinist period, 80; and Solidarity Trade Union, 93–96; martial law, 94; and religious intolerance, 321; and anti-Semitism, 322; visit by Pope John Paul II, 95, 316, 318; and atheization, 325; legal status to Roman Catholic Church, 98; and religious instruction in public schools, 315, 317; and Council of Ministers, 310; favoritism toward Roman Catholic Church, 98–99; anniversary of People's Poland, 85; 1989 legislation, 312; pacifism in, 285–291, 295–296, 297–298, 309; revision of military oath, 288, 309. See also listings under individual churches; Glemp, Jozef Cardinal; Wyszynski, Stefan Cardinal

Police (state/secret): in Czechoslovakia, 310; in Hungary, 121, 128; in Romania, 166; in Yugoslavia, 220

Polish Bible Society, 95

Polish Church of Satan. See Satan, Church of

Polish Ecumenical Council, 7, 85, 94, 98; 315; broadcasts by, 94; and Pope John Paul II, 95; and Movement of National Rebirth, 342

Polish Lutheran Church, 342

Polish National Catholic Church: formation of, 76; mission to Poland, 76

Polish Orthodox Church, 315, 321

Politika, 319

Polk, James K., 33

Polygamy: and Joseph Smith, 33

Ponet, John: appeals to Ethniks, 20; opinions about Anabaptists, 20

Pontius Pilate, 134

Popescu, Aurel, 180, 181; expulsion of, 181; criticism of Tson, 182; exile to U.S., 182

Popescu, Tudor, 187

Pope, Earl, 327, 331

Pope, Liston, 33

Popov, Haralan, 214–215; torture and show trial of, 214–215

Popov, Lyubomir, 218, 312

Pordium Folk School, 211

Pospisil, Bohuslav, 140

Pospisil, Vlastimil, 106

Post-Reformation politics, 26–28

Potsdamer Kirche, 42

Prague Spring, 78, 85–87, 291; and Charter 77, 90; comparison with Solidarity movement, 94; effect into 1980s, 96; and results, 103

Pravda, 304

Pravoslavlje, 320

Preporod, 319

Presbyterian Quarterly, 34

Presbyterians, 23; Korean Presbyterians in USSR, 274; and Puritans, 24; and John Witherspoon, 30; and Peter Hajdn, 135; and Global Mission Ministry Unit of Presbyterian Church, USA, 173

Presidential Council of Hungary, 142

Priesthood of all believers, 3

Priestly Peace Movement (Hungary), 125

Pröhle, Karoly, 137; and Theology of Diakonia, 137

Prokofiev, A. F., 245, 246, 284

Pronozin, Alexander, 304, 306

Protestant Patent (1861), 74

Protestant Review—World & Thought, 315

Protestant Student Union, 7

Contributors

Sabrina Petra Ramet (born in London, England) is Associate Professor of International Studies at the University of Washington. She is the author of *Social Currents in Eastern Europe: The Sources and Meaning of the Great Transformation, Balkan Babel: Politics, Culture, and Religion in Yugoslavia,* and *Nationalism and Federalism in Yugoslavia, 1962–1991,* 2nd ed., among others. She has edited eight books and has contributed articles to many journals, including *World Politics, Orbis,* and *Studies in Comparative Communism.*

Paul Bock (born in Beulah, North Dakota) is Professor of Religion (retired) at Doane College in Crete, Nebraska. He is the author of *In Search of a Responsible World Society: The Social Teachings of the World Council of Churches* and editor of *Signs of the Kingdom: A Ragaz Reader.* His articles have appeared in *Journal of Ecumenical Studies, Christianity and Crisis, Cross Currents,* and *Occasional Papers on Religion in Eastern Europe.* He has served as Associate Religion Editor of the daily newspaper *USA Today.*

Lawrence Klippenstein (born in Altona, Manitoba, Canada) is presently Historian-Archivist at the Mennonite Heritage Center in Winnipeg, Manitoba. He is the author of *David Klassen and the Mennonites* and editor of four books, among them *That There be Peace: Mennonites in World War II.* His articles have appeared in *Religion in Communist Lands, Occasional Papers on Religion in Eastern Europe, Mennonite Quarterly Review,* and other journals.

Paul Mojzes (born in Osijek, Yugoslavia) is Professor of Religious Studies at Rosemont College, Pennsylvania. He is the author of *Christian-Marxist Dialogue in Eastern Europe, Church and State in Postwar Eastern Europe,* and *Religious Liberty in Eastern Europe: Before and After the Great Transformation.*

He is also editor of *Varieties of Christian-Marxist Dialogue, Society and Original Sin, Attitudes of Religions and Ideologies Toward the Outsider,* and *Christian Mission and Interreligious Dialogue.* He is the co-editor of the *Journal of Ecumenical Studies* and the editor of *Occasional Papers on Religion in Eastern Europe.* He has written more than fifty journal articles.

Earl A. Pope (born in Tulca, Romania) is Manson Professor Emeritus, Lafayette College, and author of *New England Calvinism and the Disruption of the Presbyterian Church* (1987). He is a specialist on the religious situation in Romania and his articles have appeared in *East European Quarterly, Journal of Church and State, Journal of Ecumenical Studies, Occasional Papers on Religion in Eastern Europe, Ostkirchliche Studien,* and other journals. He has also contributed chapters to *Kyrkohistorisk Arsskrift* (1977) and *Religion and Communist Society* (1983).

Joseph Pungur (born in Budapest, Hungary) is Adjunct Professor of Religious Studies, University of Alberta, Calgary, Canada. He is the author of the two-volume *Theology Interpreted.* His articles have appeared in *Occasional Papers on Religion in Eastern Europe, Gesellschaft in der 2. Welt, Donau Messenger,* and other journals. He is Minister in the Reformed Church of Hungary as well as in the Presbyterian Church of Canada. He was formerly Chair of the Department of Theology and Philosophy at St. Paul's United Theological College, Limuru, Kenya.

Walter Sawatsky (born in Altona, Manitoba, Canada) is Associate Professor of Church History, Associate Mennonite Biblical Seminaries, and also East-West Consultant for the Mennonite Central Committee. He is the author of *Soviet Evangelicals since World War Two,* and has contributed chapters to *Religion and Modernization in the Soviet Union, Religion in Communist Societies,* and *Mennonites in Russia.* His articles have appeared in, among others, *Religion in Communist Lands, Occasional Papers on Religion in Eastern Europe,* and *Journal of Church and State.*

N. Gerald Shenk (born in Bridgeport, Connecticut) is Associate Professor of Church and Society at Eastern Mennonite Seminary (Harrisonburg, Virginia). He is also Adjunct Professor for the Evangelical Theological Seminary in Osijek, Croatia. He has contributed chapters to several books on religion and society in Eastern Europe, and articles to several journals, including *Occasional Papers on Religion in Eastern Europe, Mission Focus,* and *Mennonite Quarterly Review.* He is Vice President of Christians Associated for Relationships with Eastern Europe (an affiliate of the National Council of Churches).

Gerd Stricker (born near Breslau, Schlesien, Germany, now Wrocław, Poland) is Assistant Director of the Institute Glaube in der 2. Welt, in Zollikon, near Zürich, Switzerland. He is the author of *Untersuchungen zum Moskowitischen Prunkstil des 16. Jahrhunderts* (Verlag Otto Sagner, 1979) and *Die Russische Orthodoxe Kirche von ihren Anfängen bis heute*. He is also editor of *Orthodoxe Kirche in Russland: Dokumente ihrer Geschichte 860–1980, Religionen in der Sowjetunion. Unbekannte Vielfalt in Geschichte und Gegenwart*, and *Deutsche Geschichte in Russland*. His articles have appeared in *Kirche im Osten, Religion in Communist Lands, Glaube in der 2. Welt*, and other journals.

Sape A. Zylstra (born in Wassenaar, Netherlands) is Professor of Humanities at the University of South Florida. He is the author of articles on literary criticism and the history of architecture.

Library of Congress Cataloging-in-Publication Data

Protestantism and politics in eastern Europe and Russia : the
communist and post communist eras / edited by Sabrina Petra Ramet.
p.   cm. — (Christianity under stress ; v. 3)
Includes bibliographical references and index.
ISBN 0-8223-1241-7 (acid-free paper)
1. Protestant churches—Europe, Eastern. 2. Communism and
Christianity—Europe, Eastern. 3. Europe, Eastern—Church
history—20th century.   I. Ramet, Sabrina P., 1949–   .
II. Series: Christianity under stress ; 3.
BX4837.P76   1992
280'.4'09470904—dc20
                                                    92-9418
                                                      CIP